Modern Public Finance

Irwin Publications in Economics

Modern Public Finance

Bernard P. Herber
The University of Arizona

1983

Fifth Edition
RICHARD D. IRWIN, INC.
Homewood, Illinois 60430

ISBN 0-256-02808-7
Library of Congress Catalog Card No. 82-83420
Printed in the United States of America

2 3 4 5 6 7 8 9 0 K 0 9 8 7 6 5

To Jean

Preface

The fifth edition of *Modern Public Finance* retains the philosophy of the previous editions, that is, a symmetrical approach inclusive of both the revenue and expenditure sides of governmental budgetary decisions as they relate to the allocation, distribution, and stabilization functions of the economy. Meanwhile, an effort has been made to revise the contents of the book to reflect recent important conceptual and legislative developments, such as the federal tax changes enacted during 1981 and 1982. One new chapter has been added on the topic of tax reform. In this chapter, comprehensive personal income, personal consumption, and personal wealth taxes are considered along with the proposed federal value-added tax—the latter as a possible replacement for the federal social security payroll tax. The chapter on fiscal institutions has been moved to Part I in order to achieve greater continuity, and the separate chapter on welfare economics and public sector decision making has been deleted. Moreover, numerous substantive changes have been made in other chapters throughout the book. These include an expanded coverage of overall fiscal incidence, a restructuring of the two chapters on fiscal federalism, and coverage of the supply-side economics of the Reagan administration. In addition, recent proposals for a federal balanced budget amendment and a flat-rate personal income tax are considered.

Appreciation is expressed to all who have assisted me in the preparation of this edition as well as previous editions. Especially valuable for this edition have been the contributions of Julian Sayre—a man in the enviable position of knowing taxation from all directions. He is a tax attorney and certified public accountant with many years of practitioner experience and, in addition, holds a doctoral degree in business and economics with a specialization in taxation. Dr. Sayre presently teaches taxation at the university level. Alas, he is also a taxpayer! Meanwhile, others who have contributed importantly to the preparation of the fifth edition include Neal Churney, Sandy Cutter, Harry Greenbaum, J. S. H. Hunter, Peter Knez, and Paul Pawlik. However, the author alone is responsible for any inadequacies which remain. My appreciation is also expressed to my wife, Jean, for her patience as well as for her typing and other administrative assistance in the publication process. To all of these people, and to others not mentioned who have been helpful, I extend a sincere thank you.

Bernard P. Herber

Contents

PART I

Public goods and public sector decision making

1

Resource scarcity and intersector allocation

THE ECONOMIC FUNCTIONS AND
GOALS OF THE PUBLIC SECTOR

The basic economic problem of *scarcity* provides a logical point of departure for the study of public finance. The resources available to any society are limited in their ability to produce economic goods by both quantitative and qualitative constraints.[1] *Land*, which may be defined generally as natural resources, is limited in quantity by the geographical area of the nation and by the magnitude of raw material deposits within this land area. Moreover, natural resources vary in quality among nations. *Labor* faces quantitative constraints as a productive resource through the numerical size and age distribution of the society's population, and qualitative limitations through such determinants as the prevailing ethical, health, and educational standards of the society. *Capital* is limited in quantity by the society's past capital formation behavior and in quality by the relationship of its capital stock to the prevailing state of technology.

This limited supply of the productive resources available to a society leads to the *allocation function* of economics. The unlimited

---

[1] Although the traditional classification of productive resources into land, labor, and capital components will be used in this book, it should be recognized that many economists prefer an alternative classification arrangement whereby all resources are classified as *capital*, in the form of either material or human capital. However, since resource scarcity exists under either system of classification, the particular system selected will not affect the validity of the present discussion.

scope of aggregate human wants, along with the limited resources which produce the economic goods[2] capable of satisfying these wants, makes it necessary to allocate the scarce resources among alternative uses. An infinite or unlimited quantity of economic goods cannot be produced. When certain goods are produced with the scarce resources, the opportunities to produce other goods are foregone, assuming there is full employment of resources.

Thus, an *economic system* must exist to determine the pattern of production, that is, to answer the questions of which economic goods should be produced, and in what quantities they ought to be produced. The allocation function possesses an additional important dimension: It must be concerned with the *institutional means* through which the allocation decisions are processed. This requirement establishes the link between the basic economic problem of scarcity and the study of public finance, since modern society offers two institutions through which the decisions of the allocation branch of economics may be made—the *market* and the *government*. The market institution is designated the *private sector* and the government institution the *public sector*.

The forces of supply and demand and the price mechanism, as determined by consumer sovereignty and producer profit motives, characterize private sector resource allocation. Public sector allocation, on the other hand, is accomplished through the revenue and expenditure activities of governmental budgeting. In reality, of course, no economic society allocates all of its resources through a single allocational institution. Instead, each economy in the world is mixed, to one degree or another, between market-determined and government-determined resource allocation. Yet, if the market dominates, the system is usually referred to as "capitalist," and if the government dominates, it is usually termed a "socialist" economic system.

The analysis that follows will consider resource allocation in a society characterized by a preference for the private sector approach. That is, it will emphasize the allocation behavior of a public sector operating within a mixed, though market-oriented, economic system. Moreover, since both the private and public sectors of a mixed economy also determine the performance of the distribution and stabilization functions, the book will be concerned with the influence of the public sector in these economic areas too.

The *distribution function* relates to the manner in which the effective demand over economic goods is divided among the various individual and family spending units of the society. It is this effective demand that determines the distribution of real output among the

---

[2] Including intangible services.

population, through the existing patterns of income and wealth distribution in the private sector and through political voting influence in the public sector. The *stabilization function* is concerned with the performance of the aggregate economy in terms of labor employment and capital utilization, overall output and income, price levels, the balance of international payments, and the rate of economic growth.

Since the public sector will inevitably influence the performance of the national economy in terms of these three economic functions, it is reasonable to assume that society will wish to consciously formulate *fiscal policies* so as to attain given allocational, distributional, and stabilization *goals.* Hence, the three functions of economics may be viewed also as the goals, targets, or objectives of public sector economic activity. These goals cannot always be separated precisely, and a given budgetary action usually will exert an influence on more than one goal. The resulting complexity involving public finance is evident throughout this book and will be more comprehensively analyzed in Chapter 5 in the discussion of intergoal fiscal nonneutrality.

The term *public finance* is somewhat of a misnomer for the subject matter at hand. Finance, as such, suggests monetary flows as represented by the revenue-gathering and expenditure activities of the governmental fiscal, or budgetary, process. These monetary flows are a relevant component of the present analysis. Nonetheless, the more basic economic functions of the public sector are those that influence resource allocation, the distribution of effective demand and real output among the population, and aggregate economic performance. These are the direct results of public sector economic activity. Hence, the term *public sector economics* is a more accurate representation of the content of this book than is the term public finance. Moreover, since public sector economics could be said to relate to the functional economic effects of either governmental fiscal activities or of money supply control, a still more precise term for the present subject matter, due to its budgetary emphasis, would be *public fiscal economics.* However, out of respect to the orthodox nature and well-engrained popularity of the term public finance, the three terms will be used in the pages that follow on an equal basis.

INTERSECTOR RESOURCE ALLOCATION

Optimal and suboptimal intersector allocation

An economic system must determine the mix of its resource allocation between the private and public sectors. An *actual allocation division* between the two sectors will exist at any one time. Moreover, it is possible to conceptualize the existence of an *optimal allocation mix,* known also as *social balance,* given the preference patterns and

FIGURE 1-1   **Intersector resource allocation: Optimal and suboptimal points**

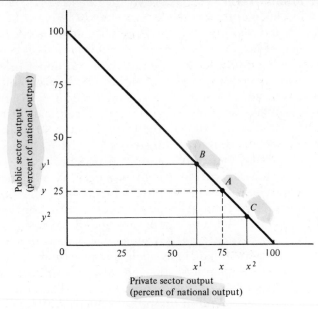

Key:
   A =   Point of optimal intersector resource allocation (assumed).
 B,C =   Points of suboptimal intersector resource allocation.

effective demand of the members of the society.[3] The points of actual and optimal intersector allocation may or may not coincide. If they do not coincide, it can be said that intersector resource allocation is *suboptimal,* or alternately, that *social imbalance* or *intersector misallocation* exists.

The relationship between optimal and suboptimal intersector resource allocation is demonstrated in Figure 1–1. In this graph, private sector output as a percentage of total national output is measured on the horizontal axis, and public sector output as a percentage of total national output is measured on the vertical axis. It is *assumed* that point *A* represents an optimal division of national output between the private and public sectors, with the private sector controlling 75 percent of resource allocation and the public sector controlling 25 percent. In a conceptual sense, this social balance point would thus be

---

[3] The question as to the proper role of government in a market-oriented economy has been in the minds of economists since at least the time of Adam Smith (1723–90). More recently, the term *social balance* has been applied to this concept by John Kenneth Galbraith in *The Affluent Society* (Boston: Houghton Mifflin, 1958).

assumed to reflect the true preferences of the people of the society for private and public goods as made effective by the distribution of income, wealth, and political voting power among the people.

If point A represents optimal intersector allocation, and if the actual mix of resources between private and public goods in the society is also at point A, then the optimal and actual points of intersector resource allocation coincide and social balance is present. Given the preference patterns of the individuals of the society, no welfare improvement would result from any reallocation between private and public output. If, however, point A represents optimal intersector allocation and the actual allocation is at point B, or at point C, then suboptimal allocation or social imbalance is present. In this instance, reallocation between the two sectors is required if societal welfare is to be maximized. The imbalance gap between points A and B represents an underallocation of resources to the private sector and an overallocation of resources to the public sector by the proportions of xx^1 and yy^1, respectively. The imbalance gap between points A and C represents an overallocation of resources to the private sector and an underallocation of resources to the public sector by the proportions of xx^2 and yy^2, respectively.

The indifference approach to optimal intersector resource allocation

The application of indifference analysis to the concept of intersector resource allocation allows the point of optimal intersector allocation to be *logically derived,* instead of merely assumed as above. The indifference approach to intersector allocation is developed in Figures 1-2, 1-3, and 1-4. In each graph, private sector output is measured along the horizontal axis and public sector output along the vertical axis. This output may be considered either in monetary value terms or in physical unit terms, though the former is more practical.

The societal production possibility curve. In Figure 1-2, the *production possibility curve* of the society, designated as P, relates the marginal rates of transformation between the production of private and public goods with the scarce productive resources available to the society. That is, it shows the various combinations of private and public goods that can be produced with the full employment of the quantitatively and qualitatively limited land, labor, and capital resources available to the society at a given time. The higher the position of the production possibility curve on the graph, the greater the production potential of the society, due to the greater quantity and/or quality of its productive resources. At point B, all of society's resources would be allocated by the private sector. At point A, all of the resources would be allocated by the public sector.

FIGURE 1-2   **The production possibility curve for a society**

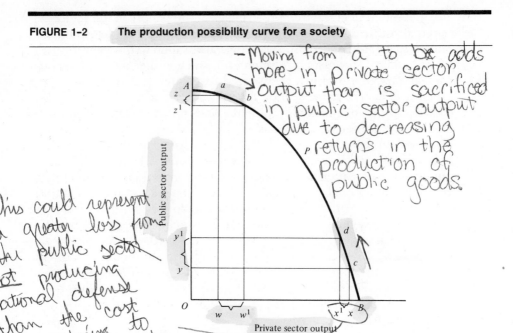

[Handwritten annotation, top right: "—Moving from a to be adds more in private sector output than is sacrificed in public sector output due to decreasing returns in the production of public goods."]

[Handwritten annotation, left: "This could represent a greater loss from the public sector not producing national defense than the cost to producing to the private sector"]

The society's production possibility curve, P, is *concave* to the origin of the graph. This reflects the fact that scarce resources cannot be substituted with equal efficiency between the production of public and private goods. Thus, in Figure 1–2, a reallocation of resources along the upper part of the P curve, as from a to b, would add more in private sector output (the distance ww^1), than is sacrificed in public sector output (the distance zz^1). This would be due to decreasing returns in the production of public goods. A movement along the lower portion of the P curve, as from c to d, however, could add more in public sector output than is sacrificed in private sector output. This would be due to decreasing returns in the production of private goods. A comparison of the distances yy^1 and xx^1, respectively, indicates this phenomenon.

The unequal trade-off between the output of private and of public goods as resources are reallocated in production between the two sectors can be explained by the following reasons. First, some economic goods, by their very nature, are produced more efficiently, with less real input costs per unit of output, by one sector than by the other. If the private sector were allocating most resources, as would be true toward the lower part of the P curve, it likely would be providing goods such as national defense. Yet, if the national defense function were transferred from federal government control to market control, production efficiency in defense would doubtless decline,[4] with a greater loss in public sector output than what would be added in private sector output. This can be seen in Figure 1–2 toward the lower end of the P curve, with the distance y^1y representing a greater loss from the public sector *not* producing national defense than the value of defense production, x^1x, that would be gained with private sector production of defense. Second, but equally important, increasing costs tend to occur when too many goods are produced by one sector, because the principles of diminishing returns and decreasing returns to scale come into operation.[5] These principles of increasing cost are applied ordinarily to the analysis of private sector production, but they may also be applied validly to public sector production. Thus, toward the upper end of the P curve, the society would be incurring increasing unit costs in the production of public goods, and toward the lower end it would be incurring increasing unit costs in the production of private goods. In either situation, the reallocation of a given bloc of resources from one sector to the other would yield greater output results in the second sector than if the same resources were retained for use in the original sector.

Social indifference curves. Having defined the production possibility curve for the society, the next step in the derivation of the point of optimal intersector resource allocation involves the use of *social indifference curves*. In Figure 1–3, each social indifference curve, S^1, S^2, S^3, and S^4, represents the marginal rate of substitution between private and public goods consumption by society in providing a *given level of satisfaction (utility)* along each curve. That is, each curve shows the various combinations of private and public goods which will provide a constant level of welfare to the society. Moreover, the higher the position of the social indifference curve, the greater the level of societal welfare it represents, since a greater aggregate output is being consumed.

The family of social indifference curves, only four of which are displayed in Figure 1–3 for reasons of simplicity, are importantly related to the state of market and political distribution in the society.[6] In other words, they reflect the aggregate preferences of the individual

---

[4] Due to the joint consumption of benefits and related issues described in Chapter 2 below.

[5] The short-run principle of *diminishing returns* states that as successive units of a variable productive resource (assume labor) are added in production to a resource constant in quantity (assume capital), real input costs per unit of output will eventually increase. The long-run principle of *decreasing returns to scale* states that as the quantities of all resources are increased by equal proportions in a production situation, real input costs per unit of output will eventually increase. Both principles may be classified as *increasing-cost* principles.

[6] The relationship between the state of distribution in the society and intersector resource allocation will be considered also in Chapter 3 in relationship to public choice theory.

members of the society for private and public goods *as made effective* by the distribution of income and wealth in the private sector and by political representation in the public sector.[7] Individual preferences for public and private goods are meaningless, of course, unless made effective by purchasing power in the private sector and by voting power or related political representation in the public sector. Clearly, an individual with a superior income and wealth base in the market can command a higher level of consumption than can a consumer of lesser means. Similarly, all individuals are not represented equally in the consumption of public goods. Instead, some individuals are more adequately represented than are others within the public sector by lobbies, pressure groups, and elected or appointed officials.[8]

Thus, it is important to note that the pattern and shape of the social indifference curves do not represent mere preferences; instead, they represent the *effective demand* of the individual members of the society for private and public goods, as this demand *can* be made operational by the state of income, wealth, and political voting distribution in the society. The degree to which such preferences *do* become operational, and thus become precise allocational realities, will be determined by the ability of the market and political processes to reveal these effective preferences accurately and efficiently.

The social indifference curves, S^1, S^2, S^3, and S^4, are *convex* to the origin of the graph in Figure 1-3. This reflects the fact that along each curve there is a *diminishing marginal rate of substitution* between private and public goods in providing a given level of societal welfare. Thus, toward the upper end of social indifference curve S^1, the quantity of public goods that the society would be willing to sacrifice to gain additional private goods is greater than it is toward the lower end of the curve. Stated alternately, it can be said that the society is willing to give up a more than proportionate amount of public goods to get a smaller quantity of private goods toward the upper end of curve S^1, and vice versa toward the lower end. For example, a movement from a to b yields the greater loss in public goods, zz^1, for the smaller gain in

---

[7] Even though an individual consumer indifference curve is independent of the level of income, it is possible to sum individual indifference curves to obtain an aggregate indifference curve under the following assumptions: If all utility functions are homogeneous of any degree (but the degree of homogeneity is the same for *all* individual utility functions); or if the utility functions are *homothetic* (not homogeneous, but still giving rise to parallel indifference curves), it is possible to construct social indifference curves by aggregation. These indifference curves would tend to change in shape, though remain convex to the origin of the graph (this convexity is explained later in the chapter), as income distribution changes.

[8] It is probable that a direct relationship exists between an individual's command over income and wealth, on the one hand, and that person's ability to influence political decisions, on the other. For an economic analysis in support of this position, *see* Randall Bartlett, *Economic Foundations of Political Power* (New York: Free Press, 1973). Also, see Chapter 3 for additional discussion of this point.

Figure 1-3   Social indifference curves

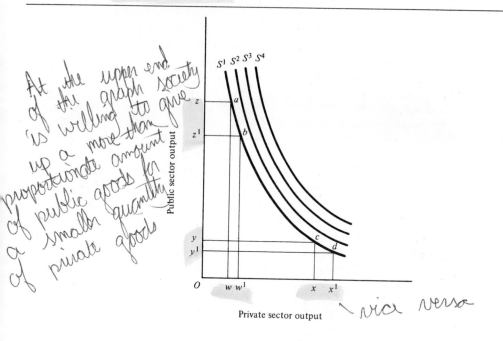

At the upper end of the graph society is willing to give up a more than proportionate amount of public goods for a smaller quantity of private goods

Private sector output

~ vice versa

private goods, ww^1. To the contrary, as the society is consuming mostly private goods toward the lower end of the curve, it would be willing to give up a less than proportionate amount of public goods to obtain a larger quantity of private goods. This is represented by a movement from c to d along curve S^1 which yields the smaller loss in public goods, yy^1, for the larger gain of private goods, xx^1, with the same overall level of societal welfare being maintained.

This declining marginal rate of substitution between the consumption of public and private goods in providing a constant level of welfare may be explained by the following reasons. First, the *more scarce* a good becomes, the greater is the tendency for its relative substitution value in relationship to another good to increase. That is, its marginal utility increases relative to the marginal utility of the other good, which now is relatively more plentiful. For example, toward the lower end of a social indifference curve, such as those presented in Figure 1-3, the marginal utility of public goods would tent to be *high*. Thus, society would be willing to give up a more than proportionate amount of private goods to obtain a smaller quantity of the now relatively more scarce public goods. By contrast, toward the upper end of a social indifference curve, the marginal utility per unit of public goods is *low*, as society has a relatively large supply of such goods. Thus, it would be willing to give up a larger amount of public goods to obtain a smaller quantity of the now relatively more scarce private goods, while maintaining the same level of total utility. More generally, it can be said that when society's consumption approaches either extreme, the marginal increments of societal welfare or satisfaction diminish as the society consumes mostly private or mostly public goods.

A second reason for the convexity of a social indifference curve is that significant losses of both political and economic freedom are incurred as government allocation becomes dominant near the upper end of the curve.[9] A society may well be willing to give up a more than proportionate quantity of public goods in order to attain a smaller quantity of private goods if, as a result, additional political and economic freedom can be gained. The convexity toward the lower (private sector) end of the social indifference curve, moreover, may be explained by the fact that an extreme degree of market allocation would likely create an undesirable state of anarchy where basic law and order does not prevail. Society would thus be willing to give up a more than proportionate quantity of private goods at this point in order to ensure government-provided law and order.

The optimal intersector allocation point. The final step in deriving the point of optimal intersector resource allocation through the indifference approach involves the placing of the societal production possibility curve and its social indifference curves on the same graph. In Figure 1-4, the relevant parts of Figures 1-2 and 1-3 are combined. Hence, the production potential of the society, as determined by its resources and technology, is brought into equilibrium with societal preferences for public and private goods, as they are made effective by the state of income, wealth, and political voting distribution. This results in optimal intersector resource allocation being established at point a in Figure 1-4, where the production possibility curve, P, is tangent to social indifference curve S^3, providing OY in public sector output and OX in private sector output.[10] At this point, social welfare is maximized.

---

[9] *Political freedom* refers to such conditions as representative government, free speech, and the free practice of religion. *Economic freedom* includes the right to own and use the property factors of production, land and capital, and one's own labor resource, without undue restraint from government.

[10] The point of tangency reflects not only optimal intersector allocational efficiency but also optimal technical efficiency, in production cost terms, since perfect technical efficiency has been assumed to be present along the production possibility curve in order to reflect the full production potential of a society's resources. To distinguish, *allocational efficiency* implies the selection of those economic goods which the society prefers to consume, as provided by the appropriate sector, in keeping with effective consumer preferences. *Technical efficiency* implies the least-cost combinations of productive resources in providing these economic goods, given a prevailing level of technology.

FIGURE 1-4   **Intersector resource allocation: Optimal and suboptimal points**

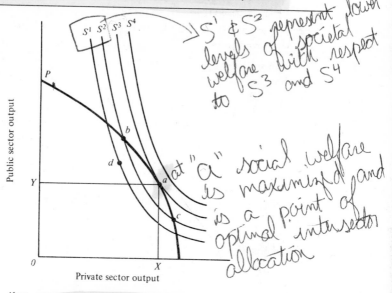

S^1 & S^2 represent lower levels of societal welfare with respect to S^3 and S^4

at "a" social welfare is maximized and is a point of optimal intersector allocation

Key:

a = Point of optimal intersector allocation.
b,c,d = Points of suboptimal intersector allocation.

It should be observed that the production possibility curve, P, and social indifference curve, S^3, have the same slope at the equilibrium point. This means that the *marginal rate of transformation* in the production of private and public goods is equal to the *marginal rate of substitution* by the society in the consumption of these goods. Effective social preferences for economic goods have been brought into equilibrium with the production capabilities of the society at point a. Thus, maximum welfare from the consumption of economic goods is attained for the society. Moreover, this point of tangency, since it rests on the societal production possibility curve P, also represents a condition of *Pareto Optimality*. That is, every reallocation of resources will have been undertaken which would make one person better off without reducing the welfare of anyone else. Furthermore, it should be noted that the optimal intersector resource allocation point would be different for every different state of societal income-wealth and political-voting distribution, since the slope (but not the convexity) of the S curves would change with each state of distribution. In addition, if the state of distribution which makes social indifference curve S^3 "effective" corresponds to the society's preferred state of distribution, as derived from a societal ethical or value judgment, both *optimal dis-*

tribution and *optimal intersector resource allocation* are attained by the society at point *a*.

It is possible, of course, that the actual intersector division of resources in a society may not be at the point of optimal allocation. The deviation of actual from optimal allocation would result from institutional defects such as the difficulty encountered in revealing preferences for public goods in the political process and from imperfect market structure distortions in the production and allocation of private goods in the market sector. The point of *actual* intersector resource allocation could be anywhere along the production possibility curve, *P,* or at any point inside *P* toward the origin of the graph. Thus, points *b, c,* and *d* in Figure 1-4 represent selected examples of points of actual allocation which deviate from the point of optimal allocation. Each reflects a condition of *suboptimal intersector resource allocation* or, in short, a condition of *social imbalance.* That is, effective societal preferences for economic goods are not being accurately revealed in the government and/or market institutions through which the allocation decisions are being made.

At point *b* there is an overallocation of resources to the public sector. At point *c* there is an overallocation of resources to the private sector. Yet, at each of these allocation points the *optimal* stabilization condition of *full resource employment* is present since both points rest on the production possibility curve, *P,* which represents full employment along its entire length. Intersector resource allocation, however, is suboptimal because points *b* and *c* provide the lower level of societal welfare represented by social indifference curve S^2 instead of S^3. Thus, even though points *b* and *c* represent full resource utilization, they do *not* represent efficient resource utilization. It should be observed, accordingly, that optimal stabilization is a *necessary, but not a sufficient,* condition for optimal intersector allocation. That is, the optimal point, *a,* must necessarily be on the production possibility curve, but actual allocation may also occur on the curve at suboptimal points such as *b* and *c*. Moreover, if allocation is at point *d* along social indifference curve S^1, the society is experiencing both social imbalance and an underemployment of productive resources (suboptimal stabilization)—the latter because output is occurring at a point inside the production possibility curve.

CHANGES IN INTERSECTOR RESOURCE ALLOCATION OVER TIME

The foregoing discussion of intersector resource allocation is static in the sense that it considers the conditions of optimal and actual allocation as they would exist at a given time. It is useful to add a *time dimension* to the discussion which allows for changes in the points of optimal and actual allocation. The possibilities of intersector allocation change over time include various types of change, which can be summarized under two primary classifications: (1) changes in actual intersector allocation, with optimal intersector allocation constant, and (2) changes in both actual and optimal intersector allocation. The changes are discussed in reference to Figure 1–4.

Changes in actual intersector allocation with optimal intersector allocation constant

1. The society can move from an actual allocation point which is optimal to a suboptimal point, such as from point *a* to points *b*, *c*, or *d*.
2. The society can move from an actual allocation point which is suboptimal to an optimal allocation point, such as from points *b*, *c*, or *d* to point *a*.
3. The society can change the degree of suboptimal allocation; that is, points *b*, *c*, or *d* could move closer to or further from point *a*.
4. The society can change the direction of suboptimal allocation. For example, it can move from point *b* to point *c*, or from point *c* to point *b*, or between points *b* and *c* and *d*.
5. The society can move from a point of full resource employment, such as points *a*, *b*, or *c*, to a point of under full employment, such as point *d*. Or, it can move from under full employment at point *d* to full employment at points *a*, *b*, or *c*.

The changes described under points 1–4 above would result largely from changes in the *institutional efficiency* of the market and the political process as these allocational institutions interpret individual preferences for economic goods. Changes under point 5 would result primarily from changes in the macroeconomic stabilization policies of the economy.

Changes in both actual and optimal intersector allocation

1. The production potential of the society can change as the quantity and/or quality of its productive resources increase or decrease. Economic growth can move the societal production possibility curve, *P*, to the right so that it will become tangent to a higher social indifference curve, such as curve S^4, thus increasing aggregate societal welfare; or a catastrophe such as war or earthquake can move *P* to the left, where it will become tangent to a lower social indifference curve, such as curve S^2, thus yielding a lower attainable level of societal welfare. In either case, the point of optimal intersector resource allocation will have changed.

2. A change in societal preferences for public and private goods, or a change in the state of income, wealth, or political voting distribution which converts these preferences into effective demand, may cause the family of social indifference curves S^1-S^4 to change their slope (though they would remain convex to the origin). Hence, they would become tangent to a given production possibility curve, such as P, at a different point of optimal allocation between private and public goods.
3. Both the P and S curves could change for the above reasons, with the very likely establishment of a new point of optimal intersector allocation.
4. The points of actual allocation can change in various degrees and directions as optimal allocation changes with a multiple number of possible results.

The final section of this chapter will consider some of the alternative instruments whereby the public sector can influence resource allocation in a mixed, private sector-public sector economy.

ALTERNATIVE PUBLIC SECTOR ALLOCATION INSTRUMENTS

Various allocational instruments are available by which government can influence resource allocation in the economy. Not all of these instruments involve outright public sector production of economic output, which would appear to be the connotation of the vertical axis in Figures 1-1 through 1-4 above. When allocational intervention is considered desirable, the public sector may, in fact, produce the economic good, but also it may only loosely influence the private allocation of the good or adopt any of a variety of intermediate techniques. Efficient resource allocation requires not only the optimal intersector solution (as discussed above), but also the selection of the appropriate allocational instruments.

A distinction should be made between public sector *organization of supply* and actual public sector *production* of an economic good. The former may consist primarily of governmental financing of the good, with the good being produced by, or purchased from, the private sector. The latter suggests both outright governmental financing and production of the good. Yet, a number of variations exist.

The selection of a particular instrument for government influence on the allocation of economic goods is often decided on *noneconomic* grounds. Considerations of freedom, along with other related social and cultural criteria, are highly relevant to the selection of an allocation instrument. The prevailing American culture prefers minimal public sector influence on resource allocation. Through the political process, American society continually weighs the relative economic efficiencies of direct or indirect, complete or partial public sector allocational influence against the existing social, cultural, and political values. Walter Heller comments that "one would be naive to think that efficiency alone dictates the choice" and notes that "the role of both economic and noneconomic constraints must be given full weight" in policy decisions as to the method of allocation.[11] Henry Wallich argues that unless the public sector has a decided edge in the technical efficiency of combining productive resources to produce the optimal output, the community may prefer indirect and partial allocation influence—and *only* when circumstances require any governmental influences at all.[12] Thus, intersector resource allocation, as discussed in the preceding section, need not be an "either-or-choice" between complete public sector or complete private sector allocational influence. Instead, instruments may be selected which commit the society to neither extreme.

Table 1-1 is a continuum showing some of the major alternative instruments the public sector can use to influence resource allocation. These range from instruments that are applied directly and completely by government to those in which the public sector's influence is very indirect and incomplete. In the former case, government power and compulsion prevail. In the latter, the instruments more closely resemble market power and individualism.

At *point 1* on the continuum, governmental allocational influence is direct and complete. The public sector both finances and produces the economic good. Moreover, it produces the component parts of the good and owns, or directly controls, all resources used in the production of these components. In addition, it supplies the good "free of direct charge" to all users. It is paid for via taxation rather than by pricing. Even national defense is not governmentally supplied to this extreme degree in the United States. Most intermediate components (missiles, planes, ships) of the final good (national defense) are produced in the market and purchased by the federal government. Furthermore, now that the military draft is no longer active, all members of the armed forces (the labor component of national defense) serve on a voluntary rather than on a compulsory basis. While national defense in the United States cannot be strictly located at the polar extreme of governmental allocative intervention, the federal government nonetheless does possess considerable financial power and authority to divert resources toward defense production and it does direct the defense operation.

---

[11] Walter W. Heller, "Economics and the Applied Theory of Public Expenditures," *Federal Expenditure Policy for Economic Growth and Stability*, Joint Economic Committee, 85th cong., 1st sess. (Washington, D.C.: U.S. Government Printing Office, 1957), pp. 106–7.

[12] Henry C. Wallich, *The Cost of Freedom* (New York: Harper & Row, 1960).

TABLE 1–1   Alternative public sector resource allocation instruments

Degree of influence		Description of instrument
100 percent	1.	The public sector finances and produces an economic good. In addition, it produces all components of the good, and it owns or directly controls all productive resources used in producing these components. Moreover, the good is financed by taxation.
	2.	The public sector finances and produces an economic good, but purchases some or all of the components or productive resources, including labor, in the market. It does not charge directly for the good but instead finances it via taxation.
	3.	Monetary system owned or basically controlled by the public sector.
	4.	The government produces or supplies an economic good, but finances it through user prices rather than by taxation (commercial principle).
	5.	Substantial subsidy plus direct (public utility) regulation of an economic good produced by private enterprise in the market.
	6.	Combined public-private ownership of a firm, or publicly and privately owned firms coexisting in the same industry.
50 percent	7.	Substantial subsidy of a market-produced good.
	8.	Direct (public utility) regulation of a market-produced good.
	9.	Tax penalty to ration consumption of a good or resource.
	10.	Product and production quality and safety standards.
	11.	Public sector licensing of private enterprise in the form of charters, franchises, and licenses, or the issuance by government of patent rights.
	12.	General antitrust regulation.
	13.	Transfer-type operations and other fiscal actions which directly redistribute income, wealth, and political voting power and thus indirectly change the pattern of allocation.
	14.	Governmental definition of property rights.
0		

Note: Positioning of numbered instruments shows percentage ranking of approximate degree of directness and completeness of public sector allocational influence. Groupings imply the same approximate degree of influence by different instruments.

Hence, the approximate directness and completeness of the public sector influence on national defense in the United States is indicated by *point 2* on the continuum. At this position the public sector finances and produces the final good, but it buys some or all of the intermediate components or productive resources on the market. The good is supplied without direct charge to all users and is paid for by taxes.

The federal government also influences the performance of the U.S. money and banking system in a significant manner. The monetary tools of the Federal Reserve System affect the supply of money and credit through their influence on the behavior of a fractional reserve commercial banking system. Moreover, the federal government issues all circulating currency and coins. However, the Federal Reserve System is, in a sense, only a quasi-governmental body. The 12 regional banks are owned by the commercial banks of their respective areas, and they are partially managed by business and banking representatives of the regions they serve. Thus, *point 3* on the continuum denotes the approximate influence of the federal government on the allocation of money and banking services in the economy. Indeed, it is a substantial influence. Yet, it is not a direct or complete one in the polar sense.

Another substantial, though not complete, intervention instrument is represented by the so-called commercial principal through which the public sector produces or supplies a privately-produced economic good, but sells it via a user charge or price rather than supplying it free to its users. The sale of water by a municipal water utility, of transportation services by the federally owned Alaska Railroad, of timber by the U.S. Forest Service, or of liquor by a state-owned liquor store illustrate a few of the numerous examples of user pricing in the American public sector. This instrument is represented at *point 4* on the continuum.

The public sector may influence resource allocation by combining subsidies and direct (public utility) regulation. Each of these instruments, of course, may also be used separately. The "combined" subsidy-direct regulation instrument of allocation would be located approximately at *point 5* on the continuum, if the subsidies and regulation are substantial.

Subsidies can take a variety of forms. A subsidy, for example, can be derived from the spending side of a government budget in the form of an outright monetary payment to a private economic agent, or as a productive resource or economic good provided to the private agent. The purchase of farm products above market price by the Commodity Credit Corporation is representative of the expenditure type of subsidy. Partial expenditure subsidies occur when government provides a productive resource or an economic good to a private economic unit at a price below the cost of providing the resource or good. Long-term, low-interest loans and commercial mailing privileges are examples of this type of subsidy. On the revenue side of the government budget, subsidies may take the subtle and disguised form of tax preferences (loopholes) designed to reduce the tax burdens of certain groups, or industries, or occupations. Regardless of their obscurity, such subsidies, known as *tax expenditures*,[13] may nonetheless be of significant monetary importance to their recipients.

Direct regulation as an instrument is best exemplified by public

---

[13] *Tax expenditures* are described in greater detail in Chapters 8 and 9.

utility regulation in the United States. All states presently have public utility commissions. In addition, many municipalities have regulatory bureaus, and the federal government sponsors such regulatory agencies as the Interstate Commerce Commission, Civil Aeronautics Board, Federal Power Commission, Federal Communications Commission, and the Securities and Exchange Commission. Public utility regulation provides direct control over private business firms in such economic facets as (1) the conditions of entry into the industry, (2) price of service, (3) quantity of service, and (4) quality of service.

Although the "combined" subsidization and public utility regulation instruments, represented by *point 5*, do not constitute the polar extreme of direct and complete public sector allocation, they do indicate a substantial influence by the public sector on the allocation of economic resources.

An allocational instrument which may be located on the continuum at approximately the same point as the combined subsidy-direct regulation instrument is the combined public-private ownership means of allocation (*point 6*). This technique can be applied to a firm or to an industry. Examples of firms include public corporations with tripartite control such as those employed in the French electricity and railroad industries. In the United States, the Communications Satellite Corporation (Comsat), as created by Congress, contains many features of joint government-market ownership and control of a firm. The development of nuclear energy under the direction of the Atomic Energy Commission (AEC) with the cooperation of private enterprise constitutes another example of such a partnership, as does the research-oriented Sandia Corporation, which is owned by the Atomic Energy Commission and operated by the American Telephone and Telegraph Company. An industrywide application of this instrument is Canada's transcontinental railroad service, in which two companies, one government-owned and the other private, provide virtually parallel routes. A similar arrangement is found in the domestic airline industry of Australia. In the United States, the Tennessee Valley Authority provides a yardstick of competition to privately-owned utilities in the Tennessee Valley region. The partnership or coexisting firms instrument thus serves as a compromise between the extremes of direct and complete public sector allocational influence and no public sector allocational influence at all.

While combined subsidies and direct public utility regulation provide substantial allocation influence, as noted above, subsidies and direct regulation sometimes exist on a largely separate basis in the American economy. When this occurs, the degree of public sector allocational influence is necessarily less than when the two instruments are used jointly. It is estimated in Table 1-1 that separate usage of the subsidy instrument and the direct regulation instrument would fall at *points 7* and *8*, respectively, along the continuum. The subsidy or direct regulation would need to be substantial, of course, in order to provide even this degree of allocation influence. Slight or unimportant subsidies and weak regulation would fall much further down the continuum.

Point 9 on the continuum represents an estimate of the relative importance of tax penalties as an instrument of allocational influence by the public sector. At times, the objective of governmental allocational intervention may be to discourage rather than encourage consumption or production. Prevailing community feelings regarding the consumption of liquor and tobacco products, for example, may result in the classification of these economic goods as vices or demerit goods whose use should be discouraged. Given such community preferences, the public sector may impose substantial excise taxes, known as *sumptuary taxes,* on the consumption of liquor and tobacco products.[14] Similarly, scarce energy supplies may lead to sumptuary energy taxes designed to discourage use. Government also sets safety standards for products such as food, automobiles, and children's toys, and for production activities such as the Environmental Protection Agency's controls over air and water pollution. *Point 10* represents private sector controls of this kind.

The public sector can restrict entry to professions and industries via the issuance of charters, franchises, or licenses. Such policies sometimes worsen rather than improve allocational efficiency because they increase or protect monopoly power within an industry. At times, however, they can improve allocation by conserving uniquely scarce or important productive resources. The issuance of charters, franchises, or licenses is located at *point 11* on the continuum. The policy of governmentally granted patent rights to the private sector constitutes a similar form of allocational intervention that also may be placed at this point.

General antitrust regulation in the United States, for the most part, has been a modest influence on private sector allocational activities. As a result, this instrument is placed toward the lower end of the continuum, at *point 12* in Table 1-1. Moreover, a subtle and indirect instrument whereby government may influence resource usage is through a change in effective demand brought about by a redistribution of private sector income and wealth or of public sector voting influence, so that a different pattern of societal allocation decisions results (see *point 13*). Examples of this technique include: (1) government transfer payments, which do not directly absorb resources, (2) the pattern in which tax burdens are distributed, (3) the manner in which an asymmetrical, or unequally distributed, public debt is main-

---

[14] See the discussion of sumptuary taxation in Chapter 12.

tained in terms of taxes collected and interest payments made on the debt, and (4) the effect of government subsidies and contracts on the distribution of private income *before* transfers and taxes. In general, the public sector budget can be employed to change a given distributional structure and, in so doing, can change the pattern of resource allocation in the society. In any event, since this technique only indirectly influences allocation while working directly on the distributional objective of public sector economics, it is classified as an indirect and incomplete governmental allocation instrument.

Finally, by its ability to define property rights, the public sector can create an environment whereby the market process will exert particular allocation outcomes. This type of influence is represented by *point 14* in Table 1-1.

It is clear that the various instruments of public sector allocation intervention described above represent a wide range of allocational influence. Unfortunately, conventional methods used to measure the size of the public sector within the aggregate economy do not fully capture the effects of the less-direct and less-comprehensive interventionary instruments, since they concentrate on more direct magnitudes such as government purchases, or on government purchases plus transfer payments, as a proportion of GNP. However, an effort toward solving this measurement problem will be described in Chapter 16. Finally, it may also be pointed out that the thrust of analysis in this book will be on those public sector allocational instruments that are primarily of a budgetary (fiscal) nature.

2

The concept of public goods:
Reasons for governmental
allocation intervention

Following a basically general-equilibrium approach, Chapter 1 considered the conditions required for optimal resource allocation between the private and public sectors of the economy. This chapter, following an essentially partial-equilibrium approach, will analyze the nature of those economic goods that are typically provided by the public sector. In so doing, it will give an economic argument for the existence of a public sector for resource allocation purposes in a market-oriented society.

Conceivably, all resource-allocation decisions could be made within the market mechanism, except for such fundamental government functions as providing minimal law and order, protecting property rights, and enforcing contracts. Moreover, the market more closely approximates the political nature of democratic governments preferred by Western nations. Why, then, do substantial public sectors exist for resource allocation purposes in *all* democratic industrial nations? This question will be answered in the present chapter.

HISTORICAL EVOLUTION OF PUBLIC SECTOR ARGUMENTS

In *The Wealth of Nations* (written in 1776), Adam Smith, the father of modern capitalism, enumerated four "justifiable" categories of government allocational activity.[1] These were:

---

[1] Adam Smith, *The Wealth of Nations* (London: Routledge, 1913), book 5, pp. 541–644.

1. The duty of protecting the society from violence and invasion by other independent societies; this, of course, is the function of national defense.
2. The duty of protecting every member of a society from the injustice or oppression of every other member of the society. This reflects the obligation of establishing an administration of justice which provides law and order within the society so that the market economy may function.
3. The duty of establishing and maintaining highly beneficial public institutions and public works which are of such a nature that the profit they could earn would never repay the expense to any individual or small number of individuals to provide them. Therefore, it cannot be expected that funds for these services would be supplied in adequate quantities.
4. The duty of meeting the expenses necessary for support of the sovereign, which vary depending on the form of political structure.

Though Smith often has been described as a bold advocate of minimal governmental activity, his writings fail to indicate significant opposition to a public sector for allocational purposes in the society. To the contrary, the four functions of government described above together would require a level of public sector resource allocation substantially greater than a laissez-faire economic system would allow.[2] The most relevant of Smith's four functions of government are the first and the third, namely, the national defense and public works functions. The second function, that of providing domestic stability in the form of law and order and the protection of property, and the fourth, that of maintaining the sovereign or executive level of government, could be logically opposed only by an avowed anarchist. Since these are not controversial functions of government, they do not require a lengthy analysis in the effort to construct an economic case for the existence of a public sector for resource allocation purposes in a market-oriented economy.

The national defense and the public works functions, however, are not so intrinsic to governmental provision as are the justice and sovereign support functions. Defense, for example, need not be as much of a collective undertaking in a primitive society as it is in modern society. Smith observed, quite accurately, that government becomes involved increasingly in the defense function as a society "advances in civilization."[3] He recognized the change introduced into the art of

---

[2] *Laissez-faire,* in this context, refers to private sector resource determination in all areas of economic activity except for the use of resources by government to provide minimal law and order, to protect private property rights, and to enforce contracts in the society.

[3] Smith, *Wealth of Nations,* p. 555.

warfare by the invention of firearms as a significant cost-increasing factor. Yet, little controversy exists in advanced nations regarding the necessary role of government in the allocation of national defense. However, the economic reasons why governmental supply control of the defense function is necessary are not immediately obvious and will be developed as part of the analysis of this chapter.

The public works function also requires further discussion. Smith observed that certain social capital items like roads, bridges, canals, and harbors would not be allocated without the influence of government because they could not be provided by private enterprise on a profitable basis. Similarly, John Stuart Mill, in his *Principles of Political Economy* (1848), argued that in the particular conditions of a given age or nation "there is scarcely anything really important to the general interest, which it may not be desirable, or even necessary, that the government should take upon itself, not because private individuals cannot effectively perform it, but *because they will not*" (italics added).[4] Thus, Mill believed that at certain times and places the public sector would be required to provide roads, docks, harbors, canals, irrigation works, hospitals, schools, colleges, printing presses, and other public works.

Many years later, John Maynard Keynes reiterated the viewpoints of Smith and Mill on the importance of public works allocation by government. Keynes commented: "Government is not to do things which individuals are doing already, and to do them a little better or a little worse; but to do those things which at the present are not done at all."[5] The position of Smith, Mill, and Keynes on public works will be developed later in this chapter as part of the discussion of the decreasing cost and imperfect market structure characteristics of public-type goods.

It has been observed that the development of economic theory in the Western world has demonstrated an appreciation of the need for governmental resource allocation in a system characterized by a basic preference for private sector economic activity. The approach of this chapter in developing a comprehensive economic case for the existence of a public sector for allocational purposes in a market-oriented society will rest on the failure of the market to optimally allocate all of society's resources. For reasons to be demonstrated below, this case must be viewed as providing a *necessary*, but not in all instances a *sufficient*, condition for public sector allocational intervention. In developing the case, the inherent characteristics of such phenomena as public goods, externalities, and natural monopolies will be demonstrated.

---

[4] John Stuart Mill, *Principles of Political Economy* (London: Longmans, Green, 1926), p. 978.

[5] John Maynard Keynes, "The End of Laissez-faire," in *Laissez-faire and Communism* (New York: New Republic, 1926), p. 67.

THE ECONOMIC CASE FOR A PUBLIC SECTOR
TO ALLOCATE RESOURCES

The economic arguments for a public sector which follow are presented in the context of the *allocation function* of economics. Though other economic arguments for the existence of government intervention may be developed in terms of the distribution and stabilization functions of an economic system, these will not be an important part of the present analysis. The allocative case for a public sector (beyond that which would supply minimal law and order, the protection of property rights, and the enforcement of contracts) will focus on problems which can cause partial failure in the efforts of the market to allocate resources and thus to produce a social-optimum output. These include:

1. Decreasing costs of production and imperfect market structure.
2. Zero marginal cost—the polar extreme of decreasing production costs.
3. Joint (collective) consumption with nonexclusion.
4. Significant economic effects (externalities) not captured by the price system.
5. Special supply phenomena which can cause failure in market efforts to allocate resources.

Decreasing costs of production and imperfect market structure[6]

A significant allocational complication arises under conditions of imperfect market structure[7] (pure monopoly, oligopoly, monopolistic competition). Such markets, of course, are prevalent in the American economy. Under imperfectly competitive conditions, the *best profit point of production* for the firm—marginal cost equal to marginal revenue—does not coincide with the *optimal social allocation* point for the society—marginal cost equal to average revenue (price). However, these points do coincide under conditions of perfect (pure) competition, where many sellers and buyers are present in the market and the product is homogeneous.

The contrast between perfect and imperfect markets in this regard is demonstrated in Figure 2–1. Figure 2–1a illustrates the case of the *perfectly competitive firm* which, while producing its best profit output (*OA*) at point *a*, where marginal cost (*MC*) equals marginal

---

[6] This concept has been developed over many years with significant contributions by Adam Smith, John Stuart Mill, Leon Walras, Alfred Marshall, A. C. Pigou, A. Bergson, H. Hotelling, Paul Samuelson, Frances Bator, and others. A thorough presentation of this concept may be found in Francis M. Bator, *The Question of Government Spending* (New York: Harper & Row, 1960).

[7] See Chapter 7 for a further description of the characteristics of imperfect markets.

FIGURE 2–1   **Pricing and output under perfectly competitive and imperfectly competitive conditions**

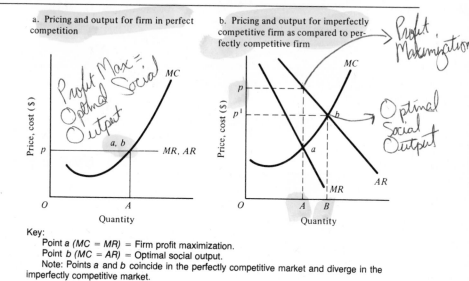

a. Pricing and output for firm in perfect competition

b. Pricing and output for imperfectly competitive firm as compared to perfectly competitive firm

Key:
Point a (MC = MR) = Firm profit maximization.
Point b (MC = AR) = Optimal social output.
Note: Points a and b coincide in the perfectly competitive market and diverge in the imperfectly competitive market.

revenue (MR), is simultaneously producing the social optimum output, where marginal cost equals average revenue (AR, price) at point b. Thus, output is carried up to the point where the additional cost of the marginal unit just equals the price that people are willing to pay for it. In this instance, consumer sovereignty determines output in a social optimum manner. Moreover, as the firm produces at the output where price (average revenue) is equal to marginal cost, it is certain in the long run that the total costs of the firm will not exceed total revenues, as the firm produces the social optimum output.

It can be seen in Figure 2–1b, however, that in an *imperfect market* (an exemplified here by a pure monopoly), the best-profit output, OA, as determined by the intersection of marginal cost and marginal revenue at point a, does not also yield the optimal social output, OB, as determined at point b, where marginal cost is equal to average revenue. Hence, the firm in an imperfect market, in achieving its profit-maximizing output, selects a price-quantity combination where marginal cost is less than average revenue. This is possible due to individual firm monopoly power (control over price). Thus, efficient social allocation in conformance with consumer sovereignty is *not* attained.

The misallocation of output in Figure 2–1b, if the firm maximizes its profits, is represented by the reduced output AB. In other words, OA is the best-profit output, OB is the optimal social output, and AB is the amount of misallocated (reduced) output in violation of consumer sovereignty. If the economic good in question is deemed socially necessary or desirable by a collective consensus of the society, an argument may be established for possible public sector influence on the allocation of the good so as to attain a quantity closer to, if not actually at, the optimum social output, *OB*.

Importantly, the optimum social quantity, *OB, cannot be produced at a profit* if the firm faces decreasing production costs at that output point. Inevitably, total costs would exceed total revenues under these conditions. This phenomenon is closely associated with the economic concept of *natural monopolies* in which long-run scale economies in production result in total supply control by a single producer, in the pure case, or by a few oligopoly producers in a variant case.

As Figure 2-2 shows, the firm could produce the social-optimum output, *OB,* only at a *loss*. This is true because under conditions of decreasing average cost, marginal cost must be below average cost, causing the intersection of marginal cost and average revenue (price) at point *b* to be where average revenue, *P¹*, is less than average cost, *C¹*. Consequently, total losses are *wxyz* when optimal social output, *OB,* is produced. Loss per unit is the vertical amount (distance) *C¹P¹*, *wx,* or *zy*. There could be no output of the good in the long run, since the losses could not be sustained during this time period by a private

---

FIGURE 2-2   **Loss at point of optimal social output under decreasing production costs in an imperfect market**

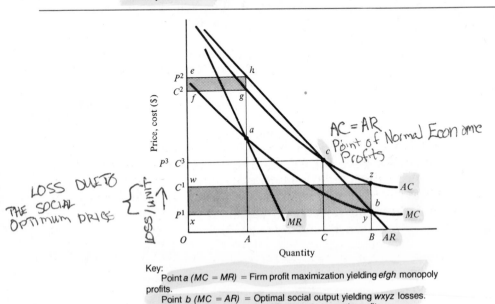

Key:
   Point *a (MC = MR)* = Firm profit maximization yielding *efgh* monopoly profits.
   Point *b (MC = AR)* = Optimal social output yielding *wxyz* losses.
   Point *c (AC = AR)* = Point of normal economic profits.

firm. This situation bears a close resemblance to the traditional historical arguments, cited earlier in the chapter, that the public sector should influence the provision of those desirable economic goods which the private sector does not provide in adequate quantities, if at all, because of its inability to produce them profitably.

Since losses cannot be sustained in the long run by a private firm, public sector allocational influence such as governmental production of the good and its sale through user prices (along with partial tax financing), or subsidization of the private firm losses, would be required if the good is to be provided in the optimum social quantity, OB.[8] Alternately, the public sector could require, through public utility regulation, that the private firm produce output, OC, as determined by the intersection of average cost (C^3) and average revenue (P^3) at point c, or a slightly smaller output yielding small monopoly profits. At point c, the firm would be earning a "normal" economic profit, with the unit price equaling the unit cost, and it would be producing an output, OC, which is closer to the optimum social output, OB, than is the profit-maximizing output for the firm, OA. The latter is determined by the intersection of the marginal cost and marginal revenue curves at point a. In any event, the combined presence of the imperfect market structure and decreasing production cost conditions for an important economic good, especially if the decreasing-cost conditions prevail over the *entire range of feasible outputs*, represents a degree of allocational failure in the market which strengthens the case for possible governmental allocative influence.[9]

Zero marginal cost

A polar or extreme case of the above phenomenon exists for those economic goods whose short-run marginal costs are zero. In Figure 2–3, the marginal cost curve (MC) coincides with the horizontal axis. At the optimum social output, OB, which is determined by the intersection of marginal cost (MC) and average revenue (AR) at point a, allocational efficiency, strictly speaking, would require that the price of the good be zero since the marginal cost is zero. In other words, this extreme variation of the decreasing-cost phenomenon would require that the good be provided *free of charge*, since it can be consumed by additional individuals without an increase in production costs.

---

[8] A detailed analysis of this subject is presented in Chapter 15.

[9] However, this does not suggest that a mandate exists for the public sector to force output to be at the $MC = AR$ level for *all* goods produced in imperfect markets. It is argued that the case for governmental allocational influence is strengthened when imperfect markets and decreasing production cost conditions coexist, but it is *not* argued that production at or near the $MC = AR$ point is to be sought in every instance.

FIGURE 2–3   **The polar case of zero short-run marginal cost**

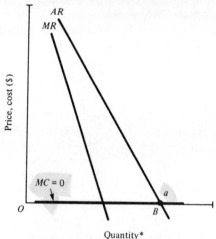

Quantity*
(number of consumers at a given level of ouput)

Note: *MC* = 0 at the optimal social output point,
point *a*, where *MC* = *AR*.
* For an explicit description of the term *quantity*,
as used here, see the discussion of Figures 2–3 and
2–5 in the text.

Francis Bator refers to this polar case of decreasing costs as involving public goods, that is, a jointly consumed good whose consumption by consumer X would lead to no subtraction from what is left over for consumption by consumers Y and Z.[10] One more radio listener, television viewer, or citizen protected by national defense need not subtract from the consumption of these activities by someone else. For example, if the marginal cost of an additional person tuning in a television program is zero, the consumption of the television program can be increased without decreasing the consumption of any other good by drawing scarce resources away from the production of the other good. Any price charged for television reception, whether a uniform price or a variable price imposed in a discriminatory manner between con-

---

[10] Bator, *Question of Government Spending,* p. 94. Some economists refer to the phenomenon of marginal cost equal to zero as a special case of *joint supply.* For example, see J. G. Head, "Public Goods and Public Policy," *Public Finance,* no. 3 (1962), pp. 197–219. However, these economists readily point out that a basic difference exists between joint supply in this sense and joint supply in the sense developed by the British economist, Alfred Marshall. The term in the Marshallian context follows the market mechanism more closely. For example, jointly supplied mutton and wool are divisible economic goods that can be exchanged through the price system. On the other hand, jointly supplied public goods are usually intangible services which are jointly consumed and impossible to resell.

sumers, would misallocate resources, since consumption would be reduced below the quantity that would be consumed at the optimum social point where price equals marginal cost. That is, if the marginal cost of an additional unit of consumption is zero, price must be zero if resources are to be allocated in accordance with the optimum social allocation rule. It is significant that private profit would be impossible with a zero price.

It is extremely important to distinguish between "quantity" in the sense of additional units of consumption and quantity in terms of a higher level of production. In Figure 2–3, the marginal cost is zero $(MC = 0)$ for supplying a given level of television transmission for *consumption* by additional viewers, within the geographical range of the transmission, who may tune in the program being transmitted. However, the marginal cost would be greater than zero $(MC > 0)$ for the *production* of a higher level of television transmission which would widen the geographical area within which potential viewers may tune in the program. Realistically, the latter may be viewed as the expansion of capacity in a *long-run* time period, while the former may be viewed as a *short-run* phenomenon within a fixed capacity. While the short-run total cost of a public good will be *constant,* the long-run total cost will *vary* with the level (scale) of output.

For example, with a fixed transmission range capable of reaching (say) 25,000 potential viewers, the marginal cost of the second viewer on up to viewer number 25,000 is zero. However, an increase in the transmission capacity so that 50,000 potential consumers, instead of 25,000, may watch the program obviously requires additional production costs. Consequently, it can be said that additional consumption of the *service* within the present short-run capacity to produce it can be enjoyed at a zero marginal cost. Alternatively, a long-run expansion in the scale or capacity to provide the *service* would be attained only after incurring additional marginal costs.

The italicizing of the word *service* in the above paragraph draws attention to the fact that an economic good which can be consumed within a given production level by one individual, without reducing the quantity available to someone else, is likely to be an intangible service.[11] Such an intangible service could be consumed at a marginal supply cost of zero (in the short-run cost sense) by two or more individuals. Hence, the *other dimension* of the supply characteristic of zero marginal cost is, indeed, the demand characteristic of joint consumption, whereby the benefits of an economic good are indivisible among two or more consumers. That is, the additional consumption of an economic good at zero marginal cost involves the important

---

[11] However, not *all* services are subject to the unique characteristics of joint consumption. The services of a doctor, dentist, attorney, or tax accountant, for example, are normally specialized for the private benefit of a particular consumer.

demand phenomenon of joint or collective consumption—a concept which will be discussed next.

The concept of joint (collective) consumption with nonexclusion

The most important component of the allocative argument for the existence of a public sector in a market-oriented society is the concept of *joint* or *collective consumption* with *nonexclusion*. The primary characteristic of jointly consumed economic goods is that they are *indivisible* in the sense that they can be consumed on a *nonrival* basis by two or more persons at the same time. That is, consumption by one person does not deny consumption to anyone else. In the extreme case of all benefits being indivisible, the good is normally called a *pure public good.*[12] When such a good is supplied in the economy, it is consumed in equal amounts by all consumers.[13] Morover, no one can be excluded from its consumption by a failure to pay for it voluntarily.[14]

A *pure private good*, however, is subject to the exclusion principle. That is, an individual can be excluded or prevented from consuming the good if he or she does not voluntarily pay for it. Such a good is completely subject to the pricing mechanism. All of the benefits are *divisible* on a private basis to the purchaser. None are jointly consumed. If one person consumes the good, another person does not consume it. The consumption is *rival* in nature.

Thus, if W reflects the total market (industry) quantity for a pure private good such as bread, and the society has two consumers, A and B, and if W_a and W_b represent the quantities of the private good consumed by A and B, respectively, then W must equal the summation of W_a and W_b. If consumer A used more of good W, consumer B must use less under conditions of full resource employment. There exists a *rivalry in consumption* between consumers A and B. For example, if the market supplies 20 units of the private good, W, and consumer A consumes 15 units, 5 units remain for consumption by consumer B. The consumption is rival, since consumer A could consume only 10 units of the good if consumer B consumes 10 instead of 5 units. Moreover, a consumer who does not voluntarily pay the price can be excluded from consuming the good.

On the other hand, a jointly consumed economic good such as

---

[12] The term *public good* may be used interchangeably with the term *social good.* In either case, the important characteristic of joint consumption is present.

[13] Consumption in an equal amount applies to *pure* public goods, but not to *quasi*-public (nonpure, intermediate, or mixed) goods, as will be explained below.

[14] Technically speaking, exclusion is possible for most economic goods, but only at such prohibitive cost in some cases that it can appropriately be said that exclusion is impossible. This topic will be discussed further in this section.

national defense is not divisible among consumers. Once supplied at a particular level or scale, it is jointly consumed on an equal basis by all consumers in the society. Here there exists a *nonrivalry in consumption* between consumers A and B. There is no way by which consumer A in consuming more can cause consumer B to consume less. Thus, Z can reflect the total quantity of the pure public good and Z_a and Z_b can refer to consumer A's and consumer B's consumption of the good Since the consumption of the total cannot be divided between A and B, the relevant equations are $Z = Z_a$ and $Z = Z_b$, respectively. If the good is supplied to one of the consumers, it must also be supplied at the same level to the other consumer regardless of any financial contribution. Hence, the exclusion principle does not apply to the collectively consumed good, and A and B each individually consume the total quantity of the economic good. The difference between a pure private good whose benefits are subject to the exclusion principle, and a good of the pure public variety whose benefits are not subject to the principle, can be demonstrated further as follows:

Assume that the total production of each good (bread and national defense, for example) is equal to 20 units. In the case of the pure private good: consumptions by A&B

$$W = W_a + W_b$$
$$20 = 15 + 5$$

W = total market (industry) quantity for a pure private good

In the case of the pure public good:

$$Z = Z_a \qquad Z = Z_b$$
$$20 = 20 \qquad 20 = 20$$

Z = total quantity of pure public good

The exclusion principle does apply to the pure private good, W, but it does *not* apply to the pure public good, Z.

Figure 2–4 demonstrates in graphic terms the conventional *horizontal* summation of individual demands to obtain industry demand under conditions where the exclusion principle applies with a divisible pure private good. A summation of the 15 units (loaves of bread) demanded by consumer A and 5 units demanded by consumer B at a price of 50 cents per unit results in a total industry demand (for bread) of 20 units. Consumers A and B can purchase the desired quantities of the good at the going industry price.

Figure 2–5 represents the unconventional *vertical* summation of the individual demand curves, Z_a and Z_b, to obtain the industry demand curve, Z, in the case of an indivisible pure public good. The exclusion principle cannot be applied to the consumption of the benefits of this good; consumers A and B each individually consume the total quantity (20 units) of the pure public good. Thus, the individual demands by consumers A and B for the pure public good have been summed vertically to obtain the industry demand, instead of horizon-

FIGURE 2-4   **Horizontal demand summation for a pure private good (exclusion principle applies)***

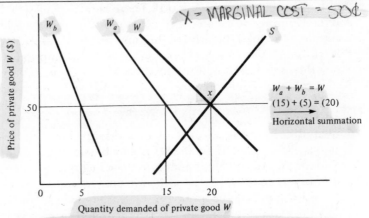

* Note that the quantity demanded by each consumer varies at a fixed price.

tally as with the pure private good.[15] The joint consumption of the indivisible pure public good precludes the individual consumer from being able to vary the quantities of the good that would be purchased at a particular market price. Instead, all individuals must consume equal amounts of the good, regardless of the price they might be willing to pay for that quantity of the good. In the case illustrated in Figure 2-5, consumer A would be willing to pay 35 cents and consumer B 15 cents for 20 units of the public good, if an exclusionary price could be worked out as it can be for a pure private good.

In comparing Figures 2-4 and 2-5, it is important to note that the market has worked better to meet consumer preferences in the private good than in the public good case. This is true because *the marginal benefit* to each consumer at the quantity each selects (Figure 2-4) is 50 cents, but this is also the *marginal cost* of the good as determined at point *x*. By contrast, the marginal benefit to each consumer in the public good case must be summed (35 cents + 15 cents) in order to equal the marginal cost of 50 cents at point *y* in Figure 2-5. Relatedly, each consumer is unable to vary the quantity purchased at 50 cents— in the public good case—unlike the private good case (Figure 2-4) in which each consumer selects the desired quantity at the prevailing

---

[15] The vertically summed industry demand curve may also be viewed appropriately as a *"pseudo*-demand curve," since joint consumption induces consumers *not* to reveal their preferences, especially under conditions of large-group consumption. Nonetheless, basic consumer preferences still exist in reference to the good, and in this generic sense it remains valid to refer to curve Z as an *orthodox* industry demand curve.

price of 50 cents. In other words, the "nonmarket" characteristic of price variance for a fixed quantity occurs in the public good case, while the traditional "market" characteristic of quantity variance at a fixed price occurs in the private good case.

It may be asked why the "more efficient" private good solution fails in the public good case. The answer is that the nature of joint consumption often induces a problem involving nonexclusion, which helps to make the pricing of jointly consumed goods difficult or impossible. Moreover, exclusion tends to become more difficult as the size of the consuming group becomes larger. This problem, called the *free-rider problem,* may be further clarified by the following example: A person with $500 might decide to spend the money for new clothes, knowing that the clothes cannot be acquired without payment. The individual can be excluded from consuming the clothes by deciding not to voluntarily exchange money for them. On the other hand, the same person would not volunteer a $500 contribution to the federal government to help finance national defense, since consumption of defense is the same for all persons in the society once it is supplied— even if a given person does not pay for it. Thus, an individual will be motivated to become a "free-rider," since he or she cannot be excluded from consuming the benefits of defense by a failure to volun-

FIGURE 2–5 **Vertical demand summation for a pure public good (exclusion principle does not apply)***

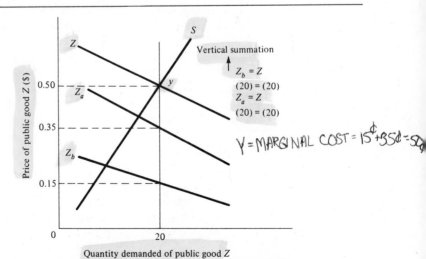

Quantity demanded of public good Z

* Note that the price which each consumer would be willing to pay varies for a fixed quantity of the economic good. This should be contrasted with the results in Figure 2-4 in which the quantity demanded by each consumer varies at a fixed price, rather than vice versa.

tarily pay for them. While conceivably only *two consumers*, (as presented in Figure 2–5 for simplicity of presentation) might be able to negotiate an agreement whereby each would share the cost of the jointly consumed good, such a solution could not be negotiated over the large national group consuming defense benefits. As a result, exclusion is impossible, and the free-rider problem would prevail. Hence, such a pure public good would not be supplied by the market since it cannot be priced, and unless the public sector finances the good through compulsory means such as taxation, it will not be supplied at all. Even a discriminating monopolist, attempting to charge differential prices based on differential preferences for the good, would be unsuccessful due to the inability to apply the exclusion principle.

It is important to distinguish further between the concepts of zero marginal cost and joint consumption. The presence of conditions whereby an additional consumer can enjoy an economic good at no additional short-run cost must involve the joint consumption of that good by two or more individuals. However, this condition of zero marginal cost does *not* necessarily mean that the good must "ultimately" be jointly consumed. Instead, it may be possible to incur additional costs and, by so doing, to supply the good on an exclusion (pricing) basis to the individual consumers.

The ability to convert a zero marginal cost—joint consumption arrangement to a pricing or exclusion arrangement is determined by such factors as the technical ability to exclude consumption of the good from nonpaying individuals, and the size of the consuming group. Free-rider efforts, which are a natural outgrowth of joint consumption, will fail if exclusion is successful. The ability to exclude, as noted, will depend partly on the technical feasibility of exclusion and, subsequently, on the costs of exclusion. The costs will tend to become greater as the consuming group becomes larger. Moreover, the pure public good, national defense, exemplifies an economic good for which the technical feasibility of exclusion is lacking and the costs of exclusion, due to the large size of the consuming group, are prohibitive. This might be contrasted to the transmission of a television program for which a technologically available scrambling device can exclude consumption if payment is not made.[16]

Supplying national defense protection thus involves both zero marginal cost for protecting an additional citizen at a given level of defense output, as well as complete joint consumption, since an individual cannot be excluded from consuming national security benefits

---

[16] Though technical exclusion is possible in this case, the cost of such exclusion, as well as other considerations of its desirability, must still be considered.

in the same amount as other individuals in the society.[17] In this case, the combined presence of both conditions, zero marginal cost and joint consumption with nonexclusion, for an important economic good provides a strong argument for public sector allocational intervention. This represents the polar case of a pure public good. The large size of the consuming group provides a firm basis for the free-rider motivation, and voluntary financing of defense from the private sector will *not* be forthcoming. As a result, tax financing of defense by government becomes a necessity.

The concept of externalities

Many economic actions undertaken by producers and consumers exert external economic effects on other producers and consumers, which effects escape the price mechanism. Such nonmarket effects are commonly known as *externalities,* but the terms *spillovers* or *neighborhood effects* are also used to refer to this phenomenon. An *externality* may be viewed as an economic gain or loss accruing to one or more recipient agents as the result of an economic action initiated by another agent—with the gain or loss *not* being reflected in a market price. The initiating or the recipient economic agent may be either a producer or a consumer.

In the producer sense, the initiating agent will normally be motivated by a *profit goal.* In the consumer sense, the initiating agent will normally be motivated by a *utility (satisfaction, welfare) goal.* If the recipient of an externality is a producer, the external gain or benefit will take the form of an improved profit or decreased loss position, while an external loss or cost will take the form of reduced profits or increased losses. If the recipient of an externality is a consumer, an external gain or benefit will take the form of increased utility (satisfaction, welfare), while an external loss or cost will take the form of reduced utility (dissatisfaction, loss of welfare). Thus, an external gain, whether of production or consumption, may be referred to as a *positive externality* or *external economy,* and an external loss, whether of production or consumption, may be designated a *negative externality* or *external diseconomy.*

Most actions initiated by an economic agent yield at least some effects which escape the price mechanism. Thus, externalities are rather commonplace, but often they are not economically significant.

---

[17] It should be noted that equal consumption of defense benefits does *not* mean equal utility derived by all persons from such benefits. For example, the utility or satisfaction would tend to be greater for a so-called hawk on defense matters as compared to a dove.

Table 2-1 summarizes the primary characteristics of externalities as discussed in this section. There are a number of possible externality combinations: (1) a consumption action may yield external production effects; (2) a production action may yield external consumption effects; (3) a consumption action may yield external consumption effects; and (4) a production action may yield external production effects. The possible combinations increase in number and complexity when both positive externalities (gains) and negative externalities (losses) are also considered. Moreover, an action undertaken by a given economic agent—such as a producer—may exert nonmarket effects on both other producers *and* consumers, while a consumer action may affect both other consumers and producers.

TABLE 2-1   Some characteristics of externalities

Initiating economic agent	Recipient economic agent
Consumer	Consumer
or	or
Producer	Producer
Type of Externality	Characteristics

Positive (external economy)	A benefit or gain
	  Increased profits or reduced losses to a
	    business
	  Increased utility (satisfaction, welfare) to a
	    consumer

Negative (external diseconomy)	A cost or loss
	  Reduced profits or increased losses to a
	    business
	  Disutility (dissatisfaction, reduced
	    welfare) to a consumer

For example, a firm manufacturing steel may acquire new blast furnaces which increase both the technical efficiency and the volume of its production. The explicit costs of acquiring this new productive capital are easily demonstrated via the price mechanism (assume an acquisition cost of $1 million). Now assume that the new blast furnaces significantly increase air pollution in the surrounding area—a result which diminishes both the profits of producers in a nearby recreational industry and the welfare of residential consumers. These other producers and consumers would incur *nonmarket costs* which are excluded from the $1 million acquisition cost of the new blast furnaces. Since these are not explicit market costs which the firm must calculate when assessing its profit position, there will be a tendency to oversupply the steel and thus to create the negative externalities; to the steel firm, the scarce resource, clean air, is not priced.

Thus, externalities are elusive, though real, and potential public interest derives from their very nature. There is no self-correcting market mechanism at work, since externalities, whether positive or negative, are not measured in price values. Moreover, it is difficult to convert many externalities to control through the market. Yet, as will be demonstrated, the mere presence of an externality does *not* provide a prima facie case for public sector allocational intervention. Nor, for that matter, does it necessarily require any corrective action at all.

The relationship between externalities and public sector allocation. The relationship between externalities and governmental allocative policy will be introduced in the terminology of the late British economist, A. C. Pigou, as developed earlier in the century.[18] Subsequent sophistication of the Pigovian analysis, especially in policy terms, will also be considered. Pigou distinguishes between private and social benefits and costs. *Private* benefits and costs represent those internal effects of an economic action which do not escape the price mechanism, and which thus are retained within the *economic calculus* of the initiating agent. *Social* benefits and costs represent both these internal private effects as well as certain external effects which do escape the price mechanism, and thus go beyond the *motivational calculus* of the initiating agent. The external benefits and costs are essentially nonmarket in character, and are the same as the externalities discussed earlier.

If social effects of a benefit variety exceed private benefits, it is said, in Pigovian terms, that an *external economy,* or *positive externality,* exists. In this instance, a private firm is likely to produce less than the social-optimum amount of an "economic good" because the firm is adding benefits to society greater than the quantity of benefits for which it is being compensated in the market. Relatedly, the recipients of these benefits have a free-rider motivation not to pay for them voluntarily. The typical Pigovian policy prescription to correct this undersupply is a governmental *subsidy* to the private producer to encourage production of the economic good which yields the external benefits.

If, however, social costs exceed private costs, it is said that an *external diseconomy,* or *negative externality,* is present. In this instance, there would be a tendency to provide an oversupply of the

---

[18] A. C. Pigou, *The Economics of Welfare* (London: Macmillan, 1920). Later important contributions to the theory of externalities include those of R. H. Coase, "The Problem of Social Cost," *Journal of Law and Economics,* October 1960, pp. 1–44; James M. Buchanan and William C. Stubblebine, "Externality," *Economica,* November 1962, pp. 371–79, and Otto Davis and Andrew Whinston, "Externalities, Welfare and the Theory of Games," *Journal of Political Economy,* June 1962, pp. 241–62. For excellent summaries of these contributions, see Ralph Turvey, "On Divergences between Social Cost and Private Cost," *Economica,* August 1963, pp. 309–13; and William J. Baumol, *Welfare Economics,* 2d ed. (Cambridge, Mass.: Harvard University Press, 1965), pp. 24–36.

"economic bad" represented in the negative externality, since the total cost of allocation is being absorbed, in part, by individuals or businesses other than the initiating economic agent. Of course, the supplier of the external costs will not voluntarily eliminate them, since they are not part of the economic maximization calculus. This is analogous to the free-rider problem in the external benefits case, in which the recipient of the benefits will not voluntarily offer payment for them. The typical Pigovian policy prescription to reduce the over-supply of the economic bad is a tax.

In economic circumstances such as these, where only partial exclusion prevails, economic goods, or positive externalities, will tend to be undersupplied, while economic bads, or negative externalities, will tend to be oversupplied. Moreover, this entails a different sort of economic good (or bad) than the polar cases of pure public good and pure private good discussed earlier. The good in this case possesses a mixture of private (priceable) and public (nonpriceable) effects. Thus it may be termed a *quasi, nonpure, intermediate,* or *mixed* good (or bad).

Figures 2–6 and 2–7 demonstrate the conditions of positive and negative externalities, respectively, and the application of the traditional corrective solutions. These solutions are frequently referred to as efforts to *internalize* the externalities, which carries the connotation of converting the external effects back into the price system. In Figure 2–6, curve D_e represents the demand for the nonpriced exter-

FIGURE 2–6   Internalization of positive externalities by means of a government subsidy

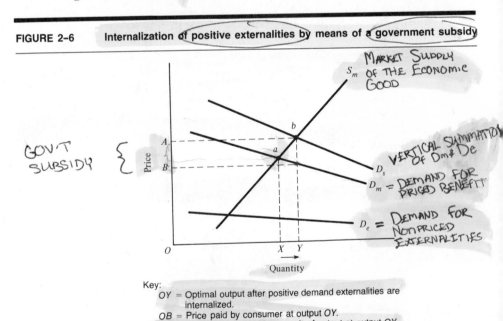

Key:
OY = Optimal output after positive demand externalities are internalized.
OB = Price paid by consumer at output OY.
AB = Government subsidy per unit of output at output OY.

FIGURE 2-7   Internalization of negative externalities by means of a government tax

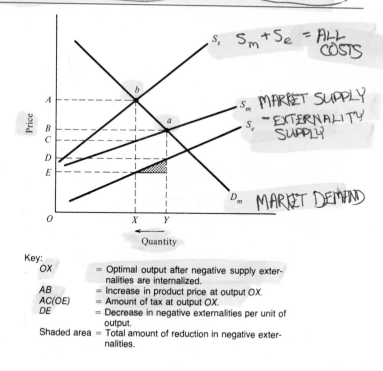

Key:

OX	= Optimal output after negative supply externalities are internalized.
AB	= Increase in product price at output OX.
AC(OE)	= Amount of tax at output OX.
DE	= Decrease in negative externalities per unit of output.
Shaded area	= Total amount of reduction in negative externalities.

nal benefits, curve D_m, the demand for the priced benefits, and curve D_s, the vertical summation of these two demand curves, since D_e involves joint consumption. Curve D_s represents social benefits, in the Pigovian sense, inclusive of *all* benefits whether priced or not. S_m represents the market (industry) supply of the economic good.

The price system calculates for only the internal benefits and costs, but not for the positive externalities contained in curve D_e. Hence, a suboptimal market equilibrium is reached at point *a*, yielding an undersupply of the good by the amount XY. It would take a government subsidy by the amount AB per unit of output to encourage the producers of the good to increase supply to the optimal output, OY.

Figure 2-7 demonstrates the traditional solution to negative externality problems such as those in the steel industry example above. D_m represents the market (industry) demand and S_m the market (industry) supply for the economic good. It is important to note that S_m includes only the direct, explicit costs incurred by the producer(s) of the good. It does *not* reflect the nonmarket costs (such as air pollution) which may be associated with the production of the good. These nonmarket costs, or negative externalities, which are not internalized in the market supply curve, are represented instead by supply curve S_e. When these nonmarket costs are added to the direct costs contained in curve S_m, supply curve S_s results. This supply curve represents social costs, in Pigovian terms, which constitutes *all costs*, that is, both internalized market costs and noninternalized external costs.

Thus, output OY of the product would result at intersection a if the external costs are ignored, but the smaller output, OX, would result at intersection b if these negative externalities are taken into account. Consequently, a tax equal to AC (OE), by reducing the quantity produced of the good from OY to OX, would also reduce the negative externalities associated with its production by the amount DE per unit of output at output OY, and overall by the shaded area indicated on the graph. Significantly, the efficient marginal solution, which equates the marginal social costs in the production of the good with marginal benefits, does not necessarily reduce pollution to zero. That is, it does not necessarily call for the elimination of all negative externalities. However, in extreme cases the efficient solution would be a reduction in the supply of the economic good to zero. For example, if one *assumes* that the construction of a nuclear power plant at a certain location will ultimately lead to the devastation of a nearby community through radiation, the equilibrium between marginal social benefits and marginal social costs might well correspond to a zero supply of nuclear energy at that location.

Next, it should be recognized that the mere existence of an externality does not in itself merit corrective action. It may be that a greater loss in welfare will occur from internalizing (correcting for) an externality through a resource reallocation than the gain in welfare to be realized from such an action. For example, the cost of internalizing a positive externality may be greater than the welfare gains acquired from the greater consumption of the good. Or the cost of internalizing a negative externality may exceed the welfare gains from a diminished supply of the economic bad. The basic economic concept of *opportunity cost* explains this fact, since any corrective action must bear a resource cost. Moreover, in some instances the externally damaged (or benefited) party may not even be motivated to seek corrective action. In this instance, the externality is not related to marginal costs, and an attempt to internalize it, such as through a governmental tax or subsidy, would have no economic influence whatsoever on its production (supply).

The cost of internalizing an externality through a resource reallocation, however, may warrant a policy adjustment in some cases. This would be true if the cost of internalization is less than the gain in welfare deriving from such an action. Yet, the public sector does not represent the only possible source of corrective policy. Moreover, public sector policy may involve regulation, tax, or subsidy and not

actual governmental production. In addition, private contractual negotiation, legal action, or other privately initiated means outside the
direct allocative intervention of government may constitute plausible
alternatives. That is, such market-oriented techniques may be capable
of internalizing the externality more efficiently than can be accomplished through the direct action of government. The opportunity for
such privately attained improvements in welfare will be enhanced
when the externalities are technologically capable of divisibility under the price system. At any one time, such divisibility will also reflect
the ability and willingness of the society to define property rights in
such a manner that the economic goods (benefits) or bads (costs) will
be salable and thus adaptable to the exchange process.

Although the definition of property rights will help to determine
the limits of product divisibility, and thus the possibility of exchange,
there remains a significant presence of economic goods and bads
under present technological constraints which are not conducive to
such divisibility. This is especially true if the externality occurs in a
large-group situation in which the motivation for a single individual to
initiate corrective action is not strong. Under such conditions, the
market or private sector exchange techniques may be incapable of
exerting corrective action, and such action, if it is to occur, must result
from the policy of the public sector.

Moreover, it should be noted that the present economic argument
for the existence of a public sector in a market-oriented society rests
on allocational efficiency considerations. Distributional considerations are only incidentally treated. However, it must be recognized
that both private and public sector efforts to internalize externalities,
an allocational goal, are likely to yield significant distributional side
effects. For example, if the steel firm which installs the polluting blast
furnaces is legally required to install pollution control devices to
protect the businesses and consumers in the surrounding area, the
distribution of the burden of pollution control will fall initially on the
steel firm and, perhaps, ultimately on the consumers of the firm's
products, who may have to pay higher prices for steel products. The
internalization of the pollution externality—an allocational consideration—would have been attained only with accompanying redistributional side effects, favorable in this case to the pollution-affected firms
and consumers in the surrounding area, but economically unfavorable, initially at least, to the steel firm and to the general consuming
public. The legal requirement that the firm is responsible for those
harmed by the pollution, which constitutes a specific definition of
property rights, is the basis for these redistributional effects. Indeed,
property rights are a strategic link between allocational and distributional activities.

In conclusion, it should be reiterated that the presence of externalities creates a necessary, but not in all cases, a sufficient, condition for public sector allocational intervention. The public sector, of course, is one of the primary institutions which may apply corrective action in order to improve resource allocation and societal welfare. Yet, it is not the only possible means of corrective action; moreover, the best policy for either the public or private sector will sometimes be "no action." Furthermore, institutional arrangements can change over time and thus provide additional techniques for welfare improvement. This is especially true to the extent that technological change may allow a changing ability to define property rights. Thus, even though the public sector must exist to influence resource allocation to an extent greater than that required to provide minimal law and order, the protection of property rights, and the enforcement of contracts, each individual case for potential governmental action should be evaluated on its own merits. No conclusive generalization can be made for governmental action in the case of *all* externalities.

Special supply causes of market failure in resource allocation

To this point in the chapter, the analysis has focused on several primary causes of market failure in resource allocation activities which can lead to an economic role for government in a market-oriented society. Several other generally less important causes also merit brief discussion. Essentially, these phenomena are of a supply nature, as were the decreasing-cost and zero marginal cost conditions already discussed.

First, *lack of adequate market knowledge* by producers may be considerable in some cases. This lack of knowledge can prevent the market from attaining sufficient output levels of an important economic good. For example, risk probabilities were assessed incorrectly by the market regarding the supply costs and the demand for electricity in rural areas of the United States prior to 1936. In that year, a series of federal government loans and subsidies was initiated through the Rural Electrification Administration (REA). This program demonstrated that rural electrification was feasible on a profit basis in many parts of the United States, since a significant potential demand existed for this economic good. Presently, almost all American farmers use electricity, which is provided by both the public and private sectors.

Other examples of a long-run payoff from such collective risk taking are the development of nuclear energy by the Atomic Energy Commission (AEC), the development of communications satellites under the substantial (though not complete) public sector influence of the National Aeronautics and Space Administration (NASA), and the development of public power through the Tennessee Valley Authority

(TVA). In the latter case, the extensive development of public power during the 1930s proved to privately owned electric utilities that the demand for electricity was not as inelastic as they had believed it to be. Hence, improvements in market knowledge, as attained through collective risk taking by the public sector, may well enhance the long-run profits of private firms and, in so doing, increase the supply of important economic goods.

Second, *immobility of productive resources* can help to prevent the attainment of efficient resource allocation. For example, labor resources may be immobile due to such factors as pension plans, seniority provisions, and entry restrictions into new job markets. When resources are not free to move to their most efficient points of usage, as indicated by market forces, the conditions of optimal long-run general equilibrium are not attained, and the ability of the private sector to allocate resources in an efficient manner is restricted. Indeed, both capital and labor resources reflect the lack of perfect mobility under market conditions in the United States. Various public sector programs may be designed to enhance resource mobility, particularly labor mobility, and thus improve resource allocation. An example of this in the federal personal income tax law is the allowance of deductions for moving expenses when job locations are changed.

Third, special efforts to *conserve resources* are sometimes necessary when the resources are particularly scarce or unique in character. While society considers the full employment (as reasonably defined) of most labor and capital resources to be desirable, it cannot consider the short-run full employment of natural resources, that is, the land factor of production, to be desirable. Thus, when short-run profit considerations would lead to overutilization of uniquely scarce or important natural resources such as the radio spectrum or 2,000-year-old redwood trees, long-run societal welfare may require governmentally directed resource conservation. Among the techniques which can be employed for the conservation of natural resources are public sector ownership of the resources, public utility regulation, severance taxes, water and air pollution standards, and effluent charges or penalty taxes.

These three phenomena—imperfect market knowledge, inadequate resource mobility, and the unique characteristics of certain resources—represent supply conditions which may suggest to society the desirability of allocative intervention by the public sector.

Moreover, one should distinguish between economic goods allocated under governmental influence that are intermediate and those that are final in nature.[19] For example, government may provide a

---

[19] For a discussion of this distinction, see Richard A. Musgrave, "Cost-Benefit Analysis and the Theory of Public Finance," *Journal of Economic Literature*, September 1969, pp. 799–801.

direct consumption item or *final good* such as national or internal security, or it may produce an *intermediate good,* typically capital in nature, which will lead to the ultimate production and consumption of a final consumer good. This final good may be either privately or publicly produced. Thus, public sector provision of an irrigation project may increase the ability of a private agricultural industry to produce food, or governmental provision of a hydroelectric project may lead to the production of electricity by either a government utility or a privately owned one. Another example would entail public sector production of roads, a capital good, which helps to improve the production of a final consumer good such as bus transportation—which again may be produced by either the private or the public sector. Both final and intermediate economic goods may be allocated under public sector influence.

In summary, the causes of partial market failure in the allocation of society's resources discussed above include:

1. Decreasing production costs in imperfectly competitive industries.
2. The polar case of decreasing costs known as zero marginal cost.
3. The phenomenon of joint (collective) consumption with nonexclusion.
4. The phenomenon of externalities.
5. Special supply causes.

The market failure which derives from any of these conditions constitutes an economic argument for the existence of a public sector for significant allocational intervention in a market-oriented system. Nonetheless, *specific* case-by-case analysis is still required. For example, it cannot be said a priori that the presence of a market failure condition provides both a *necessary* and *sufficient* condition for governmental allocational intervention. It may be that private sector allocational efforts can improve the situation better, or it may even be better not to initiate any effort to rectify the market failure. In the final analysis, both economic and noneconomic considerations will bear on society's allocation of scarce resources between the public and private sectors of the mixed economy.

CLASSIFICATION OF ECONOMIC GOODS ACCORDING TO THEIR CONSUMPTIVE CHARACTERISTICS

The final section of the chapter will now build on two major demand causes of market failure discussed above—joint consumption and positive externalities of consumption—in order to establish a classification system for the economic goods provided by a mixed economy. Figure 2–8 demonstrates this classification system.

FIGURE 2–8   **Classification of economic goods based on joint consumption and externality characteristics**

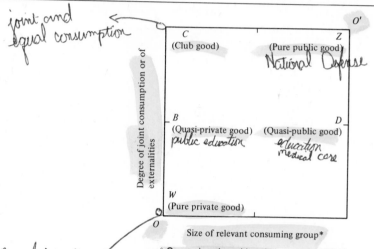

joint and equal consumption ←

* Group size along this axis is considered in the context of whether the consuming group is sufficiently large so as to induce a significant free-rider problem.

Source: Adapted from James M. Buchanan, *The Demand and Supply of Public Goods,* Figure 9-1, p. 175. © 1968 by James M. Buchanan. Reprinted by permission of author.

At this extreme there would be one individual or family unit where there is no interdependent consumption

In Figure 2–8, the size of the relevant consuming group is measured along the horizontal axis, suggesting the connotation of interdependent consumption. At one extreme, however, group size would consist of one individual or family unit, in which case there would be no interdependent consumption. Essentially, the concept of group size asks: Is the consuming unit small enough to reach a market-type agreement without encountering a serious free-rider problem? Along the vertical axis, the degree of joint consumption or of externalities, whether partial or complete, is measured. For a given economic good, the degree of joint consumption (externality) will be influenced by such factors as the prevailing definition of property rights.

At *O* (lower left corner of the diagram), the exclusion principle would apply perfectly to the *pure private good,* W. This means that the benefits of the good are completely divisible, in that none escape the price mechanism. A candy bar is an example of such a good. The exclusion principle would *not* apply at O^1 (upper right corner of the diagram) to the *pure public good,* Z. The benefits here are completely indivisible, that is, they are jointly and equally consumed at the same level of output by a large relevant consuming group. National defense is an example of such a good, which requires substantial governmental allocative influence.

An economic good of the *B* variety on the graph (*quais-private good*), in contrast to goods W and Z, possesses partial traits of both privateness and publicness, since some of the benefits are divisible and some are indivisible. It is *jointly*, but not *equally*, consumed, since the exclusion principle applies to part of the total benefits. Yet, the number of persons concerned with the good is small enough that negotiated agreements on its allocation are feasible. For example, two individuals may live as neighbors in houses on adjoining properties. They may agree that one large guard dog will provide protection from burglary and vandalism to both of them, though perhaps more to the individual on whose property the dog will be kept. The protective benefits of the dog are thus partly divisible and partly jointly consumed by the two neighbors. Yet, even though some benefits are jointly consumed, the total benefits are not equally consumed. Instead, the neighbor on whose property the dog resides receives the superior protection due to a locational factor. A market-type solution, without governmental allocative intervention, is feasible, however, since the relevant consuming group is small enough so that the two neighbors can agree on a cost-sharing plan to finance the ownership of the guard dog.

An economic good of the *C* category, a so-called *club good*, is represented by the characteristics of *both* joint *and* equal consumption. The degree of product indivisibility is complete within the group. Relatedly, the short-run marginal cost of supplying consumption to an additional individual is zero. Yet, if the size of the group is small enough, some market-type arrangement for allocating the good is feasible through the negotiating efforts of the individuals involved. This might be exemplified by a private club which, through some established decision-making procedure, decides to build a new swimming pool for the exclusive use of its members. The services of the pool are available (once it is constructed) at a short-run marginal cost of zero to the members of the club. Moreover, these benefits may be jointly and equally consumed by the members, within the capacity limits of the pool. This economic good, though it contains important traits of "publicness," is subject to a private allocational solution. This is because the size of the relevant group, as indicated along the horizontal axis, is small enough to avoid a significant free-rider problem. That is, there is no meaningful motivation among the club members to let another club member pay for the good. Hence, the exclusion principle can be applied to screen membership in the club from those who do not voluntarily pay its membership fee. Finally, it may be noted that the lower right corner of the diagram is an "empty box" since, in the absence of joint consumption, group size and a free-rider problem become irrelevant.

Thus, in the case of economic goods W, B, and C, the size of the interacting consuming group is usually small enough to avoid the need for direct governmental intervention. Market-type procedures can essentially perform the allocation function; government need provide only indirect allocational influence such as the protection of property rights, including the enforcement of contracts, the deterrence of fraud, and overall antitrust (market structure) policies.

The above conditions change significantly when the size of the relevant consuming group becomes large enough that the free-rider motivation prevails. This is true for economic goods of both the D and Z categories. Economic goods of the Z (*pure public good*) variety, for which all benefits are joint or indivisible, have been discussed. Economic goods of the D (*quasi-public good*) classification, however, contain both divisible and indivisible benefits—the latter occurring under conditions of *large-group consumption.* University education is an example of this type of good. The fact that part of the benefits are indivisible throughout the entire society leads to a free-rider motivation, since the group is sufficiently large to reduce the likelihood of voluntary payment for the joint benefits. The consumption, though joint, is *not* equal. The person who receives the university education receives greater total benefits than the person who does not, though both receive some joint benefits of a positive externality nature, which are derived by the community as a whole from a more educated population. Hence, the practice of governmental operation and partial tax financing of universities is commonplace in order to cover the cost of these joint benefits, though tuition charges are also levied to help defray the cost of the private benefits. In any event, the probable need for significant public sector allocational influence is considerably greater for goods in the D and Z categories than it is for goods in the W, B, and C categories, for which allocation can largely be conducted by the private sector of the mixed economy. Indeed, the technical feasibility and costs of exclusion become an important factor in determining whether the public or private sector should dominate the supply of a particular economic good.

In summary, once the polar limits of "privateness" have been set by the pure private good, W, and those of "publicness" have been set by the pure public good, Z, the remaining portion of the classification system is the category of *quasi goods* (or *nonpure, intermediate, mixed* goods). This category includes the in-between goods B, C, and D. Specifically, good B may be designated a *quasi-private good,* since market allocation influence prevails, and good D as a *quasi-public good,* since governmental allocation influence would tend to be substantial. Good C represents the unique case of a *club good.* Table 2–2 provides estimates of the proportions of pure public, pure private, and quasi-goods within total American consumption.

Thus, economic goods may be classified according to their con-

---

TABLE 2-2   Types of economic goods as proportions of total consumption in U.S. economy, 1972

Pure private goods = 61 percent	Pure public goods = 8 percent
Quasi-private goods = 18 percent	Quasi-public goods = 13 percent

Source: Derived from data contained in the Input-Output Accounts, U.S. Department of Commerce, and presented in Bernard P. Herber, "The Demand for Public Goods and Services: Problems of Identification and Measurement in Western Countries," paper presented at the 1982 Annual Congress of the International Institute of Public Finance, Copenhagen, Denmark, August 23–26, 1982.

sumptive characteristics—joint or private—as related to the size of the relevant consuming group. There is a tendency for the private sector to dominate allocation along the left side of Figure 2–8 and for the public sector to be importantly involved in allocation for economic goods on the right side of the diagram, but there are exceptions to these tendencies. For example, the public sector decides, at times, to involve itself importantly in the supply of certain largely divisible economic goods which would fall generally in the lower left quadrant of the graph. These governmentally supplied, or heavily subsidized, economic goods may be representative of the decreasing production cost, natural monopoly, phenomenon described earlier (postal service, railroad transportation, electricity), or they may be represented by such redistributional governmental programs as those for food stamps and school lunches. These distributionally related products are known as *merit goods*. Even though the market could totally allocate such divisible goods, they are considered so meritorious or important that a political consensus is reached whereby they are made available in certain minimal quantities to all members of the society. Political judgments of this sort are of a distributional as well as of an allocational nature.

3

Public choice
in a democracy

The problems involved in revealing societal allocational preferences through a democratic political process will be analyzed in this chapter. Given the distributional value judgments which make these preferences effective, the political process functions to varying degrees of efficiency in implementing such preferences in the form of actual allocation.

The ultimate allocational objective, of course, is the attainment of maximum social welfare. The welfare economics of the previous chapter allows for such a goal to be set in terms of public goods consumption, while the positive economics framework of this chapter is concerned with the institutional decision-making mechanism through which efforts can be made to attain such a goal. Thus, positive economics deals with the reality of the decision-making process, regardless of what the goals are or whether the welfare goals are ever fully attained. This important topic constitutes an area of political economy known by such names as *public choice theory, social choice theory, nonmarket decision making,* and *fiscal politics.*

In essence, this subject matter involves a study of the economics of political decision making. The same consumers who individually demand private-type goods through the *market* are viewed here as demanding public-type goods through a democratic *political process.* As the preceding chapter has shown, partial market failure in allocative efforts leads to an acceptance of governmental allocational intervention, despite a market-oriented culture. The political process, however, has its own problems of economic inefficiency. Differences in the nature of public-type economic goods such as the trait of joint consumption may require public sector allocation intervention if these goods are to be effectively supplied. However, interpretation of the demand for public-type goods creates problems of preference revelation that are unlike those experienced in the market sector of the economy.

Some of the difficulties encountered in revealing economic preferences in the absence of a market mechanism will be described in this chapter; moreover, some possible institutional improvements will be suggested to enhance the revelation of societal preferences for public-type goods through a democratic political process. An early contributor to this subject was the late Swedish economist, Knut Wicksell, who built his economic analysis of democratic political decision making on a voluntary-exchange theory of public goods allocation. Wicksell's insights and contributions to this area of knowledge are discussed in the next section.

THE WICKSELL APPROACH TO REVEALING SOCIAL PREFERENCES—ABSOLUTE AND RELATIVE UNANIMITY[1]

The political process is extremely important to the attainment of an efficient societal allocation of resources. Yet, even if society adopts a democratic political system based on individual choice, the institutional problems involved in revealing individual preferences for economic goods are still considerable. For example, preferences based on the concept of an equal vote for all, which is the benchmark of democratic individualism, are unlikely to be revealed and implemented effectively by a system of *simple majority voting*, whereby a majority of 50 percent plus one vote may carry a decision. In this way a minority of 50 percent minus one of the citizens may be obliged to help pay for a public-type economic good with their taxes, even though they do not desire the allocation of the good. Such costs to the "political losers" of a majority voting decision are referred to as *voter externality costs*.

It was demonstrated by Wicksell that *absolute (complete) unanimity* (100 percent approval) would be required in a democratic political system in order to have a situation analogous to the voluntary-exchange solution of the market in which no individual can be forced to

[1] See Knut Wicksell, "A New Principle of Just Taxation," in *Classics in the Theory of Public Finance*, ed. Richard A. Musgrave and Alan T. Peacock (London: MacMillan, 1958), pp. 72-118. Also see the discussion of the Wicksellian position in James M. Buchanan, *Demand and Supply of Public Goods* (Chicago: Rand McNally, 1968), and Carl G. Uhr, *Economic Doctrines of Knut Wicksell* (Berkeley: University of California Press, 1960), pp. 164-90.

pay for unwanted economic goods. This would be accomplished under the absolute unanimity rule, since the "effective size" of the group jointly consuming the public-type good would be reduced to a situation analogous to the two-party exchange condition for divisible private goods in the market. In other words, each individual may be considered to be trading with all others as a unit. By a single negative vote, one person could void a budget policy, thus not being forced to pay for and consume the good, but at the same time denying the public good to all other consumers in the society.[2] Of course, when the large-group situation is reduced to a two-party exchange, the problem of strategy is introduced as voter externality costs disappear. The motivation is thus established for the individual to engage in individual trade or exchange.

Yet, since a single negative vote would block a budget policy under conditions of absolute unanimity, the incentive for strategy would tend to allow few, if any, budget policies to be approved under the rule. Since absolute unanimity would lead to an essentially "inactive" budget system, Wicksell endorsed what he considered to be the next-best solution, namely, the concept of *relative unanimity* or *qualified majority voting*. This rule suggests that the approval percentage for a budgetary policy should be as close to 100 percent (absolute unanimity) as possible without inducing excessive vetoing strategy. For example, a majority of two thirds, three fourths, or five sixths might be required for approval of a budget policy under the relative unanimity rule. *rather than a simple majority*

This means that each individual in a large-group situation would know that his or her own negative vote, by itself, could not block a budget proposal. Consequently, a person would not be as strongly motivated to exploit others through a negative strategy as would be the case under an absolute unanimity rule. If a proposal promises some personal benefits, the individual may accept it even though otherwise tempted, under a benchmark of absolute unanimity, to strategically block the same policy. Thus, under a relative unanimity rule, it is more likely that a sufficient number of individuals in the society would follow "nonstrategic" behavior so as to allow an acceptable number of collective decisions to be made. Moreover, the rule of relative unanimity, as opposed to the simple majority rule, would tend to reduce voter externality costs, since that proportion of voters who may be losers is reduced to less than 50 percent minus 1. It could be counterargued, however, that such a rule works against the general well-being of the majority, thus creating a "tyranny of the minority," whereby a minority of (say) 34 voters can bind a majority of 66 voters to a budgetary decision under the two-thirds approval rule.

---

[2] See Buchanan, *Demand and Supply of Public Goods*, chap. 5.

Wicksell also recognized the desirability of making expenditure and tax decisions *simultaneously* in the legislature, thus entailing a symmetrical tie-in between spending and revenue decisions. The marginal benefit from a public expenditure should be related to the marginal tax cost of providing the public good—and then, the relative unanimity (qualified majority voting) rule should be applied to the joint decision. This is consistent with his preference for the voluntary-exchange approach to public goods allocation. Unfortunately, the common legislative procedure in a democracy first establishes the quantity of public goods (the level of public goods expenditure), and then selects a revenue package to finance these goods. This precludes a simultaneous benefit-tax cost decision.

THE POLITICAL INTERACTION COSTS
OF DEMOCRATIC VOTING

More recent analysis by James M. Buchanan and Gordon Tullock has added further insight concerning the economic issues involved in the process of revealing individual economic preferences through a democratic political system.[3] Figure 3–1 demonstrates some of these issues. The expected *political interaction costs* (discounted to present value) from collective democratic decision making are measured on the vertical axis, while the percentage of the group required for the approval of a collective fiscal decision is measured along the horizontal axis. The political interaction costs are twofold in nature: (1) the voter externality cost component, and (2) the decision-making cost component.

A *voter externality cost,* as described earlier in the chapter, refers to the cost incurred by a voter who has voted against a fiscal choice, which nonetheless has been approved by the required proportion of voters necessary to carry the decision for approval. Such an individual must abide by the collective decision even though his or her individual preferences did not opt for its approval. Assume a group of 100 voters. If the proportion of voters required to approve a collective action is only 1 percent, then 1 of the 100 voters can oblige the remaining 99 voters to abide by a political decision which they do not approve. Quite obviously, the potential negative voter externalities incurred by the remaining 99 voters who oppose the decision are considerable under this "dictatorship" sort of rule. However, the potential voter externalities would continually decline as the percentage required to approve a political decision increases. Ultimately, at an absolute (complete) unanimity rule of 100 percent approval, voter externality costs would reach zero, since no voter could be bound by

---

[3] See James M. Buchanan and Gordon Tullock, *The Calculus of Consent* (Ann Arbor: University of Michigan Press, 1962).

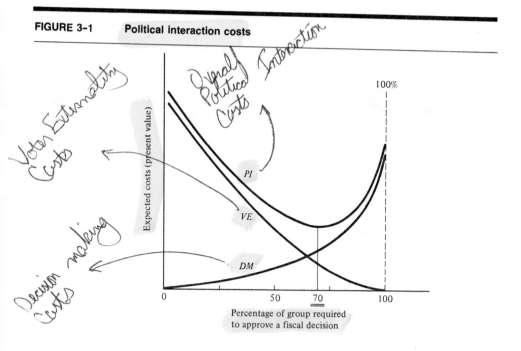

FIGURE 3-1   Political interaction costs

Overall Political Costs

Interaction

Voter Externality Costs

Decision making Costs

PI

VE

DM

100%

Expected costs (present value)

0   50   70   100

Percentage of group required
to approve a fiscal decision

the collective political decision of other voters. In other words, a single voter would retain the right to veto any proposed decision. The nature of voter externality costs is represented by curve *VE* in Figure 3-1.

A *decision-making cost,* in political interaction terms, refers to the bargaining cost required to reach a group political consensus or agreement. Essentially, these are real resource costs in terms of both direct labor, material, and capital outlay, as well as opportunity cost considerations such as the value of time spent in bargaining. Decision-making costs may be expected to increase as the proportion of the voting group required to approve a decision becomes larger. That is, under conditions requiring higher percentage approval, more effort is normally required to gain agreement. The highest cost would be expected at the point of 100 percent approval (absolute unanimity), since the potential for strategy would reach a peak at this point. This would be true because a single voter would be capable of negating a choice which conceivably every other voter would prefer. Curve *DM* in Figure 3-1 represents the nature of decision-making costs. Assuming a group of 100 voters, a 1 percent approval rule would incur little, if any, bargaining cost, since one voter (like a dictator) could approve a policy without considering the other voters. Meanwhile, approval by all 100 voters would likely incur substantial decision-making costs, as strategy among voters would become extensive.

Curve *PI* in Figure 3-1 reflects the performance of the overall political interaction costs. The curve is a summation of its two components, the voter-externality cost curve (VE) and the decision-making cost curve (DM). In this particular graph, given the character of the voter externality and decision-making cost functions, the most efficient proportion of the group required for political approval is 70 percent.[4] That is, this proportion yields the lowest political interaction cost per voter for a particular fiscal decision.

REVEALING SOCIAL REFERENCES THROUGH MAJORITY VOTING—ARROW'S IMPOSSIBILITY THEOREM

Kenneth Arrow has provided additional insight into the problems involved in making societal decisions consistent with individual preferences through group voting in a democratic political process.[5] Although Arrow's observations pertain, in general, to the problems encountered under any democratic voting rule based on individualism, their most relevant application is to the majority voting rule which is the mainstay of Western democracies. He argues that the following conditions must be met if a collective decision reached under majority voting conditions is to accurately reveal the individual economic preferences which constitute the effective social indifference curve (the social welfare function).[6]

1. Social choices must be *transitive* (consistent). That is, a *unique social ordering* must exist which will yield a clear-cut winning alternative regardless of the ordering sequence in which alternative choices are voted on.

2. The social welfare function must be *nonperverse* in the sense that an alternative policy which might otherwise have been chosen by the society must not be rejected because any individual has *changed the relative ranking* of that alternative.

3. The rankings of the choices in the social welfare function between two alternatives must be *independent of the ranking* by individuals of other alternatives which are irrelevant to the choice between the two alternatives. That is, the elimination of any one

---

[4] Note that the most efficient proportion is *not* determined by the intersection of the VE and DM curves.

[5] Kenneth Arrow, *Social Choice and Individual Values* (New York: John Wiley & Sons, 1951). Critical evaluations of the Arrow hypothesis include: Clifford Hildreth, "Alternative Conditions for Social Orderings," *Econometrica*, January 1953, pp. 81–94; Leo A. Goodman and Harry Markowitz, "Social Welfare Functions Based on Individual Rankings," *American Journal of Sociology*, November 1952, pp. 257–62; and James S. Coleman, "The Possibility of a Social Welfare Function," *American Economic Review*, December 1966, pp. 1105–22. The Coleman evaluation will be discussed later in this chapter.

[6] See Figure 1–4 and its related discussion.

alternative must not influence the ranking of the other alternatives in the social welfare function.

4. Voters must have *free choices* among all alternative policies.
5. Social choices must *not be dictatorial*. That is, they must not be based soley on the preferences of one individual, independent of the choices of other individuals.

Table 3–1a and Figure 3–2a illustrate a situation in which majority voting violates the set of conditions necessary for consumer sovereignty to be maintained in collective democratic decision making. Condition 1, the transitivity condition, in particular, is violated, leading to what is known as the *impossibility theorem* or *voting paradox*. Assume that three voters (A, B, and C) are selecting among three budgetary policies (X, Y, and Z). Policy alternative X represents a decision to build three public libraries; policy Y, a decision to build two libraries, and policy Z, a decision to build one library. Since a majority of the voters (in this example, two out of three) prefer policies X to Y, Y to Z, and Z to X, the result is *intransitive* (inconsistent) in that there is no winner. In this situation, the "sequence" in which the voting occurs would determine the final outcome—an obviously illogical result.

For example, if we first pair policy X versus policy Y, X wins since two of the three voters prefer X to Y. If we then pair policy X versus

---

TABLE 3–1   **Examples of majority voting: Individual preferences for alternative budget policies**

a. Results: Intransitive*

	Policy alternatives		
Voter	Preference 1	Preference 2	Preference 3
A	X	Y	Z
B	Y	Z	X
C	Z	X	Y

b. Results: Transitive†

	Policy alternatives		
Voter	Preference 1	Preference 2	Preference 3
A	X	Y	Z
B	Y	Z	X
C	Z	Y	X

* Summary: Voters A and C prefer policy X to policy Y; A and B prefer policy Y to Z; B and C prefer policy Z to X; thus a majority (2 of 3 individuals, in this case) prefer policy X to Y, Y to Z, and Z to X. This result is intransitive (inconsistent) and violates condition 1.

† Summary: Since voter C exhibits a Z, Y, X preference pattern, Y is preferred over X by 2 of 3 voters, Z is preferred over X by 2 of 3 voters, and Y is preferred over Z by 2 of 3 voters—thus making the median policy "Y" the winner.

FIGURE 3–2 **Examples of majority voting: Individual preferences for alternative budget policies**

a. Results: Intransitive
twin-peaked preference function for voter C

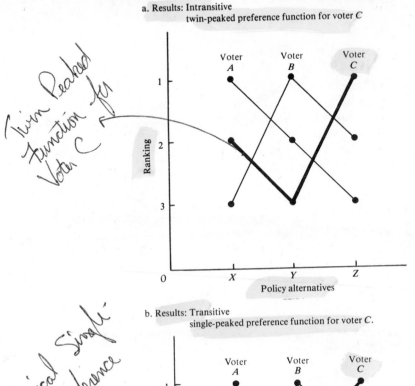

Twin Peaked
Function for
Voter C

b. Results: Transitive
single-peaked preference function for voter C.

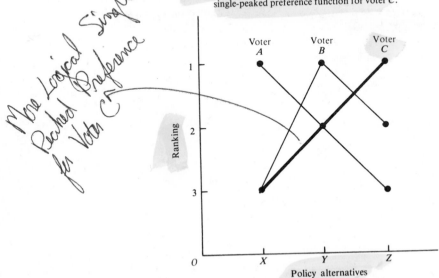

More Logical "Single"
Peaked Preference
for Voter C

policy Z, Z wins since two of three voters prefer Z to X. Thus, a pairing sequence beginning with X versus Y results in Z as the ultimate winner. On the other hand, if we first pair policy Y versus policy Z, Y is favored by two of three voters, but the subsequent pairing of Y and X finds X as the winner since it is preferred by two of three voters. Thus, a pairing sequence beginning with Y versus Z results in X as the ultimate winner.

Finally, an initial pairing of X versus Z finds Z winning over X, but the subsequent pairing of Z versus Y finds Y winning over Z—each winning vote representing a two out of three voter preference. Thus, a pairing sequence beginning with X versus Z results in Y as the ultimate winner. To summarize, the outcome is arbitrary since either Z, X, or Y will win depending on the ordering of the voting sequence.

A close inspection of the above paradox reveals that intransitivity occurs because one voter, C, prefers the two extreme policies (Z for one library and X for three libraries) over the median or intermediate alternative, Y, for two libraries. Yet, this is an unlikely position for a voter to take, that is, to prefer three libraries as a second choice instead of two libraries—which is closer to the voter's top-ranked choice of one library.[7] When graphed, the result is the *twin-peaked preference function* for voter C that is demonstrated in Figure 3–2a.

Instead, if voter C behaves in a more rational manner and prefers two libraries as a second choice, the intransitivity problem disappears and the solution becomes determinate. This transitive outcome is depicted in Table 3–1b and Figure 3–2b, with the latter showing a *single-peaked preference function* for voter C. Now, if the first pairing is X versus Y, Y defeats X and then also defeats Z. Or, if we begin with a pairing of Y versus Z, Y wins over Z and also defeats X. Finally, a pairing of X versus Z finds Z the winner, but, of course Y wins over Z as observed in the previous pairing. Thus, Y is the clear-cut winner despite the ordering of the voting sequence.

It may be observed further that the three policy alternatives in the above example consist of three different quantities of the same economic good (public libraries). However, the same results would tend to hold for overall budget considerations such as budgetary size. For example, if policy X represents a large-sized budget, policy Y a medium-sized budget, and policy Z a small-sized budget, rational voting behavior would result in the median policy, Y, as the winner. However, this example would hold to a lesser degree for heterogeneous policy alternatives such as would be the case if policy X represents one public library, policy Y represents one fire station, and policy Z

---

[7] While an occasional voter might rationalize such a decision to prefer the two extreme alternatives to the intermediate one, it seems certain that most voters would prefer as a second choice the alternative closest to the number one choice.

represents one public school—all of equal cost to the taxpayer. Nevertheless, even here the median policy could be the winner as the result of *voting coalitions* and *platforms*.

Although Arrow's requirements for rational collective decision making through majority voting are rigorous, his analysis nonetheless indicates some basic problems present in democratic political decision making. However, one condition seems unduly rigorous, condition 3, which says that the elimination of any one alternative policy shall not influence the ranking of the other alternative policies in the social welfare function.[8] There can be no interdependencies among alternative policies. Or, stated differently, the relative intensities of preference among voters for different policies cannot be a relevant consideration. Thus, in the above example, the intensities of preferences for three, two, or one library could not affect the outcome.

Or, consider another example: One half of the community prefers improved highways and streets to solve traffic congestion in an urban area, while the other half prefers a government-subsidized mass transportation system to meet the problem. Assume the cost to be equal for both traffic congestion solutions. If those who prefer the highway solution rank traffic congestion as a lower-priority program among various alternatives than those who prefer the mass transportation system, then the particular traffic congestion solution selected (provided money is to be spent for this purpose) should be the mass transportation system; those who prefer it exhibit higher relative intensities of preference. Condition 3, however, essentially stipulates that a consideration of preference intensity is irrelevant. The Arrow approach thus tends to understate the *intensity of desires* among alternative policy choices. It is difficult for a system of social choice which ignores these basic preference considerations to interpret accurately individual demands expressed in the political process.

In summary, the Arrow theorem seems too pessimistic concerning the efficiency of the democratic political process, though it does point out some weaknesses. This pessimism stems mainly from the two points described; namely, (1) the irrational voter depicted in the twin-peaked preference function (Table 3–1a and Figure 3–2a) and (2) the assumption which precludes the ability of the democratic process to reveal voters' preference intensities among policy alternatives.

REVEALING SOCIAL PREFERENCES
THROUGH POINT VOTING

The previous discussion has demonstrated some of the problems encountered in the effort to reveal individual economic preferences

---

[8] The overly rigorous nature of this condition will be analyzed in greater detail below in the section entitled "Revealing Social Preferences under Conditions of Uncertainty."

TABLE 3-2   **Examples of point voting (50-point maximum for each individual) in the revelation of social preferences**

a. Results: (1) Transitive; (2) no tie

	Points assigned to policy alternatives		
Voter	X	Y	Z
A	22	20	8
B	4	40	6
C	14	12	24
Total	40	72	38

b. Results: (1) Transitive; (2) tie

	Points assigned to policy alternatives		
Voter	X	Y	Z
A	26	15	9
B	6	30	14
C	18	5	27
Total	50	50	50

under democratic voting conditions. One prospective improvement was considered in the form of Wicksell's relative unanimity concept. Another approach provided the understanding of political interaction costs. Still another alternative in the derivation of the social welfare function is point voting.

The *point method of voting*, unlike ordinary majority voting, emphasizes the relative intensity of preferences among alternative budgetary policies. For example, under a simple majority voting rule, 51 out of a group of 100 voters can bind a minority of 49 voters to a budget policy which is not preferred by the minority. This would be so even though the welfare losses of the 49 voters may exceed the welfare gains of the majority of 51. The simple majority rule merely counts the numbers of winners and losers; the *relative preference intensities* of the voters for the budget policy are ignored. Point voting attempts to overcome this problem.

As an example, let us use our continuing voting discussion as illustrated earlier in Table 3–1 and Figure 3–2. Thus, assume in Table 3–2 that voters A, B, and C are each given 50 points whereby they can specify their relative intensities of preference among the three alternative budget policies—X, Y, and Z—on any divisional basis they prefer. Suppose that the following occurs: Voter A allots 22 points to policy X, 20 points to policy Y, and 8 points to policy Z. Voter B gives 40 points to policy Y, 6 points to policy Z, and 4 points to policy X.

Voter C allots 24 points to policy Z, 14 points to policy X, and 12 points to policy Y. Policy Y would thus be selected in a transitive decision. The margin of preference for it is obvious. The total points, as shown in Table 3–2a, are: policy Y, 72 points; policy X, 40 points; and policy Z, 38 points.

Though intransitivity is avoided under the point voting rule, a tie, though unlikely, could occur. This is demonstrated in Table 3–2b, which shows the three voters—A, B, and C—as having preference intensities that create a situation in which the total score for each policy alternative is equal to 50 points.

Consumer sovereignty, in the market sense, appears to be approximated more closely in point voting than in simple majority voting. Greater attention is also paid to preference patterns in point voting through the consideration of relative preference intensities. Why, then, should the political process not be structured so that the use of this voting method is significantly increased? In one sense, point voting does already exist in American society. Some voters, for a variety of reasons, exert greater influence on a budgetary decision than do others. Their influence may at times reflect a greater desire for particular policy alternatives, but varying degrees of influence on a governmental policy decision may also reflect the uneven ex ante distribution of political voting influence among the members of a society.

The *formal structuring* of a point voting system would entail numerous institutional and administrative problems. Moreover, strategy would come into play more prominently. Though point voting tends to reveal social preferences better than simple majority voting, the increased knowledge diffused throughout the society due to the more accurate revelation of individual preferences would encourage strategy actions by voters. The opportunity for strategy would tend to reduce the free-rider problem, whereby voluntary payments for indivisible public goods are not forthcoming, but the costs of reaching agreements in a large group may be massive when ample opportunity for strategy is present.

Thus, a paradox seems to exist: On the one hand, if strategy is neutral, point voting seems preferable because it reflects the relative intensity of desires. On the other hand, if new opportunities for strategy are introduced, simple majority voting may still be the best voting technique, even though it is far from ideal, due to the costs of negotiating large-group agreements, and especially if the latter is done without generalized political or fiscal rules (these will be analyzed later in the chapter). In any event, majority voting arrangements, as presently constituted, are an imperfect method of revealing the effective social welfare function in the political process.

REVEALING SOCIAL PREFERENCES UNDER CONDITIONS OF UNCERTAINTY

Allowing for relative preference intensities under uncertainty

The importance of relative preference intensities for various policy alternatives has been further emphasized by James S. Coleman.[9] Essentially, Coleman questions the third condition for efficient majority voting provided by Arrow, and demonstrates that the Arrow impossibility theorem is relevant only to those social choice mechanisms in which relative intensities of desire between policy alternatives cannot be expressed. In other words, the elimination of a policy alternative, even though it may be low in priority to the voter, would *not* alter the behavior of a rational individual concerning other alternatives under the Arrow assumption. Coleman avoids this unrealistic assumption by using an approach in which the problems of individualistic choice and social welfare are viewed in terms of utility maximization under conditions of *uncertainty*. Unlike the market sector, in which a consumer can purchase or reject an economic good, in the political sector a voter can only partially control a policy outcome. Thus, uncertainty and risk are especially relevant to the public sector allocational problem.

When the outcome of a policy choice is uncertain, each individual voter attaches a subjective probability to each possible outcome. This amounts to a decision regarding *expected utility* under these conditions of imperfect knowledge and risk. Thus, the voter will consider not only the ordering of utilities from alternative budget policies, as would be done for rational behavior under conditions of certainty, but also the *expected relative sizes of utility differences* between various possible outcomes, as rational behavior would require under conditions of uncertainty. The latter is an important and inherent part of the collective decision-making process; it is not externally imposed.

Table 3–3 demonstrates the collective decision making approach under conditions of expected utility and risk. In Table 3–3a, an intransitive result is shown for policy alternatives X, Y, and Z similar to the basic Arrow model applied in Table 3–1a. In Table 3–3b, three additional policy alternatives (X^1, Y^1, Z^1) are added for the three voters of the society (Voters A, B, and C), and intransitivity once again occurs. Table 3–3c gives the relative intensities of preference of the three voters for the six alternative budget policies, in terms of the relative utility differences among possible outcomes. Assume that Voter A has some knowledge of the various orderings of the other two voters

---

[9] Coleman, "The Possibility of a Social Welfare Function."

TABLE 3-3   **Collective decision making using vote exchanges under conditions of expected utility and risk**

a. Results: (1) Intransitive

	Policy alternatives		
Voter	Preference 1	Preference 2	Preference 3
A	X	Y	Z
B	Y	Z	X
C	Z	X	Y

b. Results: (1) Intransitive

	Policy alternatives		
Voter	Preference 1	Preference 2	Preference 3
A	X′	Y′	Z′
B	Y′	Z′	X′
C	Z′	X′	Y′

c. Results:* (1) Transitive; (2) no tie

	Utility expected from budget policy					
Voter	X	Y	Z	X′	Y′	Z′
A	10	5	1	10	9	8
B	8	10	9	8	10	9
C	9	8	10	9	6	10

* After voting changes based on "expected utility" differences from alternative budget policies.

Source: Part (c) of table adapted from James S. Coleman, "The Possibility of a Social Welfare Function," *American Economic Review*, December 1966, p. 1113.

among the six policy alternatives. Thus, he or she has expected utilities among a range of six possible alternatives and has the power to induce an action from another voter in response to his or her own action. Indeed, gains can be made from trade even though outcomes are probable and not certain.

As Table 3-3c shows, the utility differences for voter A among policy alternatives X, X′, Y′, and Z′ are small, while the utility differences for the same voter between these alternatives and policy alternatives Y and Z are large. Hence, voter A may well consider an *exchange of votes* with another voter, such as voter C, so that policy alternatives X and Z′ would win. Both voter A and voter C would attain a top-priority policy alternative, as well as a high-priority second policy. In fact, voter B would not be likely to oppose the vote trade either, since a substantial total of 17 units of expected utility would be received from the two policies (X and Z′), as contrasted to 18 units for voter A and 19 units for voter C.[10] In political terms, the vote exchange may be termed *logrolling*. The intransitive results of Tables 3–3a and 3–3b have been converted into a transitive situation in Table 3–3c by the application of analysis based on utility maximization under conditions of uncertainty.

An important conclusion from the above example is that when an individual is released from the restriction of voting on only one issue, and also from the restriction of a complete lack of information about the behavior of others, rational individual behavior suggests that every policy alternative which possesses some subjective probability of occurrence may affect maximizing behavior.[11] In fact, this is true even for policy alternatives of low priority. Obviously, an individual acting in a rational economic manner would be willing to give up some resources in order to achieve an expected *net gain* in welfare or utility. In the present context, this would amount to supporting a low-priority issue in order to receive a utility gain from someone else's vote in support of a higher-priority policy alternative.

Significantly, *vote trading (logrolling)* by elected political representatives does occur through various techniques in the political structure of a nation such as the United States. Yet, in a distributional sense, voting influence among the individuals of a society is often quite uneven. An equal right to vote in an election does not constitute equal political influence in the ultimate, policy determination, sense. This unevenness of influence includes the differential effects exerted on policy formation by various pressure groups, lobbies, or political action committees (PACs). The distribution of political voting power, as discussed at several earlier points in the book, takes on an especially important meaning in this discussion.

It should be recognized that a precise and formal application of the "expected utility under risk" approach would face massive costs of individual negotiation. However, elected legislatures and other political institutions can act as proxies for the individual members of a political community, and thus might well move the society closer to Pareto optimality than would hold true under the application of a simple majority voting rule on each issue, with no consideration given to relative preference intensities. In effect, logrolling provides the opportunity for a person or group to obtain what is most wanted at the expense of what is least wanted. Relatedly, minorities can establish coalitions to help attain their more intense preferences. However, one

---

[10] An effort is made in Table 3–3c *only* to demonstrate a particular vote exchange situation which is beneficial to both voters involved in the trade. No effort is made to isolate any other beneficial vote exchanges which may be implicit in the table.

[11] Even the Wicksellian absolute unanimity approach limits its direct consideration to a single-policy alternative.

conceivable unintended result of logrolling could be an overexpanded public sector within the total economy (social imbalance). This would be true if revenue constraints were largely ignored as expenditures were promoted by logrolling, and/or if logrolling is used to enact inefficient projects.

Informational costs and political outcomes under uncertainty

A recent work by Randall Bartlett provides further insight into the manner in which uncertainty can influence public sector decisions in democratic societies.[12] Uncertainty may be relevant in many ways, including the interpretation of voters' preferences and the effects of governmental decisions on various groups within the society. The mixed economy is viewed as consisting of four self-interest groups: *consumers*, who seek utility maximization; *producers*, who seek profit maximization; elected *politicians*, who seek vote maximization, and *bureaucrats*, (civil servants within government), who seek security maximization through the extension and/or expansion of governmental programs with which they are associated.[13] Neither government in general, as represented by politicians, nor the bureaucratic component of government exists merely as an extension of consumers and producers in trying to maximize their welfare; instead, each operates in its own self-interest. In other words, the mixed economy is represented by four maximizing groups, the traditional producer and consumer groups of the private sector and the politicians and bureaucrats of the public sector. Resource allocation, as well as other basic economic decisions, are said to be the result of the interaction of all of these decision-making groups. A substantial component of the post-Arrow social choice literature has pointed to this same multigroup decision-making phenomenon.

Since costs of obtaining information exist due to uncertainty, each of these four self-interest groups has an economic interest in gathering information and, relatedly, in using that information to influence public sector policy outcomes. Thus, private sector consumers and producers not only seek self-interest goals in the market, they also try to influence governmental policy in order to serve their interests. Moreover, bureaucrats have their own interests at stake in perpetuating existing programs and otherwise influencing the composition and size of governmental tax and expenditure programs. Self-interest-motivated elected officials and political parties seek vote maximization at the polls. Thus, the interacting self-interest activities of both private

---

[12] Randall Bartlett, *Economic Foundations of Political Power* (New York: Free Press, 1973).

[13] On the subject of bureaucratic self-interest, see Anthony Downs, *Inside Bureaucracy* (Boston: Little, Brown, 1967).

and public economic agents contribute to the demand and supply forces which ultimately determine the pattern of governmental fiscal decisions.

If the *expected gains* from influencing governmental policy outcomes exceed the *expected costs* of creating such influence through the gathering and use of appropriate information, the rational seeker of self-interest will be motivated to try to influence the policy outcomes. Furthermore, it is argued, there is a positive functional relationship between the distribution of economic power (income and wealth) in the private sector and the capability of influencing governmental budgetary outcomes. In other words, both the *desire* and the *ability* to influence governmental actions tend to increase as the economic power of the private economic agent (consumer or producer) increases. This applies to all types of budgetary decisions, whether they be of the expenditure or revenue-gathering variety. Thus, the fact that tax loopholes (special tax provisions) generally favor higher income and wealth classes under the federal income and estate-gift taxes may not be an accident.[14] Moreover, the correlation between private income and wealth distribution and the degree of political influence is said to lead to a long-run distributional status quo, since not only do the actions of government influence the distribution of income and wealth in society, but the distribution of income and wealth, in turn, influences the actions of government. This linkage factor between the private and public sectors of the economy in the process of collective decision making may be termed the *political influence hypothesis.*[15]

The Bartlett study can be credited with adding further insight to the ex ante distributional forces which make demand effective in the political sector of the mixed economy.

ADDITIONAL VOTING MODELS

The preceding discussion has pointed out both the de facto nonattainability of the conceptually ideal absolute unanimity model and the conceptually inefficient nature of majority voting. Certain other institutional arrangements for reaching public sector budgetary decisions, such as point voting and the various political effects created by uncertainty, have also been discussed. Several additional democratic voting models will be briefly considered in this section.

The *logrolling model* of James Buchanan and Gordon Tullock, a

---

[14] For a detailed discussion of special tax provisions (tax loopholes) relating to the federal personal income tax, see Chapter 8. For a similar discussion of federal estate-gift taxation, *see* Chapter 10.

[15] For a more extreme statement of this hypothesis, see Michael Parenti, *Democracy for the Few*, 2d ed (New York: St. Martin's Press, 1977).

simple majority voting model, considers conditions under which individuals may exchange their votes on one issue for another.[16] It is similar in this respect to the previously discussed Coleman model. It is suggested that small groups of elected officials will be motivated to exchange their votes on particular issues or policy alternatives in a manner which will assure majority support for alternatives which are of advantage to the groups or jurisdictions they represent. As in the Coleman analysis, the approach used by Buchanan and Tullock goes beyond the consideration of a single budgetary alternative.

In a general sense, a voter or elected official can array all possible budgetary alternatives according to his/her relative intensities of preference for them. Accordingly, welfare can be increased by accepting a decision counter to one's interests, in an area where preferences are *low*, in exchange for a decision in accordance with preferences, in an area where the utility assessment is *high*. Such bargains or vote exchanges can be mutually beneficial. Basically, the voter should exchange until the *marginal cost* of voting for a policy alternative which he/she disapproves, but for which the disapproval is weak, equals the expected *marginal gain* of the vote or votes obtained in return support for issues about which he/she has stronger preferences. The total bargaining or exchange mechanism should allow a *net gain* to the voter.

The rational voter would attempt to acquire the agreement of only a simple majority (50 percent plus one vote) of the voters, not all of them. He or she can initially ignore the remaining minority of the voters. However, the reverse also is true. That is, exchanges will most likely be made in which the voter does *not* participate, but for which some part of the costs of the action must be borne. In essence, these would constitute voter externality costs, as discussed earlier in this chapter. The ultimate result from the exchange mechanism of logrolling or vote trading will be to yield the individual benefits from only slightly more than half of the total exchanges made. Thus, a simple majority voting rule in group or collective decision making in the political process of a democracy will cause *external costs* as well as *internal gains* from the bargaining process. This situation would persist unless the simple majority voting rule were changed so as to allow the minority to receive compensation payments from the majority.

It should be observed that even though the logrolling model of Buchanan and Tullock provides an improved analytical framework for understanding the efficiency issues which arise under majority voting conditions, logrolling itself does not assure the attainment of a close approximation to Pareto optimality, due to such factors as institutional complexities and informational problems. Logrolling, undoubtedly, *does* tend to improve efficiency by allowing for the representation of

---

[16] Buchanan and Tullock, *Calculus of Consent.*

relative preference intensities. However, the greatest efficiency contribution would seemingly require a sort of "purely competitive"
logrolling, in which all elected politicians start out with the same
bargaining strength. This is often not the case, as exemplified by the
considerably greater influence often exerted on legislation by powerful committee chairpersons in Congress in such committees as Ways
and Means (House) and the Finance Committee (Senate). Moreover,
it is argued that logrolling may lead to an overexpansion of the public
sector. This would occur if it results in a situation in which the
aggregate costs for all voters are greater than their aggregate benefits.

Another approach to the revelation of individual preferences in the
political process takes the form of the *competitive model* of Anthony
Downs.[17] This model emphasizes the role of political parties in the
decision-making process of the public sector. Specifically, it views a
political party in terms of its *vote-maximization* motivation for the
purpose of survival in office.[18] The politicians have no direct interest
in welfare maximization, but only in vote maximization, and party
platforms are designed to conform with the consensus preference of
large groups of voters. It can be assumed that individuals will vote for
the party which best represents their welfare, or the party which
maximizes their net benefits (over tax costs) from public sector decisions. The greater the consensus of the population on major issues, the
more effective is the process. Where significant disagreement exists
on major issues, two or more major political parties are likely to exist,
with the possibility that no single party can exert a majority influence.

Adequate information is a basic requirement for the efficient operation of this system. Ideally, this would include complete knowledge of
voter preference patterns for both public and private goods, and complete knowledge of the effects of alternative budget policies. Neither
condition is likely to be present to a substantial degree.[19] Moreover,
considerable knowledge of voter preference patterns would encourage additional strategy, with significant complications for the cost of
negotiating agreements within a large group. Hence, the competitive
model, though analytically useful in broadening the understanding of
the political decision-making process, cannot be relied on to provide
conditions closely approximating Pareto optimality.

Another derivation of the concept of competition in the political
process is provided in the works of Charles E. Lindblom and Aaron

---

[17] Anthony Downs, *An Economic Theory of Democracy* (New York: Harper & Row,
1957).

[18] Vote maximization was also a feature of the Bartlett political influence analysis
discussed earlier.

[19] For a relevant discussion, see J. G. Head, "The Theory of Public Goods," paper
delivered at the Conference on Economic Policy, University of Queensland, Australia,
August 1967, pp. 21–22.

Wildavsky.[20] This approach builds on the premise of widespread *decentralization* and *differentiation* within the system of democratic political decision making. It is argued that the presence of a large number of diversified participants in the budgetary process, ranging from legislators to the employees of government agencies, guarantees representation for *all relevant viewpoints* in governmental policy-making. Thus, a form of "policy competition" is said to exist in the public sector, in a manner analogous to the widespread representation provided by competitive forces in the market sector of the economy.[21] An adjunct to this analysis is the budgetary approach known as *incrementalism*—a process by which, rather than reviewing the entire budget and each program therein in each budgetary period, the budget is only marginally changed in reference to the previous period's budgetary base.[22]

The *spatial mobility approach* to decision-making efficiency in the political process was initially developed by Charles Tiebout.[23] Its focal point is the "market-type decision" which occurs when individuals voluntarily select the particular political jurisdiction in which they wish to reside. As long as individuals can move freely among jurisdictions, they are afforded the opportunity of selecting the particular budgetary mix of expenditures and taxation which best meets their fiscal preferences. Undoubtedly, consumer sovereignty and the attendant allocational efficiency qualities are implicit in this "voting-by-your-feet" approach. Nonetheless, a choice of alternative fiscal mixes is *not* a realistic option for many individuals, because they have inflexible employment options and for numerous other reasons. Hence, the spatial mobility approach, though conceptually valid, is limited in its overall scope. It cannot serve as a general efficiency framework for making individual economic decisions within a democratic political process.

THE POLITICAL CONSTITUTION AND FISCAL RULES[24]

The *theory of public goods* should be complemented by a *theory of political institutions* within a *positive economics framework*. In polit-

---

[20] See the summary of this approach in Oliver Oldman and Ferdinand P. Schoettle, *State and Local Taxes and Finance* (Mineola, N.Y.: Foundation Press, 1974), pp. 913–16.

[21] However, it should be observed that just as monopoly forces can distort individual representation in the market, political power blocs, which are often related to such economic forces, can affect public sector representation.

[22] The incremental approach to budgeting will be further discussed in Chapter 4.

[23] See Charles M. Tiebout, "A Pure Theory of Local Expenditures," *Journal of Political Economy*, October 1956, pp. 416–24. The spatial mobility approach will also be considered in the analysis of intergovernmental fiscal relationships in Chapter 17.

[24] For a discussion of this topic, see Buchanan, *Demand and Supply of Public Goods*, chaps. 7 and 8.

ical choice there should exist a means of comparing economic benefits and costs over a range of alternative budget policies and over a period of time. Moreover, the basic theory of the demand and supply of public goods, and the political decision-making process which responds to these demand and supply forces, should also consider the means of financing these goods. Thus, various tax-sharing schemes are highly relevant to the analysis. Furthermore, it is important to recognize that considerable decision-making costs usually are incurred in reaching collective decisions in the public sector.

In the typical large-group situation, the costs of attaining "voluntary agreements" among individuals are prohibitive, and decisions ordinarily will *not be made* unless some agreement on decision-making procedures can be reached among the individual members of the society. These include: (1) the basic *political constitution,* such as the adoption of a simple majority democratic voting system which makes the political process operational, and (2) the establishment of specific *fiscal rules* within the framework of the political constitution.

If a society can predict that fiscal decisions will be made on a yearly basis, and that these decisions will be similar in a number of respects, the individual members of the society may reach an agreement to impose various *ongoing fiscal rules* upon themselves through their legislative assemblies. For example, the society may select a system of tax-sharing arrangements for distributing tax burdens, which may remain in effect over a long period of time. Such a tax structure need not be changed every time specific decisions concerning the allocation of public goods are made during a particular fiscal year. Decision-making costs are reduced if a new tax structure does not have to be set up for each successive fiscal year.

In summary, the theoretical demand and supply of public goods concept should be integrated in the real world of positive economic policies with those political conventions and fiscal institutions which help to implement the society's preferences for public goods. In other words, the individual members of a society must adopt procedures of public choice in the political process. The indivisible (joint consumption) nature of public goods prohibits the effective use of market principles in political decision making. Therefore, in order to reach group decisions and achieve the potential gains from trade which are available, society must establish a general political constitution and specific fiscal rules, including financing schemes. These make it possible for society to supply the public and quasi-public goods desired by its members. Society elects to accept compulsion in the form of coercive governmental action not only to circumvent the free-rider allocational problem, but also to reduce negotiation costs and to provide greater overall efficiency in public sector decision making.

4

Fiscal institutions

Having emphasized some of the *conceptual* issues involved in making public choice decisions in a democracy in the previous chapter, we now turn our emphasis to some of the important *institutional arrangements* by which the public choice process actually takes place in the American public sector. These include the constitutional assignment of fiscal powers—an especially important matter in a federation with its two sovereign levels of government; the major steps of federal government budgetary procedure; alternative types of government budgets, and the use of benefit-cost analysis along with a planning-programming budgeting systems (PPBS) approach.

CONSTITUTIONAL DIVISION OF FISCAL POWERS

The federal Constitution is the basic legal document which allocates the fiscal powers of taxing and spending between the federal and state levels of government in the United States. The political structure of the public sector in the United States is that of a *federation*, with a division of sovereign governmental power between the central government and the states.[1] This can be contrasted to a *unitary* system of government, such as that in Great Britain, where only the central government is sovereign. In both nations, the political structure is that of a representative democracy, and local governments are

---

[1] A sovereign government is one which possesses independent or autonomous authority. That is, it exists by its own right and not as a creation of some other unit of government.

nonsovereign. They are created through state government sovereignty in the United States and by the central government in Great Britain.

Two powers inherent in sovereign government give the public sector the authority to institute tax laws. These are the *revenue* and *police* powers of government; the former implies the basic right of government to collect revenues for the support of public sector functions, and the latter gives authority to sovereign government to control persons and property for the purpose of promoting the general welfare. Most taxes exist for both revenue and welfare purposes, but the revenue motive is usually dominant.[2]

The Constitution, by denying certain rights and powers to the federal and state governments, reserves them to the American people. Furthermore, it defines certain *enumerated powers* for the federal government. These are supplemented by other *implied powers* which have their basic origin in judicial interpretation. State governments also have certain powers reserved to them by the Constitution. In this regard, the Tenth Amendment to the Constitution states that "the powers not delegated to the United States by the Constitution, nor prohibited by it to the States, are reserved to the States respectively, or to the people."

The boundary between federal and state authority is difficult to define precisely. While a unitary system of government can rely primarily on unwritten tradition for its politico-economic direction, a federal system requires a written constitution and judicial interpretation of the laws which are legislated under the constitution. The trend in the United States during much of the 20th century has been toward a more liberal interpretation of the Constitution to provide greater central government authority in setting the political-economic direction of the society. However, at the present time the presidential administration of Ronald Reagan is leading a movement to reverse this trend. Meanwhile, a perennial conflict exists between the federal government's obligation to "promote the general welfare" and its constitutional inability to "compel coordination and uniformity" among the tax and expenditure policies of the various states.

An extremely important fiscal clause in the Constitution gives Congress the "Power to lay and collect Taxes, Duties, Imposts and Excises, to pay the Debts and provide for the common Defence and general Welfare."[3] This represents a very extensive grant of power from the Constitution to the federal government. The Constitutional Convention was called in 1787 primarily for the purpose of solving the post–Revolutionary War financial crisis of the new nation. Prior to the adoption of the Constitution, the Continental Congress, which di-

---

[2] See the relevant discussion in Chapter 5.

[3] *U.S. Constitution.* Art. I. Sec. 8.

rected the new nation, possessed no taxing authority. Instead, only the states had the authority to impose taxes. As a result, a major financial crisis occurred. This extensive fiscal clause, which was a by-product of the financial crisis, received intense discussion at the Continental Congress. The more liberal interpretation over the years of "general welfare," in terms of central governmental authority, has followed, in part, from a more liberal interpretation of the concept of interstate commerce.

Fiscal limitations on the federal government

The Constitution places several significant limitations on the fiscal activities of the federal government. First, the federal government is prohibited from taxing the export of goods to other nations. However, it is not prohibited from levying taxes (duties) on goods imported from other countries.

A second limitation placed on federal fiscal authority by the Constitution is the provision that "all Duties, Imposts and Excises shall be uniform throughout the United States."[4] This uniformity clause refers to geographical uniformity. For example, legal residence in one state rather than in another cannot be the basis for differential federal personal income tax rates. Or, the federal gasoline excise cannot be 10 cents per gallon in New York and 4 cents per gallon in California. Furthermore, the federal government could not impose a gasoline tax in one state without imposing it in all other states.

A third important federal government fiscal limitation in the Constitution is the *apportionment clause* which holds that "no Capitation, or other direct, Tax shall be laid, unless in Proportion to the Census."[5] The Constitution does not define clearly what is meant by a "direct" tax, though probably the founding fathers had property taxes and poll (lump-sum) taxes in mind. However, the clause has been used historically to question the constitutionality of a federal personal income tax. This led supporters of the income tax to seek a constitutional amendment. An income tax, of course, would be unacceptable in reference to the ability-to-pay principle if it had to be apportioned among the various states according to population. For example, two states may each possess a population of 20 million people. However, the residents of one state may have an aggregate taxable income base of $100 billion and those of the other (poorer) state may have an aggregate taxable income base of only $50 billion. If the income tax were considered to be a direct tax, the taxpayers of each state would be required to contribute the same absolute amount of tax revenues to

---

[4] *U.S. Constitution.* Art. I. Sec. 8.

[5] *U.S. Constitution.* Art. I. Sec. 9.

the federal government, in accordance with their equal populations, even though the taxpayers of one state have a much greater tax-paying ability than those of the other. Hence, the per capita amount of income tax would be the same in each state, even though the per capita incomes would be different. The tax, in effect, would be regressive against the residents of the lower-income state.

Consequently, the 16th Amendment to the Constitution, adopted in 1913, excludes the income tax from the direct tax apportionment limitation. It states: "The Congress shall have power to lay and collect taxes on incomes, from whatever source derived, without apportionment among the several States, and without regard to any census or enumeration." The constitutionality of federal income taxation using a progressive (graduated) rate structure is made abundantly clear by this amendment.

A fourth important provision in the Constitution on fiscal matters is found in the Fifth Amendment. This amendment states that "no person shall be . . . deprived of life, liberty, or property, without due process of law." The implication is that taxes and other fiscal actions cannot be so arbitrary or discriminatory as to result in the confiscation of property or the denial of fundamental personal rights. Actually, the federal courts have not employed this clause to any great extent as a limitation on federal fiscal powers, but they have stated that the use of poll taxes by lower-level governments as a "condition" for voting in federal elections is unconstitutional.

Fiscal limitations on state governments

Several significant limitations are imposed by the Constitution on the fiscal authority of state governments and, indirectly, on the local governments they create. First, state governments, like the federal government, are prohibited from taxing exports. Second, they are constrained by a due-process provision similar to that described above for the federal government, as prescribed for states in the 14th Amendment to the Constitution. As applied to taxation, this provision prohibits the imposition of taxes by state and local governments beyond their legal areas of jurisdiction, as well as prohibiting unduly arbitrary or confiscatory taxation. Third, state governments are prohibited from levying import duties without the consent of Congress. Fourth, state governments are prohibited from the levying of tonnage taxes, based on the size or capacity of boats on inland rivers and lakes, without the permission of Congress. Fifth, since states are explicitly forbidden to levy export, import, and tonnage taxes, it is implied, and also verified by judicial interpretation, that they cannot tax interstate and foreign commerce. Moreover, the Constitution directly relegates this authority to the federal government when it gives Congress the right "to regulate Commerce with foreign Nations, and *among the several* States, and with the Indian Tribes."[6] Sixth, an indirect limitation on state fiscal authority results from the fact that the Constitution gives the federal government exclusive authority to make treaties with other nations. When such treaties relate to fiscal matters, state governments are bound to set their tax and expenditure actions in accordance with the terms of the treaties.

The taxation of governmental instrumentalities

An important area of indirect legal limitation on both federal and state governments involves the taxation of governmental instrumentalities. This is not stated explicitly in the Constitution, but instead has been developed through judicial interpretation. According to this limitation (which is replete with exceptions to the rule), state governments cannot tax federal instrumentalities, and the federal government cannot tax state instrumentalities. Of course, such an "immunities" concept could exist only in a federation where sovereign state or provincial governments exist alongside a sovereign central government. *Governmental instrumentalities* are difficult to define. One public finance scholar has observed that, in its broadest sense, the term would include "all corporations (that get their charters from governments), all land (underlying title lies with state governments), banks, copyrights and patents, voting, college football games, sale to or by the government, government property, government bonds, and government enterprises."[7] In any case, governmental property, sales, and legal instruments would normally be classified as instrumentalities of government. An example of this limitation is the fact that state governments do not tax the properties of the federal government, such as national forest lands, which are located within their political jurisdictions. However, the federal government does make some "in lieu" payments to subnational governments in these cases.

Fiscal limitations imposed by state government constitutions

State government constitutions also impose fiscal limitations, though considerable variation exists among the states as to the nature and extent of these limitations. The most common limitation found in state constitutions is that which stipulates that taxes must be uniform and/or equal. For example, property tax rates and assessments should

---

[6] *U.S. Constitution.* Art. I. Sec. 8.

[7] Harold M. Groves, *Financing Government* (New York: Holt, Rinehart & Winston, 1964), p. 434.

be uniform for the same class of property within the same jurisdiction. Among the wide variety of other special fiscal provisions are the following:

1. Rate limitations on taxes, especially on property taxes, though sometimes on income and selective excise taxes.
2. Earmarked taxes, such as highway user taxes (typified by state gasoline taxes).
3. Property and income tax exemptions.
4. Origination of revenue bills in the lower house of the state legislature.
5. Specification that taxes must be for public purposes.
6. Prohibition of particular types of taxes such as income and poll taxes.

One version of rate limitations is found in the highly publicized Jarvis-Gann Amendment to the California State Constitution, known as Proposition 13 and approved during June 1978, which limited local government property taxes to 1 percent of the 1975–76 market value of real property. Moreover, this amendment restricted increases in assessments to an annual growth rate of 2 percent a year. In addition, any increase in local government nonproperty taxes would require the two-thirds approval of all eligible voters. Finally, any increase in state government taxes would require the two-thirds approval of the state legislature. These changes in California prompted numerous subsequent property tax and overall fiscal limitations to be approved in other states.

In summary, the federal Constitution and the various state constitutions place numerous limitations on the fiscal behavior of the public sector in the United States. Nevertheless, none of the constitutions (federal or state) places any significant limitation on the type of public purpose for which taxes may be imposed. As noted earlier, taxes may be imposed for revenue or for regulatory purposes or, as is usually the case, for a combination of both objectives.

FEDERAL BUDGETARY PROCEDURE

The present federal budgetary process was basically designed by the Budget and Accounting Act of 1921, with its latest important revision coming in the Congressional Budget and Impoundment Control Act of 1974. This budgetary procedure may be divided into four phases: (1) executive preparation and submission, (2) legislative review and enactment, (3) executive implementation, and (4) auditing by the General Accounting Office. These four steps in federal budgeting will be discussed in the sequence with which they are practiced.

Executive preparation and submission of the budget

The proposed budget is formulated in the executive branch of the federal government primarily under the direction of the *Office of Management and Budget* (OMB). Preliminary planning begins some 19 months before a budget goes into effect, when federal agencies prepare estimates of their desired expenditures for the fiscal year which will begin 19 months later. For example, Fiscal Year 1984 begins on October 1, 1983 and ends on September 30, 1984.[8] Expenditure estimates by federal agencies would be prepared beginning approximately in March 1982 for the 1984 fiscal year. In approximately May 1982, these estimates would be submitted to OMB for preliminary review. By this time, the executive branch would have formulated its overall fiscal philosophy for the budget year in question. This is ordinarily done by the President in consultation with the director of OMB, the Secretary of the Treasury, and the three members of the President's Council of Economic Advisors plus other key domestic and economic policy advisors. These individuals are assisted by revenue estimates and other analyses from the Treasury Department and by economic forecasts and other analyses from the Council of Economic Advisors.

It is the Treasury Department which assumes the primary responsibility for the vast amount of work involved in the preparation of the *tax recommendations* contained in a proposed budget. Within the Treasury Department, two staffs concentrate on this task. These are the Office of Tax Analysis, composed primarily of economists and statisticians, and the Office of the Tax Legislative Counsel, comprised primarily of attorneys. The Office of Tax Analysis provides revenue estimates based on tax changes, overall revenue projections based on current taxes, and a general analysis of tax issues and their effects on the economy. The Office of the Tax Legislative Counsel provides legal and accounting analyses of tax issues and, in addition, drafts tax legislation and decides on tax rulings and regulations.

Once the Office of Management and Budget receives the preliminary expenditure estimates from federal agencies, it reviews the budget requests and returns them to the agencies, accompanied by a statement of the administration's overall fiscal philosophy for the fiscal year in question, and suggested budgetary policies for the agencies. Then, in the summer of 1982, the agencies begin to recast their expenditure requests in accordance with the administration's philosophy and specific requests. The "revised formal estimates" are resubmitted during the period September–November 1982 to OMB—

---

[8] The fiscal year of the federal government takes the name of the calendar year in which the fiscal period terminates. Hence, the fiscal year which ends on September 30, 1984, is termed Fiscal Year 1984.

which reviews and discusses them in detail with the respective agencies. The agencies may then be asked to defend or change their expenditure requests. The President has the authority, operating through OMB, to reduce expenditure requests. Then, by early 1983, OMB, following the desires of the President, assembles the various estimates, after one final revision, into a unified budget document including both estimated revenues and proposed expenditures. The proposed budget for Fiscal Year 1984 would be submitted by the President to Congress within 15 days after Congress convenes in early 1983.

Legislative review and enactment of the budget

In a parliamentary system of government, the legislature usually adopts the executive budget in substantially the form in which it is presented. In the American system, the executive budget is likely to be considerably altered by Congress. In fact, Congress has always guarded its budgetary authority, especially its taxing power, jealously. After being submitted to Congress by the President, the budget is first referred to the Appropriations Committee of the House of Representatives, which in our ongoing example would be in early 1983. Then various subcommittees of the House Appropriations Committee conduct hearings at which the government agencies are asked to explain and defend their budget requests. The separate appropriations bills are subsequently returned to the House Appropriations Committee, which submits them to the floor of the House for ultimate debate and passage. The Senate Appropriations Committee follows a procedure similar to that in the House.

When an appropriations bill is passed by both houses of Congress, after differences have been ironed out, it goes to the President for signature. The chief executive does *not* have the authority of selective (item) veto, that is, the bill must be accepted totally or not at all. This encourages the attachment of riders and the practices of pork barreling and logrolling. The selective (item) veto *is* used by many states, but Congress traditionally fears that the selective veto represents a dangerous extension of presidential power.[9]

Tax bills, as well as appropriations bills, according to constitutional provisions, must originate in the House of Representatives. The research work provided by two joint committees in Congress, and by the Congressional Budget Office (established in 1974), assists in the decision-making process regarding the enactment of a budget. These committees are the Joint Committee on Taxation (formerly known as the

---

[9] For a discussion favoring the selective veto, *see Hearings before the House Expenditures Committee*, July 8 and 18, 1950, on H.R. 8054, 81st cong., 2d. sess. (Washington, D.C.: U.S. Government Printing Office, 1950).

Joint Committee on Internal Revenue Taxation) and the Joint Economic Committee. Considerable lobbying pressures are exerted to influence the final legislation by Congress, as they are on the executive branch to influence the budget submitted by the President to Congress. A large number of such pressure groups, often referred to as *Political Action Committees*, exists. They represent many segments of American society including business, labor, and state-local governments. Moreover, internal lobbying occurs within the federal government by the respective agencies of the government.

Revenue bills eventually work their way from the House Committee on Ways and Means to the floor of the House for enactment. Subsequently, Senate revenue bills are considered in the Senate Committee on Finance, go to the Senate floor, and eventually are voted on. A final revenue bill passed by Congress reflects the compromise results of the Conference Committee, composed of members of both the House and Senate, which reconciles the House and Senate bills into a single bill. The membership of this committee is appointed by the Speaker of the House and the president of the Senate, and it normally consists of three members selected from the majority side and two from the minority side in each house of Congress. The Conference Committee is capable of exerting substantial influence on the final bill enacted by Congress. Moreover, considerable authority and discretion rest with the chairperson of this committee.

Prior to enactment of the Congressional Budget and Impoundment Control Act of 1974, the legislative machinery of Congress largely prevented it from considering the budget as a whole at any one time. The 1974 legislation has provided considerable help by establishing budget committees in both the House and Senate, by creating the Congressional Budget Office (CBO), and by establishing certain formalized procedures. Moreover, it changed the official fiscal year from a July 1–June 30 to a October 1–September 30 basis.

The CBO is essentially the congressional counterpart of OMB in the executive branch. It provides budgetary information and analysis to Congress, including an analysis of the President's newly submitted budget by April 1, and possesses broad authority to obtain data from the executive branch. It is formed on a nonpartisan basis.

The legislation also requires that Congress approve two "concurrent budgetary resolutions" relating overall revenues to expenditures—one on May 15 and the second on September 15, the latter either reaffirming or revising the May 15 resolution. Furthermore, the September 15 resolution must be reconciled with the various actions of the appropriations and tax committees by September 25. Thus, some 19 months after the federal agencies and OMB began their preliminary plans for the Fiscal 1984 budget (continuing our example), the budget would finally be ready for implementation on October 1, 1983.

Executive implementation of the budget

The President has the obligation to implement (execute) the budget. The Office of Management and Budget authorizes the various agencies to spend the appropriated funds on a quarterly basis. This is to prevent an agency from spending too much of its yearly appropriation early in the fiscal year. Once the budget authorizations are received, the agencies may purchase economic goods and productive resources, as needed, to perform their various functions. The Treasury Department releases funds in accordance with vouchers that have been prepared by the spending agencies. The funds are to be spent within the legislative intent of the appropriations bills, but a reasonable amount of discretion is left to the agencies.

Auditing of the budget by the General Accounting Office

Congress has created the General Accounting Office (GAO), headed by the Comptroller General, to assure that appropriated funds are spent in accordance with provisions of the appropriations bill and to discourage fraud. This office reports directly to Congress. Several thousand accountants are employed by the GAO to help it perform its huge task. It is a quasi-judicial agency in the sense that it must interpret the intent Congress had at the time the legislation was enacted.

The broad powers of the GAO include: (1) the authority to decide most questions involving payments made by government agencies; (2) the auditing and settling of all public accounts; (3) settling, adjudicating, and adjusting all claims for and against the government; (4) describing systems and procedures for administrative appropriation and fund accounting, and (5) the investigation of all matters relating to receipts and disbursements of public funds, including the right to examine certain books, documents, papers, and records of government contractors and subcontractors. In addition to the GAO as such, the Office of the Comptroller General assists Congress by making studies and analyses of expenditure administration by the various governmental agencies.

The concepts of contained specialization and incremental decision making.[10] Despite its cumbersome nature and the presence of con-

---

[10] For an excellent discussion of these concepts as well as the overall institutional nature of public sector decision making in the United States, see Ira Sharkansky. *The Politics of Taxing and Spending* (Indianapolis: Bobbs-Merrill, 1969).

flict, the federal government "somehow" makes and implements fiscal decisions. Disputes over policy are reduced to an operational reality. Two institutional devices or fiscal rules which help to render the federal budgetary system operational are those of contained specialization and incremental decision making. *Contained specialization*, which integrates a number of separate institutions and behavioral patterns, encompasses "the assignment of specialists within the legislative and executive branches to formulate taxing and spending decisions, the capacity of these specialists to reach decisions on controversial issues with a minimum of partisan bickering among themselves, and the tendency of other members in the legislative and executive branches to accept the specialists' recommendations."[11] Though conflict over policy remains, operational policies are established. A sizable portion of the conflict is contained within institutions whose members possess the dual capacity to represent the various perspectives of a controversy, while at the same time they are able to accept a compromise position.

Incremental decision making institutionalizes decision making by reducing and simplifying the range of decisions which must be made: "The incrementalist does not attempt to write a tax or spending policy *de novo*, but accepts as given those policies already in force. He limits consideration to the *increment of change* that is proposed in taxes or expenditures."[12] This limited focus permits the decision maker to concentrate on the relevant issues involved in the decision. Moreover, previous decisions can be accepted as largely fixed parameters, and thus involvement in lingering policy disputes is avoided. Indeed, it is through such fiscal rules as contained specialization and incremental decision making that the complex federal budgetary procedure is made operational.

Zero-base budgeting. Despite the continuing overriding importance of incremental decision making, the presidential administration of President Jimmy Carter, as well as some subnational governments, have employed an essentially opposite supplemental budgetary technique. This instrument, known as *zero-base budgeting*, starts from the premise that an agency's budget base contains no programs or funding. Thus, theoretically, every agency program and program component should be evaluated vis-á-vis the agency's other programs, as well as the programs of other agencies, before being placed in the budget. Such an undertaking, of course, would be enormous. Hence, except for providing a general framework that requires all programs to be justified in some manner, zero-base budgeting does not appear to

---

[11] Ibid., p. 34.

[12] Ibid. Also, this point will be considered in Chapter 14—"Tax Reform: Alternative Tax Instruments for the American Public Sector."

be able to accomplish its nonetheless meritable objectives. Moreover, zero-base budgeting would require specific criteria for evaluating and comparing alternative programs. Thus, it would ultimately fall back on such established fiscal instruments as benefit-cost analysis (to be discussed later in the chapter).

TYPES OF GOVERNMENT BUDGETS

The unified federal budget

Until fairly recently, the federal government did not use a single official type of budget but, instead, used three different budget concepts. The unified federal budget, adopted in 1968, resulted from the recommendations of a special Presidential Commission on Budget Concepts which had been established in 1967. The new budget was designed to utilize the best characteristics of the three previously employed federal government budgets—the administrative budget, the consolidated cash budget, and the national income accounts budget. The national income accounts budget still remains in separate use, due to its value in isolating federal fiscal activity as a component of the nation's national income and product accounts. It will be further discussed in this chapter. The *administrative* and *consolidated cash budgets* differed mainly in the fact that the latter included federal trust fund activities, while the former excluded these activities.

The unified federal budget comprises an overall financial plan encompassing a set of comprehensive and integrated accounts. These accounts or subdivisions of the budget are: (1) budget authority; (2) budget receipts, expenditures, and surplus or deficit; (3) outstanding federal debt; and (4) outstanding federal loans. Table 4–1 summarizes the major subdivisions of the unified federal budget as now implemented.[13] They differ somewhat from the precise recommendations of the Presidential Commission on Budget Concepts.

The first section of the unified budget provides a statement of the new appropriations requested by the President and relates these to appropriations that will become available during the fiscal year, due to previous congressional legislative action. The summation of the newly proposed and previously approved appropriations amounts to *total appropriations* for budgetary action during the fiscal year in question.

The second, and no doubt most essential, section of the budget presents the receipts, expenditures, and the resulting surplus, bal-

---

[13] For a more detailed discussion of the application of the federal unified budget, see David J. Ott and Attiat F. Ott, *Federal Budget Policy*, 3d ed. (Washington, D.C.: Brookings Institution, 1977), chap. 2

TABLE 4–1   The unified federal budget

I. *Budget Authority*
   1. New proposals for action by Congress
   2. Continuing appropriations approved at earlier sessions of Congress
      1 + 2 = Total appropriations

II. *Receipts, Expenditures, and Surplus or Deficit*
   1. Receipts
      a. General (federal fund) receipts
      b. Trust fund receipts
         a + b = Total budget receipts

   2. Expenditures
      a. General (federal fund) expenditures*
      b. Trust fund expenditures
         a + b = Total budget expenditures

   3. Surplus or deficit
      a. General (federal fund)
      b. Trust funds
         a + b = Total budget surplus or deficit

III. *Outstanding Debt, End of Year*
   1. Gross amount
   2. Held by the public and by federal agencies

IV. *Outstanding Loans, End of Year*
   1. Direct loans
   2. Guaranteed and insured loans
   3. Government-sponsored enterprise loans

---

* Includes net lending.

ance, or deficit of the federal budget.[14] The receipts and expenditures are further subdivided into *general* (federal fund) and *trust fund* categories. However, the overall federal surplus or deficit is the result of aggregating *both* the general and trust fund activities. If federal nondebt receipts, so aggregated, exceed aggregate expenditures, the "unusual" occurrence of a federal *surplus* budget is at hand. However, if the "usual" occurrence of an excess of aggregate expenditures over aggregate nondebt receipts is the case, the federal budget is in a *deficit* position. Of course, an equality of nondebt receipts and expenditures would represent a *balanced* budget. If the general receipts and expenditures are separated from those passing through trust funds, the general account would usually show a deficit, but the trust account would ordinarily show a surplus.

The third and fourth sections of the unified budget provide data concerning outstanding federal debt and outstanding federal loans, respectively. In Section III, the effects on the federal debt of the

---

[14] Federal *intra*governmental transactions are excluded from (netted out of) the unified budget figures. An example of such a transaction would be the interest on federal bonds owned by a federal agency.

budgetary results in Section II are described. Moreover, it provides a gross debt figure and then disaggregates this amount into those portions held by the public and by federal agencies. Section IV includes data concerning direct loans by federal agencies, guaranteed and insured loans, and loans to corporations initially sponsored by the federal government, but now private in character.

Unfortunately, the data in Section II do not include all federal revenue and spending activities. There are a number of so-called off-budget programs and government-sponsored enterprises, not included in the unified budget, which nonetheless exert important fiscal and economic effects. Funding for many of the off-budget programs is handled by the Federal Financing Bank which purchases the obligations of such "on budget" agencies as the Tennessee Valley Authority and the Export-Import Bank. Meanwhile, the most important of the government-sponsored enterprises carry out loan programs and include such agencies as the Federal National Mortgage Association and the Student Loan Marketing Association. The estimated *deficit* of these off-budget programs and government-sponsored enterprises during fiscal 1981 was nearly $47 billion, but it did not even show up in the official unified budget figures.

The national income accounts budget

The national income accounts budget (NIA) is comprised of the federal government component of the national income and product accounts, as provided by the U.S. Department of Commerce. These accounts are used to measure the composition by sector and the total value of economic output (gross national product), and the income claims against that output. The NIA budget is similar to the unified budget, both in its inclusion of federal trust fund activities and in its exclusion of intragovernmental transactions. Yet, the two budgets differ in other important ways. The NIA budget, for example, considers *receipts* (except for nonwithheld personal taxes) on an *accrual* rather than on an *actual-payment* basis, and *expenditures* generally at either the time of accrual or when goods or resources are delivered—not at the time of payment. Hence, the timing of the NIA budget is more closely associated with actual productive activity than is that of the unified budget, thus making it superior for evaluating the effects of the federal budget on aggregate economic performance. Moreover, purely financial transactions of a nonproductive nature are excluded from the NIA budget.

The capital budget

A capital budget separates total government expenditure into current and capital items. This type of budget was suggested for the federal government by the Budget and Accounting Act of 1921, but it does not formally employ the concept. The *current* part of a capital budget reflects *recurring* expenditures, such as the salaries of government workers, office supplies, and annual depreciation—even though the latter does not represent an actual cash flow. The *capital* component of the budget reflects *nonrecurring* expenditure on capital assets of a durable nature. The budget would be considered balanced if current tax collections (or other receipts except those from borrowing) equal current expenditures, including depreciation allowances for existing durable goods. It is implied that long-term capital investment should be financed through borrowing (debt creation) activities rather than from current revenues.

The capital budget concept for central (national) governments was popular in Scandinavia, especially Sweden, during the 1930s and is used in other nations, such as the Netherlands, England, Canada, India, Pakistan, Republic of South Africa, and Ecuador. A number of American states and municipalities, although not strictly using a capital budget, use an implicit version of capital budgeting in the sense of having a priority list of capital projects and a philosophical preference to avoid the financing of current expenditures by debt.

The capital budget may be defended on the grounds that it shows that government spending often results in the acquisition of durable, productive capital and, thus, may be valuable to society's welfare. Relatedly, the capital budget possesses the advantage of pointing up the often-overlooked fact that the failure of current receipts to cover all expenditures, both current and capital, is not indicative, per se, of fiscal irresponsibility. The capital budget could provide a disservice to society, however, if it leads to an excessive investment in durable capital goods at the expense of current services or worthy investments in human resources. Furthermore, a complete divorcement from the orthodox idea of budget balance could lead to irrational fiscal action.[15] A relevant study recommends against the adoption of capital budgeting by the federal government.[16]

State and local government budgets

There are three major types of budget systems in use by state and local governments in the United States: the executive, committee or board, and legislative budget systems. The *executive budget* approach is similar to that employed by the federal government in that the chief executive of the state—the governor—must prepare and formally pre-

---

[15] This subject will be discussed further in Chapter 21.

[16] See Maynard S. Comiez, *A Capital Budget Statement for the U.S. Government* (Washington, D.C.: The Brookings Institution, 1966).

sent a proposed budget to the state legislature. The governor is assisted in this regard by a budgetary agency or staff. Most states use the executive budget technique, and it is used also by many large municipal governments. It is especially conducive to use by those municipalities that have a city manager format of local government administration.

The *committee or board budget* approach is used by several states and many municipalities. This budget system fits in well with governmental organizations characterized by administrative decentralization. If employed by a state government, the "committee" typically consists of the governor and the administrative heads of the major departments of state government with, in some instances, representatives from the state legislature.

The *legislative budget* is utilized primarily by smaller units of local government. In this technique, a legislative agency performs both the preparation and enactment functions. It is used mostly when the executive and legislative branches of government cannot be distinguished clearly, such as when a municipality is administered by a city council.

In general, the budgetary process tends to be somewhat less complex at the state-local level of government than at the federal level. Moreover, benefits derived from public sector expenditures tend to be somewhat easier to measure. However, there do exist greater constraints on revenues at the state-local level, due to such factors as constitutional limitations on borrowing and the overall scarcity of good revenue sources.

BENEFIT–COST ANALYSIS AND PLANNING–PROGRAMMING BUDGETING SYSTEMS (PPBS)

The benefit-cost concept

Benefit-cost analysis is a fiscal instrument intended to improve the efficiency with which public sector budgetary decisions are made. This approach attempts primarily to compare the relative economic merits of alternative governmental capital projects. All of the relevant benefits and costs of a particular project or investment are identified and, as far as possible, these benefits and costs are quantified and valued in monetary terms. In turn, projects may be compared with one another on the basis of their relative economic merits. If applied in a comprehensive manner, benefit-cost analysis would ideally guide an optimal allocation of resources between both the private and public sectors of the economy as well as within the public sector.

The selection among alternative investment projects may be

guided by reference to the *benefit-cost ratio (B/C)*, which relates the present value of the *total benefits (B)* which flow from a particular investment project to the present value of the *total costs (C)* of that project, and also by the *net benefit criterion (B − C)*, which consists of the total benefits minus the total costs of the project. Of the two efficiency criteria, the net benefit criterion is generally the more accurate indicator of the best project selection, since it works effectively under certain circumstances in which the benefit-cost ratio is less reliable. This point will be demonstrated later.

Discounting of the future benefit and cost streams from the long-run project to their present values is required because the benefits derived in some future year will tend to be worth less than benefits derived at the present time. Moreover, the same is true for costs, since opportunity costs represent the present value of foregone consumption. Thus, a *discount* or *interest* factor must be applied in order to estimate the present value of future benefits and costs.[17] The selection of a particular rate of discount (interest) will influence the relative ranking of alternative investment projects, depending on the duration of each project. A higher discount rate, for example, will tend to favor shorter-term investment projects, and vice versa.

If the benefits and costs of all investment projects were completely *divisible* into small units, and if such data were readily measurable, the task of obtaining efficient resource allocation would be relatively easy. For example, *total benefits* (ΣB) would be maximized in the *intersector* allocation of resources when the following conditions were present:

$$\frac{MB_a}{MB_b} = \frac{MC_a}{MC_b}$$

where *MB* refers to marginal benefits, *MC* to marginal costs, subscript *a* to the private sector, subscript *b* to the public sector, and where the marginal benefits and marginal costs can be measured in dollar units. Furthermore, once the size of the aggregate public sector budget is so determined, efficient *intrapublic sector* allocation would be determined by the conditions:

$$\frac{MB_x}{MB_y} = \frac{MC_x}{MC_y}$$

---

[17] The present value, *PV*, of an amount, *A*, due in a certain number of years, *n*, discounted at a particular rate of interest, *i*, is found with the following formula:

$$PV = \frac{A}{(1 + i)^n}$$

or,

$$PV = \frac{A_1}{1 + i} + \frac{A_2}{(1 + i)^2} + \frac{A_3}{(1 + i)^3} \cdots \frac{A_n}{(1 + i)^n}$$

where *MB* and *MC*, again, refer to marginal benefits and marginal costs, and the subscripts *x* and *y* refer to alternative governmental investment projects.

Unfortunately, many investment projects are not readily divisible, but instead are *lumpy* or *indivisible*. Moreover, the measurement of project benefits and costs is frequently imprecise and difficult. Thus, a commonly found condition is that of a *constrained* (or limited) government budget within which alternative expenditure projects must be compared, since marginal conditions cannot be applied for the simultaneous attainment of both the intersector and the intrapublic sector resource allocation solutions. If all such expenditure projects were of equal total cost, then the benefit-cost ratio could serve as an accurate indicator of which projects to select within the budget constraint. However, when such is not the case and the total costs differ between projects, the *B/C* criterion will not always give the best answer, that is, it would not necessarily select the project or projects which would maximize total benefits (ΣB). In this case, the net benefit criterion $(B - C)$ would be the superior criterion for indicating the best project choices, as can be observed in Table 4-2.

TABLE 4-2   **Comparison of benefit-cost ratio and net benefit criteria for best government budget choices, with budget constraint of $200,000**

	Project			
Criteria	A	B	C	B + C
Total benefits (B)*	$250,000	$190,000	$55,000	$245,000
Total costs (C)*	200,000	150,000	50,000	200,000
Benefit-cost ratio criterion (B/C)	1.25	1.27	1.10	1.225
Net benefit criterion (B − C)	$ 50,000	$40,000	$ 5,000	$ 45,000

* Discounted present value.
Results: B/C criterion: Projects B and C selected (total benefits = $245,000). B − C criterion: Project A selected (total benefits = $250,000).

In this table, the budget constraint is $200,000. The *B/C* ratio would indicate a first choice of project B, which has the highest ratio (1.27) at a cost of $150,000. The remaining $50,000 in the budget could then be allocated to Project C. However, the total benefits from this combination of projects are $245,000, which is less than the $250,000 in total benefits derived from project A. It should be noted that the net benefit criterion does indicate project A as the better choice, with a net value $50,000 above the $200,000 of total costs—a figure higher than the $45,000 net value for the combination of projects B and C. Or, stated alternately, the total benefits from project A are $250,000 while those from a combination of projects B and C are $245,000—each with a budget cost of $200,000.

An important step in benefit-cost analysis is the selection of an appropriate *social discount rate* which may be applied to the alternative projects so that their benefits and costs can be compared. The social discount rate should recognize that governmental investment decisions tend to be long run in nature, and thus it should contain a time-preference element. This is necessary because the present value of a dollar of benefits or costs would be worth more than the future value in 5, 10, or 20 years. Thus, an interest or discount factor must be applied in order to estimate the present value of future benefits and costs.

One school of thought argues that the best approximation to an ideal social discount rate is the *net yield* or *return on private investment* projects, that is, the marginal productivity of capital in private investment. Technically, this would be a weighted average of the opportunity-cost rate in private investment for *all* sectors of the economy from which the government investment would withdraw resources.[18] However, imperfections in capital markets do not allow a clear discernment of the marginal productivity of private capital investment. In practice, the discount rates utilized in the benefit-cost efforts of the federal government frequently have not approximated this version of the social discount rate. Instead, they have often moved far away from it by using the convenient government borrowing rate, that is, the *average interest rate paid by the U.S. Treasury on long-term government securities.* Formerly, most federal agencies used the *coupon rate* on federal securities, but more recently most agencies have switched to the *yield rate.*[19] The federal government borrowing rate represents an almost riskless type of investment, much unlike typical private investment. Thus, "too low" a discount rate tends to lead to the justification of "too many" governmental as opposed to private investment projects. Consequently, it tends to distort intersector resource allocation.[20] Although it is certain that the government borrowing rate is too low for social discount purposes, various adjustments can be used to blend this rate and the also imperfect marginal productivity of private capital investment rule, in order to provide a more rational social discount rate.

---

[18] See William J. Baumol, "On the Discount Rate for Public Projects," in *The Analysis and Evaluation of Public Expenditures: The PPB System,* vol. 1, Joint Economic Committee, 91st cong., 1st sess. (Washington, D.C.: U.S. Government Printing Office, 1969), pp. 497–98.

[19] The coupon rate can be represented by Annual nominal interest/Par value of bond, while the yield rate can be represented by Annual nominal interest/Current selling price of bond.

[20] This point will be discussed further in this chapter.

History of benefit-cost analysis and PPBS in the American public sector

The genesis of American public sector benefit-cost analysis began at the federal level of government in the early 1900s, when Congress required the Army Corps of Engineers to take into account the benefits to commerce as well as the costs of river and harbor projects. More pronounced attention was paid to federal water development projects, in benefit-cost terms, during the 1930s. Then, a new surge of interest in benefit-cost analysis, especially in the area of national defense expenditures, developed following World War II. This interest continued to grow during the 1950s and 1960s and, by the middle of the latter decade, the benefit-cost technique had been absorbed into the more elaborate *Planning-Programming Budgeting Systems* (PPBS) approach to federal budgetary efficiency. This occurred through an executive order by President Lyndon Johnson in 1965 which required federal agencies to utilize the PPBS technique.

The PPBS approach was intended to reduce the inefficiency inherent in conventional budgeting procedures. Conventional budgeting, for example, tends to emphasize the budget requests of government *agencies* which spend the public funds, rather than the *programs or goals* for which the funds are expended. Moreover, many programs are *interagency* in nature, which adds confusion to orthodox efforts to provide rationality in the public sector budget. In addition, the traditional stress has been on costs, in the sense of productive *inputs,* rather than on the *output* of economic goods and the benefits they provide. Furthermore, the conventional federal budgetary approach is essentially of a short, one-year duration. Yet, many programs include expenditures and benefits which cover a long time period. Thus, fiscal rationality obviously requires that the costs of a long-term program not be evaluated solely in terms of its down payment cost in the initial budget year. Finally, conventional budgeting has an inherent tendency to *perpetuate programs,* with their associated vested interests, even though the programs may yield benefits less than could be provided by alternative usage of the public sector funds. In other words, program review tends to be much too infrequent under orthodox budgeting procedures. It was hoped that PPBS would avoid these obstacles to efficiency in conventional governmental budgeting. Basically, the planning aspect of the system carried the connotation of long-term evaluation, as opposed to the short-run consideration of costs and benefits in only one or two fiscal years. The programming aspect of PPBS carried the connotation of structuring the budget in terms of goals (programs).

Efforts to utilize PPBS were made by more than 25 federal agencies, including all the primary federal departments, between 1965 and

1971. In 1971, the required use of PPBS was terminated by President Richard Nixon. The comprehensive PPBS approach was unsuccessful, for the most part, in its efforts to improve the efficiency of federal budgetary decisions. However, the more limited objectives of benefit-cost analysis retain their value. Moreover, some semblance of the application of PPBS by the federal government and, to a lesser extent, by the state-local component of the American public sector does remain in effect.

An evaluation of benefit-cost analysis

To the extent that benefit-cost analysis can enlighten the choice among alternative governmental projects, it can improve the level of efficiency in budgetary decisions. Alternative projects can be arrayed, project comparisons can be made, and alternative allocational instruments can be surveyed. Indeed, it seems very likely that the systematic evaluation of project benefits and costs as well as the inclusion of time preference considerations, by providing a greater amount of information to decision makers, should increase the quality of public sector budgetary decisions. Also, the economic calculus of opportunity costs is usefully applied to public sector economic decisions by means of the benefit-cost technique.

Yet, even though the policy results of discretly employed benefit-cost analysis should generally be positive, several problems do appear. These include: (1) the measurement of benefits and costs, (2) the selection of an appropriate social discount rate, and (3) the interaction between the allocational and the distributional effects of governmental investment projects. Ideally, the estimates of benefits and costs would be based on observable *market-type prices* for public and quasi-public goods, which would accurately reflect the social benefits of the final goods and the social costs of the resources used in their production. Yet, the very nature of public and quasi-public goods, inclusive of such traits as joint-consumption benefits and externalities, reduces the feasibility of using market-type prices for public-type goods as an overall benchmark. To an extent, *shadow prices—* either imputed from consumer behavior and supply phenomena or acquired from similar goods sold in the private sector—may be utilized in lieu of specific market prices, but they cannot be relied on in an unambiguous manner.[21]

Moreover, the problem of selecting an appropriate social discount rate is a significant one. There is a danger, as noted earlier, that the

---

[21] See the discussion of shadow prices by Roland N. McKean, "The Use of Shadow Prices," in *Problems in Public Expenditure Analysis*, Samuel B. Chase, Jr., ed. (Washington, D.C.: Brookings Institution, 1968), pp. 33–77.

Figure 4-1   Government investment expenditures at various social discount rates

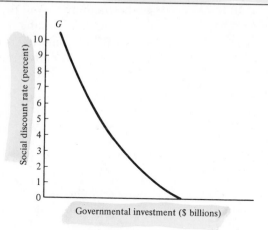

public sector will set a social discount rate lower than would be set by the market sector. This may well occur because governments generally do not need to worry about credit ratings, nonliquidity, and risk in the manner that private enterprise must consider these factors. Clearly, the lower the social discount rate applied, the greater will be the number of governmental investment projects adopted. This is evident from Figure 4-1, which measures the social discount rate on the vertical axis and the magnitude of governmental investment expenditures along the horizontal axis. The relationship between these two variables is inverse, as is indicated by the downward slope of the government investment curve, G. That is, the lower the social discount rate, the greater the volume of governmental investment expenditures undertaken, and vice versa. Thus, to the extent that the social rate of return for governmental investment is set at a lower rate than that for the market sector, a nonneutral *intersector* allocational effect will occur which favors public sector resource allocation. Moreover, by the extent to which different agencies of a unit of government use different social discount rates, a similar negative *intragovernmental* distortion will take place.

One danger of benefit-cost analysis is that its emphasis on allocational matters may cause its distributional aspects to be ignored. For example, the benefits of a government investment may primarily accrue to one group of persons, but the tax costs of financing the investment may be largely incurred by another group of persons. Yet, traditional benefit-cost analysis would focus on the allocational gains and ignore the income redistribution effects. In this regard, it has been recommended that *equity* (distribution) be included as a subset of the *efficiency* (allocation) goal in benefit-cost analysis.[22] Thus, when such equity effects are considered to be favorable, they could be included in the benefits of the program; when they are considered to be unfavorable, they could be included among the costs. Admittedly, placing a value on equity or distributional effects poses a major problem. Nonetheless, society does make collective judgments concerning these goals. Thus, it seems appropriate that:

> Until means are developed for valuing distributional effects, their importance to policy makers makes it clear that economists who undertake or advise about benefit-cost analyses should at least spell out and discuss the forms of redistributive effects of a program, even if the end product of the research fails to place a value (positive or negative) on those effects.[23]

If such precaution is undertaken, the inherent danger of an overemphasis on the allocational implications of benefit-cost analysis can be reduced.

---

[22] See Burton A. Weisbrod, "Income Redistribution Effects and Benefit-Cost Analysis," in *Problems in Public Expenditure Analysis*, Samuel Chase, Jr. ed. (Washington, D.C.: Brookings Institution, 1968), pp. 177-222.

[23] Ibid., p. 180.

5

Fiscal principles
and concepts

A number of important fiscal principles and concepts that will be applicable throughout the book are developed in this chapter. These include the traditional principle of tax neutrality as well as an expanded version of this principle which we call fiscal neutrality. This will be followed by a consideration of various fiscal concepts pertaining to government expenditures and revenues, income distribution, and intergoal fiscal nonneutrality. The next two chapters will continue the discussion by analyzing certain important fiscal principles which bear on the topics of tax equity and tax incidence, respectively.

THE TRADITIONAL PRINCIPLE OF TAX NEUTRALITY

All taxes, by nature, exert an *income effect*, since they compel the withdrawal of revenues from the private sector and, thus, reduce the level of private sector purchasing power. Moroever, all taxes (except the lump-sum tax)[1] tend to exert a *substitution effect* because they interfere with private sector allocational decisions. This effect is related in an important sense to the traditional principle of *tax neutrality*, which has been defined historically as the imposition of taxes in such a manner that they do not change private sector behavior.

---

[1] The lump-sum tax tends to avoid a substitution effect because it is not directly associated with economic decision making. That is, it is imposed on a person as such, but not on that person's income, wealth, or market transactions.

Thus, it is advocated, in a pure sense, that a tax should not influence the market decisions of either satisfaction-motivated consumers or of profit-motivated businesses. If such allocational effects do occur, nonneutrality is said to exist. In this context, neutrality is deemed desirable, while its opposite, nonneutrality, is considered undesirable. In practice, however, this translates into a preference for taxes which least interfere with market choices, since the allocationally neutral lump-sum tax (no substitution effect) is generally considered undesirable on distributional equity grounds.

Under the traditional approach, therefore, the concept of *allocational efficiency* is identified with the concept of tax neutrality. The traditional literature of public finance considers that a nonneutrality imposed by a tax will create an *excess burden* (distortion), since when allocational efficiency is reduced there is a corresponding reduction in real income in the society.[2] In fact, the reduction in real income may be considered to be a measure of the excess burden resulting from the tax. An alternative measure of excess burden could be derived by subtracting the actual tax revenues from the total costs of the tax on society—the latter inclusive of the revenue value of the tax. This difference constitutes the "excess burden" over and above the opportunity-cost sacrifice to the private sector of the tax payments. For example, if the total costs to society resulting from the imposition of an excise tax which produces $100 million of revenues are $150 million, the excess burden of the tax is $50 million ($150 million of total costs minus $100 million of tax revenues).

However, such an excess burden is assured only if the initial, pretax, allocational equilibrium is optimal. If the initial equilibrium is suboptimal, the nonneutral effects resulting from the tax may either improve or further worsen allocational efficiency. Hence, while the least tax distortion in the market should continue to serve as a general fiscal rule, it should be applied flexibly, not rigidly, because in some instances an efficiency gain will result from the nonneutrality of a given tax.

THE EXPANDED PRINCIPLE OF FISCAL NEUTRALITY

While the traditional principle of tax neutrality serves as a useful general precept for constrained intervention by government in the functioning of the market, it is nonetheless too narrow in scope since, as observed above, tax nonneutralities can at times improve allocational efficiency. Moreover, its emphasis on the *revenue* side of the fisc (government budget) results in an asymmetrical situation which

---

[2] The traditional concept of *excess burden* will be discussed in further detail in Chapter 12 when the excess burdens of excise versus income taxes are compared.

does not take into account its equally important *expenditure* side. Recently, however, substantial theoretical developments in Anglo-American public finance in the areas of public goods and public choice theory have lent some symmetry to this situation. These and other considerations suggest the desirability of expanding the traditional tax neutrality concept into a more comprehensive principle, namely, that of *fiscal neutrality*. This principle contains the following five basic considerations:

First, public sector fiscal decisions of both the revenue-gathering and expenditure varieties may yield important economic effects. Thus, the entire budget should be symmetrically considered as the starting point for analyzing fiscal decisions. Moreover, government revenue-gathering and spending activities interact importantly with one another. For example, taxes, which are the primary source of public sector revenues, impose "burdens" on those who pay them, which take the form of foregone private sector purchasing power. On the other hand, governmental expenditures yield "benefits" to those who receive them through either the consumption of government-supplied output or the flow of transfer payments. Hence, the *real income* enjoyed by each resident of a political jurisdiction necessarily reflects the pattern by which both burdens and benefits are distributed among the population. This matter will be considered further in a later section of the chapter.

Second, public sector fiscal decisions can exert effects in *any functional area* of economic activity and not solely in allocation, as emphasized by the traditional tax neutrality principle. A comprehensive fiscal rationality principle should include the capability of governmental budgetary decisions to exert nonneutral effects of an allocational, distributional, and stabilization nature in a mixed, two-sector economic system. Budgetary allocational effects are commonly referred to as *efficiency effects;* those of a distributional variety, as *equity effects,* and those of an aggregate economic or stabilization nature, as *stabilization effects.*

A *third* dimension of a comprehensive fiscal rationality approach should be appreciation of the fact that a nonneutrality effect may be either beneficial or harmful in terms of a particular economic goal. For example, as observed above, if an initial allocational equilibrium is "suboptimal", a government-induced allocational nonneutrality may actually improve efficiency, and thus increase real income. Similarly, the public sector may exert nonneutralities, given prefisc suboptimality, which either improve or make worse income and wealth distribution objectives as well as the performance of stabilization aggregates such as employment, the price level, and the rate of economic growth. Moreover, suboptimality is likely. It was demonstrated in Chapter 2 that a pure market economy cannot be expected to achieve an optimal resource allocation position, and similar evidence of market failure will be considered later in relationship to the stabilization function of the economy. In addition, a societal consensus may express dissatisfaction with an existing state of income or wealth distribution. Given these potential conditions of suboptimality, a nonneutrality may provide either beneficial or harmful results.

A nonneutrality which moves society closer to an economic goal will be designated a *positive nonneutrality*, and one which causes society to move further away from an economic goal will be termed a *negative nonneutrality*. Caution is advised, however, in the sense that excessive governmental fiscal intervention in the market, without substantial evidence of a probable net economic gain from such action, should be avoided by rational policymakers. Other things being equal, the market should be given the benefit of the doubt.

Fourth, since government in a mixed, two-sector economy will *inevitably* exert nonneutral effects in all functional branches of economic activity, whether it does so in a deliberate manner or not, it seems logical for the public sector to organize governmental economic activities along *rational* lines. Thus, it should use established economic principles, so as to promote better allocational, distributional, and stabilization performance in the economy. That is, *government should structure its economic policies so as to exert positive nonneutral effects* in terms of these major functional goals. Admittedly, specific goals of resource allocation, income redistribution, the rate of economic growth, and the like, tend to be controversial. Nonetheless, society does establish certain priorities and consensuses of action in relationship to these goals. Hence, the concept of positive nonneutral effects carries a legitimate policy inference.

The public sector can use various economic tools or instruments to create positive nonneutralities. These instruments can be placed in three primary categories related to (1) *fiscal* (budgetary) *policy,* (2) *monetary* (money and credit) *policy,* and (3) *market* (regulatory) *policy* in both product and factor, or resource, markets. The first of these—fiscal policy—is the principal subject of this book, though it should be recognized that the three instrument categories will often interact with one another in influencing economic objectives. The term *fiscal policy* can be applied appropriately to governmental budgetary policy directed toward *any* of the three functional economic goals—allocation, distribution, or stabilization. Nonetheless, popular usage of the term has often confined its meaning to *macroeconomic* stabilization goals. The following discussion will avoid this narrow interpretation as it explores the ability of governmental budgetary policy to exert positive nonneutral effects on *all* functions of the economy.

Fifth, the budgetary decisions of *all* levels and units of government in the public sector may exert allocational, distributional, and stabilization nonneutralities on the *private sector*. Moreover, governments may exert *intergovernmental fiscal nonneutralities* on one another. Realization of the three goals of an economic system will be strongly influenced, for better or for worse, by the nature of this interdependence and its resulting nonneutralities. That is, aggregate societal preferences for a particular goal may be achieved to a greater or lesser degree, depending on whether the various levels and units of government reinforce or neutralize one another's efforts to meet the preferences of the society. The appropriate placement of public sector allocational, distributional, and stabilization functions by level of government must also be determined. Aspects of this interdependence involve what is commonly referred to as the study of *fiscal federalism*.

Intergovernmental fiscal nonneutralities assume two dimensions:

1. There are intergovernmental budgetary relationships between different levels of government. This sort of relationship can be termed a *vertical intergovernmental fiscal relationship*. The fiscal interaction between the federal, state, and local levels of government in the United States pertaining to the quasi-public good, education, exemplifies this dimension.

2. The interrelationship among different segments of government can take the form of fiscal interaction among different units of government at the same level. This sort of relationship, which may be termed a *horizontal intergovernmental fiscal relationship*, can occur, of course, only at the state and local levels of government, since only one unit of government exists at the federal level. The influence of the budgetary actions of one state on other states and of one municipality on other municipalities exemplify this dimension of intergovernmental fiscal behavior. Some intergovernmental fiscal relationships are characterized by both vertical and horizontal interaction.

FISCAL CONCEPTS

Public expenditure concepts

Types of government expenditures. Public sector expenditures may be divided into two main categories, exhaustive and nonexhaustive (transfer) expenditures. An *exhaustive expenditure* is one whose initial effect is allocational in nature, since it directly absorbs resources into governmental production. Such resources, assuming full employment, would be absorbed from alternative allocational uses elsewhere in the economy. A *nonexhaustive expenditure* is one whose initial effect is on the distribution of income in the society. It does not directly absorb resources; a payment is received by an individual without an exchange of productive resources for that payment. It involves merely a transfer of tax funds between individuals in the society.

Nonexhaustive or transfer expenditures are sometimes referred to as *negative taxes,* since the government pays the individual instead of the individual paying the government. In fact, this is the source of the term *negative income tax,* a concept discussed in Chapter 13. Even though a change in income distribution does not directly change resource allocation, it is nonetheless capable of indirectly exerting such an effect when the redistributed purchasing power constituting the transfer payment is put into the spending stream. This is so because the person paying the tax which becomes the transfer payment may well possess a different preference pattern than the person who receives the transfer payment.

The income elasticity of government expenditures. A useful measurement device for evaluating public sector expenditure behavior considers the functional relationship of government expenditures to the level of income[3] over a period of time. This is known as the *income elasticity of government expenditures* (Y_e). The relevant formula is:

$$Y_e = \frac{\dfrac{\Delta E}{E_0}}{\dfrac{\Delta Y}{Y_0}}$$

where ΔE refers to the change in government expenditures between a base year and a subsequent year, E_0 refers to the level of government expenditures in the base year, ΔY refers to the change in income between a base year and a subsequent year, and Y_0 refers to the level of income in the base year. The resulting Y_e coefficient will thus relate the percentage rate of change in government expenditures to the percentage rate of change in income over a period of time. This relationship may be *elastic* $(Y_e > 1)$, *unitary* $(Y_e = 1)$, or *inelastic* $(Y_e < 1)$.

Public revenue concepts

Types of government revenues. Public sector revenues may be of either the tax or nontax variety. Typically, taxes are the primary source of governmental revenues, though the proportion of tax revenues to

---

[3] *Income* may be viewed within the framework of the political jurisdiction in question; that is, national income for the federal government, state income for state governments, and county income, municipal income, and so forth, for local governments—to the extent that such income data are available for local jurisdictions.

total governmental revenues varies considerably among levels and units of government and among nations. A *tax* can be defined as a compulsory contribution exacted from an individual for the purpose of financing governmental functions. Tax burdens are ultimately borne by individuals, even though they may be formally paid by a business entity, such as a corporation, which is owned by individuals.

Most taxes go into the *general* treasury fund of a unit of government. The federal personal and corporation income taxes, for example, flow to the general treasury fund of the federal government. Some taxes, however, are *earmarked* for a specific purpose and thus go into a separate budget or trust fund. The federal excise tax on gasoline (motor fuel), which goes into the special Highway Trust Fund, is an example of this kind of tax. Payroll (employment) taxes, such as those which finance the federal social security and federal-state unemployment insurance programs, are other important earmarked taxes in the American public sector.

Taxes generally serve more than one purpose or goal, though a single purpose typically is dominant. All taxes, by their very nature, *provide revenues* to the government which imposes the tax. In most instances, this is the primary motive for the existence of the tax. In some instances, however, a tax may exist primarily, or at least very importantly, for *regulatory purposes*.

Taxes may be regulatory in either a microeconomic or a macroeconomic sense. In the *microeconomic* context, they may influence the consumption of a particular good or the utilization of a particular productive resource. A regulatory tax designed to discourage the consumption of a particular item, such as gasoline, alcoholic beverages, or tobacco products, is termed a *sumptuary* tax. An adaptable tool of *macroeconomic* fiscal policy directed toward achievement of the stabilization goals of the society is the federal personal (individual) income tax.

Nontax revenues may take the form of: (1) user charges (user prices), (2) administrative revenues, or (3) governmental borrowing (debt). The collection of *user charges,* also known as commercial revenues, involves the sale of economic goods or resources by government for a specific charge or price. The government may both produce and sell the good, such as state toll road facilities, or it may merely sell a privately produced good, as in the case of state liquor store monopolies. User charges differ from earmarked taxes, such as those on gasoline, in that the former represent the outright sale of an economic good or resource by a unit of government, while the latter represent the application of a tax to the sale of an economic good by the market sector of the economy.

The goods to which user charges are applied under the commercial principle of government enterprise are ordinarily characterized by some internal or private benefits to the individual purchaser and, often, by significant externalities, either of a benefit or cost variety, to society. Moreover, they are ordinarily not by-products of a general administrative function of government. In most instances, those goods subject to user charges could be provided by either the public or private sectors of the economy, though not necessarily with equal economic efficiency and distributional purpose.

Allocative matters, which are related to the general administrative functions of government, produce what are known as *administrative revenues*. In some cases, the buyer has free choice concerning payment of the administrative revenue (for example, a fishing license). In these instances, the exclusion principle applies. Often, however, there is not a direct or close correlation between the payment of an administrative revenue and the receipt of a specific economic good by the purchaser. Indeed, government units collecting such revenues sometimes attempt to tie them to broad functional categories of expenditure. The relationship, however, is often loose. As a result, administrative revenues should not be confused with the much more precise quid pro quo relationships which ordinarily exist with both earmarked taxes and user charges. Administrative revenues include such revenue sources as licenses, permits, (some) fees, fines, forfeitures, and special assessments.

Another primary source of governmental revenue is borrowing or the creation of *debt*. As will be demonstrated in Chapter 22, the public sector has several means of creating and maintaining debt which are not available to the private sector. Government debt is created when the current nondebt revenues are less than current expenditures. Debt creation fills this residual deficit through borrowing.

Tax base-tax rate relationships. Taxes can be imposed on any of four primary tax bases, with hybrid or intermediate combinations also possible. The primary tax bases consist of income, wealth, sales or transactions, and people. *Income* is a flow of current factor earnings such as wages, salaries, profits, rents, royalties, and interest payments. *Wealth* refers to a stock of assets, such as land, buildings, stocks, and bonds, on which a tax may be imposed. *Sales or transactions* refer to the buying and selling of goods and/or resources in the market. *People* as such also may serve as the base of a tax, without regard to such economic considerations as income, wealth, or transactions. A tax such as the lump-sum tax, as observed earlier, is not associated with any economic activity and, accordingly, does not exert a substitution effect on private sector behavior.[4] One major type of tax, the payroll (employment) tax, utilizes a base which is essentially *intermediate* between the income and transactions bases, since it taxes labor earnings,

---

[4] See Chapter 6 for a discussion of the distributional equity performance of the lump-sum tax.

but not on a total personal income basis as does a personal income tax, and also uses a transactions base related to the monetary value of labor purchases by an employer.

Table 5-1 summarizes the primary tax bases and the particular taxes which are related to each base. All primary tax bases (except the "people" base) are used extensively in the American public sector. The taxes associated with these bases will be described in detail in later chapters. Some further conceptual distinctions and definitions related to taxation should be made at this point, however.

The *tax base* is the object to which the tax is applied. The *tax rate* is the amount of tax applied per unit of tax base. Thus, the tax base multiplied by the tax rate equals the *tax yield* to the government. The yield to the government is the same as the direct *tax burden* to the taxpayer, except for certain differentials resulting from tax administration costs to the government and tax compliance costs to the taxpayer. In addition, the *average tax rate (ATR)* is computed by dividing the total tax liability by the total tax base, and the *marginal tax rate (MTR)* is computed by dividing the change in total tax liability by the change in total tax base.

Moreover, a tax base may be either broadbased or narrowbased. A *broadbased* tax is imposed on a comprehensive base, as exemplified, by an income tax on all major sources of income or a sales (transac-

---

TABLE 5-1   Primary tax base alternatives and types of taxes

Tax bases	Major types of taxes applied to base
Primary	
Income	Personal (individual) income tax
	Corporation income tax
	Personal consumption (expenditure) tax*
Wealth	Property tax
	Death (estate, inheritance) taxes _nuisance tax_
	Gift tax
	Personal wealth (net worth) tax
Transactions or sales	General retail sales tax
	Value-added tax _Specific Tax_
	Turnover tax
	Excise tax
	Severance tax
People	Lump-sum (head, capitation, per capita) tax _used extensively in the South (poll tax)_
Intermediate	
Income/ Transactions	Payroll (employment) tax

* Classified as an *income tax* on the basis of "uses of income." This point will be more fully explained in Chapters 8 and 14.

tions) tax on a large number of diverse products purchased in the market. In contrast, a *narrowbased* tax is restricted in application, such as an income tax on only one or two sources of income or a sales tax imposed on a single product or on a limited number of products.

Furthermore, a tax may be either an *impersonal* (in rem) tax, which uses economic transactions or objects themselves as the tax base, aside from the economic circumstances of the individual taxpayer, or it may be a *personal*[5] tax which considers the individual economic characteristics of the taxpayer in computing the tax base. These individual economic characteristics are normally applied in reference to the *ability-to-pay principle* of equity in the distribution of tax burdens, to be described in the following chapter. For example, a general sales tax, which considers neither the total (net) personal income nor the total (net) personal wealth of the taxpayer, would be classified as an "impersonal" tax, since only the objects purchased constitute the tax base. On the other hand, a tax on the total (net) income or total (net) wealth of an individual would be a "personal" tax, which uses income or wealth as an indicator of the individual's taxpaying ability.

A personal tax will normally utilize an *ad valorem* (according to monetary value) base, such as dollars of income or wealth, while an impersonal tax may use either a monetary value or a *specific* base, the latter being defined in physical unit terms such as gallons of gasoline, packages of cigarettes, or tons of coal.

Three major variants of tax base—tax rate combinations are available to the government policymaker: (1) proportional, (2) progressive, and (3) regressive. These may also be referred to as *statutory* tax

---

TABLE 5–2 Example of the relationship between marginal and average tax rates and proportional, progressive, and regressive tax structures, in statutory terms

(1)	(2)	(3)	(4)	(5)
			Tax rate (percent)	
Rate structure	Tax liability	Tax base	Average (ATR) (2) ÷ (3)	Marginal (MTR) Δ(2) ÷ Δ(3)
Proportional (flat-rate)	$1,000	$ 50,000	2%	2%
	2,000	100,000	2	
Progressive (graduated)	1,000	50,000	2	6
	4,000	100,000	4	
Regressive	1,000	50,000	2	1
	1,500	100,000	1.5	

---

[5] This should not be confused with the lump-sum tax, which is devoid of direct economic considerations.

FIGURE 5–1   **Various tax base-tax rate structures in statutory terms**

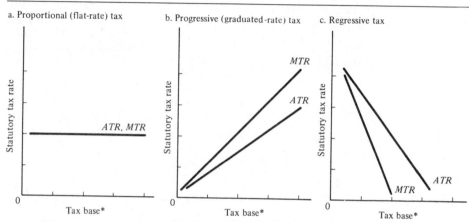

a. Proportional (flat-rate) tax   b. Progressive (graduated-rate) tax   c. Regressive tax

* Of the income, wealth, transactions, people, or payroll variety.

structures. First, the statutory (legal/technical) relationship between the size of the base and the rate structure of any particular tax would result in a tax being termed *proportional* or *flat rate,* if the statutory rate remains constant as the tax base grows larger. In this instance, MTR and ATR (as defined before) remain unchanged as the tax base expands. The general retail sales tax used by most states and by many local governments is an example of this kind of tax. If, on the other hand, the statutory tax rate increases as the tax base grows larger, the tax is known as a *progressive* or *graduated* tax. In this instance, MTR > ATR as the base increases. The federal personal income tax exemplifies this kind of tax base-tax rate relationship. A tax rate which decreases as the size of the tax base increases is *regressive* in structure. In this case, MTR < ATR as the tax base expands. Some states impose a capital stock tax on businesses incorporated within the state which is characterized by such a relationship between tax base and rate.

It is important to distinguish between these terms as used here in a *statutory* sense, and their common usage in a *distributional equity* sense. This distinction will be made in the following chapter. Meanwhile, Table 5–2 and Figure 5–1 demonstrate these tax base—tax rate relationships in their statutory context, rather than the distributional equity terms to be introduced in Chapter 6. They also show the distinction between average and marginal tax rates.

The relationship of income changes to tax revenues: The marginal propensity to tax and income elasticity of taxation concepts.[6] All

---

[6] See footnote 3 for alternative definitions of the term *income.*

taxes (except a lump-sum tax) exhibit a positive functional relationship between the amount of revenues collected under the tax and the level of income. This relationship is direct under an income tax, whose base automatically changes as income changes, and is indirect under transactions (sales) and wealth taxes. A lump-sum tax, being unrelated to any form of economic activity, does not exhibit a meaningful relationship to the level of income.

Two important concepts are relevant to this functional relationship between tax revenues and income. One concept, that of the *marginal propensity to tax (MPT)*, also known as *built-in flexibility*, is especially applicable to fiscal rationality as applied in the area of macroeconomic performance. This is considered mainly in Part IV of the book. The other concept, *income elasticity of taxation* (Y_t), is particularly applicable to the long-run revenue productivity of a tax or tax system, but it also has macroeconomic applications.

Table 5-3 demonstrates the conceptual distinction between these two useful concepts. The *marginal-propensity-to-tax* concept refers to the ratio of *absolute* change in the revenue yield from a tax (or tax system) to an *absolute* change in income, with the tax base and tax rates remaining constant (ceteris paribus). The *income elasticity of taxation* concept refers to the ratio of the *percentage rate* of change in revenue yield to the *percentage rate* of change in income, with the tax base and rates being held constant (ceteris paribus). Thus, it is the budgetary counterpart of the *income elasticity of government expenditures* (Y_e) concept described earlier in the chapter. Both the *MPT* and Y_t concepts exhibit a "positive" relationship in that tax revenues and income increase or decrease together.

The marginal propensity to tax concept will be further developed in Part Four, but some additional discussion of the income elasticity of taxation concept is appropriate here. This concept is closely associated with the long-run fiscal well-being of governments, since chang-

---

TABLE 5-3   The concepts of marginal propensity to tax and income elasticity of taxation

Marginal propensity to tax (MPT)	Income elasticity of taxation (Y_t)
$MPT = \dfrac{\Delta T}{\Delta Y}$	$Y_t = \dfrac{\dfrac{\Delta T}{T_0}}{\dfrac{\Delta Y}{Y_0}}$

Note:
T = Revenue yield (tax revenue).
Y = Income.
Δ = Change between base year and a subsequent year.
0 = Base year.

FIGURE 5-2   **Various categories of income elasticity of a tax or tax system**

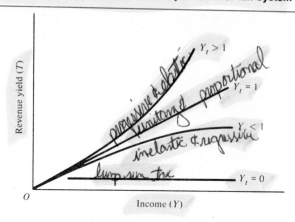

ing income brings with it varying degrees of changing governmental expenditure responsibilities. The critical question is whether revenue yields will grow in a manner commensurate with these growing expenditure obligations. Figure 5-2 demonstrates three categories of income elasticity of taxation:

1. If the change in revenue yield (T) from a tax or tax system occurs at a greater rate than changes in income (Y), the income elasticity of the tax (or tax system) is said to be *elastic* $(Y_t > 1)$. For example, a 1 percent change in income might induce a 1.1 percent change in revenue yield.
2. If the change in revenue yield (T) occurs at the same rate as changes in income (Y), the income elasticity of the tax (or tax system) is said to be *unitary* $(Y_t = 1)$. For example, a 1 percent change in income might induce an equivalent 1 percent change in revenue yield.
3. If the change in revenue yield (T) occurs at a lesser rate than changes in income (Y), the income elasticity of the tax (or tax system) is said to be *inelastic* $(Y_t < 1)$. For example, a 1 percent change in income might induce a 0.9 percent change in revenue yield.

A close relationship exists between the statutory structure of a particular tax or tax system and its resulting income elasticity. Generally, a statutorily progressive tax yields income-elastic results, a statutorily proportional tax structure provides near unitary results (with occasional exceptions), and a statutorily regressive tax yields income-inelastic results. The explanation of this behavior is that as the tax base increases, taxpayers move into higher tax rate brackets under a statutorily progressive tax, thus yielding increasingly greater revenues to government. The opposite occurs under a statutorily regressive tax, and a proportional tax yields intermediate results.

Under an income tax, the tax base *directly* increases as income increases, since income itself is the independent variable in the income elasticity formula. The association is *indirect* with wealth taxes, such as property and death taxes, and with sales (transactions) taxes such as the general sales tax. Even though increasing short-run income flows do lead to a greater long-run accumulation of wealth or assets, there is admittedly a time lag which is absent with the income tax. Also, growing income induces greater sales or transactions, but with some delay as well as with a saving leakage from income. A lump-sum tax would not yield a revenue response to increasing income, since it does not provide a significant economic linkage, either direct or indirect, between the tax base and income. In other words, the income elasticity of a lump-sum tax would tend to be zero ($Y_t = 0$), as represented by the horizontal line in Figure 5–2.

Automatic versus discretionary fiscal stabilizers. Macroeconomic fiscal policy involves the classification of budgetary instruments into automatic and discretionary fiscal stabilizers. These will be briefly defined here, primarily for use in evaluation of the stabilization performance of the various types of taxes to be discussed in Part II of the book, and described in detail in Part Four which deals with macroeconomic issues. An *automatic fiscal stabilizer* is designed to function in a countercyclical fashion to improve the performance of the economy, without the necessity of ad hoc adjustments in response to an immediate macroeconomic problem. The graduated federal personal income tax, with a given rate and base structure, will automatically withdraw revenues from the private sector more rapidly than income increases during a cyclical upswing, thus causing a net reduction in purchasing power in the private sector. Conversely, it will lag behind a decrease in income during a cyclical downswing, thus causing a net increment in private sector purchasing power. It is the elastic income elasticity characteristic of the tax ($Y_t > 1$) which provides this quality of an automatic stabilizer. A *discretionary fiscal stabilizer* refers to a direct budgetary change responding in an ad hoc fashion to a presently recognized macroeconomic problem. A reduction in federal personal income tax rates in response to a depressed economy would exemplify the application of a discretionary fiscal stabilizer.

Selecting among alternative tax sources. It is important, in terms of the revenue productivity of a tax as well as in reference to its overall economic effects, to consider the fact that several alternative tax sources may be available to a government at any given time. The public sector has an option to use one or another tax source, or a combination of sources, to varying degrees. In this sense, it is necessary to define the *capacity* of a given tax. A rational government would first use the tax with the lowest marginal social costs.[7] When this tax reaches a certain level of revenue, however, further utilization of the tax may cause it to have marginal social costs greater than those that would result from another tax. At this point, it can be said that the first tax has reached its capacity.[8] Additional revenues should be raised by a second tax until its marginal social costs become greater than those for a third tax, and so on, if alternative tax sources are used in an efficient manner at the margin in the provision of tax revenues to government.

Policymakers can learn an important lesson from such analysis. An income tax may seem to be much better than, say, an excise on sugar, but an increase in an income tax is not necessarily "better" than the imposition of that excise.[9] In other words, the addition of a new tax to the tax system will at times be preferable to an increase in the rate of a present tax.

OVERALL BUDGETARY CONCEPTS

Distribution concepts

Private income and wealth distribution. Members of an individualistic society, such as that of the United States, earn their *private incomes* from the sale of resources to be used in economic production. Since production is undertaken by both the private and public sectors of the mixed economy, either the market or the government may be the source of an income flow. Moreover, the income may stem from the provision of either labor or nonlabor (wealth, property) resources to the productive process. Meanwhile, *private wealth* refers to the stock of assets, net of claims against these assets, which a household unit (person, family) possesses at a given time. Such assets may be the cumulative result of savings from current income flows and/or from gifts or inheritances.

In turn, the concepts of *private income distribution* and *private wealth distribution,* respectively, refer to the pattern in which aggregate income or wealth is divided among the society's population. The extreme distributional possibilities, theoretically speaking, are those of "completely equal" and "completely unequal" income or wealth distribution. Thus, in the case of *completely equal income distribution,* each household unit in the society would receive the same

---

[7] Social costs, in this context, refer essentially to the opportunities foregone in private sector consumption due to the payment of taxes.

[8] See Amotz Morag, *On Taxes and Inflation* (New York: Random House, 1965), pp. 8–9.

[9] Ibid.

FIGURE 5-3   Lorenz curves demonstrating complete equality, intermediate inequality, and complete inequality in the distribution of household* income

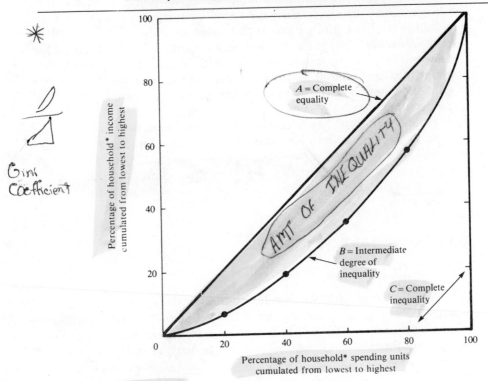

* Person, family.

amount of income during a given period of time. On the other hand, *completely unequal income distribution* would be characterized by a situation in which one household unit would receive the entire aggregate income of the society during the period, while all other household units would receive no income. Of course, neither extreme is feasible in the real world, and as a result, actual distribution consists of some *intermediate degree of income inequality*—but stopping short of complete inequality. These alternative income distribution possibilities are demonstrated in Figure 5–3 via the Lorenz-curve approach. For convenience, the two axis represent the percentage relationship between household income and household spending units, respectively, rather than numbers of persona and their absolute incomes. In the graph, the 45-degree angle line *A* depicts a completely equal income distribution; curve *B* depicts an intermediate degree of income inequality, and curve *C* represents a completely unequal distribution of income.

Redistribution of private income and wealth. Economics as a so-cial science cannot derive from its principles or theories what con-stitutes a "best state" of income or wealth distribution. That is, it cannot say whether a completely equal, or a completely unequal, or whether any particular intermediately unequal pattern of distribution is optimal. Instead, this decision is an ethically determined *value judgment* for each member of the society, and collectively for the society as a whole; the latter leading to some operational consensus which is in effect at any one point of time.

Despite its inability to prescribe an optimal state of distribution, economics is nonetheless closely involved with distributional ac-tivities. For example, as observed in earlier chapters, the *ex ante* distribution of income and wealth in the private sector, and of political representation in the public sector, are the forces which make the demand for economic output from society's scarce resources "effec-tive." Moreover, society may well decide that the existing state of unequal distribution is undesirable, and seek to change that distribu-tion to one that is either less or more unequal. If such *redistribution* is mandated, economics will likely play an important role in attaining the distributional change. In particular, the *public sector budget* is likely to play a major role in redistribution.

For example, the incidence pattern by which the "burdens" of government taxes and the "benefits" of government expenditures spread across the population will almost certainly alter the state of private income distribution. This concept of public sector fiscal bur-den and benefit incidence, as applied to the public sector as a whole, may be termed *aggregate public sector fiscal incidence*. Clearly, in a mixed economy, the incidence of public sector fiscal activities, whether rationally planned or random, can bring about changes in the distribution of private income. Thus, it will be convenient to refer to the private income distribution which exists prior to the effects of government fiscal incidence as the *prefisc distribution of income*, and to the distribution of income that exists after such effects have oc-curred as the *postfisc distribution of income*. The postfisc distribu-tion, of course, may be either less unequal or more unequal than the prefisc distribution. These concepts are demonstrated in Figure 5–4.

Redistribution as a public good. One unique approach to income (or wealth) redistribution is to view it as a public (social) good. Such an approach assumes interdependent utility functions among tax-payers of differential income (or wealth) status.[10] Thus, high-income taxpayer A may derive satisfaction not only from his own consump-tion, but also from additional consumption by low-income taxpayer B, and by other low-income taxpayers. In mathematical terms:

[10] For a relevant discussion of the interdependence of utility functions and re-distributional goals, see Harold M. Hochman and James D. Rodgers, "Pareto Optimal Redistribution," *American Economic Review*, September 1969, pp. 542–57.

FIGURE 5-4   Income redistribution: Prefisc and postfisc distribution concepts (household units*)

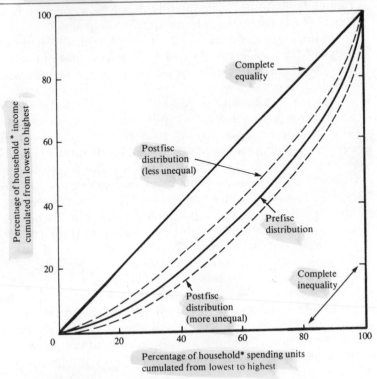

* Person, family.

$$U_A = (f) \, C_A + C_B + C_N$$

where U indicates utility, C the consumption of economic output, A and B the two taxpayers under discussion, and N additional low-income taxpayers.

Accordingly, taxpayer A may seek as part of his own demand preference schedule a redistributional process which will provide for an increase in consumption for all low-income persons such as B. However, public good qualities would tend to provide an obstacle to this in the form of free-rider behavior, since taxpayer A's taxes alone would provide an infinitesimally small contribution to a national program of redistribution in behalf of all low-income persons. It would be foolish for taxpayer A to voluntarily contribute to such a national redistribution program. Yet, he may be willing to participate in a comprehensive redistributional program which utilizes the federal government fisc to transfer some tax funds from higher-income to lower-income taxpayers. In this instance, the compulsory element of taxation, just as in the case of the pure public good, helps to overcome the free-rider problem. One advantage of the redistribution-as-a-public-good approach is that it integrates the *efficiency* considerations of the allocation branch of economics with the *equity* considerations of the distribution branch.

Intergoal fiscal nonneutrality

It is important to observe that governmental budgetary policy directed toward the attainment of a specific economic goal will often exert nonneutral effects on other public sector goals. These nonneutral effects may be termed *intergoal fiscal nonneutralities.* Fiscal policy directed toward a goal of economic stabilization, for example, may either restrict or promote the achievement of the allocation and distribution goals of the society. In the event of the restriction of a second goal, a *trade-off* would be established between the two goals. In addition, conflicting subgoals may exist within a particular functional area or goal; full-employment stabilization policy may conflict with stabilization objectives of a price level nature, for example. Governmental budgetary policy may also improve the performance of both the primary and secondary goals or subgoals. An investment credit tax subsidy for certain strategic growth industries, for example, may stimulate investment of the sort that will increase the rate of long-run economic growth as well as short-run aggregate demand in the economy.

The existence of intergoal fiscal nonneutrality makes it necessary for public sector policymakers to consider the interrelated allocational (efficiency), distributional (equity), and stabilization effects which are likely to result from a given tax or expenditure action. Social priorities should be established and social choices should be made among various budgetary alternatives. These choices should reflect the relative emphasis placed on the various economic goals by the society. In other words, a comprehensive system of priorities is required for the application of rational fiscal behavior. In addition, it is important to discern between the *normative* or value judgment considerations which help to determine societal priorities, on the one hand, and the *positive* economic methodology which is used to help implement the policies which reflect these priorities, on the other.

Table 5-4 demonstrates some of the critical areas of social choice which face public sector decision makers. These include major goals, as represented by the three functional areas of economics, as well as subgoals within the major goal areas.

In summary, we have considered in this chapter the traditional principle of *tax neutrality* and have found it to be a generally useful

TABLE 5-4   Some critical social choice areas of public sector economics

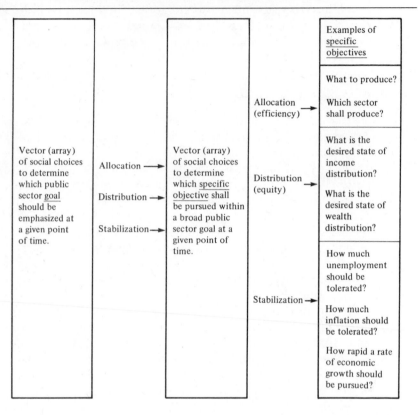

				Examples of specific objectives
Vector (array) of social choices to determine which public sector goal should be emphasized at a given point of time.	Allocation ⟶ Distribution ⟶ Stabilization⟶	Vector (array) of social choices to determine which specific objective shall be pursued within a broad public sector goal at a given point of time.	Allocation (efficiency) ⟶	What to produce? Which sector shall produce?
			Distribution (equity) ⟶	What is the desired state of income distribution? What is the desired state of wealth distribution?
			Stabilization ⟶	How much unemployment should be tolerated? How much inflation should be tolerated? How rapid a rate of economic growth should be pursued?

benchmark—though one which is nonetheless too narrow in scope. We also developed the more comprehensive principle of *fiscal neutrality* to supplement it. A number of public expenditure, public revenue, and distribution concepts, as well as the concept of intergoal fiscal nonneutrality, were also considered. This discussion will be continued in the following two chapters, which deal with the various principles of *tax equity* and *tax incidence*, respectively.

PART II

Public sector revenues

6

Distributional equity in taxation

One of the most important distributional questions to be faced in a mixed, public sector—private sector economy is how to distribute tax burdens among the individuals of the society. This question has received centuries of scholarly attention in Western public finance,[1] and the result has been the application of certain operational norms or rules for *equity* in the distribution of tax burdens. Such benchmarks, of course, are necessarily of a value-judgment nature, since distribution per se is not an economic issue.[2] Furthermore, these rules are usually interpreted in the context of the *ultimate economic incidence* of a tax, thus allowing for market reactions which may permit tax burdens to be transferred away from their initial point of impact or *statutory incidence.*

The traditional rules or norms of equity in the distribution of tax burdens will be described in this chapter, followed in Chapter 7 by an analysis of factors which allow the shifting or transference of tax burdens away from their point of initial impact. Since Part II of the book deals with public sector revenues, it views budgetary incidence in an asymmetrical manner, with no direct consideration given to expenditure incidence. However, the aggregate-public-sector-fiscal-incidence concept, inclusive of the benefit incidence of government spending—as developed in the preceding chapter, will be discussed

---

[1] Such names as Smith, Locke, Petty, Ricardo, Mill, Wagner, Edgeworth, Seligman, and Pigou are found in the impressive list of economists who have studied this issue.

[2] See the discussion of this point in Part I.

in Part III along with some appropriate data for the American public sector.

THE PRINCIPLE OF ABSOLUTE EQUALITY: UNACCEPTABLE TO SOCIETY

A very strict interpretation of equity or fairness in the distribution of tax burdens would entail application of the principle of *absolute equality*. The statistical computation of individual tax burdens would be very simple in this case, since the total spending of the government unit would merely be divided by the number of taxpaying units, the resulting quotient being the tax liability of each taxpaying unit. Under this approach, each unit would pay an equal absolute amount of tax. The term *equity* would be interpreted to mean "equality in tax payment."

Suppose that spending by the federal government, for example, is defined, for purposes of this approach, as "that amount of expenditure which appears in the official budget for a particular fiscal year." Then, suppose that taxpaying units are defined in terms of family and unmarried adult (household) spending units. If the expenditures in the total budget amount to $600 billion, and the number of spending (taxpaying) units is 100 million, the resulting quotient of $6,000 would constitute the tax liability per taxpaying unit. This approach completely ignores the differential abilities of the various units to pay taxes, as determined by such factors as income and wealth differences among them. It is conceivable, for example, that the income of a particular spending unit may not even equal the amount of tax liability.

The principle of absolute equality in taxation would be applied if the tax system relied totally on lump-sum revenues.[3] Though individual circumstances may vary as to income and wealth, taxpayers are identical in this system in the sense that each is an individual taxpaying unit, and thus each pays an equal amount of tax. American society has rejected this principle of absolute equality in its operational establishment of a public sector tax structure. *Equality*, in the sense of equal amounts of tax payment, and *equity*, in the sense of fairness in distributing tax burdens, are viewed differently by our society. Accordingly, both a universal lump-sum tax and the absolute equality approach have been rejected.

MAJOR OPERATIONAL TAX EQUITY PRINCIPLES

Since the absolute equality approach is viewed as too extreme by society, and thus unacceptable, it has been necessary to pursue alternative equity rules. Two quite diverse tax equity principles have been

---

[3] The lump-sum tax is also discussed in the previous chapter.

developed theoretically and applied institutionally in the public sectors of Western nations. These are the *ability-to-pay* and the *benefit* principles of equity in the distribution of tax burdens.

The ability-to-pay principle

While the absolute equality principle defines equity or fairness on an equal-monetary-contribution basis, the ability-to-pay principle determines equity on an *equal-sacrifice* basis. It suggests that all taxpayers should bear an equal sacrifice in the payment of taxes. The payment of taxes to the public sector constitutes a sacrifice to the taxpayer in terms of the alternative uses (in consumption or saving) of the tax monies that are foregone. Thus, the subjective *sacrifice of utility* (satisfaction, welfare) in the payment of taxes comprises the basic tenet of the ability-to-pay principle of tax equity. This tenet can be described more fully in terms of the concepts of horizontal and vertical tax equity.

According to the concept of *horizontal equity* in taxation, equal sacrifice among taxpayers will be attained if individuals of equal taxpaying ability are taxed "equally." According to the concept of *vertical equity* in taxation, individuals with unequal taxpaying ability should be taxed "unequally" in order to equalize the sacrifice. Thus, horizontal equity suggests that individuals with the same amount of taxpaying ability or capacity should bear equal tax burdens. Vertical equity, in contrast, suggests that persons of differential taxpaying abilities should pay different amounts of tax—with the greater absolute amount of tax being paid by the taxpayer with the greater ability, though just how much greater an amount of tax should be paid is still another issue.

The definition of *taxpaying ability*, of course, is highly significant to the application of these concepts. Positive economics cannot provide an explicit definition of "ability." Instead, normative value judgments, collectively reached by society through the political process, must be relied on to provide a benchmark for judging the ability to pay taxes. Western society has generally selected *income* comparisons between taxpayers as the primary indicator of ability to pay though, to a lesser extent, *wealth* comparisons have also been used. Moreover, the traditional application of the concept has defined income in a present income context rather than that of permanent or lifetime income.

The ability-to-pay approach can be viewed in terms of three other sacrifice concepts: (1) equal absolute sacrifice, (2) equal proportional sacrifice, and (3) equal marginal sacrifice (minimum aggregate sacrifice).[4]

---

[4] For an excellent discussion of these concepts, see Richard A. Musgrave, *The Theory of Public Finance* (New York: McGraw-Hill, 1959), chap. 5.

In order to attain vertical tax equity, the *equal absolute sacrifice concept* would require that a tax imposed on a higher-income individual would cause that person to sacrifice an amount of utility equal to that sacrificed by a lower-income taxpayer. For example, the tax should be designed to cause (say) 10 units of disutility to both the higher-income and the lower-income taxpayer.

The *equal proportional sacrifice concept* suggests that a tax should cause each individual to give up the same *percentage* of total utility in order to reach vertical equity. For example, if taxpayer A's higher income would yield him 200 units of consumptive utility, while taxpayer B's lower income would yield him only 100 units of utility, taxpayer A should suffer 20 units of disutility (20/200) if taxpayer B bears 10 units of disutility (10/100). Thus, both would bear equal proportions of disutility to total utility.

In the *equal marginal sacrifice* (minimum aggregate sacrifice) approach it is suggested that each taxpayer should bear an equal marginal decrease in the utility of his or her income after the payment of a tax. Thus, if the marginal tax dollar paid by taxpayer A causes him 5 units of disutility, while that paid by taxpayer B renders him 15 units of disutility, taxpayer A should pay higher taxes and taxpayer B should pay lower taxes until their marginal disutilities are equal—at, say, 10 units of disutility. If the conventional assumption of identical utility patterns among taxpayers is followed, this approach will equalize posttax incomes for both A and B, as well as for all taxpayers in the society. At the same time, minimum aggregate disutility (sacrifice) for the society as a whole will have been attained.

This concept of equal marginal sacrifice suggests a highly progres-

TABLE 6-1   **Continuum of the major theoretical approaches to equity in the distribution of tax burdens**

Absolute equality (equity in terms of equal monetary contribution)	The ability-to-pay approach (equity in terms of equal sacrifice)		
	Equal absolute sacrifice	Equal proportional sacrifice	Equal marginal sacrifice (minimum aggregate sacrifice)
←———→			
The benefit approach (based on market principles)			

Characteristics:
     Absolute equality—everyone pays an equal monetary amount of tax.
     Equal absolute sacrifice—everyone bears an equal absolute amount of disutility in paying taxes.
     Equal proportional sacrifice—everyone sacrifices the same proportion of total utility in paying taxes.
     Equal marginal sacrifice (minimum aggregate sacrifice)—everyone bears the same marginal disutility in paying taxes.
     Benefit approach—applies market criteria to the public sector, but is essentially applicable only where the exclusion principle applies to economic goods.

sive income tax rate structure. In effect, it applies a marginal tax rate of 100 percent to the highest income group for that income differential which separates it from the next highest group, and so on through successively lower income brackets, resulting in an equalization of posttax incomes for all taxpayers—if revenue needs are large enough that all income brackets except the lowest are taxed. Thus, it constitutes a polar extreme from the absolute equality theory, since it "equalizes posttax incomes" rather than requiring "equal tax payments," regardless of income size.

Table 6–1 compares the absolute equality theoretical extreme and also the equal marginal sacrifice extreme version of the ability-to-pay approach, as well as the two intermediate theoretical versions of the latter approach represented by the concepts of equal absolute sacrifice and equal proportional sacrifice. In addition, it includes the benefit principle as an alternative approach to tax equity; this will be discussed later in the chapter.

Implications for progressive taxation. When certain assumptions are accepted, the three sacrifice approaches to the ability-to-pay principle suggest the desirability of a *progressive income tax* system of taxation. These assumptions are: (1) it is possible to compare (measure) utilities among taxpayers, (2) preference schedules of taxpayers are homogeneous, that is, the utilities of individuals are the same within a particular income level, and (3) the marginal utility of income diminishes at an increasing rate as income increases. For progressive taxation to be implied under the equal absolute and equal proportional sacrifice approaches, the marginal utility of income schedule must be declining with an elasticity greater than unity. Under the equal marginal sacrifice approach, the marginal utility of income schedule must merely be declining. Moreover, a specific rate of diminution would need to be ascertained in order to justify a particular rate of tax progressivity under the first two approaches.[5]

The above assumptions are very strict. In fact, they run into a quantitative measurement roadblock, since utility cannot be measured in cardinal (absolute) measurement terms. In other words, interpersonal comparisons of utility among taxpayers are assumed, but these, in fact, cannot be made. Thus, progressive taxation, as implemented in practice, must ultimately rest on a collective societal value judgment of aggregate social utility rather than on an empirically provable economic fact.

The ability-to-pay concept, given the above assumptions, implies that the ability to make tax payments increases more than proportionately with increases in income, because the marginal utility of income declines at an increasing rate as income becomes greater. It is argued

---

[5] As noted, the equal marginal sacrifice approach, in effect, applies a 100-percent marginal rate of tax.

that, in order to maintain equal sacrifices among taxpayers of differential incomes under the vertical tax equity rule, the marginal rate of taxation must increase as the income base increases. For example, the last or marginal dollar of income to a person with a $50,000 annual income is said to provide lower marginal utility to that person than the last dollar of income earned by one with a $5,000 income. Therefore, a higher marginal tax rate above the $5,000 point is required on the income of the taxpayer with the $50,000 income if the sacrifices of the two taxpayers are to be equalized.

An analogy can be drawn between additional income, which may be used for a variety of purposes, including both consumption and saving, and the additional consumption of a particular economic good such as potatoes. Admittedly, the successive consumption of additional units of potatoes within a reasonably defined period is, after a certain point in consumption, likely to provide diminishing marginal amounts of pleasure. From the viewpoint of a person's entire income, however, the analogy is weakened. The person's consumption pattern may be switched to other economic goods with higher marginal satisfaction, or considerable pleasure may be derived from saving and investing the incremental income, or from being accorded the prestige many societies place on high incomes, large accumulations of wealth, and prestigious consumption. These are several of many alternative uses of incremental higher income which may provide substantial marginal utility to the high-income taxpayer.

Nonetheless, since low-income persons tend to allocate most or all of their incomes to the purchase of *necessity goods*, while high-income individuals spend a greater proportion of their incomes for nonessential or *luxury goods*, a reasonable judgment (though *not* an empirically provable argument) may favor the endorsement of progressive income taxation. It is not difficult, for example, to assign a greater probability of higher marginal utility to a pauper's marginal dollar of expenditure on food than to a millionaire's marginal dollar of expenditure on a yacht. Thus, despite the inability to achieve cardinal (absolute) measurement of utility, it can be argued that the diminishing-marginal-utility-of-income concept should be cautiously retained, though the pauper-versus-millionaire argument would be less persuasive if one is comparing persons above a subsistence level of income. Meanwhile, observations in the disciplines of psychology and sociology suggest that the individuals of a given society tend to possess certain similarities of behavior. These behavioral similarities may well lead to diminishing marginal income utility as income increases. Relatedly, ordinal measurement, in a behavioral sense, may substitute in part for the failure of cardinal measurement.

Progressive, regressive, and proportional taxes in the distributional equity context. The problems of empirical proof of the basic tenets of the ability-to-pay principle have not precluded Western society from reaching a value-judgment consensus in support of it.[6] Income is considered as the primary indicator of taxpaying ability, and progressive (graduated) income tax structures are generally advocated as the type which best serves the goal of equity in the distribution of tax burdens. This does not mean, of course, that all existing taxes in the Western world are progressive in relationship to the ability-to-pay norm. Nonetheless, the predominant benchmark in academic and policy circles has historically used income differences as the preferred indicator of taxpaying capacity and progressive taxation as the reference point for tax fairness or equity.

The societal consensus which allows the use of income as the indicator of taxpaying ability causes "distributional equity" semantics to differ from "statutory" semantics in regard to tax-base and tax-rate concepts. The statutory meaning was developed in the previous chapter. Now it is necessary to classify the meaning of *progressive, regressive,* and *proportional* taxation in the context of equity in the distribution of tax burdens.

In a *distributional equity context,* a tax (or tax system) is classified as *progressive* if the amount of tax paid as a percentage of income increases as income increases. This is true regardless of the type of tax in question, that is, whether it be the income, wealth, transactions, payroll, or lump-sum variety. In contrast, if the amount of tax paid (regardless of type of tax) as a percentage of income diminishes as income increases, the tax is said to be *regressive.* If the amount of tax paid (regardless of type of tax) remains a constant proportion of increasing income, it is classified as a *proportional* tax. Figure 6-1 demonstrates these distributional equity relationships in graphical form.

FIGURE 6-1   Various tax base–tax rate relationships in distributional equity terms

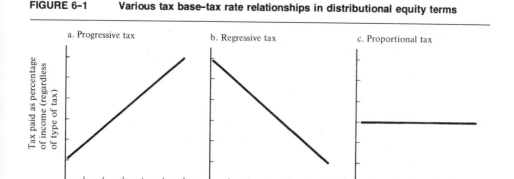

a. Progressive tax   b. Regressive tax   c. Proportional tax

Tax paid as percentage of income (regardless of type of tax)

Income ($)   Income ($)   Income ($)

---

[6] This does not suggest, of course, the complete absence of opposition to the application of the ability-to-pay principle in these nations.

A tax such as a graduated personal income tax will be in the same classification, in this case "progressive," in both statutory and distributional equity terms. This is true because income, which is the statutory base of the tax, is also the indicator of taxpaying ability under the ability-to-pay norm. However, a tax such as a general retail sales tax, whose statutory base is defined in terms of the monetary value of transactions rather than income, may yield divergent classification results. For example, the tax is "proportional," in statutory terms, since a flat rate is imposed regardless of the monetary value of purchase. Yet, it is generally considered to be "regressive," in distributional equity terms, since the primary component of its base is consumption—which tends to be a declining proportion of increasing income.[7]

The benefit principle

The benefit (benefits received) principle or tax equity rule is the primary alternative to the ability-to-pay principle used by Western society. This principle has the advantage of directly relating the revenue and expenditure sides of the budget.[8] Basically, it involves an approximation of market behavior in the allocative procedures of the public sector, thus combining both efficiency (allocational) and equity (distributional) considerations. That is, a person voluntarily exchanges purchasing power in the form of taxes for the acquisition of government economic goods—a quid pro quo arrangement whereby individual consumers pay directly for economic goods obtained from the public sector, from which goods they derive satisfaction.

The connotation of equity under this approach uses neither a monetary nor a sacrifice benchmark, but instead emphasizes the desirability of the dual facts that: (1) the exchange of purchasing power for the economic good is voluntary, as it would be in the market sector, and (2) the "payments" are made in accordance with the "benefits" received. The benefits may be priced according to either the governmental *cost* of providing the service or the *value* of the service to the purchaser, or a combination of these considerations.

The institutional application of the benefit approach is greatly restricted, however, by the inherent nature of joint (collective) consumption. That is, public-type goods are characterized by the fact that the exclusion principle cannot be effectively applied to all, if any, of the benefits of the economic goods in question. Unless *compulsion* exists to require the consumers to pay, they will benefit by free-rider

---

[7] This point will be demonstrated in Chapter 12 along with some views that challenge the regressivity conclusion.

[8] This is essentially the same approach used in the discussion of optimal intersector resource allocation that is known as the *voluntary-exchange* approach.

behavior to avoid payment. They will not pay voluntarily. Many public sector economic goods, therefore, not being subject to a market-type pricing mechanism, cannot be provided under the benefit approach. Hence, the benefit principle is not comprehensive enough in its application to serve as a general benchmark of equity in the distribution of tax burdens, though it does possess merit where it can be utilized through its application of market principles to the public sector. It is generally applicable, of course, in cases in which government applies the earmarked tax and user-charge means of raising revenues.

The benefit principle implicitly adopts the existing state of income and wealth distribution, which provides the effective demand for the acquisition of various governmentally-supplied economic goods by an individual. The higher-income individual would exert greater effective demand over these economic goods than would a lower-income individual. If the benefit principle were subject to widespread application, or even if it were applied to important economic goods such as public school education, government might well be asked by society to provide a corollary redistributional program of a tax-transfer nature. This would assure minimum purchasing power which would permit all citizens to acquire the essential goods supplied by the public sector.

OTHER EQUITY APPROACHES

The optimal income tax approach

The recently originated optimal income tax approach, like the benefit principle discussed above, also represents an effort to integrate the efficiency and equity aspects of public sector economics.[9] The thrust of the analysis under the optimal income tax concept centers on the fact that progressive income taxation causes an allocational excess burden to the taxpayer in that it introduces work-leisure and other behavioral nonneutralities. At the same time, funds transferred from such progressive income taxes will yield a distributional gain to recipient lower-income taxpayers who receive part of these revenues. Moreover, the greater the progressivity of the income tax rates, the greater is the excess burden to higher-income taxpayers, while as more tax revenues are transferred from higher- to lower-income taxpayers, the marginal utility gain from the funds being spent at that end

[9] For the initial major work in this conceptual area, see J. A. Mirrlees, "An Exploration in the Theory of Optimal Income Taxation," *Review of Economic Studies*, April 1971, pp. 175–208. For an excellent summary and evaluation of the literature on the general subject of optimal taxation, see David F. Bradford and Harvey S. Rosen, "The Optimal Taxation of Commodities and Income," *American Economic Review*, May 1976, pp. 94–101.

of the income scale decreases.[10] Hence, the *optimal income tax rate structure* is said to be that which would balance these allocational excess-burden and distributional-equity considerations at the margin. That is, the social optimum will be achieved when the marginal social cost of the tax burden from marginal income tax rates is equal to the marginal social gain of the individual who receives the funds. This would involve a series of positive and negative tax rates across the spectrum of differential income scales.

The optimal income tax concept is still in early stages of analysis, but it is receiving increasing attention in the literature of public sector economics. However, it is more complex than might appear at first glance. The optimal rate structure, for example, will depend on such factors as the distribution of income-earning skills among the population, as well as the pattern of work-leisure behavior among workers. Moreover, this approach, in placing allocational considerations on an *equal basis* with the distributional equity goal, overrides the controlling premise of the ability-to-pay principle, namely, that *income differences* alone should dictate the pattern of progressive tax rates applied in pursuit of the vertical equity goal. Thus, while an integration of efficiency and equity effects is praiseworthy in one sense, it may also unduly undermine the desirability of tax systems with an income benchmark for the attainment of vertical tax equity.

Demand elasticities and income tax rates

Another effort to integrate the efficiency and equity aspects of public sector economics focuses on the relationship between the income and price elasticities of demand for a public good (an efficiency consideration) and an appropriate income tax rate structure to finance the good (an equity consideration).[11] In effect, this analysis applies a version of the benefit principle of taxation to the determination of income tax rate structures, *without* also using the usual ability-to-pay benchmark for such rate determination.

The analysis assumes that individuals possess identical preference patterns, but different incomes. If the public good in question is a *normal* (as opposed to *inferior*) good, consumers will demand greater quantities of it at higher incomes. Thus, the *income elasticity of demand* (Y_d) for the good would possess a "positive" relationship. However, consumers will tend to demand less of the public good at higher tax prices under the *price elasticity of demand* (P_d) concept, thus yielding a "negative" relationship. Accordingly, if $Y_d > P_d$, progressive income tax rates are appropriate, since persons with higher

---

[10] The optimal income tax concept assumes a diminishing marginal utility of income.

[11] See James M. Buchanan, "Fiscal Institutions and Efficiency in Collective Outlay," *American Economic Review*, May 1964, pp. 227–35.

incomes increasingly demand, and thus benefit from, the good. If, instead, $Y_d < P_d$, regressive rates would be called for or, if $Y_d = P_d$, the appropriate income tax rate would be proportional.[12] Although such analysis is useful in demonstrating that a form of benefit taxation may be tied conceptually to income tax rates, it would be extremely difficult to apply operationally, since the various demands for specific public goods would ultimately have to be aggregated to an overall budgetary level for financing by means of general income taxation.

EQUITY AND EFFICIENCY IN TAX ENFORCEMENT

Tax equity in the enforcement sense

The term *tax equity* is perhaps as important in the enforcement sense as it is in the conceptual sense of the distribution of burdens. Tax equity must mean more than a theoretically rational tax system. It must consider also the equitable enforcement of the tax structure on all taxable subjects, seeing to it that no one illegally transfers his or her burden to other taxpayers. In this connotation, tax equity requires the consistent and unbiased imposition of taxes on all those prescribed by the law to be taxpayers. Though a good enforcement system cannot improve the rationality of an irrational tax structure, a poor system of enforcement can undo the advantages of a rational tax structure. The importance of equitable enforcement cannot be doubted.

Tax evasion, tax avoidance, and tax delinquency

It is necessary to distinguish three terms in relationship to tax enforcement: tax evasion, tax avoidance, and tax delinquency. *Tax evasion* involves a fraudulent or deceitful effort by a taxpayer to escape a legal tax obligation. This is a direct violation of tax law. *Tax avoidance,* in contrast, does not violate the letter of the law. It occurs when a taxpayer arranges his/her economic behavior in such a manner as to maximize his/her posttax economic position, that is, to minimize the amount of tax owed. This may be accomplished in the short run by the advantageous use of existing tax law provisions and, in the long run, by influencing tax legislation through the support of lobbies and pressure groups which represent the special interests of the taxpayer. Tax avoidance is lawful, while tax evasion is not. *Tax delinquency* refers to failure to pay a tax obligation on the date it is due. Ordinarily, tax delinquency is associated with inability to pay a tax because of inadequate funds, but it does cover the possibility of nonpayment even though funds are available. In any event, tax delinquency may

---

[12] Ibid., p. 230.

be only a temporary escape from tax payment, since the government unit to which the tax is owed can place liens on the property and future earnings of the taxpayer in order to secure payment eventually.

Techniques and agencies of tax enforcement

Various techniques (instruments) of tax enforcement are used in the U.S. public sector. One of the most commonly employed devices is that of *voluntary taxpayer compliance.* This technique is especially important for the collection of personal income taxes, though it seems to be eroding somewhat in the United States during recent times as the so-called *subterranean* (underground) economy, based on cash transactions and the absence of records, grows as part of an effort to escape income taxation.[13] Moreover, personal income tax administration normally utilizes the *withholding* technique, whereby tax funds are collected from wages and salaries at the income source of the taxpayer. This device was used first by the federal government during World War II, when there was critical need for immediate federal funds to finance the war, and inflationary pressures were severe.[14] The private sector thus makes a considerable contribution to tax enforcement in the United States. The use of voluntary taxpayer compliance and withholding means that both consumers and businesses bear a significant part of the explicit enforcement costs.

Auditing, whether computerized or clerical, is basic to any tax enforcement program. The federal government in recent decades has expanded its use of computers to assist tax administrators' enforcement efforts. Moreover, taxpayer account numbers are required by law as part of the federal income tax enforcement program. Tax auditing by government requires adequate information, which may be gathered in a variety of ways. Among the techniques in use, especially by the federal government, are: (1) routine checks of tax returns by a tax enforcement agency; (2) a check on large or unusual business transactions; (3) appraisal of relevant newspaper reports, court proceedings, and legal filings; (4) routine check of the business activities of gangsters and racketeers (here the revenue motive of taxation is supplemented by a regulatory motive); (5) exchange of information with other agencies within the same unit of government and also among units and levels of government; (6) using information obtained from business, as required by law, to report various information items such as wages, dividends, and interest paid to taxpayers, and (7) use of tax informers.

---

[13] See "The Fast Growth of the Underground Economy," *Business Week,* March 13, 1978, pp. 73–77.

[14] Secretary of the Treasury Henry Morgenthau and Beardsley Ruml pioneered the withholding technique during World War II.

The primary tax enforcement agency of the federal government is the Internal Revenue Service (IRS), formally called the Bureau of Internal Revenue, which was established as part of the Treasury Department during the Civil War. The IRS is responsible for the collection of *internal* (domestic) tax revenues. The other tax collection agency of the federal government, the Bureau of Customs, enforces taxes of an *external* nature, such as tariffs placed on the importation of economic goods. It also operates under the Treasury Department. At the state level of government, tax commissions or revenue departments serve as the tax collection agencies for the various state taxes such as general retail sales taxes, specific sales (excise) taxes, and state income taxes. The various units of local government use somewhat diverse tax collection techniques, though the collection of property taxes through county assessor offices is a common practice throughout the nation.

Tax enforcement efficiency

It is generally conceded that *economies of scale* exist in centralized tax collection. The central government is said to be able to collect revenue from most taxes at a lower cost per unit of revenue than can state and local governments. Though empirical studies in this regard are somewhat scarce, the argument for economies of scale in centralized tax collection is probably a valid one. Tax collection operations in the United States are considerably decentralized, while nations of similar federal structures such as Canada use techniques such as the "piggybacking" of income taxes, whereby the federal government offers to collect provincial income taxes through the federal tax administration mechanism. Most Canadian provinces have accepted this offer. The beginning of such a system for the United States was made possible by the federal revenue-sharing legislation of 1972, though no further development of this technique has yet taken place.[15] However, exchanges of tax information now increasingly occur between the IRS and the states which use personal income taxes.

For a rational tax system, the direct monetary costs of enforcement must not comprise an exceedingly high proportion of the revenues collected from the taxes. This is particularly true when reasonable tax source alternatives are available to a unit of government. In the present context, the term *enforcement costs* should be construed to include both the direct administrative costs of the public sector and the voluntary compliance costs of the private sector.

Also, it should be observed that various secondary effects, such as negative allocational nonneutralities in the form of disincentives of

[15] See Public Law 92-512, 92d cong., H.R. 14370, October 20, 1972; Title II: "Federal Collection of State Individual Income Taxes."

consumption and investment, may result from irritating or irrational tax enforcement efforts. This is undesirable. On the other hand, tax evasion—the target of enforcement efforts—is also undesirable. Thus, tax enforcement efforts, though justified, should avoid unnecessary disincentives. In deference to the danger of creating excessive disincentives from overenforcement, the degree of tax enforcement effort is normally *not* extended to the point where the marginal dollar cost of enforcement is equal to the marginal tax dollar derived from such enforcement.

Another secondary result of tax enforcement activities is that some potential evasion never occurs, because taxpayers know that an adequate tax enforcement system is in operation and they avoid or limit evasion efforts. Although the additional revenues collected directly as a result of the detection of tax evasion can be estimated, the additional revenues which indirectly accrue because potential tax evasion is discouraged cannot be determined. Yet, this may constitute a considerable amount.

7

Tax shifting
and incidence

GENERAL–EQUILIBRIUM TAX INCIDENCE ANALYSIS
AND OTHER INCIDENCE CONCEPTS

Tax equity rules and goals established through political consensus view *tax incidence* in an ultimate or final economic context. That is, they allow for market adjustments to taxes which may permit the transference of tax burdens away from their initial point of impact. In other words, the person who first bears the legal obligation to pay the tax to the government may be able to shift the burden to someone else. This chapter will review the various economic forces which bear on such potential tax burden transfers. These are commonly referred to as the *principles of tax shifting.*

Conceptually, the final incidence of a tax can best be determined within a long-run, *general-equilibrium* framework.[1] That is, the distribution of real income, as influenced by a tax, should reflect all of the

---

[1] The breakthrough article demonstrating the merits of the general-equilibrium approach to tax incidence was written by Arnold C. Harberger, "The Incidence of the Corporation Income Tax," *Journal of Political Economy,* June 1962, pp. 215–40.

For a more recent article concerning the general-equilibrium nature of taxation, see Charles E. McLure, Jr., "Tax Incidence, Macroeconomic Policy, and Absolute Prices," *Quarterly Journal of Economics,* May 1970, pp. 254–67. McLure argues that tax incidence, which is defined in terms of changes in relative product and factor (resource) prices as determined by a change in the structure of taxation, does not in itself determine a change in the absolute price of a product or resource. It is also necessary to know how the aggregate economic policies which accompany the tax change influence the general level of product or factor prices. Thus, it is argued that changes in both general

long-run price and output adjustments in both product and factor markets that result from the tax. Hence, the emphasis in the general-equilibrium approach to tax shifting and incidence is on *relative prices* among products and resources, rather than on the absolute price of a given product or resource. Normally, this would incorporate many markets and many price-output changes. Conceptually, it would involve the interaction of the entire economic system. Relatedly, effects exerted on such relevant considerations as capital/labor ratios in production functions, or work-leisure choices, also help to determine the final incidence of a tax. Thus, long-run general equilibrium tax incidence analysis involves an extreme complexity of multiple interacting variables. As a result, it faces formidable practical problems of empirical testing and measurement which may, at times, detract from its application, even though they do not detract from its conceptual purity.

In addition, other conceptual considerations, such as *interstate* or *interregional* tax incidence, which is concerned with the "exporting" of tax burdens from the citizens of one political jurisdiction or region to those of another, or *dynamic* tax incidence, which is concerned with the economic growth aspects of the subject, including changes in the overall supply of factor inputs, have significant implications for incidence analysis. However, these concepts also involve the complex interaction of many variables and resulting measurement difficulties. Moreover, the frequent assumption of perfectly competitive markets in general-equilibrium models constitutes a rigorous assumption that is not characteristic of most present-day markets.

Tax incidence studies, in general, may follow either a differential incidence or a balanced budget incidence methodology. Under the *differential incidence* approach, the level of government expenditures remains unchanged while one tax is substituted for another tax of equal yield to finance these expenditures. Hence, the redistributional effects of alternative taxes can be compared. Under the *balanced-budget incidence* methodology, the effect of the overall tax and expenditure process on the distribution of private sector income is considered as the levels of both government expenditures and taxes are increased by an equal amount.

---

price levels and relative prices determine the posttax-change price of a product or resource.

For other discussions of this topic, see Peter M. Mieszkowski, "On the Theory of Tax Incidence," *Journal of Political Economy*, June 1967, pp. 250–62, and "Tax Incidence Theory: The Effects of Taxes on the Distribution of Income," *Journal of Economic Literature*, December 1969, pp. 1103–24; Charles E. McLure, Jr., "General Equilibrium Incidence Analysis: The Harberger Model after Ten Years," *Journal of Public Economics*, February 1975, pp. 125–61; and George F. Break, "The Incidence and Economic Effects of Taxation," in *The Economics of Public Finance* (Washington, D.C.: Brookings Institution, 1974).

PARTIAL–EQUILIBRIUM TAX INCIDENCE ANALYSIS

Most tax shifting and incidence studies until recent years have been of the *partial-equilibrium* variety, which estimate incidence effects in terms of *absolute price changes.* That is, the partial-equilibrium approach attempts to measure the possible transference of tax burdens among taxpayers via the higher absolute selling price of an economic good or the lower absolute purchase price of a productive resource, but it does not consider changes in *relative product and resource prices* in the context of the interrelationship of many variables in a general-equilibrium system.

The conceptual superiority of the general-equilibrium approach to tax shifting and incidence is fully appreciated. Nevertheless, this chapter will focus on some of the traditional principles (criteria) of tax shifting and incidence as they are approached in a partial-equilibrium context. Often, the partial-equilibrium approach will prove to be the more practical methodology to employ because it entails smaller, but by no means nonexistent, empirical measurement difficulties. The most important of these partial-equilibrium criteria will be described separately as if each were the only determinant of ultimate tax incidence, though clearly together they exert a composite effect. This procedure will be followed in order to isolate the probable direction of the effects which the criterion in question would exert. Moreover, some incidence effects will be considered separately in other chapters of Part II as the fiscal performance of particular types of taxes is discussed, and in Part III as the incidence of the aggregate public sector budget is considered.

At the outset, some additional description of relevant terminology is desirable. The impact point of a tax refers to the person who bore the initial legal obligation to pay the tax to the government. This is known as the point of *statutory tax incidence.* Since persons are the fundamental claimants of all factor incomes, the point of initial burden must be on a person.[2] The concept of statutory incidence does not mean the actual administrative handover of tax funds, but instead, the persons who bear the initial financial burden of paying the tax from their income or wealth. For example, an employer may withhold taxes from the income of an employee and directly turn over the tax funds to the government. Yet, the worker from whose income the tax is withheld certainly bears the immediate impact. On the other hand, the concept of *economic incidence* can be designated as the point of the "final" placement of a tax burden. Thus, if the tax burden ultimately rests on a different person or persons than the person who first owed

---

[2] Businesses, including corporations, are correctly viewed as earning income for their individual owners. Thus, only these owners can receive the impact (initial monetary burden) of a tax.

the tax to the government, the phenomenon of tax shifting has occurred.

Thus, *tax shifting* can be demonstrated by a comparison of the statutory-incidence and economic-incidence points of a tax. If the two points are the same, the burden rests ultimately where it initially falls, and tax shifting, that is, transference of the tax burden among persons, *does not* occur. On the other hand, if part or all of the burden of the tax ultimately rests at a point or points other than the point of statutory incidence, tax shifting, at least to some extent, *does* occur. Tax shifting may be partial; it may be complete; in some instances, if the taxpayer takes advantage of unrealized profits (returns, gains), it may be said to be greater than 100 percent.[3] Thus, there is a range from zero or no tax shifting, at the one extreme, to greater than 100-percent tax shifting, given sufficient unrealized profits, at the other.

Tax shifting takes place through the market mechanism of supply and demand. Taxes induce allocational adjustments in productive and consumptive behavior which, in turn, yield redistributional results in the sense of both a real tax burden and real income distribution. These allocational adjustments, in essence, are *substitution effects*. While every tax exerts an income effect, every tax except one—a lump-sum tax—also yields some form of substitution effect. Allocationally speaking, tax shifting will occur through a change in the absolute price of an economic good or productive resource, in the partial-equilibrium sense, or through a change in the relative price of products and resources, in the general-equilibrium sense.

In partial-equilibrium terms, if the absolute price of an economic good is *increased* as the result of a new or higher tax, and this allows part or all of the tax burden to be transferred to someone else, it can be said that the burden has been shifted forward. If the result of the tax is to *decrease* the absolute price of a factor (resource) of production, and this allows transference of part or all of the tax burden, it can be said that the burden has been shifted backward. Thus, *forward tax shifting* under partial-equilibrium conditions ordinarily results from a rise in the absolute price of an economic good in a product market, and *backward tax shifting* ordinarily results from a reduction in the absolute price of a productive resource in a factor market. In the first instance, the burden of the tax has been shifted to the consumer, while in the latter case the burden has been shifted to the owner of the factor of production through the price changes.

A related technique by which a tax may be shifted is that of *tax capitalization*. Again, the shifting takes place through a change in

---

[3] The definition of unrealized profits (gains, returns), and their relationship to tax shifting and incidence, will be presented later in the chapter.

price, but in this instance the price is the capitalized value of the expected future earnings of the asset subject to the tax. This technique is particularly important in the case of a property tax involving commercial property. The following example will illustrate the possibility of transferring a property tax burden through tax capitalization.

Suppose that the average annual net income of an automobile sales agency is $100,000. Suppose also that 10 percent is the normal rate of return needed in the community to attract capital into this market. Since $100,000 is 10 percent of $1 million, the capitalized value of the auto agency may be estimated at $1 million (excluding depreciation considerations). Now, suppose the property taxes imposed on the automobile agency are increased by $5,000 per year. This tax increment lowers its posttax income to $95,000 from $100,000. Since $95,000 is 10 percent of $950,000, the capitalized value of the auto agency in terms of its posttax earning potential is decreased by $50,000 to $950,000, due to the increase in property taxes.

If the owner of the auto sales agency decides to sell the property, and is able to sell it at the pretax-increment capitalized value of $1 million, the burden of the tax increment will be shifted to the buyer. If the property is sold at the posttax-increment value of $950,000, the incremental property tax will be borne by the seller. If the owner sells at any price over $950,000, but less than $1 million, part of the tax burden will be transferred to the buyer through the process of tax capitalization and the remainder absorbed by the seller. Tax shifting, in this example, is assisted by imperfect market knowledge by the purchaser of the property after its capital value has declined. Moreover, long-run adjustments may increase the price of automobiles sold in the community as some reduction of sales capacity takes place because of reduced posttax earnings. The tax capitalization example demonstrates a peculiar market method whereby, under favorable conditions, tax shifting can occur.

Tax shifting is sometimes disguised by an implicit rather than an outward (external) price change. This would occur, for example, when the quality or size of an economic good or productive resource is reduced while price is held constant in order to shift a tax. Thus, a special excise tax levied on candy bars may be shifted forward to consumers by reducing the quality or size of the candy bar, while its price remains stable. Implicitly, and effectively, the price is raised when a reduced quality or size is sold at the same per-unit price. Thus, in an indirect and disguised manner, the burden of the tax may be transferred (at least partially) through a market adjustment involving a quality or size change rather than a direct price change.

MAJOR CRITERIA INFLUENCING TAX SHIFTING
UNDER PARTIAL-EQUILIBRIUM CONDITIONS

Several criteria or determinants may influence the ability to shift the absolute burden of a tax under partial-equilibrium conditions.[4] These incidence criteria are (1) market structure; (2) unrealized profits; (3) industry cost conditions; (4) price elasticity; (5) type of tax, and (6) political jurisdiction. There is no intent to imply that only these six determinants exist; multiple interacting variables, both these and others, are likely to bear upon the final result. However, the criteria analyzed in this chapter are among the most important determinants of tax shifting and incidence. They are not discussed in any order of relative importance; all six are considered to be significant.

Market structure

The extent to which the monetary burden of a tax is shifted, either forward or backward, may be importantly affected by the nature of the *market structure* within which the seller or buyer functions. In order to explain the effects of different market structures, let us look at the possibilities of tax shifting in both the short and long run, and under the structural conditions of: (1) pure competition, (2) monopolistic competition, (3) oligopoly, and (4) pure monopoly. In these cases, it will be initially assumed that the sellers are maximizing profits.

Pure (perfect) competition. The purely competitive (perfectly competitive) market is characterized by many sellers and buyers of homogeneous (nondifferentiated) goods.[5] Figure 7-1 indicates the initial pretax equilibrium for a purely competitive firm and for a purely competitive industry, at point *a* for the firm, in Figure 7-1a, and at point a^1 for the industry, in Figure 7-1b. The firm is producing an output of 25 units and selling at a price of $10, as determined by the intersection of its marginal cost curve, *MC*, with marginal revenue (*MR*) and price (*AR*), as the latter is set by the industry. Then, assume that an *excise tax* of $5 per unit is imposed on the good.

The individual firm can initiate no effort on its own to shift the tax forward via a higher selling price, since it has no control over price. It completely lacks monopoly power due to the homogeneity of its product and the fact that it is one of many sellers. Thus, any forward shifting which may occur can take place *only* through *industry forces*. In the *immediate* or *market period* this will not occur. Industry forces, however, may allow partial shifting of the tax in the *short run*, though

---

[4] There are also some implications for general equilibrium tax shifting in the discussion which follows.

[5] The theoretical distinction between "pure" and "perfect" competition is, for the most part, irrelevant to the analysis which follows.

FIGURE 7-1   Pure competition: Long-run tax shifting under constant cost conditions

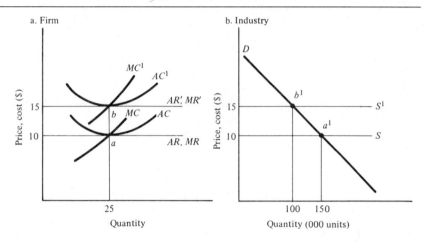

the overall possibility of shifting is reduced by the inability of the individual firm to influence price. Any shifting which does occur through industry forces in the short run would not involve the exit of firms from the industry. Yet, in the *long run*, under constant-cost supply conditions, the tax will be fully shifted forward to the consumer, due to the action of industry forces in the form of an exodus of some firms from the industry.[6]

Thus, over the long run, some marginal firms will leave the industry because the industry determined short-run price increase is not equal to the new excise tax burden. When this occurs, the industry supply schedule will shift upward until market price has risen sufficiently so that the representative firm again can earn a normal profit. This is demonstrated for the industry in Figure 7-1b at point b^1, where the industry supply schedule, S, has shifted upward by the amount of the tax to become the posttax supply schedule, S^1. Industry price increases from $10 to $15, and the firm can now sell all of its output at the higher price. The burden of the tax has thus been fully shifted forward though, significantly, this has not occurred through monopoly power by the individual firm, but instead through the operation of long-run competitive industry forces. For the purpose of the example, such forward shifting assumes constant factor prices and hence the impossibility of backward shifting. The final equilibrium price ($15) is higher than the initial price ($10) by the amount of the tax ($5).

Monopolistic competition. Monopolistic competition market structure is characterized by a substantial number of sellers and

---

[6] Only partial shifting could occur in pure competition under long-run increasing-cost conditions of supply.

buyers of heterogeneous (differentiated) goods. It provides tax-shift-ing results somewhat similar, but not identical, to those realized in purely competitive markets. As in pure competition, the firm is one of many sellers, which detracts from its ability to influence price. How-ever, product differentiation may allow the firm at times to exert a modest amount of price determination, with resulting shifting influ-ence, which could not occur under the homogenous product condi-tions of the purely competitive market. In the long run, the exit of some firms from the industry, because of the higher costs resulting from the tax, will tend to further shift the excise tax forward to con-sumers, though full forward shifting is unlikely due to the retention of some monopoly profits within the industry.

Oligopoly. Significant interdependence between a few dominant sellers characterizes oligopoly market structure. In the case of a new excise tax or an increase in the rate of an existing one, each firm recognizes that every other firm also has its costs increased by the amount of the tax. Thus, unless industry demand is elastic, or unless considerable differentiation exists between the products of the oligopoly firms, it is likely that *each* firm will add the tax to its selling price in an effort to shift the tax. In fact, the markup pricing formula commonly used in oligopolies would provide such a price increase on a virtually automatic basis. Unlike pure competition, oligopoly per-mits the individual firm to initiate such a price change on its own. Moreover, the few oligopoly firms in an industry often follow a price leader in setting price. In many ways, the price-shifting possibilities in such a cohesive oligopoly are similar to those of a pure monopoly—which will be analyzed in detail at this time.

Pure monopoly. As depicted in Figure 7-2, the pure monopoly firm, which is identical with the industry since no competitors exist, is in pretax equilibrium, producing output OX, charging price OP, and earning monopoly profits $PABC$. Assume first that an excise tax is imposed on the economic good produced by the monopoly. As a result, the marginal cost curve, MC, and the average cost curve, AC, shift upward and become MC^1 and AC^1, respectively. Thus, a new posttax equilibrium is set at output OX^1 and price OP^1, which yields monopoly profits equal to the rectangle P^1DEF. This profit rectangle is smaller than the profit rectangle $PABC$ which existed before the excise tax was imposed. Hence, the pure monopoly firm in this case *does not fully shift* the excise tax. In fact, the extent to which it can shift any part of the tax will be determined by numerous factors (some of which will be discussed below), such as industry cost conditions and the price elasticities of product demand and resource supply. Importantly, however, the pure monopoly firm could initiate a price change on its own due to the absence of competitors, and it could do so in any time period, which will tend to enhance its forward tax-

FIGURE 7-2   **Pure monopoly: Tax-shifting considerations**

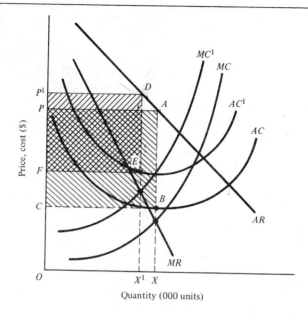

Quantity (000 units)

shifting potential since tax shifting can be attained only through a price change.[7]

In Figure 7-2, the portion of the tax borne by the monopolist is equal to the difference between the larger pretax and the smaller posttax profit rectangles. Meanwhile, the upward movement in absolute price from P to P' is an indicator of the amount of tax per unit that is shifted forward.

Unrealized profits (net income, gains, returns)

Next, assume that a *corporation* (business) *income tax* is imposed on the profits of a pure monopoly firm. In this instance, the tax is levied on a surplus or residual amount, that is, on the profits of the

---

[7] The comparative shiftability of an excise tax by a pure competition firm as opposed to a pure monopoly firm, in different time periods, may be summarized as follows:

Time period	Pure competition	Pure monopoly
Short-run	Little, if any shifting, and through "industry forces only"	Shifting, to varying degrees, possible through "firm monopoly power"
Long-run	Full shifting, and through "industry forces only" (constant cost conditions)	Shifting, to varying degrees, possible through "firm monopoly power"

firm as such. Thus, in Figure 7-2, if the pure monopoly firm is maximizing profits, the corporation income tax would be imposed on rectangle $PABC$. The corporation income tax, unlike the excise tax imposed on the good produced by a monopoly firm, does not result in an increase in the marginal and average cost curves of the firm. Thus, it does not pay for the firm to increase price to help cover the increased costs and thus attempt to shift part of the tax forward. In the case of the income tax, the firm's posttax profits are simply reduced by the amount of the tax. It is important to note that the most profitable posttax price-output point remains the same as the pretax profit-maximizing price-output point.

For example, consider a 50 percent tax on corporate profits. In Figure 7-2, 50 percent (after paying the corporation income tax) of the largest profit rectangle available $(PABC)$ leaves the firm with more net posttax income than 50 percent of any smaller non-profit-maximizing profit rectangle (such as $P'DEF$). Thus, if $PABC$ equals \$500,000 in profits and $P'DEF$ equals \$400,000, 50 percent of the former figure leaves posttax profits of \$250,000, while 50 percent of the latter figure leaves posttax profits of only \$200,000. Moreover, the posttax profits would be lower for *any* pretax profit amount under \$500,000. No increase in price, as in the response to the excise tax, can change this fact. However, the nonshiftability of a corporation net income tax is based on the strict assumption that the firm is operating in its pretax status at the profit-maximizing point where marginal cost equals marginal revenue $(MC = MR)$. If this premise is accepted, then it is only logical to conclude that the business income tax cannot be shifted.

However, an often overlooked, though significant, point relevant to tax shifting is suggested in the prior discussion. That is, a firm may *not* be operating at the $MC = MR$ point, which means that "unrealized profits" are available between the actual $MC \neq MR$ equilibrium and the potential, optimal, $MC = MR$ equilibrium. Thus, *unrealized profits* may be defined as the amount of incremental profits (or reduced losses) that could be obtained if a firm moved from a suboptimal to an optimal profit position. Yet, the concept has even wider scope since it could apply to the unrealized returns or gains that are present between an optimal and suboptimal return to *any* productive resource, including labor. However, the following discussion will focus on the concept in the form of unrealized profits to business enterprises.

Among the various types of market structure, the only place where unrealized profits cannot occur is for the firm operating under long-run, purely (perfectly) competitive conditions. In this situation, since the firm is earning only normal economic profits, it must produce at the $MC = MR$ point in order to survive in the industry in the long run. However, any imperfectly competitive firm (monopolistic competition, oligopoly, pure monopoly) may operate in both the short run and the long run apart from the *MC* = *MR* point due to the possible presence of monopoly profits. Thus, an imperfectly competitive firm which is not operating at the profit-maximizing point will be in a position to possibly shift a corporation (business) income tax, if there exists a buffer area of unrealized profits within which price-output rearrangements can be made. Figure 7–3, which is described later, demonstrates this phenomenon.

First, however, the critical question must be asked: Why would a firm choose *not* to maximize profits at the *MC* = *MR* point? Such considerations as imperfect market and production knowledge, the fear of antitrust action, the fear of an unfavorable public image, the fear of attracting new entrants into the industry, the fear of stimulating union wage demands, and public utility regulation may prevent a firm from achieving, or even attempting to achieve, an optimal profit position. Instead, the firm may follow such rules or benchmarks as: maximization of gross receipts (sales); achievement of a target rate of return on investment; maintenance of stable prices on goods produced by the firm; application of a percentage markup price over

FIGURE 7–3 Unrealized profits as a necessary condition for shifting a business income tax by a firm in imperfect competition

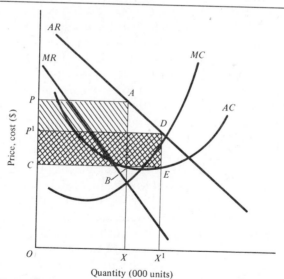

Quantity (000 units)

Explanation:
  Rectangle *PABC* = Maximum profits where *MC* = *MR* at output *X*.
  Rectangle *P¹DEC* = Profits at Output *X¹*, which is a position of suboptimal profits.
  The "excess" of *PABC* over *P¹DEC* = *Unrealized Profits*, thus allowing the "possibility" of shifting the burden of a profits tax as price is increased toward *P* and output is decreased toward the profit-maximization output *X*.

average (unit) cost, or improvement of the firm's market share position within the industry as a whole. When such rules or benchmarks are followed, the firm usually does *not* attain an optimal price-output position. Consequently, within this area of *unrealized profits* a margin is created from which tax shifting becomes increasingly possible (assuming that the other criteria permit the tax shifting). In other words, the possibility of shifting the absolute burden of a business profits tax is enhanced by the presence of unrealized profits.

In Figure 7–3, rectangle $PABC$ at the profit-maximizing point, $MC = MR$, exceeds rectangle P^1DEC at the non-profit-maximizing point shown on the graph. In this situation, imperfect knowledge, fear of antitrust action, or one of the other reasons mentioned before, causes the unrealized profits "excess" of $PABC$ over P^1DEC as a lower than profit-maximizing price (P^1) is charged and a larger than profit-maximizing output (X^1) is produced. The firm, in terms of the profit-maximization goal, would like to restrict output and utilize its monopoly power to increase price from P^1 to P at profit-maximizing output X. Then, given the imposition of a new profits (income) tax, or a rate increase in an existing profits tax, the firm may choose to set aside antitrust or other considerations which impede profit maximizing, and—given the appropriate market knowledge—move price and output toward the profit-maximizing position. In so doing, part, or all, or possibly more than 100 percent of the tax burden may be shifted.[8] Significantly, the shifting, if it occurs, is not accomplished through equilibrating market forces, as in the purely competitive case, but instead is accomplished through individual firm policy decisions as assisted by market power in an imperfectly competitive industry.

Public utility firms appear to be in a unique institutional position to shift tax burdens through the presence of unrealized profits. These privately owned, publicly regulated firms are ordinarily allowed to earn a particular rate of return on invested capital but, because of the nature of their market and production conditions, they are not allowed to charge profit-maximizing prices nor to produce profit-maximizing outputs. Thus, *unrealized profits*, operating through the institutional arrangement of public utility regulation, are built into the price-output policies of public utility firms. When additional profits (income) tax burdens are imposed, the posttax earnings on investment of these companies tend to decline, and a case is created for the firms to request higher prices (rates) from the regulatory commissions. Often, such requests are granted. The quantity demanded of the economic good, moreover, does not ordinarily decline greatly as price increases, due to the typical inelastic demand for public utility goods. Martin Farris contends that public utility firms tend to pass along increased

---

[8] Greater than 100 percent tax shifting would require extreme deviation by a firm from its pretax profit-maximization position and would likely also require both extensive forward and backward tax-shifting opportunities.

taxes through regulatory approval, but at the same time they are reluctant (and are not pressed strongly by the regulatory commissions) to lower prices following tax reductions.[9]

In summary, it may be said that the presence of unrealized profits constitutes a *necessary* condition, though not by itself a *sufficient* condition, for the forward shifting of a tax on net business income. In the final analysis, the shiftability (either forward or backward) of a business profits tax, an excise tax, or virtually any tax, will depend on numerous critical variables such as industry cost conditions and the price elasticities of demand and supply.

Industry cost conditions

A third criterion of tax shifting, in partial-equilibrium terms, derives from the cost conditions present in the industry in which the attempt to shift the tax takes place. In this regard, an industry may be classified as (1) a *constant-cost industry* if the average cost of production remains unchanged as output expands, (2) an *increasing-cost industry* if average cost rises with expanding output, and (3) a *decreasing-cost industry* if average cost declines as output expands. Industry cost conditions are a long-run phenomenon involving the concept of scale economies and diseconomies. Also, it should be noted that long-run decreasing cost conditions are not conceptually consistent with purely (perfectly) competitive markets.

Figure 7–4a represents an industry operating under *constant* aver-

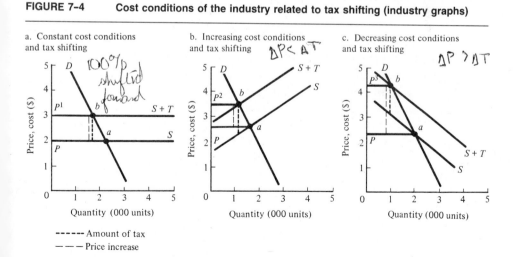

FIGURE 7–4   **Cost conditions of the industry related to tax shifting (industry graphs)**

a. Constant cost conditions and tax shifting

b. Increasing cost conditions and tax shifting

c. Decreasing cost conditions and tax shifting

------ Amount of tax

— — — Price increase

---

[9] Martin T. Farris, "Tax Reductions and Utility Rates," *Public Utilities Fortnightly,* August 27, 1964, pp. 30–36.

age costs of production. Assume the imposition of an excise tax on the product sold by this industry. The cost schedules of the firms in the industry will increase by the amount of the tax, and the supply curve, S, thus becomes $S + T$. The initial pretax equilibrium is determined at point a by the intersection of the supply curve S and the demand curve D, establishing price P. After the long-run market adjustment, the posttax equilibrium is reached at point b, resulting in price P^1. The absolute price of the economic good has increased by the amount of the tax. In this case, full forward shifting of the tax has taken place.

Figure 7–4b represents an industry operating under *increasing* average costs of production. The initial pretax equilibrium is at point a, and the posttax equilibrium is at point b. After the long-run market adjustment, the absolute price of the economic good, P^2, has increased by less than the amount of the tax. Thus, full forward shifting has *not* occurred. Figure 7–4c shows that under *decreasing* industry cost conditions, as could be the case with pure monopoly, the absolute price of the economic good, P^3, increases by more than the amount of the tax. This can be observed by comparing points a and b.[10] In this instance, more than 100 percent shifting has taken place. Thus, decreasing-cost conditions may be said to be the most conducive to tax shifting and increasing-cost conditions the least conducive.

Price elasticity

Price elasticity of product demand. Another significant partial-equilibrium determinant of tax shifting and incidence concerns the price elasticity of demand of the economic good or the price elasticity of supply of the productive resource in question. The elasticity concept relates the sensitivity of the response of a quantity (demanded or supplied) change to a change in price. Such variables as product substitutability and the price of the good in relation to the buyer's total income or outlay help determine the demand elasticity value of an economic good. By affecting the quantity demanded at various prices, thus affecting total revenue or gross income (price times quantity demanded), demand elasticity helps determine the net income level of a firm at the posttax equilibrium. The relationship of the posttax net income level to the pretax net income level will help to indicate the extent to which shifting may have occurred.

Generally, the more sensitive (elastic) the quantity demanded is to

---

[10] Equilibrium is considered here in terms of Marshallian stability. The results would differ under conditions of Walrasian stability. For an excellent discussion of the Marshallian and Walrasian conditions of the stability of equilibrium, *see* James M. Henderson and Richard E. Quandt, *Microeconomic Theory*, 2d ed., (New York: McGraw-Hill, 1971), pp. 132–36.

FIGURE 7-5   **Price elasticity of product demand related to tax shifting**

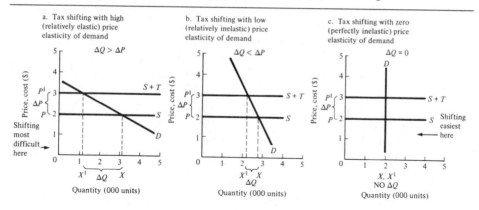

a. Tax shifting with high (relatively elastic) price elasticity of demand

b. Tax shifting with low (relatively inelastic) price elasticity of demand

c. Tax shifting with zero (perfectly inelastic) price elasticity of demand

a change in price, the more difficult it is to shift the burden of a tax forward through a higher selling price. Conversely, the more inelastic or insensitive the quantity reaction to a price change, the greater the possibility of shifting the tax forward. Suppose an excise tax is levied on a particular economic good. In Figure 7–5, the S curve represents the supply and curve D represents the demand for the good. Constant-cost conditions of supply are assumed. In Figure 7–5a, demand is *relatively elastic* throughout the relevant portion of the demand curve, while in Figure 7–5b demand is *relatively inelastic* throughout the relevant portion. In Figure 7–5c, the demand for the good is *perfectly (completely) inelastic* throughout the entire curve. When the excise tax is imposed, the price of the good is initially increased by the amount of the tax as the average and marginal cost schedules of the firms in the industry are increased by this amount. The supply curve, S, will shift upward and become the new supply curve, S + T, in each graph as the tax is added on to the original selling price of the product. Thus, the new selling price is P^1 in each graph, as opposed to the pretax selling price P. Whether the tax is successfully shifted or not will be influenced by the nature of the demand elasticity for the product.

The greatest quantity reduction to the higher price occurs in the *relatively elastic* demand case (Figure 7–5a). In this instance, tax shifting is difficult because the total revenue or gross income (price times quantity) of a firm would *decline*. Where the demand is *relatively inelastic* (Figure 7–5b), as the price increases from P to P^1 (by the amount of the tax) the quantity decrease, from X to X^1, is less than proportionate to the price increase. As a result, total revenue (gross income) to the firm *increases*, and tax shifting is more likely to take

place. The most likely occurrence of tax shifting is shown in Figure
7-5c, where the demand is *perfectly inelastic*, since there is no quantity reaction as the price increases from P to P^1. The initial quantity, X,
and the posttax quantity, X^1, are the same.

Of course, other criteria are at work in any single tax-shifting situation. However, considering the price elasticity of demand criterion
alone, it is an accurate generalization to say that the greater the price
elasticity of demand of a good, the less is the opportunity for transferring a tax burden forward. Conversely, the greater the price inelasticity of demand, the more likely forward tax shifting is to occur.

Price elasticity of resource supply. While forward shifting is ordinarily concerned with obtaining a higher selling price for an economic good, backward shifting ordinarily relates to an effort to pay a
lower buying price for a productive resource. The following general-
izations may be made concerning backward tax shifting as it would be
influenced by price elasticity of resource supply: (1) the more elastic
the resource supply, the less likely it is that the tax that can be shifted
backward to the factor of production, since the quantity of the resource supplied decreases sharply as the offer price for the resource
declines, and (2) the more inelastic the resource supply, the more
likely it is that the tax that can be shifted backward to the factor of
production, since the lower offer price induces little supply reduction.
A comparison of Figures 7-6a and 7-6b demonstrates these facts.

Moreover, in the limiting case (not shown on the graphs), a perfectly elastic resource supply could completely prevent the backward
shifting of the tax to the resource owner, since none of the resource

FIGURE 7-6   Price elasticity of resource supply related to tax shifting

a. Tax shifting with high (relatively elastic)
price elasticity of supply

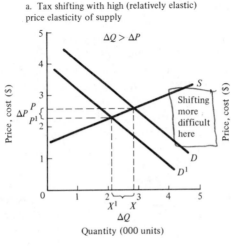

b. Tax shifting with low (relatively inelastic)
price elasticity of supply

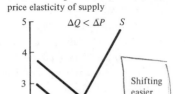
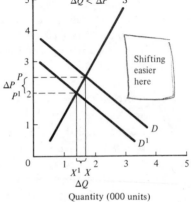

would be made available to the producer as the offer price is reduced. The ability of a strong labor union to effectively strike in reaction to a lower wage offer is a case in point. On the other hand, a perfectly inelastic supply could allow the total burden to be borne by the resource owner, since no reduction in resource availability would occur. A labor force with no union representation accompanied by the absence of alternative employment opportunities for the workers would depict such a case. However, the influence of other tax-shifting determinants could modify all of these results.

Type of tax

The nature of the tax, as determined by such characteristics as (1) whether it is direct or indirect and (2) broadbased or narrowbased, will also help to determine its shiftability and incidence. If a tax is intended by those who legislate it to largely remain at its original impact point, it is termed a *direct tax*. If it is expected that the burden is likely to be shifted, the tax is known as an *indirect tax*. What is most important here is why some taxes are regarded as less shiftable or more shiftable than others. The reason is that some taxes (direct taxes) are less adaptable than others (indirect taxes) to *market transactions*, which are the mechanism of tax burden transfers. Generally speaking, the more direct the tax, the more difficult shifting becomes, since market transactions are further removed. Conversely, the more indirect the tax, the greater the possibility of transferring its burden, since market transactions are more readily available.[11] Hence, direct taxes such as the personal income tax are not especially conducive to the further market transactions that are necessary for the successful forward shifting of a tax. In contrast, indirect taxes such as general retail sales and excise taxes are more closely associated with further market transactions and are thus more conducive to forward shifting.

In terms of the extent of the tax base, the more *broadbased* a tax, the easier it tends to be to shift the tax.[12] Oppositely, the more *narrowbased* the tax, the more difficult tax shifting becomes. For example, considering transactions taxation, when the tax base is narrow demand tends to be more elastic, since distortions in consumer decisions are more likely to occur through the operation of a substitution effect. Hence, as price is changed upward in an effort to shift the tax forward, the change downward in quantity demanded often tends to be more

---

[11] This is *not* intended to imply, however, that direct taxes are completely devoid of tax-shifting potential, but only that it tends to be more difficult to shift direct taxes as compared to indirect taxes.

[12] The reference to broadbased and narrowbased taxes under this criterion is concerned with the nature of the tax itself, and *not* with the geographical size of the political jurisdiction imposing the tax. The latter is treated below as a separate tax-shifting determinant.

than proportionate to the upward change in price, due to the availability of untaxed or lower-taxed substitute goods. This phenomenon is closely related to the price elasticity criterion already discussed. Thus, when such movement to substitutes is possible, it will be very difficult to raise the product price in order to shift the tax. That is, the demand schedule of the taxed good tends to be elastic due to the availability of the untaxed or lower-taxed substitutes. The opposite is true, of course, when the tax is broadbased, in which case demand tends to be less elastic and shifting becomes easier, since available substitutes are likely also to be taxed.

For example, a narrowbased excise tax imposed by a city government on all forms of commercial entertainment within the city (movie theaters, bowling alleys, athletic events, and the like), in the absence of a city general retail sales tax, may cause many consumers to transfer their purchases to other, relatively cheaper, untaxed items—if the sellers of entertainment increase their prices in an effort to forward shift the tax. In this instance, successful forward shifting of the tax may be difficult to attain. If, on the other hand, entertainment purchases are included as part of a broadbased city general sales tax imposed on an extensive variety of goods and services, the chances of consumer purchase transfers due to a substitution effect are reduced, and successful forward shifting by the sellers of entertainment is more likely to occur—though subject to the overall industry price elasticity of demand for entertainment. However, if a tax is direct instead of indirect, even the broadbased nature of the tax may preclude successful forward shifting. For example, a broadbased personal income tax imposed on all major sources of income may be difficult to shift due to the absence of convenient market transactions.

Political jurisdiction

The *geographical nature of the political unit* which levies a tax also helps to determine its shiftability. In this context, a political unit may be a local, state, national, or even international government. Generally, the narrower the geographical limits of a political unit, the more difficult it is to shift a tax. For example, a new (or increased) general retail sales tax in a city may lead to consumption readjustments in the form of increased purchases outside the city (in other cities or counties). The retail merchants in the city would probably absorb at least part of the tax, since they would tend to refrain from raising prices if similar taxes are not applied in nearby cities and counties. Efficient communications and transportation increase the possibility of buying outside a limited geographical or political area.

Taxes levied at the state level, since they involve a wider geographical area of political jurisdiction than those imposed at local levels of government, improve the possibility of forward tax shifting by sellers in the form of higher prices. There are reduced opportunities for buyers to purchase in no-tax or lower-tax areas. Furthermore, states normally attempt to reduce tax escape by imposing *use taxes*, whereby the residents of a state may be made subject to a tax applied in lieu of the state general sales tax which they have failed to pay because they have purchased major items elsewhere.

Since taxes levied at the national level cover a wider geographical area than do those levied by individual state governments, the chance of tax shifting is further enhanced with federal taxes. The opportunities for purchasers to move to no-tax or lower-tax jurisdictions are very limited for national taxes. In fact, this can be accomplished only by purchasing outside the national political jurisdiction, that is, within the political boundaries of another nation. A tax which was imposed and administered *uniformly* throughout the world—a true international tax—would provide the strongest potential for shifting according to the political jurisdiction criterion. In this case, there would be no political jurisdiction on this earth in which taxes might be lower or nonexistent.

Thus, the narrower the geographical limit of the political jurisdiction imposing a tax, the more difficult it is to shift a tax because there are more alternative geographical areas available where a good or resource might be purchased to escape the tax. Hence, a seller may be hesitant to raise the price by the amount of the tax, if at all. The opposite tends to occur, of course, when the geographical limit becomes broader.

SUMMARY

Many criteria influence the ability to shift the burden of a tax from its initial point of impact or statutory incidence to a different locus of final economic incidence. Some of the most important of these determinants, under partial-equilibrium conditions, relate to market structure conditions, the possible presence of unrealized profits or returns, long-run industry cost conditions, the price elasticities of product demand and resource supply, the nature of the tax, and the geographical extent of the political jurisdiction imposing the tax. Moreover, each of these determinants, and still others not discussed, are likely to simultaneously influence the final outcome. Hence, the final result will tend to be a weighted composite representing the effects of a number of causal variables. These variables might either reinforce one another in support of tax shifting or neutralize one another to prevent it. For example, a composite result in support of the probability of the forward shifting of a corporation income tax would occur in the case of the tax being imposed on a collusive oligopoly in the presence of substantial unrealized profits, and with a highly price-inelastic demand for the economic good produced by the industry.

Finally, it should be reiterated that the general-equilibrium approach to tax shifting and incidence, with its emphasis on relative prices, is conceptually superior to the partial-equilibrium approach detailed in this chapter. Whenever empirically feasible, it is desirable to supplement the study of absolute price behavior with consideration of the relative price behavior which is inherent in the general-equilibrium methodology.

8

Income taxation:
The personal income tax

ALTERNATIVE CONCEPTS OF TAXABLE INCOME

In defining income for the purpose of establishing an income tax base, both theoretical and institutional complexities are involved. Economists disagree to some extent about the theoretical ideal of what should be taxed. Moreover, accounting concepts of income, stressing the external reporting of financial information and the internal control of a business, differ from those used in economics. Government legislators and tax administrators institutionalize the concept by using a hybrid definition of income which is consistent with neither the economic nor the accounting concepts. Yet, if income is to be accepted as the primary indicator of the ability to pay taxes, and if the income tax is to be used prominently within the public sector, the definition of income selected for tax base purposes should meet the test of fiscal rationality.

The majority of economists endorse the *economic accretion* concept of taxable income as the theoretical starting point for the definition of the personal (individual) income tax base.[1] Thus, taxable income is defined as the algebraic sum of the monetary value of a

---

[1] This concept, which will be discussed much more extensively in Chapter 14, represents what is known as the Haig-Simons definition of taxable income. For the original sources of the concept, see Robert M. Haig, "The Concept of Income—Economic and Legal Aspects," in *The Federal Income Tax*, ed. R. M. Haig (New York: Columbia University Press, 1929), and Henry C. Simons, *Personal Income Taxation* (Chicago: University of Chicago Press, 1938).

person's consumption, plus or minus any change in the person's net worth, during a specified time period. The emphasis of this approach, it should be observed, is on the *uses of income* rather than on the sources of income. In fact, the notion of uses of income does seem to relate more directly to the ability-to-pay benchmark of tax equity. This benchmark attempts to "equalize sacrifice"—the sacrifice, of course, being the foregone *usage* of income for consumption or saving-investment purposes. In practice, the concept of taxable income used within the American public sector does not resemble the economic accretion approach. Instead, it emphasizes *sources of income* in terms of a current earnings flow to a taxpaying unit for labor and property resources provided in economic production.

THE FEDERAL PERSONAL INCOME TAX

Historical development

The first federal personal (individual) income tax was enacted by Congress in 1861 to help finance the Civil War. The tax was repealed in 1872, as its revenues were no longer required, and subsequently it was held to have been constitutional in an 1880 decision by the U.S. Supreme Court.[2] A second federal personal income tax was enacted in 1894, but was short lived; the Supreme Court, reversing its earlier decision, ruled it unconstitutional.[3] The question of constitutionality primarily centered on whether or not a federal personal income tax is a direct tax, which the U.S. Constitution requires to be assessed on a per capita basis among the states.[4] The constitutionality issue was eventually solved by the 16th Amendment to the Constitution, ratified in 1913. With the path thus opened, Congress enacted an income tax on individuals in 1913, and continued the corporation income tax enacted in 1909—which had been "disguised" as an excise tax. World War II revenue needs converted the federal personal income tax into a tax on the masses and established the overriding importance of personal and corporation income taxes in the federal tax structure. Specific provisions of the federal income taxes have been added or changed on numerous occasions, with the most recent major changes having been enacted in November 1978 (Revenue Act of 1978), August 1981 (Economic Recovery Tax Act—*ERTA*), and again in August 1982 (Tax Equity and Fiscal Responsibility Act—*TEFRA*).

---

[2] *Springer* v. *United States,* 102 U.S. 586 (1880).

[3] *Pollock* v. *Farmers' Loan and Trust Co.,* 157 U.S. 429 (1894); rehearing, 158 U.S. 601 (1895).

[4] This point was elaborated on in Chapter 4.

Federal personal income tax base and rate structure

The procedure required to establish tax liability under the federal personal income tax is complex, due to numerous exclusions, deductions, personal exemptions, credits, and other special provisions. These adjustments represent the source of considerable deviation between income in a conceptual sense and ultimate taxable income. The major steps involved in establishing ultimate federal personal income tax liability, and some of the most significant of these adjustments under provisions effective January 1, 1983, are the following:

1. Establish gross inflows of income and exclusions therefrom.
2. Apply deductions from gross income. The result is *adjusted gross income.*
3. Apply deductions from adjusted gross income.
4. Deduct personal exemptions. The result is the *taxable income base.*
5. Apply the rate schedule to the taxable income base.
6. Apply other special provisions, such as:
   a. Income averaging.
   b. Tax credits.
   c. Additional taxes.
   d. The alternative minimum tax rule.

These steps will be first discussed in general, and the more important provisions will then be considered in greater depth later in the chapter.

The first procedural step is to report all required gross inflows of income. A wide variety of personal receipts, however, may be treated as *exclusions from gross income* and thus need not be reported.[5]

---

[5] Exclusions from gross income include:

1. Social security benefits.
2. Up to all of unemployment compensation benefits, depending on circumstances.
3. Relief payments.
4. Payments under the Railroad Retirement Act.
5. Veterans' pensions, except retirement pay based on age or length of service.
6. Life insurance payments made upon death, with some exceptions.
7. Death benefits, up to $5,000, paid to the beneficiaries of an employee by an employer upon the death of the employee.
8. Workmen's compensation, damages for illness or injury, accident and health insurance payments.
9. Contributions by employers to qualified employee pension, profit-sharing, annuity, accident, or health plans.
10. Gifts and inheritances.
11. Interest paid on state and local government securities, with some limitations.
12. Fellowship and scholarship grants (subject to limitations).
13. Dividends received from domestic corporations, up to $100 annually per taxpayer.
14. Income earned abroad up to $75,000 (rising to $95,000 in 1986), plus certain "excess housing expenses," for a taxpayer living in another nation for 330 days in 12 consecutive months.
15. Up to $125,000 of gain from the sale of a personal residence for taxpayer age 55 or older, under certain conditions.

Moreover, most forms of income in kind, though not excluded explicitly from gross income, have not in practice been included in the gross income concept under the Internal Revenue Code. This includes such goods and services as food produced and consumed on farms and the rental value of owner-occupied nonfarm dwellings.

Once exclusions from gross income have been considered, the next step in computing tax liability under the federal personal income tax is to apply various *deductions from gross income*.[6] It should be pointed out that most deductions from gross income constitute ordinary and necessary business and trade expenses. These deductions would apply, for the most part, to professional people and those operating businesses under the proprietorship and partnership legal forms. The income concept which remains at this point of tax accounting—after exclusions and deductions from gross income considerations have been taken into account—is that of *adjusted gross income*.

The third step in determining federal personal income tax liability is to apply various *deductions from adjusted gross income*.[7] These

---

16. $750 per person of dividends from certain public utilities reinvested in the utility's common stock.
17. For 1981–83 only, certain interest from "all-saver" certificates issued by financial institutions.

[6] Deductions from gross income include:

1. All ordinary and necessary expenses paid or incurred during the taxable year in carrying on any trade or business, as a proprietor or partner. Allowable deductions include wages and salaries, depletion, depreciation, interest, and taxes.
2. Certain employee expenses incurred in behalf of an employer, including those as an outside salesman, transportation, and for travel while away from home.
3. Sixty percent of a net long-term capital gains.
4. One half of net long-term capital losses and all of the short-term capital losses up to $3,000.
5. Expenses which may be attributed to the production of rent and royalty income.
6. Certain deductions of self-employed individuals for pension, annuity, profit-sharing, and bond purchase plans (subject to various limitations).
7. The expenses of moving because of a change in job locations by new or continuing employees (subject to various limitations).
8. Alimony and separate maintenance payments, to the extent that these amounts are includable in the recipient's gross income.
9. Contributions to individual retirement accounts (IRAs) for employees (subject to various limitations).
10. A special deduction, up to a maximum of $3,000, for "two-earner" married couples amounting to 10 percent of the earnings of the lower-earning spouse.

[7] Deductions from adjusted gross income include:

1. Various taxes such as state and local personal property, real property, income and general sales taxes.
2. Interest on indebtedness (subject to various limitations).
3. Contributions to certain nonprofit institutions, such as religious, educational, scientific, and charitable organizations (subject to various limitations).
4. Various expenses associated with the occupation of the taxpayer, such as union dues, membership fees in professional associations, subscriptions to professional journals, uniforms, other types of special work apparel, and educational expenses

TABLE 8-1 **Federal personal income tax rate structure; marginal and average rates of tax for married persons filing joint returns* (effective 1984)**

	Tax rate (percent)	
Taxable income bracket	Marginal	Average†
$ 0– 3,400	(No tax)	(No tax)
3,400– 5,500	11	11.0
5,500– 7,600	12	11.5
7,600– 11,900	14	12.8
11,900– 16,000	16	13.8
16,000– 20,200	18	14.9
20,200– 24,600	22	16.4
24,600– 29,900	25	18.1
29,900– 35,200	28	19.8
35,200– 45,800	33	23.1
45,800– 60,000	38	26.8
60,000– 85,600	42	31.5
85,600–109,400	45	34.6
109,400–162,400	49	39.4
over 162,400	50	—

* Also for surviving spouses with a dependent child for the two years following the year of death of the deceased spouse.
† Calculations based on maximum figure in each taxable income bracket.

deductions, such as a portion of medical expenses and charitable contributions, are essentially of a nonbusiness or personal nature. They must be itemized on the taxpayer's return and are only deductible in excess of the *zero bracket,* a standard minimum amount given to all taxpayers in lieu of itemizing.

The fourth step in computing federal personal income tax liability is to deduct *personal exemptions.* The taxpayer receives an exemption of $1,000 and additional $1,000 exemptions for the spouse and for each dependent. Additional $1,000 exemptions are allowed for taxpayers and spouses who are age 65 or over or who are blind.

The first four steps establish the *taxable income base* of the federal personal income tax. It is to this base that the *rate schedules* are applied (Step 5). The rate structure of the federal personal income tax is graduated or progressive. Table 8–1 shows the marginal and aver-

---

　　incurred to maintain or improve skills required in the taxpayer's employment or to meet the requirements of the taxpayer's employer.
5.　Medical expenses incurred on behalf of the taxpayer, his wife, and dependents, if not reimbursed by insurance (subject to various limitations).
6.　An amount equal to the excess over $100 of each loss due to fire, theft, or other casualty, to the extent that the loss is not compensated by insurance, and to the extent such remaining amount exceeds 10 percent of adjusted gross income.
7.　Other expenses attributable to the production of passive income or to the determination of any tax.

age statutory rates of tax for married persons filing a joint return, as established under the Economic Recovery Tax Act (ERTA) of 1981— and to be fully effective in 1984. Different schedules apply for other filing statuses, such as single persons, heads of households, and married persons filing separate returns. In all, there are 15 different taxable income brackets at which the rates are applied. The average rates for taxable incomes of $162,400 and less represent a lower range of rates (11 to 39.4 percent) than do the marginal rates (11 to 50 percent), because they encompass the effects of the lower marginal rates on all previous lower-income marginal brackets as well as the higher marginal rate of the highest-income bracket attained by the taxpayer.[8] For example, on $7,600 of taxable income, the *marginal* rate of 11 percent would apply on $2,100 and the marginal rate of 12 percent on the remaining $2,100 of the $4,200 in excess of the $3,400 zero-bracket amount. The *average* rate is thus 11.5 percent on the $4,200, because half of the amount was taxed at a rate of 11 percent and the other half at 12 percent. As taxable income increases beyond $162,400, proportionally more of the income is taxed at the 50 percent marginal rate. The average rate thus increases beyond 39.4 percent and approaches, but does not reach, 50 percent. As an example, a 1984 joint return with $5,000,000 of taxable income would reflect a tax liability of $2,481,400, representing an average rate of 49.6 percent.

The tax amount determined by the application of the tax rate structure to the taxable income base in Step 5 may or may not be the final amount of tax owed by the taxpayer. Several other provisions which could alter the ultimate tax liability may apply at this point. These include: (1) *income averaging*—a tax calculation method to help compensate for the added tax liability resulting from a bunching of income in one year as compared to a prior average, thus subjecting it to higher marginal rates; (2) *tax credits*, for various purposes, which reduce the liability of the taxpayer on a dollar-for-dollar basis, up to the limit of the credit; (3) *additional taxes* such as the "self-employment tax"—a social security tax on the earnings of certain proprietors and partners, and (4) the *alternative minimum tax*, a computational method which may increase the final tax liability of some taxpayers who have received substantial amounts of so-called "preference income." Many of these provisions, as well as certain other important income tax provisions, will be described in greater detail in the next section of the chapter.

---

[8] See Table 5–2 for an additional explanation of the relationship between average and marginal rates of tax.

Special provisions of the federal personal income tax[9]

Exclusion of state and local government bond interest. Interest income received from state and local government securities is one of the major exclusions from gross income. This exclusion has been in existence, despite being reconsidered by Congress on a number of occasions, since the establishment of the present federal personal income tax in 1913.[10] The significance of the exclusion increased after World War II due to the rapid growth of state and local government debt.[11] However, the Economic Recovery Tax Act of 1981 may reduce the demand for state-local tax-exempt securities as the result of the lowering of high-bracket federal personal income tax rates and the development of various new savings incentive provisions. Nonetheless, this provision still is likely to (1) cause a substantial revenue loss to the federal government and (2) conflict with the ability-to-pay principle of equity in the distribution of tax burdens, since its tax saving value is relevant only to high-bracket taxpayers. In relation to the latter, it may be observed that an average interest yield on tax-exempt state and local government bonds of 10 percent would represent a 20 percent actual yield on a taxable security, if the taxpayer is in the 50 percent marginal-rate bracket.[12]

Additional disadvantages of the exclusion of state and local government bond interest from the federal personal income tax base include the distortion of resource allocation, both within the private sector and between the public and private sectors of the economy. If the exclusion is used by government to encourage private firms to select a particular industrial location by providing low-cost industrial facilities, an allocative distortion within the private sector occurs. When state or local governments issue tax-exempt bonds to finance their

---

[9] Certain features of federal income tax law which are applicable to business income are common both to the federal personal income tax being discussed in Chapter 8, and to the federal corporation income tax to be discussed in Chapter 9. Several of these provisions, such as those pertaining to depreciation and depletion, are described in Chapter 9, but are equally relevant to the personal income tax if the business income is that of a proprietorship or partnership instead of a corporation.

[10] A serious challenge to the full exclusion from gross income of state and local government bond interest occurred during the enactment of the Tax Reform Act of 1969. However, an avalanche of lobbying efforts on behalf of state and local governments succeeded in continuing the exclusion. Moreover, the Senate Finance Committee version of the Tax Equity and Fiscal Responsibility Act of 1982 would have included this category of interest as a tax preference item for the "alternative minimum tax," but under pressures similar to those in 1969, this proposal was deleted from the final legislation.

[11] See Chapter 22 for an elaboration on the postwar growth of state-local debt.

[12] For example, using the formula: Actual yield = $10/(1 - t)$, with t as the tax rate, and assuming a 50 percent marginal tax rate, $10/(1 - 0.50) = 10/0.50$, or 20 percent.

own commercial-type undertakings in the public utility or housing areas, intersector allocation distortion may occur.

One argument in behalf of the tax-exempt status of such interest stresses the need to preserve state and local government fiscal autonomy in a federal system. Thus, even if the exclusion were replaced by a partial or complete intergovernmental transfer or subsidy to state and local governments from the federal government, there would remain the fear that central government control over state and local governments would increase. It is clear that a policy trade-off regarding the tax-exempt security issue exists between the violation of the ability-to-pay principle of tax equity, since the loophole is primarily used by individuals with high incomes, and the political problem of a "proper" division of fiscal powers between the two sovereign levels of government (federal and state-local) in the American federation.

Preferential treatment of capital gains.   Net long-term capital gains realized on the sale or exchange of capital assets held for more than 12 months receive preferential tax treatment.[13] In contrast, net short-term capital gains realized on the sale or exchange of capital assets held for 12 months or less are fully taxable as ordinary property income. Sixty percent of the net long-term capital gains of individuals, to the extent that they exceed net short-term capital losses, may be excluded from the tax base. Thus, such gains are taxed at 40 percent of ordinary income tax rates, resulting in a maximum marginal rate of 20 percent.[14] This is much lower than the maximum marginal rate of 49⅛ percent which was in effect prior to the Revenue Act of 1978, which reduced the maximum marginal rate to 28 percent by (1) increasing the excluded portion of such gains from 50 percent to 60 percent, and (2) removing such gains as a preference item from the then-existing minimum and maximum income tax calculations. Subsequently, the Economic Recovery Tax Act of 1981 further reduced the maximum marginal rate to 20 percent as the result of lowering the maximum marginal tax rate on property income from 70 to 50 percent (income from personal services was previously subject to a maximum 50 percent rate). If the taxpayer has *capital losses*, however, only 50 percent of the long-term losses are deductible. Moreover, only up to $3,000 of ordinary income can be offset by net capital losses, with any unused

---

[13] *Capital assets* are defined by the Internal Revenue Code to include all property held by the taxpayer except certain specified categories such as: (1) stock in trade; (2) property held primarily for sale to customers in the ordinary course of the taxpayer's trade or business; (3) property used in trade or business which is subject to an allowance for depreciation; (4) real property used in trade or business; (5) a copyright, literary, artistic, or musical composition which is the product of the personal efforts of the taxpayer, and (6) accounts or notes receivable acquired in the ordinary course of trade or business.

[14] The effective maximum marginal tax rate of 20 percent is calculated by applying the 40-percent tax base remaining after the exclusion to the maximum marginal tax rate bracket for all income of 50 percent. Thus, $0.40 \times 0.50 = 0.20$ or 20 percent.

amount being available to offset capital gains and ordinary income of future years.

A controversy exists concerning the rationality of treating capital gains in a preferential manner compared to ordinary income. Indeed, a complete adoption of the economic accretion definition of income described at the beginning of the chapter would require the full taxation of all capital gains as they accrue annually. Moreover, if income is to serve as the primary indicator of taxpaying ability in reference to the ability-to-pay principle of distributional tax equity, capital gains income should be taxed on an equivalent basis with other sources of income, including labor income. In fact, at times capital gains represent an unearned increment of income in the sense that such occurrences as an increase in the site value of land, a discovery of oil, or a rise in bond prices due to changes in the market rate of interest, may be gains for which the asset holder is not directly responsible by his own initiative or actions. Hence, it is argued that such gains should be taxed on an equal basis with ordinary wage and salary income—if not taxed more heavily. Furthermore, the preferential treatment of capital gains income provides an extraordinary tax avoidance loophole which is especially attractive to higher-income taxpayers. This preferred treatment also may have a negative nonneutral effect on capital markets by encouraging the retention or plow back of profits within corporations, rather than having investment funds meet the test of the market.

Those who favor preferential treatment for capital gains, even to the point of imposing no tax at all on such gains, present a variety of arguments. One is that an investor may feel locked in if an asset or investment has increased significantly in value and is subject to full taxation if the gain is realized. On the other hand, the investor may not hesitate to sell the asset if capital gains receive preferential tax treatment. Moreover, if capital values decline, many taxpayers may be induced to sell in order to deduct the capital losses. Thus, distortion occurs in investment decision making. Furthermore, it is argued that if the capital gain is taxed in the particular year in which the gain accrues, though the gain is not realized through sale of the asset, an illiquidity burden may be placed on the taxpayer because a current cash flow is not available for payment of the tax. In addition, it is contended that the preferential tax treatment of capital gains income stimulates the accumulation of capital by individuals, who subsequently may make it available in the capital markets for investment in real productive capital. Finally, it is argued that capital gains serve as rewards, through preferential tax treatment, for those who undertake the risk of investment to promote a changing and growing economy. Since capital losses are not fully deductible, this argument is reinforced.

Personal deductions. In addition to the personal exemptions described earlier, various *personal deductions* from adjusted gross income are allowed in the computation of a taxpayer's liability under the federal personal income tax. With certain specific limitations, these deductions include medical and dental expenses, taxes paid to state and local governments, contributions to religious, charitable, educational, and other organizations, and interest expenses.

Prior to 1977, taxpayers were entitled to use a standard deduction in lieu of itemizing these personal deductions; the standard deduction was computed as a percentage of adjusted gross income within certain minimum and maximum limits. Unless the itemized deductions amounted to more than the applicable standard amount, the taxpayer was relieved from the record-keeping and reporting requirements of these personal deductions.

Commencing with 1977, the variable standard amount was replaced with flat amounts. These amounts were increased by the November 1978 legislation for 1979 and succeeding years to: $3,400 for married persons filing a joint return; $2,300 for single persons and heads of households, and $1,700 for married persons filing separate returns. This deduction is now referred to as the *zero bracket amount,* that is, instead of the standard deduction reducing taxable income as in the past, taxable income is now computed without this deduction. The resulting amount is subject to progressive schedules of rates wherein the zero bracket amount of this taxable income carries no tax liability. For taxpayers whose itemized deductions exceed these flat minimum limits, such deductions are *reduced* by the zero bracket amount, so that when such *excess* is applied to reduce taxable income, the resulting tax base, "grossed up" by the zero bracket amount, is then subject to the tax rate schedules which include the zero brackets.

For example, taxpayer A and his spouse may have itemized deductions amounting to $5,400 and a taxable income base, prior to adjustment for the deductions, of $40,000. Thus, the $5,400 of itemized deductions is reduced by the applicable zero bracket amount of $3,400, leaving an excess of $2,000 ($5,400 − $3,400 = $2,000). Taxable income is then reduced from $40,000 to $38,000 by the amount of this excess ($2,000). Hence, the tax rate applicable at this taxable income bracket level of $40,000 for taxpayer A, who itemized deductions, is consistent with that for nonitemizers who opt for the standard deduction.

Family status and taxable income. Personal exemptions allow a special preference for family size, since separate exemptions are allowed for each dependent child as well as for both husband and wife. In addition, the federal personal income tax was changed in 1948, when *income-splitting* was introduced, to provide equal treatment for persons in separate-property states with persons in community-property states, who were able to split family income between husband and wife. This brought about preferential treatment for the family taxpaying unit for married couples filing a joint tax return. They could compute their joint tax liability by applying the statutory tax rates to one half of their combined taxable income and then multiplying this result by two. With a progressive tax rate structure, married couples could enjoy tax savings with this technique as long as either spouse had a taxable income in excess of the maximum taxable income in the lowest of the marginal rate brackets.

Under this arrangement, however, discrimination was practiced against single taxpayers as well as against widows, widowers, and divorced people. Even when such an individual could be classified as the head of a household, only partial tax relief was obtained as compared to a married couple filing a joint return. The Tax Reform Act of 1969, accordingly, provided for a reduction in this preferential treatment. Under this legislation, effective in 1971, a new rate schedule for single people was initiated. This schedule allows the tax on a single person to exceed by no more than 20 percent the amount owed by a married couple with the same income filing a joint return. The unanticipated result was a penalty on marriage whereby two persons with approximately the same income would pay more tax after marriage than before. However, this so-called marriage tax on two-earner couples was reduced by the ERTA of 1981, which allows a deduction, up to a maximum of $3,000, of 10 percent of the earnings of the lower-earning spouse.

Income averaging. Fluctuating income over a period of years, as opposed to more stable earnings, may penalize the taxpayer under a progressive (graduated) statutory rate structure, in the absence of an averaging device. For example, a taxpayer with a taxable income of $20,000 per year for five consecutive years would pay less cumulative tax over the five-year period than would a taxpayer who has a taxable income of $100,000 in one of the five years, but no income in the other years—even though both taxpayers receive an identical income of $100,000 over the entire five years. This differential in tax obligations, which in this case would be substantial, is explained by the fact that the latter taxpayer, with uneven income, penetrates a higher marginal tax rate bracket under a graduated rate structure than would ever be reached during the period by the taxpayer with stable annual income.

Prior to the Revenue Act of 1964, only slight consideration was provided for fluctuating incomes. Some occupations were covered by averaging devices or other special rules, while others were not. The 1964 legislation replaced the scattered provisions with a general averaging device, which was expanded in scope in 1969. Under present law, averaging is permitted if the taxpayer's current-year taxable income exceeds the average taxable income of the prior four years by at least 20 percent—and further that this excess is greater than $3,000. Such excess is then taxed at marginal rates less than those which would apply absent the averaging calculation. Averaging applies to most kinds of income, including capital gains income. However, it is allowed only to taxpayers who receive significant increases in income; those who experience sharp decreases in income cannot backward average.

Tax credits.   A tax credit reduces the tax liability established in procedural Step 5 described earlier by the amount of the credit. Such credits may be of two types. A credit such as that for foreign income taxes paid reduces, in an actual sense, the true tax liability of the taxpayer. A credit for tax withheld at the source of income, though reducing the tax owed to the federal government when the taxpayer's return is submitted, does not represent an actual reduction in the true tax liability. It merely affects the timing of tax payments and is a "prepayment" of the tax.

Besides the foreign income tax credit, other actual credits include: (1) a credit for political campaign contributions, (2) a credit for the elderly, applicable to both retirement and earned income, (3) a credit for child-care expenses, and (4) the *earned income credit* for low-income taxpayers with children. The earned income credit for labor income allows for a payment from the federal government to the taxpayer if the credit exceeds tax liability. Thus, it represents a limited form of negative income tax. The earned income credit is 10 percent of labor income up to $5,000 and diminishes after $6,000 of the higher of earned or adjusted gross income to zero at the $10,000 income level.

Alternative minimum tax.   The Tax Reform Act of 1969 introduced the concept of a "minimum tax" on certain items of "tax preference income." The intent was to assess minimum tax liabilities on high-income taxpayers who would otherwise pay little or no federal income tax because they could take advantage of various special tax preference provisions. Such preferences include the excluded portion of net long-term capital gains, certain "excess" itemized deductions, accelerated depreciation and cost-recovery allowances on certain real and leased personal property in excess of straight-line allowances, certain excess amortizations of certified pollution control facilities, child care facilities, and railroad rolling stock, on the exercise of certain qualified stock options, the spread between the option price and the value of the stock, the excess of percentage depletion over the adjusted bases of mineral interests, and certain intangible drilling costs on productive oil and gas wells. It is noteworthy that the foregoing list of preference items does *not* include interest earnings from tax-exempt state and local bonds; this major tax-preference provision, used primarily by high-income taxpayers, remains fully in force (see footnote 10). The minimum tax was computed by totaling the items of tax preference, deducting a certain exemption, and multiplying the remainder by 15 percent (10 percent prior to 1977). The resulting tax was then added to the taxpayer's otherwise-computed, regular tax liability.

Effective January 1, 1979, the Revenue Act of 1978 removed the capital-gains and excess-itemized-deductions preferences from the minimum-tax calculation and transferred them to a new calculation termed the *alternative minimum tax*. The two preference items (the excess-itemized-deductions preference being slightly modified) were then added to taxable income (after reducing same by the applicable zero bracket amount) resulting in *alternative minimum taxable income*. After deducting an exemption of $20,000, the first $40,000 of the remaining balance was subject to a 10 percent rate and any excess to a rate of 20 percent.[15] The resulting tax, after reduction for certain credits, was then compared to the total of the taxpayer's regular tax and any add-on minimum tax (as the preexisting minimum tax, modified by the 1978 legislation, became known), also reduced by certain credits, with the larger amount being the ultimate tax liability.

The Tax Equity and Fiscal Responsibility Act of 1982 made further sweeping changes in the minimum tax rules. Starting in 1983, the original add-on minimum tax was repealed and the alternative minimum tax modified. With some changes, the remaining preferences for the add-on minimum tax have been transferred to the alternative minimum tax and some additional items included. Among the new items of tax preference is the excluded interest from all-saver certificates. While the excess-itemized-deductions preference was technically repealed, its essential effect was retained due to a modification in the mechanics of the calculation of the tax.

To the taxpayer's *adjusted gross income* (as compared to *taxable income* less zero bracket amount under 1979–82 rules) are added the various items of tax preference. Certain of the itemized deductions of the taxpayer are then allowed, such as casualty losses, charitable contributions, medical expenses (but only in excess of 10 percent of adjusted gross income as compared to 5 percent for computing regular taxable income), mortgage interest on the taxpayer's residence, other interest expense to the extent of investment income, and federal estate taxes attributable to "income in respect of a decedent." Noteworthy is the absence of any deduction—and hence of any benefit— for the alternative minimum tax of state and local taxes and of certain expenses pertaining to the taxpayer's employment, production of non-labor income, or determination of a tax. In addition, no deduction is allowed for personal and dependent exemptions. The balance remaining after deductions is termed *minimum taxable income*. Exemptions

---

[15] The maximum alternative minimum tax rate had been 25 percent on taxable income in excess of $100,000 prior to the Economic Recovery Tax Act of 1981.

are then allowed: $40,000 for married persons filing a joint return and $30,000 for single persons. The alternative minimum taxable income in excess of the exemption is then taxed at 20 percent. The resulting alternative minimum tax is then compared to the taxpayer's regular tax, and the larger is paid. Many special and complex rules apply to the above in the calculation of the various preference amounts and deductions, as well as for the application of net operating losses and in the use of credits to reduce both the regular and alternative minimum taxes.

As an example of the foregoing rules, consider the following case of a married couple with two dependent children and no credits:

Regular tax computation

Ordinary income		$78,000
Long-term capital gains	$80,000	
Less: 60 percent deduction	−48,000	
net	32,000	plus 32,000
Adjusted gross income		110,000
Less: Itemized deductions in excess of zero-bracket	46,000	
Less: Personal and dependent exemptions	+ 4,000	
Total	50,000	minus 50,000
Taxable income		60,000
Regular tax		15,168

Alternative minimum tax computation

Adjusted gross income	$110,000
Add: Items of tax preference	
Excluded capital gains	plus 48,000
Other (assumed)	plus 7,000
Total	165,000
Less: Allowable deductions (assumed)—usually less than itemized deductions in excess of zero-bracket amount	minus 35,000
Alternative minimum taxable income	130,000
Less: Exemption	minus 40,000
Taxable base	90,000
Alternative minimum tax (20 percent rate)	18,000

The taxpayers' regular tax of $15,168 is less than their alternative minimum tax of $18,000; hence, the larger alternative minimum tax would be their tax liability for the year (technically, the law adds the $2,832 excess of the alternative minimum tax over the regular tax to the regular tax of $15,168 to arrive at the final liability of $18,000).

The Economic Recovery Tax Act of 1981 (ERTA). This legislation was enacted as a major component of the Reagan Administration's economic program. While several references to the act were made earlier, it will be useful at this point to summarize the major personal income tax changes contained in the legislation. These are:

1. Reduction in the marginal tax rate range from 70–14 percent to 50–11 percent (over a three-year period). Relatedly, the reduction in the maximum marginal tax rate on property income from 70 percent to 50 percent eliminates the necessity for the previously-existing separate maximum marginal tax rate on earned (labor) income of 50 percent, as was applied through the "maximum tax on personal service income" provision.

2. Effective reduction in the maximum marginal tax rate on long-term capital gains from 28 to 20 percent.

3. Reduction in the maximum alternative minimum tax rate from 25 to 20 percent.

4. Effective increase in refund amounts under the earned income credit provision.

5. Reduction of the "marriage tax penalty" for two-earner couples via a new deduction.

6. Increase in the maximum child care credit.

7. Deduction of charitable contributions allowed, within limits, for nonitemizers who use only the zero bracket amount.

8. More liberal treatment of gains from sale of residences by taxpayers aged 55 and over.

9. Increase in the excludable portion of income earned abroad.

10. Various savings-incentive provisions including:
    a. Limited exclusion of interest income earned on new, one-year, all-saver certificates issued between October 1, 1981, and December 31, 1982.
    b. Liberalization of individual retirement account (IRA) participation and coverage for employees.
    c. An increase in the annual deduction for contributions to a self-employment retirement plan (Keogh plan).

11. Elimination of the 1982 combined interest and dividend income exclusion of $200 with a return to the $100 exclusion for dividend income only.

12. Indexing of personal income tax brackets, the standard deduction (zero bracket amount), and personal exemptions for inflation via the consumer price index—beginning in 1985.

The Tax Equity and Fiscal Responsibility Act of 1982 (TEFRA). When, in 1982, the business stimulus envisioned by the tax reductions and business incentives contained in ERTA did not fully materialize, concern over mounting federal deficits prompted legislation to cut back on some of the business provisions contained in the 1981 legislation (see Chapter 9). Moreover, to achieve more tax equity, that is, a "fairer" distribution of tax burdens, to foster better compliance with the law, as well as to mitigate the erosion of federal revenues caused by ERTA, TEFRA made a number of changes affecting the personal income tax. These changes, which went into effect January 1, 1983, mainly include:

1. Elimination of the add-on minimum tax and the restructuring of the alternative minimum tax as the sole provision in the law to tax certain preference items (see explanation above).
2. Imposing an additional floor of 10 percent of adjusted gross income before allowing any deduction for personal casualty losses.
3. Modifying the limitations on and the constituency of the medical expense deduction, such that the benefit of medical expenses in reducing tax liabilities was reduced.
4. Reducing the incentive for taxpayers to purchase and corporations to issue bonds at a discount.
5. Imposing a 10 percent withholding tax on interest and dividend payments (with exceptions) effective July 1, 1983.
6. Strengthening the requirements for the reporting to the Internal Revenue Service of payments of income, particularly with respect to income received in the form of tips.
7. Imposing a penalty for "substantial understatement of tax liability" where the Internal Revenue Service prevails in a controversy over the taxpayer's treatment of an item of income or deduction in the return. The penalty is not imposed if the taxpayer can show that there was "substantial authority" for the treatment in the return of the item giving rise to the understatement of liability, or if all the relevant facts pertaining to the item are disclosed in the return.

STATE PERSONAL INCOME TAXES

The modern era of state personal income taxation began with the progressively rated Wisconsin tax of 1911. During the 19th century, some states had permitted income taxes administered by local property tax officials, but these proved to be ineffective. Today *broadbased* personal (individual) income taxes, imposed on all major sources of income, are used by 40 states. Three other states impose *narrowbased* personal income taxes—Connecticut on capital gains and dividends; New Hampshire and Tennessee on interest and dividends. Table 8–2 summarizes the major features of the various state personal income taxes. Most states (36 out of 40) using a broadbased tax apply a progressive (graduated) rate structure at generally low marginal rates. This includes three states—Nebraska, Rhode Island,

and Vermont—which used as the tax base the taxpayer's federal personal income tax liability attributable to sources of income within the state, thus implicitly adopting the progressivity inherent within the federal tax.[16] All 40 states imposing a broadbased tax apply a withholding tax on salaries and wages at the source of income in order to improve administration of the tax.

The federal personal income tax allows the deduction of state personal income taxes from the tax base. Moreover, in 16 broadbased income tax states, deduction of the federal personal income tax from the state tax is also allowed. However, this practice tends to reduce the *effective* rate progressivity of graduated state income taxes and, at times, can even yield regressive effects at higher-income levels. The dampening effects on progressivity are especially likely to occur when the state personal income tax is characterized by low marginal rates which reach a maximum rate bracket at a relatively low taxable income level.

A majority of state personal income tax bases resemble the federal personal income tax base. The Advisory Commission on Intergovernmental Relations classifies 11 broadbased state personal income taxes as possessing bases which are either in virtually complete or substantial conformance to the federal personal income tax base, while 21 others exhibit "moderate" conformance.[17] The remaining 8 of the 40 states with broadbased personal income taxes are listed in a category of "nonconformance" with the federal base. Like the federal tax, all but one state (Pennsylvania) allow personal exemptions or a tax credit in lieu of an exemption. Moreover, a number of states, beginning in the 1960s, have added refundable tax credits against state personal income tax liability in order to minimize the alleged regressivity of general sales and property taxes against lower-income taxpayers. In fact, the use of the credit device in this manner essentially results in the existence of a state negative income tax, since the taxpayer actually receives a payment from the government when the amount of the tax credit is greater than the income tax liability.[18]

Overall, state personal income taxes exhibit a trend of increasing relative importance within state government tax structures and are exceeded today only by general sales taxes as a source of state tax revenue. For example, state personal income taxes, which provided 12 percent of overall state revenues[19] in 1960, contributed 27 percent

---

[16] The federal personal income tax reductions brought about by the ERTA of 1981 thus automatically lowered the personal income taxes of these three states.

[17] *Significant Features of Fiscal Federalism, 1979–80 Edition* (Washington, D.C.: Advisory Commission on Intergovernmental Relations, 1980), p. 109. Table adjusted for subsequent repeal of Alaska personal income tax.

[18] See the discussion of the *negative income tax* concept in Chapter 13.

[19] Excluding employment (payroll) tax revenues.

TABLE 8-2 State personal income tax rates and related data[a] (As of April 1, 1981)

State	Lowest bracket Rate (percent)	Lowest bracket To net income of	Highest bracket Rate (percent)	Highest bracket Income above	Maximum personal exemption and credit for dependents[b] Married or head of family	Single	Each dependent	Federal income tax deductible
Alabama	1.5	$1,000	5	$5,000	$3,000	$1,500	$300[d]	Yes
Arizona[f]	2	1,000	8	6,000	2,844[d]	1,422[d]	854[d]	Yes
Arkansas[c]	1	2,999	7	25,000	35[e]	35[e]	6[e]	No
California[c]	1[f]	2,630[d]	11[f]	20,450[d]	50[d,e]	25[d,e]	8[d,e]	No
Colorado[g]	2.5	1,236[d]	8	12,363[d]	2,102[d]	1,051[d]	1,051[d]	Yes[d]
Delaware	1.4	1,000	13.5	50,000	1,200	600	600	Yes[h]
Georgia	1[f]	1,000	6[f]	10,000	3,000	1,500	700	No
Hawaii	2.25[f]	500	11[f]	30,000	2,000	1,000	1,000	No
Idaho[c]	2	1,000	7.5	5,000	2,000			No
Illinois	2.5	All	—	—	Federal exemptions			No
Indiana	1.9	All	—	—	2,000	1,000	500	No
Iowa	2.5	1,023[d]	13	76,725[d]	30[d,e]	15[d,e]	10[d,e]	Yes[h]
Kansas	2[f]	2,000	9[f]	25,000	2,000	1,000	1,000	Yes[h]
Kentucky	2	3,000	6	8,000	40[e]	20[e]	20[e]	Yes[h]
Louisiana[c]	2	10,000	6	50,000	12,000	6,000	1,000	Yes
Maine	1[f]	2,000	10[f]	25,000	2,000	1,000	1,000	No
Maryland	2	1,000	5	3,000	1,600	800	800	No
Massachusetts	(j)	(j)	(j)	(j)	4,000[i]	2,000[i]	700[i]	No
Michigan	4.6	All	—	—	3,000	1,500	1,500	No
Minnesota	1.6	599[d]	16	32,890[d]	120[d,e]	60[d,e]	60[d,e]	Yes
Mississippi	3	5,000	4	5,000	9,500	6,000	1,500	No
Missouri	1.5	1,000	6	9,000	2,400	1,200	400	Yes
Montana	2	1,000[d]	11	35,000[d]	1,600[d]	800[d]	800[d]	Yes
Nebraska	(k)	(k)	(k)	(k)	Federal exemptions			No

State	Lowest bracket		Highest bracket		Maximum personal exemption and credit for dependents[b]			Federal income tax deductible
	Rate (percent)	To net income of	Rate (percent)	Income above	Married or head of family	Single	Each dependent	
New Jersey[c]	2	20,000	2.5	20,000	2,000	1,000	1,000	No
New Mexico[c]	.6[f]	2,000	6.7[f]	200,000	Federal exemptions			No
New York	2	1,000	14[f]	23,000	Federal exemptions			No
North Carolina	3	2,000	7	10,000	1,500	750	750	No
North Dakota	1	3,000	7.5	30,000	2,200	1,100	700	Yes
Ohio	.5[f]	5,000	3.5	40,000	1,500	750	750	No
Oklahoma	.5[f]	2,000	6[f]	15,000	1,300	650	650	Yes[h]
Oregon	4[f]	500	10[f]	5,000	1,500	750	750	Yes[h]
Pennsylvania	2.2[g]	All	—	—	2,000[d]	1,000[d]	1,000[d]	No
Rhode Island	([k])	([k])	([k])	([k])	—	—	—	No[h]
South Carolina	2	2,000	7	10,000	Federal exemptions			
Utah	2.75[f]	1,500	7.75[f]	7,500	1,600[d]	800[d]	800[d]	Yes[h]
Vermont	([k])	([k])	([k])	([k])	1,000	750	750	Yes
Virginia	2[f]	3,000	5.75	12,000	Federal exemptions			No
West Virginia	2.1[j]	2,000	9.6[f]	200,000	1,200	600	600	No
Wisconsin	3.4	3,300[d]	10	44,000[d]	40[e]	20[e]	20[e]	No
District of Columbia	2	1,000	11	25,000	1,500	750	750	No

[a] In addition to the states listed, three states tax limited portions of personal income. Connecticut levies a 7% tax on capital gains and a graduated 1% to 9% tax on dividends for taxpayers with Federal adjusted gross income of $20,000 or more. New Hampshire imposes a 5% tax on dividends and certain interest income. Tennessee taxes income from dividends and interest at 6% (dividends from corporations with at least 75% of their property subject to the Tennessee ad valorem tax are taxed at 4%).

[b] Does not include exemptions or credits for age or blindness, to offset sales or property taxes paid, or for any other special purpose.

[c] Community property state in which, in general, one-half of the community income is taxed to each spouse.

[d] Amount subject to annual adjustment for inflation. Amounts shown are generally for the 1980 income year. The adjustments in South Carolina become effective January 1, 1982.

[e] Credit allowed in lieu of exemptions.

[f] In California, Hawaii, Kansas, Maine, Oregon, and West Virginia for joint returns, the rates shown apply to income brackets twice as large. Rates different from those shown in the table apply to certain other categories of taxpayers in several states, as follows: California and Hawaii, heads of households; and Georgia, New Mexico, Oklahoma, and Utah, single persons and married persons filing separately.

[g] For 1980, a 20% credit against normal tax liability applies; residents pay a 2% surtax on income from intangibles in excess of $15,000.

[h] The amount of the Federal income tax deduction is limited.

[i] No tax is imposed on total income of $5,000 for husband and wife or $3,000 for a single individual. Above those amounts a 5% tax is levied on earned income and a 10% tax on interest, dividends, and capital gains from the sale of intangibles. An additional 7.5% surtax is imposed. Exemptions shown apply to earned income.

[j] A 10% surcharge on the tax is levied; surcharge repealed as of January 1, 1981.

[k] Applies to Federal income tax liability. Rates are 15% in Nebraska, 19% in Rhode Island, and 23% in Vermont.

[l] For 1981 and thereafter, the maximum rate on personal service taxable income is 10% of the amount in excess of $17,000.

Source: Commerce Clearing House; Facts and Figures on Government Finance—1981 (New York: Tax Foundation, Inc., 1981), pp. 230–31.

TABLE 8-3   Income elasticity of state and local personal income taxes:
Summary of empirical studies   *∂ income ∂tax = % ∂ income*

Study	Year published	Area covered	Elasticity coefficient
Harris	1966	Arkansas	2.40
ACIR*	1971	Kentucky	1.94
ACIR	1971	New York	1.80
Harris	1966	United States	1.80
Groves and Kahn	1952	United States	1.75
Netzer	1961	United States	1.70
ACIR	1971	Hawaii	1.47
Arizona Planning Division	1971	Arizona	1.30
Harris	1966	New Mexico	1.30

* Advisory Commission on Intergovernmental Relations.
 Studies cited above: Advisory Commission on Intergovernmental Relations, "State-Local Revenue Systems and Educational Finance," unpublished report to the President's Commission on School Finance, November 12, 1971; Arizona Department of Economic Planning and Development, Planning Division, *Arizona Intergovernmental Structure: A Financial View to 1980* (Phoenix, 1971); Harold M. Groves and C. Harry Kahn, "The Stability of State and Local Tax Yields," *American Economic Review,* March 1952, pp. 87–102; Robert Harris, *Income and Sales Taxes: The 1970 Outlook for States and Localities* (Chicago: Council of State Governments, 1966); Dick Netzer, "Financial Needs and Resources Over the Next Decade," in **National Bureau of Economic Research,** *Public Finances: Needs, Sources, and Utilization* (Princeton, N.J.: Princeton University Press, 1961).
 Source: Advisory Commission on Intergovernmental Relations, *State-Local Finances: Significant Features and Suggested Legislation* (Washington, D.C.: U.S. Government Printing Office, 1972), p. 301.

20 years later, in 1980. One reason for the growing relative importance of the tax for state (and local) governments is its "elastic" income elasticity ($Y_t > 1$). See Table 8–3 for empirical evidence of this fact.

LOCAL PERSONAL INCOME TAXES

Personal income taxes are used by local governments in 11 states and the District of Columbia. States using the tax are Alabama, Delaware, Indiana, Iowa, Kentucky, Maryland, Michigan, Missouri, New York, Ohio, and Pennsylvania. The local-government personal income tax is used most extensively in Ohio and Pennsylvania. In Ohio, 20 major cities with populations over 50,000 and over 400 cities and villages under 50,000 population impose a personal income tax. In Pennsylvania, 14 major cities or townships and nearly 4,000 other local government jurisdictions use the tax. A number of the nation's major cities impose personal income taxation. These include Akron, Baltimore, Birmingham, Cincinnati, Cleveland, Columbus, Dayton, Detroit, Kansas City, Louisville, New York, Philadelphia, St. Louis, Toledo, Washington, D.C., and Wilmington. In each of the 11 states which allow a local personal income tax to be imposed, the state government also levies such a tax. This results in the payment of three personal income taxes to three different levels of government—

TABLE 8-4   Local personal income taxes and rates by state,[a] (as of April 1, 1981)

State and locality	Rate (percent)	State and locality	Rate (percent)
Alabama		Ohio—continued	
Birmingham	1.0	Cleveland Heights	2.0
Gadsden	2.0	Columbus	1.5
3 cities under 50,000	1.0-2.0	Dayton	1.75
Delaware		Elyria	1.5
Wilmington	1.0	Euclid	1.5
Indiana		Hamilton	1.5
38 counties	.5-1.0[b]	Kettering	1.0
Iowa	(% of state tax)	Lakewood	1.0
6 school districts	1.75-4.0	Lima	1.0
Kentucky		Lorain	1.0
Covington	2.5	Mansfield	1.0
Lexington	2.0	Parma	1.5
Louisville	2.2[c]	Springfield	2.0
Owensboro	1.0	Toledo	1.5
56 cities under 50,000	.25-2.5	Warren	1.0
7 counties	.25-2.0	Youngstown	1.5
Maryland	(% of state tax)	Over 400 cities and	
Baltimore	50.0	villages[f] under 50,000	.25-2.0
23 counties	20.0-50.0	Pennsylvania[g]	
Michigan		Abington Township	1.0
Detroit	2.0	Allentown	1.0
Flint	1.0	Altoona	1.0
Grand Rapids	1.0	Bethlehem	1.0
Lansing	1.0	Erie	1.0
Pontiac	1.0	Harrisburg	1.0
Saginaw	1.0	Lancaster	.5
10 cities under 50,000	1.0	Penn Hills Township	1.0
Missouri		Philadelphia	4.3125
Kansas City	1.0	Pittsburgh	2.25
St. Louis	1.0	Reading	1.0
New York		Scranton	2.6
New York City	.9-4.3[d,e]	Wilkes-Barre	3.0
Ohio		York	1.0
Akron	1.8	Nearly 4,000 other local	
Canton	1.5	jurisdictions	.25-1.0
Cincinnati	2.0	District of Columbia	2.0-11.0[e]
Cleveland	2.0		

[a] Rates shown separately for cities with 1970 population of 50,000 or more. Where rates differ for resident and nonresident income, only rates on residents are given. In Ohio and Pennsylvania cities, rates are the same; the nonresident rate is markedly lower in New York City and is half the resident rate in most Michigan cities. In addition to the areas shown, certain local jurisdictions in Arkansas and Georgia may impose an income tax with voter approval, although none have done so to date. Also, payroll taxes are imposed on employers in San Francisco (at the rate of 1.5%) and Newark (.5%).
[b] Counties, cities, or towns may impose a 1.5% occupation income tax in addition to the county gross income tax. Cities or towns may not adopt tax if county in which they are located has levied it. Taxpayers are allowed credit for tax liability under either tax. Six localities levy the tax.
[c] Includes rates levied for Jefferson County and for school boards.
[d] Tax rates for years beginning after December 31, 1981, are scheduled to decline. An additional 2.5% tax is levied on minimum taxable income (tax to terminate December 31, 1980, or December 31 of year in which certain Federal guarantees to New York City terminate, whichever is later).
[e] In New York City and Washington, D.C., resident income tax rates are graduated.
[f] School districts may also levy a tax at rates ranging from .25% to 1% if approved by voters.
[g] Except for Philadelphia, Pittsburgh, Scranton, and Wilkes-Barre, the total rate payable by any taxpayer is limited to 1%. When other local government units such as school districts levy income taxes, the tax is usually divided equally between jurisdictions. Rates shown comprise total rate for all local taxing jurisdictions combined.

Source: Commerce Clearing House; *Facts and Figures on Government Finance–1981* (New York: Tax Foundation, Inc., 1981), p. 288.

federal, state, and local.[20] Table 8–4 summarizes the use of personal income taxes by local governments as of April 1, 1981.

Most local government personal income taxes are imposed at a low proportional rate. Important exceptions are the graduated resident personal income taxes used in New York City and Washington, D.C. Local personal income taxes are normally levied on the gross wage and salary earnings of individuals and the net profits of professions and unincorporated business. Thus, income from wages and salaries is generally taxed on a gross basis, without exemptions or deductions, and with the full amount of the tax withheld by the employer. Dividend, interest, rent and capital gains income received by individuals are normally exempt from the tax. Some states share their personal income tax collections directly with local government, but the increased usage of local personal income taxes per se represents a distinct trend. While in 1955 only 370 local units of governments used the tax, by 1981 the number had grown to over 4,500.

THE FISCAL PERFORMANCE OF THE PERSONAL INCOME TAX

The fiscal performance criteria developed in the previous three chapters relate importantly to the economic concept of *neutrality*. In examining the personal income tax in terms of its influence on resource allocation decisions, distributional equity, and aggregate economic activity (stabilization), emphasis will be placed on the performance of the *federal* personal income tax involving its *nonneutral effects*. As observed in Chapter 5, these nonneutralities may be either positive (beneficial) or negative (harmful) in terms of a given societal goal if the equilibrium prior to fiscal action is suboptimal. A general attitude in favor of minimizing tax nonneutralities seems to prevail, however, and there is a preference for the least nonneutral (most neutral) tax, especially when allocational (efficiency) effects are being considered.

The subject of the economic effects deriving from personal income taxation is a comprehensive one. Consequently, this section will present only a "selected menu" of topics concerning the performance of personal income taxes. In part, the discussion is equally applicable to both the federal personal and federal corporation income taxes, which contain a number of identical or similar provisions.

Allocational effects

Personal income taxation and the work-leisure choice. A personal income tax may alter the trade-off between *work effort* and *leisure*

---

[20] Such vertical tax overlapping involving the imposition of the same tax by three different levels of government is not undesirable per se. This point will be discussed in detail in Chapter 18 which is concerned with intergovernmental fiscal issues.

and thus may create allocational nonneutralities.[21] However, the direction of these effects will differ in that labor effort may be either discouraged or encouraged. On the one hand, personal income taxation impairs work incentives by reducing the posttax monetary reward for work effort, thus causing leisure to be "substituted" for work at the margin. In other words, the personal income tax increases the price of work relative to leisure and, conversely, lowers the price of leisure relative to work. Such a change in the relative prices of two commodities generally leads to a smaller quantity being demanded of the now relatively higher-priced commodity (work) and a greater quantity being demanded of the now relatively lower-priced commodity (leisure). This is known as the *substitution effect* component of the work-leisure trade-off; it would tend to result in a substitution of leisure for work effort.

On the other hand, income taxation reduces the posttax disposable income of the taxpayer and thus provides an incentive to increase pretax income in order to maintain a constant posttax purchasing power. This *income effect* component of the work-leisure trade-off obviously would tend to stimulate rather than reduce work effort. However, no a priori statement can be made regarding the overall dominance of either the substitution effect or the income effect. Instead, each individual case will be separately influenced depending on such factors as (1) the degree of control by an individual over time worked, (2) the desire to work for power, prestige, or other non-economic motives, and (3) the overall level of income, and thus of living standard, for the individual.

The degree of substitution effect, which is an allocational non-neutrality with efficiency implications, will tend to increase as personal income tax rates become more progressive. This is true because it is the *marginal tax rate* which directly influences the work-leisure choice, and under a progressive tax the marginal rate exceeds the average rate. Figure 8–1 illustrates this relationship and other relevant considerations. The effects of marginal tax rates on marginal increments to disposable (posttax) income as the taxpayer undertakes additional work, under various forms of personal income taxation, are measured on the vertical axis. The trade-off between work and leisure, in terms of the time available for each, is measured on the horizontal axis. In addition, the work-leisure indifference curves, WL^1, WL^2, WL^3, and WL^4, represent the taxpayer's preference pattern between work and leisure, which will interact with the different marginal tax rate effects on disposable income.

---

[21] See Richard A. Musgrave, *The Theory of Public Finance* (New York: McGraw-Hill, 1959), pp. 232–49. For pertinent discussions of the topic, also see Richard Goode, "The Income Tax and the Supply of Labor," *Journal of Political Economy*, October 1949, pp. 428–37, and George F. Break, "Income Taxes and Incentives to Work: An Empirical Study," *American Economic Review*, September 1957, pp. 529–49.

income effect predominates?

FIGURE 8-1 Work-leisure trade-offs under alternative personal income tax rate structures

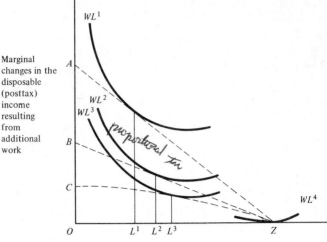

Marginal changes in the disposable (posttax) income resulting from additional work

Marginal time available for work or leisure

Explanation:
  No personal income tax (line AZ) = L^1Z work, OL^1 leisure trade-off.
  Proportional personal income tax (line BZ) = L^2Z work, OL^2 leisure trade-off.
  Progressive personal income tax with maximum marginal rate less than 100 percent (line CZ) = L^3Z work, OL^3 leisure trade-off.
  Progressive personal income tax with a maximum marginal rate of 100 percent (line OZ) = No work, OZ leisure trade-off.

First, the situation of *no* personal income tax is depicted by line AZ, which leaves the pretax disposable income OA unaffected, and thus does not distort the neutral work-leisure trade-off of L^1Z amount of work and OL^1 amount of leisure. Next, the influence of a proportional personal income tax, which taxes the incremental income resulting from additional work at a constant tax rate, is depicted by line BZ. The proportional income tax, by reducing the marginal disposable income from OA to OB, induces the taxpayer to decrease work time from L^1Z to L^2Z, and to increase leisure from OL^1 to OL^2. However, if a progressive personal income tax (with a maximum marginal rate less than 100 percent) is imposed, line CZ becomes representative of its graduated rate structure, and increments to income are now taxed at a higher rate. As a result, disposable income falls further, to OC, and the amount of work decreases to L^3Z, while leisure time increases to OL^3. Finally, the imposition of a highly progressive personal income tax with a maximum marginal rate of 100 percent (at the taxpayer's level of income) will cause a decline of marginal work effort to zero, while all time (OZ) relevant to the last marginal bracket of income is used for leisure. This is so because all of the income resulting from the additional work effort is taxed away. Thus, it may be concluded that as the marginal rate of personal income taxation increases, the substitution effect behavior of a taxpayer will tend to induce more leisure and less work.

Effect of personal income tax on risk taking and investment. The structure of a personal income tax may influence an investor's decision whether or not to invest, as well as the magnitude of the investment. For example, if an investor must pay a 20 percent capital gains tax on net long-term gains, and a tax offset for capital losses is substantially restricted, the expected net gains (yield) after taxes would be less than if a tax offset were fully allowed.[22] In effect, the degree of risk is increased when tax offsets for capital losses are curtailed. Moreover, if the investor has a liquidity preference, it is likely that a large investor has an advantage over a small investor in risk taking, since the investor of large amounts will tend to have more income left over after the limited losses are offset. Therefore, a possible policy objective, with both allocational efficiency and distributional equity in mind, would be the creation of equally favorable loss offsets for *all* types of investors and income classes.

The personal income tax, in conjunction with the lower-rate tax on long-term capital gains, may also be said to result in a bias inducing corporations to retain earnings rather than paying profits out in the form of cash dividends. This is true because stockholders in high tax brackets tend to prefer compensation in the form of price increments in their securities, which are taxed as capital gains when realized, rather than in the form of cash dividends, which are taxed at higher rates as ordinary personal income. This results in an allocation nonneutrality, in the sense that investments financed from retained earnings may be undertaken which otherwise would not have been warranted. Undoubtedly, a personal income tax will tend to affect investment incentives, risk taking, and the supply of capital. The *specific* effects, however, will depend on the existence or absence of such fiscal techniques as the preferential treatment of capital gains, loss offsets, and investment credits. Meanwhile, discussion of another allocational aspect of personal income taxation—its *excess burden*—will be deferred to Chapter 12, in which excess burdens of personal income and excise taxes are compared.

---

[22] See the discussion of capital gains earlier in this chapter for a description of the current tax treatment of capital losses.

TABLE 8-5   **Relationship of personal income to taxable income in the federal personal income tax, calendar year 1978**

Income and related concepts	Amount (billions)	Percentage distribution
Personal income	$1,717.4	100.0%
Deduct portion of personal income not included in adjusted gross income .... $-446.9		-26.0%
Add portion of adjusted gross income not included in personal income ....: +122.7		+7.1
Equals adjusted gross income of all individuals, estimated from personal income	= $1,393.2	= 81.1%
Deduct difference between Commerce Department and Treasury Department estimates of adjusted gross income .... -88.9		-5.2
Deduct adjusted gross income reported on nontaxable returns .... -61.8		-3.6
Equals adjusted gross income reported on taxable returns	= $1,242.5	= 72.3%
Deduct personal deductions on taxable returns .... -82.8		-4.8
Deduct personal exemptions on taxable returns .... -132.3		-7.7
Add tax preferences adjustment .... +1.3		+ < 0.1
Equals taxable income base (on taxable returns)	= $1,028.7	= 59.9%

Source: Department of Commerce, Bureau of Economic Analysis, and Treasury Department, Internal Revenue Service.

Distributional effects

Personal income taxation and the ability-to-pay principle. Progressive personal income taxation is the mainstay of efforts by Western society to implement the ability-to-pay principle of equity in the distribution of tax burdens. As will be observed below in Table 8–7, the federal personal income tax in the United States has effective tax rate progressivity despite the many special provisions which erode and differentiate the taxable income base. Most state personal income taxes also utilize graduated rate structures. At the same time, most, if not all, other major taxes perform rather poorly in reference to the ability-to-pay benchmark. This includes the extensively used general sales and property taxes, which are important sources of state-local government revenue in the United States. Hence, the progressive income tax stands essentially alone as a tool for implementing the societal-endorsed, ability-to-pay rule of equity in the distribution of tax burdens. Yet, the actual or effective progressivity of the federal personal income tax is considerably less than its statutory rate structure would suggest (compare Tables 8–1 and 8–7). The reasons for this important distributional phenomenon are discussed below.

Federal personal income tax base erosion and its distributional equity effects. The many special federal personal income tax provisions (preferences), some of which have been described above, exert substantial influence on the ultimate pattern of federal personal income taxation in the United States. The consequences of these tax preferences include both (1) an erosion of the potential aggregate taxable income base and (2) distributional equity effects in relation to the ability-to-pay principle, with its vertical and horizontal tax equity components.

Table 8–5 demonstrates the erosion of the federal personal income tax base. Thus, if *aggregate personal income*, as measured by the U.S. Department of Commerce, is used as the proxy for a "potential" comprehensive taxable income base "undifferentiated" by special tax provisions, and then if the *aggregate taxable income* for a given year as compiled from tax returns actually received by the U.S. Treasury Department is compared to this potential aggregate base, the difference will be an indicator of the degree of *tax base erosion*. In calendar year 1978, the potential personal income base was $1,717.4 billion and the actual aggregate base of tax returns received by the Treasury was $1,028.7 billion, which is only 59.9 percent of the potential tax base. Indeed, this represents substantial tax base erosion, the disaggregation of which may be seen by studying the table. However, it should not be concluded that all tax base erosion is fiscally irrational—a fact that will be observed in the discussion of tax expenditures.

The distributional equity effects of income tax base erosion may be viewed in reference to both the vertical tax equity and the horizontal tax equity tenets of the ability-to-pay principle. In terms of vertical equity, the federal personal income tax can be shown to have a considerably less progressive *effective* tax rate structure than its *statutory* design would suggest (as observed earlier). Moreover, the pattern of burden distribution among taxpayers is altered by special tax preferences, to the extent that taxpayers in some income classes gain relatively more tax savings from the preferential tax provisions than do those in other income classes. In terms of horizontal equity, the differentiated nature of the special provisions may mean that taxpayers with similar incomes pay considerably different amounts of tax.

Tables 8–6 and 8–7, along with Figure 8–2, present evidence of the

TABLE 8-6   Percentage distribution of features increasing the federal personal income tax base under an expanded adjusted gross income* definition, by income classes, 1972 income levels

Expanded adjusted gross income class* ($000)	All features	Capital gains‡	Features affecting the tax base†						Additional exemptions for age and blindness
			Tax-exempt interest, dividend exclusion, excess depletion, and other preference income	Life insurance interest	Home-owners' preferences§	Transfer payments	Other itemized deductions	Percentage standard deduction	
Under $3	100.0	0.8	0.5	1.1	4.4	24.0	0.5		68.9
$3–5	100.0	0.9	0.4	1.3	4.2	57.1	0.5		35.7
5–10	100.0	3.1	0.9	4.0	10.3	62.3	3.0	1.3	15.2
10–15	100.0	5.0	1.3	7.3	18.3	37.8	3.6	21.6	5.1
15–20	100.0	7.2	1.9	8.5	24.0	27.3	5.1	23.5	2.6
20–25	100.0	10.2	2.4	7.5	25.4	25.7	7.5	18.4	3.0
25–50	100.0	21.6	3.9	5.5	23.6	21.3	10.3	11.4	2.3
50–100	100.0	53.0	7.1	1.0	15.9	3.0	15.4	2.9	1.8
100–500	100.0	68.4	14.5	0.3	5.9	(#)	9.7	0.4	0.7
500–1,000	100.0	80.4	11.9	0.1	2.0		5.4	0.1	0.1
1,000 and over	100.0	88.8	6.6	0.1	0.8		3.6	(#)	(#)
All classes	100.0	15.7	3.0	5.5	17.3	33.2	5.9	12.6	6.9

* Expanded adjusted gross income is adjusted gross income as defined in the Internal Revenue Code modified to include the following additional income items: one half of realized net long-term capital gains; constructive realization of gain on gifts and bequests; tax-exempt state and local government bond interest; excess of percentage over cost depletion and accelerated over straight-line depreciation; dividend exclusion; interest on life insurance policies; homeowners preferences; transfer payments, and personal exemptions and deductions.

† Beginning with the Revenue Act of 1971 as it applies to 1972 income and going to a comprehensive tax base.

‡ Includes effects of excluding one half of realized net long-term capital gains and taxation of gains transferred by gift or bequest.

§ Includes effects of eliminating itemized deductions for mortgage interest and real estate taxes.

Less than 0.05.

Note: Details may not add to totals because of rounding.

Source: Joseph A. Pechman and Benjamin A. Okner, "Individual Income Tax Erosion by Income Classes," *The Economics of Federal Subsidy Programs,* Joint Economic Committee, 92d cong., 2d sess. (Washington, D.C.: U.S. Government Printing Office, 1972), p. 25.

TABLE 8-7   Distribution of total tax savings resulting from preference provisions
of the federal personal income tax, 1972*

(1) Expanded adjusted gross income class† ($000)	(2) Percentage increase in tax liabilities resulting from application of existing statutory rates to expanded AGI (total tax savings)	(3) Federal personal income tax paid‡ as percentage of expanded AGI (effective tax rates)
Under $3	255.6	0.5
$3–5	213.5	1.7
5–10	86.0	5.3
10–15	60.6	8.7
15–20	64.0	10.7
20–25	71.9	12.1
25–50	84.0	14.5
50–100	77.0	23.5
100–500	84.8	29.5
500–1,000	99.2	30.4
1,000 and above	97.0	32.1
All income classes	75.1	11.3

* Based on projections of personal income tax sources from 1966 levels. Assumes personal income of $925 billion in 1972.

† Expanded adjusted gross income is adjusted gross income as defined in the Internal Revenue Code, modified to include the income items listed in Table 8–6, note *.

‡ According to Revenue Act of 1971 as applied to 1972 incomes. The tax liability figures differ from those published in the U.S. budget because different estimating procedures, particularly those related to capital gains, are used.

Source: Based on data in Pechman and Okner, "Individual Income Tax Erosion by Income Classes," Table 2, p. 22, and Table 6, p. 26.

vertical equity effects which result from income tax base erosion.[23] This analysis is accomplished by expanding the adjusted gross income (AGI) concept of the federal personal income tax to include various special tax-preference provisions not included in the statutory definition of AGI. The actual tax paid by each expanded AGI class in a particular year (1972, in this case) is applied to the expanded AGI base, and the result is the range of average *effective* federal personal income tax rates.

In Table 8–6, it can be observed that the bulk of tax benefits (savings, reductions) from the preferential treatment of long-term capital gains,[24] tax-exempt interest, dividend exclusion, and excess de-

[23] Tables 8–6 and 8–7 and Figure 8–2 are based on a study, "Individual Income Tax Erosion by Income Classes," by Joseph A. Pechman and Benjamin A. Okner, which was published in *The Economics of Federal Subsidy Programs*, compendium of papers submitted to the Joint Economic Committee, 92d cong., 2d sess. (Washington, D.C.: U.S. Government Printing Office, 1972), part 1, pp. 13–40.

[24] This is defined in the Pechman-Okner study to include the tax benefits which derive from the exclusion of 50 percent (now 60 percent) of realized, net, long-term capital gains from the personal income tax base, as well as the tax benefits of unrealized capital gains that are transferred to recipients by gift or bequest.

FIGURE 8-2   **Influence of various tax preference provisions on effective rates of federal personal income tax, 1972 income levels***

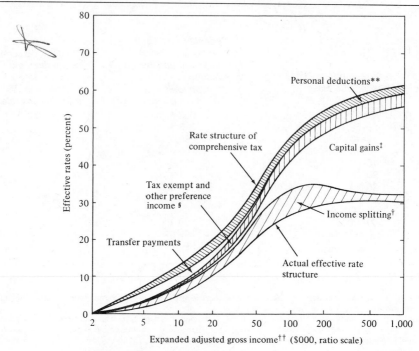

Expanded adjusted gross income[††] ($000, ratio scale)

* Rates, exemptions, and other provisions of the Revenue Act of 1971 as scheduled to apply to calendar year 1972 incomes.
  [†] Includes effect of removing maximum tax.
  [‡] Includes effect of full taxation and constructive realization of capital gains.
  [§] Includes effect of taxing of interest on state-local bonds and life insurance policies; taxing net imputed rent (including effect of disallowing personal deductions for mortgage interest and real estate taxes); disallowing excess of percentage over cost depletion; disallowing excess of accelerated over straight-line depreciation; and removing dividend exclusion.
  ** Includes effect of removing additional exemptions for age and blindness and retirement income credit.
  [††] Expanded adjusted gross income is adjusted gross income as defined in the Internal Revenue Code modified to include the income items listed in Table 8-6, note *.
  Source: J. Pechman and B. Okner, "Individual Income Tax Erosion by Income Classes," p. 28.

pletion is received at higher-income levels. That is, if these items are added back into the tax base so as to arrive at an expanded-income concept, the greatest amounts are added in near the top of the income scale. Meanwhile, the bulk of tax benefits resulting from transfer payments, including social security exclusion, and from personal exemptions for age and blindness is received at the lower-income levels. The middle-income classes receive the greatest benefits from homeowners' preferences such as the exclusion of the services (imputed rent) of owner-occupied homes and the deductibility of mortgage interest and property tax payments. Though all income classes have their own relatively most important special tax provisions, Column 2 in Table 8–7 demonstrates that the relatively greatest overall tax savings from special tax preferences are received by the very lowest and very highest income classes and the relatively least by middle-income taxpayers. Hence, the burden of the effects of income tax base erosion are unevenly distributed among taxpayers of different expanded AGI classes.

Table 8–7 and Figure 8–2 demonstrate the rapid tapering off of the increase in average *effective* federal personal income tax rates at the higher income levels in 1972. Indeed, the effective progressivity and vertical equity of the federal personal income tax, as demonstrated in Column 3 of Table 8–7, deviates considerably from the statutory rates exhibited in Table 8–1. This phenomenon of *dampened progressivity* is demonstrated also by a comparison of the bottom and top lines in Figure 8–2. The bottom line, which shows the actual income tax paid during 1972 as a percentage of expanded AGI at different expanded AGI levels, represents the *effective* average tax rate structure. Importantly, this line is considerably below the top line, which would represent the *comprehensive* tax rate structure if the existing statutory rates were actually applied to an expanded AGI base without provision for tax preferences.

Tax law changes from 1972 through 1976 tended to provide slightly greater effective progressivity, but this trend was reversed by subsequent legislation beginning in 1978 and especially by the ERTA of 1981. Regarding the latter, Table 8–8 demonstrates the redistribution-downward effects of the federal personal income tax burden as the result of law changes enacted during 1981. Further evidence of this fact, as estimated by the Congressional Budget Office for 1983, shows that households with incomes under $10,000 will pay on average about $120 less in personal income taxes due to the 1981 law changes while those with incomes over $80,000 will pay on average about $15,000 less.[25] Moreover, total federal revenue losses from the 1981 income tax law changes will amount to approximately $82 billion in 1983 with about 85 percent of these tax savings going to households with incomes over $20,000.[26]

Opponents of an extensive network of special tax preferences point out that the elimination or significant modification of these loopholes would greatly increase the revenue potential of the federal personal

---

[25] "Effects of Tax and Benefit Deductions Enacted in 1981 for Households in Different Income Categories," U.S. Congress, Congressional Budget Office, February 1982.

[26] Ibid.

TABLE 8–8   Projected federal personal income tax reductions enacted during 1981 as a percentage of income, by income class, calendar years, 1982–1985*

Calendar year	All households	Household income (in 1982 dollars)				
		Less than $10,000	$10,000– 20,000	$20,000– 40,000	$40,000– 80,000	$80,000 and over
1982	1.9	0.8	1.0	1.7	2.5	4.6
1983	3.5	1.3	1.9	3.2	4.6	6.7
1984	4.3	1.7	2.4	4.0	5.7	7.9
1985	5.2	2.3	3.0	4.9	6.7	8.4

* Personal income tax reductions resulting from the Economic Recovery Tax Act of 1981 included in this table are the rate reductions, the deduction for two-earner married couples, and indexing of the tax rates, exemptions, and zero bracket amounts for 1985.

Source: "Effects of Tax and Benefit Reductions Enacted in 1981 for Households in Different Income Categories," U.S. Congress, Congressional Budget Office, February 1982, Table 4, p. 9.

income tax under existing tax rates, and thus could allow a substantial reduction in the range of progressive tax rates applied to the tax base in order to attain a given level of tax revenue. One tax simplification plan, proposed by Fernbach, Pechman, and Gainsburgh, would have allowed the then-applicable (1966) tax rate range of 14 to 70 percent to be reduced to a range of 7 to 35 percent.[27] The proposed plan would involve the taxation of income from *all* sources. This, of course, would eliminate special treatment for certain types of income, such as long-term capital gains and state and local bond interest. Thus, it would approximate the broader concept of income represented by the *economic accretion* approach, though primarily from an "income flow" rather than from a "uses" standpoint. Deductions would be limited under the plan to such important items as large medical expenses, casualty losses, and charitable contributions above 2 percent of income. Other less important deductions, including the standard 10 percent optional deduction existing at the time of the proposal, would be removed, but the personal exemption concept would be retained. More recent proposals for a broadened federal personal income tax base include those presented in a U.S. Treasury study[28] published during 1977, as well as those contained in the extensive "flat-rate personal income tax" movement underway during 1982 (see also

---

[27] Frank Fernbach, Joseph Pechman, and Martin Gainsburgh, "What's Wrong with Our Tax System?", *Challenge*, July–August 1966, p. 17. See also the tax rate reduction alternative for the federal personal income tax as presented in Pechman and Okner, "Individual Income Tax Erosion by Income Classes," pp. 29–33.

[28] See Department of the Treasury, *Blueprints for Basic Tax Reform* (Washington, D.C.: U.S. Government Printing Office, 1977).

Chapter 14). The latter, however, differs from the more traditional proposals in that it advocates the imposition of a single, low-proportional rate, rather than a lower-range progressive rate structure, on the broadened tax base.

Proponents of an eroded federal personal income tax base contend that the difference between personal and taxable income is accounted for by items which either cannot be included in taxable income on the basis of practical administration and compliance, or which conflict with other basic objectives of public policy. Undoubtedly, there is a certain validity to these arguments. However, it seems unlikely that the overall extent of tax base erosion which now exists can be considered rational in a society that has basically espoused the concepts of horizontal and vertical tax equity as well as the use of income as the indicator of taxpaying ability under these benchmarks.

Tax expenditures: A by-product of income tax base erosion. Recent years have witnessed the popularization in fiscal circles of the term *tax expenditures*, alternately referred to as *tax reliefs*. This concept involves estimation of the value of federal personal and corporation income tax preference provisions to those individuals and corporations who are able to take advantage of them. Viewed from the federal budget standpoint, of course, these tax savings to the private sector constitute reduced revenues to the federal government. They are the direct result of the income tax base erosion caused by numerous special tax-preference provisions.

Use of the word *expenditures* here applies the word *subsidy* to the private sector beneficiaries of special tax preferences in a manner analogous to its traditional application to those in the private sector who benefit from direct federal expenditure programs. The federal budget is thus viewed in a symmetrical fashion, recognizing that economic gains to individuals (or corporations), and subsequent fiscal effects to the federal Treasury, can result from either programs which increase expenditure flows from the budget or reduce tax flows to the budget.

The estimated value of total tax expenditures, for both individuals and corporations, during fiscal year 1982 was $267 billion.[29] This total disaggregates into $215 billion of tax expenditures for individuals and $52 billion for corporations. Several of the most important of the tax expenditures for that year were: exclusion of employer pension, health, and welfare plan contributions, $49 billion; deductibility of state and local nonbusiness taxes, $34 billion; deductibility of mortgage and consumer credit interest, $31 billion; capital gains preferences, $29 billion; transfer payment exclusion $24 billion; the

---

[29] Source of data: *Special Analyses, Budget of the U.S. Government, Fiscal Year 1982.*

investment tax credit,[30] $22 billion, and the deductibility of charitable contributions, $12 billion.

Conclusions regarding tax expenditures should be drawn with discretion. For example, even though it is appropriate to consider tax preferences as private sector subsidies in the broad sense of the word, the primary reasons behind a special tax provision may *not be redistributional,* which is the normal, narrow, interpretation of a subsidy. In other words, the subsidy may be incidental to some other primary fiscal goal, such as full employment, economic growth, pollution control, energy conservation, or the encouragement of owner-occupied residences. Moreover, a tax-preference provision may simply be the result of efforts to achieve an equitable and workable definition of taxable income. Thus, tax expenditures, though representative of tax savings to their recipients and tax losses to the federal Treasury, are not always subsidies in a primary redistributional sense.

The problem of perks. A growing distributional issue relevant to personal income taxation is the accessibility of perks to certain executives and other employees of a business. A *perk* may be described as a fringe benefit form of real income which does not take on a direct monetary income form. Examples of perks include business-related meals, personal use of company automobiles, company-paid club memberships, company-paid medical examinations, low-interest or interest-free loans to an employee, company-paid life insurance, and the like. Although the law requires the disclosure for tax purposes of many perks, enforcement is often difficult, and the failure to report is not uncommon.

The distributional effects of inflation on progressive personal income taxes. Significant rates of inflation can have serious distributional effects on the pattern of progressive personal income taxation. Since personal exemptions, zero bracket amounts, tax-bracket boundaries, and certain other structural features of the federal personal income tax are stated in money (dollar) terms, a graduated rate structure can draw the taxpayer into a higher marginal tax-rate bracket if the taxpayer's money income is increasing, even though his/her real income may not be increasing. In other words, even if the *real* income of the taxpayer remains unchanged, which would be the case if the rate of inflation were the same as the rate of increase in the taxpayer's money income, the taxpayer could still be drawn into a higher marginal tax-rate bracket under these conditions. Thus, a 10 percent increase in money income could be offset by a 10 percent increase in prices, while a taxpayer is nonetheless drawn into a higher tax rate bracket.

The federal government could adjust the personal income tax for

---

[30] See Chapter 9.

this distributional effect of inflation through a variety of techniques. These include: (1) periodic tax-rate reductions, (2) periodic adjustments of those special structural features that help to define the tax base, or (3) application of "automatic" adjustment features to the personal income tax. The latter technique is commonly referred to as *indexing* the personal income tax for inflation. A number of nations, including Australia, Canada, Denmark, Luxembourg, the Netherlands, Chile, and Brazil, have adopted the indexing approach. The federal government of the United States, prior to legislation enacted in 1981, had made periodic (partial) inflation adjustments of the first and second varieties and, as observed earlier in the chapter, the ERTA of 1981 included an automatic adjustment provision effective in 1985.

Stabilization effects

The federal personal income tax also performs important stabilization functions. However, since these topics are considered in detail in Part Four, only a brief discussion will be provided at this point. Positive stabilization nonneutralities include the *automatic* countercyclical effects of the tax. Federal personal income tax revenues increase at a faster rate than national income as national income increases, and they diminish at a more rapid rate as national income declines. As a result, increasing proportions of private sector purchasing power are taken from aggregate demand as potentially inflationary prosperity approaches, while increasing proportions are left in the private sector when national income declines in a recession or depression.

Both the *marginal propensity to tax* (MPT) and *income elasticity of taxation* (Y_t) concepts, as developed in Chapter 5, illustrate the automatic stabilization qualities of the federal personal income tax. For example, the built-in-flexibility of the tax, as viewed through the *MPT* concept, finds a positive or direct relationship between changes in income tax revenues (ΔT) and changes in national income (ΔY). In addition, the $\Delta T/\Delta Y$ ratio becomes greater during inflationary prosperity, thus reducing aggregate (private) disposable income, and smaller during a depression, thus increasing aggregate (private) disposable income. The fact that the Y_t of the federal personal income tax is elastic $(Y_t > 1)$ suggests a more-than-proportionate percentage rate of response of income-tax-revenue changes to changes in national income. Moreover, the favorable automatic stabilization features of the federal personal income tax may derive from the basic features of the tax itself, namely, broadness of base, progressive rate structure, and the close linkage between changes in national income and the performance of the aggregate economy.

In addition to its automatic countercyclical characteristics, the federal personal income tax also lends itself to *discretionary* stabilization policies based on ad hoc changes in the tax itself, as stabilization objectives are pursued. Thus, changes in tax rates or in various tax-base provisions can be explicitly enacted for countercyclical purposes. These discretionary stabilization policies can be more readily understood in light of the *MPT* concept, an exercise reserved for Chapter 20.

9

Income taxation:
The corporation
income tax

FEDERAL CORPORATION INCOME TAX

Federal income tax law provides for partially different tax treatment of business and trade profits, depending on the legal form of organization under which the business functions. Businesses which are legally organized as *corporations* are taxed as separate entities and have a particular scale of tax rates applied to them. There are also numerous features of federal income tax law which apply commonly to *business income*, whether it be earned under a proprietorship, partnership, or corporate legal form. Among the provisions which are similar or identical in this regard are those pertaining to depletion, depreciation, and the investment credit. Many of the tax provisions described in the preceding chapter for personal income apply in a similar or identical manner to business income, and vice versa. Nevertheless, there is a partially differentiated tax base—tax rate structure, which constitutes the federal *corporation income tax*. Businesses organized as *proprietorships* or *partnerships* are not taxed under the federal corporation income tax, and all taxable profits are reported on the individual returns of the owners.[1]

Why a separate corporation income tax?

On theoretical grounds, it is difficult to justify the existence of a corporation income tax separate from the personal income tax. This is true because only *persons*, not legal business entities, can bear the sacrifice (disutility) of tax burdens. In other words, it is persons who forego usage in the private sector of tax funds paid to the government. If all income were taxed at the personal level in the form of a personal (individual) income tax, there would be no theoretical basis for the separate existence of a corporation income tax.

Hence, the answer as to why the corporation income tax exists as a separate revenue source must be sought on administrative and other grounds rather than in theoretical terms. One administrative argument for the corporation income tax rests on the assertion that, *without* the tax, retained (undistributed) corporate profits would completely escape income taxation. Indeed, this would be the case if the two income taxes were not integrated into a single income tax, because personal income taxation could be avoided by accumulating income in corporations. The separate existence of a corporation income tax raises another problem, however, namely that dividends (distributed profits) will be subject to "double taxation" by the coexisting personal and corporation income taxes unless the tax structures are designed to avoid this possibility, or unless the corporate tax is shifted away from shareholders to consumers and/or labor.

A means of fully integrating the two income taxes to escape these problems has been proposed in the form of the *partnership method* of income tax integration. Under this plan, undistributed corporate profits would be assigned to the personal income tax base of the shareholder on a pro rata basis, that is, on the basis of the number of shares of stock owned by the shareholder. The shareholder would then pay taxes on both dividends received as well as on the pro rata portion of undistributed profits. Problems of possible taxpayer illiquidity in the sense of being required to pay taxes on income not actually received (the undistributed profits) could largely be alleviated through a prepayment mechanism at the corporate level linked to a personal income tax credit. Accordingly, shareholders would pay personal income tax on their prorated share of undistributed corporate profits, but would receive a credit for the amount of tax prepaid at the source. Meanwhile, the corporation income tax would be abolished since all

---

[1] Some noncorporate businesses may have certain attributes of a corporation and thus be subject to the corporation income tax instead of the personal income tax.

corporate profits would be taxed under the personal income tax. Critics of the partnership approach maintain that it is administratively impractical due to the extreme difficulty in identifying the ultimate owner of stocks held by corporate hierarchies and other institutions, and also due to the frequent purchases and sales of stock and the presence of multiclasses of stock shares.

Thus, if the feasibility of full integration under the partnership method is accepted, an argument for the separate existence of a corporation income tax cannot be sustained. On the other hand, if one rejects the feasibility of full integration of the two income taxes through the partnership method, the separate existence of a corporation income tax can be justified on the grounds of preventing the escape of undistributed corporate earnings from income taxation. In this event, some "partial integration" method for eliminating the double taxation[2] of dividend income seems appropriate. Various partial integration techniques are available for this purpose. These include a dividends-received credit for individuals against personal income tax liability, the exclusion of part or all of dividends received from the base of the personal income tax,[3] and allowing corporations a deduction for dividends paid.

Another argument for the existence of a separate tax on corporation income points out that since corporations receive unique "benefits or privileges" from government, they merit a separate form of income taxation. The most important of these benefits is the *limited liability* of shareholders; that is, shareholders are not liable for the debts of a corporation beyond their investment in the corporation, unlike the partners in a partnership or the proprietor of a business, who are fully liable. Still another argument offered as justification for corporate income taxation is the view that the corporation constitutes a separate taxable entity apart from its shareholders, since most large corporations reflect minimal shareholder influence on management policies. Instead, professional officers and directors make the operational decisions for the huge amounts of capital generated by large corporations. An additional argument attempts to justify separate corporate income taxation for regulatory purposes. Hence, the corporation income tax would be accepted as a means of restraining the substantial economic power represented by the identification of large corporations with oligopolistic industries. However, only the nontaxation of undistributed profits argument, among those described here, appears to provide a possible firm basis for separate corporate income taxation, though certain secondary justification may be provided by the other

---

[2] Unless the corporation shifts the tax to consumers and/or labor.

[3] There presently exists a maximum $100 exclusion, $200 for a married couple filing a joint return, for dividends received from domestic corporations.

arguments. Finally, it is easy to overlook a pragmatic reason for the continued presence of a separate tax on the income of corporations, namely, the revenue productivity of the tax. Yet, as will be seen shortly, the revenue importance of the federal corporation income has been sharply reduced, after many years of significant revenue contribution, by the Economic Recovery Tax Act (ERTA) of 1981. Only a partial recoupment of revenue reductions has resulted from the Tax Equity and Fiscal Responsibility Act (TEFRA) of 1982.

The federal corporation income tax base and rate structure

Since 1909 the federal government has continuously imposed a tax on the net income of corporations. The tax was considered an excise tax on the "privilege" of doing business as a corporation until, in 1913, the 16th Amendment to the Constitution removed all constitutional doubts concerning income taxation. The excise tax used net income as a measure of the privilege of corporate business practice. However, as observed in the preceding section, it is difficult to provide theoretical justification for corporate income taxation on privilege or benefit grounds.

Under the present federal corporation income tax structure, *taxable corporation income* is computed by deducting from gross income the expenses which are incurred in creating that income. Such expenses must be "ordinary and necessary" to the operation of a trade or business. Among the deductible expenses are wages and salaries, remuneration of executives, rents, royalties, material costs, bad debts, casualty losses, taxes, advertising expenses, interest payments, and the depreciation cost of fixed capital for the year in question. Dividends paid to stockholders are *not* deductible as expenses, except in certain cases involving the preferred stock dividends of public utility companies. In addition, certain other expenses are deductible, though subject to rather stringent qualifications. Among these are contributions to charity, contributions to profit-sharing plans and pension funds, and entertainment expenses. In effect, the tax base of the federal corporation income tax consists of the return to equity capital in corporations.

Some corporations receive preferential treatment under the federal corporation income tax on the basis of qualification as nonprofit institutions. These include organizations organized for charitable, religious, scientific, literary, and educational purposes. No part of the net profits of these corporations may be applied to the benefit of any individual, nor can the organization substantially engage in propaganda or participate in political activity. Additional preferential treatment is provided for labor and agricultural organizations, business leagues and chambers of commerce, credit unions, recreational clubs, and fraternal organizations.

In addition, insurance companies have historically received preferred treatment under the federal corporation income tax structure, though recent decades have witnessed a significant reduction in these advantages. The first of these important modifications occurred under the Life Insurance Company Income Tax Act of 1959. Prior to this act, life insurance companies were taxed on only a portion of their net investment income. The 1959 legislation provided for taxing one half of underwriting income when earned and the other half when distributed, and also provided for the taxation of investment income under a new formula which measures the taxable margin of investment earnings on an individual company basis. Furthermore, capital gains of these companies are now taxed. Other corporate organizations receiving preferred treatment under the tax include commercial banks, mutual savings banks, savings and loan associations, cooperatives, and regulated investment companies.

Figure 9–1 demonstrates the statutory rate structure of the federal corporation income tax. It can be observed that the marginal rates increase over five tax-base brackets, thus making the tax progressive in statutory terms. The rates are 15, 18, 30, and 40 percent, respectively, on successive taxable income brackets of $25,000 each, and 46 percent on all taxable income above $100,000.

Corporate long-term *capital gains* on assets that are held more than 12 months are taxed at a lower rate than ordinary income. The maximum rate under this provision is 28 percent, as compared to the 20

FIGURE 9–1   Rate structure of the federal corporation income tax

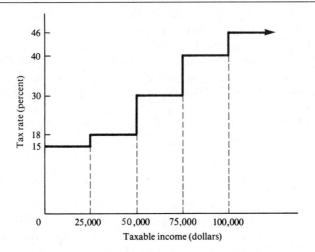

percent that applies for the long-term capital gains of individuals under the federal personal income tax. Moreover, corporations may offset capital losses only against capital gains, while individuals may deduct one half of net long-term capital losses and all short-term losses up to $3,000 from ordinary income.

Corporations, like individual taxpayers, often enjoy certain tax preferences and, accordingly, are subject to a corporate *minimum tax*. The tax is based on essentially the same preference items as for individuals, but is of the "add-on" type. The amounts of the tax preferences are totaled, and after an exemption of the greater of $10,000 or the regular corporate income tax, the remainder is subject to a 15 percent rate. The resulting minimum tax is then added to the tax regularly computed.

The Internal Revenue Code makes special provisions to inhibit the use of the federal corporation income tax by high-bracket taxpayers to avoid the higher marginal rates of the federal personal income tax on dividend distributions, but these provisions have not been fully successful. A corporation which accumulates earnings in excess of the "reasonable needs" of the business, for example, may legally be required to pay a penalty tax on the excess in addition to the regular corporation income tax. The burden of proof regarding improper accumulations can be made by astute taxpayers to fall on the Internal Revenue Service (IRS). In addition, penalty taxes apply if a corporation is a *personal holding company* and does not distribute substantially all of its posttax earnings to its shareholders as dividends. A personal holding company is a closely-held corporation whose major sources of income are from investments (for example, interest and dividends) or other personal-type income. In another vein, the mere recognition by the tax laws of the corporation as a separate entity encourages individuals to create and manipulate corporations to their tax advantage. The Internal Revenue Code is replete with provisions which circumscribe their efforts to do so. Although the incentives for the above tax avoidances were reduced by the ERTA of 1981, which lowered the maximum marginal personal income tax rate from 70 to 50 percent, the desire to utilize lower corporate income tax rates, defer the imposition of a personal income tax on income already taxed within the corporation, and convert ordinary income to long-term capital gains still remains.

Some special characteristics of the federal corporation income tax

Treatment of depreciation. Business expenditures for capital assets such as plant and equipment cannot be fully deducted, under ordinary circumstances, in the year in which they are acquired. Instead, the deduction must be apportioned over some version of asset life. The income of each year's operation is charged with a proportion of the cost of the capital asset. Allowances for depreciation may be taken only for property used in trade or business or otherwise held for the production of income. The depreciation allowance cannot exceed the original cost of the capital asset. Current rules permit depreciation deductions to occur at rates faster than the capital assets are actually used up.

Three primary methods of computing depreciation were provided by the Revenue Act of 1954. That is, a business could select from among the straight-line, declining balance, and sum-of-the-year'-digits methods of depreciation.

Under the *straight-line method of depreciation*, the acquisition cost of an asset is written off (depreciated, deducted) in equal annual installments during the useful life of the asset. Thus, a $20,000 capital asset with a useful life of 20 years would be deducted at a depreciation rate of 5 percent, or $1,000 per year.

In the *declining balance method of depreciation*, which may be 125, 150, 175, or 200 percent of the straight-line rate, a fixed percentage of the unrecovered cost (undepreciated balance) is deducted annually, and then continued at that rate on the remaining balances. The 200 percent method is referred to as the double-declining-balance method. Thus, for the same capital asset as in the above example, a double-declining depreciation rate of 10 percent of $20,000, or $2,000, would be applied in the first year, with the rate being 10 percent of the unrecovered cost of $18,000, or $1,800 in the second year, and so on.

The *sum-of-the-year's-digits method of depreciation* produces a depreciation pattern somewhat similar to that of the double-declining balance method, but without leaving an undepreciated balance sometimes in excess of salvage value at the end of the useful life of the asset. Using the same example, this method would sum the useful years of life of the asset $(20 + 19 + 18 + 17 \ldots 1 = 210)$ and then calculate depreciation allowances in each year, beginning with the highest number year, as that year is a proportion of the sum of the years $(20/210, 19/210, 18/210 \ldots 1/210)$. This fraction is then multiplied by the cost of the asset ($20,000). Thus, $20/210$ $(2/21)$ times $20,000, or (approximately) $1,905, is deducted during the first year, with $19/210$ times $20,000, or (approximately) $1,810, in the second year, and so on.

The declining balance and the sum-of-the-years'-digits methods allow a capital asset to be written off in greater proportions in the earlier years of the life of the asset. This is known as *accelerated depreciation*. In 1962, following an extensive study of depreciation rules, methods, and existing practices, the Treasury Department issued an administrative ruling which substantially reduced suggested asset lives for tax purposes, thus allowing for still greater accelerated depreciation. The practice of accelerated depreciation increases the amount of money capital available (in the shorter term) for reinvestment by a business, since it allows a cost write-off for a capital asset that is more rapid than the actual physical using up or obsolescence of the asset. Thus, the net taxable income of the corporation is reduced and its capital expenditure potential increased in the short run by the use of accelerated depreciation. In effect, it constitutes a noninterest-bearing loan from the government to the taxpaying business.

However, accelerated depreciation may be justified, in part, to offset the general investment retardation effects of the corporation income tax and, in part, to encourage business investment in a direct manner. Also, it may be used to provide a more realistic measure of taxable income, since capital assets tend to use up value faster in the early years of their useful lives than in later years. In addition, accelerated depreciation can help to adjust the depreciation base for inflation.

Legislation in 1969 placed limitations on the accelerated depreciation of real estate. However, in 1971, depreciation procedures in general were significantly liberalized with the introduction of the *asset depreciation range (ADR)* system. This system allowed a taxpayer to select a tax life for an asset up to 20 percent shorter than the liberal guideline lives previously in effect. The ADR technique applied to tangible personal property, such as machinery, but not to real property, such as buildings.

The ERTA of 1981 provided further significant liberalization of accelerated depreciation provisions. This was accomplished by the establishment of an *accelerated cost recovery system (ACRS)* to replace the existing ADR system of depreciation. ACRS asset lives are much shorter than ADR lives, the number of asset classes is sharply reduced (to five), and the concept begins a movement away from the length-of-economic-life concept of depreciation. The basic recovery (write off) periods for tangible personal property are divided into four asset classes, and a fifth class applies to real property. Thus, *tangible personal property,* such as autos, light trucks, and research and development equipment, may be recovered in three years; most other machinery and equipment, furniture, and fixtures in five years; 18–25 year ADR public utility property in 10 years, and public utility property with a longer-than-25-year ADR life in 15 years. Meanwhile, the general recovery period for *real property* is 15 years.[4] These new, shorter depreciation periods apply to both old and new assets. Moreover, the speed of depreciation within the recovery periods is in-

---

[4] Longer asset recovery periods, utilizing a straight-line method, are optional for both personal and real property.

creased by the utilization of various accelerated methods during the early years of the asset lives, and then switching over to the sum-of-the-years'-digits or straight-line methods, so that the full cost of the asset is recovered within the class life. Under ERTA, the faster "speeds" were phased-in over the years 1981–86. However, it was discovered that the 1985 and 1986 schedules, coupled with the investment tax credit (see below), gave more tax advantages than if taxpayers were permitted to expense, or write-off immediately, the cost of capital assets. Accordingly, the TEFRA of 1982 cancelled the 1985 and 1986 schedules and froze the recovery speeds for post-1984 acquisitions at the 1984 rates. A provision in the law to benefit small businesses permits the immediate expensing of part of the cost of personal property used in a trade or business, up to $5,000 per year in 1982 and 1983, $7,500 per year in 1984 and 1985, and $10,000 per year thereafter. Of course, no additional cost recovery allowances or investment tax credits are available on the amounts so expensed. The enormous expansion of accelerated depreciation brought about by the ERTA of 1981 will greatly reduce the revenue productivity of the federal corporation income tax and, in the minds of some experts, will essentially remove the corporation income tax from the federal revenue structure.

The investment tax credit. In order to promote economic stabilization objectives, businesses are allowed an *investment tax credit* (*ITC*). As liberalized by ERTA, the credit is equal to 10 percent of the purchase price of new capital equipment with an ACRS class life of five or more years, or a 6 percent credit for new capital equipment in the three-year ACRS class.[5] Moreover, some real property (for example, blast furnaces and grain and petroleum storage facilities) is also eligible for a credit. The maximum credit limit is 85 percent of tax liability above $25,000 with a 100 percent credit applicable to the first $25,000 of tax liability. The credit, in effect, amounts to a discount paid by the federal government on the cost of capital investment. Although the ITC has been in existence since 1962 (with various amendments, suspensions, and reinstatements over the years), the amount of the credit has not affected the basis or cost of the property for purposes of depreciation and gain or loss realization on sale. However, under the TEFRA of 1982, commencing in 1983, the basis of acquired property for depreciation and gain or loss is reduced by one half of the credit. In lieu of such reduction, however, taxpayers may elect to reduce the otherwise-available credit by two percentage points. Thus, three-year ACRS property would allow a 4 percent credit and other property an 8 percent credit.

---

[5] A credit may also be applied for the acquisition of used property up to a value of $125,000 per year.

The faster depreciation deductions under ACRS, together with the liberalized ITC rules above, came into being in 1981 (under ERTA) when the nation's economy was in a recession and many businesses were suffering losses. Concerned that such businesses would not respond to the incentives to invest in new productive plant and equipment as envisioned by ERTA, as they could not take advantage of the depreciation and ITC benefits, Congress added the "safe harbor leasing" provisions to the 1981 legislation. Under these rules, retroactive to January 1, 1981, businesses not able to use their eligible tax credits and depreciation benefits are able to "sell" them to other businesses who can use them to reduce their own tax liabilities. This would be profitable, of course, to the business purchasing the tax benefits as long as the price paid for them is less than the amount of tax savings which the benefits bring about. Essentially, the arrangement consists of the purchaser of the benefits, a profitable company, becoming the owner of the property and leasing it to the seller of the benefits. The lease terms are structured such that the investment tax credit and depreciation benefits are shared with the user of the property. Thus, an unprofitable or low-profit company can reduce its cost of investment in property under the leasing arrangement and, simultaneously, the high-profit company can reduce its tax liability. While the resulting economic assistance given to lower-profit businesses seems defensible, the reduction of tax liabilities for higher-profit businesses seems questionable.

The safe-harbor leasing provisions proved quite successful in fostering new investment by low-profit or loss businesses—in fact too successful! Federal tax revenues in 1981 and early 1982 from the "profitable" businesses were substantially reduced. Accordingly, the Tax Equity and Fiscal Responsibility Act of 1982 imposed substantial cutbacks on the benefits to be obtained under safe harbor leasing effective July 1, 1982, and eliminated the availability of the arrangement for 1984 and subsequent years. However, commencing in 1984, a new "finance lease" arrangement will be available containing most of the benefits of the restricted, post-July 1, 1982, safe-harbor-lease rules.

Taxation of income from natural resources. Various special provisions for the taxation of income derived from natural resources are provided by the Internal Revenue Code. For example, *depletion allowances* may be applied to capital sums invested in the development of natural resource properties. For mineral properties, depletion allowances are computed by either a cost depletion or a percentage depletion method.

Under the *cost depletion method,* which must be used for timber resources, the *adjusted basis* (original cost plus any additional capital costs less the total of all depletion allowed) of the property is divided by the total number of units estimated to remain in the deposit or property (for example, tons of ore or board feet of lumber), and the result is multiplied by the number of units sold during the year. When the adjusted basis of the property is lowered to zero, the cost depletion allowance ceases. For example: If the adjusted basis is $100,000, and the number of recoverable units is 100,000, and 5,000 units were sold during a final year, the total depletion allowance would be ($100,000/100,000 × 5,000) = $5,000.

Under the *percentage depletion method,* depletion is computed as a specific percentage of the annual gross income from the property. It cannot, however, exceed 50 percent of the net taxable income from the property. Percentage depletion usually exceeds cost depletion. Moreover, it can continue to be claimed—and deducted—*after* the cost of the mineral deposit has been completely recovered! The percentage depletion rates for various minerals are as follows:

1. 22 percent for sulfur and uranium and, if mined in the United States, for asbestos, bauxite, cobalt, lead, manganese, mercury, nickel, platinum, thorium, tin, titanium, tungsten, zinc, molybdenum, and numerous other minerals.
2. 15 percent for (domestic) gold, silver, oil shale, copper, and iron ore.
3. 14 percent for certain clays, rock, asphalt, and vermiculite.
4. 10 percent of asbestos, coal, lignite, salt, and certain other minerals.
5. 7.5 percent for clay, shale, and brick used for specified purposes.
6. 5 percent for gravel, sand, peat, pumice, scoria, some shale and stone, and certain brine well minerals.
7. 14 percent for all other minerals except soil, sod, dirt, turf, water, or mosses or minerals from sea water, the air, or similar inexhaustible resources, or oil and gas wells.

Formerly, oil and gas wells enjoyed the benefits of percentage depletion as with other minerals. However, starting in 1975, only independent or small producers and royalty owners are entitled to percentage depletion on oil and gas revenues, the rates for which have decreased from 22 percent in 1975 to 16 percent for 1983 and 15 percent for 1984 and thereafter. An independent producer or royalty owner is defined as a person whose share of average daily production does not exceed 1,000 barrels of oil or 6 million cubic feet of gas. At 365 days of production per year and assuming a price of $30 per barrel of oil, an owner of interests in oil wells has to exceed $10,950,000 in annual revenues before losing the ability to claim percentage depletion. For persons entitled to claim percentage depletion on oil and gas wells, the deduction is subject to a limitation of 65 percent of taxable income (before depletion) as well as the general limitation of 50 percent of the net income from the mineral property.

The Internal Revenue Code provides special treatment, other than depletion allowances, for certain capital expenditures incurred in bringing mineral properties into production. A taxpayer is allowed, for example, to write off as "incurred" the costs of *exploring* for mineral deposits (except oil and gas wells, which are treated preferentially under separate provisions), or to set these costs up as deferred expenses to be deducted ratably as the deposit is exhausted. These expenses include expenditures to determine the existence, location, extent, and quality of mineral resources. Another special provision permits a taxpayer either to write off as incurred the costs of *developing* a mineral deposit (except oil and gas wells, which again are treated separately), or to set these up as deferred expenses to be deducted ratably as the mineral deposit is exhausted. Expenditures for development include the costs of mine shafts, tunnels, and strip mine activities. No dollar limitation is placed on deductions for development costs.

The statutes also grant a special provision to oil, gas, and geothermal well operators by providing an option of either capitalizing or charging as current expenses certain *intangible* drilling and development costs of such wells. These deductible expenses include costs of fuel and power, labor, materials, tool rental, repairs of drilling equipment, and the like. The costs, however, are treated as "tax-preference items" subject to the corporate minimum tax and the personal alternative minimum tax.

Taxation of income from foreign sources. Income earned by U.S. corporations through their foreign subsidiaries is subject to the federal corporation income tax when these profits are returned as dividends to the parent company in the United States. At the same time, a credit against tax liability is allowed for income tax paid to a foreign government on these profits up to the amount of U.S. corporation income tax liability on such income. Thus, double taxation of the income is avoided.

Another federal corporation income tax feature relevant to international economics encourages a U.S. corporation to create a *domestic international sales corporation* (DISC) to handle its export business. DISCs are allowed to defer corporation income tax on a designated part of their earnings until those earnings are returned to the parent company. This proportion, though reduced in 1976 and again in 1982, remains a significant favorable tax provision for American corporations who engage in considerable export activity. The objective of the DISC technique—improved U.S. balance of payments performance—is served in a positive manner by this special tax provision.

STATE AND LOCAL CORPORATION INCOME TAXES

States began to charge fees for business incorporation and to levy capital stock taxes during the 19th century. The period of state corporation income taxation, however, began essentially with the enactment by Wisconsin of comprehensive personal and corporation income taxes in 1911. Today 45 states and the District of Columbia impose corporation income taxes. A number of cities also levy corporation income taxes, though these cities are concentrated in a small number of states. These local government corporation income taxes are usually "supplemental" to the low-rate personal income taxes and taxes on the net profits of unincorporated businesses imposed by the cities. In terms of their income elasticity performance, state and local corporation income taxes in the nation as a whole appear to be slightly income elastic. One study (Harris) estimates the income elasticity coefficient to be 1.16 ($Y_t = 1.16$), while another study (Netzer) estimates the income elasticity value to be 1.10 ($Y_t = 1.10$).[6]

Table 9–1 summarizes state corporation income tax rates and certain other characteristics. It can be observed that 31 out of 45 states using the tax, plus the District of Columbia, apply a proportional (flat) rate structure.[7] The mean proportional rate for these 31 states averages out to the rather low figure of 6.7 percent, with a range from 2.35 percent (Michigan) to 12 percent (Minnesota). The progressive rates in the other 14 states range from a minimum marginal rate of 1 percent (Arkansas) to a maximum of 10.5 percent (Arizona). In six states, the federal corporation income tax is deductible from the state tax base for taxes paid on that part of income subject to the state tax.

Local government corporation income taxes are also usually low, proportional-rate taxes. In this instance, the rates tend to be even lower than for the state corporation income taxes; typical local rates are 1, 1.5, or 2 percent. New York City, however, applies a relatively high rate of 9.5 percent[8] of net income. Local corporation income taxes overlap state corporation income taxes in a number of major cities, including Cincinnati, Cleveland, Detroit, Kansas City, New York City, and St. Louis.

Many state corporation income taxes have been converted to the

---

[6] Robert Harris, *Income and Sales Taxes: The 1970 Outlook for States and Localities* (Chicago: Council of State Governments, 1966); Dick Netzer, "Financial Needs and Resources over the Next Decade: State and Local Governments," in National Bureau of Economic Research, *Public Finances: Needs, Sources and Utilization* (Princeton, N.J.: Princeton University Press, 1961), pp. 23–65.

[7] Includes Alaska, Kansas, and Massachusetts taxes with their special "surtax" characteristics.

[8] The tax is either 9.5 percent of net income or a tax on three alternate bases, whichever is highest.

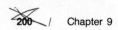

TABLE 9–1   State corporation income tax rates[a] (as of April 1, 1981)

State	Flat rate or lowest bracket		Highest bracket		Minimum tax	Federal income tax deductible[b]
	Rate (percent)	To net income of	Rate (percent)	Net income over		
Alabama	5.0	All	–	–	–	Yes
Alaska	5.4 of taxable income plus 4.0% surtax		–	–	–	No
Arizona	2.5	$1,000	10.5	$6,000	–	Yes
Arkansas	1.0	3,000	6.0	25,000	–	No
California[c]	9.6	All	–	–	$200	No
Colorado	5.0	All	–	–	–	No
Connecticut	10.0 [d]	All	–	–	50	No
Delaware	8.7	All	–	–	–	No
Florida	5.0	All[e]	–	–	–	No
Georgia	6.0	All	–	–	–	No
Hawaii	5.85 [f]	25,000	6.435	25,000	–	No
Idaho	6.5 [f]	All	–	–	–	No
Illinois	4.0 [g]	All[e]	–	–	–	No
Indiana	3.0 [h]	All	–	–	–	No
Iowa	6.0 [i]	25,000	10.0	100,000	–	Yes
Kansas	4.5 [i]	All	–	–	–	No
Kentucky	3.0	25,000	6.0	100,000	–	No
Louisiana	4.0	25,000	8.0	200,000	–	Yes
Maine	4.95	25,000	6.93	25,000	–	No
Maryland	7.0	All	–	–	–	No
Massachusetts	8.33[j]	(j)	(j)	(j)	–	No
Michigan	2.35	All	–	–	–	No
Minnesota	12.0	All	–	–	–	No
Mississippi	3.0	5,000	4.0	5,000	–	No
Missouri	5.0	All	–	–	–	Yes
Montana	6.34	All	–	–	50[k]	No
Nebraska	3.75	25,000	4.125	25,000	–	No
New Hampshire	8.0	All	–	–	–	No
New Jersey	9.0 [l]	All	–	–	–	No
New Mexico	4.0 [m]	1,000,000	6.0	2,000,000	–	No
New York	10.0 [m]	All	–	–	250	No
North Carolina	6.0	All	–	–	–	No
North Dakota	3.0	3,000	8.5	25,000	–	Yes
Ohio[n]	4.11	25,000	8.22	25,000	50	No
Oklahoma	4.0	All	–	–	–	No
Oregon	7.5	All	–	–	10	No
Pennsylvania	10.5	All	–	–	–	No
Rhode Island	8.0 [o]	All	–	–	–	No
South Carolina	6.0	All	–	–	–	No
Tennessee	6.0	All	–	–	–	No
Utah	4.0	All	–	–	25	No
Vermont	5.0	10,000	7.5	250,000	50	No
Virginia	6.0	All	–	–	–	No
West Virginia	6.0	All	–	–	–	No
Wisconsin	2.3 [p]	1,000	7.9	6,000	–	No
District of Columbia	9.0 [p]	All	–	–	25	No

[a] A special tax on financial institutions is levied in all states, based either on net income or generally on value of shares of capital stock.
[b] In general, states permitting Federal income tax deduction limit deductions to taxes paid on that part of income subject to own income tax.
[c] For calendar or fiscal years ending after 1980, rate will vary between 9.6% and 9.3%, depending on the state's collections from the tax.
[d] Additional tax imposed on capital stock and surplus to extent that it exceeds net income tax.
[e] For Florida an exemption of $5,000 and for Illinois $1,000 of net income allowed each corporation.
[f] Each corporation pays additional $10.
[g] An additional 2.5% personal property replacement tax is levied.
[h] A supplemental 3% net income tax is imposed.
[i] Surtax of 2-1/4% imposed on taxable income in excess of $25,000.
[j] Corporations pay excise tax equal to greater of following: (1) $2.60 (includes surtax) per $1,000 of value of Massachusetts property not taxed locally or net worth allocated to Massachusetts, plus 8.33% (excludes surtax) of net income; or (2) $200 (excludes surtax). Surtax of 14% imposed.
[k] Minimum tax for small corporations is $10.
[l] All corporations pay additional tax on net worth. A 7-1/4% corporation income tax is imposed on entire net income of corporations deriving income from New Jersey other than those subject to or exempt from general income tax.
[m] Corporations are subject to 10% net income tax on three alternative bases, whichever produces the greatest tax.
[n] Alternate tax is 5 mills times the value of stock, whichever is greater.
[o] Tax on 8% of net income or 40¢ on each $100 of net worth if tax yield is greater.
[p] A 10% surtax is imposed.

Source: Commerce Clearing House; *Facts and Figures on Government Finance–1981* (New York: Tax Foundation, Inc., 1981), p. 234.

federal corporation income tax base. This improves the overall administrative efficiency of the tax. However, one serious problem resulting from the multistate imposition of corporation income taxes is the allocation of the taxable income base among states for corporations whose income originates on an interstate basis.[9] There are still a number of states that do not follow the Uniform Division of Income for Tax Purposes Act and/or have not adopted the Multi-State Tax Compact, both of which represent efforts to achieve greater administrative efficiency in interstate tax matters.

FISCAL PERFORMANCE OF THE CORPORATION INCOME TAX[10]

Allocational effects

The overall effect of corporate income taxation on investment decisions. It is often asserted that the corporation income tax has serious disincentive effects on the decision to invest. Indeed, an unshifted corporation income tax does reduce net posttax profits on new investments, which would tend to reduce investment incentives. Moreover, such profit reduction occurs, whether the investments are for the expansion of present capacity or for the replacement of existing facilities. Yet, there are certain important forces which tend to reduce or neutralize the retardation effect of the corporation income tax on business investment.[11] The corporation income tax, for example, is *not* the only tax corporations must pay. Since other taxes also require consideration when investment decisions are made, the relative impact of the corporation income tax on decisions is reduced. Furthermore, the assumption that the corporation income tax is not shifted is an uncertain one, especially if nonshiftability is assumed in the sense that not even partial shifting of the tax occurs.[12]

Still other forces or conditions may help to neutralize the retarding

---

[9] For a detailed discussion of this subject, see Charles E. Ratliff, Jr., *Interstate Apportionment of Business Income for State Income Tax Purposes* (Chapel Hill: University of North Carolina Press, 1962). See also, Charles E. McLure, Jr., "The State Corporate Income Tax: Lambs in Wolves' Clothing," in Henry J. Aaron and Michael J. Boskin, eds., *The Economics of Taxation* (Washington, D. C., Brookings Institution: 1980), pp. 327–46.

[10] Many points developed in this section will also be applicable to the personal income tax, due to the numerous identical or similar features of the two taxes. Moreover, the discussion pertains primarily to federal income taxes, though much of it is applicable to state income taxes.

[11] Gerhard Colm, "The Corporation and the Corporate Income Tax," *American Economic Review*, May 1954, pp. 486–503.

[12] See the following discussion concerning the incidence of the corporation income tax.

effects on investment of a corporation income tax.[13] These include the following: (1) in many instances, investment demand is inelastic; (2) many businesses use the pretax rate of return as an earnings goal; (3) many businesses look to the loss potential as well as the rate of return from an investment; (4) businesses may have other goals, in addition to the earnings goal; and (5) the volume of investment is determined, in many instances, by "bottleneck factors" such as management size and the availability of internal funds. For example, for a company to expand beyond a point, a subsidiary staffed with its own management hierarchy may have to be established.

No definite conclusions can be reached regarding the degree of overall reduction in investment incentives that may be caused by the corporation income tax. The variables mentioned, and many others, will help determine the result in any one case. Moreover, these parameters may be expected to change over time. Thus, only general observations can be made, and specific conclusions cannot be reached. Among the most relevant of these general observations are:

1. A shiftable corporation income tax is less likely to reduce aggregate investment incentives than one that cannot be shifted.
2. Investment incentives are less likely to be harmed by a corporation income tax during a cyclical upswing than during a cyclical downturn since, when the demands for their products are relatively high, stronger motivation exists for businesses to modernize equipment and to expand output and inventories.
3. High personal and corporation income tax rates, combined with a lower rate on capital gains, encourage the retention and reinvestment of earnings by corporations.
4. Certain special provisions of the corporation income tax, in addition to capital gains, such as accelerated depreciation and the investment credit, may also provide offsets to the investment disincentive effects of corporation income taxation.

The effect of alternative corporation income tax depreciation and rate structures on investment decisions. The following example explores how various corporation income tax depreciation and rate structures can exert investment nonneutralities on the decision by a firm to purchase real capital assets. The example, which is summarized in Table 9–2, is based on the following assumptions about the firm in question:

1. The firm has a short-run profit maximization objective.
2. It wishes to increase rapidly in size so as to gain a larger share of the market.

---

[13] John Lintner, "Effect of Corporate Taxation on Real Investment," *American Economic Review*, May 1954, pp. 520–34.

TABLE 9-2 Investment nonneutralities as influenced by the method of depreciation and the rate structure of a corporation income tax*

Income, asset, and tax parameters	Item	Depreciation method used			
		Straight line	Double-declining balance	Sum-of-the-years'-digits	No depreciation
A. Proportional tax rate					
Annual pretax and predepreciation income from asset = $10,000					
2. Life of asset = 5 years					
3. Cost of asset = $24,000					
4. Proportional tax rate = 28.8%	Depreciation	$4,800	$9,600	$8,000	0
	Taxable income	5,200	400	2,000	$10,000
	Income tax	1,498	115	576	2,880
	Remaining funds	8,502	9,885	9,424	7,120
B. Progressive tax rate					
Annual pretax and predepreciation income from asset = $10,000					
2. Life of asset = 5 years					
3. Cost of asset = $24,000	Depreciation	$4,800	9,600	8,000	0
4. Progressive rate schedule:†	Taxable income	5,200	400	2,000	10,000
0–$1,500 .... 20%	Income tax	1,630	80	450	3,950
1,500– 3,000 30	Remaining funds	8,370	9,920	9,550	6,050
3,000– 6,000 40					
6,000 up 50					
C. Regressive tax rate					
Annual pretax and predepreciation income from asset = $10,000					
2. Life of asset = 5 years					
3. Cost of asset = $24,000	Depreciation	$4,800	9,600	8,000	0
4. Regressive rate schedule:†	Taxable income	5,200	400	2,000	10,000
0–$1,500 .... 50%	Income tax	2,010	200	950	3,050
1,500– 3,000 40	Remaining funds	7,990	9,800	9,050	6,950
3,000– 6,000 30					
6,000 up 20					

* Nonneutral effects (nonneutralities) are based on the first year of use of a capital asset by a firm.

† The tax rates represented here are marginal, not average, rates. For example, under the progressive tax rate schedule and a $5,200 taxable income, the first $1,500 of taxable income is taxed at a rate of 20 percent, the next $1,500 at 30 percent, and the remaining $2,200 at 40 percent—yielding an income tax of $1,630.

3. It wishes to utilize all possible internal sources to finance its capital acquisitions.
4. The relevant capital asset has a cost of $24,000 and a useful life of five years.
5. The income generated by the use of the asset is $10,000 annually.
6. All funds remaining after the payment of taxes are invested.

The alternative depreciation methods are straight line, double-declining balance, sum-of-the-years'-digits, or no depreciation at all. The alternative tax rate schedules are proportional, progressive, and regressive.[14]

First, if a proportional tax rate of 28.8 percent is applied, the firm will have $8,502 remaining for investment after the corporation income tax is paid if the straight-line method of depreciation is used. However, the more rapid the depreciation write-off during the first year, the more the firm will have left over to invest after paying the first year's taxes.[15] As Table 9–2 shows, $9,885 would be left over for investment under the double-declining balance method of depreciation, and $9,424 under the sum-of-the-years'-digits method. Only $7,120 would remain out of the $10,000 income for investment if *no depreciation* is allowed and a proportional tax rate is applied.

Next, it can be observed in Table 9–2 that both the progressive and regressive tax rate schedules diminish the first-year investment funds under the straight-line method of depreciation, as compared to the results of the proportional tax. On the other hand, under double-declining balance depreciation, the progressive tax rate schedule increases the amount of posttax investment funds, as compared to the proportional tax, but the regressive rate schedule leaves fewer posttax investment funds than the proportional tax. Similarly, under sum-of-the-years'-digits depreciation, progressive taxation leaves more investment funds than the proportional tax, but regressive taxation leaves fewer funds than the proportional tax. With no depreciation, the most investment funds are left under the proportional tax schedule and the least under the progressive tax schedule. In *all* of the examples, regardless of the tax rate structure, the posttax first-year investment funds are largest under the double-declining balance method, second largest under the sum-of-the-years'-digits method, third largest under the straight-line method and, of course, least when no depreciation is allowed. Thus, it has been demonstrated that the

---

[14] These assumptions are made for pedagogical purposes only, and do not reflect the actualities of the federal accelerated cost recovery system (ACRS) nor the existing federal corporation income tax structure.

[15] It should be noted that a larger depreciation and smaller tax *at present* result in a smaller depreciation and larger tax in the *future*, in the absence of other offsets.

method of depreciation and the rate structure of a corporation income tax may be expected to exert nonneutral effects on the decision of a firm to purchase real capital equipment.

Distributional effects

Corporation income tax base erosion and distributional equity issues. The many special tax provisions that are present in the federal corporation income tax structure (as with the federal personal income tax) contribute to significant *tax base erosion*. Moreover, these special provisions, along with the dual system of both personal and corporation income taxation, cause serious distributional equity issues in relation to the horizontal and vertical tax equity tenets of the ability-to-pay principle.

The concept of tax expenditures can be used as an indicator of tax base erosion, as was done in the preceding chapter. The tax savings to corporations from special tax provisions amounted to $52.3 billion during fiscal year 1982, according to the U.S Department of the Treasury. The most substantial of these corporate tax expenditures and their estimated values were: the investment credit, $18.3 billion; the reduced rates on the first $100,000 of taxable income, $7. 6 billion; the exclusion of interest on state and local debt and the deferral of interest payments, $7.5 billion; and accelerated depreciation, $4 billion.

The special tax provisions and the presence of the two federal income taxes distort both horizontal and vertical tax equity. For example, significant horizontal equity effects may result from the double taxation of dividend income under the two taxes. As compared to an equivalent amount of wage or salary income, the dividend income would be taxed twice except for the modest $100 exclusion provision. Of course, the double taxation would be modified by the extent to which the corporation may be able to shift the tax forward to consumers and/or backward to labor. Nonetheless, the horizontal equity issue for dividend income remains a potentially serious one. Yet, without a separate corporate income tax, and in the absence of integration of the two income taxes, undistributed corporate profits would go untaxed, which would cause serious horizontal and vertical inequities of its own. Moreover, many other special provisions of the corporation income tax structure, in addition to the double taxation issue, result in taxpayers of similar income circumstances paying considerably different amounts of tax (horizontal inequity).

In terms of observing vertical equity effects, the estimated *effective* rate structure of the federal corporation income tax, as it applies to individuals, can be compared to the *statutory* rate of structure of the federal personal income tax. It is estimated that the effective rate structure of the federal corporation income tax (under 1976 law) ranged between 2.6 percent on (individual) incomes[16] up to $5,000 and 41.9 percent on incomes over $1 million.[17] This compares to the 14–70 percent marginal statutory range of the federal personal income tax at that time. Moreover, the average effective rate for all income was only 15.9 percent.[18]

Any improvement in the ability-to-pay performance of the federal corporation income tax must ultimately rest on a simplification of the tax code in reference to its many special provisions and, relatedly, on efforts to integrate the two income taxes through techniques such as the partnership method described earlier in the chapter. Meanwhile, the distributional effects of the present income tax structure, as well as those of any reformed structure, will be closely related to the *incidence* of the corporation income tax. For example, if the tax is unshifted and remains on the shareholders, the tax would be *progressive* since capital (K) as a source of income (Y), or (K/Y), tends to increase as an individual's income increases in American society. However, if the tax is totally shifted backward to labor, it would be *regressive* since labor (L) as a source of income, or (L/Y), tends to decrease as an individual's income increases. Moreover, if the tax is totally shifted forward to consumers, it would also be *regressive,* since the consumption (C) to income (Y) ratio, or (C/Y), tends to decrease as an individual's income increases in American society. Of course, a hybrid combination of these possibilities may occur.

Incidence of the corporation income tax. A renewed interest in the incidence of the corporation income tax during the 1960s led to a number of significant empirical studies.[19] Some of these studies have considered corporation income tax incidence in a general-equilibrium sense rather than in the more narrow framework of a partial-equilibrium analysis. Although the studies as such have not been conclusive concerning corporation income tax incidence, they have expanded knowledge concerning the topic and, furthermore, have improved the methodology for studying overall tax and budgetary incidence.

Some earlier corporation income tax incidence studies during the

---

[16] Income is defined here in an expanded context similar to that used for the federal personal income tax in the preceding chapter.

[17] Joseph A. Pechman, *Federal Tax Policy,* 3d ed. (Washington, D.C.: Brookings Institution, 1977), Table 5–13, p. 179.

[18] Ibid.

[19] For an appraisal of these studies, as well as of the state of incidence theory in general, see Peter Mieszkowski, "Tax Incidence Theory: The Effects of Taxes on the Distribution of Income," *Journal of Economic Literature,* December 1969, pp. 1103–24. Also, see Balbir S. Sahni and T. Mathew, *The Shifting and Incidence of the Corporation Income Tax* (Rotterdam: Rotterdam University Press, 1976) for an analysis of various corporation income tax incidence studies.

1950s provided analyses of the relationship between *corporate income tax rates,* on the one hand, and *corporate rates of return* and *factor shares* (the proportion of the income originating in the corporate sector which is received by capital in the form of profits), on the other. These include studies by E. M. Lerner and E. S. Hendrikson in 1956 and those by M. A. Adelman in 1957.[20] The Lerner-Hendrikson study attempted to determine the relationship between federal corporation income tax rates and the *rates of return* to capital in various American industries for the period 1927–52. The authors consider that a decline in the posttax rate of return following a tax increase would suggest the absence of complete short-run shifting of the tax, whereas a constant or rising posttax rate of return would indicate substantial shifting of the tax. The Lerner-Hendrikson study concludes from its evidence that complete short-run shifting of the federal corporation income tax did *not* take place during the period.

The Adelman study focused on *factor shares* in that it compared the proportion of pretax corporate profits to total income originating in the corporate sector of the economy for the periods 1922–29 and 1946–55. The proportion of pretax corporate profits was approximately 23 percent during both the prosperous, *low-tax,* 1922–29 period and also during the prosperous, *high-tax,* 1946–55 period. Adelman concludes that substantial shifting of the federal corporation income tax had *not* occurred, since the ratio of pretax corporate profits to total income originating in the corporate sector remained constant. A higher pretax proportion in the later, high-tax period would be required if the higher tax were to be offset through shifting.

Both studies, though useful, are generally conceded to have failed to account for the significant *nontax forces* which affect corporate rates of return or factor shares. That is, they fail to separate the nontax variables from the federal corporation income tax as forces which determine corporations' profit-making behavior.

An important study by Arnold Harberger, which broadened the scope of corporate income tax incidence analysis into the *long-run, general-equilibrium* context, appeared in 1962.[21] The Harberger study emphasizes long-run capital flows from the corporate sector to the noncorporate sector of the economy, under an assumption of perfect competition. It concludes that the tax is fully borne by capital in general, both corporate and noncorporate, with no shifting to labor nor to consumers taking place.

---

[20] E. M. Lerner and E. S. Hendrikson, "Federal Taxes on Corporate Income and the Rate of Return on Investment in Manufacturing, 1927–1952," *National Tax Journal,* September 1956, pp. 193–202; M. A. Adelman, "The Corporate Income Tax in the Long Run," *Journal of Political Economy,* April 1957, pp. 151–57.

[21] Arnold Harberger, "The Incidence of the Corporation Income Tax," *Journal of Political Economy,* June 1962, pp. 215–40.

This process can be summarized as follows: the imposition of a tax on corporation net income lowers the posttax rate of return on corporate capital, thus making noncorporate capital investment relatively more attractive. As a result, capital flows will occur from the relatively less profitable (after taxes) corporate sector of the economy to the relatively more profitable noncorporate sector. These capital flows will eventually establish a new long-run equilibrium with a posttax rate of return that is the same for both sectors, but lower than the pretax equilibrium rate. As a result, *all capital*—not only corporate capital—is said to bear the burden of the tax. The study is sometimes criticized for its unrealistic assumption of perfect competition, a condition which does not apply to the American economy. However, an important implication which may be derived from the Harberger general-equilibrium study is that even if some *short-run* forward shifting of the tax does occur, the overall burden of the tax in the *long run* might still fall on capital.

M. Krzyzaniak and R. A. Musgrave presented a much-discussed *short-run, partial-equilibrium* study of corporation income tax incidence in 1963.[22] This study considered the influence of the federal corporation income tax on the *rate of return*, using multiple regression analysis and a profit behavior model. Data were tested for the years 1935–59, with the war and early postwar years, 1943–47, excluded. An attempt was made to determine the extent of short-run shifting by comparing the actual behavior revealed by existing data with the behavior that would be indicated by the profit behavior model when the tax determinant is excluded. If successfully implemented, the model would thus isolate the functional relationship between the federal corporation income tax and profit behavior as it influences the rate of return; the other (exogenous) determinants would be separated from this main functional relationship. A correlation between *high* prettax corporate profits (rates of return) and *high* corporate tax rates would thus indicate forward shifting of the tax.

On this basis, these authors conclude that the federal corporation income tax is shifted by more than 100 percent in the short run.[23] That is, for every $1 increment in corporate tax liabilities per unit of capital, pretax corporate profits would increase by $1.34. The authors acknowledge that such a ratio represents some "overstatement" of the extent of shifting, due to the lack of initial correction for factors such as inflation and governmental expenditure effects in the standard, all-manufacturing case they develop. When these forces are considered, however, it is still concluded that a high degree of short-run shifting

---

[22] M. Krzyzaniak and R. A. Musgrave, *The Shifting of the Corporation Income Tax* (Baltimore: Johns Hopkins Press, 1963).

[23] The presence of unrealized profits or gains would be required for forward shifting to exceed 100 percent.

to consumers exists.[24] Needless to say, the policy implications of substantial short-run shifting of the federal corporation income tax would be significant.[25]

A number of studies have challenged the conclusions reached in the Krzyzaniak-Musgrave analysis. Among these are studies by R. Goode, R. E. Slitor, and R. J. Gordon, and one by J. G. Cragg, A. C. Harberger, and P. Mieszkowski.[26] The basic criticism in these reactions to the Krzyzaniak-Musgrave model is that it fails to adequately reflect *aggregate* or *cyclical changes* in the national economy during the period under study (1935–59). This was a period characterized by both depression and prosperity as well as by wartime mobilization (the years 1943–47 related to World War II are excluded from the Krzyzaniak-Musgrave study). Thus, it is argued that the correlation between high corporate tax rates and high pretax corporate profits (rates of return) may be explained by *nontax cyclical variables* rather than by the shifting of the federal corporation income tax. That is, high tax rates are usually associated with periods of economic prosperity and wartime mobilization, for inflation-control reasons. Moreover, corporate profits also tend to be higher during prosperity. Hence, it may be the prosperity rather than successful tax-shifting efforts that causes higher corporate profits to occur when corporate tax rates are high. The critics believe that the Krzyzaniak-Musgrave model did not adequately adjust for this possibility.

The Cragg-Harberger-Mieszkowski study, in order to adjust for the alleged inadequacies of the Krzyzaniak-Musgrave model, introduces a cyclical variable in the form of the *employment rate* and a dummy variable to represent *wartime mobilization* for the years 1941, 1942, 1950, 1951, and 1952—all war-related years covered in the Krzyzaniak-Musgrave study. The results of these adjustments led Cragg et al. to conclude that capital bears approximately 100 percent of the tax. The studies by Goode and Slitor, in an effort to adjust for

---

[24] Moreover, studies by Roskamp and Spencer, using the Krzyzaniak-Musgrave model, indicate 100 percent shifting of the corporation income tax in West Germany and Canada, respectively. K. W. Roskamp, "The Shifting of Taxes on Business Income: The Case of West German Corporations," *National Tax Journal*, September 1965, pp. 247–57; B. G. Spencer, "The Shifting of the Corporation Income Tax in Canada," *Canadian Journal of Economics*, February 1969, pp. 21–34.

[25] See R. J. Gordon, "The Incidence of the Corporation Income Tax in U.S. Manufacturing, 1925–62," *American Economic Review*, September 1967, pp. 731–58, for a list of these important policy implications.

[26] R. Goode, "Rates of Return, Income Shares, and Corporate Tax Incidence," in *Effects of Corporation Income Tax*, ed. M. Krzyzaniak (Detroit: Wayne State University Press, 1966); R. E. Slitor, "Corporate Tax Incidence: Economic Adjustments to Differentials under a Two-Tier Tax Structure," in Krzyzaniak, *Effects of Corporation Income Tax;* Gordon, "Incidence of the Corporation Income Tax"; J. G. Cragg, A. C. Harberger, and P. Mieszkowski, "Empirical Evidence on the Incidence of the Corporation Income Tax," *Journal of Political Economy*, December 1967, pp. 811–21.

aggregate economic conditions, add the ratio of actual to potential GNP to the Krzyzaniak-Musgrave model. None of these studies yields results consistent with the short-run forward shifting conclusion reached in the Krzyzaniak-Musgrave study. However, a subsequent study by R. Dusansky—using a rate-of-return approach and a cyclical variable proxy—estimated 100 percent forward shifting of the tax in the short run.[27]

Other nontax variables which should be considered in relation to the Krzyzaniak-Musgrave study, and which are also relevant to any study of corporation income tax incidence, include those effects exerted by increases in *capital productivity* and by changes in the *capital-output ratio* in firm production functions. For example, the higher pretax return which allows posttax rates of return to remain constant, after higher tax rates are in effect, may be due to an increase in the productivity of capital rather than to tax shifting. Or, under the factor shares approach, a higher pretax share of corporate profits out of total income originating in the corporate sector, after higher corporate income tax rates are in effect, may be due to an increase in the capital/output ratio in the corporate sector.

In terms of methodology, it should be noted that the study by Gordon integrates the rate of return and factor share approaches. Thus, in addition to its point of disagreement with the Krzyzaniak-Musgrave conclusions, it also provides methodological sophistication to the study of corporate income tax incidence by combining the two approaches. In addition, reference should be made to the *production function* approach used by C. A. Hall, which relates changes in the productivity of capital to corporate rates of return, and also to the study by R. W. Kilpatrick, which attempts to establish a positive relationship between *industry concentration* in a market structure sense and the forward shifting of the corporation income tax.[28]

In summary, it may be said that there exists an active interest in the incidence of the corporation income tax, even though the various studies have left unresolved the actual direction of that incidence.[29] Despite the absence of a definitive conclusion from these studies, an a priori position on the short-run incidence of the tax can still be

---

[27] R. Dusansky, "The Short-Run Shifting of the Corporation Income Tax in the United States," *Oxford Economic Papers*, November 1972, pp. 357–71.

[28] C. A. Hall, "Direct Shifting of the Corporation Income Tax in Manufacturing," *American Economic Review*, May 1964, pp. 258–71; R. W. Kilpatrick, "The Short-Run Forward Shifting of the Corporation Income Tax," *Yale Economic Essays*, Fall 1965, pp. 355–420.

[29] For a later version of one part of the corporation income tax incidence controversy, see M. Krzyzaniak and R. A. Musgrave, "Corporation Tax Shifting: A Response," *Journal of Political Economy*, July–August 1970, pp. 768–73, and J. G. Cragg, A. C. Harberger and P. Mieszkowski, "Corporation Tax Shifting: Rejoinder," *Journal of Political Economy*, July–August 1970, pp. 774–77.

adopted. Thus, if one considers the primary tax-shifting criteria developed in Chapter 7, there seems to be a considerable a priori suggestion of possible forward shifting of the corporation income tax. For example, it is certain that imperfect knowledge as well as several other causes, such as the fear of attracting new competitors, lead to the presence of substantial *unrealized profits* or *gains* in American industries. Moreover, predominantly *imperfect market structures,* especially oligopoly at the national level, assure the presence of some degree of individual firm monopoly power over price in many industries. Furthermore, it is known that industry price elasticities of product demand are relatively *inelastic* in many major industries. In addition, the corporation income tax is essentially a *broadbased* tax. All of these characteristics point in the direction of probable forward shifting, in at least the short run, of some, possibly substantial, part of the corporation income tax burden through higher selling prices. Moreover, this does not consider the additional possibility of some backward shifting to labor, especially where labor is nonunionized or weakly unionized. Admittedly, a priori evaluations lack empirical proof. However, it seems appropriate to make such cautious observations in light of the nondefinitive conclusions resulting from the various empirical studies.

Stabilization effects

The federal corporation income tax is an important fiscal tool for use in aggregate economic policy. For example, *discretionary* (ad hoc) budgetary policy directed toward production, employment, price level, balance of payments, and economic growth objectives may be implemented through such corporate income tax devices as (1) a change in corporation income tax rates, (2) the investment credit, (3) accelerated depreciation, and (4) the preferential treatment of domestic international sales corporations (DISCs). Moreover the income-elastic character of the tax lends it some value as an *automatic* countercyclical stabilizer. A full discussion of the application of various stabilization techniques through the federal corporation income tax will be presented in Part Four, which is concerned with the relationship of the public sector to aggregate economic performance.

10

Wealth taxation:
Death and gift taxes

DEATH AND GIFT TAX STRUCTURES

Death and gift taxes are *wealth-transfer taxes*. They differ from sales taxes in that the transference of wealth (property) which constitutes the tax base is not the result of property being exchanged for a market price. Death and gift taxes necessarily complement each other; the latter could provide a means of avoiding the former, unless the two are related to each other in a meaningful fashion. Moreover, a death tax can limit tax avoidance by complementing an income tax which does not tax unrealized capital gains. In general, death and gift taxes apply personal wealth as an indicator of taxpaying ability in reference to the ability-to-pay benchmark of equity in the distribution of tax burdens. Furthermore, the holding of wealth tends to be positively correlated with income in American society.

There are two main varieties of death taxes—the estate tax and the inheritance tax. An *estate tax* uses the entire property which is transferred at death as its tax base. An *inheritance tax* uses a base consisting of only the portion of the property that is received by an individual heir.[1] The estate tax is normally imposed with a progressive (gradu-

---

[1] Property under both the estate and the inheritance taxes is ultimately taxed in a *net* sense, after certain appropriate adjustments of an exemption or credit nature are made.

ated) rate structure. The inheritance tax also normally utilizes progressive rates, but rather than applying them to the total estate, it applies them instead on the basis of (1) the size of the bequest to a particular heir, and (2) the closeness of the relationship between the decedent and the heir. Larger bequests are assessed at higher marginal rates. Moreover, an heir who is a brother or sister of the decedent would normally pay a higher rate of tax on a bequest than would a spouse, and a nonrelative would pay a still higher rate.

A *gift tax* is imposed on property transferred among living people by means other than a market transaction. The tax is normally the obligation of the donor, that is, the person who gives the property. It is not imposed on the donee, or recipient, of the gift. Gift taxes normally utilize progressive rate structures.

The history of federal estate and gift taxes[2]

The federal government has imposed death taxes on estates of decedents intermittently since 1798, but the present estate taxation practice dates from 1916. A sizable segment of Congress viewed the federal estate tax of 1916 as a temporary measure. Competition between states for wealthy residents during the early 1920s, however, provided support for its continuance. Some states had advertised in national publications that immunity from death taxation was provided for in their jurisdictions, and several states had amended their constitutions to guarantee freedom from death taxes to those who established residence within their political boundaries. The Revenue Act of 1926 took an important step toward continuance of the federal estate tax within the federal revenue structure by permitting an 80 percent *credit offset* of federal estate tax liability for death taxes paid to the states. This helped to reduce interstate competition for wealthy residents, since each state could collect death taxes, up to 80 percent of the federal tax liability, without increasing the overall death tax burden. For example, if the federal tax on an estate were $40,000, and no state tax were imposed on the estate, the overall death tax burden would be $40,000, even though the state receives no death tax revenues. However, the state could have collected $32,000 in death tax revenues (80 percent of the $40,000 federal estate tax liability) without increasing the overall (federal plus state) death tax burden, since the 80 percent credit would reduce the federal estate tax liability to $8,000 ($40,000 − $32,000). Thus, any state not levying a death tax up to the limit of the credit would be sacrificing revenues to the federal

---

[2] For an excellent discussion of federal estate and gift tax history, see Advisory Commission on Intergovernmental Relations, *Tax Overlapping in the United States—1964* (Washington, D.C.: U.S. Government Printing Office, 1964), chap. 10.

treasury which it otherwise could realize.[3] The federal tax credit achieved its initial goal of reducing interstate competition for wealthy residents by providing an adequate incentive for increased state government utilization of death taxes.

The first federal gift tax, imposed on the donor of the gift, was levied for two years, 1924 and 1925. In 1932, the federal gift tax was established on a continuous basis. More recent legislation, in 1976, unified the existing federal estate and gift taxes into a single tax structure, effective January 1, 1977.

The present federal estate and gift tax

The present unified estate-gift tax was achieved essentially in the 1976 legislation through three means: (1) the consideration of the passage of property at death as a person's *final gift*, (2) the adoption of a *uniform set of tax rates* for both bequests and gifts, and (3) the introduction of a *uniform (unified) credit* for both bequests at time of death and gifts among the living. Previously, each tax had possessed different tax bases primarily due to different exemption structures. These were replaced by the new uniform credit except for the continuation of an annual $3,000 (now $10,000) gift exclusion per donee. Moreover, each tax previously had its own rate structure though they were related through a common bracket structure. The unified tax is calculated by accumulating all taxable gifts of prior years and adding them to the taxable gifts of the current year. Applying a progressive rate structure, the tax is calculated both on the total of prior years' gifts and the cumulative total through the current year. The current year's liability is the difference between the two taxes. The uniform credit is gradually applied to the taxes so calculated until used up.

The uniform credit,[4] introduced in 1977, was scheduled forward in stages with increasing annual values leading to full implementation by 1981. In 1981, the credit value reached $47,000 and possessed an equivalent exemption value of $175,625.[5] In addition, a new uniform

---

[3] The tax credit technique used by the federal government to help coordinate state death tax activity resembles the approach used in the Social Security Act of 1935 to encourage states to adopt payroll taxes for the unemployment insurance program. See Chapter 13 in this regard.

[4] Other credits against the estate tax include those for state death taxes paid (an effectively reduced version of the 1926 credit), for taxes paid on prior transfers, for foreign death taxes paid, and for death taxes on life tenents in generation-skipping trusts (described later).

[5] A tax credit has a greater tax-saving value than an exemption or deduction of like amount since it constitutes a dollar-for-dollar remission of tax liability after the tax rates have been applied to the tax base, while an exemption or deduction merely reduces the tax base prior to the application of the tax rates to the base. Thus, a smaller credit would need to be matched by a larger exemption or deduction in order to yield the same amount of tax saving.

tax-rate range from 18 to 70 percent was implemented in 1977. There-after, the Economic Recovery Tax Act (ERTA) of 1981 significantly liberalized the uniform credit and significantly lowered the uniform rate structure. Effective in 1982, the credit was raised to $62,800 with an exemption equivalency of $225,000. Moreover, it will increase to $192,800 with a $600,000 exemption equivalency by 1987. The 70 percent maximum marginal tax rate, in turn, is scheduled to be re-duced by 5 percent per year until reaching 50 percent in 1984. The minimum marginal rate will remain at 18 percent. The ERTA of 1981 also increased the annual gift tax exclusion from $3,000 to $10,000 per donee per year. Still further reductions in the estate-gift tax burden were provided by an expansion of the "marital deduction" from 50 percent to 100 percent of the gift or estate, thus making it possible to make a gift or leave the entire estate tax free to one's spouse.

In all, the 1981 legislation virtually eliminated the federal estate-gift as a viable tax source and further reduced its already limited capacity to redistribute wealth as an equity goal. This previous limita-tion stemmed largely from the numerous special tax provisions (pref-erences) which sharply lowered the effective rate progressivity of the tax as compared to its statutorily-progressive rate range.

The *gross estate* for inclusion in the tax base under the federal estate-gift tax refers to the total amount of property which, according to tax law, is deemed to have been transferred by the decedent at death. The *value* of the property may be determined, for tax purposes, either as of the date of death or at a later date, up to six months after death, at the option of the executor of the estate. Gifts made during the decedent's lifetime are also included in the calculation of the tax on the total of lifetime and testamentary transfers. The *net estate tax base* consists of such cumulative "lifetime" and "deathtime" transfers of property, less certain deductions, such as charitable bequests, admin-istrative expenses, funeral expenses, debt claims against the estate properties, and the marital deduction.

State death and gift taxes

The first state death tax—an inheritance tax—was imposed by Pennsylvania in 1825. Subsequently, several other states enacted death taxes. Most of these fell into disuse following the Civil War, but a revival in their importance was initiated by New York in 1885 with its adoption of a 5 percent tax on the transfer of property to collateral heirs. In 1903, Wisconsin adopted an inheritance tax which set a pattern followed by many other states on such matters as progressive rates and central administration. Presently, all states except Nevada impose death taxes.

The majority of state death taxes use the inheritance tax rather than the estate tax form. Moreover, the typical rate structure is progressive. Death taxes can be further classified as summarized in Table 10–1. Thirteen states levy only a *pick-up tax,* which "picks up" the federal credit for the state tax. A combination of inheritance and pick-up taxes is used by 28 states and the District of Columbia. Meanwhile, a combination of estate and pick-up taxes is used by eight states while Nevada, as noted, levies no death tax.

A considerable variation exists among state death tax structures; there are differences in deductions, exemptions, and rates. Rates and exemptions even vary sharply among states that impose the same type of death tax. Among the states with estate taxes, for example, exemptions range from $5,000 to $200,000. Gift taxes are imposed by 12 states, where they are generally integrated with the state death taxes. However, all states with death taxes do not impose gift taxes, despite what would seem to be an open invitation for tax avoidance, because federal gift taxation provides an "umbrella protection" to the states in this matter. In other words, the federal taxation of gifts is sufficient to discourage extensive avoidance of state death taxes by means of lifetime gifts.

FISCAL PERFORMANCE OF DEATH AND GIFT TAXES

The analysis which follows will concentrate primarily on the economic effects of *federal estate-gift taxation,* though it has implications also for state death and gift taxes. The most important economic effects of death and gift taxation are likely to be of an allocational and

TABLE 10–1   Type of state death taxes, July 1, 1980

Type of tax	State
Pick-up tax only	Alabama, Alaska, Arizona, Arkansas, Colorado, Florida, Georgia, Missouri, New Mexico, North Dakota, Utah, Vermont, Virginia
Estate tax and pick-up tax	Massachusetts, Minnesota, Mississippi, New York*, Ohio, Oklahoma*, Rhode Island*, South Carolina*
Inheritance tax and pick-up tax	California*, Connecticut, Delaware*, District of Columbia, Hawaii, Idaho, Illinois, Indiana, Iowa, Kansas, Kentucky, Louisiana*, Maine, Maryland, Michigan, Montana, Nebraska, New Hampshire, New Jersey, North Carolina*, Oregon*, Pennsylvania, South Dakota, Tennessee*, Texas, Washington*, West Virginia, Wisconsin*, Wyoming
No tax	Nevada

* Also has gift tax (12 states).
Source: Advisory Commission on Intergovernmental Relations.

distributional nature. The influence of death and gift taxation on the economic stabilization goal generally tends to be modest. However, economic growth could be significantly influenced in a society where highly progressive death taxes bear heavily on the formation of real productive capital.

Allocational effects

The work-leisure choice. One possible area of allocational non-neutrality is the effect of death taxation on the choice between work and leisure. For example, a progressive death tax may affect a person's decision to stay on the job or to retire, or to work more or to work less, in a manner similar to that of the income tax.[6] On the one hand, the price of leisure in terms of the posttax net estate is reduced by the amount of the marginal rate of tax on the estate. The individual may thus desire to purchase more leisure by retiring or by working less, since leisure is now a comparatively cheaper commodity than work. As a result, the *substitution effect* is adverse to work effort. On the other hand, the *income effect* will encourage work effort if the individual is motivated to work more in order to leave the same posttax amount of wealth to his or her survivors. Since the income effect might lead to greater work effort at a time when the substitution effect would retard it, a determinate answer is not forthcoming.

It is unlikely that the work habits of many people are significantly affected by death taxes, because the contemplation of death taxes is likely to affect only the older segment of the population. Moreover, a substantial proportion of this group will not have a choice concerning the date of retirement, and some of those who do have a choice will enjoy their work and not wish to retire. Hence, the possibility of death taxation affecting the work-leisure choice in a significant manner can be dismissed as being unlikely.

The consumption-saving decision. Another possible allocational effect of progressive death taxes is their influence on the choice between consumption and saving.[7] As with the work-leisure choice, both the substitution effect and the income effect are relevant. By reducing the cost of a dollar of consumption in terms of its estate consequences, the marginal tax rate will have a *substitution effect* favorable to consumption and unfavorable to saving. However, a strong desire to leave a certain amount of property to survivors could lead to an *income effect* which would decrease consumption and increase saving. Again, we are left with an indeterminate answer.

---

[6] See the discussion in Earl R. Rolph and George F. Break, *Public Finance* (New York: Ronald Press Co., 1961), pp. 264–65.

[7] Ibid., pp. 265–66.

It would appear, however, that the overall influence of death taxation on the consumption-saving decision is insignificant, since by the time most people have reached the age when estate considerations bear heavily on their thinking, they will not depart radically from their established modes of living. In addition, it is generally agreed that death taxes have less of an effect on the incentive to save and invest than income taxes do. This is because income taxes reduce the return for effort and risk taking from current income, while death taxes are "postponed" to a later date and are paid by the estate and its beneficiaries rather than by the person who earns the income. However, it is possible that extremely high progressive death tax rates, especially in *effective* rather than in *statutory* terms, could significantly reduce aggregate saving in the economy. Moreover, this allocational effect of reduced saving would likely introduce a serious long-run stabilization effect in the form of reduced economic growth due to insufficient capital formation. Finally, in view of the sizable reduction in the federal estate-gift tax burden brought about by the ERTA of 1981, the allocational nonneutralities discussed above are also likely to be reduced.

Distributional effects

Progressive death taxes have long been advocated in Western society. During the 19th century the famous British economist John Stuart Mill argued for a strict limit on the amount of wealth any individual might receive through inheritance. He thus called for *progressive death taxes.*[8]

Assuming a societal consensus for greater equality in the distribution of wealth, the performance of death and gift taxation in the United States is poor in relationship to this goal. Of course, since the rate structures of the federal estate and gift tax and of state death and gift taxes are typically progressive, some redistribution of wealth in the direction of greater equality can be expected. However, the progressivity of the statutory rate structure of the federal estate–gift tax is sharply reduced by the many special tax preference provisions that, in particular, tend to help higher-wealth categories. In addition, the significant overall tax-burden reductions enacted during 1981 further weaken the redistributional effects of the tax. In fact, as one expert observed:

> ... because estate tax avoidance is such a successful and yet wasteful process, one suspects that the present estate and gift tax (in 1979) serves no purpose other than to give reassurance to the millions of unwealthy

---

[8] John Stuart Mill, *Principles of Political Economy* (New York: Longmans, Green, 1909), book 2.

that entrenched wealth is being attacked. The attack is, however, more cosmetic than real and the economy is paying the price of fettered capital and distorted property ownership for this tax cosmetology. Unless the system can be significantly reformed, consideration should be given to scrapping it or at least replacing it with a more effective means of accomplishing its perceived goals.[9]

The ERTA of 1981 came close to scrapping the tax, but it did not substitute an alternative fiscal means to pursue the wealth redistribution goal.

To the extent that it remains effective, the federal estate–gift tax contributes to distributional equity by helping to close some implicit tax-avoidance loopholes. That is, the estate-gift tax base can include certain items which escape the federal personal income tax base. Interest on state and local government securities, for example, is exempt from the federal personal income tax base, but the value of the securities which earn this interest and the accumulated, unconsumed, interest earnings are includable in the federal estate-gift tax base. In addition, the gift-tax component of the base can serve to control tax avoidance by those who would escape income and death taxes by giving property away.

Despite some small distributional gains in reference to the goal of greater posttax wealth equality, death and gift taxes also yield certain negative distributional effects. For example, the impact of death taxes will depend largely on the amount of legal skill and effort applied to the planning of an estate. Yet, many individuals—for a variety of reasons, including a relative lack of financial capability and early death—do not have an opportunity to minimize death taxes through planning. Moreover, horizontal and vertical tax equity may be violated in federal estate-gift taxation through specific techniques employed in the transfer of property. These include the use of trusts and the providing of gifts to charitable foundations. In fact, trusts have historically been a major moderating force on the effective rate of progressivity of the federal estate tax.

A *trust* is a legal arrangement whereby funds are administered for an individual or organization. Federal tax law permits trusts to pay income to one or more successive generations of heirs, while the property is given ultimately to a still-later generation. For example, a wealthy man may establish a trust at the time of his death naming his wife and children as successive *life tenants* entitled to receive income from the trust, and his grandchildren as the ultimate owners of the property (known as *remaindermen*). When the trust is terminated, the property in the trust legally passes to the remaindermen. However,

---

[9] George Cooper, *A Voluntary Tax? New Perspectives on Sophisticated Estate Tax Avoidance* (Washington, D.C.: Brookings Institution, 1979), p. 82.

the transfer of the property by successive life tenants (such as by the wife to the children and by the children to the grandchildren) was not subject to the estate tax. In fact, an estate (or gift) tax was not paid again unless the remaindermen transfer the property.

Such generation skipping in estate taxation has constituted a major tax avoidance loophole within the structure of the federal estate tax. Moreover, this loophole has been utilized primarily by wealthy individuals capable of transferring large segments of property at the time of death. However, the legislation of 1976, which integrated the then-existing federal estate and gift taxes, also restricted, but did not eliminate, the generation-skipping trust loophole. This was accomplished by imposing a tax on such trusts which is substantially equivalent to the estate-gift tax that would have been imposed if the property had been transferred outright between generations. While the provision of a $250,000 exclusion for transfers to all of the children of each child of the grantor greatly eases the tightening of this provision, nonetheless a potential tightening does occur for very large wealth transfers in excess of the exclusion amount.

Stabilization effects

Wealth-transfer taxes such as death and gift taxes are not conducive to the realization of aggregate economic policy. Their inherent nature, which largely removes them from current income-earning and transactions activities, precludes their effective application as either automatic or discretionary fiscal stabilizers. This is true despite the fact that national governments utilize these taxes, and central government is the most efficient point of departure for aggregate economic policy. The only major application of these taxes to macroeconomic performance would appear to come not in the direct policy sense but, instead, in the indirect sense of avoiding extremely progressive wealth-transfer taxes that would endanger long-run capital formation, and thus would restrict economic growth.

Death and gift taxes were reliable, but extremely modest, revenue producers for the American public sector even before the ERTA of 1981. Their long-run revenue reliability is suggested by an estimated income elasticity, for state governments, of 1.2 ($Y_t = 1.2$).[10] However, they yielded only slightly more than 1 percent of the tax revenues of the federal government, and also of the states, in fiscal year 1979. Indeed, the primary justification for wealth-transfer taxes cannot be found in the direction of allocation, stabilization, or revenue productivity objectives. Instead, it falls, though very modestly, within the realm of distributional policy.

---

[10] See Selma J. Mushkin and Gabrielle C. Lupo, "Project 70: Projecting the State-Local Sector," *Review of Economics and Statistics*, May 1967, p. 243.

11

Wealth taxation:
The property tax

HISTORY OF THE PROPERTY TAX

The property tax dates from the colonial period in the United States and from at least as far back as the feudal period in Europe. Historically, the property tax has been used in one form or another by all levels of government in this nation, but primary usage has been reserved for state and local units of government. In the 20th century state governments have sharply reduced their reliance on property taxation and have turned to other tax sources such as sales and income taxes. The states derive only 1.5 percent of their total tax revenues from property taxes at the present time, as compared to more than 50 percent at the beginning of the century. Meanwhile, local governments continue to rely heavily on property taxation, though to a diminishing extent, as indicated by the fact that 74 percent of their total tax revenues presently come from this source.

The nature of the property tax in the United States has changed considerably during its more than 200 years of usage.[1] Initially, it was largely a *classified* (or differentiated, or selective) tax imposed on specified classes of wealth. Then, over a period of some 100 years, the tax gradually evolved toward the status of a *general* property tax, applying broadly to most or all classes of real and personal property.

---

[1] Jesse Burkhead, *State and Local Taxes for Public Education* (Syracuse, N.Y.: Syracuse University Press, 1963), p. 20.

Since the Civil War this trend has been reversed, however, and the tax base has been gradually narrowed so that classified property taxes have tended, once again, to replace the general tax. The states have exempted some classes of property by constitutional amendment or statute. Moreover, personal property, both tangible and intangible, has been increasingly excluded from the tax base—if not by specific exemption, then by the implicit action of assessors who have difficulty discovering this type of property. In addition, differential tax rates have been applied to various types of property in some states.

PRESENT STATUS OF THE PROPERTY TAX IN THE UNITED STATES

The property tax base

The American property tax is an impersonal (in rem) tax. It is *not* a personal wealth tax, which would consider the total net wealth of the taxpayer as the tax base.[2] There is considerable variation among the property tax bases of the many units of state and local government using the tax in the United States. In other words, there is no single nationwide system of property taxation. Instead, there are many different systems in the 50 states and the District of Columbia. Moreover, there are differential procedures for imposing the tax within each state, because much of the administration of the tax is performed at the local level of government by numerous counties, cities, and special districts. Nonetheless, there is a meaningful similarity among the various property taxes in the sense that the property tax, as employed within the U.S. public sector, tends to be a classified or differentiated property tax rather than a general property tax. Moreover, as observed earlier, it is in all cases an impersonal wealth tax.

A *general property tax,* in the pure or complete sense, would be imposed on all classes or types of property in an identical manner, regardless of the nature of the property or the circumstances of its ownership or use.[3] Regarding the nature of the property, a general property tax may be classified into two major categories: realty, known as real property, and personalty, known as personal property. *Realty* may be further classified into *land* and *improvements* segments. *Per-*

---

[2] The personal wealth (net worth, net wealth) tax is described and evaluated in Chapter 14.

[3] In reality, it is the *degree of differentiation* which distinguishes a classified from a general property tax, since neither a "completely comprehensive" nor a "completely differentiated" property tax is feasible. Unfortunately, there is no general agreement as to the particular degree of differentiation which may serve as the demarcation line between a classified and general property tax.

sonalty may be further classified into *tangible* and *intangible* segments. Table 11–1 lists these classifications and subclassifications and gives examples of each class or type of property.

A general property tax can be converted into a *classified property tax* through a variety of differentiating techniques. Differentiation can be achieved by:

1. The partial or complete exemption of a certain class or classes of property. For example, intangible personal property, such as stocks and bonds, may be exempt from the base of the tax.
2. Consideration of the circumstances surrounding the ownership of the property. For example, property owned by veterans, widows, or nonprofit religious, educational, and charitable institutions may be partially or totally excluded from the base of the tax.
3. Application of differential ratios of assessed value to market value, depending on the use of the property. For example, business property may be assessed at 40 percent of its market value, while residential property may be assessed at 20 percent of market value.
4. Application of different tax rates to different properties, depending on their class or use. For example, a rate of $2 per $100 of assessed valuation may be imposed on realty and a rate of $1 per $100 of assessed valuation on personality.

The first three techniques classify or differentiate the property tax by affecting the *base* of the tax, while the fourth technique directly affects the *rate* structure of the tax. Nonetheless, all four techniques tend to convert a general into a classified property tax. Moroever, each of the four techniques is used in at least one state, and many states employ a combination of two or more of them.

Typically, the property tax base is predicated on the ownership of property, regardless of any liens that may exist against it, and is

---

TABLE 11–1   Property classifications for tax purposes

Realty (real property)	Personality (personal property)
A. Land	A. Tangible
1. Farm	1. Farm machinery
2. Residential	2. Furniture
3. Commercial	3. Merchandise (business inventories)
4. Forest	4. Motor vehicles
B. Improvements	B. Intangible
1. Farm buildings	1. Stocks
2. Homes or residences	2. Bonds
3. Business buildings	3. Mortgages
4. Fences, sidewalks, etc.	4. Bank deposits

measured in monetary terms. In several states, the tax base consists exclusively of realty. In the remaining states, the tax is imposed on varying combinations of both realty and personalty, though intangible personalty is often exempt, and the important tangible personalty category of motor vehicles produces revenues separately through motor vehicle license fees. Moreover, not only is realty of dominant importance in the American property tax base, the tax is also characterized by the considerable importance of property used for housing. These two facts are indicated by the data in Table 11-2, which shows property tax revenues by source in 1977. It may be observed that realty in households (for housing) produced 48.6 percent of total property tax revenues in that year, realty in business firms produced another 18.7 percent, and vacant lots yielded 3.1 percent (total = 70.4 percent). This does not include the revenues produced by public utilities and acreage and farms, much of which came from property in the form of realty. In the meantime, including revenues from personalty, along with those from realty, households produced 52.7 percent of all property tax revenues. Thus, a descriptive profile of the American property tax base would point to the dominance of realty and housing in the aggregate tax base.

TABLE 11-2   Estimated property tax revenues by source, 1977

Source	Amount (millions)	Percentage distribution
Households* (total)	$32,982	52.7%
Realty‡	30,447	48.6
Personalty‡	2,535	4.1
Businesses* (total)	21,642	34.6
Realty§	11,672	18.7
Personalty‖	6,405	10.2
Public Utilities	3,565	5.7
Acreage and farms	5,973	9.6
Vacant lots	1,938	3.1
Grand total	62,535	100.0

* Excluding acreage and farms, and vacant lots.

† Includes both single-family dwelling units and apartments. In 1977, an estimated $26 billion or 41 percent of all property tax revenue was derived from single-family homes; about $5 billion or 8 percent from multifamily units.

‡ The collections produced through the taxation of furniture and other household effects and from the property tax on motor vehicles and intangibles.

§ Commercial and industrial real estate, other than public utilities.

‖ Collections from the taxation of merchants' and manufacturers' inventories, tools, and machinery, and so on (other than public utilities).

Source: Advisory Commission on Intergovernmental Relations.

The property tax rate structure

The property tax is shared by two levels of American government—state and local. The latter includes county, municipal, school district, road district, and other special district governments. Hence, the owner of property typically pays *several different property taxes,* levied on the same tax base. In some instances, the property tax rate is *limited* explicitly by constitution or statute, or implicitly by popular tax consciousness which attaches great importance to holding down the rate. Under such circumstances, pressure for additional revenues is likely to find an outlet in increased assessment levels, unless the property tax payment is limited as a proportion of the market value of the property as in the Jarvis-Gann Amendment to the California State Constitution (Proposition 13), approved by voters in June 1978.[4] Also, the availability of other revenue sources, such as federal or state grants to local government or the use of nonproperty taxes such as general sales and income taxes, can help to reduce the amount of revenue that must be raised through the property tax. With all nonproperty revenue factors taken into account, the decision then turns on the expenditures required for desired services as weighed against the requirements such expenditures place on the property tax rate. As one expert comments, "this judgment reflects the socio-economic variables—income, attitudes toward government, elements of strategy, bargaining, and conflict—that characterize public sector decisions."[5]

At this point, a distinction should be made between nominal (statutory, mill) and effective property tax rates. The *nominal* rate is the annual tax liability assigned to the property expressed as a percentage of the *taxable assessed value* of the property (the value of the property for tax purposes—which is usually less than its market value). The *effective* rate, on the other hand, is the annual tax liability assigned to the property expressed as a percentage of the *estimated market value* of the property. Table 11–3 provides an example of this distinction and demonstrates other relevant concepts.[6]

Because of substantial interstate variation in the ratios of the taxable assessed value of property expressed as a percentage of market value, nominal rates cannot be compared among states in a meaningful fashion. However, valid interstate property tax comparisons can be

---

[4] See the additional discussion of this amendment in Chapter 4.

[5] Burkhead, *State and Local Taxes for Public Education,* p. 23.

[6] As an alternative to the effective property tax rate, the reader may wish to think in terms of a *real mill rate,* which can be expressed by the ratio: Property tax liability/$1,000 of market value. Using the example presented in Table 11–3, the "real mill rate" would be 15/1,000, or $15 per $1,000 of market value.

TABLE 11-3   Example of distinction between nominal (statutory) and effective property tax rates

a.	Market value of property	= $100,000
b.	Gross assessed value of property	= 30,000
	Assessment ratio ($b \div a$) = 30 percent	
c.	Exemptions (such as homestead or home ownership and veterans' exemptions)	= 5,000
d.	Taxable assessed value of property ($b - c$)	= 25,000
e.	Annual property tax liability	
		= 1,500

Nominal tax rate ($e \div d$) = 6 percent
Effective tax rate ($e \div a$) = 1.5 percent

made by relating the property tax liability in a state to the market value of the property taxed in the state. This constitutes, of course, the effective property tax rate concept defined earlier. Table 11-4 provides estimates of such average effective property tax rates on existing single-family homes with FHA-insured mortgages in the 50 states for selected years from 1975 to 1980. It can be observed that in 1980 the effective rates varied widely, from a low of 0.26 percent in Louisiana to a high of 2.75 percent in New York. The overall average effective property tax rate on such single-family homes for the nation in 1980 was 1.28 percent. It is interesting to note the decline in such effective property tax rates on single-family dwellings during the latter half of the 1970s, and especially after California's ratification of Proposition 13 in 1978—an action which prompted similar property tax-burden reductions across the nation.

Property tax administration

Administration of the property tax consists of the threefold tasks of assessment, rate setting, and collection.

Assessment.   The first of these three functions, assessment, involves the discovery and evaluation of the property subject to tax. Discovery of realty such as land and buildings is relatively easy; discovery of personal property is much more difficult. In most states, the taxable value of railroad and public utility property is determined by the central tax agency of the state. Usually this agency will arrive at a unit value on the entire operating property of the railroad or public utility company, and then distribute the total valuation on some equitable basis among the taxing jurisdictions within which the properties of the company are located. The state agency in some states, in addition, appraises other types of specialized business property such as mines and business inventories.

TABLE 11-4   Average effective† property tax rates, existing single family homes with FHA-insured mortgages, by state and region, selected years 1975–1980

State and region	1980	1977	1975‡	State and region	1980	1977	1975‡
United States	1.28	1.67	1.89	Southeast:			
				Virginia	1.26	1.21	1.32
New England:				West Virginia	0.43	n.a.	0.78
Maine	1.25§	1.65	1.86	Kentucky	1.19	1.25	1.23
New Hampshire	1.73‖	n.a.	(2.38)	Tennessee	1.27	1.40	1.31
Vermont	1.60#	n.a.	(2.21)	North Carolina	0.95	1.35	1.51
Massachusetts	2.51	3.50	3.26	South Carolina	0.81	0.82	1.07
Rhode Island	1.93	n.a.	(2.27)	Georgia	1.24	1.27	1.33
Connecticut	1.55	2.17	1.94	Florida	1.02	1.13	1.18
				Alabama	0.56	0.74	0.75
Mideast:				Mississippi	0.93	1.10	1.12
New York	2.75	2.89	2.56	Louisiana	0.26	0.61	0.64
New Jersey	2.60	3.31	3.15	Arkansas	1.53	1.49	1.41
Pennsylvania	1.57	1.85	1.71				
Delaware	0.85	0.88	0.92	Southwest:			
Maryland	1.61	1.69	2.01	Oklahoma	0.91	0.95	1.27
Dist. of Columbia	1.30	n.a.	1.78	Texas	1.57	1.84	2.06
				New Mexico	1.12	1.65	1.56
Great Lakes:				Arizona	1.16	1.72	1.54
Michigan	2.54	2.63	2.38				
Ohio	1.08	1.26	1.29	Rocky Mountain:			
Indiana	1.19	1.66	1.64	Montana	1.11	1.31	1.60
Illinois	1.50	1.90	2.21	Idaho	0.96	1.46	1.86
Wisconsin	1.67	2.22	2.63	Wyoming	0.50	0.87	1.12
				Colorado	1.05	1.80	1.99
Plains:				Utah	1.02	1.03	1.20
Minnesota	0.93	1.39	1.58				
Iowa	1.48	1.76	2.20	Far West:			
Missouri	1.00	1.59	1.85	Washington	1.06	1.75	1.86
North Dakota	1.00	1.26	1.53	Oregon	1.72	2.25	2.18
South Dakota	1.70	1.79	2.14	Nevada	1.22	1.71	1.53
Nebraska	2.37	2.48	2.50	California	0.98	2.21	2.08
Kansas	0.94	1.37	1.55	Alaska	1.35	n.a.	1.73
				Hawaii	0.42	n.a.	(0.95)

Note: These effective rates are for existing FHA-insured mortgages only, which represent small and varying percentages (by state) of total single-family homes. These rates may or may not be representative of the rates applicable to all homes in a particular state. The United States average tax rate for 1980 (1.28) indicates that, on average, the property tax on a home with a market value of $100,000 would be $1,280.

n.a. = Data not available.

† Effective property tax rates are computed by dividing the annual property tax liability by the market value of the taxed property.

‡ Figures in parenthesis are for 1974, data for 1975 not available.

§ Fourth quarter of 1977, increased to 1980 on the basis of the U.S. average percentage change.

‖ ACIR staff estimates based on 1974 (latest year readily available), increased to 1980 on the basis of the U.S. average percentage change (75 percent) and the 1977 Census of Government's, "Taxable Property Values and Assessment/Sales Price Ratios" (25 percent).

ACIR staff estimates based on 1974 (latest year readily available), increased to 1980 on the basis of the U.S. average percentage change.

Source: Advisory Commission on Intergovernmental Relations.

Local assessors determine the vast majority of the taxable assessed value of property. Typically, local assessors are selected through either election or appointment by elected government officials. There is considerable interstate variation in local assessment organization. In a majority of states, the county is the primary assessing jurisdiction, while in others, hundreds of cities, villages, and townships use assessors to discover and evaluate the property subject to tax. In a few states, the primary assessment function is undertaken by state-employed assessors. All other states influence the administration of the tax by determining how the assessment and collection machinery is organized, including the division of responsibility between state and local government officials. Some states with efficient state tax agencies provide considerable direct assistance and guidance to local officials, but in others the quality of administrative guidance leaves much to be desired.

Ordinarily, property is assessed at a value less than its current market or sales value. This policy, of course, cannot be defended on logical grounds. Lower assessment levels simply mean that tax rates must be higher in order to provide the same revenue yield. Clearly, the tax liability to the taxpayer would be unchanged, for example, if property tax rates were lowered by one half while the assessed value of the property was doubled in amount. The administrators of some local units of government, such as counties, may deliberately evaluate property within their jurisdictions at lower ratios of market value than the ratios used by other counties, in order to lower their shares of state property tax collections. This is referred to as *competitive underassessment;* it can be controlled only by an effective state tax agency which will *equalize the assessment ratios* used by the local units of government within the state. Efficient enforcement procedure also entails the need for an adequate system of local review to equalize assessments of particular parcels of property within a given classification, in accordance with the applicable property tax law. Many of the abuses attributed to the property tax arise because of inadequate assessment procedures, particularly inadequate equalization procedures, among different parcels of property of the same class or use. The state laws are clear—assessments must be uniform within the same class or use of property. The 14th Amendment to the Constitution stipulates, moreover, that fair treatment must be provided in the apportionment of the tax burden. Yet, review and equalization procedures are sometimes ineffective.

Rate setting.   First, a government must determine the amount of its planned expenditures. Next, it must determine the amount of revenues available from nonproperty taxes and other sources. The residual amount which then remains is to be financed by the property tax. This amount is divided by the total assessed valuation of all taxable property in the jurisdiction in order to determine the nominal rate to be applied to the taxable property.[7] This rate may be expressed either as a percentage (see Table 11–3), or as so many dollars of tax per $100 or per $1,000 of assessed valuation. If the amount to be financed

---

[7] Unless rate differentiation exists in the form of applying different tax rates to different properties on the basis of their class or use.

is $4 million, for example, and the assessed valuation is $400 million, the tax rate is equal to 1 percent, or $10 per $1,000 of assessed valuation. It should be noted that there are numerous state-imposed constitutional and statutory restrictions on local government property tax revenue-raising power, however.

Collection. Once the tax rate is set, the assessment roll which lists the assessed valuation of each parcel of taxable property in the jurisdiction is provided to the tax collector. Collection officials then multiply the assessed valuation of each parcel of property by the tax rate in order to determine the tax liability attached to the parcel. In some states, property tax collection is exclusively a function of the county, and the county collector bills the taxes for all other jurisdictions within it, such as municipalities and school districts. Certain other states provide for centralized county collection, but allow cities to collect their own property taxes, with the option of contracting with the county for tax-collection services.

Delinquent property taxes require the imposition of penalties. Normally, a monetary penalty is imposed immediately after the tax payment becomes delinquent. In addition, interest charges at the legal rate are imposed on unpaid taxes for as long as they remain unpaid. In most states, if the tax is unpaid for a specified period, the government may foreclose on the tax lien and assume the property, in essentially the same manner that a private mortgageholder can foreclose if the debtor fails to meet payment obligations. The government later may sell the tax lien. If not redeemed, the purchaser can procure a deed, normally referred to as a *tax deed* or *treasurer's deed,* after a specified period of time.

Table 11–5 summarizes the various steps of property tax administration—assessment, rate setting, and collection—which have been described.

Site-value taxation

The famous 19th-century British economist, David Ricardo, noted that a tax on the "nonreproducible properties of the soil" is a tax on *economic rent* and, thus, cannot be shifted forward through a higher selling price. This would be true because land at any given location is fixed (constant) in supply (see curve S in Figure 11–1) and, yet, supply would have to be reduced in order to shift a tax forward through a higher selling price.

Later, Henry George, in his well known book, *Progress and Poverty* (written in 1879), applied the Ricardian analysis to *urban land.* It was suggested that the economic rent or *site value* of urban land could be taxed without creating "direct" allocational nonneutralities, since the supply of land at a given urban location cannot be changed in

TABLE 11-5   **Example of the determination of local government property tax revenue from realty (real property)**

1982	assessment roll
+	New taxable construction
−	Demolition of taxable property
=	Physical roll
±	Revaluations induced by:
	Market forces
	Public policy
=	1983 assessment roll
1983	expenditure requirements
−	Nonproperty tax revenue plus federal and state aid
=	Property tax requirements for revenue
÷	1983 assessment roll
=	1983 tax rate (frequently subject to legal limitations)
+	Special district assessments
=	Nominal (mill) tax rate for specific properties
1983	assessment roll × 1983 tax rate = 1983 tax levy
	(potential property tax yield)
−	Delinquencies
=	1983 property tax collections (actual property tax yield)

Source: Adapted from Jesse Burkhead, *State and Local Taxes for Public Education,* Economics and Politics of Public Education Series, vol. 7 (Syracuse, N.Y.: Syracuse University Press, 1963), Figure 1, p. 21.

FIGURE 11-1   **Example of site-value taxation**

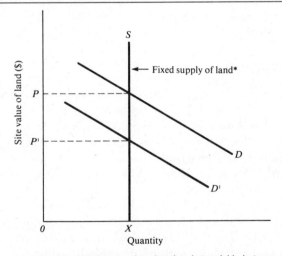

* Fixed in quantity at a given location, but variable in terms of alternative uses at that location.

response to the imposition of a tax. Thus, such a tax would be optimally efficient in the sense of *perfect allocational neutrality*. On the other hand, it was argued that the taxation of reproducible improvements (for example, buildings) should not take place because direct allocational nonneutralities would be likely to result from such a tax. However, it should be pointed out that even though land itself cannot be changed in quantity at a given location, the use of land can be changed and, in this sense, a tax on land might "indirectly" create an allocational nonneutrality or substitution effect.

The Georgian argument also emphasizes that the site value of land is determined exclusively by societal economic forces, which impute different degrees of importance to land at different locations. As a result, two identical parcels of land at different locations may have considerably different site values, depending on the locational importance placed on the land by the societal economic forces. Thus, in Figure 11–1, demand curve D represents a higher locational value for land than does demand curve D^1, with a resulting higher site value—OP as compared to OP^1. Moreover, it is argued that the higher tax amount paid on the higher site value is justified because society as a whole, not individual labor effort, has created this greater value. In a related manner, it is contended that economic rent (site value), being an unearned value created by society, serves as an appropriate basis for distributional equity in taxation. The proposed *site-value tax*, with its alleged allocational and distributional merits, became known as the *single tax on land* during the late 1800s, since it allegedly could have provided all of the tax revenue required by the American public sector at that time.

Economic rent or site value should not be confused with the *net income* from land. *Idle land*, for example, creates no net income, but it still would have a market value (or site value, or economic rent). In addition, *land in use* may be poorly managed and yield no net income, yet such land would have a market value. A practical disadvantage of site-value taxation involves the difficulty of distinguishing the *land rent* from the *business rent:* In other words, how much of the value is derived from the site or location value, and how much from reproducible assets and entrepreneurial expertise? Moreover, in order to be equitable, the tax should be applied when land is first acquired. Otherwise, unearned wealth is diffused through the purchase and sale of property and also through inheritance.

A concerted effort was made to introduce the single-tax notion into the public sector of the United States during the latter years of the 19th century. This effort met with only limited success, but its basic concept lives on today in those who advocate differentially higher property taxes on land as compared to improvements. This is especially tied, at the present time, to the problem of *urban sprawl,* which is encouraged by the considerably heavier taxation of improvements as compared to undeveloped land under the American property tax. Thus, a tax incentive exists for the owner of land *not* to develop it in growing urban areas, so as to minimize taxes and maximize land value appreciation.

FISCAL PERFORMANCE OF THE PROPERTY TAX

Allocational effects

The property tax and intergovernmental nonneutrality. Many instances of intergovernmental nonneutral effects resulting from property taxation could be cited. The fact that the tax is not a uniform national tax but, instead, is disaggregated across many state and local government jurisdictions helps lead to many nonneutralities. The Advisory Commission on Intergovernmental Relations, for example, observes that several negative nonneutralities result from the use of constitutional or statutory property tax *rate limitations*.[8] The Commission suggests that while property tax restrictions initially may have had some influence in limiting tax rates, local governments have managed to increase their property tax revenues in the long run by other means. Meanwhile, the negative allocational distortions placed on the structural and fiscal operations of local governments have been substantial. Property tax rate limitations, for example, have stimulated the creation of special assessment districts for the primary purpose of gaining additional taxing authority. This has caused a distortion by needlessly adding to the proliferation of local governments—some without rational economic and political justification. In addition, financial distortions have been introduced in the sense that rate limitations have made necessary the use of short-term debt financing in order to meet operating deficits. Such debt ultimately has to be funded. The rate limitations, furthermore, have encouraged long-term borrowing for activities which may have been financed more efficiently from current revenues.

Influence of the property tax on residential and industrial location. The property tax can also influence allocational efficiency through its effects on residential and industrial location. For example, persons in metropolitan areas may *select their residence* on the basis of property tax differentials. While this may lead to greater efficiency through individual choice, as discussed in relation to the concept of spatial mobility in Chapter 3, it may also lead to inefficient choices in

---

[8] See the Advisory Commission on Intergovernmental Relations, *State Constitutional and Statutory Restrictions on Local Taxing Powers* (Washington, D.C.: U.S. Government Printing Office, 1962).

the face of imperfect information. For example, an individual may select a residential location on the basis of tax liability disparities rather than on differences in the quantity and quality of governmental services in the various political jurisdictions. The property tax, moreover, is increasingly becoming a tax on improvements to real estate. As such, it tends to discourage investment in heavily taxed real estate improvements and to encourage the speculative purchase of lower-taxed, unimproved, land—a point made under the discussion of site-value taxation and urban sprawl. Such distorted behavior may exert significant effects in rapidly growing communities, where it can result in the existence of large tracts of unimproved land within the metro-politan community, making necessary additional miles of streets; gas, electric, and telephone lines; extensive areas of police and fire protection; and increased commuting costs and travel time. This is an out-standing case of a negative allocative nonneutrality resulting from the structure of the property tax with its heavy emphasis on the taxation of improved realty.

Moreover, property tax differentials are increasingly being used by state and local governments to *induce industry* to locate within their political jurisdictions. Two basic approaches are undertaken in this regard. One, which is quite direct, is simply to *exempt* the property of the invited industrial firm from state and/or local property taxes. The exemption may be either partial or complete. Normally, the exemption is for a specified period of time. The second approach involves the sale of *industrial development bonds* by a state or local unit of government. These bonds provide funds for the acquisition of land and the construction of plant facilities, which are usually exempt from state and local property taxes since they are governmentally owned and only leased to the private firms. Under either approach, non-neutral effects (distortions) are introduced into the selection of business sites and patterns of allocative behavior are thus influenced. These allocational nonneutralities may be either positive or negative, depending on whether they attract resources to a location of greater or lesser production efficiency than would have prevailed in the absence of the property tax inducement. The allocational distortions are further intensified by the fact that interest earned on the state and local bonds used to finance the industrial complex is exempt from the federal[9] personal and corporation income taxes and, frequently, from state income taxes as well. Hence, the financing is accomplished at a lower cost than the firm could have acquired by itself. Moreover, if the company buys a part of the new bond issue, it receives tax-free income from what amounts to an investment in itself. Despite the possible

---

[9] Since 1968, however, there have been restrictions on the amount of such bonds qualifying for the interest exemption. See the *Internal Revenue Code,* Sec. 103(b).

negative nonneutralities that can result from such industry attraction efforts, it should be noted that other variables such as the availability of labor and the level of wage rates may often play a more important role than tax inducements in the decision of a business on where to locate.

General versus classified property taxes and allocational nonneutralities. A general property tax equally applied to all assets will reduce the expected income from each asset and thereby tend to reduce the overall capitalized values of capital assets in general. A general property tax, moreover, tends to discriminate against income from nonhuman sources, such as capital equipment, as opposed to income derived from human sources through the labor factor of production, since the latter is not included in the property tax base.

A classified (selective) property tax, in contrast, will produce differential results, depending on the pattern of selectivity. The present de facto exemption of intangible personal property, for example, tends to encourage some individuals to hold their wealth in this form rather than to invest it in property that is includable in the property tax base. In addition, the homestead exemption, combined with federal income tax deductions for interest payments and for property taxes, has encouraged owner-occupied housing, though admittedly the exemption of certain other types of property from the tax tends to increase the overall tax burden on buildings. Another noteworthy differentiation under the property tax is the exemption typically granted to the property of nonprofit religious, educational, and charitable organizations. This exemption tends to encourage the holding of property by such institutions more than by profit-oriented institutions. However, such allocational effects may be accepted by society because of the social objectives that can be pursued through this type of exemption.

Distributional effects

The ability-to-pay principle: Traditional viewpoint. In reference to the ability-to-pay principle, the property tax is considered to be regressive in that it takes a higher proportion of income from lower-income taxpayers than it does from higher-income taxpayers. This conclusion is based on the following points:

1. A definition of income in current or present terms rather than a permanent or lifetime connotation.[10]

---

[10] *Present-income* data consist of data from a cross-sectional, vertical cut across income classes, from high- to low-income, using data from a short period of time such as one year. On the other hand, *permanent-* or *lifetime-income* data would consist of time-series data over a large number of consecutive years. The latter data are the more difficult to obtain in sufficient sample size to be empirically useful.

2. The related facts that the property tax falls heavily on owner-occupied residential and rental housing, while housing expenditures, both owner-occupied and rental, tend to represent a greater proportion of income for lower-income than for higher-income taxpayers.
3. The assumption that landlords shift the property tax on improvements (buildings) in rental housing forward to tenants, via higher rents.[11]
4. The assumption that the business property tax on improvements (buildings) is shifted forward to consumers via higher product prices.

Thus, since the tax on both the land and improvements segments of owner-occupied dwellings is borne by the consumer of housing, as is the tax on the improvements segment of rental housing if the tax is forward shifted, the fact that the housing consumption/income ratio declines as income increases renders the property tax on housing regressive. Moreover, the forward shifting of the tax on improved business realty to consumers would accentuate this regressivity because consumption as a whole is a diminishing function of increasing income (under a current or present definition of income).

In addition, it should be noted that wealth in itself does not reflect an immediate monetary capacity, in terms of liquidity, to pay the tax. Property such as vacant lots, for example, may have present value in a tax assessment sense, but may not yield income until some future date. Moreover, the ownership of a particular parcel of property does not necessarily indicate the overall taxpaying ability of the property owner in a *total wealth* sense.[12] Furthermore, the value of a particular item of property does not necessarily correlate with the *income* measure of taxpaying ability. For example, elderly people on fixed incomes may own properties which have appreciated in value during periods of sustained inflation, so that they are assessed at high values, but there may be no corresponding increment in the owner's ability to pay property taxes in an income sense due to the retirement of the owner. Or, two businesses may have properties assessed at identical values, but one business may be profitable while the other is operating at a loss. Hence, the assessed value of property fails to serve as an

---

[11] The tax on land, as opposed to improvements, is assumed to remain on the property owner—whether business, owner-occupier of residence, or landland—due to the perfectly inelastic supply of land at a given location (see the discussion prior of site-value taxation).

[12] This problem would be eliminated if the tax used a "net personal wealth" base, which would take into account the total personal wealth of the taxpayer net of claims against that of wealth. Such a tax, known as a *personal wealth (net worth, net wealth)* tax, will be described in Chapter 14.

accurate indicator of the ability to pay taxes in relationship to an income measure of ability.

Further deterioration of distributional equity results from the many problems associated with the *administration* of the property tax. This is particularly true in jurisdictions where higher-value property is assessed at a lower percentage of market value than is lower-value property. Inflation, combined with poor administration, may also introduce inequities into the distribution-of-property tax burdens, because tax officials often fail to adjust the property tax base in a manner consistent with changing property values. For example, an assessor may increase the tax roll by adding new construction, while at the same time failing to adjust the valuation of old property for inflation. Hence, the ratio of assessed value to market value may vary significantly among properties of different ages. In addition to creating residential inequities, this can also lead to serious competitive distortions among businesses.

As observed earlier, the traditional conclusion of property tax regressivity rests, in part, on certain incidence assumptions: Property taxes imposed on capital (improvements) in both business and rental housing are shifted forward to consumers of business products and to tenants, respectively.

Table 11–6 sheds additional light on this subject by demonstrating the distribution of property tax burdens in the United States by income class on the basis of three alternative incidence assumptions:

1. Column 1 assumes that the property tax on improvements (mainly buildings) is borne exclusively by their owners (capital). This is assumed to be true for business, rental housing, and owner-occupied dwellings. Thus, since property taxes on land are assumed to be nonshiftable, capital bears the entire property tax burden (on both land and improvements) under this assumption.
2. Column 3 assumes that the property tax on improvements in business and in rental housing is fully shifted forward to consumers and renters, respectively.
3. Column 2 takes an intermediate position and assumes that businesses and landlords partly absorb (one half), and partly shift forward (one half) the property tax on improvements.

Column 3, which represents the traditional viewpoint, shows the tax on improvements to be regressive throughout the entire range of incomes. However, if the tax is assumed to be borne entirely by capital, as shown in Column 1, the burden distribution is U-shaped, with the tax being regressive on incomes up to $15,000. Moreover, the intermediate assumptions, as shown in Column 2, also exhibit a U-shaped result; progressivity, of a generally smaller magnitude than in Column 1, becomes effective at the higher $20,000 income level. It is

TABLE 11-6   Incidence of the property tax under alternative assumptions, 1972

	Property tax burden as percentage of income, assuming tax on improvements is borne by:		
	(1) Capital only*	*(2)* Intermediate case	*(3)* Renters and consumers only†
Income class			
$ 0– 2,999	7.2	10.1	13.0
3,000– 4,999	5.4	6.7	8.0
5,000– 9,999	3.6	4.8	5.9
10,000– 14,999	2.6	3.8	4.9
15,000– 19,999	2.9	3.8	4.7
20,000– 24,999	3.7	4.1	4.4
25,000– 49,999	5.7	5.1	4.4
50,000– 99,999	14.1	8.9	3.7
100,000–499,999	22.4	13.0	3.5
500,000–999,999	24.5	13.8	3.0
1,000,000 and over	18.2	10.2	2.1
All incomes	5.0	5.0	5.0

Note: Property taxes include all levies by state and local governments on automobiles; livestock; commercial, industrial, and residential property; and so on. *Income is equal to the sum of federal adjusted gross income, transfer payments, state and local government bond interest and long-term capital gains excluded from federal income taxation.* The tax on land is distributed on the basis of income from capital under all sets of assumptions. (The exclusion of imputed income from owner-occupied homes from the definition of income somewhat overstates the estimated progressivity of the tax in Columns (1) and (2). Imputations in the national income accounts for interest, net rent, and proprietors' income associated with owner-occupied homes amount to some 18 percent of total proprietors' income, rents, dividends, and interest.)

* Property taxes other than levies on nonfarm motor vehicles and agricultural property are distributed on the basis of total property income; the tax on cars is distributed using the value of cars owned by the family; and agricultural taxes are distributed on the basis of gross farm value.

† It is assumed that the tax on owner-occupied homes falls on the owner-occupier and that the tax on apartments rests on tenants in proportion to rents paid. The tax on commercial and industrial improvements is allocated on the basis of general consumption, and the tax on farm improvements is allocated among farmers and consumers in general.

Source: Advisory Commission on Intergovernmental Relations, *Financing Schools and Property Tax Relief* (Washington, D.C.: U.S. Government Printing Office, January 1973), Table 13, p. 34. This table is derived by the Advisory Commission from the following additional source: Charles L. Schultze, Edward R. Fried, Alice M. Rivlin, and Nancy H. Teeters, *Setting National Priorities: The 1973 Budget* (Washington, D.C.: Brookings Institution, 1972). Columns 1 and 3 are from p. 445. Column 2 from ACIR staff computations based on p. 445 and p. 447.

important to note that the tax was still regressive for a majority of American families, even if no forward shifting is assumed, as in Column 1, since 70 percent of the families earned annual incomes of $15,000 or less in 1972.

The ability-to-pay principle: Alternative viewpoints. The traditional conclusion regarding property tax incidence under the ability-to-pay rule is challenged by so-called revisionists who adhere to a *permanent* as contrasted to a *present* or *cross-sectional* definition of income. For example, it is argued that if housing expenditures are considered as ratios of lifetime income over a successive period of years, the alleged regressivity concluded under the traditional viewpoint is either significantly reduced, made proportional, or even possibly rendered progressive. The latter would be the case if the income elasticity of housing expenditures to permanent income is greater than unity. In addition, it is argued that the "imputed income" of owner-occupied dwellings should be added to an expanded definition of income, thus lowering the proportion (burden) of property tax collections to income at all income levels.

Another revisionist counterargument to the traditional argumentation stems from the application of the Harberger (corporation income tax) model to the question of property tax incidence.[13] Several rigorous assumptions such as perfectly competitive conditions in all product and factor markets, inelastic aggregate factor supplies, perfect factor mobility, and the absence of unrealized gains underlie this general equilibrium model. It is concluded that a uniform national property tax would be borne by all owners of capital in the long run, since capital would flow from taxed to untaxed (exempt) property. Importantly, the tax would remain on all capital through a reduced overall posttax rate of return, but it would *not* be shifted forward to consumers nor backward to labor. Since capital (property) as a source of income increases in proportion to total income as income increases, it is concluded that the property tax is progressive.[14]

However, the American property tax is not a uniform national tax, a fact that is recognized by those who apply the Harberger model to the subject of property tax incidence. Effective property tax rates vary among the many subnational political jurisdictions that impose the tax. As a result, some mobility of capital from the relatively higher-taxed to the relatively lower-taxed jurisdictions will occur. Complex changes in product prices, wages, and land rent take place (so-called excise tax effects) which are advantageous to these income groups in the low-tax areas, but disadvantageous in the high-tax areas. Accordingly, the economic incidence of the property tax will ultimately depend on: (1) the degree of diminished posttax returns to capital (property) in general, that will result from the average effective rate of property tax imposed across all political jurisdictions using the tax—a diluted effect from the uniform national tax assumption; and (2) the distributional pattern of the particular excise tax effects on product prices, wages, and land rents which result from differential effective property tax rates.

In conclusion, it appears that the traditional arguments need to be modified to account for the newer revisionist viewpoints. However, the traditional arguments still retain considerable validity. The tax on

---

[13] See Peter Mieszkowski, "The Property Tax: An Excise Tax or a Profits Tax?" *Journal of Public Economics,* April 1972, pp. 73–96, and Henry J. Aaron. *Who Pays the Property Tax?* (Washington: Brookings Institution, 1975).

[14] Labor as a source of income diminishes in proportion to total income as income increases.

owner-occupied dwellings remains substantial, and the regressivity effects of this would appear to be importantly modified only if one accepts a permanent-income definition. However, such an acceptance is tenuous, since some individuals do not experience a meaningful real income growth during their lifetime, and the present sacrifice of paying taxes in terms of foregone consumption seems to be more appropriately a matter of present income foregone rather than of foregone lifetime income.

Moreover, the application of the Harberger model to the subject of property tax incidence involves the acceptance of certain rigorous assumptions, such as perfectly competitive markets and perfect factor mobility, which do not correspond to actual economic circumstances. The assumption of perfect competition, for example, precludes the ability of businesses and landlords in imperfect markets to exert monopoly power in the form of higher selling prices in order to forward shift the tax on improvements. Finally, reference should again be made to Column 1 of Table 11–6, which demonstrates that even if capital is assumed to bear the total incidence of the tax on improvements, the tax was still regressive for 70 percent of the population (in 1972). Hence, the traditional position of property tax regressivity seems to be sustained, but probably with less regressivity than was originally considered to be the case. Finally, considerable political belief that the property tax is regressive appears to exist, since a number of states allow refundable state personal income tax credits for property taxes paid by low-income, especially elderly low-income, taxpayers.

The benefit principle. The property tax does *not* perform well in relationship to the benefit principle of tax equity. The payment of property taxes, in many instances, does not follow a quid pro quo relationship with the benefits received from the consumption of public-type goods financed by the taxes. A childless couple, for example, will pay school property taxes on an identical basis to one with several children to be educated. Fire and police protection, moreover, usually does not correlate closely with the assessed value of property and the taxes paid on that property. A modern, fireproof apartment building of high assessed value, for example, may require less actual fire protection effort than an old fire-trap apartment, but its owner will pay much higher property taxes, based on the assessed value of the respective properties, than the owner of the firetrap will pay. Indeed, distributional equity in the bearing of tax burdens tends to be inadequately achieved by the property tax, whether viewed in terms of the ability-to-pay or the benefit norms.

Property tax circuit breakers. State governments offer a number of tax policies which reduce the property tax burden of low-income taxpayers. Each of the 50 states offers some form of *property tax relief* for elderly taxpayers—a segment of the population which has many poor people due, among other things, to the extreme vulnerability of fixed incomes to inflation. One of the most interesting fiscal devices used for this purpose is the so-called *circuit-breaker system* used by a number of states. This technique gets its name from the electrical device that cuts off electricity when an electrical circuit is overloaded. Circuit-breaker property tax relief normally "cuts in" when the property tax percentage of family income reaches a specified proportion defined by the state government as the "point of overload."

Most of the state-financed property tax circuit-breaker systems allow for *rebate* payments from the state government to homeowners and renters. In effect, a rebate amounts to a tax credit against the state personal income tax liability of the taxpayer which, if the credit exceeds the amount of personal income tax owed, makes the taxpayer eligible to receive a cash payment from the state. In practice, this constitutes the payment of a *negative income tax* by the state government to the taxpayer. Traditionally, state efforts to reduce property tax regressivity have also included *exemption* from the property tax base of low-value, owner-occupied dwellings (homestead exemptions) and of homes owned by widows.

The property tax and the distributional equity of public school financing. The use of the property tax as a primary source of *public school finance* in the United States has important implications for the distribution of educational benefits. The public school educational benefits issue was precipitated in August 1971 when the Supreme Court of the State of California, in the case of *Serrano v. Priest,* ruled that the public school financing system in that state, by making the quality of a child's education a function of the wealth of his parents and neighbors through its financial reliance on local government property taxes, was unconstitutional. The unconstitutionality was judged on the basis of a violation of the equal-protection clause of the 14th Amendment to the federal Constitution, in the sense that public school education is a "fundamental right" not to be dependent on wealth. This significant court decision was quickly followed by similar rulings in Minnesota, Texas, New Jersey, and a number of other states.

The essence of these judicial decisions is the contention that *unequal* local government property tax bases contribute to *unequal* educational opportunities for students attending public elementary and secondary schools, since the local property tax is the dominant means of public school financing in the United States. Moreover, existing state foundation programs for the purpose of equalizing these educational quality disparities have been largely unsuccessful. Two local school districts with different wealth endowments can provide equal educational expenditures per pupil only if the poorer district levies a higher property tax rate on its smaller property tax base. The equally disturbing alternative is for the poorer jurisdiction to provide a lower level of educational spending per pupil, while maintaining a property tax rate similar to that imposed by the wealthier district. In practice, some combination of both undesirable results is likely to occur. That is, property tax burdens per student may be higher and educational expenditures per student may be lower in the poorer school districts. Moreover, relevant data suggest a widespread differentiation in the distribution of per-pupil school district wealth and of per-pupil public school educational benefits among the various local government school districts.

This important issue found its way to a U.S. Supreme Court decision in the Texas (*Rodriguez* v. *San Antonio Independent School District*) counterpart of the California (*Serrano*) case during 1973. In a 5-4 vote, the U.S. Supreme Court ruled that the equal-protection clause of the federal Constitution, at least where education is involved, does not require absolute equality or precisely equal advantages. In effect, the Court has said that even though all citizens have a fundamental constitutional right to public school education, they do not have a fundamental constitutional right to "equal" public school education.

Despite this adverse judicial ruling, advocates of public school fiscal reform seem to be achieving some success. A number of states have reviewed the role of the local government property tax in reference to its overall distributional equity problems and, in particular, its relationship to public school financing. A trend seems to be developing whereby a higher proportion of the financing of local public schools is assumed by state governments, and reliance on the local government property tax for this purpose is subsequently diminished. Such actions are likely to reduce to some degree the existing extreme variation in the distribution of public school educational benefits. Meanwhile, a 1977 California Supreme Court decision ruled, as it had in the 1971 *Serrano* case, except that the constitutional violation this time was said to be of the California rather than of the U.S. Constitution.

Stabilization effects

The property tax is *not* a major economic stabilization tool. There are several reasons for this, the most important being that (1) it is primarily a local government tax, while stabilization policy is best directed at the national government level, and (2) its income elasticity, according to the majority of estimates, tends to be inelastic. The absence of national government application of the tax rules out the effective application of *discretionary* fiscal policy. Moreover, the in-

TABLE 11-7 Income elasticity of state and local property taxes: Summary of empirical studies

Study	Year published	Area covered	Elasticity coefficient
ACIR*	1971	New York City, N.Y.	1.41
Mushkin	1965	United States	1.30
ACIR*	1971	Baltimore City, Md.	1.25
Netzer	1961	United States	1.00
Bridges	1964	United States	0.98
ACIR*	1971	Honolulu Co., Hawaii	0.89
ACIR*	1971	Multnomah Co., Oreg.	0.84
McLoone	1961	United States	0.80
Rafuse	1965	United States	0.80
ACIR*	1971	Jefferson Co., Ky.	0.50
ACIR*	1971	Newark, N.J.	0.38
ACIR*	1971	Albany City, N.Y.	0.34

* Advisory Commission on Intergovernmental Relations.
Other sources: Benjamin Bridges, Jr., "The Elasticity of the Property Tax Base: Some Cross Section Estimates," *Land Economics,* November 1964, pp. 449–51; Eugene P. McLoone, "Effects of Tax Elasticities on the Financial Support of Education," unpublished Ph.D. dissertation, College of Education. University of Illinois, 1961; Selma Mushkin, *Property Taxes: The 1970 Outlook* (Chicago, Council of State Governments, 1965); Dick Netzer, "Financial Needs and Resources over the Next Decade," in National Bureau of Economic Research, *Public Finances: Needs, Sources, and Utilization* (Princeton, Princeton University Press, 1961); Robert W. Rafuse, "Cyclical Behavior of State-Local Finances," in *Essays in Fiscal Federalism,* ed. Richard A. Musgrave (Washington, D.C.: Brookings Institution, 1965).
Source: Advisory Commission on Intergovernmental Relations, *State-Local Finances: Significant Features and Suggested Legislation* (Washington, D.C.: U.S. Government Printing Office, 1972), p. 301.

elastic income elasticity of the tax renders it ineffective as an *automatic* stabilization instrument. Meanwhile, Table 11–7 summarizes several studies of the income elasticity of the property tax.

Since property tax revenues do not respond to changes in the aggregate performance level of the economy with the same sensitivity that income tax revenues respond, a revenue advantage is created for governments which use the tax, in the sense that property tax revenues, except in a time of a major depression like the 1930s, remain relatively stable during downward phases of the business cycle. There is also a revenue disadvantage in that the relative inelasticity of the tax with respect to national income often causes it to lag behind the rapid growth of local government expenditures which, in turn, are responding to an elastic demand for local government economic goods in a growing economy. This leads to the frequent observation that the property tax is being "overworked."

12

Sales taxation:
Narrowbased and
broadbased
sales taxes

DIFFERENT TYPES OF SALES TAXES

Nature of the sales tax base

Sales taxes are in rem taxes imposed on a market transactions base. They are impersonal in character, unlike a personal consumption (expenditure) tax[1], since they do not consider the overall expenditures of the taxpayer. Instead, a sales tax uses only a particular market transaction as its base.

The imposition of sales taxes may be placed at various stages of economic activity. Among the alternative points of placement are the natural resource extraction (mining), manufacturing, wholesale, and retail levels of production. If it is placed at only one of these transaction points, the tax is referred to as a *single-stage sales tax*. A tax imposed at two or more stages of production is known as a *multistage* or *multiple sales tax*. A single-stage sales tax placed on the extraction of a natural resource is called a *severance tax*. One imposed on an

---

[1] See Chapter 14 for a detailed discussion of the *personal consumption (expenditure) tax.*

economic good at the manufacturing level is referred to as a *manufacturer's sales tax*. A tax levied on a commodity when it is sold by a wholesaler to a retailer is called a *wholesale sales tax,* while one levied on the final sale of the commodity to its ultimate purchaser is known as a *retail sales tax*. Multistage sales taxes are best represented by *turnover* and *value-added taxes*.

In addition to being differentiated by means of the various levels of economic activity at which they may be placed, sales taxes also can be differentiated in terms of their tax bases, which are either narrow or broad in scope. A sales tax applied to one or to a few economic goods (resources) is considered *narrowbased,* while one levied on a wide range of goods (resources) is called a *broadbased* sales tax. A sales tax base can be further classified in terms of whether it measures the monetary value or the physical number of units purchased. If the tax base is defined in terms of the monetary value of the purchased item or items, like the broadbased state general retail sales taxes, the tax is said to be *ad valorem* in nature. If the tax base is defined in terms of the number of units of the commodity purchased, like gallons of gasoline under the federal and state gasoline taxes, the tax is termed a *specific* tax.

Narrowbased sales taxes

A narrowbased sales tax may also be known as an *excise* or *selective* sales tax. Such a tax can be imposed either externally or internally. An *external excise tax* is applied to the movement of an economic good or resource across an international boundary.[2] External excise taxes are commonly known as *customs duties* or *tariffs*. Such taxes may be imposed by either the nation exporting or by the nation importing an economic good or resource. Thus, an external excise can be either an export duty or an import duty.

An *internal excise tax* may be applied to one or a small number of items involving market transactions within the political boundaries of a sovereign nation. Many different commodities are, or have been, subject to excise taxes in the United States: for example, tobacco products, alcoholic beverages, motor fuels, jewelry, cosmetics, luggage, and transportation. Internal excises may be imposed for a variety of reasons other than the primary reason (in most cases) of providing revenue. For example, some excises are applied on luxury goods with an *income redistribution* motive in mind. Other excises, known as *sumptuary* taxes, are intended to discourage the consumption of certain so-called undesirable or *demerit* commodities, such as liquor and

---

[2] External sales taxes may also be broadbased in nature.

tobacco products, or the consumption of scarce resources such as petroleum.

Another use of internal excise taxes involves the benefit principle of taxation. Here an attempt is made to tie the payment of the excise to the consumption of a particular quasi-public good. Federal gasoline tax payments, for example, go into a special trust fund where they are earmarked for the interstate highway system. It should thus be noted that the revenues from an excise tax may go either into a *general treasury fund* for nonspecific purposes or into a *particular trust fund,* where they are earmarked for a specific purpose, normally related to the good on which the excise tax is imposed.

Broadbased sales taxes

Sales taxes which are applied to a wide variety of economic goods, known as broadbased sales taxes, generally have a tax base which is ad valorem in nature because of the difficulty in applying a specific tax to a large number of diverse economic goods or resources. Broadbased sales taxes may be imposed at one or more than one level of economic activity. Hence, they may be either single-stage or multistage in nature.

The primary type of single-stage broadbased sales tax used in the United States is the *general retail sales tax.* The typical American state or local government general sales tax is imposed at the *retail* level and applies a flat percentage rate to a broad base of purchases (with certain exemptions). Primary types of multistage broadbased sales taxes are the turnover tax and the value-added tax *(VAT).*[3] A *turnover tax* is imposed on the *gross* monetary value of a product at each stage of the production process. The *value-added tax* is also applied at multiple stages of business activity, but it differs from the turnover tax in that it defines the tax base at each level only in the *net sense* of the value added at that particular stage of production.

The *revenue productivity* of a sales tax, either narrowbased or broadbased, imposed by a state or local unit of government may be threatened by the possibility buyers will purchase taxable economic goods in another political jurisdiction. In order to discourage such tax avoidance efforts, all states levying broadbased retail sales taxes also impose a *use tax,* which applies a special sales tax to economic goods which are purchased outside the state but which are subsequently brought into the state. The use tax is somewhat difficult to enforce because of the problems involved in discovering out-of-state purchases.

---

[3] *Value-added* and *turnover taxes* are discussed in greater detail in Chapter 14.

NARROWBASED SALES (EXCISE) TAXATION
IN THE UNITED STATES

Federal excise taxes

The federal government has collected both internal and external excises since the early days of the Republic. In fact, external excise taxes served as the primary source of federal tax revenue between 1790 and the beginning of World War I. Legislation passed by Congress during 1965 substantially reduced the federal excise tax burden on American taxpayers when a number of federal excise taxes were either repealed or substantially reduced. Prior to this, federal excise taxes had been applied to a fairly wide variety of economic goods. Several excises were increased during 1982.

Today, the list of products subject to federal excise taxes includes alcoholic beverages, tobacco products, gasoline, and telephone service. Table 12–1 shows the statutory rate structures of these and other federal excise taxes as of 1982. As Table 12–2 indicates, in 1980 alcoholic beverage excises were the greatest revenue producer among the federal excise taxes ($5.7 billion), followed by the gasoline excise ($4.2 billion), the windfall profits tax ($3.1 billion), and various other excises. The windfall profits tax is an important new federal excise tax related to the deregulation of federal government control over oil prices. It became effective in 1980. Total federal excise tax revenues amounted to $24.6 billion that year.

The federal excise tax on gasoline represents a major example of earmarked tax financing. Though the federal government has been continually assisting the states in highway development since 1916, a marked policy change occurred with the passage of the interstate highway legislation of 1956. This legislation not only provided for the long-term development of a 42,500-mile interstate highway system, it also changed the philosophy of federal highway financing. Previously, federal assistance to the states had been derived from general tax funds. Federal gasoline tax revenues went to the general treasury, just like any other nonearmarked tax. The legislation of 1956 *earmarked* various highway user tax revenues, including those of the federal gasoline tax, for a special highway trust fund which would be used to finance highway construction. Specific excise taxes on gasoline, tires, trucks, and other economic goods closely connected to highway use thus became the revenue sources for the separate federal highway trust account. The trust fund provides 90 percent of the costs of interstate highway construction, the remaining 10 percent being contributed by the states. Legislation enacted by Congress during 1973 "opened" a limited portion of the highway trust fund revenues for use in the development of urban mass transit systems.

TABLE 12–1   **Federal excise tax rates* on selected items (includes changes enacted in the Tax Equity and Fiscal Responsibility Act of 1982)**

Item taxed	
Liquor taxes	
Distilled spirits (per proof or wine gallon	$10.50
Still wines (per wine gallon 14% alcohol or less)[a]	17¢
Champagne and sparkling wines (per wine gallon	$3.40
Fermented malt liquors (per 31 gallon barrel)	$9.00
Tobacco taxes	
Cigars, large (per thousand)[b]	8-1/2% of wholesale price to $20.00
Cigarettes (per thousand weighing not more than 3 lbs.)[c]	$8.00
Tobacco (per pound)	([d])
Stamp taxes, documentary, etc.[ef]	
Manufacturers' excise taxes[g]	
Lubricating oil (per gallon)	6¢[h]
Gasoline (per gallon)	4¢[h]
Tires used on highways and other tires (per pound, respectively)	10¢[i], 5¢
Inner tubes (per pound)	10¢[j]
Tread rubber (per pound)	5¢[k]
Trucks and buses (sale price)	10%[l]
Automobiles (sale price)	([m])
Truck parts and accessories	8%[l]
"Gas Guzzler"	$200–$650[n]
Coal	50¢, 25¢[o]
Sporting goods (sale price)	([p])
Firearms, shells, and cartridges (sale price)	11%
Pistols and revolvers (sale price)	10%
Bows and arrows	11%
Fishing equipment	10%
Airway user taxes	
Annual registration	([q])
Poundage fees (aircraft over 2500 lbs.)	
Propeller-driven (per pound)	([r])
Turbine-powered (per pound)	([s])
Highway motor vehicle use tax (for each 1,000 lbs. of gross weight over 26,000 lbs.)	$3.00
Miscellaneous excise taxes	
Local and toll telephone service and teletypewriter service (amount charged, respectively)	3%[u], 3%[u]
Miscellaneous excise taxes (Continued)	
Air transportation[v]	
Persons (domestic flights, amount paid)	8%[w]
Persons (international flights, amount paid)	$3.00
Wagers (amount wagered; except parimutuel)	2%
"Windfall profit"	30%, 60%, 70%[x]
Deep seabed hard mineral (imputed value of resource removed)	3.75%
Petroleum (barrel)	79¢
Chemicals (per ton)	Various, $.22–4.87

TABLE 12-1 *(concluded)*

Retailers' excise taxes[y]	
Diesel fuel (per gallon)	4¢[h]
Gasoline used in noncommercial aviation (per gallon)	12¢[h]
Jet fuel used in noncommercial aviation (per gallon)	14¢
Gasoline substitute fuels	4¢[h]
Inland waterways users fuel	4¢[z]

* Also, cites various repealed excise taxes.

[a] On beverages of 14 to 21% alcohol content: 10¢ in 1939, 67¢ from 1951–1976; 21 to 24% alcohol content: 20¢ in 1939, $2.25 from 1951–1976; over 24% alcohol: $2.25 in 1939, $10.50 from 1951–1976.

[b] Rates graduated with wholesale prices of cigars. Small cigars (not more than 3 lbs. per thousand) have been taxed at 75¢ per thousand throughout the period.

[c] Was $4.00 prior to 1982 legislation.

[d] Repealed effective January 1, 1966. Prior to repeal, rate was 10¢ per pound.

[e] Taxes on issuance and transfer of stocks and bonds expired January 1, 1968.

[f] Taxes on playing cards repealed effective June 22, 1965.

[g] Taxes on ordinary matches; musical instruments; records; phonograph; electric, gas, and oil appliances; photographic film in rolls; radios, televisions, and air conditioners; fountain pens, mechanical pencils, and mechanical lighters repealed effective June 22, 1965. Taxes on electric light bulbs and tubes and automobile parts and accessories repealed effective January 1, 1966.

[h] For lubricating oil, credit if not used in highway vehicles. For gasoline, credit if used for farming or for nonhighway uses other than noncommercial aviation. Tax was 4¢ prior to 1982 legislation.

[i] Scheduled to drop to 5¢ on October 1, 1984.

[j] Scheduled to drop to 9¢ on October 1, 1984.

[k] No tax on or after October 1, 1984.

[l] To be reduced to 5% on October 1, 1984.

[m] The Revenue Act of 1971 repealed the tax effective after August 15, 1971.

[n] The Energy Act of 1978 imposed a tax on automobiles under 6,000 lbs. whose fuel economy fails to meet certain standards. For the 1981 model year, automobiles with mileage rating (per gallon) of greater than 16 but less than 17, tax is $200; under 13, $650. Tax became effective in 1980 model year.

[o] 50¢ per ton on underground mined coal and 25¢ per surface mined coal.

[p] Taxes on most sporting goods repealed effective June 22, 1965.

[q] Expired September 30, 1980. Previously, rate was $6.25 for July 1, 1980 to September 30, 1980; and $25.00 prior to July 1, 1980.

[r] Expired September 30, 1980. Previously, rate was 1/2¢ for July 1, 1980 to September 30, 1980; and 2¢ prior to July 1, 1980.

[s] Expired September 30, 1980. Previously, rate was 7/8¢ for July 1, 1980 to September 30, 1980; and 3.5¢ prior to July 1, 1980.

[t] Taxes on telegraph service and telegraph and wire equipment repealed effective January 1, 1966. Taxes on bowling alleys and pool tables repealed July 1, 1965. Taxes on lease of safe deposit boxes, general admissions, cabarets, and club dues and initiation fees repealed July 1, 1965; December 31, 1965; and January 1, 1966, respectively.

[u] To drop to zero after 1985.

[v] Also, imposed tax of 5% on air freight waybills (in 1982).

[w] Was 5% prior to 1982 legislation.

[x] Tier three, tier two, and tier one crude oil, respectively. Effective February 29, 1980.

[y] Taxes on jewelry, furs, toilet preparations, and luggage repealed effective June 22, 1965.

[z] Scheduled to increase to 6¢ per gallon, October 1, 1981 to September 30, 1983; 8¢ per gallon, October 1, 1983 to September 30, 1985; and 10¢ per gallon (maximum) after October 1, 1985.

Source: Commerce Clearing House; Treasury Department; *Facts and Figures on Government Finance–1981* (New York: Tax Foundation, Inc., 1981), pp. 138–39, as amended to include 1982 law changes.

TABLE 12-2   **Major federal excise tax revenues, fiscal year 1980**

Type of tax	Amount (billions of dollars)
Alcoholic beverage excises	$ 5.7
Gasoline excise	4.2
Windfall profits tax	3.1
Tobacco excises	2.4
Air transportation	1.6
Telephone and teletypewriter	1.1
Other excises	6.5
Total	$24.6

Source: U.S. Department of the Treasury.

State and local excise taxes

The use of excise taxes by state and local governments has largely been a 20th-century phenomenon. The gasoline tax was initiated by five states, led by Oregon, in 1919. State cigarette excises were introduced during the 1920s and alcoholic beverage excises during the 1930s. Some of the most important state and local government excises are discussed in this section.

Gasoline excise taxes are imposed by all 50 states and the District of Columbia. As of 1981, the rates ranged from as low as 5 cents per gallon in one state (Texas) to as high as 13.9 cents per gallon in another (Nebraska). Local governments in several states and the District of Columbia also impose gasoline excise taxes.

All 50 states and the District of Columbia levy excise taxes on *cigarettes*, and a number of states also impose excises on *other tobacco products*. These range between 2 cents per standard pack of 20 cigarettes in North Carolina to 21 cents per pack in Connecticut, Florida, and Massachusetts. Local governments impose cigarette excises in several states and the District of Columbia.

All states and the District of Columbia either impose excise taxes on *beer* and *alcoholic beverages* (distilled spirits), or they mark up the prices of these products as they are sold in government retail outlets. Liquor is distributed in government retail stores in 17 states. In addition, alcoholic beverages are subject to local government excise taxes in a few states.

Both state and local governments levy gross receipts taxes on the sale of *public utility services*. The majority of states, and some local governments, impose documentary taxes on the *transfer of real estate*. *Parimutuel betting* on thoroughbred and harness horse racing and on dog racing is also subject to excise taxation in a large number of states.

State severance taxes

The *severance tax,* an excise tax imposed on the extraction of natural resources, is an increasingly important tax at the state level of government in the United States. More specifically, it may be defined as a *gross receipts* or *gross production* tax levied on the transaction in which natural resources are removed from land or water. Examples of resources to which it might be applied include oil, gas, coal, timber, and fish. Severance taxes imposed on timber-cutting operations are usually ad valorem *gross receipts* taxes based on the stumpage value of the cut timber, such as 10 percent of the monetary value of the timber. Some of the state severance taxes on other natural resources are also gross receipts taxes. Most state severance taxes, however, are *gross production* taxes, which impose *specific* rates such as 1 cent per ton of coal, or 5 cents per barrel of oil, multiplied by the gross number of resource units extracted from the land or water.

Severance taxes contributed $686 million in state revenues in 1970. However, by 1980 they were contributing $4.2 billion in revenues to 34 states. This constituted 3 percent of all state nonemployment (non-payroll) tax revenues—more than double the 1.4 percent proportion in 1970. Importantly, the severance tax was proving to be an important revenue source to several states that are rich in energy resources, at a time of high and rising energy prices. The intergovernmental fiscal implications of this phenomenon will be considered in Chapter 18.

In a sense, severance taxes are a rationing device which ideally would help establish an optimal societal rate of use of the resource in question. They have been levied at times in lieu of property taxes, which have a built-in tendency to encourage natural resource usage. For example, the actual cutting of timber would lower the assessed value of land under a property tax, thus reducing property tax liability, while there would in fact not even be a severance tax liability if the timber is not cut. Hence, the owner of the property would tend to cut the timber in order to reduce a property tax liability, but to leave it uncut to avoid a severance tax liability. Although severance taxes as replacements for property taxes could involve a short-run revenue loss, they may well also cause a long-run revenue gain by helping to conserve natural resources for economically rational long-term usage. Moreover, it should be noted that severance taxes offer a high potential for *exportability* to the residents of other political jurisdictions in a decentralized public sector, since they occur at an early stage of the productive process and may well, on occasion, be added into the downstream price of the final product.[4]

---

[4] See Chapter 18 for an elaboration of the concept of *tax exporting.*

Under certain conditions, severance taxes, if unevenly applied among several states and among several types of substitutable resources, could yield undesirable allocational and distributional nonneutralities. For example, a severance tax levied on copper ore but not on bauxite, which is the source of aluminum and a competitor of copper for many residential and industrial uses, would cause an allocational distortion; some users would substitute aluminum for copper because of the tax-induced price differential. Moreover, the owners of copper mines would bear a posttax income distribution bias, as compared to the owners of bauxite property.

BROADBASED SALES TAXATION IN THE UNITED STATES: THE GENERAL RETAIL SALES TAX

The federal government has never employed a broadbased general retail sales tax, though Congress has considered the matter on a number of occasions. However, most states (45), and local governments in 25 states plus the District of Columbia, use the tax at the present time. Use by the *states* of broadbased general sales taxes developed in the 20th century; specifically, the retail sales tax movement grew out of the Great Depression of the 1930s. Though some states had imposed taxes on gross business receipts in the 1920s, the first permanent general retail sales tax was enacted by Mississippi in 1932. In the next few years, there were many more adoptions of the tax. By the end of the depression, approximately one half of the states were using the tax, though several states which had adopted it earlier in the 1930s had discontinued it by that time. The use of general sales taxes by *local* governments derives primarily from their desire to relieve pressure on the property tax. Only two major cities, New York City and New Orleans, used the tax prior to World War II. Following the war, a local general sales tax movement was initiated in California and spread to a number of other states.

State general sales tax rates are applied ordinarily to the retail sales of tangible personal property and specific services. Table 12–3 lists the various state sales tax rates for the 45 states (and the District of Columbia) that impose the tax. All rates are proportional in statutory design, and they range from 2 percent in Oklahoma to 7.5 percent in Connecticut.

Local governments impose general sales taxes in 25 states. In all, more than 5,000 local governments use the tax. The taxes are locally administered in some states and are administered through cooperation between the state and local, or between county and municipal, governments in others.

TABLE 12-3   State general sales tax rates[a] (as of April 1, 1981)

State	Rate[b] (percent)	Taxation of food and drugs[c]		Local sales taxes levied[d]
		Food[e]	Prescription drugs[f]	
Alabama	4	T	T	Yes
Arizona	4	E	E	Yes
Arkansas	3	T	E	Yes[k]
California[h]	4.75	E	E	Yes
Colorado[h]	3	E	E	Yes
Connecticut	7.5	E	E	No
Florida	4	E	E	Yes
Georgia	3	T	T	Yes
Hawaii	4	T	T	No
Idaho	3[j]	T	E	Yes
Illinois	4[i]	T	T	Yes
Indiana	4	E	E	Yes
Iowa	3	T[j]	E	Yes
Kansas	3	T[j]	E	Yes
Kentucky	5	E	E	Yes
Louisiana	3	E[k]	E	Yes
Maine	5	E	E	No
Maryland	5	E	E	Yes
Massachusetts[h]	5	E	E	No
Michigan[h]	4	E	E	No
Minnesota	4	E	E	Yes
Mississippi	5	T	T	No
Missouri[h]	3.125	T	T	Yes
Nebraska[h]	3[j]	T	E	Yes
Nevada	3[l]	E	E	Yes
New Jersey[h]	5	E	E	Yes
New Mexico[h]	3.75[l]	T	T	Yes
New York	4	E	E	Yes
North Carolina	3	T	E	Yes
North Dakota	3	E	E	No
Ohio	4	E	E	Yes
Oklahoma	2	T	T	Yes
Pennsylvania	6	E	E	Yes
Rhode Island	6	E	E	No
South Carolina	4	T	E	No
South Dakota	5	T[f,m]	E	Yes
Tennessee	4.5[n]	T	E	Yes
Texas	4	E	E	Yes
Utah[h]	4	T	E	Yes
Vermont[h]	3	E	E	No
Virginia	3	T	E	Yes
Washington	4.5	E	E	Yes
West Virginia	3[o]	E[o]	E	No
Wisconsin	4	E	E	No
Wyoming	3	T	E	Yes
District of Columbia	6	E	E	—

[a] In all but two of the states listed, tax is confined to retail, or final sales; Hawaii and Mississippi also tax certain preretail sales at special low rates. Every sales-tax state levies an accompanying use tax on imports from other states at a rate identical to that of the sales tax.
[b] Certain states tax retail sales of automotive vehicles and/or aircraft at lower rates.
[c] E = Exempt; T = Taxable.
[d] See Table 237 for information on local sales taxes.
[e] Exemptions generally apply only to food for consumption away from place of sale; all states tax restaurant meals, although Massachusetts and Vermont do it under separate taxes. Several states which are listed as taxing food exempt farm products sold directly to consumers by producers.
[f] Certain states exempt persons over 65 (60 in Kansas; 50 in South Carolina) and/or disabled persons from the tax. In South Dakota, senior citizens and disabled persons on Social Security may claim a sales tax refund dependent on income.
[g] Authorization restricted to one or a few localities.
[h] A personal income tax credit is allowed against the sales tax.
[i] Effective July 1, 1981, food and drugs will be taxed at 2%.
[j] Food purchased with food stamps is exempt.
[k] Food and drugs are taxed at 2%.
[l] From May 1, 1981, through June 30, 1983, rate rises to 3.5% in Nevada. Effective July 1, 1981, rate drops to 3.5% in New Mexico.
[m] Levy on food is 4%.
[n] After June 30, 1982, rate drops to 3%.
[o] Effective June 1, 1981, rate rises to 5%. Effective July 1, 1981, food exempt; from July 1, 1980, to June 30, 1981, food taxed at 1%.

Source: Commerce Clearing House; *Facts and Figures on Government Finance–1981* (New York: Tax Foundation, Inc., 1981), p. 236.

FISCAL PERFORMANCE OF SALES TAXES

Allocational effects

Broadbased versus narrowbased sales taxes. Broadbased sales taxes tend to be less distortive of allocational behavior in the choice among products than narrowbased sales (excise) taxes. The latter, of course, change the relative prices between taxed and nontaxed economic goods. Hence, the product taxed by the excise becomes relatively more expensive than the untaxed good. The greater the substitutability between the two products, the greater will be the resultant allocational nonneutrality in the form of an increased quantity demanded of the now relatively less expensive untaxed product. However, in the choice between consumption and saving, a broadbased sales tax is more likely to change the allocational behavior of the taxpayer, unless the narrowbased tax bears directly on the consumption-saving decision.

Does an excise tax or a personal income tax exert the greater excess burden? For many years economists concluded that a proportional personal income tax was preferable to an excise tax on efficiency grounds, since it was "more neutral" in its influence on allocational behavior in the private sector than was the excise tax.[5] That is, it was said to yield the lesser excess burden. This position was challenged subsequently by other economists and, as a result, the issue has been further clarified.[6] The traditional analysis was said to be weakened by its partial-equilibrium orientation, which led to (1) omission of the possible diversion of resources to the production of other goods besides those whose relative prices are affected by the excise tax, and (2) failure to consider the fact that excise tax receipts may be used either to subsidize the production of one of the goods affected by the excise tax or for general consumer subsidies, or they can be impounded and held idle.

The present, more sophisticated consideration of the issue of personal income versus excise tax neutrality has resulted in the following observations:

1. A personal income tax is preferable, in neutrality terms, to an excise tax on one of two economic goods.

---

[5] This viewpoint is represented in M. F. W. Joseph, "The Excess Burden of Indirect Taxation," *Review of Economic Studies*, June 1939, pp. 226–31, and in several other sources.

[6] See Milton Friedman. "The Welfare Effects of an Income Tax and an Excise Tax," *Journal of Political Economy*, February 1952, pp. 25–33, and *Price Theory* (Chicago: Aldine, 1966), pp. 56–67; I. M. D. Little, "Direct vs. Indirect Taxes," *Economic Journal*, September 1951, pp. 577–84; Richard A. Musgrave, *The Theory of Public Finance* (New York: McGraw-Hill, 1959), pp. 140–48.

2. Identical excise taxes on two economic goods are preferable to a personal income tax superimposed on an excise tax on one of the two goods.

3. A personal income tax or identical excise taxes on two goods will yield equally preferable neutrality results.

The obvious conclusion is that it is impossible to state categorically whether a personal income or an excise tax is superior in terms of allocational neutrality (minimizing excess burden). The most that can be generally inferred is that the broader the tax base and the more equal its incidence, the less likely it is to distort the relevant marginal rates of substitution which characterize the private sector reaction to taxation. However, other considerations such as the rate of substitution between work and leisure are outside the direct scope of the above analysis, but the relevance of the work-leisure trade-off to the personal income tax is considered in Chapter 8.

Earmarked taxes. Economists disagree concerning the economic efficiency effects of earmarked taxes such as the federal excise tax on gasoline. Some researchers suggest that earmarking tends to reduce the willingness of taxpayers to approve expenditures on specific products,[7] while others maintain that earmarking tends to increase taxpayer support for a particular product.[8]

James Buchanan, in a study on the economics of earmarked taxes,[9] reaches the following conclusions in support of earmarking:

1. Earmarking may increase allocational efficiency by ensuring more rational individual choice since, with earmarking, the individual can appraise more closely the relevant costs and benefits of a particular project. A person is thus able to adjust the amount consumed of each quasi-public good in order to attain his or her most preferred consumption level. This is not true in general-fund financing, which is similar to a joint-product sale in the sense that to get one commodity the consumer must also purchase another. The individual consumer of quasi-public goods is subject to an allocational distortion with general-fund financing, since his or her independence of choice is reduced.

2. General-fund financing tends to be distortive since it will at-

---

[7] Julius Margolis. "Metropolitan Finance Problems: Territories, Functions, and Growth," in *Public Finances: Needs, Sources, and Utilization* (New York: National Bureau of Economic Research, 1961), pp. 261–66; Walter Heller, "CED's Stabilizing Budget Policy after Ten Years," *American Economic Review*, September 1957, pp. 634–51.

[8] Earl Rolph and George Break, *Public Finance* (New York: Ronald Press Co., 1961), p. 62; Jesse Burkhead, *Government Budgeting* (New York: John Wiley & Sons, 1956), p. 469; Tax Foundation, Inc., *Earmarked State Taxes* (New York, 1955).

[9] James M. Buchanan, "The Economics of Earmarked Taxes," *Journal of Political Economy*, October 1963, pp. 457–69.

tract more publicly-supplied economic goods with "elastic" demands than will earmarked financing. A person without children, for example, is likely to vote against funds which are earmarked *only for education* (thus an elastic demand for education by this person), but is more likely to vote for a *bundle of additional goods* to be financed from a general fund, which happens to include education along with other goods for which he/she has a strong preference. Thus, when general-fund financing is used, society receives a greater proportion of those economic goods with highly elastic demands, since they are tied in with the acquisition of other goods, and it receives a smaller proportion of goods that have less elastic demands.

Sumptuary taxes. Excise taxes imposed for the purpose of reducing the consumption of certain goods are known as *sumptuary excise taxes.* Society makes a political judgment that the consumption of these products, or *demerit goods,* is undesirable. To be successful, a sumptuary tax must be imposed on a good for which the increase in price created by the excise tax falls on an elastic portion of the relevant demand curve. This can be observed in Figure 12–1, in which the presumptuary tax equilibrium at point *a* consists of price *P* and quantity demanded *X*. After the sumptuary excise tax is imposed, in an

FIGURE 12–1   Successful and unsuccessful sumptuary excise taxes

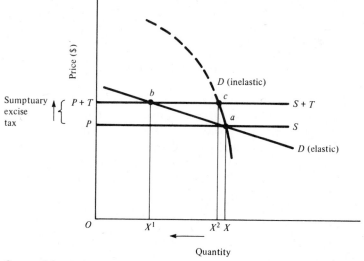

Successful sumptuary tax:
 Price change ↑ (*P* to *P* + *T*)
 Quantity change ↓ (*X* to X^1)
Unsuccessful sumptuary tax:
 Price change ↑ (*P* to *P* + *T*)
 Quantity change ↓ (*X* to X^2)

effort to reduce significantly the quantity consumed of the good, price increases from P to $P + T$ as supply curve S shifts upward to become $S + T$, and quantity demanded decreases sharply from X to X^1 at the new post-sumptuary tax equilibrium point, b. However, if the relevant demand for the product in that price range had been inelastic, the post-sumptuary tax equilibrium would have been at point c, quantity demanded would have decreased only slightly from X to X^2, and the attempt to reduce the consumption of the product significantly would have been unsuccessful.

Interestingly, major sumptuary excise tax applications in the United States, at least at the present time if not perhaps at the time of original imposition, are on products (alcoholic beverages and tobacco products) that are essentially price inelastic in demand in the relevant portion of the demand curve. Hence, the continued use of excise taxes on alcoholic beverages and tobacco products by American governments apparently represents a pragmatic *revenue objective*, rather than reliance on the tax as a means of constraining the consumption of these so-called *demerit goods*. However, as shown by the *elastic* dotted line on the upper portion of the otherwise price-inelastic demand curve in Figure 12–1, at some relevant point a sumptuary excise tax of sufficient magnitude would ultimately reach a portion of the demand curve at which significant consumption decreases would occur. Undoubtedly, there *is* such a point for the sumptuary excises imposed on the alleged vices, alcohol and tobacco, and on the scarce energy good, gasoline, in the United States.

Distributional effects

The ability-to-pay principle: Traditional viewpoint regarding the general sales tax. The traditional analysis of the general retail sales tax, the most important sales tax revenue source in the United States, concludes that it is *regressive* in reference to the ability-to-pay benchmark. In statutory terms, of course, the general sales tax is a proportional or flat-rate tax. Its regressivity, in ability-to-pay terms, results from the fact that consumption tends to be a declining proportion of increasing income.[10] Thus, the average propensity to consume (C/Y) becomes lower as income becomes greater. Since the general sales tax is a broadbased consumption tax, and since the C/Y ratio declines with rising income, general sales tax payments as a proportion of income will also decline with rising income. The result is a regressive tax. Table 12–4 and Figure 12–2 demonstrate this fact by means of a hypothetical example.

The orthodox conclusion that the general retail sales tax is regres-

---

[10] This is based on a "present period" definition of income.

TABLE 12–4   **Example of general sales tax* regressivity: Traditional argument**

	Consumer A	Consumer B
Income (Y)†	$10,000	$50,000
Consumption (C)	$ 9,500	$35,000
Average propensity to consumer (C/Y)	$\frac{\$9,500}{\$10,000} = 0.95 = 95\%$	$\frac{\$35,000}{\$50,000} = 0.70 = 70\%$
Sales tax (S) paid on consumption at 5 percent rate	$\begin{array}{r} \$\ 9,500 \\ \times 0.05 \\ \hline \$\quad 475 \end{array}$	$\begin{array}{r} \$35,000 \\ \times 0.05 \\ \hline \$\ 1,750 \end{array}$
Sales tax to income ratio (S/Y)	$\frac{\$475}{\$10,000} = 0.0475 = 4.75\%$	$\frac{\$1,750}{\$50,000} = 0.035 = 3.5\%$

* Example also essentially applies to a value-added tax of the consumption variety (see Chapter 14).
† Current (present) income.

sive has prompted many states to exempt necessity goods such as food and prescription medicine from the base of the tax, in order to reduce its regressivity. As Table 12–3 presented earlier in the chapter, shows, 25 states exempt food "purchased for consumption away from the place of sale" from the general sales tax base, while 38 states exempt prescription drugs from the base. Moreover, all 25 states which exempt food also exempt prescription drugs. In addition, the District of

FIGURE 12–2   **Example of general sales tax* regressivity: Traditional argument**

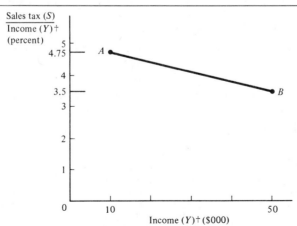

* Example also essentially applies to a value-added tax of the consumption variety (see Chapter 14).
† Current (present) income.

Columbia exempts both of these products. Of the 45 states which impose the general sales tax, 7 exempt neither food nor prescription medicine from the tax base. Interestingly, the occasional exemption of *clothing* from the general sales tax base, as contrasted to food and prescription drugs, tends to increase rather than decrease sales tax regressivity, since low-income taxpayers spend a smaller proportion of their incomes for clothing than do those with higher incomes.[11]

The effort to offset general retail sales tax regressivity also is represented in four states by a sales tax *credit* against state personal income tax liability. Such a credit, if in excess of the income tax liability, results in a negative income tax payment to the low-income taxpayer.[12] One state, New Mexico, which exempts neither food nor prescription medicine, nonetheless does provide a refundable (to low-income taxpayers) credit against state personal income tax liability for *all* taxes paid to the state and local governments.

The ability-to-pay principle: Alternative viewpoint regarding the general sales tax. The traditional conclusion of general sales tax regressivity has been challenged recently by a so-called *revisionist* viewpoint which argues that "permanent" or "lifetime" income is a more relevant basis than present income for evaluating the relationship between consumption and income (C/Y at different income levels).[13] In this line of reasoning it is argued that some taxpayers who are temporarily at low-income levels, after having been at higher levels, may adhere to their previous higher consumption behavior, thus increasing their present C/Y ratios as compared to others at that lower-income level who have not previously earned higher incomes. This tends to overstate the overall C/Y ratio, in present-income terms, at the lower-income levels. In addition, it is pointed out that the elderly, who may have low present incomes, often consume at an unusually high C/Y proportion as they "use up" capital accumulated during their lifetime. This also would tend to overstate the C/Y ratio at the lower-income levels. In general, it is argued that a long-run income perspective will provide a C/Y ratio which will not diminish significantly, if at all. However, there are many taxpayers whose real incomes remain permanently low or permanently high during an entire lifetime, and for them the cross-sectional analysis would be more appropriate.

The revisionist position thus appears to lead, at best, to a conclu-

---

[11] Two sources which demonstrate the fact that "clothing exemptions" increase sales tax regressivity are Jeffrey M. Schaefer, "Sales Tax Regressivity under Alternative Tax Bases and Income Concepts," *National Tax Journal,* December 1969, pp. 516–27, and David G. Davies, "Clothing Exemptions and Sales Tax Regressivity: Note," *American Economic Review,* March 1971, pp. 187–89.

[12] Also, see the general discussion of negative income taxation in Chapter 13.

[13] See the similar application of the permanent-income hypothesis to property taxation in the preceding chapter.

sion of *less* general sales tax regressivity, but not to one of proportionality or progressivity. Besides the fact that some individuals never experience meaningful real income growth, others who do experience it are considered under the permanent income concept to pay taxes on the basis of past or expected future income. Yet, *present income,* which is the immediate source of general sales tax payments, seems to more closely fit the ability-to-pay goal of equal sacrifice from foregone consumption than does consumption sacrificed over an entire lifetime. The fact remains that the sacrifice of a present period tax payment is initially felt in the present period. In addition, if a person's income rises above subsistence during lifetime, it is unlikely that his or her C/Y ratio would remain constant since the relative importance of necessity to luxury consumption is then likely to decline. Finally, the traditional viewpoint of regressivity is sustained by the fact that most states exempt necessities such as food and prescription medicine from the sales tax base—which seems to suggest that the basic structure of the tax tends to be regressive in the minds of political decision makers.

Excise taxes. Regarding narrowbased sales (excise) taxes, the overall incidence of these taxes in the United States is *regressive*—though a few placed on luxury consumption are progressive.[14] However, some excise taxes which fail to meet the ability-to-pay benchmark still perform adequately in reference to the benefit criterion such as the earmarked federal excise tax on gasoline.

Equity and sales tax enforcement. Ultimately, equity in the distribution of tax burdens must encompass the ability to enforce and collect the tax in question effectively. The general sales and excise taxes used in the United States generally meet this criterion in an adequate fashion. For example, collection costs incurred by the states for the general retail sales tax average about 1.5 percent of the total revenues collected. The total cost of enforcement, however, is increased further by taxpayer compliance costs, which often entail additional labor and equipment inputs. To compensate for these business-incurred collection expenses, a number of states allow discounts to retailers on the total amount of general sales tax revenues paid to the

---

[14] A study of the incidence of federal excise taxes by T. W. Calmus shows a regressivity index of -2.8 for all federal excises prior to the comprehensive federal excise tax revisions of 1965, and a -2.9 regressivity for excises repealed that year. (Note: A negative value indicates regressivity, a positive value indicates progressivity, and zero indicates proportionality. Moreover, a larger negative or positive value reflects greater regressivity or progressivity, respectively.) A wide range of results was demonstrated for particular excises. For example, the individual items varied from an extremely regressive -37.1 for the excise on smoking tobacco to a progressive $+14.2$ for the excise on furs (now repealed). For the detailed study, see Thomas W. Calmus, "The Burden of Federal Excise Taxes by Income Class," *Quarterly Review of Economics and Business,* Spring 1970, pp. 17-23.

government. These discounts generally range from 1 to 5 percent of total tax receipts. Moreover, vendors often collect more than the tax liability based on their total sales through use of the bracket system of tax assessment, whereby small sales bring in more than the established rate. In a number of states, vendors are allowed to retain these excess receipts, which are known as *breakage*. Most states not providing discounts to vendors allow them to keep the breakage.

Federal, state, and local excises are collected with varying degrees of efficiency. The Alcohol and Tobacco Tax Unit of the Internal Revenue Service is responsible for collecting the federal sumptuary excises on alcoholic beverages and tobacco products. Federal taxes on tobacco are collected directly from the manufacturer, while state tobacco taxes are collected from wholesale distributors of tobacco products. Obviously, the federal enforcement approach is more easily accomplished, because there are relatively few manufacturers of tobacco products as compared to the number of wholesale distributors of tobacco products within a state. No discount for collection efforts is allowed to manufacturers for the federal tobacco excise, but most states do allow discounts to distributors. These discounts generally range between 1 and 10 percent of sales.

In general, it can be concluded that the *enforcement efficiency* of sales taxes, both broadbased and narrowbased, meets the test of adequacy, since a satisfactory ratio exists between collection costs and total revenues collected. Moreover, the enforcement of general sales and excise taxes in the United States successfully avoids widespread evasion efforts.

Stabilization effects

Sales taxes are not important fiscal stabilizers in the United States. One major explanation is the fact that the federal government does not impose a broadbased sales tax, and the related fact that national government is the most efficient locus for the direction of aggregate economic policy. Even if a broadbased sales tax were imposed by the federal government, it still would be inferior to the personal income tax for stabilization purposes for two reasons: (1) the less-elastic income elasticity of taxation (Y^t) for the general sales tax as compared to the personal income tax, and (2) the functional dependence of consumption expenditures on income as the basic source of purchasing power, thus rendering income tax policy a more direct fiscal instrument.

The approximate *unitary elasticity* of general sales taxes, is demonstrated in Table 12–5, in which the 11 studies cited yield an average elasticity of approximately *one* within a range of 0.80 to 1.27. This unitary elasticity limits their countercyclical performance as an *auto-*

TABLE 12–5   **Income elasticity of state and local general retail sales taxes: Summary of empirical studies**

Study	Year published	Area covered	Elasticity coefficient
Davies	1962	Arkansas	1.27
Rafuse	1965	United States	1.27
ACIR*	1971	Maryland	1.08
Peck	1969	Indiana	1.04
Netzer	1961	United States	1.0
Harris	1966	United States	1.0
Davies	1962	United States	1.0
Friedlaender-Swanson-Due	1973	United States	<1.0†
ACIR*	1971	Kentucky	0.92
Arizona Planning Division	1971	Arizona	0.87
Davies	1962	Tennessee	0.80

* Advisory Commission on Intergovernmental Relations.

† An average general sales tax income elasticity for *all states* is not presented in this study. However, the income elasticities of general sales taxes presented for the *individual states* are generally inelastic, with only one state displaying an elastic coefficient.

Studies cited: Advisory Commission on Intergovernmental Relations, "State–Local Revenue Systems and Educational Finance," unpublished report to the President's Commission on School Finance, November 12, 1971; Arizona Department of Economic Planning and Development, *Arizona Intergovernmental Structure: A Financial View to 1980* (Phoenix, 1971); David G. Davies, "The Sensitivity of Consumption Taxes to Fluctuations in Income," *National Tax Journal,* September 1962, pp. 281–90; Ann F. Friedlaender, Gerald J. Swanson, and John F. Due, "Estimating Sales Tax Revenue Changes in Response to Changes in Personal Income and Sales Tax Rates," *National Tax Journal,* March 1973, pp. 103–110; Robert Harris, *Income and Sales Taxes: The 1970 Outlook for States and Localities* (Chicago: Council of State Governments, 1966); Dick Netzer, "Financial Needs and Resources over the Next Decade," in National Bureau of Economic Research, *Public Finances: Needs, Sources, and Utilization* (Princeton, N.J.: Princeton University Press, 1961); John E. Peck, "Financing State Expenditures in a Prospering Economy," *Indiana Business Review,* July 1969, pp. 7–15; Robert W. Rafuse, "Cyclical Behavior of State-Local Finances," in *Essays in Fiscal Federalism,* ed. Richard A. Musgrave (Washington, D.C.: Brookings Institution, 1965).

Source: (Except for Friedlaender-Swanson-Due study) Advisory Commission on Intergovernmental Relations, *State-Local Finances: Significant Features and Suggested Legislation* (Washington, D.C.: U.S. Government Printing Office, 1972), p. 301.

matic fiscal stabilizer, since their receipts do not expand more rapidly than income during inflationary booms, nor do they contract more rapidly than income during economic downturns. The application of ad hoc *discretionary fiscal stabilizers* in the form of sales tax changes, both broadbased and narrowbased, could be of some positive counter-cyclical value, though the absence of a broadbased federal sales tax in the United States again limits this capability. Nonetheless, the imposition of narrowbased excise taxes during periods of war-induced inflation and consumer goods scarcity does tend to discourage the effective demand for these goods. In addition, the use of an *interest-equalization tax* to discourage the outflow of domestic capital to foreign nations represents a technique employed for the purpose of improving the nation's balance of international payments. The federal government imposed such an excise tax on foreign stocks and bonds acquired by Americans (Canada excepted) between 1963 and 1976.

The more insensitive income elasticity of sales taxes, as compared to income taxes, also restricts the long-run revenue productivity of these taxes. This can have significant fiscal implications for jurisdictions relying on sales taxation, since long-run demands for public-type economic goods may grow at a more rapid rate than sales tax revenues.[15] Table 12–5, as noted above, summarizes the results of several studies of the income elasticity of the general sales tax in the United States. Although the results vary, the mean (average) result approximates *unitary* income elasticity, that is, $Y^t = 1$. While no table is presented here for the income elasticity of narrowbased excise taxes, each of 18 separate studies surveyed suggests an *inelastic* income coefficient ($Y^t < 1$) for the motor fuel and tobacco excises.[16]

---

[15] See Chapter 18 for an elaboration of this point.

[16] See Advisory Commission on Intergovernmental Relations, *State-Local Finances: Significant Features and Suggested Legislation* (Washington, D.C.: U.S. Government Printing Office, 1972), p. 301.

13

Payroll taxes,
social insurance, and
public assistance
programs

Government-sponsored *income maintenance programs* in the American public sector fall into two major categories: *social insurance* programs, financed through payroll taxation, and *public assistance* (welfare) programs, financed through general revenues. Table 13-1 summarizes some of the major income maintenance programs of each variety. Overall, total income maintenance expenditures have increased significantly in the United States during recent decades.

The first section of this chapter will discuss the social insurance programs financed by payroll taxes. Then, public assistance programs will be described, and after some of their major weaknesses have been pointed out, the final section will evaluate the proposed negative income tax solution to the welfare issue.

PAYROLL TAXES AND SOCIAL INSURANCE PROGRAMS

Payroll (employment) taxes represent the most rapidly growing major tax source in the American public sector at the present time. In one sense, these are excise taxes imposed on a transactions base consisting of wage and salary payments to the labor factor of production. In another sense, they resemble income taxes, but the payroll tax base differs from that of the personal income tax, since the total

TABLE 13-1   Major government income maintenance programs (fiscal year 1979)

Program	Form of aid	Source of funds	Benefit payments (billions)
Social insurance:			
Social Security			
Old-Age and survivors			
Insurance	Cash	Federal	$ 87.6
Medicare*	In-kind	Federal	28.2
Disability Insurance	Cash	Federal	13.4
Federal Employee Benefits†	Cash	Federal	24.8
Unemployment Insurance	Cash	Federal-state	11.3
Workers' Compensation	Cash	Federal-state	11.1
Veterans Benefits	Cash	Federal	11.0
Railroad Retirement	Cash	Federal	4.2
Disabled Coal Miners	Cash	Federal	1.0
Total			192.6
Public assistance:			
Medicaid	In-kind	Federal-state	23.4
Aid to Families with			
Dependent Children	Cash	Federal-state	14.3
Supplemental Security Income	Cash	Federal-state	7.5
Food Stamp Program	In-kind	Federal	6.4
Child Nutrition	In-kind	Federal	3.4
Housing Assistance	In-kind	Federal	2.8
Total			57.8

* Includes Hospital Insurance and Supplementary Medical Insurance.
† Includes Military Retirement Benefits.
Source: U.S. Department of Commerce.

income of the taxpayer from all sources is not considered in the computation of the base. Furthermore, they are taxes only on labor, not on capital, income. Their revenues are normally earmarked for special trust funds to be used for designated purposes. The statutory incidence of such employment taxes may fall on either the employer or the employee or both.

Payroll taxes are most important at the federal level of government, where their growth has been extremely rapid. Federal payroll taxes in 1954 amounted to only $7 billion, as compared to $22 billion in 1964 and $127 billion in 1979 (fiscal years). This represents a growth from 10 percent of total federal nondebt revenues in 1954 to 25 percent in 1979. The major payroll taxes used in the American public sector will be discussed in terms of the social insurance programs they finance.

Social security payroll taxes:
The Old-Age, Survivors, Disability, and
Hospital Insurance Program (OASDHI)

The most important American payroll taxes were created by the Social Security Act of 1935. This depression-era measure was far more than an antidepression instrument. The initial legislation was divided into three sections providing for *old-age and survivors insurance* (OASI), for *unemployment insurance* (UI), and for certain *welfare payments* to the poor. Provisions for *disability insurance* (DI) were added to OASI in 1956, and for *hospital and health insurance* (HI) for the aged in 1965. Thus, the present social security program is represented by the name Old-Age, Survivors, Disability, and Hospital Insurance (OASDHI).

The earmarked payroll taxes collected under this program go into four separate trust funds: the *old-age and survivors, disability, hospital,* and *supplemental medical care trust funds.* Amounts equivalent to collections of OASDHI taxes are appropriated to these trust accounts, which are invested in securities of the federal government until used to pay benefits. Both employers and employees pay the taxes in equal amounts.[1] The taxes are levied on a base consisting of wage or salary earnings up to a certain maximum known as the *wage base ceiling.* In addition, since 1951 self-employed persons have paid taxes under a different formula to obtain coverage by the program. The original legislation had exempted from coverage various categories of employment, such as agricultural labor; domestic service in private homes; casual labor; services performed for religious, charitable, scientific, literary, and educational organizations; and services performed for the United States, a state, or political subdivisions. Many of these exemptions have since been eliminated.

In fiscal year 1979, some 68 percent of OASDHI benefits were distributed under the old-age and survivors insurance component, 22 percent under the hospital and supplemental medical insurance (Medicare) component, while the remaining 10 percent were distributed for disability insurance.

Old-age and survivors insurance in some ways resembles a private insurance system, but it differs in several important respects, including the fact that its "premiums" are really taxes; that is, they are *compulsory.* These compulsory premiums (payroll taxes) are calculated on a very rough actuarial basis, and reserves are accumulated to strengthen the trust fund and to assure payments when the claims of policyholders are due. Because a private insurance company operating on strict, actuarially computed principles would have to charge more annually for such benefits and privileges, the comparison between social and private insurance on an actuarial basis is somewhat loose.

However, the program is in close accord with certain other private insurance principles. For example, only insured or covered workers (whose pay has been taxed) are eligible to receive the nonhealth

---

[1] The *supplemental medical care* program is voluntary and is financed by equal contributions from participants aged 65 and over and the federal government.

benefits of the program. The benefits, moreover, belong to the workers by right. The programs are operated as separate financial operations with earmarked taxes (analogous here to premiums) going into special trust funds to help provide the benefits. It must be acknowledged, nonetheless, that the scale of benefit payments is not strictly proportional to the size of the tax payments. Present beneficiaries as a group are receiving benefits much larger than their payroll tax contributions would entitle them to, since an effort is made to keep the benefits consistent with rising prices in the economy. In fact, a poorly planned formula, introduced in 1972, caused an overindexation of benefits, which resulted in overcompensation for inflation until later repealed.

Disability insurance benefits are payable to a worker under age 65 who is unable to engage in any substantial gainful work because of a physical disability which can be expected to last for a long, indefinite period of time, or can be expected to result in death. This coverage does not relate to "job-caused" disability, which is covered under separate *workers' compensation* programs set up largely by the states. The dependents of a disabled worker covered by social security disability insurance receive benefits under the same conditions as the dependents of retired workers. Disability payments are made until an individual recovers and can return to work or until age 65, when retirement benefits would begin.

Congress amended the Social Security Act in the mid-1960s to provide for certain health insurance coverage, including the Medicare program. *Medicare* provides the aged, regardless of income, with a hospital insurance plan as well as an optional supplementary medical insurance (SMI) plan, at low rates, which covers doctors' fees. The monthly premium paid for the voluntary insurance plan is matched by the federal government. Most of the nation's aged have subscribed to this voluntary insurance plan. Certification by a physician is required before benefits will be paid. Hospitals and doctors are free to select their own collection agencies. The program, moreover, remains individualistic in the sense that the doctor may charge more than the fee listed on the reasonable-customary-charge schedule provided by the government. The doctor's fee is negotiated between the doctor and the patient, as customary, and the patient can go to the doctor of his or her choice.

The employer and the employee pay identical *payroll tax* rates to finance the various old age, survivors, disability, and hospital insurance benefits.[2] As of 1983, the employer and the employee each pay a tax rate of 6.7 percent on a maximum wage base of $35,700; thus, the

---

[2] Technically speaking, OASDHI consists of separate payroll taxes. However, since these taxes are collected simultaneously under one combined rate, they will usually be referred to here as a single tax.

combined employer-employee rate is 13.4 percent. The tax rate for self-employed persons covered by social security is somewhat greater than the separate employer or employee rate alone. In December 1977, Congress enacted a bill which greatly increased social security taxes into the future, primarily through a considerable expansion of the taxable wage base rather than a substantial tax rate increase. These programmed future increases in the taxable wage base and tax rates of the social security payroll tax are presented in Table 13-2.

Table 13-2 **Federal Old-Age, Survivors, Disability, and Hospital Insurance tax rates and bases, 1937-1990**

| | | Combined OASDHI tax rate (percent) | | |
Year	Taxable wage base ceiling	Employer and employee each (percent)	Combined employer and employee (percent)	Maximum amount paid each by employer and by employee
1937–49	$ 3,000	1.0	2.0	$ 30
1950	3,000	1.5	3.0	45
1951–53	3,600	1.5	3.0	54
1954	3,600	2.0	4.0	72
1955–56	4,200	2.0	4.0	84
1957–58	4,200	2.25	4.5	94
1959	4,800	2.5	5.0	120
1960–61	4,800	3.0	6.0	144
1962	4,800	3.125	6.25	150
1963–65	4,800	3.625	7.25	174
1966	6,600	4.2	8.4	277
1967	6,600	4.4	8.8	290
1968	7,800	4.4	8.8	343
1969–70	7,800	4.8	9.6	374
1971	7,800	5.2	10.4	405
1972	9,000	5.2	10.4	468
1973	10,800	5.3	10.6	572
1974	13,200	5.85	11.7	772
1975	14,100	5.85	11.7	825
1976	15,300	5.85	11.7	895
1977	16,500	5.85	11.7	965
1978	17,700	6.05	12.1	1,071
1979	22,900	6.13	12.26	1,404
1980	25,900	6.13	12.26	1,588
1981	29,700	6.65	13.3	1,975
1982	32,400	6.7	13.4	2,171
1983	35,700	6.7	13.4	2,392
1984	*	6.7	13.4	†
1985	*	7.05	14.1	†
1986–89	*	7.15	14.3	†
1990 and later ...	*	7.65	15.3	†

* Amount is adjusted automatically for increase in average earnings level of American workers.
† Subject to adjustable taxable wage base ceiling in second column of table.

Unemployment insurance payroll taxes:
The Unemployment Insurance Program

The Social Security Act of 1935, as observed earlier, also established an unemployment insurance (UI) program to be financed via payroll taxes. This program, unlike OASDHI, involves a combination of both federal and state fiscal action. The initial legislation provided an incentive for state government participation in the program by imposing a federal payroll tax of 1 percent to be paid by employers, with the stipulation that if a state unemployment insurance law and administration meets certain requirements, the federal government will pay 100 percent of the administrative expenses of the program and will permit employers to *credit* a state payroll tax against 90 percent of the federal tax. Thus, for every dollar of federal tax, the existence of a state unemployment tax would reduce the dollar of federal tax liability for the employer to 10 cents via the *tax credit* technique (if 90 cents is being collected under a state-imposed tax). Within a short time, all states passed unemployment insurance laws providing for state employment taxes on payrolls. Though all states participate in the program, some differentiation exists among the programs of the 50 states. For example, states may determine such basic features of their programs as coverage, benefits, the rate of the state tax, eligibility, and disqualification provisions.

The original legislation imposed the tax on the payrolls of employers of eight or more workers, but this has now been reduced to employers of one or more workers. Moreover, beginning in 1939, the tax was applied to only the first $3,000 of each covered employee's annual earnings, but by 1978 the taxable wage base had been increased to $6,000.[3] The federal tax rate was raised from 1 to 3 percent in 1938 and remained at that level until 1961. In 1961, the tax was increased to 3.1 percent, in 1970 to 3.2 percent, and in 1977 to 3.4 percent. The tax of 0.4 percent above the 3 percent rate is designated for the federal share of the tax to assist in meeting rising administrative costs and to provide additional financing for the loan fund. The latter supports advances made to states whose unemployment reserves become depleted. Credits for state taxes paid by employers continue to be computed on the basis of a 3 percent (not the actual 3.4 percent) federal tax. Thus, 90 percent of a 3 percent rate, or 2.7 percent, may be credited against the federal tax for state taxes paid by employers.

Although no federal tax is levied on employees, a few states impose unemployment insurance payroll taxes on employees. All states use *experience-rating systems* to determine the degree of unemployment risk of particular employers. Some low-risk employers pay taxes of

---

[3] A state may elect to exceed the federally established wage base of $6,000.

less than 2.7 percent on their federally covered payrolls to the states, though they still retain the full 2.7 percent credit against the federal tax. Taxes collected by the states are deposited in a separate unemployment trust fund. The individual states have their own accounts in the fund, against which they draw as required for the payment of unemployment benefits. During periods of recession or sustained stagflation, some states deplete their funds and must rely on loans from the federal Treasury to finance their benefit payments.

Most wage and salary earners (85 percent) are covered by unemployment insurance, primarily under the federal-state system described before. In addition to the regular benefits, Congress passed ad hoc legislation in 1958, and again in 1961, and permanent legislation in 1970, to extend benefits to those who have exhausted their regular benefit rights during periods of serious recession.

In addition to the social insurance programs described earlier, various other social insurance services are provided by state and local governments independently of federal support. These include the state-sponsored *workers' compensation* (industrial compensation) programs, used in all states, which provide medical services and cash benefits to a worker injured in connection with his/her job. More than three fourths of all nonagricultural employees are covered by such laws. The essence of most of the state workers' compensation laws is that the employer is responsible for injuries resulting from any accident "arising out of or in the course of employment," and thus for insuring workers in the event that such injuries occur. The quality of program coverage, however, varies greatly between the states. Some of the programs are inadequate in terms of their coverage, the length of the benefit period, and the amount of benefits. Also, they are often biased in favor of employers. For example, they limit the liability of employers by placing specific ceilings, often unreasonably low, on the amount of cash compensation that an employee can receive for a particular type of on-the-job injury.

Fiscal performance of payroll taxes and social insurance programs

The performance of the major payroll tax programs, OASDHI and unemployment insurance, in reference to the three primary branches of economic activity—allocation, distribution, and stabilization—will be evaluated in this section.

Allocational effects. In reference to the allocation function, OASDHI exerts considerable nonneutrality on private sector behavior in relation to voluntary saving. This nonneutrality is mainly the result of the fact that OASDHI is a "compulsory" savings and insurance program, and thus may bring about different savings behavior than would have been the voluntary, private savings choice of individual participants in the program. Moreover, an allocational nonneutrality can result from the fact that OASDHI is a tax on wages but not on capital. Thus, it is suggested that payroll taxes, by increasing the cost of hiring new employees, may encourage the substitution of capital for labor, since capital is not subject to the tax.

The unemployment compensation program, though generally less nonneutral than the OASDHI program, may also be expected to exert some nonneutral allocation effects. For example, a labor supply disin-centive may be exerted on secondary workers, such as wives who become unemployed, who may find it economically more advan-tageous to receive unemployment compensation and to work more in the home (not hiring help for child care, cleaning, and the like), rather than actively seeking reemployment with its accompanying payroll and income taxes. The greater the value of unemployment benefits, the more likely it is that such a trade-off would become important to the secondary worker.

Distributional effects. The performance of the OASDHI payroll tax structure is largely unsatisfactory when tested by the established principles of distributional equity, but especially in relation to the ability-to-pay principle. The proportionally rated OASDHI tax is dis-tinctly regressive when income is used as the indicator of taxpaying ability. In 1983, the OASDHI payroll tax applied to only the first $35,700 of annual wages and salaries. Thus, a worker who earned that amount (the taxable wage ceiling) would, at the rate of 6.7 percent in 1983, pay a tax of $2,392, the same amount of tax as would be paid by an individual with a salary of $100,000. Yet, the *effective* tax rate, in ability-to-pay terms, would be 6.7 percent of the wages of the first wage earner, but only 2.39 percent for the individual with $100,000 of wage income. This regressivity occurs because of the existence of a taxable wage base ceiling, at which point the tax rate falls to zero on additional wages. On wages up to the ceiling, the tax is essentially proportional, but beyond the ceiling, it becomes regressive. More-over, as some experts believe, if part or all of the *employer's* matching tax of 6.7 percent (in 1983) is shifted backward to the wage earner, the regressivity may be further accentuated.

Thus, the OASDHI payroll tax, which exempts income (wages) *above* a maximum level from the tax base, works in an exactly opposite manner to the federal personal income tax, which exempts income *below* a certain level from the base of the tax. The regressive effects of the former arrangement, and the contrasting progressive effects of the latter, are obvious. Since the tax exempts nonwage (property, capital) income from its base, still greater regressivity tends to result. This is so because property, as opposed to labor, as an income source be-comes a greater proportion of total income as income increases. More-over, the tax discriminates against multiworker families and in favor of single-worker families, since the former pay additional taxes for benefits which are partially redundant.

Efforts to alleviate the regressivity of the federal OASDHI payroll tax may take a number of different directions. For example, a *low-income exemption* could be affixed to the employee portion of the tax. Moreover, additional upward movements in the taxable wage-base ceiling would reduce the regressivity of the tax, or the ceiling could be entirely removed, thus allowing the imposition of a lower rate of tax. However, if the wage base ceiling is increased with a constant tax rate, overall tax burdens will increase accordingly.

A more basic reform would involve *general-fund financing* of part, or all, social security benefits from the progressive, federal personal income tax revenues. This course of action would not only reduce the tax regressivity, it would also reflect the long-term trend away from the private-insurance analogy that was earlier applied to the social security program. Instead, it would recognize that today's benefit structure, in some important ways, represents a *redistributional* program favoring low-income groups rather than providing an approximate quid pro quo between costs and benefits. Of course, if one considers the "pro-poor" nature of the benefit structure in a symmetrical fashion alongside the regressivity of the OASDHI payroll tax structure, the regressivity of the tax does not seem to be as serious an issue.

Relatedly, there appears to be a growing propensity among policymakers to coordinate various tax programs in such a manner as to offset the undesirable effects that one tax may exert. This tendency has been associated with payroll taxation in the sense that the refundable *earned income credit*[4] for low-income-family taxpayers, enacted in 1975, was made a part of the federal personal income tax structure primarily for the purpose of offsetting the burden of high OASDHI tax payments on low-income taxpayers. Moreover, the added burdens on taxpayers, especially those in the middle-income and upper-middle-income categories, resulting from the social security tax increases enacted in late 1977, were mitigated by subsequent legislation during 1978, and in 1981, which reduced federal personal income taxes with the offset to the higher social security taxes being one of the purposes of the tax reductions.

Meanwhile, taxes and benefits under the unemployment insurance program are not closely correlated to either the benefit or the ability-to-pay principles of distributional equity. The employer-paid taxes do not allow for a quid pro quo relationship between the earnings of the worker and the compensation benefits received by the worker if unemployment occurs. Furthermore, the ability to pay of the worker,

---

[4] See the discussion of the earned income credit in Chapter 8.

in income terms, is irrelevant, since it is the employer and not the employee who pays the tax at its statutory impact point though, admittedly, shifting considerations could in the long run bear more closely on the ability-to-pay benchmark. In all, it would seem that the most appropriate distributional equity criterion for an unemployment insurance program, rather than being a specific application of the benefit or ability-to-pay principles, would derive from the general social attitude that employment, or compensation for the involuntary absence of employment, is a guaranteed "right" of all individuals in the society.

Stabilization effects. As a social insurance program, OASDHI was not established, of course, for the primary purpose of serving as a stabilization policy instrument. However, it does bear some indirect benefits as a macroeconomic tool by providing a "floor" of purchasing power to retired persons, survivors, and the disabled. Since these groups are likely to possess relatively high average propensities to consume (C/Y), the effects of such spending certainly will be felt in the determination of greater effective demand and aggregate output.

In contrast, the primary purpose of the unemployment insurance program falls directly within the realm of macroeconomic policy. The unemployment insurance trust fund operates as a major *automatic fiscal stabilizer* for the national economy.[5] This occurs because benefit payments tend to exceed payroll tax collections during periods of recession, while tax payments tend to exceed benefit payments at times of high employment in the economy. An *expansionary* multiplier effect is thus initiated by the unemployment insurance program during recession, and a *contractionary* multiplier effect is provided during times of inflationary pressure. This result occurs without ad hoc *discretionary* changes in tax rates or benefits. The magnitude of the stabilization effects resulting from the unemployment compensation program may be increased, of course, if deliberate rate or benefit changes are enacted.

Social security financing: The future outlook

Congress enacted major long-term social security tax base and rate increases in December 1977, as a response to the projected insolvency of the system by the early 1980s. Yet, despite these sizable tax increases, insolvency still threatened to occur in the early 1980s. In fact, during 1982, a special federal commission was conducting a thorough study of the social security system, leading to proposed legislative changes. Meanwhile, the changes of 1977 failed to consider some of

---

[5] See Chapter 20 for further discussion of the unemployment insurance program as an automatic fiscal stabilizer.

the major contributing causes of the financing problem. The development of the social security financing crisis during the 1970s may be linked to the following causal forces: (1) the across-the-board 20 percent increase in social security benefits during 1972, accompanied by a faulty indexing formula which caused future benefits to be doubly adjusted for inflation (this double indexation now has been repealed); (2) the effect of the recession element of sustained stagflation on the level of payroll tax revenues; (3) demographic changes in the age distribution of the population toward relatively more older and fewer younger, work-age, people, and (4) the growing use of social security as an income redistribution mechanism.

Regarding the last point, it is very questionable whether earmarked payroll taxes are an efficient instrument for income redistribution. The hospital insurance coverage of Medicare is a case in point, since coverage is available even to persons who have not paid into the program through payroll taxes. Even though such redistributional objectives may have much merit, their financing should likely come from general-fund financing, especially income taxes, rather than from social security payroll taxes, since redistribution is by nature a broad national social objective separate from the more specific objectives of the social security system.

Moreover, as noted, even though the social security tax increases will diminish the regressivity of the tax by increasing the wage base ceiling, it will also sharply increase social security payroll tax liabilities for a large segment of middle- and upper-middle-income workers. It is doubtful that the subsequent federal personal income tax reductions enacted since 1977 will alleviate the tax burdens proportionately for these wage earners. Moreover, to the extent that the payroll tax increases support national redistributional objectives, there would appear to be no logic in having one segment of labor income bear a major portion of the burden while high-wage labor and property income sources bear a lesser burden. This disproportionate placement of taxation for financing the redistributional elements of social security could be alleviated, of course, by the partial conversion of social security financing to a *general-revenue source*, such as income tax funds, or the adoption of a *new broadbased federal tax*, such as the value-added tax, to help finance social security.

PUBLIC ASSISTANCE PROGRAMS

Several of the most important income-maintenance programs of the public assistance variety, which are not financed by payroll taxes, will be discussed in this section. These programs for the needy will be considered in the order of their benefit payment magnitude, as indicated in Table 13–1 at the beginning of the chapter.

Medicaid

The public assistance program providing Medicaid was introduced in 1965 by legislation which also established the Medicare component of the OASDHI social insurance program. The Medicaid legislation offers federal revenues to the states to cover a portion of the cost of an "approved" program for providing free medical services to specified needy persons. No maximum spending limitation is imposed on a state's outlay for such a program. In order to qualify for the federal aid, a state is required to establish a new medical assistance program to replace and liberalize the coverage under previous public assistance programs.

Benefits vary considerably among the states. The federal government covers at least 50 percent of the cost of such programs in all states, but may cover a substantially higher proportion in states with low per capita incomes. In 1979, nearly 8 million households received Medicaid benefits. The magnitude of Medicaid payments during fiscal 1979 was $23.4 billion (see Table 13-1)

Aid to Families with Dependent Children

The Aid to Families with Dependent Children (AFDC) program, like Medicaid, is a combined federal-state endeavor. The AFDC program provides monetary (cash) assistance to families with children under 18 years of age who need support due to the death, prolonged absence, or incapacity of one or both parents. A state also has the option of providing assistance, under certain circumstances, to families where both parents are present but the father is unemployed. Slightly more than one half of the states and the District of Columbia have elected this option.

Each state determines its own payment standards for basic needs. However, these differ greatly among the states, as is evidenced by the fact that in 1980, the average monthly payment per family ranged from $88 in Mississippi to $399 in California. Average monthly benefits nationally were $280. Nearly 3.6 million families (10.4 million persons) received AFDC payments during 1979. AFDC benefit payments amounted to $14.3 billion in that year (see Table 13-1). The federal share of total AFDC expenditures is slightly above 50 percent; the states finance most of the remainder, though a few local governments also help.

Supplemental Security Income

The Supplemental Security Income (SSI) program is a monetary (cash) assistance program of the federal government for the aged, blind, and disabled. It was established during 1972 to replace the then-existing combined federal-state programs for these groups. The basic SSI benefit is the same nationally and is financed by the federal government, but states have the option to provide additional assistance to SSI recipients. Many states have elected this option. Benefit payments in 1980 averaged $198 to disabled persons and $128 to aged persons.[6] During fiscal 1979, SSI benefit payments amounted to $7.5 billion (see Table 13–1).

Food Stamp Program

The Food Stamp Program, established in 1964, is a federal program of in-kind assistance to the needy in the form of a monthly allotment of coupons that can be used to purchase food. It is available to all low-income individuals without regard to family or employment status. In 1977, the maximum annual food stamp allotment for a family of four with no other income was $2,088. This amount is reduced, if net income is received, by 30 cents of each dollar of net income. In most instances, able-bodied adult food stamp recipients must register for work and accept suitable employment, in order to be eligible. Food stamp benefits amounted to $6.4 billion in fiscal 1979 (see Table 13–1) with approximately 5.9 million households receiving the benefits.

Fiscal performance of public assistance programs

Undoubtedly, the public assistance programs described above, along with certain redistributional effects derived from social insurance programs, help to reduce poverty in the United States. For example, it was estimated by the Congressional Budget Office that 21.4 million families would have had incomes below the poverty level for a nonfarm family of four ($5,815) during fiscal 1976 if no income-maintenance programs had been in effect. This number would be reduced to 10.7 million families if the monetary (cash) benefits of the social insurance and public assistance programs were added to the income from other sources for that year. Moreover, if in-kind benefits are also counted as income, the number of families below the poverty line would decrease to 6.6 million.

Yet 6.6 million families, which was 8.3 percent of all American families in that year, still represents a sizable pocket of "postfisc" poverty—even after a very comprehensive definition of expanded income, inclusive of both monetary and in-kind benefits from governmental programs, has been applied. In addition, numerous specific

---

[6] Data do not include state SSI payments that are administered by state governments, but do include payments administered by the federal government.

serious problems exist in the maze of present income-maintenance programs. For example, some programs provide considerably different benefits to individuals with similar needs. This is especially true of the Medicaid and AFDC public assistance programs, which are essentially controlled by the states even though federal funds provide substantial proportions of the financing of the programs. Benefit levels, as a result of state determination, vary widely among states, though federal food stamps do tend to alleviate the effects of this somewhat for the AFDC program.

Moreover, differentials exist among demographic and family groups in some public assistance programs. For example, AFDC benefits are restricted to fatherless families or, in about one half of the states, unemployed fathers. The present system also is biased against childless couples and nonelderly single persons. In addition, the incentive to work is reduced in a number of ways. In many states, for example, earnings from a minimum-wage job plus food stamps would be less than the assistance payments to a family of equal size with no one working. Another related issue stems from the so-called *benefit reduction rate* (marginal tax rate), which refers to the loss in benefits per dollar of additional earnings. Although no single program has a benefit reduction rate on earned (labor) income greater than 70 percent, the cumulative rate from more than one program may be considerably higher than that figure.

Furthermore, the presence of so many, largely uncoordinated, public assistance programs being directed by three levels of government breeds widespread administrative inefficiency. Thus, administrative expenses take up unnecessarily large proportions of total program budgets, and error rates are high. In addition, the system tends to be slow in response to the needs of recipients. Unquestionably, the public assistance programs of the American public sector have spent enough taxpayer money during recent decades to have done a much better and more equitable job of eliminating poverty than has been the case. No small part of this outcome has been the result of an overdecentralization of program determination, despite the centralization at the federal level of the bulk of program financing.[7] One often-advocated fiscal instrument for improving the nation's public welfare system is that of a comprehensive federal negative income tax. This proposed technique will be discussed in the final section of the chapter.

---

[7] It will be demonstrated in Chapter 17 that central (national) government, as opposed to subnational governments, has a comparative advantage in directing national redistributional programs.

THE NEGATIVE INCOME TAX CONCEPT

Since the 1960s, widespread interest has been apparent regarding the possible use of a federal negative income tax (NIT) to alleviate poverty.[8] Under this concept, an individual with personal income in excess of the poverty level is considered to be capable of making "positive" tax contributions to the government, but a person with personal income below the designated poverty level is considered as eligible to receive the "negative" transfer of funds from the government. Since both tax and transfer payments are non-resource-absorbing fiscal activities, a transfer payment may appropriately be considered as a *negative tax,* that is, the government transfers funds to an individual rather than exacting them from the individual in the form of a tax.

The reasoning behind the proposed extension of the NIT concept to the presently existing federal personal income tax structure includes the basic fact that an individual with little or no income is unable to take full advantage of personal exemptions and personal deductions otherwise available to persons with greater income. Thus, it can be said that such individuals are being doubly penalized for being poor, and monetary compensation by the government in the form of a negative tax payment is appropriate. A rational negative income tax program should be coordinated with job training and other assistance designed to make it possible to find employment, or better employment, and thus for individuals to obtain greater positive income by themselves. However, there are instances when it is either very difficult, or impossible, for individuals to increase their positive incomes above the poverty level.

Table 13-3 and Figure 13-1 demonstrate both a 100 percent NIT, which is assumed to fully assure the taxpaying unit (here a family of 4) an income sufficient to eliminate poverty, and a 50 percent NIT, which will partially eliminate poverty. Under the 100 percent rate,

---

[8] For various discussions of this concept, see Milton Friedman, *Capitalism and Freedom* (Chicago: University of Chicago Press, 1962), chap. 12, and "The Case for the Negative Income Tax: A View from the Right," *Proceedings of the National Symposium on the Guaranteed Income,* Chamber of Commerce of the United States, December 1966, pp. 49–55; Robert J. Lampman, "Prognosis for Poverty," *Proceedings of the Fifty-Seventh Annual Conference of the National Tax Association,* 1964, pp. 71–81, and "Approaches to the Reduction of Poverty," *American Economic Review,* May 1965, pp. 521–29, and "Negative Rates Income Taxation," Office of Economic Opportunity (unpublished paper), 1965. See also Robert Theobald, *Free Men and Free Markets* (New York: Clarkson N. Potter, Inc., 1963); James Tobin, "Improving the Economic Status of the Negro," *Daedalus,* Fall 1965, pp. 889–95, and "The Case for an Income Guarantee," *The Public Interest.* Summer 1966; James Tobin, Joseph Pechman, and Peter Mieszkowski, "Is a Negative Income Tax Practical?", *Yale Law Journal,* November 1967, pp. 1–27.

TABLE 13-3 Examples of 100 percent and 50 percent negative income taxes for a poverty income level of $6,000*

	100 percent NIT		50 percent NIT	
Pre-NIT income	NIT payment	Post-NIT income	NIT payment	Post-NIT income
$6,000	$ 0	$6,000	$ 0	$6,000
4,500	1,500	6,000	750	5,250
3,000	3,000	6,000	1,500	4,500
1,500	4,500	6,000	2,250	3,750
0	6,000	6,000	3,000	3,000

* Based on the pretax income of a family of four.

any deficiency between pre-NIT income and the designated poverty-level income of $6,000 will be made up through an NIT payment. Under the 50 percent rate, however, only one half of this deficiency is offset via an NIT payment. It is important to note that the 50 percent rate will always result in more post-NIT income for taxpayers who have earned some income of their own, as compared to someone who

FIGURE 13-1 Examples of 100 percent and 50 percent negative income taxes for a poverty income level of $6,000*

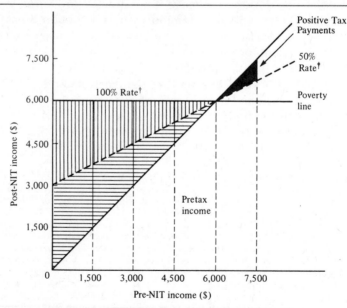

† Negative tax payments received under 100 percent rate = ≡ + ||| .
‡ Negative tax payments received under 50 percent rate = ≡
* Based on the pretax income of a family of four.

only receives an NIT payment. In fact, this would be true for any negative income tax with a rate below 100 percent. Conversely, the 100 percent rate will guarantee the same $6,000 income to all taxpayers, regardless of whether they have earned any income of their own.

Clearly, the 100 percent NIT rate will discourage work incentives for those who would be able to earn some part of the $6,000 poverty–line income. On the other hand, it does fully protect against poverty. The below-100 percent rate will not fully eliminate poverty, but it will help to preserve work incentives by always allowing a greater post-NIT level of purchasing power if the taxpayer has earned some income. Of course, the objectives of both full poverty alleviation and preserving work incentives could be realized, but with considerable additional treasury costs, if the poverty-income line were increased to $12,000 and a 50 percent rate were applied. Although this is not shown in Table 13–3 or Figure 13–1, it can be readily understood that a 50 percent rate up to a $12,000 poverty line would allow $6,000 to a taxpayer with no income, thus fully eliminating poverty, but at the same time would allow greater post-NIT income for those taxpayers with earnings above zero. However, it would also provide NIT payments to individuals above the poverty line. In any event, regardless of the rate applied or the poverty-income level, it would seem that any effective NIT would need to be coordinated with reasonable, and enforceable, work-requirement rules for those individuals who are able to find employment.

In conclusion, it might be observed that the widespread interest in and support of the federal negative income tax concept, along with the serious problems present in the existing public assistance approach, may ultimately lead to the adoption of a comprehensive version of this redistributional fiscal instrument. Meanwhile, the beginning of negative income taxation already exists in the American public sector in the form of the federal earned income credit and the Supplemental Security Income Program as well as the various state income tax credits for sales and property taxes paid by low-income taxpayers.

14

Tax reform: Alternative tax instruments for the American public sector

---

THE POLITICS OF TAX REFORM

Why new tax sources?

The *fiscal systems* of government should reflect the economic and social conditions of a given period of time. Since such conditions are likely to change over time, so also should public sector taxes and expenditures be subject to change in reflection of these changing economic and social parameters. One relevant example in the United States at the present time is provided by the problems of social security financing.[1] While the federal social security payroll tax has been adequate for carrying this financial responsibility for most of the history of the social security system—following its inception in 1937, more recent demographic and other changes have reduced the capability of the payroll tax to perform this role. As a result, alternative financing schemes are presently being considered. One of these, the possible use of a federal value-added tax to replace part, or all, of the payroll tax revenues, will be evaluated in a later section of the chapter.

Other reasons presently being given for American tax reform include:

1. The threat of huge federal deficits over the next few fiscal years.
2. Severe state and local government financial problems.

---

[1] See Chapter 13.

3. The need to stimulate saving and investment activities, so as to expand aggregate supply, increase labor productivity, and promote economic growth.
4. The desirability of attaining greater equity in the distribution of tax burdens.[2]

Intergoal trade-offs and the redistributional effects of tax reform

Thus, some reasons for tax reform may be unique to the present time, such as the issue of social security financing, while other reasons may be more of a traditional nature, such as distributional equity. The latter traditional type of argumentation in behalf of tax reform also mentions such specific goals as allocational neutrality, economic growth or other stabilization objectives, and administrative simplification. Yet, conflicts invariably arise between the various objectives of tax reform, whether traditional or otherwise. For example, allocational neutrality and administrative simplification would normally be enhanced by a more comprehensive, less differentiated, tax base and rate structure. However, specific tax provisions may be enacted in order to encourage such activities as energy conservation or saving and investment (to promote economic growth) which, in fact, differentiate or erode the tax base and rate structure. As a result, the neutrality and administrative simplification objectives may be largely offset.

Importantly, all specific tax provisions which *reduce* tax liabilities exert distributional effects in favor of persons who receive the tax reduction benefits. However, unless the composite of specific tax provisions or loopholes reduces the taxes of persons in equal proportions to their incomes, the consequent redistribution of tax burdens will favor some taxpayers relative to others. Similarly, tax *increases* that are unevenly distributed in proportion to incomes will also exert redistributional effects. Hence, tax reform or change is inextricably involved with distributional considerations, even when these considerations do not outwardly appear to be the explicit or primary reason for a particular tax provision being adopted.[3] Moreover, if one accepts the validity of the political-influence hypothesis,[4] the ability to influence such redistribution would be positively related to the amount of a person's income and/or wealth.

---

[2] In recent years, however, the equity goal has received less emphasis than in former times.

[3] For a discussion of this point, see Bernard P. Herber, "Personal Income Tax Reform and the Interaction Between Budgetary Goals: A UK and USA Comparison," in *Reforms of Tax Systems*, ed. Karl W. Roskamp and Francesco Forte (Detroit: Wayne State University Press, 1981), pp. 55–71.

[4] See Chapter 3.

Incremental tax changes

The multiple effects and goals of tax reform often help cause a political impasse against comprehensive tax reform at a given point of time. Thus, tax changes are normally *incremental* or *marginal* rather than comprehensive in character. However, there are some exceptions to this point. For example, major social or economic disturbances may so disrupt a politico-economic system that the aftermath will provide an environment within which comprehensive tax and/or intergovernmental fiscal changes may be accomplished. Such was the case in the Federal Republic of Germany (West Germany) and in Japan following World War II. Yet, more often than not, the conflicting interests affected by tax reform, and various other political realities, create a situation whereby the entire tax system is usually *not* subject to review and change at a given point of time. Instead, the changes that are introduced are more of an incremental or marginal nature.[5]

ALTERNATIVE TAX INSTRUMENTS

Personal Taxation

Comprehensive income tax. Tax reformers have often advocated a *comprehensive income tax (CIT)* as the best tax instrument. This tax is associated with the so-called *accretion concept* of taxable income.[6] Under this concept, emphasis is placed on the *uses* of income rather than on the *sources* or *flow* of income as the relevant income tax base. This contrasts to the operational income tax systems in the United States and other Western nations which, both theoretically and administratively, focus on the flow of earnings.

Table 14–1 demonstrates the nature of the CIT base with its "uses-of-income" orientation. All three taxpayers—A, B, and C—spend the same amount, $25,000, on consumption. Yet, taxpayer A is said to have the *greatest* "ability to pay taxes" since his economic power to use income is the greatest. That is, taxpayer A is able to consume at a $25,000 level and still conduct $5,000 in saving and investment ac-

---

[5] The Reaganomics "tax revolution" may well stand as a peacetime exception to this behavioral norm. For example, the federal corporation income and estate-gift taxes were greatly reduced as revenue sources in 1981 and, along with the pattern of federal personal income tax reductions, helped to redistribute federal tax burdens downward along the income scale. In other words, several major federal taxes were simultaneously changed by the Economic Recovery Tax Act of 1981, with important redistributional effects ensuing.

[6] The theoretical development of the accretion concept was pioneered in Germany by Georg Schanz and in the United States by Robert M. Haig and Henry Simons. Essentially, the concept would define the income tax base in terms of the accretion or accumulation of economic power.

TABLE 14–1   **A comprehensive income tax following the "uses-of-income" approach (tax period equals one year)**

(1) Taxpayer	(2) Consumption (C)	(3) Change in net worth (ΔNW)	(4) CIT base ($C \pm \Delta NW$)
A	$25,000	$+5,000	$30,000
B	25,000	0	25,000
C	25,000	−5,000	20,000

tivities, as indicated by the increase in his net worth of $5,000 during the year. Meanwhile, taxpayer C exhibits the *least* "ability to pay taxes" under this approach, since he actually dissaved by $5,000 as his consumption exceeded his income during the year. On the other hand, taxpayer B, who spent all of his income on consumption, ranks *second* in the ability to use income and, hence, in the "ability to pay taxes."

Importantly, income is defined in broad or comprehensive terms, with no important exceptions. Thus, factor earnings such as wages, interest, rents, or profits are viewed as increasing the economic power to consume and to save as do transfer payments, gifts, inheritances, and gambling winnings. In practice, such a nondifferentiated income tax base (and rate) structure with a "uses of income" orientation would be difficult to attain, just as have been attempts to achieve a comprehensive base with the conventional "flow-emphasis" income taxes, since the tax system is often used to pursue various allocational, distributional, and stabilization objectives. The special tax provisions created by the efforts to attain these objectives, by their very nature, differentiate and erode the income tax base (and rate) structure.

A U.S. Treasury study,[7] published in 1977, suggests a possible structure for an American CIT, combining both theoretical and administrative considerations. This hypothetical CIT is summarized in Table 14–2 (which also summarizes the features of a proposed personal consumption or expenditure tax, as will be discussed later). It may be observed that even though the CIT theoretically emphasizes the *uses* of income, it must be administered from a *flow* of income standpoint. In effect, the Treasury-proposed CIT would first integrate the existing federal personal and corporation income taxes in order to acquire a more comprehensive tax base. Moreover, interest income earned from state and local government debt, now tax exempt, would be included in the tax base. In addition, the CIT would tax earnings

---

[7] U.S. Treasury Department, *Blueprints for Basic Tax Reform* (Washington, D.C.: U.S. Government Printing Office, 1977).

TABLE 14–2   Comparison of the major features of the United States comprehensive income tax and personal consumption (expenditure)* tax proposals

Tax item	Treatment under comprehensive income tax	Treatment under personal consumption tax
Corporation income Retained earnings	Included in tax base as income to individual shareholder	No tax unless spent for consumption
Dividends	Included in tax base as received by individual shareholder	No tax unless spent for consumption
Capital gains	Fully included in tax base upon realization	No tax unless spent for consumption
Capital losses	Fully deducted from tax base upon realization	No tax offset unless consumption is reduced
State and local government bond interest	Included in tax base	No tax unless spent for consumption
Other interest income	Included in tax base	No tax unless spent for consumption
Rental value of owner-occupied homes	Excluded from tax base, but property tax deduction would be eliminated	Implicitly included in tax base since home purchase is treated as consumption
Contributions to retirement pensions	Excluded from tax base	Excluded from tax base
Interest earnings on pension funds	Fully taxed as accrued—tax paid by either employer or by individual	Excluded from tax base
Retirement benefits from pension funds	Included in tax base	Included in tax base unless saved
Social security contributions	Excluded from tax base	Excluded from tax base
Social security retirement income and unemployment compensation	Included in tax base	Included in tax base unless saved
Wage and salary income	Included in tax base	Included in tax base unless saved
Deposits in qualified investment accounts	No tax consequences	Excluded (deducted) from tax base
Withdrawals from qualified investment accounts	No tax consequences	Included in tax base
Tax rate structure	Progressive	Progressive

* Specifically referred to as a *cash flow tax* in the Treasury study.
Source: Adapted from U.S. Treasury Department, *Blueprints for Basic Tax Reform,* Table 1, pp. 17–20.

on pension funds as they accrue and retirement benefits as they are received, while allowing employer and employee contributions for pensions to be deducted from the tax base. Progressive tax rates would be applied to the CIT base.

The primary advantage of the comprehensive income tax is its distributional equity performance in relationship to the ability-to-pay benchmark.[8] It also would provide greater allocational neutrality and administrative simplicity due to its comprehensive, minimally differentiated, base structure. On the other hand, since it taxes economic power in both its consumptive and saving uses, it raises the relative price of saving by taxing the future income which it will earn. In so doing, it will tend to reduce the level of saving in the economy unless this substitution effect is offset by a comparable income effect which increases saving.[9] If saving is reduced, of course, economic growth is likely to be retarded. Thus, even though overall allocational neutrality would be improved, the specialized "saving-decision" component of allocation would become more nonneutral.

Personal consumption tax. Recent years have witnessed growing support for the adoption of a *personal consumption tax (PCT),* also commonly known as an *expenditure tax.*[10] A PCT, like the CIT, would follow a uses of income definition of the tax base. However, it would include in the tax base only the use of income for consumption. It would *not* tax income used for saving and investment purposes. Thus, in terms of Table 14–1, the PCT base for taxpayer A would be $25,000 instead of $30,000, as it would be under the CIT.

Further understanding of the structure of a PCT can be obtained by reference to Table 14–2, which summarizes a hypothetical PCT as proposed for consideration by the U.S. Treasury Department. Again, a flow of earnings approach would be required for the administration of the tax, as with the CIT, even though its conceptual orientation is on the uses of income. However, the flow of income would be taxed only

---

[8] For a detailed discussion of the merits and demerits of the CIT, see the following works: Joseph A. Pechman, ed., *What Should be Taxed: Income or Expenditure?* (Washington, D.C.: Brookings Institution, 1980); Richard Goode, *The Individual Income Tax,* rev. ed. (Washington, D.C.: Brookings Institution, 1976), and also his "The Economic Definition of Income," in *Comprehensive Income Taxation,* ed. Joseph A. Pechman (Washington, D.C.: Brookings Institution, 1977), Chapter 1; *The Structure and Reform of Direct Taxation,* Report of a Committee chaired by Professor J. E. Meade (London: Allen & Unwin, 1978); U.S. Treasury Department, *Blueprints for Basic Tax Reform* (Washington, D.C.: U.S. Government Printing Office, 1977), and Bernard P. Herber, "Personal Income Tax Reform and the Interaction Between Budgetary Goals: A UK and USA Comparison," in *Reforms of Tax Systems,* ed. Karl W. Roskamp and Francesco Forte (Detroit: Wayne State University Press, 1981), pp. 55–71.

[9] See the discussion of the effects of marginal tax rates on saving and investment activities in Chapter 20.

[10] Such a tax has been used historically, with limited success, in two developing nations—Ceylon (now Sri Lanka) and India.

on that part of the flow spent for consumption. Taxpayers, under the Treasury-proposed PCT, could select from between two alternative investment procedures. Under *one* method, asset purchases could be deducted from the flow of earnings, if made through qualified accounts. These accounts would keep formal records of the taxpayer's net investment activities via annual saving and dissaving adjustments. Increases in net worth (positive net investment) would reduce the tax base, and decreases in net worth would increase the tax base. Under the *second* method, saving not deposited in a qualified account would be included in the tax base, but the subsequent income from such invested saving would be excluded from the tax base. All consumer durable goods, including automobiles and homes, would be treated as assets purchased outside a qualified account. Progressive rates would be applied to the PCT base under the Treasury proposal.

The primary advantage of the personal consumption tax is its favorable treatment of saving, so as to encourage such activity, leading to increased real capital formation and economic growth.[11] Its distributional equity defense usually takes the form of the "limited-resource-pool" argument, which points out that consumption activity uses up scarce resources while saving and investment activity increases such resources. Thus, an altruistic advantage is said to accompany the use of income for saving, and thus it is only "equitable" not to tax this activity. Another equity argument in defense of the PCT would point out that with the appropriate minimum consumption exemption and statutorily progressive tax rate structure, the burden distribution of a PCT could be made progressive relative to income.

Personal wealth tax. Rather than focusing on the current income or consumption of an individual, the *personal wealth tax (PWT)* looks toward an individual's stock of wealth or assets as the basis for personal taxation.[12] Such wealth may either be self-accumulated or inherited. A PWT, which is alternately known as a *net wealth tax* or *net worth tax,* is imposed in a number of nations, but is not used in the United States. Economically developed nations such as Austria, Denmark, Finland, Japan, Luxembourg, the Netherlands, Norway, Sweden, Switzerland, and West Germany use the tax. Moreover, it is also used in developing nations such as India and Pakistan. It is levied on the aggregate wealth (assets, property) of the individual owner rather

---

[11] For a detailed discussion of the merits and demerits of the PCT, see the same sources cited for the CIT in footnote 8.

[12] For detailed analyses of personal wealth taxation, see Organization for Economic Cooperation and Development, *The Taxation of Net Wealth, Capital Transfers and Capital Gains of Individuals* (Paris: OECD, 1979); Alan A. Tait, *The Taxation of Personal Wealth* (Urbana: University of Illinois Press, 1967); Lester C. Thurow, *The Impact of Taxes on the American Economy* (New York: Praeger Publishers, 1971), and also his "Net Worth Taxes," *National Tax Journal,* September 1972, pp. 417–23.

than on a specific item of wealth itself. Thus, it is a personal rather than an impersonal, *in rem*, tax. In this sense, it contrasts sharply with the property tax which does not concern itself with the overall wealth status of the owner of the property. Moreover, it contrasts with the property tax in the important sense that it is a *net* rather than a gross tax. That is, the PWT allows the deduction of liabilities (claims) against the property from the base of the tax, while the property tax does not allow such deductions.

The personal wealth tax is a comprehensive levy on most property, but household and personal effects are normally exempt as are pension rights. The usual taxpaying unit is the family. Some nations place a ceiling on the combined amount of tax payable from the dual imposition of both personal income and personal wealth taxes. This ceiling is expressed as a percentage of income. Rates in some nations—such as Austria, Luxembourg, the Netherlands, and West Germany—are proportional. In other nations—such as Denmark, Finland, Norway, Sweden, and Switzerland—the rate structure is graduated or progressive. The central government imposes the tax in most nations, but in Norway it is also used by local governments, and in Switzerland, it is imposed by the cantons or states. In some nations, the PWT is levied on incorporated businesses as well as on individuals.

Ideally, a person's net wealth should be determined anew each year, but practically this is not possible except for property such as shares of corporate stock. For most other property, so-called *expedients* are used to help administer the tax.[13] These expedients either remove the need to make annual valuations or they simplify the process of making such valuations. Under one expedient, an individual's net wealth may be considered as fixed over a period of years. Under another expedient, the values of particular classes of assets may be fixed by periodic official valuations, which then remain in force over a period of years. Under a third expedient, set rules or formulae for the valuation of certain classes of property may be applied. In all, the administration of the personal wealth tax is reasonably efficient in nations which use it, and moreover, it provides additional information to tax enforcement agencies which facilitates the collection of personal income taxes.

The personal wealth tax serves the goal of distributional equity better than does the property tax. As observed, it defines the tax base in terms of the "overall" wealth of the taxpayer, not only the *in rem* value of a "single item" of wealth—which says nothing about the overall taxpaying ability of an individual. Moreover, it achieves greater distributional equity by allowing liabilities or claims against

---

[13] See the Organization for Economic Cooperation and Development, *The Taxation of Net Wealth.*

property to be deducted from the tax base, thus creating a *"net wealth"* base. Hence, if two persons each possess gross wealth of $50,000, but one person has claims of $25,000 against that wealth while the other has no claims against his wealth, the greater net wealth of the person with no claims ($50,000 as compared to $25,000) clearly suggests a greater taxpaying ability for that person. Moreover, wealth can be used as a substitute for income in the application of the ability-to-pay principle. For example, it may be said that vertical tax equity can be served by a tax which provides a positive relationship between tax payments and a person's net wealth. Moreover, if one assumes a diminishing marginal utility of wealth as the amount of a person's wealth increases, a progressively rated personal wealth tax could be justified. Furthermore, since wealth or capital as a source of income tends to increase relative to labor as an income source as income increases, a tax on personal wealth rather than on labor income may also be said to serve the interests of vertical tax equity.

In terms of allocational performance, a PWT would tend to be neutral in terms of the choice between work and leisure, since income is taxed only if it is saved and invested in assets, not as it is earned. On the other hand, the tax is nonneutral in relationship to the consumption versus saving choice, since it has the effect of increasing the relative price of saving as compared to consumption. Thus, it does not serve the capital formation and economic growth objectives in a satisfactory manner.

Recent flat-rate personal income tax proposals. During the middle of 1982, a widespread discussion was underway in American society concerning the possible conversion of the federal personal income tax, with its existing progressive rate and highly-differentiated base structure, into a flat-rate (proportional-rate) tax levied on a much more comprehensive tax base than presently exists. Although a number of schemes were being proposed to accomplish this end, the various proposals had certain common general features, namely, the elimination of many existing, tax-reducing special tax provisions, and the adoption of a relatively low, flat tax rate on the broader tax base. The primary conceptual focus, unlike the CIT discussed above, would remain on the "sources of income." These newer proposals differ from the more traditional, sources-of-income-oriented, comprehensive income tax proposals, such as the Fernbach-Pechman-Gainsburgh proposal described in Chapter 8, in that they advocate a proportional rate rather than a progressive rate schedule. All of these proposals, however, whether present-day or historical, would adopt a comprehensive tax base, the broader base subsequently allowing a reduction in tax rates for the attainment of a given tax revenue yield.

It is important to sort out several different fiscal goals in discussing these various proposals. On the one hand, a more comprehensive income tax base would tend to increase allocational neutrality, at least in the long run, and also increase administrative simplicity. Both the conventional progressive-rate and the new flat-rate proposals would meet these goals. On the other hand, the conventional comprehensive income tax would better meet the ability-to-pay norm of distributional equity, since it retains a progressive rate schedule. On the other hand, the flat-rate approach would violate this norm in its rate schedule.[14] Thus, if one assumes a societal consensus for greater allocational neutrality, for administrative simplication, as well as for an adherence to the ability-to-pay distributional norm, all three goals can be attained *only* by the comprehensive income tax that utilizes progressive rates. Meanwhile, only the first two of the goals can be attained by a flat-rate comprehensive income tax.

In any event, the political reality of attaining a comprehensive income tax base, regardless of rate structure, seems tenuous, since the actual legislation of such a tax base would threaten to "upset" many entrenched tax preference "applecarts." Moreover, even though improved allocational neutrality would be attained in the long run through a more comprehensive tax base, many short-run allocational instabilities would be introduced as existing, special tax preferences, are eliminated. For example, if the base-broadening legislation were to eliminate the deduction of homeowner mortgage interest payments and property tax payments, the owner-occupied housing market could be thrown into chaos. All of which goes to suggest that comprehensive income tax reform is not easy to accomplish, even though its long-run merits may be considerable.

Impersonal taxation

Value-added tax. The discussion will now turn from personal income, consumption, and wealth taxation to *impersonal* (*in rem*) taxation. Specifically, attention will be given to a form of broadbased sales tax, the *value-added tax* (*VAT*), now prominently used in western Europe and frequently recommended for prominent use in the United States. In particular, the VAT will be considered here as a partial, or complete, replacement for the federal social security payroll tax as a means of financing social security benefits.

Unlike the *general retail sales tax* (*GRST*) as used in the United States, but similar to the *turnover tax* (*TT*) as formerly used in western Europe, the *value-added tax* is a broadbased sales tax that is imposed

---

[14] However, some effective progressivity could be introduced toward the bottom of the income scale through a large personal exemption. Yet, such a large exemption would work against the attainment of a comprehensive tax base, and would not have the same potential for progressivity as can be achieved through a graduated rate mechanism.

at different levels of production. Table 14–3 compares the primary characteristics of the GRST, TT, and VAT. It may be observed that the GRST is imposed on the value of the good at only the final, retail, stage of production, while the TT and VAT are imposed both at the final, retail, stage plus various upstream stages of production. However, the latter two differ in that the TT base entails the total or gross value of the economic good at each stage of production, while the VAT base consists of the increment to the value of the good added at each production stage. The cumulative multistage base of the VAT is the same as the single-stage base of the GRST, but the cumulative multistage base of the TT is greater than that of the VAT. Thus, at the same tax rate, the TT would yield more tax revenue than would the VAT, or as is the case in the example of Table 14–3, a lower-rated TT can yield the same tax revenue as a VAT.

One criticism of the turnover tax is that it is more likely than either a VAT or a GRST to encourage vertical integration of firms in manufacturing and distribution, with resulting market structure distortion. In Table 14–3, for example, assume (as is usually the case) that internal transactions or transfers within a given business are exempt from the tax. In this case, the tax base under the TT for a firm with full vertical integration would be $300—the gross monetary value of the final good. Yet, if the overall production process involves a number of separate business firms (in the absence of vertical integration), the cumulative base of the TT would be $600. However, the cumulative tax base is $300 under a VAT, whether or not vertical integration exists. Clearly, there is a motivation to seek vertical integration in the case of the TT.

Meanwhile, the value added base of the VAT is ascertained conceptually by subtracting the purchase cost of a taxable good from its selling price. That is, each firm would pay a tax on the increase in value of an economic good for which its productive or distributive activities are responsible. In practice, however, administrative con-

TABLE 14–3   Comparison of general retail sales tax (GRST), turnover tax (TT), and value-added tax (VAT) structures

Stage of production	Value of economic good	Tax base under			Rates and amount of tax revenue under		
		GRST	TT	VAT	GRST (12% rate)	TT (6% rate)	VAT (12% rate)
Manufacturing	$100	$—	100	100	$—	6	12
Wholesale	200	—	200	100	—	12	12
Retail	300	300	300	100	36	18	12
Cumulative base and tax revenue	—	300	600	300	36	36	36

TABLE 14–4   Example of the income and consumption varieties of value-added tax

Tax base of income-type VAT (VAT_i)
$VAT_i = S - I - D$
$50,000 = 100,000 - 40,000 - 10,000$

Tax base of consumption-type VAT (VAT_c)
$VAT_c = S - I - C$
$40,000 = 100,000 - 40,000 - 20,000$

Key:
S = Sales = \$100,000.
I = Cost of intermediate goods = \$40,000.
D = Depreciation costs = \$10,000.
C = Capital costs or new investment =
  \$20,000.

siderations induce nations using a VAT to levy the tax on the basis of the sales value of the good at a particular stage of economic activity, not directly on the value added at that stage, with the firm then receiving a tax credit for the value-added tax imbedded into the price of the purchased input or intermediate good (see following definition). Of course, the overall results are the same as they would be if the tax were levied directly on the value added at each stage of production. However, the credit approach has an administrative advantage in that it entails separate itemization of the tax on all invoices, and this reduces the opportunities for evasion of the tax.

Value-added taxes may be of either the income (VAT_i) or of the consumption (VAT_c) variety, the difference resulting from the manner in which capital goods are treated in computing the tax base (see Table 14–4). Under an *income-type* VAT, the tax base for a firm consists of sales, S, minus both the cost of purchasing factor inputs or intermediate[15] goods, I, and depreciation costs, D. Under a *consumption-type* VAT, the tax base for a firm consists of sales, S, minus both the cost of purchasing intermediate goods, I, and the cost of capital goods, C. Thus, a consumption-type VAT would deduct capital costs (new investment) immediately, while a VAT of the income variety would allow the capital offset to be applied only as the capital assets depreciate. Most, if not all, nations using the VAT have opted for use of the consumption-type VAT. Among other advantages, it is administratively more simple. The comparative administrative simplicity of VAT_c results largely from the fact that it does not require detailed depreciation schedules.

Evaluation of the substitution of a federal VAT for the federal social

---

[15] For example, an automobile acquired by a dealer for sale at the retail level constitutes an intermediate good for that dealer.

security payroll tax.[16]   In many ways, the existing federal social security payroll tax is *allocationally neutral*. For example, it covers most employment and, thus, only minimally distorts the allocation of labor among various occupations. However, the payroll tax does produce a disincentive for investment in human capital as opposed to physical capital, since the latter is not taxed. A VAT without appreciable exemptions would probably be slightly more neutral than the existing payroll tax. Yet, such a comprehensive VAT is unlikely to be adopted, as is suggested by the western European experience.[17] Hence, the substitution of a VAT for the payroll tax would probably yield a modest sacrifice in allocational neutrality as various necessity goods are either exempt from the tax base and/or are taxed at lower rates than luxury-type goods.[18]

A broadbased VAT of the consumption variety, with few exemptions and with a uniform rate on the various classes of goods, would tend to be regressive, in ability-to-pay terms, and thus in violation of this norm of *distributional equity*. In this regard, its performance would be similar to that of a GRST with few exemptions for necessity goods. However, a payroll tax also tends to be regressive for a number of reasons (see Chapter 13). These include the fact that it applies only to labor income, which is a declining relative source of income, as compared to capital as an income source, as income increases. Moreover, the payroll tax exempts labor earnings above the wage base ceiling and, furthermore, provides no minimum exemption at the bottom of the income scale.

Nonetheless, a VAT can be made proportional or progressive in its ability-to-pay performance through several adjustments. These include: (1) the exemption from the tax base of certain necessity goods such as food, housing, and medical services, and/or (2) the application of preferential rates to such goods, and/or (3) the application of a personal income tax credit for value-added taxes paid by low-income taxpayers. In fact, the use of the first two instruments by various western European nations has led to the conclusion that, depending on the particular nation in question, the potentially regressive VAT has actually been rendered either proportional or progressive, in ability-to-pay terms.[19] Yet, this distributional equity improvement has been obtained at a cost of reduced allocational neutrality. In turn,

---

[16] For a detailed analysis of these effects, see Charles E. McLure, Jr., "VAT versus the Payroll Tax," in *Social Security Financing*, ed. Felicity Skidmore (Cambridge, Mass.: MIT Press, 1981), chap. 4.

[17] See Henry Aaron, ed., *The Value-Added Tax: Lessons from Europe* (Washington, D.C.: Brookings Institution, 1981).

[18] See McLure, "VAT versus the Payroll Tax," and Aaron, *The Value-Added Tax: Lessons from Europe*.

[19] Aaron, *The Value Added Tax: Lessons from Europe*.

many observers argue that the same improvement in distributional equity could have been attained without such allocational non-neutrality if other more equitable taxes and transfer payments had been used to achieve the desired distributional effects.[20]

Thus, on general allocational and distributional grounds as well as on other grounds beyond the scope of the present discussion, the proposed substitution of a federal VAT for the existing federal social security payroll tax would appear to yield mixed results. However, one important intergovernmental fiscal issue should not be over-looked, namely, the fact that the adoption of a federal VAT in the United States would add another layer of broadbased sales taxation on American taxpayers—unlike the Western European situation in which subnational governments do not impose important broadbased sales taxes. In the United States, most states and several thousand local governments do impose broadbased general retail sales taxes. Hence, the *vertical fiscal balance* implications for the American federation that would result from the adoption by the federal government of a broadbased value-added tax, which would be imposed on top of already-existing broadbased state-local government general retail sales taxes, may be considerable.[21]

---

[20] Ibid.

[21] See Chapters 17 and 18, and also Bernard P. Herber, "A Federal Value-Added Tax in the 1980's: An Idea Whose Time Has Not Yet Come," *Western Tax Review*, January 1981, pp. 43–52, for discussions relevant to this point.

15

User charges

USER PRICING IN THE AMERICAN PUBLIC SECTOR

The user-charge (user-price, commercial) technique for the financing of government-supplied economic goods (or resources) involves the "sale" of the good to a private buyer in a manner analogous to that of the market. That is, the good is priced and the exclusion principle becomes operational, thus denying consumption of the product to those who do not voluntarily pay for it.

Examples of user charges at the *federal* level include pricing by the postal service; Alaska Railroad; various power and reclamation projects, such as the Tennessee Valley Authority and the Rural Electrification Administration; national forests and parks; various loan and insurance programs, such as the Commodity Credit Corporation and the Federal Housing Administration; and the sale of surplus military goods. A good example of the commercial principle being applied at the *state* level is the tuition charged for attendance at state universities. Tuition may be appropriately viewed as a user price charged for the purchase of educational services, though the tuition, as is typical with many other user charges by American governments, only partially covers the cost of providing the education. Another example of state commercial activity is found in the operation of toll roads, bridges, and tunnels. The commercial principle is also found in state-government ownership of retail liquor stores in a number of states. American *local* governments make significant usage of the commer-

TABLE 15–1   Major categories of user-charge revenues* by level of government, absolute amount, and as a proportion of total revenues, 1980

User-charge category	Absolute amount of user-charge revenues (millions of dollars)				User-charge revenues as a percentage of total revenues			
	All governments	Federal	State	Local	All governments	Federal	State	Local
Charges and miscellaneous general revenue† ..	$142,385	$66,555	$32,190	$43,640	15.3%	11.8%	11.6%	16.9%
Utility revenue	22,359	—	1,304	21,055	2.4	—	0.5	8.2
Liquor store revenue	3,201	—	2,765	435	0.3	—	1.0	0.2
Total	$167,945	$66,555	$36,259	$65,130	18.0%	11.8%	13.1%	25.3%

* Figures represent gross revenues without offsets for operational costs and purchases.
† This category consists mainly of current charges received from the performance of specific services and from sales of commodities (other than utility and liquor store proceeds) benefitting those persons charged. It also includes such miscellaneous items as special-assessment revenues, the sale of property, and interest earnings on governmental loans.
Source: Bureau of the Census, U.S. Department of Commerce.

cial principle in the sale of such products as water, electricity, gas, transit services, and hospital services.

In recent years, a number of American states have engaged in the "sale of risk" through the establishment of *public lotteries*.[1] In effect, this constitutes a *user price* being charged by government for the voluntary purchase of a lottery ticket by an individual. Public lotteries are employed in many nations of the world to provide government revenues. In the United States, New Hampshire initiated a public lottery in 1963, followed by New York in 1967, New Jersey in 1970, and by a number of other states since that time.

Table 15–1 provides a summary of the user-charge revenues received by American governments during 1980. Total such revenues for all governments combined amounted to approximately $168 billion during the period. The greatest amount of user-charge revenues ($66.5 billion) was collected by the federal government, followed closely by local governments with $65.1 billion of such revenues. The states obtained $36.2 billion in user-charge revenues. Altogether, 18 percent of total public sector revenues during fiscal 1980 came from the user-pricing technique, with the highest proportion being the 25.3 percent figure for local governments.

---

[1] For a discussion of state government lotteries, see Frederick D. Stocker, "State Sponsored Gambling as a Source of Public Revenue," *National Tax Journal*, September 1972, pp. 437–41.

FISCAL PERFORMANCE OF USER CHARGES

The choice between public and private supply
of quasi-public goods[2]

Since user charges are an important fiscal instrument in the American public sector, the question arises as to the *economic justification* for governmental production or sale of such goods whose benefits are at least partially subject to the exclusion principle.

A government may undertake commercial activities for a variety of reasons. The most obvious would appear to be the need to obtain *revenue* for the support of governmental functions. Yet, in a society which collectively prefers the market allocation of quasi-public (quasi-private) goods, this motivation cannot be considered the dominant reason for the American public sector to engage in commercial activities. Moreover, many user-charge activities operate on a net loss basis, with gross revenues being exceeded by the costs of supplying the product.[3]

Instead, the primary reasons for governmental participation in such activity derive from the overall characteristics of quasi-public goods which, in certain cases, confer substantial degrees of "publicness" on particular economic goods considered important by society. Publicness may be conferred on a particular economic good by such circumstances as the presence of decreasing production costs at relevant output scales, elements of joint consumption, or important externalities. Such conditions warrant the consideration of possible public sector allocational influence on the good, in order to assure an adequate supply. Moreover, society may choose to allocate certain priceable *merit goods* through the public sector, because of their particular importance, even though substantial traits of publicness such as externalities are absent. Certain so-called *demerit goods*, such as alcoholic beverages, also may be sold by government monopolies with the intent of regulating the consumption of the good. Another demerit good example would be the imposition of an effluent charge on pollutants being dumped into a river. Finally, a charge may be employed to "ration" the short-run capacity of a product, such as a price charged for the use of a public campground, a municipal swimming pool, and the like.

Figure 15-1 provides a framework for analyzing the question of

---

[2] The discussion in this chapter will concentrate on government supply of *final economic goods*, not the provision of resources which may be employed to produce these goods. *Supply* is defined to mean both goods that are produced by government and those that are sold at a later stage of economic activity, such as the sale by state government liquor stores of privately produced alcoholic beverages.

[3] A major exception is found in governmental liquor monopolies, whose gross revenues substantially exceed costs.

FIGURE 15-1 Various price-output alternatives for a firm operating under decreasing production costs in an imperfect market

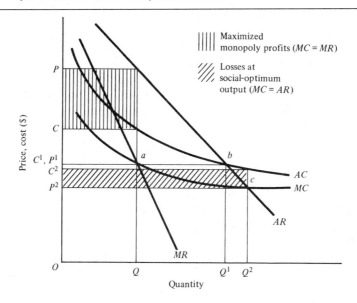

government versus market allocation of quasi-public goods. Since imperfectly competitive market structures, particularly of an oligopolistic nature, characterize American industry, the graph depicts monopolistic elements. Furthermore, since many instances of governmental allocation influence on the supply of quasi-public goods exist in decreasing-cost industries, the graph also depicts economies of scale in production—leading to a so-called natural monopoly situation.[4] The price-output combination at point *a* is set under conditions of *profit maximization pricing (MC = MR);* that at point *b*, under circumstances of *average cost pricing (AC = AR);* and that at point *c*, under conditions of *marginal cost pricing (MC = AR).*

The major alternatives available for the allocation of such quasi-public goods include: (1) unregulated (except for antitrust) private sector provision of the good; (2) private provision of the good under *direct* governmental (public utility) regulation, (3) private sector production of the good with both public utility regulation and governmental subsidy,[5] or (4) public sector production of the good.

---

[4] See Francis M. Bator, *The Question of Government Spending* (New York: Harper & Row, 1960). Bator estimates that approximately 97 percent of federal administrative budget expenditures (a budget no longer officially used by the federal government) are for economic goods with significant decreasing cost/public good characteristics.

[5] Government subsidy alone, without regulation, is not a viable alternative since no corrective mechanism would exist to adjust supply upward toward the optimal level.

If economies of scale exist over a wide range of output scales, the *unregulated private industry* likely will consist of either one pure monopoly firm or a few oligopoly firms which dominate the industry. The pure monopoly firm, or the oligopoly firms if substantial collusion exists, prefer to produce at or near the profit-maximizing price and output determined by the intersection of marginal cost and marginal revenue at point *a* in Figure 15–1.[6] Thus, output *OQ*, price *OP*, and cost *OC* reflect the relevant magnitudes at the profit-maximizing position. No direct governmental regulation exists to compel lower prices and greater output. Distributional distortion will result from the exploitative monopoly price, and allocation distortion will result because output is restricted below the optimal social allocation point where marginal cost equals average revenue (price).[7] Moreover, the condition of exploitative monopoly price will tend to be accentuated if the economic good is characterized by a highly inelastic price elasticity of demand. Yet, if the good does not possess important externalities or other important traits of publicness, and/or is not deemed by the political process to be a socially necessary good, the best *allocation* approach (though not theoretically optimal) will likely be that of unregulated private production (except for antitrust regulation). This is especially true for a society whose preferences favor market allocation and where most markets are imperfect, so that output is *not* typically carried to the social-optimum allocation point where marginal cost is equal to average revenue.

A second alternative for allocating the quasi-public good in question is application of the *public utility concept*. This approach, while continuing to allow private production of the good, provides for *direct regulation* of the private producer or producers of the good in such basic matters as price, quantity, and quality of output. In Figure 15–1, the firm subject to public utility regulation ordinarily would be allowed to produce at a price-output combination in the vicinity of point *b*. At this output (*OQ*[1]), average revenue equates average cost, giving price *OP*[1] and cost *OC*[1]. This is known as *average cost* or *full-cost pricing*. The firm in this instance is earning a normal return on invest-

---

[6] The firm may choose not to maximize profits for fear of attracting new entrants to the industry, an antitrust crackdown, or a public image deterioration, or it may be unable to maximize them because of inadequate production and market knowledge. It seems reasonable to assume, however, that the firm will ordinarily come as close to point *a* as possible in its price-output combinations.

[7] It is not argued that the public sector should compel output at or near the $MC = AR$ point for all economic goods produced in a world of imperfect markets. For a comprehensive model which precludes overall application of the marginal cost pricing technique ($MC = AR$) to all industries (as in a socialist economy in which all industry has been "nationalized"), and which substitutes an alternative rule, see William J. Baumol and David F. Bradford, "Optimal Departures from Marginal Cost Pricing," *American Economic Review*, June 1970, pp. 265–83.

ment, since alternative uses of the self-employed factors are compensated in a manner consistent with their opportunity-cost values elsewhere. A public utility firm frequently is allowed to operate at a price-output combination slightly to the left of point b, thus earning modest monopoly profits.

In comparison to the unregulated case, public utility regulation provides a greater output at a lower price, $OQ^1 - OP^1$, as compared to the unregulated output-price combination, $OQ - OP$. Thus, if the good possesses substantial traits of publicness, direct governmental regulation likely will increase welfare by increasing output from OQ to OQ^1—the latter output being closer to the social-optimal output, OQ^2. At any output to the left of OQ^2, the price consumers are willing to pay for the good exceeds the marginal cost of supplying the good, thus distorting the ability of the market to meet consumer preferences. In addition to its beneficial allocational effects, public utility regulation may also reduce distributional nonneutrality because it does not allow the full exploitative monopoly price to be charged.

A third major alternative for the allocation of quasi-public goods is for the private sector to produce the good, under public utility regulation, at the social-optimum output, OQ^2 (or at least somewhere between quantities OQ^1 and OQ^2), charging the "competitive" price, OP^2, and with government subsidizing the loss (the vertical excess of OC^2 over OP^2 for each unit produced). This would represent a "mixed form" of *marginal cost pricing* in which there is present both *private sector production and public sector regulation and subsidization.* If the fourth alternative—*government production of the good*—is selected, production by the public sector ordinarily must be justified by some strong traits of publicness in the good itself, or by the ability of the public sector to supply the good at lower costs than the private sector. In this instance, a "pure government" form of marginal cost pricing would exist as output is carried to OQ^2, where $MC = AR$, with exclusive governmental control over supply. Moreover, if price, OP^2, is charged, the government would likely cover the losses at OQ^2 output through general tax revenues.

A private firm, of course, could not earn a profit producing optimal social output OQ^2 and charging price OP^2 because average cost exceeds price (average revenue) at that output. This *always* would be the case when decreasing production costs are being realized at the output where marginal cost equals price, since marginal cost must be below average cost when average cost is declining. Government production of the good, or the subsidization of private production, is thus required if the good is to be allocated in optimal quantities.

At times, a quasi-public good which possesses certain undesirable or demerit characteristics may be supplied by government if, by doing so, price will be kept high and quantity exchanged will be reduced.

This is analogous to the case of sumptuary excise taxation (see Chapter 12), except that here government produces and prices the good itself instead of imposing a tax on a privately supplied good. Private allocation at the $MC = AR$ point is purposefully avoided because of a higher priority social interest of a regulatory nature. A uniquely scarce good or resource with social importance also may be allocated by government with a high price so as to ration its use. Of course, such rationing could also be performed by direct governmental mandate without charging a user price.

In conclusion, if strong traits of publicness are present, and/or if considerable importance is attributed to a particular economic good, either outright governmental production of the good, government regulation and subsidization of private production, or government regulation of private production, without subsidy, may be desirable. If either of the first two choices is elected, the allocation efficiency gains would be accompanied by significant distributional implications if the expanded output is financed from general tax revenues.

The choice between general-fund and user-charge financing of quasi-public goods

If government production or supply of a quasi-public good is considered desirable, a variety of financing techniques is available to the government providing the good. Emphasis in the analysis to follow will center on the choice between the *general-taxation (general-fund)* and *user-charge* techniques as means of paying for quasi-public goods. Other possible financing techniques, such as earmarked excise taxes, administrative revenues, and debt financing, are discussed elsewhere.

Pure public goods, which are not subject to the exclusion principle, cannot be allocated by the commercial principle. Quasi-public goods, in contrast, can often be priced, because their benefits are often partially subject to the exclusion principle. Yet, quasi-public goods can also be allocated and financed through general taxation. The choice between general taxation and user charges as financial allocative techniques is thus relevant for quasi-public goods, but irrelevant for pure public goods.

The case for *general taxation* as the means of financing quasi-public goods rests on several related points. First, general tax financing seems preferable to user pricing in those instances where the short-run marginal cost of an additional unit of output is very low or zero, and the price elasticity of demand for the good is highly inelastic. The low or zero short-run marginal cost means that additional units of the good do not withdraw resources in any substantial way from alternative uses. For example, the marginal cost of additional usage of a park or playground up to capacity is negligible, and user-charge financing thus seems unnecessary unless there is a serious problem of congestion in the use of the facility. Moreover, if the demand for an economic good is highly inelastic, there would be little purpose in charging a price for rationing the use of the good within its short-run capacity, since the quantity demanded of the good would be largely insensitive to price changes.

Another argument in behalf of the general tax financing of quasi-public goods emphasizes the fact that pricing quasi-public goods with important joint consumption or externality characteristics may cause a seriously short supply of these goods. Thus, if the total cost of a university education were financed through tuition charges, with no general-fund financing, there would likely be an undersupply of this important economic good since no payment would be forthcoming for the external (social) benefits due to the free-rider problem. This result would be assured further by the economies of scale which seemingly exist in the provision of higher education. As a result, even though the user charge may initially be set equal to marginal cost, providing a socially optimal output, the decreasing-cost nature of the industry would not allow this price to cover unit costs of production. If costs are to be covered fully, and if general fund financing is not to be used, a higher tuition price would have to be charged. The higher price, of course, would tend to reduce the quantity demanded and the output of educational services below the social optimum.

A further argument in favor of the general tax financing of quasi-public goods concerns the cost of administering a user-charge system. If collection costs for user charges are substantial, general taxation, from this standpoint, may be a better method of financing. Severe inconvenience to users from the collection system, moreover, may be looked on as an important reduction in the utility derived from the consumption of quasi-public goods financed by user charges. If tolls were collected for the use of *all* streets, roads, and highways, for example, the inconvenience would cause considerable consumptive disutility to their users, not to mention the added resource costs of administration and the opportunity costs of wasted time.

The pursuit of certain distributional objectives provides another argument in defense of the general-fund financing of certain quasi-public goods. The community may decide, for example, to make its postfisc income and wealth distribution more equal by means of either *direct* cash transfer payments, or the *indirect* method of concentrating on the reallocation of resources. Transfer payments, of course, are incompatible with the user pricing technique, since they do not involve resource-absorbing activities. There is no opportunity to apply the exclusion principle. Direct redistribution through transfer payments thus would have to depend on some form of general financing (either tax or debt). Moreover, the indirect redistribution of income and wealth, as achieved by the reallocation of resources toward the provision of additional amounts of certain desirable quasi-public goods for low-income persons, would also tend to require at least partial dependence on general financing techniques. For example, if these goods are priced above the purchasing-power means of low-income individuals, such people will be unable to acquire the goods in adequate quantities unless they are financed, at least in part, from other sources such as general tax revenues. Medical services or school lunches thus may not be available in adequate quantities to certain low-income people, if they are available only on a direct-pricing basis. The argument again suggests a preference for the general tax financing of quasi-public goods as opposed to the user-charge alternative, though user charges can be jointly employed with general tax financing when such indirect redistributional efforts are undertaken.

For the most part, the arguments in support of user pricing rest on the converse of the above points. The free provision of goods without the involvement of a pricing mechanism, for example, loses sight of any long-term investment criterion or guide. User charges, on the other hand, provide at least a partial benchmark for long-run changes in supply capacity. Moreover, use of the commercial principle provides prices which help to prevent overuse of short-run capacity. In addition, general-fund financing may induce an oversupply of those quasi-public goods that are characterized by highly-elastic price elasticities of demand.[8]

Another argument in behalf of user charges is found in those quasi-public goods whose economic effects are mostly subject to the exclusion principle. This is true of electricity consumption, for example, as compared to education. In the absence of significant *positive* externalities or joint consumption, the argument for general tax financing loses strength, and user pricing may be preferable. In addition, the presence of substantial *negative* externalities accompanying an economic good may call for user charges at high levels to discourage consumption of the good—to the extent that the exclusion principle can be applied.

In addition, if the costs of collecting user charges are lower than the expenses of general tax administration for the same revenue yield (other things equal), the former means of financing is to be preferred. Certain distributional goals, moreover, may be better met through user pricing than through tax financing. Since the consumption of

---

[8] See the discussion of the similarity between general fund financing and joint product sale, as developed in James M. Buchanan, "Economics of Earmarked Taxes," *Journal of Political Economy*, October 1963, pp. 457–69, and described in Chapter 12.

electricity primarily benefits the purchaser, for example, the application of user charges conforms to the overall distributional philosophy accepted in American culture and demonstrated through the obvious community preference for market-type allocation and pricing. That is, the benefit principle of tax equity is approximated.

User pricing of quasi-public goods by government: Pricing alternatives

As observed earlier in the chapter, the commercial principle may be implemented through profit-maximizing pricing, average cost pricing, or marginal cost pricing. It was also observed that negative allocational and distributional nonneutralities tend to be reduced as output is expanded toward the marginal cost—average revenue equality (the social-optimum allocation point). However, the reader should be reminded that isolated examples of *marginal cost pricing* in a society where imperfect markets prevail do not necessarily constitute an optimal allocation solution, though in many cases they likely would constitute an improvement in allocational efficiency. The strongest case for marginal cost pricing would likely center on an important good possessing both significant joint and private consumption characteristics and the presence of decreasing production costs at the relevant output scales.

In allocating a quasi-public good, the use by government of the *profit-maximizing price,* as determined by the intersection of marginal cost and marginal revenue $(MC = MR)$ (see point a in Figure 15–1), would best serve only the revenue goal, unless the society is trying to reduce consumption of an "undesirable" economic good. *Average cost pricing,* the alternative shown in Figure 15–1 at point b, is generally preferable to profit-maximizing pricing, since it helps to reduce negative allocational and distributional distortions. However, marginal cost pricing (point c) appears to be the most desirable of the three alternatives for governmental pricing of very important quasi-public goods. While it has several problems, some of which were mentioned before, the impediments to efficient marginal cost pricing may be reduced by certain modified (hybrid) financing techniques.

One important economic problem which occurs when marginal cost pricing is used is that the government enterprise operating under decreasing production costs will incur a *loss* at the social-welfare optimum allocation point where $MC = AR$. The point c conditions of Figure 15–1 demonstrate this fact. Since the user charge does not cover the cost of production at this output, general tax revenues could be used to make up the difference. Under certain conditions, *mixed financing,* utilizing both user charges and general tax revenues, would seemingly constitute the most rational alternative for financing quasi-public goods. Under other circumstances, it may provide negative allocational and distributional nonneutralities. The use of mixed financing may be rational if the good possesses both substantial joint consumption effects, which benefit the society as a whole and which remain outside the exclusion principle, and also important private benefits. Tax funds would finance the social benefits, while user prices would finance the individual or private benefits. Moreover, the use of general-fund financing paid for by progressive income taxation, to cover the loss at the $MC = AR$ point, is rational if society chooses to redistribute real income by increasing the allocation of the quasi-public good in question to the benefit of low-income persons. The combined use of general-fund financing and user pricing to finance public university education in the United States seems to meet both of the above rationality criteria, since the benefits of education are both social and private in nature, and improving the education of the poor is an effective means of improving their long-term real income position.

On the other hand, the absence of sufficient joint consumption benefits to justify general-fund subsidization of the loss incurred at the $MC = AR$ point, or the absence of a sufficient community-approved redistribution objective, would make the mixed financing technique irrational. This would be true because private users would derive most or all of the benefits from the consumption of the good, and few, if any, social benefits would exist. Yet, general tax funds collected from the society as a whole would subsidize part of the cost of the private consumption. The results would be both a redistribution of income in favor of the private consumers of the quasi-public good and an allocational distortion.

Another related problem present in the decreasing-cost case is the fact that subsidized output at the optimal social allocation point *distorts long-run investment planning.* There is no profit test to indicate the appropriate long-run allocation of resources for production of the good, since the price does not cover full costs. A partial solution to this problem is offered by the *multipart* or *peak-load pricing approach.* Under this approach, the price schedule is divided into two parts: one part for the opportunity to acquire the commodity, and the other for the actual quantities demanded. A *flat price* may thus be charged for the standby opportunity to use a quasi-public good, and an *incremental price* can be charged for each specific usage, to cover short-run marginal costs as well as to suggest long-run investment needs. Such multipart pricing techniques are uniquely applicable to industries which produce nonstorable commodities, such as electricity and transit services, and whose product demands are uneven over the relevant period. It is here, in particular, that multipart pricing takes on the name of peak-load pricing.

Peak-load pricing suggests that prices charged at periods of maximum or peak use of capacity should be higher than those charged at off-peak hours. The reasoning behind this approach is that higher prices will more effectively ration short-run use of the capacity at peak-load periods of demand and, at the same time, will help determine future capacity requirements as well as to help cover the costs of these requirements. Both short-run rationing and long-run investment criteria are thus served by this technique. Though such an approach involves differential prices, this does not necessarily mean that price discrimination exists, since the differential prices may be proportional to differences in marginal costs. If so, true price discrimination, which consists of charging different purchasers different prices for the same economic good when such price differentials are not justified by cost differences, is not present.

The following example demonstrates the peak-load pricing approach: Consider the case of a government-owned electric utility. Assume that the peak demand is "firm," that is, it will not change as the multipart prices under consideration are introduced. The marginal cost of electricity consumption in off-peak periods is merely the cost of the energy itself. On the other hand, the marginal cost in peak periods is the sum of the energy cost and the cost of capacity. Suppose that the demand is divided into two equal parts, that is, one half of the day represents peak demand for electricity, and the other half represents off-peak demand.

The long-run solution to the problem is demonstrated in Figure 15–2. There is no need to increase capacity to meet the energy cost in the off-peak period. In Figure 15–2a, the marginal energy cost is

FIGURE 15–2   **Peak-load pricing of a government-supplied quasi-public good**

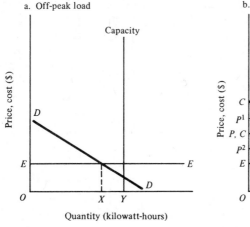
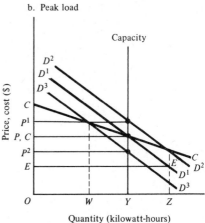

represented by line EE and the off-peak demand is represented by demand curve DD. At the intersection of the marginal energy cost and the off-peak demand curves, the quantity of off-peak electricity purchased is determined. This quantity is equal to OX on the horizontal axis, which is less than the capacity quantity OY.

In Figure 15–2b, the long-run capacity cost is added to the energy cost for the peak demand situation. Capacity, of course, must be greater to meet the peak demand as opposed to the off-peak demand for electricity. Hence, line CC represents the long-term marginal cost for electricity, inclusive of both energy and capacity requirements. It is a downward-sloping curve to characterize a decreasing-cost industry, as is frequently associated with quasi-public goods. Line EE again represents marginal energy costs. Line D^1D^1 represents the peak demand for electricity. It should be observed that line D^1D^1 in Figure 15–2b is higher than line DD in Figure 15–2a, because of greater peak than off-peak demand. At the intersection of peak demand curve D^1D^1 and long-run marginal cost curve CC, the quantity purchased of peak-demand electricity is determined. This quantity is equal to OY on the horizontal axis.

The determination of *long-run capacity requirements* in Figure 15–2b is attained through the following adjustments: If the price at peak demand (P) is equal to the sum of the marginal energy cost and the marginal capacity cost (C), and the entire available capacity is allocated (*quantity OY*), *optimal capacity* exists, and there is no reason to change capacity ($P = C$ at quantity OY). However, if the price *exceeds* the sum of the marginal energy cost and the marginal capacity cost ($P^1 > C$ at quantity OY), as under the high-demand conditions represented by peak-demand curve D^2D^2, the results constitute a long-run investment signal that capacity should be *expanded* to quantity OZ. If the price is *less* than the sum of the marginal energy and capacity costs ($P^2 < C$ at quantity OY), as under the low-demand conditions represented by peak-demand curve D^3D^3, the loss per unit of electricity signals the need for a long-run *reduction* in capacity to quantity OW. Hence, peak-load (multipart) pricing, under certain conditions, may improve allocational efficiency when user charges are imposed by government.

ADMINISTRATIVE REVENUES

Administrative revenues are collected by a government in the performance of its general governmental functions. These functions are primarily regulatory in nature. For example, government must protect persons and property, and it must provide a certain basic framework within which private economic activity will take place. In the performance of these and other general functions, government frequently charges a fee, levies a fine, receives an escheat (defined later), or otherwise collects revenue from individuals. The correlation between the payment of an administrative revenue by an individual, and the subsequent service or right acquired by the individual, is often broad and imprecise. Only in a general sense, therefore, may it be said that a quid pro quo relationship exists in the case of administrative revenues. On this basis, a definitional line is drawn between *administrative revenues* and *user charges*.

Fees, licenses, and *permits* are very similar in nature. They all provide administrative revenues to government as part of a regulatory function, and they all involve the granting by government to the individual of permission to act in a particular way. A fishing license, for example, allows a person to fish in public waters within the political jurisdiction of the grantor. A business license allows an individual or firm to participate in a particular trade. Admittedly, permission to act in a particular manner can be regulated without requiring a monetary payment to government. However, the revenue motive may be used by government to justify the required payments. Collection costs are usually low and are frequently exceeded by the revenues collected. Yet, since the fees are often uniform to all taxpayers, they do not perform well in reference to the ability-to-pay principle of tax equity. Moreover, since the quid pro quo relationships generally are less than precise, the charges also fail to meet the benefit principle satisfactorily.

Fines and *forfeitures* clearly involve the performance of a regulatory function by government. Fines are monetary charges levied by a governmental unit as a penalty for a violation of law. Forfeitures similarly are penalties. They include the sacrifice of bail or bond for failure to appear in court or to complete contracts as prescribed. Except for isolated local government examples (such as "traffic-trap" cities), the relative revenue importance of fines and forfeitures to the American public sector is slight.

According to the American legal system, the state level of government has the legal right to be the ultimate claimant of property left by deceased persons who have no legal heirs. This right of the state to absorb such property is known as an *escheat*. Escheats constitute another source of administrative revenues. As with fines and forfeitures, the overall revenue importance of escheats to the public sector is slight.

Special assessments, though sometimes classified as administrative revenues, are also similar to user charges. Moreover, they contain certain characteristics of the property tax. However, it is not inconsistent to classify them as administrative revenues, since they often are closely related to the overall governmental regulatory function of administering community development programs. A special assessment charge for the installation of sewers, street lights, or paved streets, as part of the development plan of a community, may thus be viewed as a by-product of the general administrative function of government. Special assessments normally are characterized by the allocation of costs and benefits resulting from the improvement of land. The basis for assessment is usually not in terms of property value, but in terms of area or frontage. Considerable procedural variation exists among the various levels and units of government which utilize the special-assessment technique for allocating quasi-public goods.

PART III

The aggregate public sector
and fiscal federalism

16

Fiscal incidence and profile of
the aggregate public sector

The aggregate public sector of the United States is composed of nearly 80,000 separate governments, each of which performs the basic fiscal functions of revenue gathering (mainly taxation) and spending.[1] The overall allocational, distributional, and stabilization effects exerted by the American public sector thus will reflect the combined budgetary decisions of all of these governments, though obviously some units exert greater influence than others do. This chapter will provide a *symmetrical fiscal profile* of the aggregate public sector in the United States, including both revenues and expenditures for all levels and units of American government. Moreover, special attention will be paid to the *overall fiscal incidence* of public sector budgetary activities in the United States, including the concepts of prefisc and postfisc income distribution, as developed in Chapter 5. The chapter will not, however, specifically consider intergovernmental fiscal relations, which is the subject of Chapters 17 and 18.

THE 20TH–CENTURY GROWTH
OF THE AMERICAN PUBLIC SECTOR

The overall economic activity of American governments has increased significantly in both relative and absolute terms during the

---

[1] In 1977, the Bureau of the Census, U.S. Department of Commerce, reported the existence of 79,913 governments in the United States, including the federal government, the District of Columbia, 50 state governments, and 79,861 local governments.

20th century. A number of indicators are available for measuring this growth but, for fiscal purposes, governmental *expenditures* and *revenues* may be deemed the most appropriate indicators. The following discussion will select public sector expenditure behavior to demonstrate the 20th-century growth of American government, as well as certain important fiscal changes within the aggregate public sector.

Table 16–1 shows that total public sector expenditures (*G*), both exhaustive and nonexhaustive, have more than quadrupled as a percentage of gross national product (*GNP*) during this century. In addition, a more than threefold increase in this G/GNP ratio may be detected between 1929, the end of the prosperous 1920s, and 1980. During the height of World War II (1944) the expenditures of American governments were nearly one half of GNP. In 1980, the G/GNP stood at 33.1 percent, with evidence of a steady upward trend following the immediate post-World War II decline (indicated by 1947) until the mid-1970s. Since that time, however, the G/GNP trend has been downward, with the strong possibility of a continuation of this downward trend during the 1980s as a mood of fiscal conservatism and government retrenchment has swept over the nation. Meanwhile, the greater portion of public sector expenditures is for government allocational activities. For example, government exhaustive spending was 20.4 percent of GNP in 1980, while nonexhaustive (transfer) spending was 12.7 percent of GNP.

Absolute public sector expenditures (in current prices) increased from a total of $1.6 billion in 1902 to $942.4 billion in 1980 (see Table 16–2a and b). The federal government accounted for $618.2 billion, or 65.6 percent, of total government spending in 1980, while state and local government expenditures accounted for 19.9 percent and 14.5 percent, respectively. Significantly, federal government expenditures have increased from about one third to nearly two thirds of total public

---

TABLE 16–1 Total public sector expenditures as a percentage of GNP, selected calendar years, 1902–1980

Year	Percent	Year	Percent
1902	8.0	1947	18.2
1913	8.5	1950	21.3
1929	9.9	1960	26.9
1940	18.4	1970	31.6
1944	48.9	1975	34.5
		1980	33.1

Note: Expenditures are from the U.S. Department of Commerce's national income and product accounts. These are presented on an accrual basis and include government trust fund transactions, but exclude those capital transactions not representing current production. Duplication from intergovernmental transfers has been eliminated.

Source: U.S. Department of Commerce; author's estimates for data prior to 1929, with reference to national product data from Simon Kuznets, *National Product since 1869* (New York: National Bureau of Economic Research, 1946).

TABLE 16-2   **Federal, state, and local government expenditures, by level of government, selected fiscal years, 1902-1980**

a. **Absolute dollar terms (millions of dollars)**

		Government level		
Year	Total	Federal	State	Local
1902	$ 1,660	$ 572	$ 179	$ 909
1913	3,215	970	372	1,873
1927	11,220	3,533	1,882	5,805
1932	12,437	4,266	2,562	5,609
1940	20,417	10,061	4,545	5,811
1944	109,947	100,520	4,062	5,365
1950	70,335	44,800	12,774	12,761
1960	151,289	97,284	25,035	28,970
1970	332,985	208,190	64,665	60,130
1980	942,400	618,206	187,154	137,040

b. **Percentage distribution**

		Government level			
Year	Total	Federal	State	Local	Combined state-local
1902	100.0	34.4	10.8	54.8	65.6
1913	100.0	30.2	11.6	58.3	69.9
1927	100.0	31.5	16.8	51.7	68.5
1932	100.0	34.3	20.6	45.1	65.7
1940	100.0	49.3	22.2	28.5	50.7
1944	100.0	91.4	3.7	4.9	8.6
1950	100.0	63.7	18.2	18.1	36.3
1960	100.0	64.3	16.5	19.2	35.7
1970	100.0	62.5	19.4	18.1	37.5
1980	100.0	65.6	19.9	14.5	34.4

Note: Expenditures are treated in terms of the financing rather than the final spending level of government; that is, by treating amounts represented by intergovernmental transactions as expenditures of the originating rather than the recipient government. Total expenditures are shown as defined by the Bureau of the Census.

Source: U.S. Department of Commerce, Bureau of the Census; Tax Foundation, Inc.

sector spending during the 20th century. At the same time, state government expenditures have nearly doubled in importance, but local government spending has decreased sharply, from more than one half to less than one sixth of the total. Hence, the combined state-local component of the public sector, under the influence of the significantly diminished importance of local government, has declined during the century from roughly two thirds to slightly more than one third of total government spending. Nonetheless, the relative proportions of the federal and state-local components have remained essentially unchanged during the period following World War II.

The reasons for the relative expansion of the public sector within the American economy may be classified into two broad categories:

(1) the more *intensive* application of governmental economic activity within areas provided previously by the public sector, and (2) the lateral or *extensive* movement of government into new areas of economic activity. The latter, for example, may involve the performance of activities previously performed by the private sector, or newly developed activities previously performed by neither sector.

The 20th-century growth of national defense expenditures provides a major example of government's more intensive supply of a traditional product. The nation's growing involvement in international affairs, and the increasing sophistication of the weaponry of defense, further explain this area of expenditure growth. As war and defense were causing the federal government to perform more intensively its time-honored function of national security, state and local governments were expanding their expenditures to meet the growing demands of an urban-industrial population for such traditional functions as education, highways and streets, police and fire protection, public health, and other public-type output. Ever-improving technology, and related cultural adjustments associated with an urban-oriented society, help to explain the growing demands for these governmental economic products.

Three areas of extensive or lateral expansion during the 20th century also deserve comment: social insurance and public assistance programs, macroeconomic stabilization policies, and microeconomic regulatory policies. Since the 1930s, government in the United States has played a primary role in providing social insurance and public assistance programs (see Chapter 13). These include plans for retirement, survivors' insurance, unemployment compensation, medical care for the aged, industrial accident benefits, and transfer payments to the needy.

The public sector has also moved during this century to deliberately influence aggregate economic activity in terms of macroeconomic production, employment, price level, balance of payments, and economic growth goals (see Part Four). The application of Keynesian economics has been the foundation of this movement in the Western world.

In addition, American government has moved laterally into new areas of microeconomic regulation during the late 19th and 20th centuries. This expansion takes the form of such market structure policies as antitrust law and public utility regulation.

PROBLEMS OF PUBLIC SECTOR MEASUREMENT

The data utilized in the previous section to indicate public sector size within the mixed, private and public sector, American economy present some inherent measurement difficulties. For example, the combination of both government exhaustive (G_e) and nonexhaustive (G_n) expenditures as a ratio of GNP (G/GNP) is somewhat inconsistent, since exhaustive expenditures represent actual economic production, as does GNP, but nonexhaustive expenditures are transfers, which are not related to economic output in a direct sense. Yet, nonexhaustive spending is directly important from an income redistribution standpoint, and does reflect a function of governmental economic activity, even though it is not of the resource allocation variety. Thus, a combination of $G_e + G_n$ tends to *overstate* public sector economic activity, in allocational terms, but G_e alone, which excludes government spending directed toward the distribution function of economics would, on the other hand, *understate* overall public sector economic activity inclusive of the distribution function.

Moreover, if one does concentrate on resource allocation activity as encompassed in the exhaustive expenditure data, allocational influence itself is understated since the data measure only government purchases of economic resources (inputs) used in production. Yet, they ignore the myriad of indirect allocational influences that the public sector may exert on the pattern of economic output. For example, some private industries are regulated as public utilities with direct price, output-quantity, and output-quality prescriptions imposed by government. Or, the public sector may influence private sector output decisions via health and safety regulations, antitrust laws, or numerous other governmental interventionary procedures. Yet, the conventional government purchases data simply do not take such indirect, though very real, resource allocation influence into consideration.

In order to adjust for this measurement deficiency in estimating the public sector's allocational role within the mixed economy, a specialized use of data from the input-output accounts of the U.S. Department of Commerce has been developed.[2] The considerable disaggregation of output data in these accounts makes possible a closer scrutiny of GNP and, as a result, some ability to estimate indirect public sector resource allocation effects in addition to the conventional direct output effects. Thus, with the value of O representing the complete absence of public sector allocational activity (a no-government economy) and 3 representing complete output domination by government, it is estimated that public sector allocational influence possessed a "publicness value" of 1.29 in 1972. This repre-

---

[2] See: Bernard P. Herber, "The Demand for Public Goods and Services: Problems of Identification and Measurement in Western Countries," paper presented at the annual Congress of the International Institute of Public Finance, Copenhagen, Denmark, August 23–26, 1982.

sented a considerable growth in influence as compared to the estimated value of 0.90 for 1947.[3] Although such an initial effort to measure overall governmental allocative involvement in the mixed American economy may be improved on in terms of sophistication, it nonetheless does serve to recognize the need to consider the ability of government to affect economic output in ways other than through the direct purchase of resources to be used in production.

THE COMPOSITION OF PUBLIC SECTOR EXPENDITURES AND REVENUES

Public sector expenditures

Table 16–3 indicates the *functional composition*[4] of government expenditures in the United States during fiscal year 1979. If the public sector is viewed as a whole, the single most important functional expenditure category is social insurance, as evidenced by the fact that 21 percent of all expenditures are made from insurance trust funds. This is followed by educational expenditures, which constitute 16 percent, and defense-related expenditures, which constitute 15 percent of the total spending of all American governments combined.

Meanwhile, social insurance expenditure constitutes 33 percent and national defense expenditure 28 percent of the *federal* budget. The single most important functional item of *state* government expenditure is education (21 percent of the total), followed by public welfare (19 percent), social insurance (13 percent), and highways (12 percent). Education is also the leading functional expenditure category for *local* governments with 38 percent of total spending. In the meantime, during the early 1980s, the absolute and relative magnitude of defense spending seems likely to increase within the federal budget and, thus, within the public sector as a whole.

Public sector revenues[5]

Table 16–4 displays the composition, by *type of tax*, of public sector tax revenues in the United States in fiscal year 1979. It can be observed that the single most important revenue-producing tax in the American public sector is the personal income tax, which yields 37

---

[3] Ibid.

[4] This refers to *specific* economic goods or programs rather than to the *broader* functions of economics: namely, allocation, distribution, and stabilization.

[5] This discussion pertains to governmental tax and user-charge revenues. The relationship of *debt* revenues to the aggregate public sector is discussed in Chapter 22.

TABLE 16–3   **Percentage distribution of direct functional expenditures, by level of government, fiscal year 1979**

	Percentage distribution of total expenditures, by function			
Function	Federal	State	Local	All governments
General	67%	84%	87%	75%
National defense and international relations	28	0	0	15
Education	2	21	38	16
Highways	<1	12	5	4
Public welfare	4	19	5	7
Hospitals	1	7	5	3
Health	1	2	1	1
Police	<1	1	5	2
Natural resources	6	3	<1	4
Housing and urban renewal	1	<1	2	1
Air transportation	1	<1	1	1
Water transport and terminals	<1	<1	<1	<1
Social insurance administration	1	1	<1	<1
Financial administration	1	4	4	2
Interest on general debt	11	4	3	7
Other	10	10	18	12
Utility and liquor stores	0	3	12	4
Insurance trust (social insurance)	33	13	1	21
Total	100%	100%	100%	100%

Note: Intergovernmental transfers are represented by the recipient governments, which directly spend the funds for a functional purpose.

Source: U.S. Department of Commerce, Bureau of the Census.

percent of the tax revenues collected by all American governments combined. Moreover, if the corporation income tax is included (11 percent of total tax revenues), income taxation accounts for 48 percent of the total. Payroll taxes of a social insurance nature are second in importance (24 percent of all government tax revenues), followed by sales taxes (15 percent) and property taxes (9 percent).

At the *federal* level, the personal income tax produces 49 percent of all tax revenues, with the corporation income tax adding another 15 percent—making overall income tax revenues 64 percent of all federal tax revenues. Social insurance payroll taxes rank second in importance, contributing 28 percent of all federal tax revenues in 1979. Sales taxes of the domestic excise and customs varieties contributed only 6 percent, and death-gift taxation, only 1 percent, of federal tax revenues.

For American *state* governments, the most important revenue-producing tax category is sales taxation, which contributed 40 percent of total state tax revenues. This 40 percent figure disaggregates into 25

TABLE 16-4   **Percentage distribution of tax revenues from own sources, by type of tax and by level of government, fiscal year 1979**

| Type of tax | Percentage of total tax revenues | | | |
	Federal	State	Local	All governments
Property	—	2	74	9
Personal income	49	20	5	37
Corporation income	15	8	*	11
Sales and gross receipts	6	40	13	15
Customs duties	2	0	0	1
General sales and gross receipts	0	25	8	7
Selective sales and gross receipts	4	15	4	7
Motor fuel	1	6	<1	2
Alcoholic beverages	1	2	<1	1
Tobacco products	<1	2	<1	1
Public utilities	1	2	3	1
Other	1	3	1	2
Motor vehicle and operators licenses	—	3	1	1
Death and gift	1	1	†	1
Payroll taxes (insurance trust, social insurance)	28	22	4	24
Other	1	4	3	2
Total	100%	100%	100%	100%

* Minor amount included in personal income tax category.
† Minor amount included in "other" category.
Source: U.S. Department of Commerce, Bureau of the Census.

percent for general (broad-based) sales taxation and 15 percent for selective (narrow-based, excise) sales taxation. Meanwhile, a sizable 22 percent of all state tax revenues was collected in the form of social insurance payroll taxes. Personal income taxes furnished 20 percent, and corporation income taxes another 8 percent, thus making income tax contributions an important 28 percent of the total. Property taxes contributed only 2 percent of total state tax revenues in 1979, but they are the primary *local* government tax source, contributing 74 percent of total local tax revenues. Sales taxes (13 percent) and personal income taxes (5 percent) follow in importance at the local level.

Recent trends in American taxation (not demonstrated in Table 16-4) include, at the federal level, a significant relative decline in the importance of the corporation income tax and a sharp relative growth in payroll tax revenues. The personal income tax has essentially maintained a status quo position as an important federal tax source. However, the Economic Recovery Tax Act of 1981, which sharply reduced federal personal and corporation income taxes and the estate-gift tax, may further affect federal tax revenue distribution. Meanwhile, general sales taxes and personal income taxes have exhibited substantial relative growth for state governments and modest relative growth at the local government level.

Table 15-1 in the preceding chapter demonstrated the importance of user charges as a governmental revenue source. It was observed that user charges are most important to local governments, where they provide over 25 percent of total revenues. Meanwhile, state governments obtain over 13 percent and the federal government nearly 12 percent of their total revenues from user charges. The public sector as a whole derives 18 percent of all revenues from this source.

INCIDENCE OF THE AGGREGATE PUBLIC SECTOR BUDGET

As previously indicated, it is often useful to consider the total economic effects of governmental budgetary activities in a symmetrical fashion, including both expenditure and revenue-gathering flows. This is true whether one is considering the fiscal activities of individual governments, entire levels of government, or the aggregate public sector, inclusive of all governments. An important application of this symmetrical approach to the aggregate public sector is found in the concept of *fiscal incidence.* This concept considers the overall distributional incidence of the tax burdens and expenditure benefits of governmental budgetary activities, by income class, throughout the entire society. In other words, it compares the prefisc distribution of private income to the postfisc distribution of income which results from the pattern of governmental fiscal activities.[6]

Although *fiscal incidence* represents a difficult research undertaking, several important studies have emerged. These include those by Irwin Gillespie; the Tax Foundation; Richard Musgrave, Karl Case, and Herman Leonard, and by Morgan Reynolds and Eugene Smolensky.[7] Measurement difficulties in such studies arise from a number of sources, including the need to estimate the degree of tax shifting which occurs under various taxes, as well as the need to assign the benefit incidence of pure public goods such as national defense across income classes. The studies cited earlier, largely using intermediate assumptions regarding such measurement difficulties, draw similar

---

[6] See the discussion of these concepts in Chapter 5.

[7] Irwin Gillespie, "Effects of Public Expenditures on the Distribution of Income," in *Essays in Fiscal Federalism,* Richard A. Musgrave, ed., (Washington; D.C.: Brookings Institution, 1965); Tax Foundation, Inc., *Tax Burdens and Benefits of Government Expenditures by Income Class, 1961 and 1965* (New York: 1967); Richard A. Musgrave, Karl E. Case, and Herman Leonard, "The Distribution of Fiscal Burdens and Benefits," *Public Finance Quarterly,* July 1974, pp. 259–311; Morgan Reynolds and Eugene Smolensky, "The Post Fisc Distribution: 1961 and 1970 Compared," *National Tax Journal,* December 1974, pp. 515–27, and *Public Expenditures, Taxes, and the Distribution of Income* (New York: Academic Press, 1977).

FIGURE 16–1   Fiscal incidence of the U.S. aggregate public sector in the United States

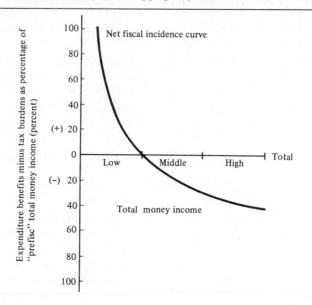

conclusions; namely, that the overall incidence of aggregate public sector fiscal activities in the United States is redistributional toward (in favor of) lower-income classes.[8]

This phenomenon is exemplified in Figure 16–1, which uses the data in the studies cited to show that the *fiscal incidence* of the American public sector is "positive" up to an approximate upper-lower-income to lower-middle-income range.[9] That is, the benefits of governmental expenditures exceed the burdens of governmental taxes in that range of income for which the results are positive. Moreover, if the public sector is disaggregated into federal and state-local components, a similar pattern emerges for each component. The incidence of tax burdens, however, is essentially proportional,[10] and thus not im-

---

[8] It should be noted that such redistribution per se does not assure the elimination of poverty.

[9] For example, overall budgetary incidence becomes a negative value at approximately $4,000 of income in the Gillespie study (using 1960 data), at approximately $6,000 of income in the Tax Foundation study (using 1965 data), at approximately $8,000 of income in the Musgrave Case-Leonard study (using 1968 data), and at approximately $12,000 of "income" (as represented by net national product data) in the Reynolds-Smolensky study (using 1970 data). These income figures are in current dollar terms and, thus, would be closer to each other in magnitude if adjusted for inflation. Clearly, they represent an upper-lower to lower-middle segment of the income range for their respective years.

[10] For additional evidence of this fact, see Joseph A. Pechman and Benjamin A. Okner, *Who Bears the Tax Burden?* (Washington, D.C.: Brookings Institution, 1974).

portantly redistributional, since the modest progressivity of federal taxes is offset by the modest regressivity of state-local taxes. This means that the primary contributor to redistribution is found in the pro-poor incidence of the other side of the budget, namely, governmental expenditures. Once more, this redistribution results from the pattern of both federal and state-local government expenditures.

Moreover, a study by Reynolds and Smolensky, published in 1977, in comparing the redistributional effects of the aggregate public sector budget between 1950 and 1970, reaches the following interesting conclusions:[11]

1. The distributional inequality of prefisc factor income increased slightly between 1950 and 1970.
2. The distributional inequality of final postfisc income, after the incidence of governmental tax and expenditure programs, remained essentially the same over the period.
3. Even though the redistributional effects of the aggregate public sector budget remain considerable, the redistributive effect of each dollar passing through government budgets declined, since government represented a much larger proportion of the total economy in 1970 than it did in 1950.
4. The incidence of government taxes moved from progressive in 1950 to proportional, or even slightly regressive, by 1970. However, the effect of this on the postfisc distribution was neutralized by the rapid growth in government transfer payments, and government spending overall, during the period.

Important fiscal legislation enacted by the federal government during 1981 is likely to reduce the degree of pro-low income redistribution in the American public sector. Evidence of this is provided in Table 16-5, which summarizes the results of recent research conducted by the Congressional Budget Office. It may be seen that *cash benefit reductions* as a percentage of income, resulting from social program (nondefense) spending cuts enacted in 1981, are greatest in the lowest income category, and then decline as income increases. This is true for all calendar years shown (1982 through 1985). Moreover, *personal income tax reductions* as a percentage of income, resulting from the 1981 legislation, are least for the lowest income category, and then increase as income increases—again, for all years shown. Furthermore, when the net effects of the cash benefit and personal income tax reductions are considered, the tax reductions exceed the cash benefit reductions for all income classes, except the lowest. In addition, if the effects of federal revenue sharing (grants-in-aid) reductions were included in the data, it is likely that the pro-poor

---

[11] Reynolds and Smolensky, *Public Sector Expenditures,* p. 92.

TABLE 16–5 Net change in personal income taxes* and cash benefits† as a percentage of income, by income category, resulting from 1981 legislation, for calendar years 1982–1985

		Household income (in 1982 dollars)				
	All households	Less than $10,000	$10,000-20,000	$20,000-40,000	$40,000-80,000	$80,000 and over
1982:						
Cash benefits	−0.4	−2.7	−0.5	−0.2	−0.2	−0.1
Taxes	1.9	0.8	1.0	1.7	2.5	4.6
Net	1.5	−1.9	0.5	1.5	2.3	4.5
1983:						
Cash benefits	−0.5	−3.0	−0.6	−0.3	−0.2	‡
Taxes	3.5	1.3	1.9	3.2	4.6	6.7
Net	3.0	−1.7	1.3	2.9	4.4	6.7
1984:						
Cash benefits	−0.4	−2.9	−0.5	−0.2	−0.1	‡
Taxes	4.3	1.7	2.4	4.0	5.7	7.9
Net	3.9	−1.2	1.9	3.8	5.6	7.9
1985:						
Cash benefits	−0.4	−2.6	−0.4	−0.2	−0.1	‡
Taxes	5.2	2.3	3.0	4.9	6.7	8.4
Net	4.8	−0.3	2.6	4.7	6.6	8.4

* Estimates the tax reductions resulting from the rate reduction, two-earner married-couple deduction, and indexing provisions. (see Chapter 8)

† Food stamp, in-kind, benefit reductions are included with the cash benefit reductions. However, other in-kind benefit reductions are not included in the data.

‡ Less than 0.05.

Source: *Effects of Tax and Benefit Reductions Enacted in 1981 for Households in Different Income Categories,* Congressional Budget Office, February 1982, Table 12.

redistributional pattern would be further weakened. Finally, though not shown in the table (except for food stamps), the Congressional Budget Office study also concludes that in-kind benefit reductions would fall heaviest on the lower-income segment of the population.

A study of *fiscal incidence* in the public sector of Canada produces results largely similar to those found in the United States during recent decades.[12] In Canada, for the year 1969, fiscal incidence was positive to approximately the $10,000 family income level, thus indicating that lower-income persons were net gainers from the redistributive mechanism. The general fiscal incidence pattern, again as in the United States, was redistributional toward lower-income persons as the result of a pro-poor expenditure pattern of benefits. It was not the result of the tax incidence pattern which, in fact, is estimated to be regressive in Canada. Finally, no significant additional postfisc

---

[12] W. Irwin Gillespie, "On the Redistribution of Income in Canada," *Canadian Tax Journal,* July–August 1976, pp. 419–50.

income redistribution toward lower-income classes occurred in Canada during the period 1961–1974. This is similar to the essential status quo in the United States for the period 1950–1970, as pointed out by Reynolds and Smolensky.[13]

THEORETICAL ANALYSIS OF PUBLIC SECTOR GROWTH

The experience of the Western world during the last half of the 19th century and in the 20th century has been one of growth in the public sectors of most industrial nations. This growth has been evident not only in the *absolute* sense—which would be expected in an environment of expanding population, output, and complexity in economic activity—but also on a *relative* basis. Thus, while the resources allocated by both the public and private sectors have increased in absolute terms, a higher proportion of total resources is now being allocated through the influence of government. Some of the theoretical efforts to explain this growth phenomenon, as well as to explain the pattern of such growth, are discussed in this final section of the chapter. They involve what are commonly referred to as positive theories of public expenditure, that is, efforts to find a predictable, long-run, functional relationship between certain causal variables and relative public sector growth. Even though they are classified as positive theories, several of the important studies were not intended as such by their authors.

The Wagner hypothesis of increasing governmental activity

Statement of the hypothesis. Adolph Wagner, a famous German political economist (1835–1917), argued that a functional, cause-and-effect relationship exists between the growth of an industrializing economy and the relative growth of its public sector. According to Wagner, relative growth of the government sector is an inherent characteristic of industrializing economies. He referred not only to Britain, which essentially had completed its industrial revolution before Wagner's time, but to nations such as the United States, France, and Germany (in the West) and Japan (in the East), whose industrial revolutions were contemporary to Wagner's life. Hence, the Wagner hypothesis of increasing governmental activity holds that as per capita income and output increase in industrializing nations, the public sectors of these nations necessarily grow as a proportion of total economic activity.[14]

---

[13] Reynolds and Smolensky, *Public Sector Expenditures.*

[14] Adolph Wagner, *Finanzwissenschaft,* 3d ed. (Leipzig: 1890). For a comprehensive analysis of the Wagner hypothesis, see Richard M. Bird, *The Growth of Government Spending in Canada* (Toronto: Canadian Tax Foundation, 1970), chap. 4.

Wagner believed that social progress was the basic cause of the relative growth of government in industrializing economies. The chain-reaction circumstances described by Wagner are that social progress leads to a growth in government functions which, in turn, leads to the absolute and relative growth of governmental economic activity. The hypothesis is clearly secular (long-term) in nature.

In his attempt to validate the hypothesis, Wagner distinguished certain types of governmental activities or functions. One function is that of providing the law and order essential for the market to operate. Second, Wagner described governmental participation in the material production of economic goods, including the provision of certain social, public-type, goods such as communications, education, and monetary-banking arrangements.

It is argued that need for the first type of public sector activity, *law and order,* increases along with economic growth and increasing per capita output, because the inevitable accompanying growth in centralized administration results in an impersonalization and automation of many social and economic institutions. Economic growth and centralization of administration thus increase labor specialization and cause greater complexities and interdependencies in economic and social life. Efficient performance of the economy, given the existence of these interdependencies and the desirability of maintaining qualitative governmental services, suggests the need for additional public sector economic influence.

Wagner believed, second, that *government corporations* must produce certain economic goods requiring large fixed investment, because private corporations cannot undertake such investment on a profitable basis. The similarity of this viewpoint to those of Smith, Mill, and others is obvious.[15] These industries often are characterized by natural monopoly conditions of production, which involve heavy fixed costs, or by joint consumption conditions, or by significant consumption externalities (*not* Wagner's terminology), which give the goods an income-elastic demand during the period of industrialization. Such goods take on important characteristics of publicness and thus incur a social (collective) interest in their allocation.

Graphic presentation of the Wagner hypothesis. The Wager hypothesis of increasing governmental activity is demonstrated in Figure 16–2. In this graph, the real[16] per capita output of public goods (*PG*) is measured on the vertical axis, and real[16] per capita income (*Y*) is measured on the horizontal axis. Time is an important third dimension implicit in the graph, because the growth in the real per capita output of public goods and in real per capita income is realistically

---

[15] See Chapter 2.

[16] Adjusted for price-level changes.

FIGURE 16-2 **Wagner hypothesis: The relative expansion of public sector economic activity over time**

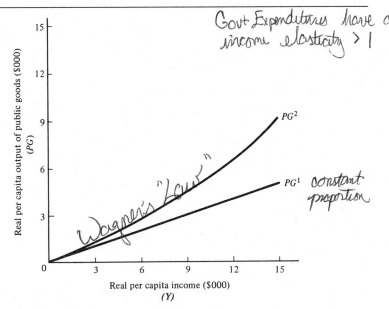

assumed to take place on a historical basis over an extended period of time. In the equations following, which correspond to various aspects of the graphical analysis, the subscript a refers to a "later" and the subscript o to an "earlier" point of time.

Line PG^1 in Figure 16-2 represents a circumstance in which the public sector maintains a *constant proportion* of the total economic production of the society over time. In other words, as real per capita income increases, due to economic development of the society, the real per capita output of public goods remains at the same proportion of total economic activity. Thus,

$$\frac{PG_a}{Y_a} = \frac{PG_o}{Y_o},$$

The constant-proportions line, PG^1, can be used as a reference point for the presentation of the Wagner hypothesis in Figure 16-2. Thus, along line PG^2, the proportion of resources devoted to the output of public goods is expanding over time. That is,

$$\frac{PG_a}{Y_a} > \frac{PG_o}{Y_o}.$$

In other words, the income elasticity of expenditure for public goods (Y_e) is *elastic*.

FIGURE 16–3 **Relative changes in public sector economic activity during preindustrialization, industrialization, and postindustrialization periods of economic development**

no analysis supports this

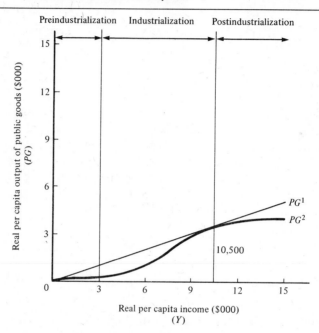

Preindustrial and postindustrial maturity stages of a society's economic development. Since the Wagner analysis was directed toward industrializing nations, a discussion of the hypothesis should delimit the industrialization era in a nation's history from a possible earlier preindustrial stage, and also from a possible later period of postindustrial maturity when living standards are affluent not only on an *average* basis, but on a *distributional* basis as well.[17] Figure 16–3, which is based on the terminology of Figure 16–2, provides, in line PG^2, an example of how the proportion of the real per capita output of public goods to real per capita income may change, depending on the particular stage of development in a nation's economy. It can be conjectured that the proportion PG/Y will tend to decline in the preindustrialization and postindustrialization stages of a society's economic evolution. Thus,

$$\frac{PG_a}{Y_a} < \frac{PG_o}{Y_o}$$

---

[17] For a discussion of the preindustrial and postindustrial maturity stages of a society's economic development, see Walt Whitman Rostow, *Economic Growth* (New York: Cambridge University Press, 1960).

would represent both of these stages. The reasons why this may occur are described below.

First, most subsistence wants and goods have traditionally been provided by the private sector through market-type arrangements, since food, clothing, and shelter are divisible goods to which the exclusion principle can be applied. Consequently, the gradual economic expansion of a preindustrial society well may cause the real per capita output of private goods to become a greater proportion of real per capita income, which would mean that the real per capita output of public goods would become a declining proportion of real per capita income.

As real per capita income continues to increase, however, the relative allocative importance of each sector may be expected to change. For example, investment in social capital items such as communications, transportation, and education must take place as part of the economic development process. Since these goods tend to have heavy fixed costs of production and joint consumption or externality characteristics, they are often provided by the government sector of the economy rather than by the market. Thus, let us say that as real per capita income rises above $3,000 in Figure 16–3, the economy enters an industrialization stage and the real per capita output of public goods now becomes a greater proportion of real per capita income over an extended period of time. This stage, which represents the Wagner hypothesis, is largely explained by the fact that important social capital items provided by the public sector have now become part of aggregate demand. Ultimately, these social overhead items will be provided in sufficient quantities, and the society will attain postindustrial maturity at a real per capita income level of (say) $10,500.

All spending units are now assumed to possess an adequate standard of living in the postindustrial society.[18] It seems plausible to suggest that, at this stage of economic development, government may already be providing adequate quantities of those economic goods with decreasing production cost and joint consumption or externality characteristics, and so society will increasingly turn to additional private sector output.[19] Moveover, society may be resisting a "too large" public sector, in relative terms, due to a cultural preference for market activity, with its greater individual freedom and the absence of compulsory taxation. Hence, the real per capita output of private

---

[18] It is possible, of course, for a nation to choose to enter stage 3 even though its poverty (distribution) problem has not been solved.

[19] For evidence of a slowdown in relative public sector growth in Western industrial economies, see Morris Beck, "The Expanding Public Sector: Some Contrary Evidence," *National Tax Journal*, March 1976, pp. 15–21, and also his "Toward A Theory Of Public Sector Growth," *Public Finance*, Vol. 37, No. 2 (1982), pp. 1–15. Meanwhile, a mood of fiscal conservatism in the early 1980's suggests further such constraint in the United States.

goods may well become, once again, a larger proportion of real per capita income during the postindustrial maturity stage. Oppositely, the relative importance of the public sector may be expected to decline.

Critique of the Wagner hypothesis.   Although the Wagner hypothesis has many attributes, it also has several defects. Primarily, the hypothesis deals with interdisciplinary phenomena, even though it is not sufficiently interdisciplinary in its analytical framework. Political science, economics, and sociology are among the several disciplines which must be involved in any theory of public sector expenditure. Such theories must consider the cultural characteristics of a society. It thus seems unlikely that the causal conditions described by Wagner, which are primarily of an economic nature, constitute *all* of the primary determinants of a relatively expanding public sector during industrialization and economic growth. Although the Wagner hypothesis does accumulate and partially explain important historical facts, lack of a comprehensive analytical framework causes it to fall short in these explanations. Yet, it does provide a convenient framework for discussion and for further research.

Alan Peacock and Jack Wiseman have observed that the Wagner argument contains three important defects: (1) it is based on an organic self-determining theory of the state, which is not the prevailing theory in most Western nations; (2) it omits the influence of war on governmental spending; and (3) it stresses a long-term trend of public economic activity which tends to overlook the significant time pattern or process of public expenditure growth.[20]

The displacement, inspection, and concentration effects

Peacock and Wiseman, in their early 1960s work, emphasize the time pattern of public spending trends rather than striving for a genuine positive theory of public sector growth.[21] Their general approach includes three separate, though related, concepts. These are the displacement (threshold), inspection, and concentration (scale) effects.

Using empirical data for the British economy after 1890, they observe that the relative growth of the British public sector has occurred on a steplike rather than a continuous-growth basis. Government fiscal activities, in other words, have risen step by step to successive new plateaus during the period studied. Moreover, the absolute and relative increases (steps upward) in taxing and spending by the British government have generally taken place during periods of major social

---

[20] Alan T. Peacock and Jack Wiseman, *The Growth of Public Expenditure in the United Kingdom* (Princeton, N.J.: Princeton University Press, 1961), p. xxiii.

[21] Ibid.

disturbance or crisis such as war and depression. These crises cause the previous lower tax and expenditure levels to be replaced by new, higher, budgetary levels. After the social crisis has ended, the new levels of tax tolerance which have emerged make the society willing to support a higher level of public expenditure, since it realizes it can carry a heavier tax burden than it previously had thought possible. In other words, the tax threshold has increased. Thus, there is no strong motivation to return to the lower precrisis level of taxation. Greater governmental revenues are used, instead, to support a permanently higher level of public sector activity. Hence, a permanent public sector *displacement* takes place of a portion of society's economic resources which had been allocated previously through the private sector. Over the secular period 1890–1955, this displacement procedure occurred several times in Great Britain.

Figure 16–4 demonstrates the *displacement effect* with its accompanying tax threshold behavior. Time (in years) is measured along the horizontal axis, while public sector revenues (mostly taxes) and public expenditures as a percentage of gross national product (GNP)[22] are measured along the vertical axis. The equation G/GNP will be used to symbolize the relative importance of the British public sector to the aggregate economy at different points of time. It is suggested that as social crises cause a relative expansion of the public sector, the displacement effect which occurs helps to explain the time pattern by which the governmental growth took place. This displacement effect

---

[22] Or the European equivalent of GNP known as gross domestic product (GDP).

FIGURE 16–4   **The displacement effect**

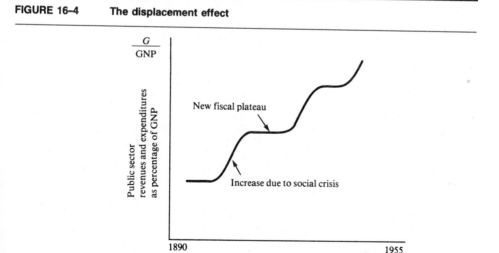

does not require that the new higher plateau of expenditure continue the same expenditure composition that was created by the social disturbance. Although some of the increased expenditures, such as veterans' benefits and debt interest, are direct results of a social disturbance, other expenditure items frequently involve the expansion of government into new areas of economic activity. Some of these new areas may have been provided formerly by the private sector, while others may be the result of technological advancement which allows new goods to exist which have no previous allocational history. Moreover, war or other social disturbances frequently force people and their governments to seek solutions to important problems which previously had been neglected. This is referred to as an *inspection effect*.

In addition to the displacement and inspection effects, Peacock and Wiseman also describe a *concentration (scale) effect*. This concept refers to the apparent tendency for central (national) government economic activity to become an increasing proportion of total public sector economic activity when a society is experiencing the above phenomena. This means, of course, that subnational government necessarily will decline in relative importance within the public sector. Empirical data for the British economy are consistent with this hypothesis during the 20th century.

The doubtful existence of a positive theory of public expenditure

A comprehensive review and analysis of the public expenditure literature, including an examination of the positive theory issue, has been provided recently by Ved P. Gandhi.[23] In this study, Gandhi concludes that the existence of a general positive theory of public expenditure cannot be established. The inability to establish a positive theory, of course, could result merely from measurement problems (which are well documented by Gandhi). Or, it could reflect the intrinsic absence of pervasive independent variables to explain public expenditure behavior over a heterogeneous range of nations. Gandhi tends to support the latter reason, and such a conclusion seems tenable.

Indeed, it is difficult to expect that complex public expenditure behavior can be reduced to a single primary explanatory variable, or set of primary explanatory variables, capable of accurately predicting trends in public sector size and output composition in societies char-

---

[23] Ved P. Gandhi, "Trends in Public Consumption and Investment: A Review of Issues and Evidence," in *Secular Trends of the Public Sector,* ed. Horst C. Recktenwald (Paris: Editions Cujas, 1978), pp. 85–110.

acterized by important economic and noneconomic differences.[24]
Economic differences exist among democratic, mixed, political economies despite their common core of market orientation. Furthermore,
noneconomic differences of a social, cultural, institutional, and historical nature may be of even greater significance. In addition, the parameters of a nation's decision-making matrix may be subject to
change *over time*. It is recognition of this time factor that explains the
tendency in much of the recent public expenditure literature to assign
methodological superiority to time series as opposed to cross-sectional analytical techniques.

On an a priori basis, a number of possibly relevant variables can be
suggested to explain the part of a positive theory which is represented
by the Wagner hypothesis, namely, that the real per capita output of
public goods (PG) will grow more rapidly than real per capita income
(Y) during the period of industrialization. A sampling of such "likely"
independent variables would include:

1. The process of industrialization itself (Wagner).
2. An increasing tolerance level of taxation following periods of
    national economic crisis (Peacock-Wiseman).
3. A productivity growth lag in the public sector behind that of the
    private sector (Baumol).[25]
4. The monopolization of factor markets selling resources to the
    public sector.
5. The bureaucratic entrenchment of existing programs, depart-
    ments, and personnel, and political vote-maximizing by elected
    government officials.
6. Sufficiently strong preferences by society for public and quasi-
    public goods to cause an income-elastic demand for these goods.
7. An increasing demand by society for improved quality in pres-
    ently supplied governmental output.
8. Distributional policies of either a tax-transfer or merit-goods
    variety.
9. Macroeconomic stabilization and economic growth policies.
10. The process of urbanization and, relatedly, of suburbanization.
11. Environmental and other resource-related policies of govern-
    ment.
12. A changing age distribution of the population.
13. Diminishing opposition to taxation as society becomes more
    affluent.

[24] See the discussion in Bernard P. Herber, "Positive Theories of Public Expenditure," paper presented at the 1977 annual meeting of the Western Economic Association, Anaheim, California, June 20–23, 1977.

[25] See William J. Baumol, "Macroeconomics of Unbalanced Growth: The Anatomy
of the Urban Crisis," *American Economic Review*, June 1967, pp. 415–26.

14. Graduated (progressive) national government income taxes and a resultant elastic income elasticity of national government tax revenues.
15. The predominant use of general-fund as opposed to earmarked tax financing.[26]

To be sure, the perusal of such a list does not make one optimistic concerning the existence of either a single independent variable, or a set of independent variables, capable of universal predictive application to public sector behavior across the broad spectrum of democratic mixed economies. Moreover, as the above list suggests, the issues under consideration are not confined to the expenditure side of the fisc. Instead, financing alternatives should be symmetrically considered alongside public expenditure decisions. Thus, a theory of taxpayer behavior may be regarded as equally important to the secular PG/Y ratio as is a theory of expenditure behavior. In fact, one could argue that a truly superior *theory of public sector fiscal behavior* would need to integrate both the expenditure and revenue sides of the budget, in an eclectic fashion.[27] Even then, it is doubtful whether the relevant independent variables for one nation will be common with those of other nations. Thus, a genuinely international (general, universal) positive theory of public expenditure behavior, or of fiscal behavior in general, may simply not exist. The previously cited problem of changing parameters over time would cast additional doubt on the existence of a genuine positive theory.

---

[26] See James M. Buchanan, "The Economics of Earmarked Taxes," *Journal of Political Economy*, October 1963, pp. 457–69.

[27] One advantage of the Peacock-Wiseman analysis and its accompanying displacement (threshold) effect is an effort at such integration.

17

The theory of
fiscal federalism

ECONOMIC RATIONALE FOR FEDERALISM

The federal form of democratic government, commonly known as *federation* or *federalism,* consists of two, coexisting, sovereign[1] levels of government—one at the national or central level and the other at the subnational level. This is generally considered to be more efficient than a *balkan* arrangement, in which the subnational states or provinces of a federation would, instead, each operate as a separate nation. Yet, a *unitary* democracy, with only a sovereign central government and no sovereign subnational governments, might appear to be a better alternative to balkanization than federation, since it would avoid certain intergovernmental problems that arise in a federation as the result of its dual levels of sovereignty. Such a unitary system, for example, is used in Great Britain. However, an operationally efficient unitary democracy would be difficult to attain in the United States, due to the large magnitude of the geographical area to be governed. Governmental adaptability to differential regional preferences would be a problem and, in addition, the American cultural preference for individualistic involvement in the political process would likely be weakened. Thus, it will be assumed that the American people prefer

---

[1] *Sovereign* refers to original and independent government authority. It should be noted that in a system of "dual levels of sovereignty," a written constitution to allocate fiscal and other rights and responsibilities takes on special importance.

federation to a unitary democracy on both efficiency and cultural grounds.

Moreover, strong justification for federalism may be derived from economic analysis relevant to the three basic economic functions: allocation, distribution, and stabilization.[2] Thus, in the analysis to follow, the central theme will be the comparative advantage of *centralized (national)* versus *decentralized (subnational)* governments in "performing"[3] these basic functions, or significant components thereof. It will be demonstrated that central government possesses the comparative advantage in the performance of the distribution and stabilization functions as well as part of the allocation function. However, it will also be demonstrated that decentralized government decision making is the most efficient point for performing the remaining significant portion of the allocation function. As a result, both sovereign levels of government have basic economic justification for coexistence and, thus, for federation. Meanwhile, before further development of this line of thought, additional analysis is required concerning the economic characteristics of the various types of public goods typically allocated through the government sector of the economy.

Types of public goods

The public goods and externality concepts developed in Chapter 2 can be usefully applied at this point. Accordingly, public goods may be classified as national, quasi-national, and nonnational (subnational, local) in nature. A *national* public good may be defined as one whose benefits are consumed on a joint and equal basis by all residents of a nation. An economic good such as national defense fits these consumptive characteristics. Meanwhile, a *quasi-national* public good is characterized by joint, but unequal, consumption of the good's benefits across political jurisdictions. In effect, this means that externalities spill over from the political jurisdiction which initially supplies the good to the residents of other jurisdictions. Moreover, the spillover effects might be bad rather than good. Just as with private externalities, there will be a tendency to undersupply the good or oversupply the bad. Education exemplifies such a quasi-national public good and government-caused water pollution such a quasi-national public

---

[2] For a thorough development of this functional approach, see Wallace E. Oates, "The Theory of Public Finance in a Federal System," *Canadian Journal of Economics*, February 1968, pp. 37–54, and *Fiscal Federalism* (New York: Harcourt Brace Jovanovich, 1972).

[3] *Performance*, in this context, refers to the primary direction of a function by a particular level of government, but does not exclude another level of government from playing some secondary role.

bad. Finally, a *nonnational* public good is characterized by joint and essentially equal consumption on a subnational basis, that is, within a state or local government political jurisdiction. The protective benefits provided by a state highway patrol or by a local fire department would exemplify such a nonnational public good with minimal interjurisdictional externalities.

Arguments for centralized government

The fact that certain economic goods have joint consumption benefits or externalities, which are either national or intergovernmental in scope, suggests that the efficient *allocation* of *national* and *quasinational public goods* may require substantial central government allocational influence. The benefits of national public goods are consumed collectively on a national basis, while those of quasi-national public goods tend to be only partly assignable to particular state or local governments. National defense, for example, involves a common consumptive interest among all individuals in the nation. Moreover, there exists a *correspondence* between the set of persons who consume the benefits, on the one hand, and the persons who finance/supply the good, on the other. Thus, it is not surprising that the federal government supplies national defense as a public good, since this correspondence is national in scope. In contrast, the jointly consumed benefits of a quasi-national public good are diffused unevenly among a number of governmental jurisdictions. In this case, the consumptive benefit population and the finance/supply population do *not correspond* within a given political jurisdiction. When such quasi-national public goods are judged by society to be important, the public interest becomes involved to the extent that the goods should be allocated in acceptable quantities. Thus, a case for central government allocational influence can be argued, so that the supply of these economic goods may be provided at the desired overall level among the various political jurisdictions (states or localities) that are involved. Yet, if the primary level of supply of a quasi-national public good is at the local government level, it may be better for a state government rather than the federal government to provide the appropriate intergovernmental coordination of the relevant externalities.

Another argument for central government economic activity focuses on the fact that *only* a geographically comprehensive central government can effectively equalize significant interstate differences in fiscal capacities and per capita tax (revenue) burdens among the states. In other words, central government holds the comparative advantage in directing any *interstate redistribution policy* that society may desire. The same comparative advantage also rests with central government for programs directed toward the *redistribution of private sector income or wealth*. Otherwise, population mobility between jurisdictions would be self-defeating to any subnational government that would take upon itself to implement a major redistributional program. For example, if a given state were to impose highly progressive personal income tax rates in order to finance a major welfare program for the poor, while other states did not follow suit, higher-income and -wealth persons would tend to migrate from that state and lower-income and -wealth persons would tend to migrate to the state. The obvious result would be an erosion of the state's tax base in the face of many needy persons.

Central government also holds the comparative advantage to perform the *stabilization* function. For example, effective fiscal policy directed toward the problem of a national recession would be unlikely to come from state and local governments since the problem is national in scope, and many of the benefits resulting from any subnational fiscal policy would flow outside the political boundaries of the government initiating the fiscal policy. For example, consider the possibility of one state undertaking a deficit budget policy, resulting from reduced taxes and/or increased spending, in order to increase private sector purchasing power with the intention of increasing output and employment. In an open-trade economy such as the United States, many of the expansionary benefits would escape the economy of the initiating state and would pass to other states. Hence, the motivation to initiate such macroeconomic stabilization policy at the subnational level would be lacking. Under these circumstances, stabilization policy—if deemed desirable—should be directed primarily by the central government which, in effect, can "internalize" the flow of output and employment benefits.

Still another advantage of central government fiscal activity is that a national government can often *collect tax revenues* more efficiently than state-local governments. The comparative advantage which higher levels of government, and especially central government, have in collecting tax revenues stems from several factors. First, a level of government with broad political jurisdiction is in a preferred position to discover items relevant to the tax base and to enforce the tax rates imposed on that base. Broad jurisdictional authority, moreover, discourages migration of the tax base to locations with lower taxes. If a municipality, for example, levies a comprehensive personal income tax on all types of income and does not receive any enforcement assistance from the state or federal government, it would be at a comparative administrative disadvantage with the higher levels of government. Some income earned outside the political limits of the city would be difficult to discover. Moreover, in the long run, economic activity could migrate to other municipalities with lower, or no, income tax burdens. Obviously, the discovery of a personal income tax base is easier, and the opportunities to transfer economic activities to other jurisdictions are fewer, the broader is the scope of the political jurisdiction levying the tax. Finally, the comprehensive nature of central government budgeting avoids the distortive *intergovernmental competition for industry* that exists between state and local governments, as brought about by various tax preferences or expenditure subsidies (see Chapter 11).

In summary, it may be said that the case for central government fiscal activity in a federation rests on the following grounds:

1. The allocation of national public goods.
2. Coordinating the allocation of certain quasi-national public goods.
3. Implementing intergovernmental equalization or private income/wealth-redistribution policies.
4. Directing aggregate stabilization policies.
5. Achieving economies in tax administration.
6. Discouraging intergovernmental competition for industry.

Arguments for decentralized government

The strongest arguments in support of fiscal decentralization and federation rest on the *allocation* of *quasi-national* and *nonnational public goods.* There is little, if any, economic justification to allocate nonnational public goods at the national level of government, though some allocational coordination by the central government may be desirable as states and localities supply certain quasi-national public goods. The jointly consumed benefits of the nonnational public good can be enjoyed by the same residents who finance/supply the goods within a given state or local government jurisdiction. That is, a demand and supply correspondence exists.

Relatedly, it is reasoned that decentralized governmental decisions approximate those of the *market* more closely than do those of central government. This argument focuses on the relationship in the market between the benefits received from the consumption of an economic good and the voluntary monetary outlay for the good. The correlation between payments and goods received is partially approximated at the state-local level of government, in the sense that revenues collected in a particular state or locality can be designated to supply benefits within that political jurisdiction rather than in another jurisdiction. By contrast, members of Congress at the federal level do not usually relate the taxes collected from their particular jurisdictions to the benefits received in these jurisdictions, because so many revenues are collected from so many states and districts that a diffusion effect exists which makes it easy to say: "Why not give my state or my district a larger portion of the revenue pie, since the same amount of taxes will be collected from it in any case?" Federal expenditures, thus, tend to be justified, *not* by a particular tax collection, but by an attempt to obtain more of the diffused aggregate of tax revenues. Moreover, since lower-level government decisions are *closer* to the individual, in terms of a smaller political jurisdiction, than are those of a national government, it is asserted that a representative of the people at the subnational government level will be under greater pressure to establish a meaningful relationship between the benefits received and the tax cost of a project. In addition, it is argued that the local government representative will be in a better position to *interpret* the preferences of the community.

Another argument in behalf of decentralized government points out that the existence of some 80,000 units of state and local government in the United States allows individuals an opportunity to select residence in the community whose fiscal characteristics best meet their preferences (see Chapter 3).[4] Such a selection approximates consumer sovereignty and choice in the market, since extensive fiscal variations exist among these many units of state and local government. As a result, individuals, via *spatial mobility,* are (sometimes) able to select the state and community which best fit their fiscal tastes in tax structure and expenditure patterns. Obviously, there is no similar choice at the central government level—the only remote comparison being the right of an individual to move from one nation to another national jurisdiction.

Decentralized government is also advocated on the grounds that state and local governments allow the recognition of *regional* and *local (subnational) values* rather than an across-the-board application of uniform standards on a national basis. Preferences will tend to differ as the cultural habits and attitudes of the people vary across regions, states, and communities. Yet, national government policy usually contains considerable uniformity. This uniformity can be partially offset, however, when the federal government uses its tax-collecting power to transfer additional funds to the state-local levels of government in an unconditional manner without specifying the uses to which these funds are to be applied.[5]

An additional argument favoring decentralized government asserts that individuals attain *greater freedom* and *responsibility* when public goods are allocated by local government. In this regard, George Stigler comments:

> If we give each governmental activity to the smallest governmental unit which can efficiently perform it, there will be a vast resurgence and revitalization of local government in America. A vast reservoir of ability

---

[4] Charles M. Tiebout, "A Pure Theory of Local Expenditures," *Journal of Political Economy,* October 1956, p. 416–24.

[5] See the following discussion of unconditional (general) revenue sharing grants.

and imagination can be found in the increasing leisure time of the population, and both public functions and private citizens would benefit from the increased participation of citizens in political life. An eminent and powerful structure of local government is a basic ingredient of a society which seeks to give to the individuals the fullest possible freedom and responsibility.[6]

Though Stigler favors a maximum of fiscal decision making by lower-level governments, he acknowledges that certain fiscal areas require central decision making.

In summary, it may be said that the case for decentralized government fiscal activity, and hence for federation, rests on the following grounds:

1. The allocation of nonnational public goods.
2. Coordinating the allocation of certain quasi-national public goods.
3. Similarity to the market principle of benefit-cost linkage, and the related proximity to the interpretation of consumer preferences.
4. Spatial mobility.
5. Allows the meeting of subnational preferences where these may vary from national preferences.
6. Allows greater individual freedom and political responsibility.

INTERGOVERNMENTAL FISCAL INSTRUMENTS

In a multilevel government system, especially one in which sovereign governments coexist as in a federation, intergovernmental fiscal problems are certain to arise. This section of the chapter will describe several of the *intergovernmental fiscal instruments* which may be used to help solve such problems. In turn, the following chapter will describe these problems in specific terms and will apply the appropriate policy instruments for the solution of each problem.

Intergovernmental grants

An important instrument of intergovernmental fiscal policy takes the form of the intergovernmental transfer of funds among governments. These *intergovernmental grants* are a form of revenue sharing. Normally, they flow vertically from a higher-level to a lower-level government. They may be *conditional, block,* or *unconditional* in nature. Each of these will now be considered.

Conditional grants. A *conditional (categorical) grant* involves the specific application of restrictions by the grantor (disbursing) govern-

---

[6] George J. Stigler, "The Tenable Range of Functions of Local Government," *Federal Expenditure Policy for Economic Growth and Stability.* Joint Economic Committee, 85th cong., 1st sess. (Washington, D.C.: U.S. Government Printing Office, 1957), p. 219.

ment concerning how the funds may be used by the grantee (recipient) government. For example, the grantor government may require that the grantee government use the funds for education in a specific sense such as school books or teacher salaries, with still further specifications likely.

A conditional grant may be provided with either a matching or nonmatching formula. Under a *matching* conditional grant, the grantee government must meet from its own funds some proportion of the funds received from the grantor government. Thus, if the matching proportion is 100 percent or 1 to 1, the grantee government must supply $1 of its own funds in order to receive $1 of funds from the grantor government. Or, if the matching proportion is 50 percent, the grantee government would provide 50 cents of its own funds in order to receive $1 of funds. Some matching formulas contain a *variable matching component* which allows economically poorer governments to match at a lower matching proportion than wealthier jurisdictions. *Nonmatching* conditional grants allow the eligible recipient government to receive funds for the particular program without a matching requirement.

Matching conditional grants, in turn, come in closed-end and open-end varieties. A *closed-end* matching grant would place a dollar ceiling on the total amount that may be received under the grant program by a grantee government. On the other hand, an *open-end* matching grant places no upper limit on the total amount of funds that may be received.

A conditional grant will tend to exert both income and substitution effects. The *income effect* resulting from the provision of money to a recipient government will encourage that government to reduce revenue collections from its own sources. On the other hand, the *substitution effect* will tend to encourage the recipient government to increase spending from its own sources, since the cost of supplying the economic good is reduced by the grant. If the price elasticity of demand for the good, as interpreted through the political process, is elastic, the substitution effect will assume greater significance than it will in the case of price-inelastic demand. Moreover, the substitution effect can be intensified, leading to still greater expenditure for the economic good in question, by a *matching* formula since the recipient government will receive the funds only if it provides some revenues of its own.

Block grants. A *block grant* is similar to a conditional grant in that the grantor government designates how the funds are to be used by the grantee government. However, this designation normally would stipulate only the functional area of expenditure for which the funds must be used, and would not prescribe the specific use of the funds within that functional area. For example, the grantor government may require that the funds be used for education but, beyond that prescription, the grantee government may elect to use the funds for school books, teacher salaries, school lunches, or any other activity related to the educational process.

Unconditional grants. As the title suggests, an *unconditional grant* is characterized by the absence of significant restrictions on the use of funds transferred to a grantee government. The higher-level grantor government simply provides funds for the discretionary use of the recipient government. There are a number of reasons for the possible use of this intergovernmental fiscal instrument. They include: (1) economies of scale in tax administration, (2) the differential fiscal capacities of various states and localities, and (3) the tendency for subnational governments in a federation to possess inferior tax sources as compared to those of the national government. However, a full appreciation of the ability of unconditional grants to deal with these issues must wait for the next chapter, which describes specific intergovernmental fiscal problems and their solutions.

Meanwhile, certain other characteristics of unconditional grants may be considered. One of these characteristics, often looked upon as a defect of this instrument, is the fact that a higher-level, grantor government bears the burden of imposing the taxes, while a lower-level, grantee government decides how to use the money. Such an "asymmetry" between the political unpopularity of imposing taxes and the political popularity of spending money is said to foster fiscal irresponsibility. This asymmetry would be avoided, however, if the same government that makes the taxing decision also, in a symmetrical fashion, makes the spending decision. Relatedly, it may be noted that such asymmetry is less of a problem with conditional and block grants, since the grantor government does designate something about the use of the tax funds that it has collected.

Finally, it may be observed that unconditional grants, like all grants, exert an *income effect,* which motivates the recipient government to reduce its own revenue-gathering activities. However, since unconditional grants do not assign expenditures to a specific economic good or program, they do not exert a direct *substitution effect.* Yet, they could exert an indirect allocational change, which would increase the supply of a particular economic good, if the income effect does not result in a reduction in own-source revenues that is equal to the amount of the grant. In this case, a net increase in revenues would occur which, assumedly, would be expanded for an economic good or program with high price elasticity. Hence, the expenditure pattern of the recipient government would have been indirectly changed.

Income tax credits

The *income tax credit* instrument, when used for intergovernmental fiscal purposes in a federation, allows people to reduce their tax liability owed to one unit of government by means of taxes paid to another unit. Intergovernmental tax credits may be applied vertically between two governments at different levels, or horizontally between two governments at the same level.

Vertical income tax credits may represent an effort by a higher-level government to encourage a lower-level government to use a particular tax source or sources. For example, the federal government could allow a credit against federal personal income tax liability for a particular tax or taxes paid to a state and/or local government, or a state government might do likewise with its personal income tax for a certain tax or taxes paid to a local government.[7] Thus, if the federal government were to allow a credit of 25 percent against federal personal income tax liability for personal income taxes paid to a state government, a $1,000 federal tax liability could be reduced to $750, as long as at least $250 of personal income taxes are paid by the taxpayer at the state level. This would encourage a state to utilize personal income taxation, at least up to the limit of the credit, since the total tax liability of the taxpayer would remain unchanged, that is, he/she would pay either $1,000 to the federal government without the credit, or $750 to the federal government and $250 to a state government with the credit.

By contrast, horizontal income tax credits usually represent an effort to improve distributional equity among taxpayers, rather than to induce a greater tax effort by lower-level governments. For example, horizontal multiple taxation in the form of the imposition of income taxes by two different states, or nations, on a person or business may require use of the horizontal tax credit technique in order to avoid double taxation of the income. Thus, ideally, income tax payments to one state (nation) would be credited against those owed to another state (nation), according to some interstate or international income allocation formula. Although such horizontal income tax credits are important, the discussion which follows deals mainly with income tax credits in a vertical intergovernmental context.

Vertical income tax credits come in a variety of forms.[8] These include:

1. An *unlimited credit subject to a proportional ceiling.* This would be characterized by the 25 percent personal income tax credit example described before, whereby a person could fully credit all of

---

[7] This type of income tax credit, with the intention of expanding a lower-level government's tax base, is not importantly used in the American public sector. Nonetheless, its potential for encouraging lower-level governments to develop their own tax sources is considerable.

[8] For a discussion of tax credits as well as other intergovernmental fiscal instruments, see George F. Break, *Intergovernmental Fiscal Relations in the United States* (Washington, D.C.: Brookings Institution, 1967), chap. 2.

the tax paid to a lower-level government(s) up to some percentage limit or ceiling of the tax liability owed to a higher-level government. For example, all personal income taxes paid to state and local governments could be credited, up to 25 percent of the taxpayer's federal personal income tax liability.

2. An *unlimited credit subject to a declining ceiling*. For example, personal income taxes paid to state and local governments would be fully credited against federal personal income tax liability, up to (say) 40 percent of the first $500 of such liability, 20 percent of the next $1,000, and 5 percent of the remainder. This approach, which reduces the value of the credit as taxpaying ability (as measured by income tax liability) increases, introduces progressivity into the credit in accordance with the ability-to-pay principle of distributional equity.

3. A *limited proportional credit*. Under this form of vertical tax credit, a specified percentage of the tax paid to the lower-level government, but not the full amount of the tax, may be credited against the tax owed to a higher-level government. For example, a taxpayer may be allowed to subtract 25 percent of the personal income tax paid to state and local governments from his or her federal personal income tax liability.

4. A *limited declining credit*. Under this form of vertical intergovernmental credit, decreasing specified percentages of taxes paid to a lower-level government may be subtracted from the tax owed to a higher-level government. For example, 40 percent of state-local personal income taxes might be subtracted from the first $500 of federal personal income tax liability, 20 percent from the next $1,000, and 5 percent from all remaining liability. This approach, similar to that of the unlimited credit subject to a declining ceiling, introduces progressivity into the credit in accordance with the ability-to-pay concept.

The discussion below will focus on the first of these vertical tax credit forms—the *unlimited credit subject to a proportional ceiling*—though the analysis will be largely applicable to the other forms. First, it will be useful to distinguish among single, block, and global tax credits. A *single tax credit* exists when the credit is allowed for only one type of tax paid to another unit of government. A *block tax credit* exists when the credit is allowed for several, but not all, types of taxes paid to another government unit. A *global tax credit* represents a credit for all taxes paid, regardless of type, to another unit of government. The control over *revenue instruments* exerted by the higher-level government utilizing a single tax credit is analogous to the control over *expenditure patterns* exerted by a higher-level government utilizing a conditional grant. Similarly, a block credit and block grant are analogous, as are a global credit and an unconditional grant. The global credit and unconditional grant, of course, allow the lower-level government to select whatever revenue sources and expenditure patterns it desires.

Income tax deductions

An *income tax deduction* differs from a credit in that it represents a subtraction from the tax base prior to the application of the tax rate to that base, while the credit represents a subtraction from the tax liability after the application of the rate to the base. The deduction technique, just as the credit, may be used by higher-level governments to encourage lower-level governments to develop their own tax sources. The "tax-saving" value of an income tax deduction (against, say, federal personal income tax liability) will vary significantly, depending on the marginal tax rate bracket of the taxpayer. For example, assume that taxpayers A and B each pay $1,000 in state-local taxes, but taxpayer A is in a 50 percent federal personal income tax marginal rate bracket, while taxpayer B is in a 25 percent bracket. In this instance, the deduction of these taxes is worth more in tax saving ($500) to taxpayer A, than it is to taxpayer B ($250), as the following calculations indicate:

Federal personal income tax base reduction due
  to the deductibility of $1,000 in
  state-local taxes   = $1,000

Federal personal income tax that would have
  been owed on this amount of federal tax
  base without the deduction of the state-local
  taxes — hence, the *amount of tax saving* resulting
  from their deduction:

        Taxpayer A = $500 with a 50 percent marginal
                  tax rate ($1,000 × 0.50 = $500)
        Taxpayer B = $250 with a 25 percent marginal
                  tax rate ($1,000 × 0.25 = $250)

The tax-deduction approach to intergovernmental fiscal coordination is used between all levels of the American public sector. The most significant use, however, involves the various deductions from the federal personal income tax for such state-local taxes as the personal income tax, general sales tax, and property tax. These deductions are subtracted from adjusted gross income. Many state personal income tax structures, moreover, allow a deduction for the federal personal income tax.

Comparative intergovernmental effects of the income tax credit and deduction instruments. The primary contribution to intergovernmental fiscal policy provided by the income tax credit and deduction instruments, as observed earlier, is their ability to encourage lower-level governments to develop their own tax sources. However, the income tax credit tends to contribute more effectively in this regard than does the income tax deduction instrument. This is demonstrated by the fact that the total public sector tax liability of a taxpayer generally tends to be *less*, and hence the tax saving tends to be *greater*, when the tax credit device is used rather than the tax deduction method (see Table 17–1). This occurs because the credit is an off-the-top substitution of one tax liability for another. A tax deduction, on the other hand, reduces the taxable income base prior to tax computation, but does not reduce tax liability on a dollar-for-dollar basis. Thus, an income tax credit ordinarily provides a greater *stimulant* for a government to adopt a new tax, or to intensify the application of an already-existing tax, than does an income tax deduction. The reason is that the credit would be politically more popular than the deduction, since it tends to result in a relatively lower tax liability to the higher-level government which offers the credit or deduction.

In effect, an income tax credit and, to a lesser extent, an income tax deduction, redistributes tax funds among levels of government within the public sector. For example, a federal income tax credit for personal income taxes paid to a state government, if ignored by the state, would amount to a needless loss of funds that it could otherwise collect without increasing the tax burdens of its taxpayers. Moreover, the income tax credit, as does the income tax deduction, allows a symmetrical, *quid pro quo*, relationship in the sense that the government which spends the money also has the responsibility for raising the tax revenues. Indeed, the income tax credit and deduction instruments can serve as important intergovernmental fiscal instruments. However, they do possess the possibly unpopular facet that the central government is able to influence the structure of the tax system of the lower-lever government unless the credit or deduction is of the global variety.

In 1966, the Advisory Commission on Intergovernmental Relations[9] recommended federal government adoption of the income-tax-credit device to encourage state government usage of the personal income tax. Even today, 10 states do not use a comprehensive (broad-based) personal income tax. Moreover, most states which do impose the tax apply it with a modest rate structure. The commission suggested the adoption of a federal personal income tax credit (such as 40 percent) for personal income taxes paid to state governments. This amount would then be subtracted from the total federal personal income tax liability of the taxpayer. As observed, a state would thus be able to collect additional personal income tax revenues, up to the limit of the tax credit, without increasing the tax liabilities of its taxpayers. Although such a credit was not adopted, an implicit income tax credit, in effect, was included in the State and Local Fiscal Assistance Act of

---

[9] A special research body created by Congress in 1959.

TABLE 17-1   Example of the tax saving for a hypothetical taxpayer from the income tax credit and income tax deduction instruments*

Income tax credit		Income tax deduction	
Federal personal income tax of taxpayer	= $4,000	Federal personal income tax of taxpayer	= $4,000
State personal income tax of taxpayer	= $1,000	State personal income tax of taxpayer	= $1,000
Value of credit for state personal income taxes paid	= 25% of federal personal income tax liability (unlimited credit, subject to a proportional ceiling)	Value of deduction for state personal income taxes paid (assume a 25% marginal tax-rate bracket on the federal tax)	= Reduction of taxable income base by the amount of the deduction: ($1,000) times the marginal tax rate (25%)
	$4,000		$1,000
	×0.25		×0.25
	$1,000		$ 250
Federal personal income tax liability following application of credit	= $4,000	Federal personal income tax liability following application of deduction	= $4,000
	−1,000		−250
	$3,000		$3,750
Total public sector tax liability without credit: $4,000 (federal) + $1,000 (state)	= $5,000	Total public sector tax liability without deduction: $4,000 (federal) + $1,000 (state)	= $5,000
Total public sector tax liability with credit: $3,000 (federal) + $1,000 (state)	= $4,000	Total public sector tax liability with deduction: $3,750 (federal) + $1,000 (state)	= $4,750
Tax saving	= $5,000	Tax saving	= $5,000
	−4,000		−4,750
	$1,000 (tax saving)		$ 250 (tax saving)

* Credit or deduction is for personal income taxes paid to a state government.

1972, since one of the two formulas for distributing general (unconditional) revenue-sharing funds among the states includes a factor preferential to those states that utilize personal income taxation.[10]

Tax supplements

The *tax supplement* instrument for improving intergovernmental fiscal performance in a federation involves the application of separate tax rates to an identical (or essentially identical) tax base by governments at different levels. A higher-level government normally imposes the basic tax under this arrangement. That is, a state government adopts the base of a federal tax or a local government adopts the base of a state tax. There are two primary variations of this approach: (1) a *pure tax supplement,* which occurs when a lower-level government adopts the tax base of a higher-level government, applies its own tax rates to this base, and then collects the tax itself; and (2) the *tax piggyback* variation, in which a lower-level government adopts the tax base of a higher-level government and applies its own tax rates to this base, but allows the higher-level government to collect the tax for it instead of collecting the tax itself. Moreover, a form of revenue sharing known as *source revenue sharing* also has certain similarities to tax supplements. Source revenue sharing involves the return of some part of the revenues collected by a higher-level government from its own taxes to a lower-level government which was the geographical source of the funds. However, this form of revenue sharing differs somewhat from the basic tax-supplement concept in that the two tax bases are formally merged into one base, instead of remaining two formally separate tax bases utilized by two different governments. Source revenue sharing resembles an unconditional grant, but does perform better than the unconditional grant in attaining "symmetry" between tax sources and spending decisions within the same political jurisdiction.

The tax piggybacking and source revenue-sharing techniques have the advantage of reducing tax enforcement costs, due to the economies of scale inherent in centralized tax collection. Moreover, to the extent that different state or local governments are encouraged to use the same tax base, tax supplements reduce horizontal fiscal competition via the tax structure, with its attendant allocational distortions. However, some interstate or interlocal tax variation could still remain due to differential tax rates being applied to the uniform tax bases.

The tax-supplement approach is used between both the federal and state and the state and local levels of government in the United States. Moreover, both variations of tax supplements described here, as well

---

[10] The general revenue sharing program will be discussed further in Chapter 18.

as source revenue-sharing, are employed in the American public sector. Primary examples of tax supplements between the federal and state governments include payroll and income taxes. Regarding the former, both federal and state unemployment taxes are levied on the same tax base. Regarding the latter, three states—Nebraska, Rhode Island, and Vermont—use a state personal income tax which applies a fixed percentage rate to the taxpayer's federal personal income tax liability. In other words, the state personal income tax uses the federal personal income tax base, with slight modifications, and collects for the state an amount equal to a percentage of the taxpayer's federal tax payment. Moreover, the State and Local Fiscal Assistance Act of 1972 makes it possible for state personal income tax collection to be piggybacked on top of the collection of the federal personal income tax by the Internal Revenue Service, though the policy has never been implemented.

The general sales tax provides an example of use of the tax supplement instrument between a number of state and local governments in the United States. The receipts of state and local general sales taxes are frequently collected on the same tax base by the state government. Under this piggyback form of tax supplement, the revenues derived from the local tax are then returned by the state government to the local government. On the other hand, local governments collect most of their own property tax revenues, even though both state and local governments typically use the same property tax base. The main exception to local government collection of property taxes exists in the case of public utility or transportation industry properties, which cross county boundaries and, thus, are administered centrally by a state government.

Interstate redistribution through the federal budget

Figure 17-1 demonstrates the ability of the federal budget to redistribute funds among the states. This map relates the estimated federal revenues originating in a state to the estimated federal expenditures flowing from the federal budget to that state. The quotient (r) which results constitutes the *net impact* of the federal budget on a state.[11] If the ratio of expenditures received to revenues paid exceeds unity ($r > 1$), a net inflow of federal funds to a state is indicated. That is, more funds have flowed into the state than have been taken out of the state through the federal budget. If the ratio is less than unity

---

[11] See I. M. Labovitz, "Federal Expenditures and Revenues in Regions and States," *Intergovernmental Perspective,* Fall 1978 (Washington, D.C.: Advisory Commission on Intergovernmental Relations), pp. 16–23. For an earlier study of the period 1965–67, see The Conference Board, *The Federal Budget–Its Impact on the Economy* (New York, 1969), pp. 38–43.

FIGURE 17-1 Ratio of estimated federal government expenditures in each state to estimated federal revenues from residents of the state: Fiscal years 1974–1976 (average ratio for all states equals 1.00)

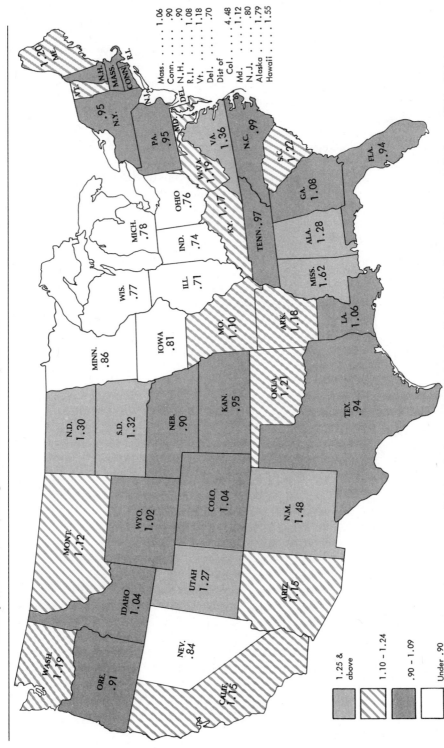

Mass.	1.06
Conn.	.90
N.H.	.90
R.I.	1.08
Vt.	1.18
Del.	.70
Dist of Col.	4.48
Md.	1.12
N.J.	.80
Alaska	1.79
Hawaii	1.55

ME. 1.20
VT.
N.H.
MASS.
CONN.
R.I.
N.Y. .95
N.J.
PA. .95
MD.
DEL.
W.VA. 1.19
VA. 1.36
N.C. .99
S.C. 1.22
FLA. .94
GA. 1.08
ALA. 1.28
KY. 1.17
TENN. .97
MISS. 1.62
ARK. 1.18
LA. 1.06
OHIO .76
MICH. .78
IND. .74
ILL. .71
WIS. .77
IOWA .81
MINN. .86
MO. 1.10
OKLA. 1.21
TEX. .94
N.D. 1.30
S.D. 1.32
NEB. .90
KAN. .95
N.M. 1.48
COLO. 1.04
WYO. 1.02
MONT. 1.12
UTAH 1.27
ARIZ. 1.15
IDAHO 1.04
WASH. 1.19
ORE. .91
NEV. .84
CALIF. 1.15

1.25 & above
1.10 – 1.24
.90 – 1.09
Under .90

Source: Advisory Commission on Intergovernmental Relations. Table appears in I. M. Labovitz, "Federal Expenditures and Revenues in Regions and States," *Intergovernmental Perspective*, Fall 1978 (Washington, D.C.: Advisory Commission on Intergovernmental Relations), p. 19.

($r < 1$), a net outflow of funds from the state has taken place. That is, fewer funds have flowed into the state than have been taken out of the state through the federal budget. During the fiscal period 1974–76, only 18 states fell within a range of moderate deviation from unity (0.90–1.09). This demonstrates the fact that most states (32) received a substantial redistributional effect from the federal fisc. The leading gainers consisted mostly of states with fairly small populations, while the losers were primarily agricultural-industrial states in the upper Midwest.[12]

One important cause of this interstate redistribution is the fact that most federal revenues come from progressive personal and corporation income taxes, especially the former.[13] Thus, states with high per capita incomes normally contribute revenues to the federal budget above the per capita national average contribution, and vice versa. Overall, 11 of the 14 states with per capita incomes under 85 percent of the national average per capita income had net impact ratios considerably above unity (1.17 or greater), while the remaining 3 had net impact ratios ranging from 0.97 to 1.06.[14] It is safe to say that such interstate redistribution through the federal budget is due partly to design, but also due partly to accidental circumstances. Nonetheless, the federal budget does *in fact* yield an important redistributional influence.

---

[12] Labovitz, "Federal Expenditures and Revenues in Regions and States," p. 19.

[13] However, this is not to suggest that grant-in-aid programs as well as the overall pattern of federal expenditures did not exert redistributional effects of their own.

[14] These results are computed on the basis of the 1975 (calendar year) state average per capita personal income figure of $5,902.

18

The problems of
fiscal federalism
and their solution

Having established an economic rationale for the existence of federalism in the previous chapter, we now turn our attention to some of the *intergovernmental fiscal problems* that tend to arise under this form of government.[1] In turn, the intergovernmental fiscal instruments developed earlier will be applied as solutions to these problems. It should be noted that an *eclectic* policy approach is advocated, since the various fiscal instruments each have their respective comparative advantages in alleviating particular problems. Finally, the actual intergovernmental fiscal performance of the American federation will be assessed, along with recent intergovernmental fiscal trends, in the last two sections of the chapter.

INTERGOVERNMENTAL FISCAL PROBLEMS AND INSTRUMENTS FOR THEIR SOLUTION

Primary problems

Vertical fiscal imbalance. It must be decided which level of government in the federation will perform the *specific functions* required to meet societal preferences. Moreover, the *revenue sources* neces-

---

[1] Nonetheless, the benefits of federalism are considered to outweigh its problems.

351

sary to finance these expenditure functions must be allocated in some manner among the various levels of government.[2] *Vertical fiscal imbalance* refers to a disproportionate alignment of these revenue sources vis-á-vis expenditure obligations by level of government. That is, one sovereign level of government often tends to possess relatively superior revenue (mainly tax) sources to finance its spending functions as contrasted to the other sovereign level. Such imbalance normally follows a pattern whereby the central (national) government holds the superior fiscal position, while sovereign state governments and their local government offspring possess inadequate tax sources to finance their spending responsibilities. This primarily results from the dominant use of *progressive income taxes* by central governments—leading to an income-elastic tax structure. Meanwhile, the income elasticity of subnational government tax systems tends to be less elastic than that of the central government, due to their greater reliance on statutorily proportional rather than progressive taxes.

Further insight into the reasons why central governments have dominated the income tax field seems warranted. These reasons may be viewed in allocational, distributional, and stabilization terms. First, the 20th century has witnessed an enormous growth in the complexity of the national defense function and, relatedly, in the *allocation* of resources to perform this function. As a result, central government, which holds the comparative advantage in allocating this national public good, has had to develop a productive tax source, such as progressive income taxation, to help finance this extremely costly function. Moreover, central government also holds the comparative advantage in directing *distributional (redistributional)* policies, which are often closely tied to progressive income taxes due to their superior performance in relationship to the ability-to-pay norm. Finally, increased attention has been given to *stabilization* policies since the chaotic Western world depression of the 1930s, and central government also holds the comparative advantage in meeting this function. As will be seen in Chapter 20, progressive income taxes serve as important instruments of macroeconomic stabilization policy. Meanwhile, other factors which may lead to central government revenue superiority include (in some federations) a constitutional allocation of fiscal powers which deny appropriate tax sources to state (and local) governments. In addition, the sheer size and political clout of a larger central, versus smaller, subnational governments may enable it to dominate the superior tax sources.

Various intergovernmental fiscal instruments may be used to help

---

[2] This does not suggest that each level of government should possess exclusive rights to a particular type of revenue, but it does mean that overall consideration should be given to the *combined* effects of the revenue-gathering activities of *all* components of the public sector.

solve the vertical fiscal imbalance problem. Ranked in order of effectiveness, these are:

1. *Income tax credits.* A central government personal income tax credit for taxes paid to state (or to state and local) governments, as described in the preceding chapter, will provide an incentive for these governments to develop their own tax systems to a satisfactory point. Moreover, this will be done in a manner that provides fiscal symmetry, since each subnational government will be making both the *tax imposition* as well as the *expenditure* decisions. If the central government wishes to avoid any influence on the type of tax instruments adopted by the subnational government, a *global credit* would be in order. Moreover, in order to take advantage of scale economies in tax administration, an income tax credit could be accompanied by a *piggyback* form of tax supplement.

2. *Income tax deductions.* A central government personal income tax deduction for taxes paid to state (or to state and local) governments will also provide an incentive for these governments to develop their own tax systems. However, this incentive will be less than that of an income tax credit due to its relatively smaller tax-saving potential for taxpayers. However, like the income tax credit instrument, the income tax deduction also allows for fiscal symmetry between the power to tax and the power to spend. Also, like the credit, it could be *global* in nature in order to permit subnational government discretion in tax system design and, in addition, could encourage efficient tax administration if accompanied by a *piggyback* form of tax supplement.

3. *Unconditional grants.* Under this approach, central government would provide no-strings-attached grants to state (or to state and local) governments to help alleviate their revenue shortages. These grants would preserve the discretion of the recipient subnational governments to spend the funds as they see fit. However, a disadvantage of this instrument is that it violates the principle of fiscal symmetry, since the central government bears the "onus" of imposing the taxes while the subnational governments enjoy the political "pleasure" of spending the funds.

4. *Conditional and block grants.* These restrictive central-government grants would provide revenues where they are needed—to the subnational governments. However, they impose unnecessary restrictions on their use and, thus, distort spending patterns through substitution effects. The problem of vertical fiscal imbalance, of course, is not one of "how to spend the funds," but instead, is one of "inadequate funds" at a particular level of government.

Horizontal fiscal imbalance. When fiscal imbalance occurs between different units of government at the same level of government in a federation, it is known as the problem of *horizontal fiscal imbalance.* For example, considerable differences exist in the distribution of economic resources among the various states. This means that the sources of taxation, when converted to a per capita basis, differ among the states. Thus, per capita income, wealth, and sales (the three primary tax bases) take on an interstate dimension and result in horizontal fiscal imbalance among the various states. Furthermore, similar variations may occur among local units of government within a given state. These differences in the resource endowments of communities, similar to those among the states, cause the per capita revenue collection potentials of the communities to vary. Admittedly, one advantage of decentralized fiscal decision making by state and local governments is the fact that a particular revenue structure can be adapted to the unique resource characteristics of a given state or locality. Nonetheless, since resource endowment is the ultimate source of governmental revenue collection capacity, a given state or community enjoying considerable income- and wealth-producing ability and a strong sales base is capable of providing *either* a greater per capita output of public and quasi-public goods than a resource-poor jurisdiction, at the same revenue effort (RE), *or* the same output of such goods at a lower revenue effort than the poorer jurisdiction.

For example, let $RE = R_p/Y_p$ provide the measure of *revenue effort,* with R_p representing per capita revenues from own sources and Y_p representing per capita income.[3] Then, assume that state A possesses an annual per capita income of $5,000, while that of state B is $2,500. Moreover, assume that the costs of supplying public-type goods are the same in each state. Thus, if state B supplies $500 per capita in public and quasi-public goods from its own revenue sources, it does so with a revenue effort of 0.20, since $R_p/Y_p = 500/2,500 = 0.20$. However, with the same revenue effort (0.20), state A could supply $1,000 of public-type goods, since $R_p/Y_p = 1,000/5,000 = 0.20$. Moreover, if state A decides to supply only the same output of public goods as state B ($500 per capita), it can do so with a lower revenue effort (0.10) than that of state B (0.20), since $R_p/Y_p = 500/5,000 = 0.10$. It is very possible that the worst of all worlds will be the result; that is, an intermediate position will occur whereby the residents of the poorer jurisdiction will experience both a lower per capita consumption of public and quasi-public goods and a higher per capita revenue effort than the wealthier jurisdiction.

Revenue effort, of course, consists of both the tax and nontax payments made to government by the residents of a jurisdiction though, in most jurisdictions, tax revenues are by far the more important source of governmental revenues. Thus, revenue effort is primarily an

---

[3] Per capita income is commonly used as a measure of *fiscal capacity,* and thus as the base of the revenue effort formula, due primarily to its easy attainability. It is not theoretically "the best" measure of fiscal capacity that could be selected.

indicator of the tax burdens of the members of a political jurisdiction. However, it is possible for some taxes to be ultimately paid to a jurisdiction by taxpayers who are not residents of that jurisdiction. This is known as the phenomenon of *tax exporting*.[4] The ability to transfer or export a tax to the residents of another political jurisdiction will vary depending on, among other things, the nature of the tax itself. For example, a state severance tax on the extraction of natural resources is conducive to exporting, given such factors as price-inelastic demand, because it is a tax on transactions at an early stage of the productive process. Thus, it is certain to be followed by a number of further productive transactions, which transactions may allow the shifting of tax burdens to the residents of other states or nations.

Since states with lower per capita personal incomes tend to have either lower per capita public-type goods consumption than wealthier jurisdictions, or higher revenue effort (and tax effort) burdens, or both, the relevant question thus becomes: Should federal budgetary policy be deliberately undertaken to equalize the per capita consumption of public and quasi-public goods and of tax burdens among the various states (and localities)? Such a policy, if adopted, may be termed *equalization policy*.[5]

A yes answer to the above question could be based on distributional, allocational, or stabilization grounds. For example, it can be argued, on *distributional* grounds, that a group of states which chooses federation over balkanization necessarily accepts a "common interest" in the living standards of all the citizens of the federal nation. Each citizen, as it were, has dual citizenship; that is, a person is simultaneously a resident both of a sovereign nation and of a sovereign state. The coincidence of residency in a poor state should not penalize that person. Accordingly, the collective consensus of a democratic society might choose to reduce inequality in the interstate (and interlocality) consumption of public-type goods and of tax burdens.[6] Thus, equalization policies of a budgetary nature would be introduced. Moreover, this reasoning often is extended to include a governmental responsibility to alleviate private sector poverty, as well as poverty in the consumption of public-type goods and the equalization of tax burdens, since the dual citizenship argument can

---

[4] Two excellent articles which deal in depth with the issue of tax exporting are Charles E. McLure, Jr., "Tax Exporting in the United States: Estimates for 1962," *National Tax Journal*, March 1967, pp. 49–77, and "The Inter-regional Incidence of General Regional Taxes," *Public Finance*, no. 3 (1969), pp. 457–83.

[5] "Equalization policy" refers to the *reduction* of public goods consumption and tax burden differentials, but not necessarily to the complete elimination of such differentials.

[6] All federations of the world have adopted equalization policies, but with widely varying degrees of equalization being sought in the different federations.

be applied to both private and public economic activity. However, the interaction of private sector and public sector poverty is very complex. For example, a poor person living in a rich state will tend to "gain" from his/her location, in a redistributional sense, but a rich person living in a poor state will tend to "lose".

Society may also wish to adopt equalization policies due to *allocational* considerations, which focus on the concept of intergovernmental externalities.[7] In an advanced industrial society, for example, high-quality communications and transportation systems allow the conditions imposed by the public sector of one state or locality to diffuse into the comsumptive and productive activities of other jurisdictions. In other words, a poorer state or community, through its budget policy, is likely to affect negatively the allocational patterns of production and consumption in wealthier states or localities in an interdependent, specialized society in which intergovernmental externalities are common. Thus, fiscal policy of an equalization nature may, once again, be desirable.

Finally, the quality of productive resources in a poor state or community is likely to be lower than in an area capable of providing a higher level of public consumption. Labor, for example, may be less educated and health standards lower in a poor as opposed to a wealthy state or community. The aggregate *stabilization* implications of this situation suggest that lower volumes of short-run output and lower long-run rates of economic growth may result for the economy as a whole. Thus, horizontal intergovernmental inequalities in resource quality may serve as an argument for the institution of intergovernmental equalization programs in order to promote the stabilization goal.

Not only does central government hold the comparative advantage in directing private income- and wealth-redistribution policies, it is also the logical point for directing the majority of intergovernmental redistribution (equalization) policies. However, state governments may nonetheless play some role in equalizing public goods consumption and tax burdens among local governments in their jurisdictions. Meanwhile, various intergovernmental fiscal instruments may be used to help solve the horizontal fiscal imbalance problem. Ranked in order of effectiveness, these are:

1. *Unconditional grants.* Central government may provide "no-strings-attached" grants to relatively poor states, or to relatively poor state and local, governments. Or, a state could provide such grants to the poorer governments within its jurisdiction. Unlike the vertical

---

[7] The concept of *intergovernmental externalities* constitutes a major fiscal issue in a federation—one far beyond the scope of only equalization considerations. Hence, this concept is treated later, in greater detail, as a separate intergovernmental fiscal problem.

fiscal imbalance problem in which all subnational governments need revenue assistance, only the poorer governments, in *fiscal capacity* terms, require assistance. Unconditional grants are an ideal form of such assistance, since they allow the central government budget to be used as a mechanism whereby per capita grants, financed from the taxes of the higher fiscal capacity states, are provided to the poorer, lower fiscal capacity, states. The recipient states may use the funds at their own discretion, which is appropriate since the horizontal imbalance problem is not linked to the deficient supply of any particular economic good. Although the fiscal symmetry of taxing and spending powers is not attained, such symmetry is simply unattainable due to the nature of the horizontal fiscal imbalance problem.[8]

2. *Conditional and block grants with variable matching formulas.* While not ideal, grants of this type, from the central or state governments, nonetheless do supply funds to the poorer jurisdictions. Moreover, they place less pressure on the poorer government's own tax sources by requiring a lower matching ratio than is required for the wealthier recipient governments. However, a disadvantage of this instrument is the unnecessary restriction placed on how the recipient government can use the funds. It is the overall fiscal capacity deficiency of the recipient government, not any particular deficient good or function, that is the root of the horizontal fiscal imbalance problem.

3. *Interstate redistribution resulting from progressive central government income taxes.* A central government, by imposing progressive income taxes, tends to collect higher per capita tax amounts from the wealthier, as opposed to the poorer, states. Thus, even with a proportional per capita expenditure incidence across the states, an income redistribution effect favoring the poorer states would result from the tax side of the budget. The interstate redistribution brought about by the federal budget that was described in the previous chapter may be partly explained by progressive income taxes.

Finally, it should be noted that the income-tax credit and income-tax deduction instruments are of *no use* against the problem of horizontal fiscal imbalance. This is because such instruments merely encourage a lower-level government to develop its own tax sources more intensively. They do not, however, alter the relative fiscal capacity differences between the various governments, nor the effects of these differences. Hence, they do not attack the root, nor due to the absence of revenue transfers, even the symptoms, of the horizontal fiscal imbalance problem.

Intergovernmental externalities. It was observed in Part I that economic effects initiated in the private sector sometimes escape the

---

[8] Except in the long run, at which time various *economic development policies* may be used to expand the resource base, and thus the revenue (tax) capacity, of the poorer states.

price mechanism. That is, consumers or producers may receive benefits or costs initiated by the allocational activities of other private consumers or producers, over which there is no direct market control. This is known as the concept of *externalities.*

An analogous situation may occur in the public sector of the economy, since government-initiated benefits and costs sometimes escape the internal budgetary control of the unit of government whose residents either initiate or receive these economic effects. This concept in the public sector may be referred to as either *intergovernmental externalities* or *intergovernmental spillovers.* It means that the fiscal action of one unit of government can exert either beneficial or harmful allocational[9] effects on the residents of another governmental jurisdiction, in a manner which escapes budgetary control. Thus, a public school education system financed by one city may bring benefits to the residents of a nearby city (*positive* intergovernmental externality), or the dumping of poorly treated sewage into a river by one city may harm the drinking water of the residents of a downstream city (*negative* intergovernmental externality). Moreover, an intergovernmental externality may involve governments at different levels (*vertical* intergovernmental externality), or at the same level (*horizontal* intergovernmental externality), though the latter are the more important and will receive emphasis in the present discussion.

Quasi-national public goods (bads), as defined earlier, reflect the intergovernmental externality phenomenon. Importantly, there is a tendency to undersupply quasi-national public goods, since the residents of the supplying jurisdiction do not consume all of the benefits which they pay for. Moreover, there is a tendency to oversupply quasi-national public bads, since the supplying jurisdiction is creating costs which do not show up in its budget.

Thus, if the goods or bads involved are deemed important, internalization efforts are required to increase the supply of the goods and to reduce the supply of the bads. Such internalization must be coordinated by a higher level of government. If the externalities are mainly interstate in nature, a coordinative role by the central government would be appropriate. However, if they are primarily interlocal in scope, state governments may play a major role in the internalization effort. If interstate coordination by the central government is undertaken, the sovereign states would need to give their legal consent. Such would not be the case, however, when a state coordinates its local governments, since the latter are not sovereign, but instead are the nonsovereign legal creations of the sovereign state government.

Conditional and *block grants* are ideal instruments for dealing with

---

[9] Although externalities, both private and intergovernmental, are basically allocational in nature, they may nonetheless exert distributional side effects.

the intergovernmental externality problems. Whether one or the other instrument is selected would depend largely on the degree of precision required for a successful internalization effort, with the conditional grant, of course, being the more closely prescriptive. Such grants can isolate the quasi-national public good or bad in question, and adjust its supply upward or downward accordingly. Moreover, at times, an *earmarked tax* related to the allocation of the good or bad can be imposed, with its revenues flowing to a trust fund to help finance the internalization effort. Furthermore, *direct supply mandates* can be legally imposed on local governments by states in their coordination of interlocal externalities.

Secondary problems

Multiple taxation (tax overlapping). Various situations arise in a federation whereby the same tax base is taxed more than once. This *multiple* or *overlapping taxation* may be imposed (1) by different levels of government (vertical multiple taxation), (2) by different units of government at the same level (horizontal multiple taxation), or (3) by the same unit of government (intraunit multiple taxation).[10]

Examples of *vertical multiple taxation* by different levels of government include federal, state, and local government imposition of a personal income tax on a common income base, and the imposition of state and local property taxes on the same property base. *Horizontal multiple taxation* by different government units at the same level is exemplified by the imposition of property taxes by several units of local government such as counties, municipalities, and school districts. *Intraunit multiple taxation*, with the same tax base being taxed more than once by the same unit of government, also exists within the American public sector. The best example occurs in the dual imposition of federal income taxes—both corporation and personal—on corporate dividend income, with only a slight exclusion offset provided by law.[11] Another example of intraunit multiple taxation involves the dual imposition by some states of a selective excise tax and a general sales tax on motor fuel.

The fact that multiple taxation is not undesirable per se should be emphasized. Only intraunit multiple taxation appears to present an inherent problem of equity. However, some circumstances of horizontal multiple taxation, which lead to such issues as intergovernmental competition for industry and the income allocation basis of interstate

---

[10] Multiple taxation (tax overlapping) is often referred to as *double taxation*, though clearly the latter term is inferior because the same tax base may be taxed more than twice.

[11] However, as was observed in Chapter 9, the magnitude of such multiple taxation may be reduced through the process of tax shifting.

business income, are also questionable. Overall, multiple taxation
tends to become troublesome when it is practiced by one unit or level
of government without concern for its aggregate effects within the
public sector and between the public and private sectors. This includes the interacting effects of multiple taxation on the allocation,
distribution, and stabilization goals of economic activity.[12] The
cumulative tax burden created by multiple taxation, for example, may
distort the society's concept of equitable distribution. Appropriate
constitutional design, *ex ante*, can reduce the risk of such problems, as
can periodic, formalized, meetings between the two sovereign levels
of government in a federation.

Intergoal nonneutrality. The aggregate public sector of the
United States, consisting of *three levels* and nearly *80,000 units* of
government, will inevitably exert composite allocational, distributional, and stabilization effects on the economy. Moreover, the revenue-gathering and spending activities of these multitudinous governments may either complement or contradict each other in the pursuit
of any particular societal economic goal. This fact is well demonstrated by both the pattern of tax sources used by American governments and the pattern of economic effects which these tax sources
exert.

Table 18-1 is presented in order to focus attention on such *intergoal nonneutralities* of the *tax* variety within the American public
sector. In this table, each of the major tax sources employed by federal, state, and local governments is evaluated in terms of its ability to
serve four different economic objectives—allocational neutrality, distributional equity, aggregate stabilization performance, and long-run
revenue (income) elasticity. The tax sources considered at the federal
level of government are the personal income tax, corporation income
tax, and OASDHI payroll tax.[13] In addition, federal and state unemployment insurance payroll taxes are considered. The state-local tax
sources evaluated in the table are the general retail sales, (various)
selective sales, personal income, corporation income, and property
taxes.

The evaluations in Table 18-1 are based on various principles and
empirical studies, and especially those which deal with taxes and
their economic effects. Each tax is evaluated in relationship to its

---

[12] The problem of *intergoal nonneutrality* resulting from intergovernmental fiscal
behavior is treated here as a separate intergovernmental fiscal problem.

[13] The federal income taxes are evaluated on the basis of their statutory structures
prior to the Economic Recovery Tax Act of 1981. In general, this recent legislation is
likely to have: (1) increased the allocational nonneutrality of the corporation income
tax; (2) reduced the distributional equity, in ability-to-pay terms, of both income taxes;
(3) increased the stabilization performance of both income taxes, in a capital formation
sense; and (4) reduced the long-run income (revenue) elasticity of the two income taxes.

TABLE 18-1   Estimated intergoal effects of major American taxes*

Type of tax	Performance pertaining to economic goal			
	Allocational neutrality†	Distributional equity‡	Stabilization§	Long-run (revenue) elasticity‖
Federal personal income tax	Fair	Excellent	Excellent	Excellent
Federal corporation income tax	Fair	Good	Good	Good
Federal OASDHI payroll tax	Fair	Poor	Fair	Fair
Federal-state unemployment insurance payroll tax	Fair	Fair	Excellent	Fair
State-local general retail sales taxes	Good	Poor	Poor	Fair
State-local selective sales (excise) taxes#	Poor	Poor	Poor	Poor
State-local personal income taxes	Fair	Good	Fair	Good
State-local corporation income taxes	Fair	Fair	Fair	Fair
State-local property taxes**	Fair	Poor	Poor	Fair

Note: Estimates for federal taxes are based on law existing prior to the Economic Recovery Tax Act of 1981.

* Taxes are appraised on the basis of their actual base and rate structures as used in the American public sector, including consideration of the level of government at which each tax is imposed.

† It is assumed that the pretax allocational equilibrium approaches optimality. Hence, all nonneutral allocational effects are assumed to be negative in character.

‡ Distributional equity is appraised in accordance with the ability-to-pay principle, with income as the indicator of taxpaying ability.

§ This involves an overall appraisal of the effectiveness of each tax as an aggregate economic stabilizer in both automatic and discretionary fiscal policy terms.

‖ Each tax is evaluated here on the basis of its estimated long-run income elasticity (Y_t).

Includes excise taxes on motor fuel.

** Follows the traditional viewpoint that the property tax is shifted forward to renters and consumers.

actual rate and base characteristics as present in the American public sector and *not* as it might appear in some pure, conceptual form. In addition, the level of government imposing a tax will, in itself, tend to have a bearing on the results of a tax. Thus, a national government might be able to achieve significant stabilization policy results from a general sales tax, while a subnational government would achieve inferior results. The performance of each tax in relationship to a particular goal is rated as *excellent, good, fair,* or *poor.* Admittedly, these are broad categories, and it should not be concluded, for example, that an excellent rating precludes any defects in the tax nor that a poor rating precludes any merits.

The table demonstrates that some tax instruments achieve multiple goals with less intergoal conflict than do others. In particular, the balanced performance of the federal personal and corporation income taxes in relation to the four economic goals considered in Table 18–1 stands out as a primary feature of the table. Also, the table clearly suggests that the various goals are influenced, either positively or negatively, by the different taxes imposed by the different levels and units of government. Thus, an aggregate public sector consisting of three levels and some 80,000 units of government will yield, in its intergovernmental interaction, a composite of intergoal economic effects from its varied tax structure. Although the present discussion has focused on *taxation,* it is obvious that similar intergovernmental economic effects will follow from the nontax fiscal decisions of the federal, state, and local governments which comprise the American public sector.

Urban economic problems. There has been no more significant trend in American history than the movement whereby the nation has been transformed from a basically rural to a basically urban society. The growth of urban areas in the United States, for the most part, has been a function of industrialization. The growth of cities, moreover, has been supported by the population decline in rural areas made possible by the income-inelastic demand for most farm products and the fact that improving technology allows much greater farm output per unit of labor input. The social, political, and economic complexities of *urbanization* are substantial. Indeed, the economic benefits which derive from industrialization, and from the urbanization which it sponsors, are to some extent neutralized by problems which also result from these phenomena. These problems, many of which are of an intergovernmental fiscal nature, are not insoluble. Nevertheless, the failure to meet some of them adequately in recent decades has been alarming.

The concentration of people in cities is not the sole dimension of the complex social, political, and economic problems of an urban-industrial society. Equally important is the shift of population and industry away from the heart of the city into the suburbs, a phenomenon which may be called *suburbanization.* New and complex problems arise with this dimension of urban living. Though three fourths of the American population presently resides in metropolitan areas, less than one half of this population lives in the central city, the remainder living in the surrounding area. Thus, a central city must provide governmental services for a population greater than that which resides within its political boundaries, while at the same time suburban political jurisdictions are faced with the pressing needs of a growing area, including such requirements as new schools, water systems, sewage disposal systems, streets, fire protection, and police protection. Each new house in the suburbs requires, on the average, several thousand dollars of incremental governmental services. The movement of people and industry from the central city to the suburbs tends to decrease the property and income tax bases of the central city, while the suburban governments often are inadequate for the performance of the complex functions required of them. The tax burdens on those remaining in the central city, moreover, will tend to increase as the tax base declines, thus stimulating an additional exodus to the suburbs. Since many people who live in the suburbs work in the central city, an extreme demand for transportation facilities, particularly roads for highway transportation, often faces the central city.

Substantial intergovernmental externalities—both benefits and costs—exist among the multitude of political jurisdictions comprising urban areas in the United States. Yet, the decentralization of decision making causes a noncorrespondence between the revenue sources and the expenditure decisions of these various political jurisdictions. This noncorrespondence exists despite the fact that the problems to be solved and the governmental economic goods to be provided are common to the entire urban area because of the externalities. There is an inability to pool financial resources and to coordinate decision making to meet the problems which face the entire urban complex.

A comprehensive consideration of urban economic problems, and of policies for their solution, is beyond the scope of the present book. Yet, many of the principles and concepts developed herein can be applied to particular aspects of the overall urban problem area. Moreover, policies to alleviate such primary intergovernmental fiscal problems as vertical fiscal imbalance, horizontal fiscal imbalance, and intergovernmental externalities are also relevant to the urban discussion. Furthermore, even though the *federal* government in recent decades has been playing an increasing role in dealing with urban economic problems, it is frequently recommended that the *state* level of government play a more decisive role in alleviating urban fiscal problems. In this regard, Roy Bahl[14] comments that state government seems to be in a good position to provide fiscal coordination and balance among local governments within SMSAs[15] because:

1. It has a broader tax base than any local government.
2. A state government can institute an aid policy capable of reducing resource-requirement gaps, while simultaneously equalizing tax burdens.
3. The state can control the proliferation of local governments within an SMSA, and thereby reduce horizontal fiscal imbalance among local governments.
4. The state can (and already does in many states) administer a planning agency which controls intergovernmental variations in public service levels.
5. Federal aids can be passed through the state level to local governments to assure conformity with a comprehensive plan to maintain fiscal balance among the various units of local government.

---

[14] Roy W. Bahl, "Public Policy and the Urban Fiscal Problem: Piecemeal vs. Aggregate Solutions," *Land Economics*, February 1970, p. 50.

[15] SMSA refers to *Standard Metropolitan Statistical Area*, a commonly used federal government measure of urban areas.

Finally, it should be observed that any program directed toward the solution of *urban transportation problems* should utilize areawide planning rather than decentralized decision making among a multitude of political jurisdictions. Urban transportation problems can be solved in the long run only if economic rationality is applied to the issues. Social and private costs must be considered for each alternative mode of urban transportation, and the existence of externalities between modes is also a highly relevant consideration. Furthermore, if a given mode of transportation cannot meet all costs (both social and private) on a pricing basis, the degree of governmental subsidization should be approximately equal among the various transportation modes. Otherwise, investment and consumption distortions will result. The degree of automobile subsidization, thus, should likely be reduced and that for public transportation facilities increased. Since the entire society, not the urban area alone, receives significant benefits from efficient transportation, the federal government can legitimately bear part of the responsibility for improved urban transportation.

THE INTERGOVERNMENTAL FISCAL PERFORMANCE OF THE AMERICAN FEDERATION

The chapter to this point has considered the important intergovernmental fiscal problems that tend to develop in a federation and, in addition, has applied the various intergovernmental fiscal instruments toward the solution of these problems. It has been apparent that an *eclectic* policy approach, using a set of appropriately selected instruments, is desirable in dealing with this multiple set of problems. Using the first part of this chapter as a normative reference, the discussion will now turn to an overall evaluation of the performance of the American federation in relationship to such problems.

The problem of vertical fiscal imbalance

The American federation performs reasonably well in relationship to the vertical fiscal imbalance problem. One of the primary factors contributing to this result is the fact that the *Constitution* does not preclude access by the sovereign states, and their local government legal creations, to any major source of tax revenue. Moreover, the federal government has not used its powerful political position to make it difficult for subnational governments to develop their own tax sources. In fact, it has done just the opposite through the *income tax deduction* instrument whereby most state and local taxes may be deducted from the tax base of the federal personal and corporation income taxes. While the income tax credit instrument would have been an even more powerful incentive device for the development of subnational government tax systems, the deduction approach has nonetheless been highly effective.[16] Strong evidence of the successful performance of the American federation in regard to the pursuit of vertical fiscal balance is the fact that each level of American government has dominant (though not exclusive) use of each of the three major tax bases. Thus, the federal government collects the majority of income tax revenues, states collect the majority of sales tax revenues, and local governments collect most wealth tax revenues in the form of the property tax.

To a limited extent, the American federation uses what is ranked above as the third best instrument for dealing with the problem of vertical fiscal imbalance, namely, *unconditional grants.* Except for one ad hoc application in the last century,[17] the federal government did not adopt this instrument until 1972 under the State and Local Fiscal Assistance Act of that year. Two formulas for distributing the *unconditional (general) revenue-sharing funds* to the recipient governments are used under the legislation.[18] Thus, a state may choose either the Senate or the House formula to determine its share of the overall revenue-sharing appropriation, as constrained by the overall *appropriation limit* for the period in question. The *Senate formula* weighs *population* by both the *inverse of per capita income* and by *tax effort,* the latter consisting of total state and local government taxes divided by state personal income. The *House formula* adds to these factors an *urbanized population* factor, plus a factor based on *state personal income tax collections.* A two thirds required pass-through of state revenue-sharing funds to local governments is apportioned among the local governments on the basis of population, per capita income, and tax effort, but in a manner favoring the lower-income urban areas of a state.[19]

The five factors which comprise the two formulas used for the disbursement of general revenue-sharing funds serve, in a differential manner, the various goals of the multipurpose revenue-sharing program. Vertical fiscal adjustment (reducing vertical fiscal imbalance), for example, is influenced via the population factor which is common

---

[16] An *implicit tax credit* factor is present in one of the two general (unconditional) revenue sharing formulas used under the State and Local Fiscal Assistance Act of 1972. Under this factor, a state government receives greater revenues, the more intensively it uses the personal income tax as a revenue source.

[17] A federal fiscal surplus was distributed to the states, with no strings attached, during one fiscal year of the presidential administration of Andrew Jackson (1829–37).

[18] For a more detailed description and evaluation of the 1972 legislation, see Bernard P. Herber, *Fiscal Federalism in the USA* (Canberra: Australian National University, 1975), pp. 59–77.

[19] During recent years, the state government segment (one third) of the funds has not been appropriated by Congress.

to both formulas. Moreover, the population factor also provides a favorable horizontal fiscal adjustment (reducing horizontal fiscal imbalance) for large, metropolitan inner cities through the heavy weight it receives, along with the tax effort factor, in the three-factor formula. The urbanized population factor in the five-factor formula, in contrast, tends to favor the suburban areas. The tax effort factor in each formula encourages vertical fiscal adjustment by providing an incentive for state and local governments to utilize their own tax sources more intensively. Moreover, the personal income tax collections factor in the five-factor formula is intended to encourage state governments either to adopt, or to utilize more intensively if they already have adopted, the most revenue-productive, income-elastic tax available—the personal income tax.[20] The per capita income factor bears the major role for providing horizontal fiscal adjustment in recognition of the differential fiscal capacities of the various state and local governments.

Thus, the State and Local Fiscal Assistance Act of 1972 constitutes a multifaceted approach to several different intergovernmental fiscal problems. Moreover, the fact that all 50 states and 38,000 general-purpose local governments—not only those governments with relatively poor fiscal capacities—receive shared revenues under the program demonstrates that it is not solely a horizontal equalization program—though the general revenue-sharing instrument clearly best serves the equalization goal. Yet, the dollar magnitude of the vertical fiscal adjustment in the new legislation should not be overestimated. For example, it may be seen from Table 18–2 that unconditional grants constituted only 8 percent of all federal grants to state and local governments during fiscal year 1980.

The lowest-ranking fiscal instruments for alleviating vertical fiscal imbalance—*conditional* and *block grants*—are extensively used between the federal and state-local governments (see Table 18–2), and between state and local governments in the American federation. However, since these grants, especially those of the conditional variety, restrict use of funds by the recipient governments, they are not considered to be optimal instruments of vertical fiscal adjustment. However, they do increase the amount of revenues available to the recipient governments and, in this way, do something to alleviate the symptoms of vertical fiscal imbalance.

In sum, the American federation meets the vertical fiscal imbalance challenge in a satisfactory fashion. Much of this success results from two factors, as discussed, namely, (1) the *ex ante* prevention of serious vertical imbalance stemming from the manner in which fiscal powers

---

[20] However, the incentive is proving to be a rather weak stimulus for the more intensive usage of state personal income taxes.

Table 18-2   **Federal aid to state and local governments by type of grant and function (fiscal year 1980)**

Type of grant and function	Millions of dollars	Percentage of total grants
Total grants	$89,708	100%
Conditional and block grants		
Federal Funds Accounts	72,904	81
Veterans benefits and services	90	<1
Health	15,758	17
Education, employment training, and social services	21,152	24
Agriculture	569	1
Natural resources and environment	5,362	6
Commerce and housing credit	3	<1
Transportation	3,822	4
Community and regional development	6,486	7
Income security	18,495	21
General government	160	<1
Administration of justice	530	1
National defense	93	<1
Energy	384	<1
Trust Funds	9,975	11
Airport and airways	590	<1
Highway	8,675	10
Unemployment	710	1
Unconditional grants	6,829	8

Source: Office of Management and Budget.

are apportioned among the sovereign federal and state governments by the *Constitution* and (2) the positive attitude of the federal government in encouraging subnational governments to develop their own tax sources—especially as implemented by the income tax deduction instrument. Finally, secondary vertical fiscal adjustment contributions have been made by the modest federal unconditional (general) revenue sharing program that was instituted in 1972 and by the extensive use of conditional and block grants.

The problem of horizontal fiscal imbalance

How well the American federation meets the problem of horizontal fiscal imbalance is dependent on a preliminary assumption. If one assumes that extensive interstate (and interlocal) equalization should be undertaken as a basic political responsibility in a federation, then the performance record is not good. This is especially true if a comparison is made between the United States and other federations, such as Australia and Canada, which have formal and extensive interstate (interprovincial) equalization programs. On the other hand, if one assumes that extensive equalization is not a political mandate for a federation, but instead is dependent on a societal value judgment as to the degree of equalization (if any) that is desirable, the performance of the American federation looks much better. In other words, it may be concluded that the political consensus is in favor of only a modest degree of horizontal intergovernmental equalization. This appears to be a logical point of argument. Relatedly, the nation's traditional emphasis on states' rights would historically validate such a decision.

What, in fact, has been done to pursue the horizontal equalization goal in the American public sector? For one thing, the optimal equalization instrument—*unconditional grants*—has been used only sparingly, as noted in the previous section. Moreover, when used, as has continuously been the case since 1972, the unconditional grant (general revenue-sharing) program is a multipurpose program, only partly dedicated toward the pursuit of horizontal fiscal equalization. Yet, some horizontal equalization does occur, as Table 18–3 demonstrates. However, the next best instruments—*variable-matching conditional* and *block grants*—have been used rather extensively, especially the variable conditional grant variant. Furthermore, the progressive *federal personal income tax*, and to a lesser extent—the *federal corporation income tax*, yield automatic interstate redistributional results. Finally, the federal government has historically undertaken a number of long-run programs which seek to promote *economic development and redevelopment* of relatively poor urban governments and regional

---

TABLE 18–3   Relationship between state general revenue-sharing (unconditional grant) entitlements per $1,000 of personal income and state per capita personal income*

	General revenue-sharing entitlement (allocation) per $1,000 personal income		
States ranked by per capita personal income	Median	Average, unweighted for population†	Population-weighted average
Highest-income state (Connecticut)		$ 4.15	
Ten states with highest income	$4.97	5.48	$5.49
Second 10 states	5.27	5.29	5.29
Third 10 states	5.73	5.58	5.58
Fourth 10 states	7.24	6.33	6.35
Ten states with lowest income	8.41	8.46	8.50
Lowest-income state (Mississippi)		12.70	

* For Entitlement Period 4, July 1, 1973, to June 30, 1974.

† These averages represent the summation of the individual state per capita figures in each group and then a division of this amount by the number of states (10) in each group. In other words, it is an average unweighted for the population of each state respective to the population of the entire group.

Source: Advisory Commission on Intergovernment Relations, *General Revenue Sharing: An ACIR Re-Evaluation* (Washington, D.C.: U.S. Government Printing Office, October 1974), p. 5.

areas. In sum, the performance of the American federation in relationship to the problem of horizontal fiscal imbalance is satisfactory, if one accepts the assumption of a societal value judgment in favor of only modest redistributional results.

The problem of intergovernmental externalities

The American federation has performed well in its efforts to internalize important intergovernmental externalities. One example of this is provided by the present *interstate highway system*. This combined federal-state program finds the federal government applying the appropriate coordination while the state governments, subject to minimal federal standards, serve as the main supplying agents of highway services. The coordinative effort involves a federal excise tax on motor fuel, which is earmarked for the Highway Trust Fund, from which conditional grants flow to the states to finance the interstate highway system.

Public school education in the American federation provides further evidence of satisfactory performance in relationship to the intergovernmental externality issue. Regarding the quasi-public good, the primary supplying agents are at the local government level while the necessary coordination of the externalities is provided by the state level of government. This is accomplished through a variety of instruments including conditional grants, earmarked revenues, and the imposition of various rules and regulations by the sovereign states on the non-sovereign local governments, such as school districts, which they have created.

Meanwhile, the federal government has undertaken a strong effort during recent decades to internalize negative externalities appearing in the forms of air, water, and noise *pollution*. The Environmental Protection Agency of the federal government has primarily directed this effort, but state and local governments also participate in the control activities. In sum, the performance of the American federation in its efforts to adjust for intergovernmental externalities has been a satisfactory one.

Secondary problems

One of the secondary problem areas, *multiple taxation*, has been generally met in an unsatisfactory fashion by American governments. For example, intraunit multiple taxation exists in the form of the statutory double taxation (except for a small exclusion) of dividend income under the federal personal income tax. Moreover, with a proliferation of subnational governments (some 80,000), the potential for negative effects from vertical and horizontal multiple taxation is increased. Furthermore, unlike federations such as Australia and Canada, the American federation does not possess a formal arrangement whereby the sovereign federal government and the sovereign states periodically meet to work out solutions to existing intergovernmental fiscal problems, including that of multiple taxation. Also, allocation of the corporation income tax bases of interstate corporations among the various states is handled in a fashion that leaves much to be desired. Whatever effective procedures that do exist to meet this problem are primarily the result of the Multistate Tax Commission, established in 1967 on a voluntary basis, but which only part of the states recognize.[21]

In relationship to problems of *intergoal nonneutrality,* the American federation performs in a mixed fashion. One positive factor is the performance of the federal personal income tax, as exhibited in Table 18–1. However, the complex *urban economic problem* area leaves much room for public sector improvement. In addition, scale economies in *tax administration* are largely not taken advantage of, as is exemplified by the fact that the federal government does not collect state income taxes.

To conclude, it may be observed that the American federation employs an *eclectic* combination of intergovernmental fiscal instruments in its pursuit of an effective federalism. These include income tax deductions, unconditional grants, conditional-block grants, and trust fund earmarking of revenues, among other fiscal instruments. While the overall intergovernmental fiscal performance is not optimal, it is nonetheless satisfactory. Yet, room clearly remains for improvement and better policies, where required, should be adopted. Relatedly, important intergovernmental fiscal trends have recently arisen in the American federation and, moreover, significant additional changes are being proposed by the presidential administration of Ronald Reagan. These will be discussed in the final section of the chapter to follow.

RECENT INTERGOVERNMENTAL FISCAL TRENDS[22] AND THE PROPOSED NEW FEDERALISM

The most significant new *trend* in the American federation is the reversal of the long-term growth of the state and local government segment of the public sector. Between the years 1942–1976, state-local expenditures, including those financed by federal grants, increased nearly three times as fast as the aggregate economy, that is,

---

[21] For an evaluation of the interstate tax issue and its solution, see C. R. Cahoon and William R. Brown, "The Interstate Tax Dilemma—A Proposed Solution," *National Tax Journal,* June 1973, pp. 187–97.

[22] For detailed evidence of these trends, see *Significant Features of Fiscal Federalism: 1980–81 Edition* (Washington, D.C.: Advisory Commission on Intergovernmental Relations, December 1981).

from 7.5 percent of personal income in 1942 to 20.3 percent in 1976. Further evidence of this growth is demonstrated by the fact that per capita state-local government spending, in constant dollar terms, increased by 2.9 times during a comparable period, 1939–1976. However, the long-run growth trend began to reverse itself after 1976, with state-local expenditures failing to keep pace with either the growth of the aggregate economy or the rate of inflation after that year.

The reversal of the long-run state-local growth trend is interrelated to a fundamental change in attitude toward the appropriate level of subnational government economic activity. In other words, there was a fundamental grass roots change in public attitude even prior to the highly publicized Proposition 13, which reduced California taxes in 1978 and which started a wave of state-local budget constraints across the nation.[23] In fact, after adjustment for inflation, the growth in local government spending actually ended in 1974, and that of the state government sector followed suit in 1976. An important aspect of the subnational government spending reversal is the behavior of many state legislatures, which began to oppose further tax increases and often introduced tax reductions.

Meanwhile, the restrictive effects of these state legislative changes were about to be reinforced by a reversal in the long-run growth of federal financial assistance to state and local governments. This latter reversal began in 1978. Table 18–4 demonstrates the long-run growth of federal grants to state and local governments prior to fiscal year 1978, as well as the trend reversal which began in that year. Federal grants, which in 1955 had amounted to 11.8 percent of state-local government revenues from their own sources, increased to 31.7 percent in 1978, but are projected to fall sharply to 20.8 percent by 1983. Moreover, the recent decline of the state-local public sector may be sustained by a number of factors. These include: (1) the fact that many states placed constitutional and legislative restrictions on revenue-raising and spending activities during recent years; (2) public education is no longer a growth industry due to demographic changes; and (3) the prospect of huge future federal government deficits will further limit the ability of the federal government to provide financial assistance to state-local governments.

These fiscal trends, which began prior to the administration of President Ronald Reagan, carry important implications for the philosophy of fiscal federalism which his administration espouses. This philosophy reflects an overall attitude of limited government, at all levels, along with the transfer of a significant segment of decision making from the federal to state-local governments—which seems to run counter to the declining state-local public sector. In 1981, the first year of the Reagan presidency, initial efforts were made in this regard

---

[23] See the discussion of Proposition 13 in Chapters 4 and 11.

TABLE 18-4   Federal grants-in-aid in relation to state-local receipts from own sources, total federal outlays, and gross national product, 1955–1983 (dollar amounts in billions)

Fiscal year*	Federal grants-in-aid (current dollars)		as a percentage of			Federal grants in constant dollars (1972 dollars)	
	Amount	Percent increase or decrease (−)	State-local receipts from own sources†	Total federal outlays	Gross national product	Amount	Percent increase or decrease (−)
1955	$3.2	4.9	11.8	4.7	0.8	$5.8	5.5
1956	3.7	15.6	12.3	5.3	0.9	6.6	13.8
1957	4.0	8.1	12.1	5.3	0.9	6.9	4.5
1958	4.9	22.5	14.0	6.0	1.1	8.2	18.8
1959	6.5	32.7	17.2	7.0	1.4	10.6	29.3
1960	7.0	7.7	16.8	7.6	1.4	11.5	8.5
1961	7.1	1.4	15.8	7.3	1.4	11.3	−1.7
1962	7.9	11.3	16.2	7.4	1.4	12.1	7.1
1963	8.6	8.9	16.5	7.8	1.5	12.4	2.5
1964	10.1	17.4	17.9	8.6	1.6	14.4	16.1

Year							
1965	10.9	7.9	17.7	9.2	1.7	15.7	9.0
1966	13.0	19.3	19.3	9.6	1.8	18.1	15.3
1967	15.2	16.9	20.6	9.6	2.0	20.3	12.2
1968	18.6	22.4	22.4	10.4	2.2	23.5	15.8
1969	20.3	9.1	21.6	11.0	2.2	24.2	3.0
1970	24.0	18.2	22.9	12.3	2.5	26.9	11.2
1971	28.1	17.1	24.1	13.3	2.7	29.6	10.0
1972	34.4	22.4	26.1	14.8	3.1	34.4	16.2
1973	41.8	21.5	28.5	16.9	3.3	39.7	15.4
1974	43.4	3.8	27.3	16.1	3.1	38.1	−4.0
1975	49.8	14.7	29.1	15.4	3.4	39.7	4.2
1976	59.1	18.7	31.1	16.2	3.6	43.9	10.6
1977	68.4	15.7	31.0	17.1	3.7	47.2	7.5
1978	77.9	13.9	31.7	17.4	3.7	50.3	6.6
1979	82.9	6.4	31.5	16.9	3.5	49.4	−1.8
1980	91.5	10.4	31.7	15.9	3.6	50.0	1.2
1981	94.8	3.6	29.4	14.4	3.3	47.8	−4.4
1982 Est.	91.2	−3.8	25.7	12.6	3.0	42.6	−10.9
1983 Est.	81.4	−10.7	20.8	10.7	2.4	35.5	−16.7

* For 1955–1976, years ending June 30; 1977–83 years ending September 30.
† As defined in the national income accounts.
Source: Advisory Commission on Intergovernmental Relations.

including a related attempt to consolidate a number of existing conditional grant programs into block grants. However, the primary components of President Reagan's proposed *New Federalism* were not announced until early 1982. These proposals fall into two segments, both of which would become effective during fiscal year 1984.

1. A *major reallocation of responsibility for income-transfer (welfare) programs* would take place. Under this proposal, the federal government would assume full responsibility for *Medicaid.* It now partially finances the program. Meanwhile, state governments would assume full responsibility for the *Aid to Families with Dependent Children (AFDC)* and *Food Stamp* programs. AFDC is currently a federal-state program, with substantial federal financing, and the Food Stamp program is exclusively federal.

2. There would be a *transfer of 43 existing conditional-block grant programs*, estimated to total $30.2 billion in expenditures during fiscal year 1984, from the federal government to the states. These include sewage treatment, water systems, transportation, urban development, school lunch and child nutrition, energy assistance for the poor, and vocational rehabilitation programs. In order to help the states finance these programs, a temporary trust fund of earmarked tax revenues would be established. This trust fund, financed mainly from excise tax revenues, including the windfall profits tax, would be phased out by fiscal year 1991. From 1984 on, the states would have the discretion to conduct these programs as they wish, or even repeal them.

The new-federalism proposals were made during the deepest recession since World War II and, as a result, were initially given secondary political consideration. In fact, only a month after their announcement, the Reagan administration made it known that the introduction of legislation for the transfer of the three major welfare programs would be deferred. However, it indicated that legislation for the transfer of the 43 conditional-block grant programs would be introduced in the then-current session of Congress.

If the new-federalism proposals are evaluated in light of the theory of fiscal federalism, as developed in the previous chapter, certain problem areas would seem to arise. For example, if one accepts the economic rationale that the central government best performs the redistribution function, then segment (1) of the proposals comes into question since it would remove the federal government from two of the three major welfare programs. Moreover, a number of the conditional-block grant programs, to be transferred to the states under segment (2), are also redistributional programs. However, a number of other conditional-block grant programs are of an allocational nature, and it is possible that some, or all, of these might be performed better by subnational governments.

PART IV

Fiscal policy and economic stabilization

19

Aggregate fiscal
policy goals

DEVIATIONS FROM OPTIMAL AGGREGATE
ECONOMIC PERFORMANCE

Recession and inflation

Part IV of the book is concerned with the economic *stabilization* function. Prior to the 1930s, economic theory, based on Say's Law,[1] held that forces inherent to a market economy would automatically direct it toward a full-employment equilibrium. The British economist, John Maynard Keynes, proved otherwise, as modern macroeconomic theory was developed during the 1930s.[2] Keynesian analysis indicated that market economies do *not* automatically attain an optimal full-employment, noninflationary, aggregate economic equilibrium. Although such an optimal aggregate performance is possible, Keynes demonstrated that either of two "suboptimal equilibria," with *deflationary gap* or *inflationary gap* conditions, is more likely to occur.

Figure 19–1 demonstrates both optimal and suboptimal performance in a pure market economy, as depicted in the Keynesian model.

---

[1] *Say's Law* was formulated by the French economist, Jean Baptiste Say (1767–1832).

[2] Keynes' pioneering work in this regard is *The General Theory of Employment, Interest, and Money* (London: MacMillan, 1936).

FIGURE 19-1   Deflationary and inflationary gap conditions in a pure market economy

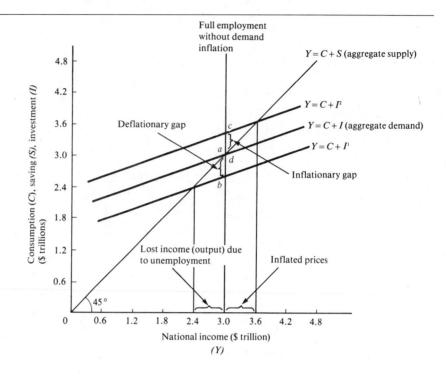

Private consumption (C), saving (S), and (autonomous) investment (I) are measured on the vertical axis; and national income (Y), used as the indicator of aggregate economic performance (income, output), is measured on the horizontal axis. Optimal results are attained in the graph at a $3 trillion level of national income, since at this point labor and capital resources are fully employed and demand (monetary) inflation does not exist.

In order to apply this theory, *full employment* must be defined in some acceptable manner. Traditionally in the United States, full employment usually has been said to exist if 4 percent or less of the civilian labor force is involuntarily unemployed, and manufacturing plant capacity is utilized at a rate of approximately 90 percent. However, the entry of many women into the labor force during recent years, and the resultant emergence of many two-worker families, suggests that a higher (say 5 percent) full-employment figure is more realistic. Thus, we will define full employment of labor as existing at the 5 percent unemployment point. Furthermore, a distinction must be made between *demand (monetary) inflation* and *structural*[3] *inflation.* Although demand inflation does not exist at the $3 trillion equilibrium level of aggregate economic performance in Figure 19–1, due to the absence of "excessive" aggregate demand, structural inflation, as caused by supply imperfections in product and resource markets, could exist. Thus, if optimal performance is defined to include complete price stability, then even this level of performance is not optimal if structural inflation is present.

In any case, where the intersection of aggregate supply $(C + S)$ and aggregate demand $(C + I)$ sets an aggregate performance level of $3 trillion in Figure 19–1, the society suffers neither from lost output due to unemployment nor from demand inflation resulting from excessive aggregate demand. This condition would be only accidentally attained under the operational process of a pure market economy, however, so *suboptimal* conditions are likely to occur instead. Aggregate demand thus may be deficient to aggregate supply at the full-employment income level of $3 trillion $(C + I^1 < C + S)$, creating a *deflationary gap,* or it may exceed aggregate supply at the full-employment income level $(C + I^2 > C + S)$, thus creating an *inflationary gap* situation characterized by excessive aggregate demand.

Any of these three conditions may exist; the pure market economy will not automatically tend toward any one of them. The *deflationary gap, ab,* would cause reduced income, or output, by the amount of $.6 trillion ($600 billion)—which is the difference between the full-employment income of $3 trillion and the under-full-employment income of $2.4 trillion. This would be a case of *deficient* aggregate demand. The *inflationary gap, cd,* would lead to inflated income by the amount of $.6 trillion ($600 billion)—consisting of the difference between the full-employment, but inflationary, income of $3.6 trillion and the noninflationary full-employment income of $3 trillion. This would be a case of *excessive* aggregate demand.

The ratios between *ab* and the lost income and output, and between *cd* and the inflated prices, reflect the value of the *multiplier.* Thus, for example, if the deflationary gap *ab* is equal to $360 billion, and the reduced income (output) is $600 billion, the *multiplier value* is 1.66 ⅔ ($360 billion × 1.66 ⅔ = $600 billion). Specifically, the multiplier is the relationship between the change in investment (I^2 or I^1 compared to I at the optimal equilibrium) and the resulting change in income.

The value of the multiplier is itself determined by the marginal

---

[3] *Structural* inflation will be described in greater detail in the next section of the chapter.

propensities to consume *(MPC)* and to save *(MPS)*.[4] *MPC* refers to a change in consumption *(ΔC)* in relationship to a change in income *(ΔY)*, or *ΔC/ΔY*. *MPS* refers to a change in saving *(ΔS)* in relationship to a change in income, or *ΔS/ΔY*. Since *Y* is said to be equal to *C + S* in the Keynesian model, *ΔC + ΔS = ΔY*.

The dilemma of stagflation

As noted, aggregate demand *(C + I)* and aggregate supply *(C + S)* may be in equilibrium at a full-employment, no-demand inflation point, such as \$3 trillion of national income in Figure 19-1, but inflation of a structural variety may still exist. This phenomenon is demonstrated in Figure 19-2, in which the so-called *Phillips curve*[5] depicts the difficulty of a market economy, given substantial market structure imperfections and related impediments, to simultaneously attain the objectives of both full employment and price stability. Thus, in effect, *full employment* and *price stability* become conflicting aggregate economic goals, even though the achievement of one goal is

---

[4] The derivation of the investment multiplier, as depicted in Figure 19-1, may be stated as follows:

$$\Delta I + \Delta C = \Delta y \text{ (true by definition)}$$

Dividing through by *Y:*

$$\frac{\Delta I}{\Delta Y} + \frac{\Delta C}{\Delta Y} = 1$$

$$\frac{\Delta I}{\Delta Y} = 1 - \frac{\Delta C}{\Delta Y}$$

$$\frac{\Delta Y}{\Delta I} = \frac{1}{1 - \dfrac{\Delta C}{\Delta Y}}$$

but

$$\frac{\Delta Y}{\Delta I} = K \text{ (multiplier)}$$

and

$$\frac{\Delta C}{\Delta Y} = MPC \text{ (marginal propensity to consume)}$$

Therefore,

$$\text{Multiplier } (K) = \frac{1}{1 - MPC}$$

or, since

$$MPC + MPS \text{ (marginal propensity to save)} = \Delta Y \text{ or } 1,$$

$$\text{multiplier } (K) = \frac{1}{MPS}.$$

[5] See A. W. Phillips, "The Relation between Unemployment and the Rate of Change of Money Wage Rates in the United Kingdom, 1862–1957," *Economica,* November 1958, pp. 283–99.

FIGURE 19–2   Trade-off between inflation and labor unemployment (short run)
as depicted by Phillips curve

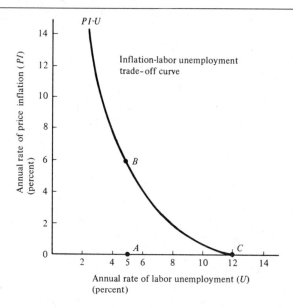

Annual rate of price inflation (*PI*) (percent)

Inflation-labor unemployment
trade-off curve

Annual rate of labor unemployment (*U*)
(percent)

not the direct cause of the failure to achieve the other. Instead, tertiary factors such as market structure imperfections cause the trade-off to occur.

In Figure 19–2, the annual percentage rate of *price inflation* (*PI*) is measured along the vertical axis, and the annual percentage rate of *labor unemployment* (*U*) is measured along the horizontal axis. The *short-run* trade-off between price stability and labor unemployment along curve *PI-U* is apparent. However, some economists take the position that a trade-off between labor unemployment and inflation does not exist in the *long run*. For example, Milton Friedman argues that the economy tends toward a long-run natural rate of labor unemployment, and any attempt to obtain a lower rate will result in an accelerating rate of inflation.[6] In other words, aggregate demand policies can affect only prices and not the rate of unemployment in the long run, thus eliminating the trade-off between the two objectives. Still other economists suggest that a labor unemployment-inflation trade-off does exist in the long run at high labor unemployment levels, but vanishes at some critical level approaching the full-employment

[6] See Milton Friedman, "The Role of Monetary Policy," *American Economic Review*, March 1968, pp. 1–17.

[7] See James Tobin, "Inflation and Unemployment," *American Economic Review*, March 1972, pp. 1–18.

point.[7] In any event, there appears to be at least a short-run trade-off between the two macroeconomic objectives, so the discussion to follow will focus on this time frame.

Ideally, the society would prefer to be operating at point A in Figure 19-2, where full employment exists at the 5 percent labor unemployment rate and there is no inflation. This would be consistent with the $3 trillion income (output) level in Figure 19-1, in which there would be full employment and no demand inflation. Moreover, at point A there would also be no inflation of the structural variety. However, several factors, especially imperfectly competitive product and factor markets (as exemplified by oligopolistic manufacturing industries, monopolistic labor unions, and effectively monopolistic professional associations), tend to prevent the attainment of an aggregate performance level at point A. Instead, the graph would indicate an inflation rate of 6 percent if full employment is achieved at the 5 percent unemployment rate (point B), or a 12 percent rate of labor unemployment if price stability is attained (point C).[8] Most likely, some intermediate point between B and C would be attained, and *stagflation*—the coexistence of both recession and inflation—would become a reality. Increases in aggregate demand do tend to move prices upward, but structural forces may cause inflation to set in prematurely before full employment is reached. Unfortunately, orthodox *fiscal* and *monetary* policies are unable to attack directly the basic causes of structural inflation. That is, even though they can help move the economy along curve *PI–U*, such policies cannot directly shift the curve toward point A. This important fact will be discussed further in the following chapter.

It should be recognized that *inflation* is a complex, eclectic phenomenon which can result from a number of causal variables, any one or combination of which may be operational at a given time. Undoubtedly, the expansionary *aggregate demand effects* of federal deficit budgets, and the occasional monetization financing of these deficits, as well as various *structural forces*, have been important contributing factors to the prolonged inflation experienced in the U.S. economy since the mid-1960s. Yet, the sustained nature of this inflation has also created *inflationary expectations* among businesses, workers, and consumers, which has tended to reinforce the upward movement in prices. Relatedly, the failure of governmental policies to restrain inflation significantly has stimulated an expectation of future inflation by private interests who, therefore, take actions of both a demand and

---

[8] The precise trade-off percentages depicted by the Phillips curve in Figure 19-2 are assumed. However, the substance of the analysis is that some inflation will exist under conditions of "full employment," and the elimination of inflation will be accompanied by "under full employment," given the presence of structural inflation forces in the economy.

supply nature which further increase prices. One form which these actions take is the *indexing* of wages to the rate of inflation even though labor productivity may be lagging behind at a lower rate of increase or, similarly, the *indexing* of retirement benefits, pensions, and other benefits not directly related to the production of current output in the economy. In addition, occasional short-run resource shortages develop in some industries when aggregate demand expands rapidly, leading to a so-called *bottleneck inflation* reflecting the inflated prices of these resources. Also, the rapidly increasing scarcity of important basic resources such as oil can be an important *exogenous* inflationary factor. Furthermore, *taxes*, through the process of forward tax shifting, can add to the inflationary pressures of an economy.

Finally, it may be pointed out that inflation tends to be a *redistributional process*. That is, unless the nominal incomes of all economic sectors (for example—agriculture, manufacturing, mining), and of all occupations (for example—teachers, farm workers, business executives), increase at a rate equal to the rate of inflation, there will be both "winners and losers" in the inflationary game. Those sectors and occupations whose nominal incomes increase more rapidly than the rate of inflation will see their real income (purchasing power) increase, while those experiencing a less-rapid (or no) growth in nominal income will incur a reduction in real income (purchasing power). Only if all nominal incomes grow at the same rate as the rate of inflation, which is extremely unlikely, would there be no redistributional effects. Hence, given the presence of such forces as inflationary expectations and market power deriving from imperfect market structures, an inflationary trend can be further reinforced by the pricing activities of those who can gain during a period of inflation. Clearly, as discussed in the next chapter, an eclectic policy approach to inflation is warranted, since its interacting causes are eclectic, and fiscal policy can only perform part of the corrective effort.

The problem of inadequate economic growth

Not only does the pure market economy fail to assure full employment without inflation, but there is no evidence that it will automatically tend to achieve a satisfactory rate of economic growth. The forces which determine economic growth in a market-directed economy are at least as complex as those analyzed above for short-run aggregate performance. In addition, they involve significant noneconomic as well as economic variables. No attempt will be made here to develop a comprehensive theory of economic growth. Though economic science has contributed many useful theories of economic growth, no single theory is comprehensive enough to be used as a general analytical reference point.[9] Hence, our analysis of fiscal procedures to assist economic growth will be based on certain widely accepted general aspects of the growth process rather than on a single definitive theory.

There is no question, for example, that both the quantitative expansion of productive resources, particularly capital, and the qualitative improvement of these resources are essential to the maintenance of a satisfactory growth rate. In addition, the importance of noneconomic factors such as political stability, particularly in developing nations, stands out as a proven fact. There is also no doubt as to the importance of the dual role of investment in the growth process, namely, that investment not only continues its short-run function of utilizing the saving generated at full-employment equilibrium in the economy, but that it also involves the long-run problem of absorbing the incremen-

---

[9] Some of the more important writings which provide insight into the economic growth process are: Roy F. Harrod, "An Essay in Dynamic Theory," *Economic Journal*, March 1939, pp. 14–33; Evsey Domar, "Expansion and Employment," *American Economic Review*, March 1947, pp. 34–55; James S. Duesenberry, *Business Cycles and Economic Growth* (New York: McGraw-Hill, 1958); Robert M. Solow, "Technical Change and the Aggregate Production Function," *Review of Economics and Statistics*, August 1957, pp. 312–20, and "Technical Progress, Capital Formulation, and Economic Growth," *American Economic Review*, May 1962, pp. 76–86; William Fellner, *Trends and Cycles in Economic Activity* (New York: Holt, Rinehart & Winston, 1956); John R. Hicks, *A Contribution to the Theory of the Trade Cycle* (Oxford: Clarendon Press, 1950).

FIGURE 19–3   **Long swings in U.S. aggregate production, 1860–1961, annual estimates and nine-year moving averages**

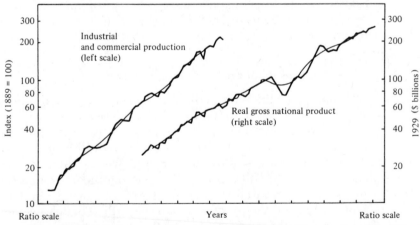

Source: Adapted from Bert G. Hickman, "The Postwar Retardation: Another Long Swing in the Rate of Growth?" *American Economic Review*, May 1963, Chart I, p. 491.

TABLE 19-1 **Growth of real* gross national product in the United States, 1929–1981 (percentage change from preceding year; quarterly data at seasonally adjusted annual rates)**

Year	Real gross national product	Year	Real gross national product
1929	—%	1960	2.2%
1933	−2.2	1961	2.6
1939	7.8	1962	5.8
1940	7.6	1963	4.0
1941	16.3	1964	5.3
1942	15.3	1965	6.0
1943	15.1	1966	6.0
1944	7.1	1967	2.7
1945	−1.5	1968	4.6
1946	−14.7	1969	2.8
1947	−1.7	1970	−0.2
1948	4.1	1971	3.4
1949	0.5	1972	5.7
1950	8.7	1973	5.8
1951	8.3	1974	−0.6
1952	3.7	1975	−1.1
1953	3.8	1976	5.4
1954	−1.2	1977	5.5
1955	6.7	1978	4.8
1956	2.1	1979	3.2
1957	1.8	1980	−0.2
1958	−0.4	1981[P]	1.9
1959	6.0		

* In constant (1972) dollars.
[P] = Preliminary.
Source: *Economic Report of the President–1982*, p. 239.

tal output resulting from net additions to the nation's capital stock.[10] Indeed, if the economy is to grow steadily it must have a continually rising level of productive capacity.

The fact that the American economy has not always experienced steady economic growth, or even satisfactory growth rates, is indicated in Figure 19–3 and Table 19–1. In Figure 19–3, the cyclically interrupted pattern of American economic growth during the 100 years following 1860 is evident. The graph is presented with particular emphasis on the long-swing variety of business cycle, but cycles of shorter duration also occurred during the period. Table 19–1 demonstrates the considerable variability in the growth rates of *real gross national product*[11] during the 1929–81 time period. It is interesting to

---

[10] This concept is developed in the Harrod-Domar growth models presented in the references cited in footnote 9.

[11] Real gross national product refers to gross national product expressed in terms of "constant" dollars.

note that *negative real growth* has occurred on 10 occasions during this time span.

Problems with the balance of international payments

The nation's balance of international payments performance can also raise serious aggregate economic issues. This is particularly true in an open economy, such as that of the United States, which participates significantly in international product and resource markets. Moreover, when monetary exchange rates between nations are less than fully flexible, an expanding domestic economy, especially if accompanied by price inflation, can lead to an expansion of imports and a contraction of exports. This helps cause a serious balance-of-payments deficit, such as generally occurred from the late 1950s through the 1960s, but which was eased somewhat by the introduction of more flexible exchange rates during the 1970s. Yet, balance of payments remain a potentially serious problem area at the present time.

FISCAL POLICY AND ECONOMIC STABILIZATION GOALS

In the same way that market failure of an *allocational*[12] nature helps to establish an economic case for the existence of government in a market-oriented system, so also does market failure in relationship to the economic *stabilization* function. If market economies did automatically tend toward an optimal stabilization performance, then the role of government in aggregate economic matters should be one of being as "neutral as possible" in reference to the optimally equilibrating market forces. However, if such is *not* the case, as has been demonstrated, then the public sector may be in a position to improve the performance of the aggregate economy. Thus, an economic case for aggregate economic policy, inclusive of aggregate *fiscal* policy, can be established in the pursuit of aggregate economic objectives. Of course, governmental economic policy in relation to these goals might at times be irrational. Nonetheless, since governmental fiscal decisions cannot be separated from the whole in a mixed economy, a deliberate direction of such decisions so as to *avoid* actions which would *increase* suboptimality, and to *encourage* actions which would *reduce* suboptimal aggregate performance, can be supported on the basis of economic rationality.

The goals of aggregate fiscal policy are multiple, since the major problems are several in number. As observed in the preceding section, they include the *full employment* of labor and capital resources

---

[12] See Part I.

(as reasonably defined), in order to combat the undesirable conditions of recession or depression. Aggregate fiscal policy may also be applied in the pursuit of *price stability,* in order to help prevent inflation. Finally, fiscal policy may be directed toward the promotion of *economic growth* and improvement in the nation's *balance of international payments.*

It is important to note that a fiscal policy in the form of fiscal effects exists whether or not one is desired, because government cannot act in budgetary matters without influencing the various economic goals, including aggregate economic objectives. Hence, the fiscal impact of government might just as well be rationalized in terms of deliberate policy. The primary responsibility for aggregate economic policy rests with the federal government, as the federalism theory of Chapter 17 suggests. It was not until 1946 that Congress formally recognized this fact and passed legislation providing a mandate for federal economic policy to help improve the aggregate performance of the economy.

THE EMPLOYMENT ACT OF 1946: A LEGISLATIVE MANDATE FOR AGGREGATE FISCAL POLICY

The year 1945, in which World War II ended, found the nation's economy operating under severe *inflationary gap* conditions. The enormous federal spending in support of World War II had exerted tremendous inflationary pressures during the preceding several years. Aggregate demand was considerably greater than aggregate supply at full-employment output during the period. Once the war was over, the long-postponed demand for consumer goods such as cars, refrigerators, and houses, along with the postponed business demand for peacetime capital goods, threatened to provide continued inflationary pressures. Moreover, this high volume of aggregate demand was made effective by wartime savings. In addition, the war had allowed the economy to escape the severe, decade-long *deflationary gap* (depression), which had begun with a cyclical downturn just prior to the stock market collapse of late 1929. The lingering fears of depression in the minds of members of Congress, business managers, professional economists, and others, along with the then-existing conditions of inflation, laid the groundwork for the passage of the Employment Act in the following year, 1946. The essence of this extremely important legislation is as follows:

> The Congress hereby declares that it is the continuing policy and responsibility of the Federal Government to use all practicable means consistent with its needs and obligations and other essential considerations of national policy, with the assistance and cooperation of industry, agriculture, labor, and State and local governments, to coordinate and utilize all its plans, functions, and resources for the purpose of creating

and maintaining, in a manner calculated to foster and promote free competitive enterprise and the general welfare, conditions under which there will be afforded useful employment opportunities, including self-employment, for those able, willing, and seeking work, and to promote maximum employment, production, and purchasing power.[13]

With the passage of such legislation, the central government of the United States joined the national governments of other Western industrial nations in stipulating a governmental responsibility to promote aggregate economic performance through *rational economic policy.* Such a policy normally takes the form of *monetary* and *fiscal* tools. The act clearly authorizes federal government economic activity to influence aggregate economic performance favorably. The federal government, however, is given the mandate to conduct such policy only in cooperation with the considerations of the market sector of the economy, as is evident in the part of the above statement which says that the federal government is to act "in a manner calculated to foster and promote free competitive enterprise."

The Employment Act of 1946 directly specifies the maximum employment goal, but it is somewhat less direct, though by no means unclear, in its mandate to maintain reasonable price-level stability. The latter goal is implicit in the phrase which authorizes efforts to promote "maximum purchasing power," and it was also evident in the congressional debate prior to the passage of the bill. Less precise is the mandate for federal fiscal policy to promote satisfactory rates of economic growth. There has been an increasing emphasis on the growth objective, however, and the interpretation of the act has clearly been broadened to include the economic-growth objective. Similarly, it has also been broadened in interpretation to include the goal of improvement in the nation's balance of international payments.

The act requires that a report regarding the state of the American economy be submitted to Congress by the executive branch early each year. The first report under the act was submitted in January of 1947. The *Economic Report of the President* describes such matters as the employment, output, and price-level conditions and trends of the economy, a review of federal fiscal and monetary policies, and other relevant economic considerations.

The legislation also established a Council of Economic Advisers (CEA) to assist and advise the President on economic matters. The Economic Report of the President is based in part on analytical work provided by the CEA, which consists of three members. The act also established in Congress the Joint Committee on the Economic Re-

---

[13] The Employment Act of 1946, February 20, 1946, P.L. 304, 79th cong., 2d sess. (60 Stat. 23).

port. This group was first created for the purpose of conducting economic studies pertinent only to the Economic Report of the President. The analysis conducted by the committee, however, has been gradually extended over a wide range of economic issues and is no longer soley for the Economic Report. Furthermore, the name of the committee has been changed to Joint Economic Committee (JEC). The JEC consists of 16 members, 8 each from the Senate and the House, and is assisted by a specialized professional staff. To a large extent, the committee provides broad economic analyses for the direct benefit of Congress and indirectly for the benefit of academicians, business people, labor union leaders, and others interested in the performance of the aggregate economy. It does so in a manner analogous to the role performed by the CEA, whose studies directly benefit the executive branch of the federal government and indirectly benefit many other interested parties.

The final section of this chapter will describe the *measurement* of the goals of aggregate fiscal policy which, in effect, are also the goals of the Employment Act of 1946. Satisfactory data are required for the implementation of effective fiscal (and overall economic) policy. It will be observed that the existing measurement techniques are satisfactory, for the most part, but clearly allow for further improvement and greater sophistication.

MEASURING THE GOALS OF AGGREGATE FISCAL POLICY

The full-employment and maximum output goal

Full employment. The aggregate performance of the economy may be alternately measured in terms of *resource employment,* the *income* earned by the owners of these resources, or the *output* which these resources produce. Regarding the employment of resources, it is common to define *full employment of resources* in terms of some reasonable proportion of the total amount of a particular resource being utilized in production during a certain period of time.[14] Although there is no official definition of either labor or capital full employment, reasonable figures must be selected for operational purposes. As noted above, we consider *full labor employment* to exist when no more than 5 *percent* of the civilian labor force is involuntarily unemployed (and thus at least 95 percent is gainfully employed). Thus, an allowance is made for the modest amount of involuntary labor unemployment which would be consistent with a generally healthy economy, due to such factors as workers changing

---

[14] It is not rational, of course, to expect that all, or even most, units of the land factor of production (natural resources) would be utilized in a given time period.

occupations, temporary seasonal layoffs, layoffs resulting from technological change, and unemployment caused by the changing composition of product demand. *Full capital employment* is commonly defined as a 90 percent rate of utilization of existing manufacturing capacity.

Labor force data for measuring employment and unemployment are provided by four federal agencies. These include the Bureau of Employment Security and the Bureau of Labor Statistics in the U.S. Department of Labor, the Bureau of the Census in the U.S. Department of Commerce, and the Bureau of Agricultural Economics in the U.S. Department of Agriculture. Statistics on the *employment status* of the population, that is, the personal, occupational, and other characteristics of those who are employed, the number of unemployed, and persons not in the labor force, and related data, are compiled by the Bureau of the Census on a monthly basis for the Bureau of Labor Statistics. These monthly surveys use a scientifically selected sample designed to represent the civilian noninstitutional population 16 years of age and over.

The *unemployment rate* compiled with the above approach is widely used as an indicator of aggregate economic activity. Specifically, this represents the number of workers unemployed, as defined above, as a percentage of the civilian labor force. The data also provide disaggregated unemployment rates according to classifications within the labor force, such as sex, age, marital status, color, and the like. Such disaggregated rates sometimes vary sharply from the aggregate national rate.

Maximum output. The U.S. Department of Commerce, through its national income and product accounts, provides the primary means of measuring *output,* and the *income* earned in producing that output, in the American economy. These accounts are built on a premise similar to the income statements used by business enterprises, in the sense that they are constructed in a double-entry manner. They emphasize the related flows of income and output in the economy during a particular period. One calendar year divided into four quarters constitutes the time period. Money is used as the common denominator of value for the aggregates.

On the one side, the accounts measure the *value of output (product)* as constituted by the major categories of purchasers of national output. Total American production of new goods and services in a given year is purchased by consumers, businesses, and governments within the nation and by foreign purchasers. The output referred to is *final* output, thus eliminating double counting in the various value-added stages of production. In addition, output refers only to currently produced items. On the other side of the national income and product accounts, *claims* against the value of national output are measured.

Income for the productive resources which produced the output, indirect business taxes, and capital depreciation allowances are important items on this side of national income and product accounting.

The Department of Commerce provides four subclassifications which comprise the composite national income and product accounting system. These are: (1) the *personal income and outlay account,* which demonstrates the income and expenditure totals for households (consumers) during a specific period; (2) the *gross savings and investment account of business operations,* which shows the nation's savings, and the disposition thereof, during the period; (3) the *government receipts and expenditures account,* which shows the public sector's resource-allocating activities during the period; and (4) the *foreign account,* which shows purchases by the United States from foreign nations (imports) and purchases by foreign nations from the United States (exports) during the period. Thus, a personal sector, a business sector, a government sector, and a foreign sector comprise the comprehensive national income and product accounts which reveal the value of total current production, and claims against that production, for the entire economy during a specified time period.

Among the aggregate concepts derived from these accounts, which may be useful for information and policymaking purposes, are gross national product, net national product, national income, personal income, and disposable income. *Gross national product* (GNP) refers to the money value of all final goods produced by the nation's economy in a certain time period, usually one year. *Net national product* (NNP) relates to the money value of all final goods production, as defined above, minus estimated business capital depreciation allowances during the period. *National income,* which derives from the claims side of the accounts, refers to the factor earnings which accrue to the owners of the resources used to produce national output (GNP) during the period under consideration. *Personal income* measures the spending power that individuals and families actually receive, as opposed to what they have earned (national income). For example, some earned income, such as social security deductions, corporation income taxes, and undistributed corporation profits, is not actually received by households. Moreover, some purchasing power is received through transfer payments, though they do not represent current earnings. *Disposable income* represents what remains of personal income after various personal taxes, such as personal income taxes, have been paid. The selection of any one of these five aggregate economic indicators will depend, of course, on the purpose in mind.

The GNP data can be statistically adjusted so as to project the value that GNP would have *if* the economy were fully employing its resources, at a time when it is *not* operating under full-employment conditions. This amounts to a measure of the "lost (reduced) output" that results from deflationary gap conditions in the economy. Such a *GNP gap* is the difference between actual and potential gross national product. *Potential GNP* refers to the volume of economic goods which the nation's economy can produce at reasonably stable prices, using the best available technologies, least-cost combinations of inputs, and rates of utilization of both capital and labor consistent with the prevailing full-employment norms of the economy. *Actual GNP* refers to the existing level of GNP. Actual and potential GNP are synonymous if the full-employment goal has been attained. The existence of the gap suggests that resources are being underutilized.

The price stability goal

The price stability goal is related in an important sense to the control of inflation. The term *inflation* refers generally to an increase in a level or index of various relevant prices. *Deflation,* of course, is the opposite of inflation and occurs as price levels decline. In recent decades, there has been far more reason to be concerned with rising than with declining prices. The United States does not have a completely adequate measure of general price-level behavior, though the techniques in use do possess overall favorable qualities. The primary price measurement devices are the consumer price index (CPI), the producer price index (PPI), and the GNP deflator index (GPI).

The consumer price index (CPI) measures the average change in prices over time in a fixed market basket of goods and services. It is compiled on a monthly basis by the Bureau of Labor Statistics of the U.S. Department of Labor. In fact, the CPI is provided for two population groups: (1) the all urban consumers CPI (CPI-U), which covers approximately 80 percent of the total noninstitutional civilian population, and (2) the urban wage earners and clerical workers CPI (CPI-W), which represents about one half of the population covered by the CPI-U. The additional population coverage provided by the CPI-U includes professional, managerial, and technical workers, the self-employed, short-term workers, the unemployed, retirees, and others not in the labor force.

Among the prices included in the CPI are those for food, clothing, shelter, fuels, transportation fares, and charges for medical and dental services. Prices are collected in 85 urban areas nationwide from over 18,000 tenants, 18,000 housing units for property taxes, and approximately 24,000 business establishments. Taxes directly associated with the purchase and use of items are included in the index. Price changes for the various items in each location are averaged together with weights representative of their importance in the spending patterns of the appropriate population groups. The designated reference date is 1967, which is equal to 100 percent or 100.0. Thus, an increase in prices of 30 percent relative to 1967 prices would be shown as 130.0.

The CPI is currently being adjusted to better measure the price of home ownership, which has tended to overstate the rate of inflation in the CPI. The CPI thus should include the price of the shelter provided by the home, but should *exclude* the change in the asset value of the house. The new approach will make this exclusion.

The producer price index (PPI), which was formerly known as the wholesale price index, is also compiled by the Bureau of Labor Statistics of the U.S. Department of Labor. This index measures the average changes in prices received in primary U.S. markets by producers of goods in all stages of processing. In fact, the PPI consists of more than one index. The sample used for constructing these indexes is approximately 2,800 commodities and some 10,000 price quotations representative of all commodities produced in the manufacturing, agriculture, forestry, fishing, mining, gas and electricity, and public utilities sectors of the economy.

Producer price indexes are organized by stage of processing (finished goods, intermediate or semifinished goods, and crude materials), or by the type of commodity (similarity of end use or material composition). In calculating the PPI, price changes for the various commodities are averaged together with weights representative of their importance in the total net selling value of all commodities as of 1972. The detailed data are aggregated to provide indexes for stage-of-processing groupings, commodity groupings, durability of product groupings, and a number of special composite groupings. Each PPI index uses a 1967 price level reference point equal to 100.0.

The *GNP deflator index (GPI)* is another indicator of price-level performance in the American economy. This index is obtained by dividing the GNP figure in current prices by the GNP figure in constant prices. The latter figure is obtained by disaggregating current-price GNP into the major components (and various subcomponents) of aggregate demand—consumption, investment, government expenditures, and exports net of imports—and deflating each component by its own price index. The resulting constant-dollar components are then added together to get a total constant-dollar GNP. Thus, the GNP deflator is a weighted average of price changes in the components of aggregate demand.

The GPI is provided on a quarterly basis by the U.S. Department of Commerce. It is a more comprehensive measure of national price-level performance than are either the CPI or PPI indexes. For example, it considers all components of GNP, with double counting eliminated, including government resource-absorbing activities. However, all major price indexes used for the American economy have one common defect stemming from measurement difficulties, namely, the inability to adjust satisfactorily for changes in product and resource "quality" over time.

The economic-growth goal

The data provided by the national income and product accounts of the U.S. Department of Commerce, as adjusted for price level and demographic (population) changes over time, provide the best information for estimating the economic-growth performance of the economy. Such intertemporal performance may be viewed from either the output or the income side of aggregate economic activity. Concepts such as gross national product, net national product, and national income may prove useful in the measurement of economic growth but, in order to get the best available measure of growth, these data must be adjusted for population changes over time, thus yielding a per capita concept, and also for intertemporal price-level changes, thus converting the values to real or constant-dollar terms. As a result, comparisons over time of *real per capita GNP, real per capita NNP,* and *real per capita income* provide the most useful indicators of the economic-growth performance of the economy.

The goal of international balance of payments

One measurement approach for international balance-of-payments performance is *international balance-of-payments accounting.* This approach measures the income, product, and financial transactions between the United States and the rest of the world. International balance-of-payments accounting is more comprehensive than the foreign sector component of the national income and product accounts, since it includes financial transactions as well as measurement of the value of goods and services output and the various claims against this output.

Current account transactions in international balance-of-payments accounting measure the total of goods and services available for consumption by Americans, and capital account transactions are concerned with dealings in real property or debt instruments. Both current and capital account transactions are reflected normally by changes in the cash account. Transactions which increase American cash holdings of foreign currency appear in the current and capital accounts preceded by a plus (+) sign. Those transactions that decrease American cash holdings are preceded in each account by a minus (−) sign. In the cash account itself, however, double-entry bookkeeping requires that increases in American cash holdings of foreign currency be preceded by a minus sign, while increases in foreign holdings of American currency are preceded by a plus sign.

The Department of Commerce collects the data and formulates the international balance-of-payments accounts. This measurement technique is clearly important to governmental economic policies which seek to improve the balance of international payments.

In conclusion, it has been observed in this chapter that the public sector will inevitably influence aggregate economic performance in a mixed economy. Moreover, a pure market economy possesses no inherent mechanism to assure optimal employment, output, price, economic-growth, and international balance-of-payments performance. It is only rational, therefore, in light of this market failure, to structure the economic actions of the public sector deliberately so that they will improve performance in relation to these goals. Congress recognized such a responsibility for the federal government by passing the Employment Act of 1946. Effective administration of the act requires adequate definitions and measurement of the aggregate goals. *Fiscal policy* is one important means of pursuing these goals.

20

Aggregate fiscal
policy instruments

DEMAND-SIDE FISCAL POLICY

The basic Keynesian explanation of macroeconomic malperformance focuses on deficient or excessive aggregate demand as the primary culprit. Consequently, it also emphasizes "demand-side" policies in its instruments for correcting such malperformance. The fiscal policies discussed in this section of the chapter will reflect such an orientation.

Meanwhile, the discussion of demand-side fiscal policy instruments requires a more elaborate multiplier concept than the one used in the simplified model of the preceding chapter. The Keynesian model presented in Figure 19–1 was concerned primarily with the functioning of a pure market economy operating in a closed environment with no international economic transactions. A more realistic analysis of how the American economy functions requires the introduction of both a government sector and international economic transactions to the model. When these are added to the analysis, there are significant new leakages from the private sector spending stream.

Thus, tax and import leakages, in addition to saving leakages as reflected in the marginal propensity to save concept discussed in Chapter 19, must be considered as limitations to the value of the multiplier. Saving, tax revenue, and import purchases all assume a functional relationship with the level of income. Although the relevance of the foreign trade leakage, which may be termed the *marginal propensity to import,* will not be totally ignored, the relatively more important saving and tax leakages will receive greater emphasis in the present discussion.

Fiscal stabilization instruments, as observed in Chapter 5, may be built into the budgetary structure as *automatic* responses of a countercyclical nature, or they may consist of ad hoc *discretionary* policy decisions directed toward a current aggregate malfunction in the economy. The former instruments are known as *automatic fiscal stabilizers,* while the latter are called *discretionary fiscal stabilizers.* Both of these sets of stabilization instruments are importantly related to the functional relationship between changes in income and the resulting changes in tax revenue.

The important functional relationship which exists between an absolute change in tax revenue and an absolute change in income is known as the *marginal propensity to tax (MPT).* This concept, which was discussed in Chapter 5, may be expressed as $MPT = \Delta T/\Delta Y$, with T representing tax revenue, Y representing income,[1] and Δ referring to change. Thus, as consumption and saving are considered as functions of income in the marginal propensity to consume and marginal propensity to save concepts, tax revenue is treated as a function of income in the marginal propensity to tax concept. The marginal propensity to consume (MPC), the marginal propensity to save (MPS), and the marginal propensity to tax (MPT) all represent positive functional relationships with income. That is, the dependent variables of consumption, saving, and tax revenues move in the same direction as changes in the level of income.

In addition, a related concept—the *income elasticity of taxation* (Y_t)—is also relevant to fiscal stabilization policy. The concept, which was also described in Chapter 5, is represented by the formula:

$$Y_t = \frac{\dfrac{\Delta T}{T_0}}{\dfrac{\Delta Y}{Y_0}}$$

with T representing tax revenue, Y representing income, Δ indicating change, and the subscript 0 referring to the base year. These two tax revenue-income concepts differ in that MPT represents the ratio between an absolute change in tax revenue and an absolute change in income, while Y_t represents the ratio between the percentage rate of change in tax revenue and the percentage rate of change in income.

---

[1] For purposes of later analysis, it is significant to observe that the tax yield from a federal tax is a function of *national income,* while consumption, in the consumption function, is more appropriately considered to be a function of *disposable income.*

The two concepts apply somewhat differently to stabilization policy. For example, an income change might induce a low Y_t, but a high *MPT*, if the tax is of major importance in the government budget. In this instance, the absolute revenue yield emphasis of the *MPT* concept is more relevant. If, however, two taxes of equal relative importance in the budget are considered, but one possesses a higher Y_t coefficient than the other, the tax with the higher Y_t is more likely to be the superior fiscal instrument for stabilization policy purposes.

Automatic fiscal stabilizers

The three primary automatic fiscal stabilizers of a demand-side nature are the *federal personal income tax*, the *federal corporation income tax*, and the *federal-state unemployment insurance program*. Each of these instruments automatically responds in a countercyclical manner to undesirable changes in aggregate economic performance.

For example, if the tax revenue extracted from the private sector increases more rapidly than national income, there will be a net decrease in private sector purchasing power and an accompanying decline in aggregate demand. This dampening effect on private sector purchasing power occurs when full employment is approached and the threat of inflation increases. On the other hand, when national income declines in a recession, tax revenue declines more rapidly than the decline in national income. The resulting net increase in private sector purchasing power would expand aggregate demand and thus provide a cushion underneath the cyclical downturn of the economy. Both the progressive federal personal and corporation income taxes work in these ways as automatic fiscal stabilizers. Yet, the federal corporation income tax is not as important as automatic stabilizer as the personal income tax, since its effect on disposable income is less direct and less complete, and its overall revenue importance is less.

The third major automatic fiscal stabilizer, the unemployment insurance program, provides a countercyclical program inclusive of both taxation and expenditure effects operating through a special trust fund. Payroll tax collections increase and unemployment compensation payments decline as labor employment expands toward full employment, thus creating restraint against demand inflation through a "net reduction" in private sector purchasing power. Oppositely, payroll tax collections decline and unemployment benefits increase as a greater number of workers are involuntarily unemployed, which provides a cushioning effect against recession through a "net increase" in private sector purchasing power. These net changes in private sector purchasing power thus exert either a contractionary or an expansionary multiplier effect on the economy, depending on the desired direction of improvement. As a result, the federal-state unemployment insurance program serves, along with the federal income taxes, as an important automatic fiscal stabilization instrument.

A study by Peter Eilbott lends support to the anticyclical effectiveness of automatic fiscal stabilizers.[2] It is estimated, on the basis of a multiplier model, that the percentage by which the stabilizers reduced the potential change in income in each of the three expansions and recessions during the period 1948–60 was significant. The analysis, which stresses the anticyclical and not the growth impact of the stabilizers, concludes that, even if one assumes fairly low values for the marginal propensity to consume out of disposable income and for the marginal propensity to invest out of retained corporate earnings, the automatic stabilizers prevented an average of over *one third* of the potential "income declines" during the first three postwar recessions. The effectiveness of the automatic stabilizers in restraining the three expansions between 1948 and 1960 was also sizable, though slightly less effective than for the contractions. Even though it cannot be expected that automatic fiscal stabilizers will be capable, by themselves, of returning a suboptimally performing economy to an optimal point, there can be little doubt that they exert important countercyclical effects in the appropriate direction of improvement in aggregate economic performance.

Discretionary fiscal stabilizers

The instruments of fiscal policy are essentially implemented through the budgetary procedures of taxation and expenditure. In the case of automatic stabilization tools, the taxes and expenditures are of such a nature that countercyclical results will occur *without* an additional ad hoc policy adjustment. Yet, stabilization policy may also involve the *deliberate, ad hoc* alteration of taxes or expenditures, so as to achieve aggregate economic goals. When fiscal policy is approached in this manner, it is termed *discretionary fiscal policy*.

Deliberate changes in either tax rate or tax bases, or the adoption or deletion of a tax, or deliberate changes in governmental spending, or in both taxes and spending, can be rationally directed toward the improvement of the aggregate performance of the economy in terms of such important objectives as full employment and price stability. The discretionary *government fiscal multipliers* that will be discussed have a demand-side orientation in that they exert their countercyclical effects, either directly or indirectly, through changes in aggregate demand. They are importantly related to the MPT concept.

---

[2] Peter Eilbott, "The Effectiveness of Automatic Stabilizers," *American Economic Review*, June 1966, pp. 450–65.

The following algebraic example of an *exhaustive expenditures multiplier* demonstrates the interaction between the marginal propensities to consume and save and the marginal propensity to tax, with a resulting influence through the multiplier effect on aggregate economic performance:

$$\Delta G = \$10 \text{ billion} \quad K = \frac{1}{1 - b + b(d)}$$

$$MPC(b) = 0.80 \quad K = \frac{1}{1 - 0.80 + 0.80(0.20)}$$

$$MPT(d) = 0.20 \quad K = \frac{1}{0.20 + 0.16} = \frac{1}{0.36} = 2.77$$

Legend

Δ = Change.
K = Multiplier.
G = Level of government exhaustive expenditures.
MPC = Marginal propensity to consume.
MPT = Marginal propensity to tax.
MPS = Marginal propensity to save $(1 - MPC)$.

Observe that changes in consumption and saving depend on changes in disposable income which, in turn, does not change as much as national income because of the automatic dampening influence of the increasing level of tax collections.

Thus, an increase in federal exhaustive expenditures of $20 billion, with other variables constant, would exert an increase in national income of $20 billion times the multiplier of 2.77. The result would be an ultimate growth in national income of $55.4 billion. The restraining influence of the marginal propensity to tax is obvious, since the multiplier value would be 5 instead of 2.77 when only the saving leakage is considered. With a multiplier of 5, a $20 billion increase in governmental spending would lead to a $100 billion increase in national income, as compared to the much lower figure of $55.4 billion when the tax leakage is also considered. This differential exists because the $55.4 billion increase in government exhaustive expenditure does not represent a $20 billion increase in disposable income when the tax leakage enters the picture. This leakage, plus the saving leakage of $1 out of every $5 of income change, reduces the value of the multiplier effect. Thus, just as the marginal propensities to consume and save help to determine the potential impact of a governmental budget multiplier, so will the value of the marginal propensity to tax influence the result. This should be kept in mind as we now discuss the various *discretionary* fiscal multipliers (stabilizers).

The tax multiplier. A change in the tax rates or tax base, or the adoption or deletion of a tax—and the resultant change in the level of tax revenue—will create a *multiple* change in national income (aggregate economic performance). This phenomenon is known as the *tax multiplier.* In Figure 20–1, S refers to saving, T to tax revenue, I to business investment, and G to governmental exhaustive (resource-absorbing) expenditures. S and I represent the private sector, while T and G represent the public sector of the mixed, private and public sector, economy. A change in tax revenue resulting from such discretionary actions as a change in tax rates must be distinguished, of course, from the marginal propensity to tax. This difference can be observed in Figure 20–1. A change in tax rates and the resulting change in tax revenue will cause the $S + T$ curve to shift, while the marginal propensity to tax merely refers to a movement along the $S + T$ curve since, even with a given set of tax rates in effect, tax collections will continue to vary as a function of the level of income.

The graph has netted out *consumption* from both the aggregate supply $(C + S + T)$ and the aggregate demand $(C + I + G)$ flows in order to simplify the presentation and allow greater emphasis on the rudiments of the tax multiplier itself. A similar procedure will be followed in the other relevant graphs which follow in this chapter.

FIGURE 20–1   The tax multiplier

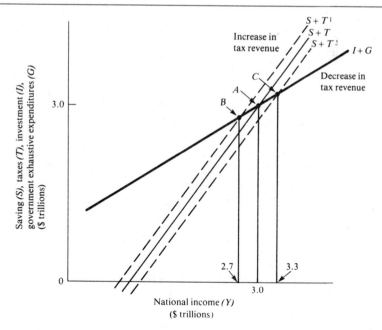

Also, for purposes of simplification in presentation, the initial increase or decrease in tax revenue resulting from a discretionary fiscal action is assumed to be by the same amount at all income levels.

The initial equilibrium level of aggregate economic performance in Figure 20-1 is at a national income level of $3 trillion. This is determined by the intersection at point A of the $S + T$ and $I + G$ curves. If tax revenue is increased via higher tax rates, and/or a broader tax base, and/or by the addition of a new tax, with both government transfer and exhaustive expenditures constant, the $S + T$ curve will shift to the left, as from $S + T$ to $S + T^1$, and the new equilibrium performance level will be at point B. It is important to note that national income has decreased from $3 trillion at point A to $2.7 trillion at point B after tax revenue is increased. Thus, if a tax revenue increase of $100 billion ($0.1 trillion) leads to the contraction in national income of $300 billion ($0.3 trillion), that is, from $3 to $2.7 trillion, the tax multiplier has a value of 3.

In contrast, a reduction in tax rates, and/or the narrowing of the tax base, and/or the repeal of an existing tax, with government transfer and exhaustive expenditures constant, will cause the $S + T$ curve to shift to the right, as from $S + T$ to $S + T^2$, and the new equilibrium performance level will be at point C. The reduction in tax revenue in this case has led to a new higher national income level at $3.3 trillion. If these actions cause tax revenue to decline by $100 billion ($0.1 trillion), and this leads to the expansion in national income of $300 billion ($0.3 trillion), that is, from $3 to $3.3 trillion, the value of the tax multiplier again is 3.

Thus, a variation in tax revenue may be either *contractionary* or *expansionary* in its influence on the economy, depending on the direction of the tax revenue change. Moreover, the tax multiplier exhibits an *inverse*, or *negative*, relationship between a discretionary change in tax revenue and the resulting change in aggregate economic performance. In other words, changes in national income move in the opposite direction from changes in tax revenue. An increase in tax revenue, for example, causes national income to fall, and a decrease in tax revenue causes national income to rise. This is true, of course, because higher tax revenue reduces the purchasing power of the private sector, thus reducing aggregate demand, while lower tax revenue yields a net increase in private sector purchasing power, which leads to a higher level of aggregate demand. The latter expansionary effect could be neutralized, of course, by restrictive monetary policy—as was the apparent case in 1981–1982 (see the discussion of Reaganomics below). The following formula depicts the tax multiplier (K_{tx}):

$$K_{tx} = \frac{-b}{1 - b + b(d)}$$

where

$$b = MPC$$
$$d = MPT.$$

If the existing aggregate economic performance problem is that of a *deflationary gap*, resulting from "deficient" aggregate demand, the appropriate implementation of the tax multiplier would be to decrease the amount of tax revenue extracted from the private sector, as represented by a move from curve $S + T$ to curve $S + T^2$ in Figure 20–1. That part of the reduced taxes that is not saved would, in turn, lead to expanded private sector expenditure and, thus, to expanded aggregate demand. The resulting multiplier expansion would alleviate the deflationary gap problem caused by the deficient aggregate demand.

Meanwhile, the appropriate use of the tax multiplier to alleviate *inflationary gap* conditions, which result from "excessive" aggregate demand, would be to increase the collection of tax revenue, as represented by a shift from curve $S + T$ to curve $S + T^1$ in Figure 20–1. The higher taxes will diminish private sector purchasing power leading to diminished aggregate demand and diminished upward pressure on prices.

It should be observed that the initial (direct) effect of the tax multiplier, whether used to combat a deflationary or an inflationary gap, is to change aggregate supply $(S + T)$. Yet, this is only a means to the primary, though indirect, objective of either *increasing aggregate demand* via expanded private sector purchasing power in order to alleviate deflationary gap conditions, or *decreasing aggregate demand* via reduced private sector purchasing power in order to alleviate inflationary gap conditions. In other words, the demand-side orientation of the Keynesian approach remains in effect.

The transfer expenditures multiplier. The spending as well as the tax side of the budget is capable of exerting a multiplier effect. In this regard, government expenditures may be either transfer or exhaustive (resource absorbing) in nature. A change in the level of transfer payments by government to the private sector, and the resulting multiplier change in national income, or aggregate economic performance, is known as the *transfer expenditures multiplier*. This is demonstrated in Figure 20–2. The initial equilibrium level of aggregate economic performance is again at a $3 trillion level of national income (point A). If transfer expenditures are *decreased*, with tax rates, base, the number of taxes used, and exhaustive expenditures remaining constant, the $S + T$ curve will shift to the left, as from $S + T$ to $S + T^1$, and the new equilibrium performance level will be at point B, which represents a decrease in national income from $3 trillion to $2.7 trillion. On the other hand, an *increase* in transfer expenditures, with tax rates, base, the number of taxes, and exhaustive expenditures

FIGURE 20-2   **The transfer expenditures multiplier**

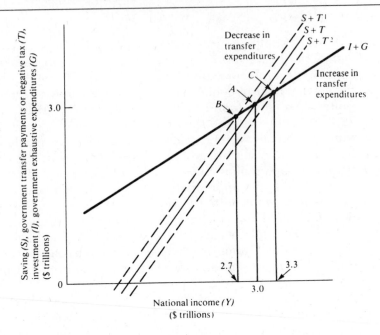

remaining constant, will cause the $S + T$ curve to shift to the right, as from $S + T$ to $S + T^2$, and national income expands from \$3 trillion to \$3.3 trillion at point C. The multiplier has a value of 3 in either case if the transfer spending change is \$100 billion (\$0.1 trillion). The transfer expenditures multiplier is *positive* in the direction of its relationship between a change in transfer spending and the resulting multiplier change in national income, that is, transfer expenditures and national income both rise and fall together. The following formula depicts the transfer expenditures multiplier (K_{tr}):

$$K_{tr} = \frac{+b}{1 - b + b(d)}$$

where

$b = MPC$
$d = MPT.$

In order to combat a *deflationary gap*, transfer expenditures should be increased so as to "increase" aggregate demand, and thus remove the aggregate demand "deficiency." Alternately, an *inflationary gap* can be alleviated by a decrease in transfer expenditures so as to decrease aggregate demand and, thus, remove "excessive" aggregate demand.

It may be observed that the *transfer expenditures multiplier*, just as the *tax multiplier*, exerts its multiplier effects in an indirect manner, since it represents the type of governmental budgetary behavior that does not directly absorb resources, but instead merely changes private sector purchasing power. Subsequent resource-using and saving decisions are then made by the private sector. This is not true of the government exhaustive expenditures multiplier, which directly absorbs resources in production instead of influencing spending indirectly by altering private sector purchasing power. Graphically, this is why the *S + T*, or aggregate supply curve, shifts to depict the *tax* and *transfer expenditures* multipliers, while the *I + G*, or aggregate demand curve, shifts to depict the operation of the *exhaustive expenditures* multiplier (as demonstrated later). However, the primary objective of the tax and transfer expenditures multipliers, even though indirectly attained, remains demand side in nature, that is, a change in aggregate demand.

The exhaustive expenditures multiplier. Federal exhaustive, or resource-absorbing, expenditures may also serve as the basis for aggregate fiscal policy. This was demonstrated earlier as the formula for the exhaustive expenditures multiplier was presented. The *exhaustive expenditures multiplier* represents a relationship between a change in the level of governmental resource-absorbing expenditures and the resulting multiple change in the level of national income. This multiplier approach is demonstrated in Figure 20–3.

A *decrease* in exhaustive expenditures, with tax revenue and transfer expenditures constant, will cause the *I + G* curve in Figure 20–3 to

FIGURE 20–3   The exhaustive expenditures multiplier

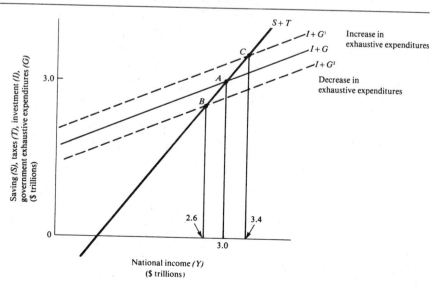

shift downward, as from $I + G$ to $I + G^2$, and national income will decline from $3 trillion at point A to $2.6 trillion at point B. This result occurs because private sector purchasing power, and thus aggregate demand, has been directly diminished. In contrast, an *increase* in exhaustive expenditures, with tax revenue and transfer expenditures constant, will cause the $I + G$ curve to move upward, as from $I + G$ to $I + G^1$, and national income will increase from $3 trillion at point A to $3.4 trillion at point C. This result occurs because private sector purchasing power, and thus aggregate demand, has been directly increased by the incremental exhaustive spending of government.

The exhaustive expenditures multiplier, like the transfer expenditures multiplier, represents a *positive* relationship between the direction of a change in spending and the resulting change in national income, since the variables move upward and downward together. In other words, an increase in exhaustive spending exerts an expansionary influence, and a decrease in exhaustive spending exerts a contractionary influence on aggregate economic performance. Thus, an increase in exhaustive expenditures would tend to increase national income, and thus would be the appropriate policy to combat a *deflationary gap*. Meanwhile, a decrease in exhaustive expenditures would tend to decrease national income, and thus would be the appropriate policy to combat an *inflationary gap*.

It is significant that the size of the multiplier effect will tend to be greater in the case of the exhaustive expenditures multiplier than for the tax and transfer expenditures multipliers.[3] This is demonstrated by comparing Figures 20–1, 20–2, 20–3. These graphs show that a $100 billion ($0.1 trillion) increase in tax revenue, or a similar decrease in transfer expenditures, will cause national income to decline from $3 trillion to $2.7 trillion, while a $100 billion ($0.1 trillion) decrease in exhaustive expenditures will cause national income to decline from $3 trillion to $2.6 trillion. Furthermore, a $100 billion ($0.1 trillion) reduction in tax revenue, or a similar increase in transfer expenditures, will cause national income to increase from $3 trillion to $3.3 trillion, while a $100 billion ($0.1 trillion) increase in exhaustive expenditures will cause national income to increase from $3

---

[3] In comparing the ultimate multiplier potential of the *tax* and the *transfer expenditures multipliers*, it should be observed that by the extent to which the taxes collected to make the transfer payments come from higher-income spending units than those who receive the payments, the transfer expenditures multiplier would possess the greater multiplier potential of the two. This would be true because higher-income groups tend to have a higher marginal propensity to save, and thus a lower marginal propensity to consume, than lower-income groups. Hence, the saving leakage would be smaller for the transfer expenditures multiplier as opposed to the saving that would result from a comparable tax rate reduction for the higher-income group brought about through a tax multiplier. Nonetheless, the fact remains that neither the tax nor the transfer expenditures multiplier would possess the multiplier potential of the *exhaustive expenditures multiplier*, which has no initial saving leakage whatsoever.

trillion to $3.4 trillion. Why does the exhaustive expenditures multiplier tend to have a greater multiplier value than the tax and transfer expenditures multipliers?

The relatively larger exhaustive expenditures multiplier effect exists because a change in exhaustive government spending involves no initial (first-round) change in saving (the *MPC* of government equals 1), while a change in private sector spending resulting from either a tax or transfer payment change is subject to the *MPS* behavior of individuals.[4] An increase of $100 billion in exhaustive governmental expenditures, for example, will directly increase national money income by this same amount (and output if resource unemployment permits it), and none of the $100 billion will be initially saved. A tax *reduction* of $100 billion, or a transfer expenditure increase of that amount, will lead to a less than $100 billion increase in consumption, because some of the incremental purchasing power will normally be *saved* by the private sector. Private sector purchasing power (and *not* resource-absorbing activities) is directly affected by the tax and transfer spending changes. Hence, the amount of additional aggregate demand on which the ultimate multiplier expansion depends will be less with the decrease in taxes or the increase in transfer payments than it will be with the increase in exhaustive expenditures. In other words, the initial round of exhaustive government expenditures is a total direct component of gross national product, while the initial round of the tax reduction or transfer spending increment is merely a transfer of purchasing power, some of which will be saved before it enters the spending stream.

The phenomenon described in the above paragraph may be enlightened by the following example:

> If the federal government cuts taxpayer A's taxes by $1,000, the operation of the *tax multiplier* is indicated.
> If the federal government makes $1,000 in welfare payments to taxpayer A, the *transfer expenditures multiplier* is indicated.
> If the federal government purchases $1,000 of labor input from taxpayer A, the *exhaustive expenditures multiplier* is indicated.

Assume that taxpayer A has a marginal propensity to consume of 0.80 and a marginal propensity to save of 0.20. The tax and transfer expenditures multipliers are thus subject to an initial 20 percent, or $200, saving leakage out of the expanded purchasing power ($1,000 − $200 = $800). However, the exhaustive expenditures multiplier possesses no such initial saving leakage. Instead, resources (labor input)

---

[4] This discussion is related to the earlier discussion which explained the fact that the direct, though not primary, effect of the tax and transfer expenditures multipliers is on aggregate supply.

are directly absorbed by the full value of the exhaustive expenditure ($1,000 − 0 = $1,000).

SUPPLY–SIDE FISCAL POLICY

The basic approach

The primary objective of the fiscal instruments which constitute supply–side fiscal policy is to expand aggregate supply with a resulting expansion in the rate of economic growth. In comparison to the demand-side fiscal policy discussed in the previous section, supply-side fiscal policy takes on an essentially long-run connotation. Furthermore, the supply-side approach rejects the basic Keynesian demand-side contention that the federal government can manage the aggregate economy through discretionary fiscal stabilizers applied in the form of tax and expenditure changes. For example, it argues that an increase in federal expenditures to combat recession, at a time when tax rates are high, will spur inflation by increasing aggregate demand without a corresponding increase in aggregate supply. In historical terms, supply-side fiscal policy is nothing new. In fact, it dates back to the time of Adam Smith and is represented in Say's Law,[5] which contends that supply creates its own demand since price reductions[6] in the face of excess aggregate supply will stimulate the purchasing of economic output. The counterpart Keynesian argument would be that demand creates its own supply. Demand-side fiscal (and economic) policy replaced supply-side fiscal policy as the primary orientation during the great Depression of the 1930s and continued throughout most of the post-World War II era.

Specifically, the supply-side fiscal approach attempts to change the relative prices of (1) work versus leisure and (2) consumption versus saving and investment by means of marginal tax rate reductions. Thus, if marginal tax rates—especially personal income tax rates—are reduced, posttax real wages will increase. As a result, there will be a tendency to substitute work for leisure, and a resulting increase in aggregate supply, since the price of work relative to leisure declines. A similar effect is said to exist for the choice between consumption and saving-investment. That is, a marginal tax rate reduction would reduce the relative price of future versus current consumption and, as a result, would stimulate present-period saving and investment activities as consumption is postponed.

The aggregate supply expansion that is said to result from marginal

---

[5] See Chapter 19.

[6] However, the dominance of oligopoly markets may restrict price flexibility downward.

tax rate reductions is not without theoretical challenge.[7] For example, an increase in posttax real wages resulting from a tax reduction could cause people to work less rather than more, since a person could now maintain a constant real income and living standard while working fewer hours and enjoying more leisure. Thus, an income effect which reduces work effort may counteract the substitution effect which increases work effort. Moreover, after taxes are reduced, a person may save less and still maintain, or increase, future consumption. This is possible due to an income effect resulting from the higher posttax rates of interest that are brought about by the tax reduction. Such higher posttax interest rates, even if applied to a lower level of saving, could yield an increase in future consumption. Hence, on theoretical grounds, substitution effects favoring more work and more saving-investment activities may be neutralized by income effects which reduce such activities.

However, at this point in our continuing discussion of supply-side fiscal policy, we will assume that the substitution effects discussed here outweigh the income effects. Thus, aggregate supply will tend to expand as marginal tax rates are reduced. Relatedly, the modern supply-side approach argues that the expansion in aggregate supply, and the resulting increase in economic growth, may lead to an *increase in total tax revenue*. This has become known as the Laffer curve[8] when presented in graphical form as in Figure 20–4. Thus, total tax revenue may be inversely related to a reduction in tax rates. That is, along one portion of the curve (*CA*), a reduction in tax rates will actually increase tax revenue, as the tax base expands due to economic growth.[9] Tax revenue, of course, would be zero at point *B*, when the marginal tax rate is zero, and also would be zero at point *C*, when a marginal tax rate of 100 percent destroys all incentives for market economic activity. Meanwhile, in the *AB* segment of the curve, the

---

[7] For theoretical arguments *in support* of aggregate supply expansion resulting from marginal tax rate cuts, see: Martin S. Feldstein, "Tax Incentives, Corporate Saving, and Capital Accumulation in the United States," *Journal of Public Economics* 2 (1973), pp. 159–71, and Michael J. Boskin, "Taxation, Saving, and the Rate of Interest," *Journal of Political Economy,* April 1978, pt. 2, pp. S3–S27. For theoretical arguments which *reject* the aggregate supply expansion conclusion, see E. Philip Howrey and Saul H. Hymans, "The Measurement and Determination of Loanable-Funds Saving," in *What Should Be Taxed: Income or Expenditure?* ed. Joseph A. Pechman (Washington, D.C.: Brookings Institution, 1980). For a *general discussion* of the subject, see James R. Barth, "The Reagan Program for Economic Recovery: Economic Rationale," Federal Reserve Bank of Atlanta *Economic Review,* September 1981, pp. 4–14.

[8] Named after economist, Arthur Laffer, who has popularized the concept during recent years.

[9] The termination of the revenue-expansion portion of curve CA at a 50 percent marginal tax rate is arbitrarily selected. The basic argument merely contends that there *is* such a portion of the curve, but does not stipulate the exact marginal tax rate range at which revenue expansion would occur.

FIGURE 20–4   **Elastic revenue response to marginal tax rate reductions***

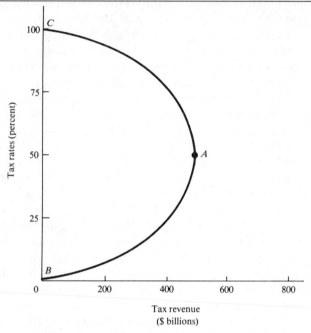

Tax revenue
($ billions)

* Also known as the Laffer curve (see footnote 8).

more conventional result applies whereby a reduction of tax rates reduces tax revenue, in part because important public goods, complementary to private sector economic activity, are now being undersupplied. However, in the *CA* segment, tax rate reductions—by increasing work and saving-investment activities—would yield expanded tax revenue through expanded aggregate supply, economic growth, and the resultant expanded tax base.

Reaganomics: The supply-side fiscal (and economic) policy of the Reagan Administration

The *Reaganomics* aggregate economic program has these basic components:

1. Substantial federal tax reductions, especially personal and corporation income tax reductions, designed to be relatively greater as one moves up the income scale.[10]

_____

[10] See Chapters 8, 9, 10, and 16 for further evidence of this fact.

2. Substantial federal social and other nondefense expenditure reductions.
3. Substantial federal defense expenditure increases.
4. Substantial deregulation of the private sector from various federal controls.
5. A restrictive monetary policy to control inflation until the anticipated expansionary fiscal policy takes effect.

The various income and estate-gift tax reductions enacted by Congress in response to the Reagan Administration requests have been documented in earlier chapters, which have described the Economic Recovery Tax Act of 1981. Moreover, Congress also has met the basic Reagan administration spending requests by significantly decreasing, in real terms, social and other nondefense expenditures, while significantly increasing defense expenditures. In addition, the pace of federal deregulation has expanded and monetary policy has been restrictive through the first 18 months of the Reaganomics program.

However, as of mid-1982, the hoped-for economic expansion and growth had not developed, but the rate of inflation was moderating as recessionary conditions deepened. The some $750 billion in federal tax reductions enacted for the next several years, accompanied by an essential expenditure *status quo* since defense spending increases have offset nondefense spending decreases, have created a scenario of large present, and prospective future, federal budget deficits. Meanwhile, interest rates reflective of a restrictive monetary policy have remained high, thus helping to neutralize the anticipated fiscal-induced economic expansion. Nonetheless, since supply-side fiscal (and economic) policy is inherently long-run in nature, the ultimate success of the Reaganomics program cannot yet be judged. However, one may note that the program deviates in one important way from the traditional supply-side approach. The latter would first seek a short-run federal budget balance—if necessary even by an increase in taxes as spending is reduced—and then would reduce taxes in the long run only *after* economic expansion has occurred.

In any event, the Reagan administration fiscal (and economic) program represents a sharp change in direction away from the demand-side orientation which began during the Depression of the 1930s. In so doing, it returned to the traditional supply-side focus of economic policy dating back to Adam Smith and J. B. Say. However, this does not suggest a total absence of supply-side policies between the 1930s and the present time. For example, the federal corporation-income tax reductions of the Kennedy-Johnson administrations during the early-1960s featured such supply-side instruments as the introduction of the investment tax credit (ITC) and the liberalization of business depreciation provisions.

TECHNIQUES OF DEFICIT FINANCING
AND SURPLUS DISPOSAL

The deficit budget

The use of tax and expenditure changes to promote aggregate economic goals will often help to create either a *deficit* or a *surplus* budget (usually the former). There are various means, moreover, by which the federal govenment may finance a *deficit* budget (when expenditures have exceeded tax and other revenue collections) and dispose of a surplus (when tax and other revenue collections have exceeded expenditures). Depending on the particular deficit financing and surplus disposal techniques selected, however, substantially different *secondary effects* may be exerted on aggregate economic activity. These secondary effects may either reinforce or neutralize the initial expansion or contraction resulting from the deficit or surplus. Of course, a *deficit* budget resulting from reduced tax revenue and/or higher government spending, or both, tends to be *expansionary,* and a *surplus* budget resulting from higher tax revenue and/or reduced government spending, or both, tends to be *contractionary.* In Keynesian terms, the expansionary and contractionary results involve the multiplier effect that the public sector exerts on the private sector when government provides *either* a *net increment* in private sector purchasing power through a deficit budget, or a *net decrement* in private sector purchasing power through a surplus budget.[11] Yet, once these multiplier effects are set in motion, the particular means of financing a deficit or disposing of a surplus takes on considerable importance because of its ability to exert secondary economic effects.

We will consider five alternative methods of financing a federal deficit budget:

1. The Treasury Department sells securities to the private sector (excluding commercial banks and the Federal Reserve System).
2. The Treasury Department sells securities to commercial banks at a time when they do *not* have excess loanable reserves.
3. The Treasury Department sells securities to commercial banks at a time when they do possess substantial excess reserves.
4. The Treasury Department sells securities to the nation's central bank—the Federal Reserve System.
5. The federal government creates or prints fiat money.

The least expansionary means of financing a federal deficit are

---

[11] The net increment and net decrement in private sector purchasing power, as observed earlier, may vary in size depending on whether the exhaustive expenditures multiplier, the transfer expenditures multiplier, or the tax multiplier is being considered.

methods 1 and 2. A sale of Treasury securities (debt instruments) to private individuals and businesses in the market sector of the economy, equal in volume to the amount of the deficit, for example, would withdraw purchasing power from the private sector equal to the amount introduced into the private sector by the deficit budget itself. This, indeed, must be classified as a restrictive means of financing a deficit budget, since the secondary effects of the financing technique selected tend to neutralize the primary effects of the initial multiplier.

Another highly restrictive means of financing a deficit budget occurs when the Treasury Department sells securities to the commercial banking system at a time when the banks do *not* possess excess loanable reserves. Under such conditions, commercial banks would necessarily restrict their loans to the private sector or to state and local levels of government in order to finance the purchase of the securities. This would cause a reduction in aggregate demand, which would also tend to neutralize or offset the primary expansionary effects of the initial multiplier.

If, however, Treasury securities equal to the amount of the deficit are sold to the commercial banking system at a time when the banks *do* possess substantial excess reserves, the initial multiplier expansion need not be severely neutralized, if neutralized at all, by restrictive secondary effects, because the banks can purchase the securities from their excess reserves without reducing their volume of loans to the private sector or to state-local governments. Moreover, an expansion of the money supply, as the excess reserves are put to work through the operation of a fractional reserve banking system, will allow the greater economic activity made possible by the expansionary multiplier to take place. The expanding money supply will reinforce, not neutralize or offset, the multiplier-caused expansion and, in addition, may prove to be inflationary. A form of *debt monetization* has occurred.

An additional expansionary means of financing a deficit budget is to sell Treasury securities to the Federal Reserve System. This process involves an even purer version of the concept of *debt monetization*. The effect, in this case, is at least as expansionary as that of the sale of securities to commercial banks at a time when they have substantial excess reserves. The following paragraph provides a description of the debt monetization process derived from the sale of Treasury securities to the Federal Reserve System.

The Treasury Department sells government securities (debt instruments) to the Federal Reserve banks. The Federal Reserve banks then create new Treasury deposit accounts, or expand present Treasury deposit accounts, at the banks. These deposit accounts are liabilities to the Federal Reserve System, but the securities purchased by the Federal Reserve System are classified as assets. The government then spends the funds to purchase economic goods and productive resources from the private sector or as transfer payments. Subsequently, checks are drawn by the Treasury Department on its deposit accounts in the Federal Reserve System as the money is spent. Individuals and business firms in the private sector who sell productive resources and economic goods to the federal government, and individuals who receive transfer payments, receive these checks. Ordinarily, the checks will be deposited in the commercial banking system and the commercial banks, on receiving the checks as deposits, will credit the deposit accounts of the private individuals and business firms. The commercial banks, in turn, send the checks to the Federal Reserve banks, and the commercial bank reserve accounts within the Federal Reserve System are subsequently increased by the full amount of the checks. The commercial banking system thus possesses new excess reserves over and above the reserve amount required legally behind the new demand deposits. This monetary expansion, or debt monetization, will reinforce the expansionary influence of the original multiplier and may yield inflationary results.

The federal government, of course, need not resort to ordinary debt creation to finance a budget. It could simply print *fiat money* equal to the amount of the excess of government spending over revenue collections. This technique of financing a deficit, once again, is expansionary and does not neutralize the primary multiplier expansion through the imposition of any offsetting secondary effects. Moreover, it is likely to be inflationary.

The surplus budget

When the federal government collects more in taxes and other revenues than it spends, which has been an extremely rare occurrence, the resulting surplus may be utilized in a variety of ways. An increase in tax revenue and/or a reduction in government spending, for example, may lead to a surplus budget. Depending on the particular surplus disposal technique selected, the contractionary effect of the surplus budget working through the multiplier may be either reinforced or neutralized. If maximum economic contraction is desired, the surplus funds should be held idle and not allowed to reenter the private sector. Under such conditions, no neutralization of the contractionary multiplier occurs, since a net decrease in private sector purchasing power has taken place. If some degree of neutralization is desired, the surplus can be (1) distributed among groups who will spend most of it immediately, which would yield a substantial offset to the contractionary effects of the surplus, or (2) used to retire already-existing government debt. In the latter case, depending on who holds the debt to be retired, varying degrees of partial neutralization will result.

Thus, not only do unbalanced budgets provide *primary* multiplier effects through tax rate and spending changes, but also important *secondary* economic effects may result, depending on the particular technique used to finance a deficit or to dispose of a surplus. The specific technique selected, however, will necessarily depend on policy objectives and the overall conditions of the economy. The huge federal deficits of World War II were inevitable, for example, and the proper fiscal policy under these conditions—a surplus budget—could not be used, despite the inflationary gap conditions which prevailed. The next best approach was to finance the deficit in the most restrictive way possible in terms of secondary effects. Consequently, an enormous effort was made to sell war bonds to the private sector of the economy as well as to the banking system, while at the same time monetary policy attempted generally to restrict private credit. It is seen in this example that fiscal and monetary policy cannot be totally divorced from each other. Instead, they require coordination to achieve mutual economic objectives. It is perhaps noteworthy, in terms of improving future policy, to observe that the institutional arrangement for monetary policy working through the quasi-independent Federal Reserve System is considerably different from the institutional arrangement for federal fiscal policy. The latter often works much more slowly, since the federal government budget-making process requires the action of both the executive branch of the federal government and of Congress. The important relationship between fiscal and monetary policy will be explored further in the following chapter, as various fiscal policy norms or rules are discussed.

THE STAGFLATION PARADOX AND THE NEED FOR AN INCOMES POLICY

As observed in the preceding chapter, conventional fiscal and monetary policy is unable to attack directly the root causes of structural inflation. This is so because structural inflation is not directly caused by excessive aggregate demand but, instead, is the result of pricing behavior in imperfectly competitive resource and product markets. Moreover, related forces such as the indexing of wages for inflation can also contribute to the inflationary process. This leads to a paradox whereby it becomes extremely difficult, if not impossible, for the economy to simultaneously achieve the aggregate economic goals of full employment and price stability. Instead, an intermediate mixture of both underfull employment and inflation—or *stagflation*—is usually the result, often over an extended period of time. Relatedly, the long-run persistence of the recessionary element of under full employment translates into inadequate rates of economic growth.

Since the dilemma stems largely from structural conditions of monopoly power in resource and product markets, the practice of such economic power leads to continuing rounds of wage and price (or price and wage) increases.[12] Moreover, the wage increase component is often tied to a cost-of-living index, as well as containing an increment in real wages, even though labor productivity increases may not have kept pace. Or, oppositely, product price increases may be implemented in excess of real production cost increases. This involves an important *income redistribution process,* as observed in Chapter 19. In the absence of conventional fiscal (and monetary) policy capabilities to mitigate structural inflation, a serious need arises for alternative policy instruments. The search for such instruments in the Western industrial world so far has met with very limited success. This area of policy is commonly referred to as *incomes policy* because of the redistributional effects which result from structural inflation and related forces.

Figure 20–5, which is adapted from Figure 19–2 in the preceeding chapter, can be used to demonstrate the objective of an effective incomes policy. A successful incomes policy would move the inflation-unemployment (stagflation) trade-off curve *PI-U* downward and to the left, thus moving the aggregate performance of the economy toward the optimal full employment of labor and noninflation point— point A.[13] We will briefly evaluate several of the alternative instruments of incomes policy that may be directed toward the stagflation dilemma.

Antitrust policy

This may be used in an effort to increase price competition in product and resource markets. Such an approach, if successful, would be very desirable from the standpoint of the society's orientation toward a market economy. Unfortunately, the achievement of more competitive markets in major national industries would in itself introduce a paradox; namely, the danger in many industries of negating scale economies in production if a large number of smaller producers is to supply an industry's output. Indeed, one major historical reason for the emergence of oligopoly and monopoly market structures is that available technology made possible important scale economies.

---

[12] There is no convincing evidence that either wages or prices lead the inflationary spiral, with the other the follower. Thus, it is no more accurate to call the phenomenon a wage-push spiral than it is to refer to it as a profit-pull spiral.

[13] Empirical evidence for the 1960s and 1970s suggests that the PI-U curve has actually shifted in the opposite direction, that is, upward and to the right, during the period.

FIGURE 20–5   **The stagflation paradox and the need for an incomes policy**

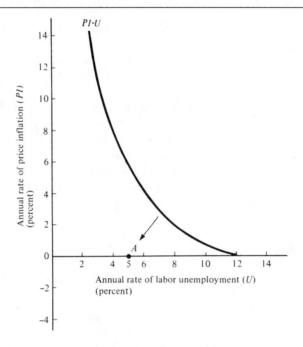

Thus, a trade-off would arise between either retaining scale economies in production or attaining significant price competition. Moreover, any efforts to "demonopolize" labor unions, while leaving large oligopoly and monopoly producers unaffected by such policy, would be irrational, in that the historical development of labor unions was largely a necessary countervailing reaction to the emergence of large, essentially nonprice-competitive businesses. Nonetheless, despite the pessimistic appraisal of a total solution to stagflation from the antitrust approach, antitrust policies should be actively pursued with the view of making markets *more* competitive. Undoubtedly, they are capable of exerting at least a marginal improvement in the reduction of inflation. Finally, deregulation in certain (but not all) industries characterized by public utility (or similar) regulation may introduce greater price competition. Presently, such an approach is being implemented in the commercial aviation industry.

Manpower policy

Another approach to shifting the *PI-U* curve closer to point *A* in Figure 20–5 may take the form of policies which increase the employability of certain persons in the labor force who lack the appropriate skills or opportunities to earn substantial income. Again, manpower policy cannot be viewed as a total solution to the stagflation problem. However, it appears capable of exerting at least marginal improvement in the position of the *PI-U* curve, in reference to its optimal position at point *A*.

Federal programs of a manpower nature were actively pursued during the 1960s and 1970s, but are being deemphasized at the present time. Such programs should be designed to train workers in occupations where a legitimate need exists for an additional supply of labor. It should be recognized that manpower policies can serve as a selective, or disaggregated, attack on particularly acute segments of unemployment. For example, a national labor unemployment figure of 6 percent, if disaggregated, would normally reveal several classifications of workers (such as nonwhite, teenagers, etc.) with significantly higher unemployment rates.

Direct or formal wage and price controls

Although direct, formal wage and price controls are capable of moving the *PI-U* curve toward point *A* in Figure 20–5, at least in the short run, the stagflation improvement is obtained at a high social cost. This is so because such direct intervention in the wage- and price-setting decisions of the private sector is in conflict with the inherent character of a market economy. Drastic action of this sort might be acceptable, and even desirable, during times of major national emergency such as war. However, this instrument cannot be considered a viable peacetime solution within the framework of a market-oriented society. The possibility of direct wage and price controls, therefore, will not be pursued further in this discussion of antistagflation policy instruments.

Indirect or informal wage and price controls

Another approach to incomes policy takes the form of indirect or informal wage and price instruments. Yet, this is a largely undeveloped area of policy in the Western industrial world at the present time. Various forms of indirect controls have been suggested, and a few have been adopted, but other feasible alternatives await formulation.

For example, during the administrations of Presidents John Kennedy and Lyndon Johnson, the executive branch of the federal government attempted to use persuasion as a short-run means of combating structural inflation. This technique, known also as "jawboning," primarily took the form of a *wage-price guidelines* or *guideposts* policy based on an estimated annual labor productivity increase in the economy of 3.2 percent. It was suggested that an increase in wages should not exceed the national trend rate of increase in output per man-hour of labor. Moreover, it was suggested that product prices should remain stable in those industries that experience the same productivity growth as the national average, but should rise in industries with below-average productivity growth and should decline in industries with above-average gains in productivity. This guidelines policy was only semiregulatory in nature, since it carried no absolute authority to compel compliance. It merely employed persuasion. However, it did appear to attain modest success before its termination early in the Nixon administration. No significant indirect incomes policy efforts were undertaken during the Nixon-Ford administration. However, the Carter administration introduced wage-price guidelines during October of 1978, but these were largely unsuccessful.

Another indirect incomes policy instrument that has been proposed is the creation of a special federal agency or body with the responsibility of reviewing wage and price actions, especially in major industries. As an arbitrator, such an agency would seem to require some degree of enforcement capability or at least a strong recommendation influence, with the interest of the general public in mind. Otherwise, it would revert to the largely ineffective "moral suasion" efforts of a federal agency such as the Council on Wage and Price Stability (COWPS), as it existed in the Carter administration.

Tax-based incomes policy as an indirect antistagflation instrument

The tax-based incomes policy (TIP) technique was first formally proposed by Henry Wallich and Sidney Weintraub in 1971, and it has been the object of considerable discussion since that time.[14] This proposed fiscal instrument, which constitutes an effort to integrate relevant macroeconomic and microeconomic considerations, would first set an average annual wage-increase benchmark, based on labor productivity trends in the economy. Then, for the approximately 1,000 largest corporations to which TIP would apply, a federal corporation income tax surcharge would be imposed if a given corporation's average wage bill (for all employees) increased annually by more than the national average wage-increase benchmark. Moreover, the surcharge would increase in a graduated fashion as the deviation from the benchmark becomes greater. An average wage increase equal to or below the benchmark would not incur the penalty tax. The penalty tax

---

[14] See Henry C. Wallich and Sidney Weintraub, "A Tax-Based Incomes Policy," *Journal of Economic Issues,* June 1971, pp. 1–19, for the original presentation. For an example of a later evaluation and supportive article, see Abba P. Lerner, "Stagflation— Its Cause and Cure," *Challenge,* September–October 1977, pp. 14–19.

revenues would be subsequently returned to the corporate sector as a whole through a reduction in federal corporation income tax rates, thus preserving the corporate income share of total national income, and hopefully mitigating any tendency of corporations to forward shift the penalty tax. Some later modified versions of TIP have added a tax credit provision for those corporations whose average wage bill in- creases by less than the national wage-increase benchmark, with the credit diminishing as the deviation draws closer to the benchmark.[15]

The basic intent of TIP is to constrain product price increases by first holding wage increases in line with national productivity trends. To be successful, of course, TIP would have to break the "indexing syndrome" whereby wages are indexed for the rate of inflation regard- less of productivity trends. A primary attraction of TIP is that it does not intervene directly in the price-setting mechanism of the market. It simply adds another relevant factor to be considered by a business in its wage and profit calculations. Yet, it does not specify the wage that must be paid. Each corporation may choose its own course of action, depending on its own supply and demand characteristics. These *mi- croeconomic* decisions remain in the hands of the business on a *relative price* basis, thus avoiding the excessive *absolute price* inter- vention in the market of direct wage and price controls. At the same time, TIP reflects the *macroeconomic* costs of stagflation through its tax surcharge and credit provisions. Furthermore, the tax features of TIP provide an economic incentive which would induce results un- like the wage-price guidelines or guideposts, which lack both enforce- ment power and economic incentives.

Other inflation issues

Before concluding this discussion of stagflation and the need for an effective incomes policy, several additional inflation phenomena, which were mentioned briefly in the preceding chapter, will be dis- cussed in somewhat greater detail. These are (1) the role of price expectations in the inflationary process, (2) the matter of bottleneck inflation, and (3) the fact that taxes themselves can result in inflated prices.

Regarding *price expectations*, lack of public confidence in the abil- ity of government policy to control inflation tends to create an *infla- tionary psychology*, which makes efforts to control inflation even more difficult. For example, the sellers of products and of resources may conclude that significant inflation will continue into the foresee- able future. Consequently, the spiral of higher product prices, as well

---

[15] For example, see Arthur M. Okun, "The Great Stagflation Swamp," *Challenge*, November–December, 1977, pp. 6–13, and Lerner, "Stagflation."

as higher wages and other factor costs, will accelerate, and this will lead to still more inflation. Furthermore, intensified efforts may be undertaken by businesses to acquire a larger inventory of nonlabor inputs and by consumers to acquire durable economic goods now instead of later, when it is feared their prices will be higher. This pushes prices up still further. The best way to reduce such an inflationary psychology appears to be to restore public confidence by applying effective and consistent federal government economic policies toward inflation, including an effective incomes policy.

Bottleneck inflation results from temporary resource shortages that occur in certain industries during periods of rapidly-expanding aggregate demand in a less than full-employment economy. The temporary input shortages tend to increase resource prices and, subsequently, the prices of the economic goods that the resources are used to produce. Fortunately, this is a temporary phenomenon and not a basic cause of inflation. However, once resource and product prices have increased, they may later be "somewhat sticky" on the downward side under imperfectly competitive market conditions, even though the shortages may have ended. Marginal improvement of bottleneck inflation can be expected to result from policies which increase resource mobility, including those that increase the level of information concerning resource availability.

Tax inflation can result to the extent that taxes are forward shifted into product and resource prices. Inflation from this source has not received much attention, but there have been recent signs of a growing interest in it. For example, in early 1978 Congress reconsidered the substantial social security payroll tax increase enacted in late 1977, partly on the basis that any shifting of the tax increase by employees through obtaining higher wages or by employers through charging higher product prices would be inflationary. It is important to note that broadbased, indirect taxes, such as the general retail sales tax and the value-added tax, are among the most likely to be forward shifted. As a result, one way to reduce price inflation may be to change the composition of the tax system toward a greater usage of direct taxes such as the personal income tax.

In summary, the inability of conventional fiscal (and monetary) policy to directly combat structural inflation points up the need to develop an effective incomes policy. Such a policy undoubtedly should be comprehensive in nature, since improvement can be expected to result from properly designed antitrust, manpower, and indirect wage and price instruments. In particular, the latter would seem to hold promise for reducing structural inflation and constraining the indexing problem through such techniques as the proposed tax-based incomes policy (TIP), which attacks the problem while respecting the inherent importance of the price mechanism in a market economy. Meanwhile, direct wage and price controls are justified only under severe emergency conditions. The attainment of a successful incomes policy directed toward stagflation will allow conventional fiscal and monetary policies to be applied more effectively to aggregate demand deficiencies or excesses without trading off between the twin evils of recession and inflation.

21

Aggregate fiscal policy norms

NORMS OR RULES OF FISCAL POLICY

It is customary to relate the instruments of aggregate fiscal policy discussed in the preceding chapter to specific norms or rules. The array of possible norms extends over a wide range. At one extreme is the *annually balanced budget norm,* while the *functional finance norm* is at the other extreme. Intermediate positions include the *cyclically balanced budget* and the *high-employment budget* rules.[1]

The annually balanced budget norm

Since the early days of the sovereign history of the United States, a strong preference has existed for an annually balanced federal government budget. In fact, the philosophy favoring an *annually balanced budget* has also been extended to the public sector as a whole, as is indicated by the various state government restrictions on unbalanced budgets and on spending by state and local governments. The belief

---

[1] The discussion of fiscal policy norms in this chapter necessarily includes frequent reference to *government debt,* since each of the important norms bears at least indirect implications for public sector debt. Government debt creation, for example, is a necessary corollary to a discussion of the annually balanced budget rule, because the failure to maintain budget balance by allowing expenditures to exceed revenue collection creates a condition of deficit spending which is likely to be financed through debt creation. Since government debt is the subject of the next chapter, it will be discussed in this chapter only to the extent necessary for a proper evaluation of the various fiscal policy norms.

that annually balanced government budgets are desirable per se is apparently based on the cultural notion that a balanced budget indicates fiscal responsibility for government just as it allegedly does for the household and business segments of the private sector. Yet, many households and businesses carry debt in a financially stable fashion. Hence, the long-established notion that *only* a balanced budget can be fiscally responsible, it would seem, does not apply to the private sector. Thus, a requirement of an annually balanced federal government budget, based on a private sector budget balance principle, may also be open to question. However, this important issue will be considered more closely in a later section of the chapter which discusses a proposed constitutional amendment to require an annually balanced federal budget.

The annually balanced budget principle was generally espoused by the classical economists and has been continued as a guideline for governmental fiscal behavior. Government debt, which results from government deficit budgets, had not existed on a widespread basis, of course, until the establishment of the monetary-exchange type of economy under capitalism and with it, classical economics.[2] The classical case for the annually balanced budget was based on the following arguments: (1) private sector economic development is reduced by the sale of government debt to the private sector since fewer capital funds are then available for the acquisition of private capital goods; (2) government deficit spending allows an expansion of the public sector relative to the private sector, in intersector resource allocation terms, and (3) deficit spending necessarily leads to inflation. However, considerable moderation of this antidebt and pro-balanced budget position occurred between the early days of classical economics and the early 20th century. Yet, significant opposition in economics to the annually balanced budget principle did not arrive until the emergence of Keynesian economics and of demand-side fiscal policy during the 1930s.

Franklin D. Roosevelt was elected president during the Great Depression in 1932 on a political platform which included an annually balanced budget plank. However, the effects of Keynesian economic analysis were beginning to be felt in the political and economic circles of the Western world, leading to the discretionary use of fiscal policy by the Roosevelt administration to pursue the economic stabilization objective. Since the advent of modern macroeconomics, most economists have accepted the legitimacy of the use of the federal government budget to promote the economic stabilization objective, though politicians have accepted it to a somewhat lesser extent. Nev-

---

[2] For an excellent discussion of the classical and neoclassical position on government debt, see Jesse Burkhead, "The Balanced Budget," *Quarterly Journal of Economics,* May 1954, pp. 191–216.

ertheless, a pronounced trend toward greater political acceptance of these fiscal tools has occurred during recent decades.[3]

The annually balanced budget fiscal rule may be unnecessarily restrictive in a mature democratic political economy. The fact that it may represent an unacceptable extreme on a continuum of fiscal benchmarks, however, does not suggest that it possesses no merit whatsoever. In a society which holds a preference for the market allocation of resources, the notion that the annually balanced budget norm exerts *control* over excesses by government, and thus over the relative expansion of the public sector, contains definite merit. Hence, some of the compromise benchmarks we will discuss accept certain aspects of the control function of the annually balanced budget, though such acceptance remains secondary to the acceptance of deliberate budget manipulation as a fiscal tool.

Even if the annually balanced budget rule were a totally acceptable fiscal norm, certain institutional impediments exist which would tend to prevent its realization, unless mandated by the Constitution or by legislation. For example, the lobbying influence of pressure groups or political-action committees (PAC's), which is encouraged by American political institutions, leads to a bias in favor of deficit budgets. This occurs because lobbies attempt to improve the economic status of those whom they represent by either increasing the flow of government expenditures to, or decreasing the tax payments of, these constituents, or both. Obviously, higher governmental spending and lower taxes result in a movement toward deficit spending and resultant debt. The individual pressure groups may separately decry deficit spending, but their collective actions frequently add up to this result. Moreover, politicians campaigning for office often contribute to deficit budgeting by promising to provide benefits from government spending while holding the line on taxes.

The functional finance norm

The complete antithesis to the annually balanced budget norm is the *functional finance* fiscal rule. While the balanced budget norm stresses the importance of *control* over governmental fiscal activities, the functional finance norm advocates that the government budget be used to promote macroeconomic *goals*, without regard to budget balance. Relatedly, it is less concerned than the annually balanced budget with allocational and distributional considerations and more concerned with the stabilization objective.

The functional finance concept was developed rather early in the

---

[3] For an excellent description and analysis of the evolutionary acceptance of stabilization policy (both fiscal and monetary) in the United States, see Herbert Stein, *The Fiscal Revolution in America* (Chicago: University of Chicago Press, 1969).

Keynesian era and represents an extreme application of Keynesian economic theory. The most famous statement of the functional finance norm was provided by Abba Lerner in 1943.[4] Lerner observed that World War II had proven the ability of government fiscal action to maintain full employment. The chronic depression conditions that preceded World War II had been relieved as defense-supported aggregate demand expanded. Lerner thus argued that the essential idea of government economic policy—which involves governmental spending, taxing, borrowing, the repayment of loans, the issue of new money, and the withdrawal of money from circulation—should be undertaken with the effects of these actions on the national economy in mind. Attachment to any established fiscal doctrine, such as the annually balanced budget rule, should not receive priority consideration. The principle of judging fiscal measures by the way they work or function in the economy is called *functional finance.*[5]

The first law (governmental responsibility) of functional finance, according to Lerner, is that the government budget should be directed toward the achievement of full employment and stable prices. It should *not* concern itself with whether tax receipts and governmental expenditures are balanced or unbalanced. In other words, tax collections need not equal the level of government spending, as advocated by the annually balanced budget norm, and taxes need to be imposed only to prevent inflation. The second law of functional finance states that the government should incur debt by borrowing money from the private sector *only* if it is desirable that the private sector have less money to spend and more government bonds to hold. This would be a desirable goal if, in the absence of debt, the rate of interest were too low, thus inducing an inflationary excess of private investment. Third, functional finance would prescribe that any excess of governmental money outlays over the money revenues accruing to government, which cannot be met out of private money hoards for the purchase of government debt, should be met by the printing of new money. Conversely, any excess of governmental revenues over outlays can be either destroyed or used to replenish private sector money hoards. In effect, the printing, hoarding, or destruction of money should be conducted as required for the achievement of full employment and price stability.

Comparison of the annual balanced budget and functional finance norms

Although the functional finance fiscal norm is extreme in its complete noncommitment to budgetary control, thus ignoring intersector

---

[4] Abba P. Lerner, "Functional Finance and the Federal Debt," *Social Research,* February 1943, pp. 38–51.

[5] Ibid., p. 39.

resource allocation considerations, it contributes importantly to the recognition of the fact that government budgetary action is capable of promoting macroeconomic goals in a market-oriented economy. Hence, just as *control* generally should be recognized as a desirable element of the annually balanced budget rule, so also should the ability of fiscal policy to help attain employment, price level, economic growth, and balance-of-payments *goals* be recognized as an advantage of the functional finance norm. A rational fiscal norm thus should contain some reference to both control and macroeconomic objectives.

Undoubtedly, undue emphasis on the intersector allocational and control goal can seriously impede attainment of the stabilization objective, and vice versa. The annually balanced budget rule, for example, would require such policies as a reduction in government spending and/or an increase in tax revenue when national income declines, and an increase in government spending and/or a decrease in tax revenue when national income expands. This is so because tax revenue (except for a lump-sum tax) is a positive function of the level of income. Thus, assume a federal government budget "balanced" with $700 billion in both expenditures and tax revenue. Then, a decline in national income causes tax revenue to decline, say by $100 billion, with the result being a *deficit* budget of 100 billion ($700 billion in expenditures minus $600 billion in taxes). This deficit would tend to be expansionary—a desirable effect in times of recession and declining national income. However, adherence to a balanced budget rule would necessitate the elimination of the expansionary deficit by means of either reduced spending or increased tax revenue, each of which would tend to neutralize the expansion. Moreover, destabilizing effects of an opposite nature would occur at times of expanding national income if the federal budget is to remain balanced. For example, even though the contractionary effects of a federal budget surplus may be desirable in terms of the stabilization goal, an effort to balance the budget via an expenditure increase or tax reduction would tend to neutralize these contractionary effects.

Furthermore, Musgrave observes that even though no conflict exists at the "normative level" between the allocation and stabilization functions of budget policy, since the allocation budget is planned ideally to meet individual preferences on the basis of a full-employment income, "fiscal politics" may create a conflict between the allocation and stabilization objectives.[6] If a deficit budget is called for by the stabilization objective, for example, in order to promote the expansion of employment and income, some people may erroneously conclude that the extension of additional public (and quasi-public)

---

[6] Richard A. Musgrave, *The Theory of Public Finance* (New York: McGraw-Hill, 1959), p. 522.

goods is virtually costless which, in turn, can lead to an overallocation of public (and quasi-public) goods and a resulting intersector allocation distortion. Taxes thus would not be serving their function as an index of opportunity cost.[7]

Thus, an adequate fiscal norm should attempt to meet, to some degree, *all major fiscal objectives.* It should not totally ignore one goal for the attainment of another unless the preferences of the community clearly dictate such action. Relatedly, a sound fiscal rule should contain some recognition of both the *control* and *goal-achievement* objectives.

The intermediate fiscal rules to be discussed here represent compromise positions between the annually balanced budget and the functional finance extremes. Each intermediate norm recognizes both the importance of budgetary control for allocation purposes as well as the ability of governmental budgetary behavior to pursue the various goals of aggregate economic performance through rational fiscal policy.

The cyclically balanced budget norm

One intermediate approach to fiscal rationality—the *cyclically balanced budget* norm—advocates budget balance over the course of a complete business cycle rather than in a particular fiscal year. Thus, tax receipts and expenditures would be equal over the course of the cycle—whether measured from peak to peak or from trough to trough. Figure 21-1 displays the cyclically balanced budget fiscal rule. The policy prescription under this norm calls for the central government, primarily through discretionary fiscal policies, to establish a surplus budget at the time of a cyclical peak or prosperity in order to restrain the pressures of demand (monetary) inflation, and to establish a deficit budget to expand the economy under conditions of cyclical recession or depression. Ideally, the surpluses and deficits would offset each other in equal magnitude over the period of the cycle, thus providing budget balance over the cycle rather than for a single fiscal year. It is argued that both the aggregate performance and control goals would be well served by this compromise rule.

Many practical difficulties, however, would arise in the application of the cyclically balanced budget norm. These obstacles include, first, the unlikelihood that a given cycle will be symmetrical, in the sense that the size of the surplus necessary to restrain demand inflation will be equal to the size of the deficit necessary to reverse a downturn and stimulate expansion. Only by great coincidence would an exact cyclical balance occur. There is no built-in mechanism to assure a

---

[7] Ibid.

FIGURE 21-1   Cyclically balanced budget fiscal norm

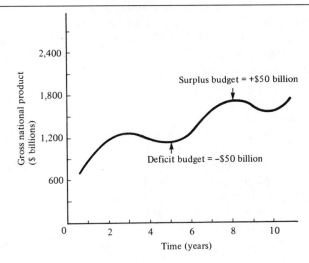

symmetrical cycle. In addition, the peak of a cycle need not be inflationary, in demand inflation terms. In fact, the peak may not even provide full-employment output, in which case a surplus budget would only worsen the conditions of recession.

A further drawback of the cyclically balanced budget rule rests on the institutional fact, observed earlier, that in a democratic political structure, such as that of the United States, lobby or pressure groups exert considerable influence over legislation. As a result, there exists a built-in bias in favor of deficit budgets and opposed to surplus budgets, since the various lobbies ordinarily support higher spending and lower taxation policies for those whom they represent. Thus, even if the cycle were symmetrical, the institutional impediment to surplus budgets would make it very difficult to apply the norm precisely. In general terms, however, the cyclically balanced budget benchmark contains some merit in that it accepts the best element of functional finance, namely, recognition of the fact that deliberate fiscal policy can favorably affect macroeconomic goals and; yet, it still retains consideration of budgetary control in reference to the intersector resource allocation goal.

The high-employment budget norm

The compromise fiscal norm represented by the cyclically balanced budget has received only modest acceptance. An alternative intermediate approach exists in the form of the *high-employment budget* benchmark. Initial support for this fiscal norm came from the Committee for Economic Development (CED) in 1947.[8] The CED proposal, which was conceptually structured in terms of the former federal consolidated cash budget concept, recommended that federal tax rates be set not only to balance the budget, but also to provide a modest surplus for debt retirement purposes at agreed upon high-employment and national income levels.[9] Once these rates are set, they should be left alone as automatic stabilizers, unless there is some major change in national economic conditions. It should be pointed out, however, that inflation of a structural form may still exist at full employment, and this inflation cannot be directly affected by automatic changes in aggregate demand.

The high-employment budget rule, as noted above, is based on the use of *automatic fiscal stabilizers*, and thus avoids *discretionary* changes in tax rates except under conditions of major national emergency. In this regard, the high-employment budget norm is significantly different from the functional finance and the cyclically balanced budget rules, which allow the use of discretionary fiscal actions. Since the major components of the federal tax base (income, payroll, and excise taxes) are functionally related to the level of national income, tax collections tend to rise and fall in positive relation to changes in the level of national income. This occurs automatically and does not depend on discretionary changes in tax rate or bases. Thus, rising national income will be accompanied by increasing tax revenue and by a declining volume of unemployment compensation payments. Conversely, declining national income will be accompanied by declining tax revenue and by an increased volume of unemployment compensation payments. Moreover, the federal personal and corporation income taxes are characterized by significantly elastic *income elasticities*, which means that revenue yields change at a more rapid rate than do changes in the level of national income. Thus, built-in features in the budget work in a rational countercyclical manner, since aggregate demand is automatically restrained during expansion and reinforced during a downturn in the national economy.

The stabilizing budget principle of the CED emphasizes automatic tax and expenditure responses because, it is argued, such devices do not depend heavily on an "impossible accuracy" in forecasting economic fluctuations. Moreover, it is argued that automatic stabilizers do not require "impossible speed" in making tax and expenditure decisions in the legislature and then implementing them into meaningful fiscal action through the executive branch. The CED enumer-

---

[8] See Committee for Economic Development, *Taxes and the Budget: A Program for Prosperity in a Free Society*, (New York: 1947.)

[9] The former federal consolidated cash budget included *all* federal revenues and expenditures, inclusive of both general and earmarked (trust fund) transactions and, in this regard, was similar to the federal unified budget in current use.

ates three exceptions to its nondiscretionary approach, that is, three conditions requiring discretionary fiscal actions.[10] These are:

1. A growing population and increasing productivity may increase national income and labor employment levels, and relatedly, *increase tax capacity.* However, the discretionary readjustments of tax rates made necessary by such long-term growth in the tax base would need to be made only at reasonable intervals, say, five years apart.

2. Occasionally, an urgent need may arise, as in a war, for *extraordinary expenditures,* large in amount but temporary in nature. Often, it would be undesirable under such circumstances to raise tax rates sharply in order to finance the expenditures on a current basis, and then reduce tax rates sharply when the expenditures cease. Under such circumstances, the expenditures can be met through incremental taxes collected over a period of time longer than one year, instead of marginally balancing the additional tax collections and expenditures in a single fiscal year.

3. If the recommendations of the CED are combined with appropriate measures in other fields, it is believed that economic fluctuations can be confined to "moderate departures" from a high performance level. Yet, in the case of *severe depression or inflation,* discretionary fiscal action should be undertaken. Under such extreme emergencies, it is suggested that the best approach is to change tax rates.

Walter Heller doubts that a genuinely automatic fiscal mechanism can exist, because any such mechanism would require that its very establishment, continuance, modification, and abolishment be accomplished through "discretionary decisions."[11] Under the CED proposal, of course, discretion is allowed to determine when a recession or inflation is severe enough to merit deliberate budgetary action. In any event, while a case can be established for the use of automatic fiscal stabilizers as part of a comprehensive set of fiscal tools, it would be foolish to conclude that "non-automatic policy is uncertainly managed by fallible men while an automatic fiscal policy is divinely guided by infallible rules."[12]

THE PROPOSED CONSTITUTIONAL AMENDMENT TO BALANCE THE FEDERAL GOVERNMENT BUDGET

Recent years have witnessed a major effort to revise the federal Constitution to require an *annually balanced federal budget.* Still another, less-stringent but similarly motivated, attempt is being made

---

[10] Committee for Economic Development. *Taxes and the Budget.*

[11] Walter W. Heller, "CED's Stabilizing Budget Policy after 10 Years," *American Economic Review,* September 1957, pp. 634–51.

[12] Ibid., p. 640.

to restrict the level of federal expenditures to a specified proportion of GNP. The latter approach, of course, would directly limit only federal expenditures, while the first approach would directly restrain both revenues and expenditures.[13] Such proposed federal budgetary restrictions normally make exception for conditions of war and, in addition, would allow an override of the restriction rule by a qualified majority vote of Congress—such as three fifths.

A summary of major arguments both for and against a constitutionally imposed balanced-budget requirement, or similar federal fiscal restriction, will now be presented:[14]

Arguments for a balanced budget amendment

1. *Deficit spending exerts negative effects on the economy.* It is the major cause of inflation and contributes to a large federal debt which crowds out private sector access to investment funds.

2. *Keynesian demand-side fiscal instruments constitute an excessive use of discretionary economic policy.* Automatic monetary instruments and other less distortive instruments are capable of stabilizing the economy. Moreover, if emergencies require discretionary fiscal activities, the "escape clauses" of the proposed amendment would make this possible.

3. *The amendment would check the long-term growth of the federal government within the economy.* In so doing, the historical private sector orientation of American society would be preserved.

4. *Political pressures will prevent Congress, on a year-to-year basis, from taking the necessary steps to attain annually balanced budgets.* Spending increases and tax decreases are politically popular, and elected officials seeking reelection will thus be biased toward deficit budgets unless required by law to balance the budget.

Arguments against a balanced budget amendment

1. *The amendment will not eliminate inflation, but instead will increase recession and unemployment.* Inflation is caused by a number of forces and not primarily by federal deficits. Meanwhile, the termination of flexible fiscal policy would obstruct the discretionary ability to increase aggregate demand in order to combat recession.

---

[13] Of course, as some federal-budget constraint advocates have done, it is possible to merge the balanced-budget and ratio-of-GNP proposals into a single, more complicated, proposal.

[14] See *Proposed Constitutional Amendment to Balance the Federal Budget,* hearings before the Committee on the Constitution of the Committee on the Judiciary, U.S. Senate, 96th cong., 1st sess., March–November, 1979, Statement by the Association of the Bar of the City of New York, pp. 239–52.

Moreover, it would invalidate the performance of automatic fiscal stabilizers during cyclical changes in the economy.

2. *A balanced-budget amendment is unenforceable.* Congress could transfer numerous programs into the unofficial, off-budget category, thus circumventing the intent of the amendment.

3. *A mandatory balanced budget could cause major economic and social distortions.* For example, programs least represented by political lobbying, even though possibly with great merit, would tend to lose out as the inevitable dogfight for limited funds occurs.

4. *The balanced-budget amendment will prevent the appropriate responses to economic and other crises.* An economic crisis, for example, may develop to major proportions before the necessary qualified majority of Congress can be mustered to approve corrective fiscal policies.

THE NEED FOR A COMPREHENSIVE AND
FLEXIBLE ECONOMIC POLICY

The most effective and rational economic policy approach for the attainment of macroeconomic stabilization objectives, as well as for achieving the microeconomic goals of allocation and distribution, is the one that incorporates an *eclectic* combination of the best elements of the various specific norms and instruments of economic policy.[15] Both the control objective of the annually balanced budget rule and the goal objective of the functional finance norm should be included in such an approach, with the result being that an intermediate norm is to be preferred. In addition, the combination of both discretionary and automatic economic stabilizers, along with the coordinated use of both fiscal and monetary policy, is desirable. Moreover, both demand-side and supply-side instruments can be simultaneously used in appropriate combination. Finally, an effective incomes policy is required to deal with structural inflation. These points will now be discussed in greater detail.

The best elements of the functional finance and annually balanced budget norms should be combined to help form an acceptable intermediate fiscal norm. An effort is made in this regard by the *cyclically balanced budget* benchmark. This rule recognizes the control (discipline) function of the budget, while at the same time acknowledging the ability of the budget to promote macroeconomic goals. Nevertheless, it is not a refined approach and is subject to the rather severe

---

[15] See the arguments in behalf of an *eclectic* approach for macroeconomic policy in Jan Tinbergen, *On the Theory of Economic Policy* (Amsterdam: North Holland, 1952); Bent Hansen, *The Economic Theory of Fiscal Policy* (London: Allen & Unwin, 1958), and Leif Johansen, *Public Economics* (Amsterdam: North Holland; Chicago: Rand McNally, 1965).

limitations discussed earlier in the chapter. Meanwhile, the *high-employment budget rule* which, though it overemphasizes the relative importance of automatic stabilizers, also importantly emphasizes the obvious need to rationalize the impact of the public sector on aggregate economic performance. Moreover, it is not subject to the inherent weaknesses of the cyclically balanced budget approach, such as the unlikelihood of matching upswing and downswing phases of the business cycle with resulting matching surpluses and deficits over the period of a cycle. By contrast, the high-employment budget norm has some capability of helping to achieve a budget balance (or small surplus) at a full employment, no-demand inflation, equilibrium. Unfortunately, however, structural inflation may still persist at this equilibrium point.

The high-employment budget approach, in the form proposed by the Committee for Economic Development, suggests that automatic rather than discretionary fiscal stabilizers be emphasized to achieve stabilization objectives. Automatic stabilization efforts alone, however, though extremely valuable, do not constitute a complete fiscal policy approach. There is no reason, given adequate sophistication in data collection and in forecasting, why discretionary fiscal efforts should not be used in an intelligent and rational manner, along with the automatic stabilizers.

A comprehensive and rational economic policy approach also should include the coordinated use of both *fiscal* and *monetary* instruments which, of course, may interact with each other. For example, an expansionary fiscal policy may be partly neutralized by an increase in the rate of interest which may accompany the economic expansion. The need for a *coordinated fiscal and monetary approach* is also indicated by the various stabilization policy lags. The *recognition lag*, which relates to the detection of undesirable unemployment and inflationary trends, depends on the quality of the data and the analytical quality of their interpretation for forecasting. Since fiscal and monetary policy equally face the economic forecasting problem, no preference between fiscal and monetary policy may be detected on this point. However, when we consider the *administrative lag,* which refers to the time taken to make policy decisions after the need for action is detected, discretionary monetary policy carries the advantage over discretionary fiscal policy in its ability to make decisions more quickly, due to the semi-autonomous nature of the Federal Reserve System. Fiscal policy holds the advantage when the *operation lag* is considered, in terms of the length of time between policy decisions and their actual impact on the economy. This is true because fiscal policy can deal directly with resource usage and income flows, while monetary policy affects these flows through the indirect manner in which it influences the structure of liquidity and assets in the economy. In the monetary policy case, the operational impact on the economy tends to be spread over a longer period of time.

Optimal macroeconomic policy should also be flexible enough to include both *demand-side* and *supply-side* components, though one or the other may receive the primary thrust of the policymaking effort. For example, personal income tax rate reductions at the lower- and middle-income levels may be used to spur aggregate demand while, at the same time, selective supply-side instruments may be used to stimulate investment and an expansion in aggregate supply.

Finally, the serious problem of stagflation cannot be averted unless an effective *incomes policy* is in use. In this regard, several approaches (as suggested in the preceding chapter) may be considered. These include antitrust, manpower, and indirect wage-price policy, but especially the latter. The recently proposed tax-based incomes-policy (TIP) instrument would appear to possess considerable merit as an indirect antistagflation technique. In any event, once an effective incomes approach is established, conventional fiscal (and monetary) policies can attack the twin evils of recession and inflation more successfully, while averting the Phillips curve paradox. In conclusion, the desirability of a *comprehensive and flexible economic policy approach* directed toward the attainment of the various macroeconomic goals in an eclectic fashion should be recognized.

22

Public sector debt

Public sector debt is interrelated with the basic governmental fiscal flows of taxation and spending. If the volume of governmental expenditures exceeds the volume of tax and other (nontax) revenues, a deficit budget exists. Such a deficit budget provides the fundamental precondition for debt creation. Yet, it is not synonymous with debt creation. Instead, debt creation should be viewed as one of several alternative financial arrangements for the provision of public and quasi-public goods by government. If deficit financing were not used, for example, these economic goods could have been financed through other techniques. That is, taxes, user charges, or administrative revenues could have been collected in lieu of the sale of debt. Having once been created, debt requires interest payments to maintain the debt, and refinancing operations if the debt is to continue beyond the maturities of existing securities.

AN ECONOMIC ANALYSIS OF PUBLIC SECTOR DEBT

Government debt misconceptions

Probably no economic concept is subject to more misunderstanding regarding its true nature than government debt. There are several sources of such confusion. One is the false parallel often drawn between government debt and private debt.[1] However, certain important dissimilarities exist between public sector and private sector debt. These differences are at greatest variance when federal government debt is compared to private consumer debt, as will be demonstrated.

A second area of debt misconception is the confusion between the fiscal flows of taxing and spending and the separate, though related, phenomenon of government debt. Taxing and spending, of course, are the nucleus of the fiscal or budgetary process. Debt is merely a means of meeting a particular budgetary situation, namely, a deficit budget caused by the excess of government spending over receipts. The fiscal flows of taxation and spending as such, as well as debt creation and retirement, alike may exert effects on the basic economic functions of allocation, distribution, and stabilization. It is important to remember, however, that fiscal flows, on the one hand, and debt, on the other, may exert such influences in somewhat different ways because they are essentially different phenomena.

A third source of confusion regarding public sector debt is the attempt to solve the optimal intersector resource allocation (social balance) issue by means of a debt-oriented analogy. Government debt, whether large or small or nonexistent, has no *direct* implication for the proper size of the public sector relative to the size of the private sector. Conceivably, government could allocate most of society's resources and still have no interest-bearing debt. Or, the public sector could allocate a relatively small percentage of total productive resources and still build up a sizable debt over time.

Internal versus external debt

The need to distinguish between public and private debt leads also to a necessary distinction between internally and externally held debt. *Internal debt* may be defined as a situation whereby the borrowing unit acquires the money from itself (lends to itself). *External debt* is a condition whereby the borrowing unit acquires money from some other lending unit or units. The borrowing unit may be a unit of government, a business, or a consumer. Size of political jurisdiction essentially determines the internal borrowing limit of government debt, while market conditions determine the internal borrowing limit of private debt. Government borrowing may be termed *public borrowing,* while business and consumer borrowing may be termed *private borrowing.*

---

[1] Public and private debt, of course, are similar in the generic sense that each involves a creditor-debtor relationship with corresponding debt instruments, such as securities and promissory notes.

The only possible case of *purely internal debt* within a nation exists in the category of public borrowing, and then only for a *central* or *national* government. However, this is a necessary, but not a sufficient, condition of purely internal debt. In other words, only a central government debt can be purely internal, but it *need not* be an internal debt. Our entire federal debt, or part thereof, could be owed to foreigners though, actually, only a relatively small portion of it is. If the gross federal debt of the United States were financed totally by the sale of securities to *American* governmental agencies, financial institutions, businesses, and individuals, the debt would be a purely internal debt. No claims against the borrowing unit would arise from outside the borrowing unit, that is, from outside the political boundaries of the United States. The United States as a sovereign nation, and composed of the people within the nation, would be borrowing money from itself. The lenders would all be part of the borrowing unit. There would be no outside or external claim against American productive resources or against the income and output these resources create. In reality, most federal debt in the United States is held internally. By legislation, the nation could have forbidden the sale of *any* debt outside the political boundaries of the United States, in which case the debt could have been 100 percent internal.

Since only the federal government possesses the power to issue money, it has a unique ability to maintain or repay debt. State and local governments do not possess the power to issue money, but they do share with the federal government the power to compel payment of taxes for purposes of maintaining or repaying debt. In addition, all three levels of government often acquire offsetting productive assets when they incur debt. Hence, the public sector has important fiscal advantages as compared to the private sector in borrowing. The private sector cannot issue money nor collect taxes. Moreover, private borrowing of a consumptive sort does not ordinarily result in offsetting assets of a real productive nature. Thus, public borrowing, particularly by the federal government, tends to create a debt which is not only more internal in nature than that resulting from private borrowing, but which also is easier to carry, since additional financing devices and offsetting productive assets are more readily available.[2] Table 22-1 summarizes the above points.

Despite the fact that a central government is in the best relative position to carry a debt burden, it can be argued that an externally held central government debt is not necessarily more burdensome on

---

[2] However, the relatively greater ability of government, and especially national government, to carry debt, as contrasted to the private sector, might lead to intersector resource allocation (social balance) problems in terms of "too large" a public sector.

TABLE 22–1   **Continuum of internal and external debt categories and offsets to debt burdens**

Type of debt	Categories of borrowing	Offsets to debt burdens
Pure internal ↑	Public: by federal, state, and/or local governments	1. Money issuance power 2. Tax power 3. Many expenditures provide offsetting productive assets
	Private: by business and/or consumer	1. No money issuance power 2. No tax power 3. Expenditures may be for consumptive goods
Pure external		

Note: Direction of arrow indicates increasing offsets to debt burdens.

the people of the society than one which is internally held.[3] This would outwardly seem to be the case, since the taxes which pay interest to the foreign holders of the debt must be withdrawn from the private sector of the domestic economy. However, the fact is that the tax payments collected to make interest payments on central government debt held by foreigners may *not* constitute a greater burden than those collected for payments on debt held by domestic citizens. The reason is that the national income of the society tends to be larger in the external debt case, since resources do *not* need to be withdrawn from the private sector of the domestic economy when the debt is initially issued, but instead can be acquired in international markets. Hence, the greater amount of resources available to the society when the debt is externally financed should yield a greater national income. From this greater national income, the taxes can be collected which provide the source of the interest payments made to the foreign holders of the debt. Thus, the debt burden would not necessarily be greater when the debt is externally held than it would be if the debt were internally held. This does not suggest, of course, that an external central government debt does not incur greater institutional difficulties than one which is internally held. These greater institutional difficulties for external debt arise from the fact that the prevailing system for processing international payments is more complex and less perfect than the typical domestic payments mechanism, especially in mature economies.

---

[3] See James M. Buchanan, *Public Principles of Public Debt* (Homewood, Ill.: Richard D. Irwin, 1958) for the genesis of this argument.

Real versus financial debt burdens and symmetrical versus asymmetrical debt burden distribution

Overall budgetary incidence was considered in Chapter 16. Meanwhile, the distributional implications of public sector debt as such are considered in this chapter. Thus, a distinction between real and financial debt burdens, and between symmetrical and asymmetrical debt burden distribution, will now be made. The burden of debt may be viewed in *real terms* when the nonusage of the private sector "resources foregone" because of the debt-creating activity is emphasized, and in *financial terms* when the monetary flows of interest payments and the taxes to finance these payments are considered. Furthermore, both the real and the financial aspects of debt burden are concerned with the distinction between symmetrical and asymmetrical debt burden distribution.

A financial debt burden is *symmetrical* when the debt instruments are held equally by the various spending units of the population, who likewise pay equal amounts of taxes to finance the debt. In this instance, no redistribution of money income results from the existence of the debt. The symmetrical distribution of the debt burden takes on a real burden connotation when the actual economic goods financed with the debt are divided among the population in proportion to the payment of taxes to service the debt. Under these circumstances, no real income redistribution occurs. In contrast, an *asymmetrical* debt burden is characterized either by a disproportionate distribution between tax and interest payments, in financial burden terms, or by a lack of proportionality between the consumption of debt-financed economic goods and the payment of taxes to finance the debt which paid for these goods, in the real-burden sense. In either case, a redistribution of income would take place. Thus, it can be said that debt burden symmetry is a case of *distributional neutrality,* and debt burden asymmetry involves *distributional nonneutrality,* due to its income redistribution effects among the population.

Some of the distinctions between real and financial burdens and between symmetrical and asymmetrical debt burden distribution are indicated in the following example:

Suppose that the present federal debt is $1 trillion.[4] Suppose also that the securities held against this debt are divided equally among some 100 million family (or unmarried adult) spending units in the United States. Thus, every spending unit would possess $10,000 in treasury securities. If the annual interest paid on the securities is 8 percent, each spending unit will receive $800 ($10,000 $\times$ 0.08) in annual interest payments. The federal government could tax every

---

[4] In fact, the actual federal debt at the end of 1981 was $1.05 trillion.

spending unit $800, and then turn around and pay each spending unit $800 in interest. Since the debt is held and tax-financed in a *symmetrical* manner, no income redistribution effects of the *financial burden* variety occur. The only possible redistributive effects that would result would be in a *real-burden sense,* from a disproportionate (unequal) relationship between the payment of taxes to service the debt and the receipt of the goods provided with the debt-created funds.

Intergeneration transfer of debt burdens

A question arises as to whether a government debt burden is borne by the generation which creates the debt, or instead is passed on to future generations. The classic economic viewpoint regarding the *intergeneration transfer of debt burdens,* which was later adapted to Keynesian economic theory, has been challenged by James Buchanan and numerous other scholars.[5] The orthodox position holds that a debt burden rests largely with the present generation which creates the debt, and that it may be shifted to future generations *only* if the present generation reduces its rate of saving as a result of the debt creation activity. This argument, which descends from David Ricardo, was stated brilliantly by A. C. Pigou and later adapted to Keynesian terms by economists such as Abba Lerner and Paul Samuelson.[6]

The traditional argument thus suggests that the present generation will bear the burden of government debt, *except* in the following case: Reduced saving by the present debt-creating generation causes future generations to inherit a smaller amount of real productive capital (that is, plant and equipment), with consequent reduced income for the future generations. Present saving may be reduced when debt instead of tax financing is used, because tax obligations are seen *clearly* by the present generation, while debt obligations involve future rather than present tax payments (as the debt is financed and repaid) which are less certain in the eyes of the present taxpayers. Hence, the purchasers of bonds may pay for them more out of saving than out of

---

[5] Buchanan, *Public Principles of Public Debt;* William G. Bowen, Richard G. Davis, and David H. Kopf, "The Public Debt: A Burden on Future Generations?" *American Economic Review,* September 1960, pp. 701-6; Richard A. Musgrave, *The Theory of Public Finance* (New York: McGraw-Hill, 1959), chap. 23; Franco Modigliani, "Long-Run Implications of Alternative Fiscal Policies and the Burden of the National Debt," *Economic Journal,* December 1961, pp. 730-55.

[6] Abba P. Lerner, "The Burden of the National Debt," in *Income, Employment and Public Policy* (New York: W. W. Norton, 1948), pp. 255-75, and review of James A. Buchanan's *Public Principles of Public Debt* in the *Journal of Political Economy,* April 1959, pp. 203-06, and "The Burden of Debt," *Review of Economics and Statistics,* May 1961, pp. 139-41; Paul A. Samuelson, *Economics* (New York: McGraw-Hill, 1964), chap. 18.

consumption, because they consider their net wealth position better under loan finance than under tax finance. As a result, the reduced level of saving causes less real productive capital to be inherited by future generations, and thus a real burden in the form of a reduced output potential is passed along through this indirect means to future generations.

Buchanan supplied the opening volley against the traditional position in 1958 in his *Public Principles of Public Debt.*[7] He denies that the present generation bears the burden of public debt, since individuals who purchase government securities do so on a voluntary basis. These individuals acquire present assets in lieu of present consumption—with future earnings from these assets and repayment of the assets in mind. In other words, they do not realize a present burden because they are merely postponing present consumption to the future, when they will redeem their securities. Meanwhile, these individuals earn interest compensation on their bonds.

Since the government securities are purchased voluntarily, those in the present generation who purchase them do not consider themselves to be undergoing a sacrifice, whereas those in future generations who pay the interest and redeem the bonds do experience a sacrifice through compulsory tax payments. It is contended that the taxes are an actual net burden to future generations, since they would not have been collected from the future generations if the present generation had met its expenditures through taxation, while the bondholders of the present generation would have received income anyway from whatever other assets in which they might have invested their savings.

Though the Buchanan argument carries a certain real-burden connotation, its primary emphasis is on burden in a *financial* (monetary) sense. It is asserted, for example, that the monetary contributions of taxes by subsequent generations to maintain or retire the debt created by an earlier generation constitute an intertemporal burden transfer to the later generations, because the generation which created the debt voluntarily purchased the financial assets (securities). Thus, in a market or exclusion principle sense, these purchases were freely chosen and were based on a time preference financial decision for present earnings and for future consumption. Also, the Buchanan approach focuses on the *disaggregation* of the burden among individuals instead of on the aggregate or total debt burden of the society.

As E. J. Mishan points out, a basic weakness in many of the dissenting arguments is the failure to consider that the gross debt burden may be offset by secondary effects in the form of the future returns derived

---

[7] Buchanan, *Public Principles of Public Debt.*

from the present public expenditures.[8] Relatedly, the failure of inter-generation debt burden analysis to consider as important the aggregate of both public and private sector investment and their returns is said to be a defect which could mislead the general public and government policymakers.[9] This matter can be looked on as a failure of intergeneration debt-burden discussants to distinguish adequately between the *primary* and *secondary results* of debt and, indeed, to define *debt burden* as distinct from *debt effect*.

Earlier in this chapter, real burden was distinguished from financial burden. The former was said to relate to the real productive resources foregone in terms of consumer and capital goods, and the latter to the monetary arrangement whereby government debt is financed through tax revenues. In either context, it was observed that redistributional effects may occur. Significantly, many effects of debt financing, as contrasted to tax financing, bear on the nature of the real and financial burdens of debt. For example, changes in consumption-saving patterns, capital formation, inheritance patterns, net worth positions, the types of governmental expenditures which are financed with the debt, and the like, essentially are effects which, through market adjustments, help to determine the ultimate real and financial burdens.

Closely related to the desirability of some distinction (though possibly rough) between the terms *burden* and *effect* is the need to distinguish primary from secondary results. Essentially, *primary results* refer to *burdens*—real and financial—and *secondary results* refer to the *effects* of debt financing which will influence the nature of the burdens. Although the literature on debt does not make this precise distinction, the terms *primary burden* and *secondary effect* will be applied here.

Seemingly, the orthodox debt position regarding intergeneration transfers has largely withstood the arguments which have been made against it. The dissenting arguments essentially consist of special cases involving specialized assumptions and definitions. Buchanan,[10] for example, stresses freedom of choice for the individual and, in so doing, tends to define burden as an individual burden instead of an aggregate societal burden. The Bowen-Davis-Kopf[11] and Musgrave[12] approaches involve special, somewhat unrealistic assumptions re-

---

[8] E. J. Mishan, "How to Make a Burden of the Public Debt," *Journal of Political Economy,* December 1963, pp. 537–42.

[9] Ibid., pp. 540–42.

[10] Buchanan, *Public Principles of Public Debt.*

[11] Bowen, Davis, and Kopf, "The Public Debt: A Burden on Future Generations?"

[12] Musgrave, *The Theory of Public Finance,* chap. 23.

garding inheritance. All of these dissenting arguments are logically consistent. However, in an overall sense, they do not appear to be comprehensive enough, nor realistic enough in terms of their assumptions, to repudiate the traditional analysis.

In retrospect, the present generation does tend to bear the *direct, real-resource* burden of debt-financed expenditures, but the secondary effects may well allow some *indirect* transference of the *real* burden through reduced capital stock, inefficient government investment, and the like. However, it is unlikely that any significant *net real burden* will be transferred under these circumstances, because many government expenditures are for public and quasi-public goods which contain important benefits which accrue to future generations. Thus, even though the intergenerational transfer of the *financial burden* of debt may occur, the later generations are likely to be consuming some of the *real benefits* from earlier, debt-financed governmental investments. Failure to use a comprehensive approach to intergenerational debt equity, that is, failure to fully consider important secondary effects, including the social returns from public and quasi-public goods to later generations, has been a weakness in contemporary debt analysis. Thus, the dissenters to the orthodox approach, though increasing the sophistication of the intergenerational debt burden discussion as well as forcing its proponents to state their position more precisely, have not contributed a superior approach.

PUBLIC SECTOR DEBT IN THE UNITED STATES

Federal, state, and local debt data and trends

Table 22-2 presents 20th-century debt data and trends for all three levels of American government. First, absolute debt as well as per capital debt are presented in current dollars for each level of government. Then, the percentage distribution of debt between the federal, state, and local components of the public sector is provided. The table clearly demonstrates the enormous growth of absolute public sector debt, in current dollar terms, for all levels of government during this century.

Although the per-capita government-debt burden has also risen during this century, it has not risen as rapidly as absolute government debt because of population growth during the century. For example, column 9 shows that total public sector per capita debt was $42 in 1902 and $5,584 per person in 1980, or nearly 133 times greater in the latter year. However, during this same period, total public sector debt in absolute terms increased from approximately $3.3 billion to over $1.24 trillion (column 5), which is nearly 379 times greater in the latter year. Meanwhile, the general ability of government to carry a greater

TABLE 22-2   Gross debt,* per capita debt, and percentage distribution of debt for federal, state, and local governments, selected years, 1902–1980

(1)	(2)	(3)	(4)	(5)	(6)	(7)	(8)	(9)	(10)	(11)	(12)	(13)
	Absolute amount of debt (current dollars in millions)				Per capita debt (current dollars)				Percentage distribution of debt			
Year	Federal	State	Local	Total	Federal	State	Local	Total	Federal	State	Local	Total
1902	$ 1,178	$ 230	$ 1,877	$ 3,285	$ 15	$ 3	$ 24	$ 42	35.9%	7.0%	57.1%	100%
1913	1,193	379	4,035	5,607	13	4	42	59	21.3	6.7	72.0	100
1922	22,963	1,131	8,978	33,072	209	10	82	301	69.4	3.5	27.1	100
1932	19,487	2,832	16,373	38,692	156	23	131	310	50.4	7.3	42.3	100
1940	42,968	3,590	16,693	63,251	326	27	127	480	67.9	5.7	26.4	100
1946	269,422	2,353	13,564	285,339	1,924	17	97	2,038	94.4	0.8	4.8	100
1950	257,357	5,285	18,830	281,472	1,702	35	125	1,862	91.4	1.9	6.7	100
1955	274,374	11,198	33,069	318,641	1,670	68	201	1,939	86.1	3.5	10.4	100
1960	286,331	18,543	51,412	356,286	1,591	103	286	1,980	80.4	5.2	14.4	100
1962	298,201	22,023	58,779	379,003	1,604	118	319	2,041	78.6	5.8	15.6	100
1964	311,713	25,041	67,181	403,935	1,629	131	351	2,111	77.2	6.2	16.6	100
1968	347,578	35,663	85,492	468,733	1,739	178	428	2,345	74.2	7.6	18.2	100
1972	426,435	54,453	120,705	601,593	2,048	261	580	2,889	70.9	9.0	20.1	100
1976	620,432	79,556	160,278	860,266	2,890	371	747	4,008	72.1	9.3	18.6	100
1977	709,136	90,200	167,332	966,668	3,269	416	771	4,456	73.4	9.3	17.3	100
1978	780,423	102,569	177,864	1,060,856	3,567	469	813	4,849	73.5	9.7	16.8	100
1979	833,750	111,740	192,363	1,137,853	3,778	506	872	5,156	73.3	9.8	16.9	100
1980	914,317	123,968	206,644	1,244,929	4,101	556	927	5,584	73.4	10.0	16.6	100

* Gross debt includes both interest-bearing and non-interest-bearing debt, including debt held by federal government agencies and trust funds.

Source: U.S. Department of Commerce; U.S. Treasury Department; adapted from Tables 12 and 13, pages 24–25, *Facts and Figures on Government Finance, 1981* (New York: Tax Foundation, Inc., 1981).

per capita debt burden has increased during the century as the nation's productive power and wealth have grown on a real per capita basis.

Table 22-2 also reveals some additional significant debt trends. Intergovernmental trends are particularly discernible in the data showing changes in the percentage distribution of public sector debt between the three levels of American government. A cursory glance at this part of the table, comparing 1902 and 1980, shows that the *federal* debt has approximately doubled as a percentage of total public sector debt. During the 78-year period, the relative importance of *local* debt has decreased sharply, to a ratio of less than one third what it had been at the beginning of the century. *State* debt, however, increased slightly in relative importance during the same period. Thus, while combined *state-local* debt was 64.1 percent of total government debt in 1902, it was only 26.6 percent of the total in 1980. However, the present *state-local* share is several times greater than the 5.6 percent state-local distribution in 1946 and the 8.6 percent distribution in 1950. In other words, since the close of World War II (1945), there has been a downward trend in federal debt as a percentage of total public sector debt, and an upward trend in state and local government debt. This is true whether the two subnational levels of government are combined or considered separately.

The primary cause of growth in federal government debt has been national defense and war. This is also evident from Table 22-2. The large increases in federal debt from 1913 to 1922, and again between 1940 and 1946, reflect World War I and World War II expenditures, respectively. A sizable portion of the post-World War II absolute growth in federal debt also can be attributed to defense-related spending and to interest on war- or defense-related debt. A growing population and the derived demand for education, roads, and the like represent the major source of growth in state and local government debt.

Despite the substantial growth of public debt in the United States during this century, private debt is still much larger than public debt. For example, total private debt in 1980 amounted to $2.829 trillion, of which $1.045 trillion was corporate debt and the remaining $1.784 trillion was individual and noncorporate debt. Total government debt amounted to $1.244 trillion in 1980.

Federal, state, and local debt in relation to GNP

The ability to carry private debt is determined largely by the wealth and earning power of the consumer or business debtor. These considerations are less crucial for public debt owed by a sovereign national government with the fiscal powers of taxation and money issuance. Nevertheless, the resource base of a nation, and the aggregate level of economic performance which results from that base, do reflect something about the ability of a nation to carry debt. Clearly, a nation with 220 million people can make interest payments and refinance a $1 trillion national (federal) debt more safely if its productive resources allow it to produce a national output of $3 trillion as opposed, say, to one of $1.5 trillion.[13] It should be kept in mind, however, that the ability to carry central government debt may depend also on such considerations as whether the debt is internally or externally held and the way that the debt is managed.

Table 22–3 demonstrates the ratios of federal, state, and local government debt to gross national product (GNP) for selected years between 1929 and 1981. Interestingly, it can be observed that the national (federal) debt was actually a lower proportion of GNP in 1981 than it was in a pre-World War II year such as 1939, or a post-World War II year such as 1949. In fact, even during the 1970s it was not a growing ratio, though recent fiscal events may reverse this trend.

While the federal government debt/GNP ratio has declined since

---

[13] This does not preclude, however, the fact that federal deficits and debt creation may create undesirable inflationary and other economic effects.

TABLE 22–3 Public sector debt* as a percentage of gross national product, selected years, 1929–1981

Year	Gross federal debt	Total state debt	Total local debt	Total public sector debt
1929	16.9%	2.3%	14.2%	33.4%
1939	46.1	4.0	18.9	69.0
1949	96.6	1.5	6.5	104.6
1954	74.5	2.6	8.1	85.2
1959	60.4	3.6	10.0	74.0
1964	51.4	4.1	10.9	66.4
1969	40.6	4.4	10.4	55.4
1970	39.8	4.4	10.6	54.8
1971	40.2	4.7	10.9	55.8
1972	39.3	4.9	10.9	55.1
1973	37.8	4.8	10.4	53.0
1974	35.8	4.8	10.4	51.0
1975	37.5	5.0	10.3	52.8
1976	38.9	5.2	9.6	53.7
1977	38.0	5.1	9.4	52.5
1978	37.4	5.1	8.8	51.3
1979	35.4	4.9	8.4	48.7
1980	35.6	4.8	8.5	48.9
1981†	34.9	4.8	8.5	48.2

* Outstanding debt at end of year.
† Estimated.
Source: Advisory Commission on Intergovernmental Relations.

1949, the ratio has increased for both state and local governments. However, the overall debt/GNP ratio for all governments combined, under the prevailing influence of federal debt performance, declined during this period. Meanwhile, interest payments on government debt as a proportion of GNP, at all levels of American government, are following an increasing trend since 1949. (See Table 22–4).

Composition and institutional uses of the federal debt

In order to evaluate the influence of the federal debt on the economy, it is important to consider the composition of the debt with respect to ownership categories. In other words, who holds the federal debt? Table 22–5 provides these basic data. First, it can be noted that only 14 percent of the debt is *external debt* owed to foreign and international investors. Thus, the remaining 86 percent of the federal debt is *internal debt*. This is relevant to the earlier discussion concerning the ability of a nation to carry a large central government debt. The fact that most of the federal debt in the United States is held internally helps to validate the ability of the nation to carry the debt.

An institutional breakdown of the composition of the federal debt, moreover, reveals that 35 percent of the debt is held within the federal government, if the Federal Reserve System is classified as federal government. Furthermore, even if a strict definition of gross and net

TABLE 22–4   Interest payments on government debt, selected years, 1929–1981

Year	Amount (in $ millions)			As a percent of GNP		
	Federal	State	Local	Federal	State	Local
1929	$ 678	$ 95	$ 550	0.7	0.1	0.5
1939	941	129	534	1.1	0.1	0.6
1949	5,339	97	330	2.0	0.1	0.1
1954	6,382	193	525	1.8	0.1	0.1
1959	7,592	453	963	1.6	0.1	0.2
1964	10,666	765	1,590	1.7	0.1	0.3
1969	16,588	1,275	2,457	1.8	0.1	0.3
1970	19,304	1,499	2,875	2.0	0.2	0.3
1971	20,959	1,761	3,328	2.1	0.2	0.3
1972	21,849	2,135	3,894	2.0	0.2	0.4
1973	24,167	2,434	4,351	2.0	0.2	0.4
1974	29,319	2,863	4,803	2.2	0.2	0.4
1975	32,665	3,272	5,511	2.2	0.2	0.4
1976	37,063	4,140	6,129	2.3	0.3	0.3
1977	41,900	5,136	6,257	2.3	0.3	0.3
1978	48,695	5,268	6,714	2.4	0.3	0.3
1979	59,837	5,790	7,197	2.5	0.3	0.3
1980	74,860	6,763	7,984	2.9	0.3	0.3
1981	90,600	7,700	8,800	3.2	0.3	0.3

Source: Advisory Commission on Intergovernmental Relations.

TABLE 22-5   Composition of the federal debt, end of fiscal year 1980

Debt concept	Debt ownership	Absolute value (billions of dollars)	Percentage of gross (total) federal debt
Gross debt		$914.3	100%
Minus	Securities held by U.S. government agencies and trust funds	− 197.7	22
Minus	Securities held by federal reserve banks	− 120.7	13
Equals		= 595.9	65
		914.3	100
		− 595.9	− 65
		$318.4	35%
Net debt		$595.9	65%
Securities held by:			
Commercial banks		$100.9	11%
Mutual savings banks		5.3	< 1
Insurance companies		14.4	1
Corporations†		25.5	3
State and local governments		73.4	8
Individuals‡		123.0	13
Foreign and international investors		126.0	14
Miscellaneous		127.4	14

† Exclusive of banks and insurance companies.
‡ Includes partnerships and personal trust accounts.
Source: Federal Reserve System; U.S. Treasury Department.

debt is followed, and the Federal Reserve System is excluded from the federal government component, the percentage held within the federal government by federal agencies and trust funds is still a substantial 22 percent of total federal debt.

The existence of federal debt is useful in several ways to the federal government. Treasury securities, for example, serve as an ideal investment source for federal trust funds. They allow no conflict of interest such as would inevitably occur if the federal trust funds were invested in the securities of private businesses. Moreover, these securities serve the federal government importantly in their usage by the Federal Reserve System, the nation's central bank, since they are used as backing for Federal Reserve notes, the nation's principal currency. Treasury securities, in addition, are used by the Federal Reserve System as the vehicle for conducting open-market operations, an important technique used to affect the volume of money and credit in the economy. By buying and selling Treasury securities on the open market, the Federal Reserve System can affect purchasing power and interest rate levels in the economy in a manner consistent with the aggregate economic objectives of the Employment Act of 1946. Since the federal debt became large during World War II, open-market operations have emerged as an important monetary policy tool of the Federal Reserve System.

The individual-investors category heads the list of specific federal debt holders outside the federal government (except for foreign and international investors) with 13 percent of the gross federal debt. Commercial banks hold 11 percent. Lesser amounts, in order of relative importance (except for miscellaneous investors), are held by state and local governments, business corporations, insurance companies, and mutual savings banks. Treasury securities serve the private sector as ideal investment assets, particularly for financial institutions, because of their tendency to be relatively stable in value, low in risk, and highly liquid.

Should public debt eventually be retired?

A highly relevant question is whether public debt should ever be completely retired. This question can generally be answered no, especially if the debt is an internal debt of the central government. Indeed, the public sector, like businesses and individuals, should repay *specific* obligations at maturity, plus all interest obligations. However, just as businesses and individuals can refinance, and thus maintain or raise, their total outstanding debt under the appropriate circumstances, so also can units of government refinance and continue to carry or expand debt. In fact, a sovereign national government such as the federal government can carry and expand debt more readily than can either private businesses, individuals, or state-local governments, since the federal government alone possesses the important financial power of issuing money. Meanwhile, the public sector as a whole possesses the power to tax, which gives it a considerable debt-carrying advantage over private sector borrowers, including large corporations such as the American Telephone and Telegraph Company (A.T.&T.)

Although AT&T's total outstanding debt has increased many times over during recent decades, no one is suggesting that the company is threatened with bankruptcy and that part of its debt should now be retired. The company has much greater earning power today than it did several decades ago, because it possesses a much larger stock of more technically efficient capital. In addition, AT&T's markets are more lucrative in terms of potential demand, due to the higher level of aggregate economic activity in the nation at the present time and population growth. Yet, the debt of AT&T is an external debt—it is owed to lenders outside the company. If AT&T need not retire its debt to prevent bankruptcy—and, indeed, it need not—why should the federal government retire its debt, particularly when it is largely an internal rather than an external debt, and when the nation's economic ability to carry it in the form of productive resources and income-creating power is substantial?

Despite the considerable ability of the federal government to carry and maintain its debt, Congress has long imposed a maximum limit on the size of the federal debt. This debt limit, known as the federal debt ceiling, was first established in 1917 at a maximum of $11.5 billion. The ceiling has been increased on numerous occasions since that time. It is argued by proponents of the debt ceiling that it discourages excessive spending by the federal government. On the other hand, it can be argued that policymakers should be free to select the best alternative means, given the economic circumstances of the time, to finance incremental governmental expenditures. It might well be that the best financing alternative under prevailing economic conditions will be debt financing rather than tax or user-price financing. In this event, fiscal rationality would be distorted by the operation of a rigid debt ceiling.

Debt management issues

The existence of a large federal debt places considerable responsibility on the U.S. Treasury Department to maintain the debt in an economically rational fashion. That is, a continual problem of refinancing maturing issues and making interest payments on current issues must be faced. Moreover, net additions to total federal debt caused by deficit federal budgets require the sale of additional new securities. Furthermore, the maturities on the various outstanding issues must be staggered so excessive pressure for refunding is not created at any one time. In this regard, it is in the interest of the Treasury to have a debt structure in which the maturities are as long term as possible. It is important to note that the various debt management activities will inevitably exert economic effects on the three functional areas of economic activity—allocation, distribution, and stabilization. Such activities should be rationalized so as to promote, rather than retard, the economic goals of the society.

The most direct influence of debt management policy is exerted on the *distributional* and *stabilization* branches of economic activity. As observed earlier in the chapter, the pattern of debt ownership, and its relationship to the taxes collected to maintain and repay the debt, are capable of yielding *redistributional* effects within the society. Debt management, of course, participates in this influence primarily through debt ownership, since it is not directly related to the tax structure of the federal budget. Such redistribution may yield either a more-equitable or a less-equitable distribution of income and wealth in the society.

Although the potential distributional effects of debt management are worthy of attention, the primary influence of debt management policy appears to be exerted in the realm of *aggregate economic performance.* In terms of its own primary function, it is only logical that debt management policy attempt to fund the federal debt at the lowest possible interest cost. Moreover, it is equally logical to attempt to lengthen the maturities of the securities composing the debt structure. Yet, such policies may influence the employment, price-level, balance-of-payments, and economic-growth goals of the society in either a favorable or unfavorable manner. Furthermore, as discussed in Chapter 20, the manner in which securities are sold, that is, whether they are sold primarily to the federal reserve system, to commercial banks with or without excess loanable reserves, or to the general public, can result in secondary economic forces which may either neutralize or reinforce the expansionary multiplier effects of a deficit budget.

Moreover, regarding economic stabilization, the assertion is often made that the creation of debt by the central government is per se *inflationary.* Although this is not a necessary consequence, under certain conditions the full effect of the issuance of the securities may tend to produce upward price movements. The conditions required for price inflation to occur under debt creation are complex. There are two general cases against which the alleged inflationary effects of debt creation must be examined—the case in which there is unemployment, and the case in which full employment (or a reasonably close approximation) exists.

In the case of *unemployment,* the issuance of new debt by the federal government may not tend to produce significant inflationary pressures. However, the issuance of the new securities will tend to produce interest rate changes which, given highly elastic supply elasticities in a number of important industries, could cause the general level of prices to rise. The price rise, however, would likely be slight, and the probability of the requisite conditions existing is slight. When the proceeds of the debt creation are spent, however, there are likely to be price changes, though a major portion of the adjustment will be in the direction of increased output and increased employment. In the case of approximate *full employment,* the issuance of the debt instruments generally will tend to cause a rise in interest rates and, unless there is a decrease in other spending equal to the increase in expenditure from the proceeds of the loan, the likely result will be a general price increase. Even in the full-employment case, however, it should be noted that significant price inflation does not necessarily follow as a consequence of debt creation.

Moreover, an already-existing debt, as contrasted to a newly issued debt, could be inflationary through a redistribution effect, under full-employment conditions, if the government obtains the funds for debt services by taxing those with a lower marginal propensity to consume than those who receive the interest payments.[14] This redistribution effect, however, is unlikely to serve as a substantial cause of inflation, particularly since the evidence on ownership of the debt suggests that units with relatively high income (and hence relatively low marginal propensity to consume) are the primary recipients of the debt interest payments. A complete answer to this question demands knowledge of the income-wealth status of interest-receiving units and the structure of the tax system. In any event, it is extremely unlikely that this effect is of any great consequence in the United States.

Management of the federal debt is at times at odds with the monetary policy of the Federal Reserve System. An important objective in the Treasury Department's management of the federal debt is to finance and refinance it at the *lowest possible interest rates*. At the same time, the economic stabilization objective of Federal Reserve monetary policy may dictate *high interest rates,* especially during times of demand inflation.[15] This conflict was resolved in favor of low Treasury interest costs from the end of World War II until March 1951. Since that time, the Federal Reserve System has had greater, but not complete, discretion in conducting its monetary policy along proper stabilization lines. Meanwhile, debt management policy was performed rather poorly during the 1950s by the Treasury. The low-interest goal was emphasized, and the lengthening of maturities in debt structure was largely ignored.

Ideally, the Treasury would like to sell long-term securities at cyclical troughs or depressions, when interest rates tend to be low, and it would like to sell short-term securities at peak periods of the cycle, when interest rates tend to be high, in order to minimize interest costs over a period of time. This conflicts, once again, with Federal Reserve monetary policy because extensive Treasury borrowing during a depression would make money capital more scarce, thus raising interest rates and making private investment—which lags during a depression—even less attractive. In a period of demand inflation, moreover, the Treasury would prefer to minimize long-term

---

[14] Even if full employment does not exist, given appropriate elasticities of supply in the industries in which the two groups spend their incomes, inflation could occur.

[15] Monetary policy tends to be ineffective against the basic causes of structural inflation.

borrowing because of high interest rates. Yet, appropriate stabilization policy would require the Treasury to do considerable long-term borrowing in order to reduce the capital funds available to the private sector and thus reduce aggregate demand. At times, this dilemma has been resolved in favor of low interest costs to the Treasury rather than optimal stabilization policy.

A development in debt management policy which has assisted the Treasury at times in its ever-present problem of debt refinancing is the technique of *advance refunding.* In this approach, security holders are given the opportunity to exchange intermediate or long-term securities for newly issued securities at higher rates of interest several years before their present securities would mature. This helps to reduce the likelihood of shifts from Treasury debt to other assets when the Treasury securities become due. In addition, advance refunding helps to lengthen the maturity structure of the federal debt.

Another possible approach for the United States would be to convert the debt structure of the federal government to "nonmaturing" debt. Such a debt instrument, known as a *consol,* may be defined as an obligation to pay a certain annual rate of interest on a debt instrument into perpetuity, that is, with no maturity date at all. A number of nations, including Great Britain, use this technique extensively. If the central government wishes to redeem a consol, it merely enters the security market and purchases it, or it could sell additional consols in the face of continuing deficit budgets. However, if the debt were to remain at a fixed aggregate level, the only action the Treasury would need to take would be to maintain the interest payments on the outstanding consols. There would be no necessity to redeem maturing debt or to sell new debt.

In general, it can be said that *debt management policy* in the United States has not been completely satisfactory in its relationship to aggregate economic goals. In other words, it has tended at times to exert negative nonneutral effects on the various stabilization goals of the society. Minimally, debt management policy should be neutral in its influence on these goals. Ideally, it would promote these goals by exerting positive nonneutral effects.

Index